Survival
in Marriage

Gail Putney Fullerton

San Jose University

Survival in Marriage

Introduction to family interaction, conflicts, and alternatives

Second edition

The Dryden Press
Hinsdale, Illinois

Preface to the first edition

A few years ago at a panel discussion on the campus where I teach the subject was sex and marriage. A man asked, half in jest and half in bitterness, why it was that there were books on how to adjust in marriage, on how to be happy in marriage, on how to succeed in marriage, but no book on how to *survive* in marriage. I hope that this book will help to fill the gap.

The question presumably was asked in the narrow context of marital conflict. There are, of course, chapters in this book on marital adjustment and marital conflict that attempt to deal with this interpretation of the question. Simply stated, the first rule of survival in marriage is to recognize that it *is not* a romantic situation; the second is to perceive that marriage *is* a unique setting for the satisfaction of human needs, an opportunity not to be lightly dismissed in our increasingly dehumanized society.

But the broader sense of the question is whether marriage can provide a context for the survival of the individual in our society. In its origins, the American conjugal family was quite literally the basis for physical survival on the frontier. This book attempts to answer the question of whether the marital institution that fit the agrarian society of an earlier America can continue to function in our mass society. The loss of specific functions to other institutions, the intensification of some functions that remain to marriage and family, can best be understood in an historical context. And so can the innovations that are appearing. Seen in context, the communal "families" are more than esoteric phenomena; they represent an alternative life-style that a growing minority of young Americans are choosing.

We live in a time of social change so rapid that it approaches chaos. Values and institutions that were considered the epitome of goodness and hope only a short while ago are now under attack as agents of repression. During the coming years, marriage and the family seem destined to be the target of much the same kind of social criticism that has been directed toward the educational institutions of America for more than a decade. Before the 1960s, most Americans shared Jefferson's veneration of education and perceived the public schools as nothing less than the guardians of the future. In the decade past, the public schools and colleges were attacked by both Left and Right. They were decried by some as agents of racial discrimination of the most insidious kind and by others as the source of left wing ideas that had spoiled our youth. Political movements have swirled around our campuses and schoolyards, and even the familiar yellow school bus has become a political symbol.

Some of the same social forces now seem to be pressing in around the institutions of marriage and family. Monogamous marriage is seen by some as the focal point of the exploitation of women, the source of sexual hypocrisy, and the institution responsible for the population explosion. Yet others perceive marriage and the family as the last bastion of morality, now in danger of being abandoned as parents fail to provide the strict upbringing of children that alone can secure the future. Between the two extremes are a large group of troubled women who know that they do not wish to forego marriage in the name of liberation, yet are seeking some definition of woman's roles as wife and mother that can carry dignity and that can approach equality with the roles of men.

In such a social climate, any book about the family becomes a book with an ideological focus: to claim to be detached and objective is itself to make an ideological statement—one that denies that each of us must inevitably make value assumptions as we write or talk about marriage and the family, and that there is today a value crisis in our society.

The ideological position underlying this book is summarized in its title. I believe that conjugal relationships do provide the means for the emotional survival of the individual in our mass society and that the conjugal family is a flexible and viable institution. I do not believe, however, that it is the only possible basis of social organization. In other societies, kinship ties or age-group ties have provided the structure, and if marital ties seem the only acceptable basis to most of us, we might do well to remember Tocqueville's observation that "what we call necessary institutions are often no more than institutions to which we have grown accustomed."

The inclusion of extensive case study data gathered by tape recorder is intended to emphasize that we are dealing with real people, not "irrelevant" theory, and to put flesh on the abstract descriptions of contemporary family structure and function. In all instances I have tried to protect the identity of the persons involved by altering their names, locations, and other data that might identify them. No person interviewed is depicted in any photograph appearing in the book. I want to thank all the persons who so graciously consented to be interviewed. They are not presented as typical, or as a random selection of families and people, but as illustrative cases in point. In my student days I usually read the case studies first and then went back to the surrounding text; it is probable that this is one aspect of student behavior that has not changed.

Finally, in view of the strains that writing a book places on a marriage, I want to thank my husband, Stanley, for his patience and equally for his impatience; for knowing when to guard the study door against intrusion and for knowing when to take me from my typewriter to the beach or the mountains, or simply out to dinner.

G.P.F.
San Jose, California
January 1972

Preface to the second edition

In the few years since the first edition of this book appeared, there have been a number of significant changes in the legal, medical, and social situation in which American marriages are formed, function, and dissolve. Improved medical techniques have made abortion safer and reduced the undesirable side effects of contraceptives. In 1973, the U.S. Supreme Court ruled that within the first two trimesters of pregnancy, therapeutic abortion is a matter for a woman and her doctor to decide, not a matter for state legislation. A number of states have enacted some version of "no-fault" divorce. The age of majority has been lowered from twenty-one to eighteen, which in many states means a younger age at which persons can marry without parental consent.

The communal life-style of the counter-culture seems to have lost its glamor, and the pair bond has survived as the strongest human emotional tie. The growing number of couples living together before marriage, along with the trend toward informal weddings, with a ceremony in which couples exchange vows they have written themselves, suggests that marriage in America is becoming a more personal union, and less a religious or social institution. The conjugal contract is an experimental and tentative response to the desire of a growing number of couples to restructure marital roles, one of the ways in which the women's movement has affected marriage and the family in America.

This edition of *Survival in Marriage* has been extensively revised to take into account these and other changes in American marriage and family life. There are also chapters added in response to the requests of professors who used the first edition, but asked if there could be chapters added dealing with the physical aspects of the sexual relationship and with the problems of handling family financial resources. I thank these professors for their suggestions, and hope that the revised edition will meet their needs.

And again, I want to thank my husband, Stanley, who knew what he would be getting into this time, but still encouraged me to return to writing (and who had the wisdom to know when to go fishing).

G.P.F.
San Jose, California
August 1976

Contents

6
Marriage as a parental union: sex roles and socialization   **165**

Part Two
Marital choice and marital roles

7
Love as myth: the quicksilver foundation   201

8
Premarital bargaining and the sexual revolution   221

12
Marriage and money 333

Part Three
Marital conflict and marital dissolution

13
Marital conflict: hostility in intimacy 361

14
Divorce: legal fictions and social realities 391

15
Bereavement: the widow's role

16
Postmarital roles

Part Five
Emerging marital patterns and some alternatives

17
The corporate "family": man, wife, and corporation

18
Middle-American families

19
The family in poverty

20
Interracial marriage

21
The communal "family"

22
The conjugal contract 613

Acknowledgments 635

Photograph Credits 637

Index 639

Part One

The changing functions of marriage in the mass society

1

Marriage as an economic union: the providers

Time was, and it was all time up to 200 years ago, when the whole of life went forward in the family, in a circle of loved, familiar faces, known and fondled objects, all to human size. That time has gone forever. It makes us very different from our ancestors.

Peter Laslett (1960:609)

W hen time began for the human race, there was the family. Not always in the form contemporary Americans know, it was still the family. Men and their brothers formed hunting parties; women scavenged for roots and birds' eggs, with their children grubbing beside them. The family was the only economic institution and provided for its members, or they died. The family was also the only educational institution. Older boys hunted beside their father, brothers, and uncles, learning what they had to know to survive and to help provide for the others. Girls learned from their sisters, mother, aunts, and grandmother how to make animal skins and plant fibers into clothing, which plants were edible and which were poisonous. A lesson poorly learned could be fatal.

The family revered its ancestors, less for what they had done in life than for what they might do for the family as its representatives in the spirit world, where they might intercede with spirits believed to send the rain or herds of game. In the household shrine, the family honored those ancestors or worshipped gods whose preoccupation was supposed to be the protection of members of that particular family and its branches. Each extended family viewed itself as the chosen people of its own Creator.

The family governed itself—or was enslaved by another family. The prototype of all later governmental authority was the relationship between parent and child: the loyalty and respect, and sometimes fear, that flowed between the generations. The family defended itself and sought redress for wrongs done to its members or drove trespassers from its hunting grounds. Family feuds leading to bloodshed have become illegal as the state has assumed the sole legitimate power to protect rights and redress grievances, but in time of war the nation often assumes the trappings of a pseudo-family: men go into battle to defend the Fatherland or the Motherland. The media often report that "American blood was spilled at . . ." as if the soldiers were kinsmen as well as fellow citizens.

Social institutions form around social functions. The family is the prototypical social institution, and for thousands of generations performed all social functions. Kinship was the thread of which the entire fabric of human life was woven. The rise of cities and civilization—perhaps ten thousand years ago, only recently when viewed against the perspective of several million years of human existence—made it necessary to create new social institutions. These social institutions have made it possible for persons who are not kindred to work together and live beside one another in peace.

It is possible to view the history of social development from tribe to modern civilization as a continuing process by which social functions have been peeled away from the family to become the basis of new institutions: church, state, military, corporation, educational institutions, medical institutions, penal institutions, welfare agencies. We are witnessing the transfer of yet another family function today: the shift of responsibility for the care of the aged from the family to the nursing home. We may witness the transfer from the family of some remaining functions, such as child care.

But because the world as we knew it in our childhood seems the world that always used to be, most of us may not realize how recently many fundamental social functions left the family.

Less than a hundred years ago—only some three generations back—such a fundamental function as economic production was still predominantly a *family* function in America. Many of the changes that are presently occurring in American family life are the result of the transfer of the basic productive function from the family to corporate industry. The effects on the roles and responsibilities of husband and wife, on the relationship between parents and children, have been profound. If we would understand what is happening to marriage and family in America today, we must begin with the change from the family as a producing unit to the family as a consuming unit.

The household enterprise: where the family lived and worked

Home was once the place where people made a living. Few American men went out of the home to work for a wage before the Civil War. In 1850 only 16 percent of the American labor force was employed in manufacturing and construction (U.S. Bureau of the Census 1960). Most men were self-employed, and most goods were produced in the home. Nails were still hand-forged at the smithy less than a century ago in the United States, and the smith was likely to have his forge in a shed behind his house. Families owned and operated most business enterprises: sawmills, livery stables, general stores, creameries. Typically, the family lived in the back of, or over, the place of business (as the few remaining owners of "Mom and Pop" enterprises often do today). The family business enterprise, like the family farm, did not often make a profit. No one really expected that it would. What people hoped was that it would enable the family to make a living.

If the family enterprise was unusually successful, it might provide a living for the founder and several grown sons and their families, with each son formally taken into the partnership at an appropriate time. But most family enterprises were marginal operations, able to provide only for the owner-operator of the business, his wife and children, and perhaps an aged parent. The conjugal family—the family group that has as its central axis the relationship between husband and wife—has been the major family form throughout American history, and the conjugal family was the locus of most American economic enterprise until the recent past.

When most men worked at home, a man typically worked beside his family, and his subordinates included his wife and children. The family was a productive unit. A man's role as head of the family was fused with his role as the owner and operator of the family business or farm. Because the place of business was also the place of residence, because his children were workers and any workers he could afford to hire became a part of the household (often taking room and board as a major part of their wages),

5

a man's family responsibilities and his business concerns overlapped almost completely. A woman was her husband's business partner as well as his wife: the junior partner, for she was a woman, but a partner nonetheless.

Marriage was a union that made possible the survival of both husband and wife, for each was dependent on the skills of the other. The basic division of labor in America in the seventeenth, eighteenth, and nineteenth centuries was the division between man's work and woman's work. Each sex required the presence of the other. A single or widowed woman could survive in the city by running a boardinghouse and hiring the maintenance skills of a man. But on the frontier a woman could not have existed for long without the labor and skills of a husband, father, brother, or son. (The eldest son of a widow often had to take his father's place, and become the responsible male of the family.)

Traders and trappers opened the frontier, but families settled it. Writing in the 1830s of "the greater part of the adventurers who migrate every year to people the Western wilds" (which at that time were somewhere near Cincinnati), Alexis de Tocqueville said that "many who rush so boldly onwards . . . take their wives along with them, and make them share the countless perils and privations" (1956 ed.:237). He greatly admired the character and courage of these American women:

> I have often met, even on the verge of the wilderness, with young women who . . . had passed, almost without any intermediate state, from the wealthy abode of their parents to a comfortless hovel in a forest. Fever, solitude, and a tedious life has not broken the springs of their courage. Their features were impaired and faded, but their looks were firm; they appeared to be at once sad and resolute.   (Tocqueville 1956 ed.:237)

The division between man's work and woman's work was sharp on the frontier. If a woman fell ill, or was in childbed, her husband seldom took over her tasks. If there were no daughters old enough to assume responsibility, the wife's sister, or aunt, or a neighbor woman came to "help out" until the woman of the house was well. (The help would be returned one day, when the other woman fell ill.) A man had his own demanding work, and had neither the time nor the skills to take on his wife's tasks. Moreover, the line between man's work and woman's work was a line between more and less honorific tasks, to borrow a phrase from Thorstein Veblen. The isolated trapper or cowhand could cook for himself and mend his own coat without loss of dignity, but a married man was head of a household, and thus had a status that precluded "woman's work."

But if the husband's tasks were clearly delineated from his wife's, the skills of both were essential to their common livelihood. A woman's productive skills complemented those of her husband, in the literal sense of *complement:* that which completes. Sometimes husband and wife worked side by side; more often their labor was divided so that he began and she

6

completed the process of producing food, clothing, and shelter for the family. Their skills were different, but the lives of both were centered on the same small world. Whether on the frontier farm or within the confines of the family-owned enterprise in town, husband and wife were tied together in a union of mutual dependence.

Providers and homemakers: the dual roles of husband and wife

Today, the working wife is often assumed to be violating traditional roles, for in contemporary American culture the husband is regarded as the provider, the wife as the homemaker (despite the fact that nearly half of all American wives work outside the home). It is part of the conventional wisdom—what "everybody" knows—that there was a traditional division of conjugal roles between "provider" and "homemaker" in the past. But that is not the way it was. Although the line between "man's work" and "woman's work" was sharply drawn, *both* roles were a blend of domestic and productive functions. Both husband and wife were providers, and both were homemakers.

Most Americans lived on family farms until well into the present century. It was not until 1920 that the U.S. Census recorded more than half of the American population living in towns of 2,500 persons or more. Until late in the nineteenth century, most family farms were subsistence farms. This meant that little was grown as a cash crop and that the family lived on what it could raise, make, or acquire through barter with another family.

In his history of the sod-house frontier, Everett Dick (1954) describes the life of a young couple living on a homestead in Cloud County, Kansas, in the 1870s. This young couple, in many ways typical of the settlers who went west to homestead the plains after the Civil War, recorded a total cash expenditure of sixteen dollars for the entire first *year* of their married life (Dick 1954:236). This meager cash outlay was in part a reflection of the poverty in which most American families lived a hundred years ago. But it also reflected the fact that this young married couple were subsistence farmers.

On a subsistence farm, the husband and wife were both involved in providing for the household, and both were involved in maintaining it. A settler's bride brought a few vegetable seeds west in her jewel box, and those seeds were as much a part of the couple's investment capital as the ax and team of oxen that her husband brought. The vegetable garden that the young wife planted, tilled, harvested, and preserved provided not only food for the family table, but produce to barter. Dick records the labors of one Nebraska settler's bride, Mrs. LeRoy Otis, who may not have been unusual for an American farm wife of the 1880s. Mrs. Otis raised *ten acres* of "pumpkins, squashes, watermelons, muskmelons, and other garden truck" in one season. "In the fall she put up a forty gallon barrel of

7

cucumber pickles. She traded a load of pumpkins for a runty pig one day while her husband was away, cut saplings, and built a pen for her newly obtained property" (Dick 1954:238).

There was no clear line between a wife's productive functions and her domestic functions. Laundry—a domestic maintenance chore—began with soapmaking—a productive task. The settler's wife collected kitchen fat of all kinds: meat drippings, bacon rinds, and bone marrow, which made excellent soap grease. She saved hardwood ash from the kitchen stove or fireplace and placed it in a wooden hopper, called a leach. (On the plains, where there were few hardwood trees, the ashes from burned cornstalks had to do.) The woman began the soapmaking process by pouring water over the ashes and catching it in a pail as it soaked through the leach. If the resulting lye water was to make good soap, according to tradition it had to be "strong enough to hold up an egg." The woman then poured the lye water in a great iron kettle along with the moldering fat, rinds, and bones, and boiled the mixture for hours until it formed a gelatinous mass known as lye soap or soft soap.

On wash day the woman carried laundry to the bank of the nearest creek, gathered firewood to heat water from the creek in her iron kettle, dipped the hot water into a wooden keg, added lye soap and dirty clothes and stirred with a long stick, lifted the hot clothes out and pounded them clean, then rinsed and hung them to dry on the brush along the creek bank. Although washing the family's clothing was defined as a woman's task, it was heavy labor, requiring the woman to lift tubs of boiling water and handle dangerous substances, such as lye. It was also a long and tedious task. Not surprisingly, when a family began to prosper it was likely to hire a neighbor woman to do the laundry, and "taking in washing" was one of the means by which a woman could earn a few dollars, or exchange her labor for things her family needed. The industrious Mrs. Otis "earned the first peck of seed potatoes by washing for a neighbor . . . Once more by washing she secured some turkeys and chickens and went into the poultry-raising business" (Dick 1954:238). The wife's role thus involved the production of goods and the acquisition of capital for which she traded her produce or her labor.

The settler's life was as much a blend of domestic and productive tasks as was his wife's. He cleared the land and planted crops, built and mended fences, but a great deal of his time and energy were spent hauling fuel and water for household use. Digging a well was a long and dangerous job when done by hand. The digger had to be lowered on a rope and windlass, and the earth was removed in buckets raised on the same pulley. There was the danger of being killed by a falling bucket of earth, or by a cave-in, or if the well went deep, by the odorless but deadly gases that could accumulate in the bottom of the well. Until a well was dug, the husband hauled water in wooden barrels from the nearest river or spring.

Fuel was a constant problem on the plains, where winters were bitter and trees were scarce. Men sometimes drove a wagon twenty miles in search of firewood. Buffalo chips (sun-dried droppings) were used as fuel, and after the buffalo were gone, cow chips were used. Boys gathered cow chips and stacked them beside the house for winter use. Twisted prairie hay made a hot fire, but one that required nearly constant tending by a man or boy. Corncobs and cornstalks were saved for fuel, and sometimes the corn itself was burned: compact and oily, corn burned better and longer than twisted hay.

Corn was fuel, food, and bedding. The dried husks were used to stuff mattresses, fresh ones each season. Corn was the basic food staple. An article in the *Nebraska Farmer* in January of 1862 listed thirty-three ways of cooking corn, but cornbread and cornmeal mush were the daily fare. A century ago, the men who settled the plains raised corn more for domestic use than as a cash crop. A man's labors in the cornfield were parallel in function to his wife's work in her vegetable garden.

Another of the husband's domestic chores was providing oil for the lamps, filling them, and trimming the wicks. Until the kerosene lamp was introduced at the end of the nineteenth century, the common means of illumination was an oil lamp of a type that sod-house settlers called an "old hussy." Lard could be burned in such lamps, but lard was edible and scarce. The husband hunted ground hogs, opossums, raccoons, and similar animals whose fat could be rendered for use in the lamps. Dick records that Mr. Otis once killed "a fat skunk which gave two quarts of oil. This made an excellent odorless light when used in the 'old hussy'" (Dick 1954:252).

Whether hauling fuel and water, tending the fires, and filling the lamps were part of the husband's provider role or part of his homemaking role is a matter of definition, and it does not really matter where the line is drawn. The point is that on the subsistence farms of the American frontier there was no way to distinguish between productive labor and household maintenance. Economic life and family life were one, and the work of most American men, like that of their wives, was an inextricable blend of domestic and economic functions.

The railroad made the first major change in the pattern of life on the farm. The grain elevator beside the new railroad spur marked the transition from subsistence farming to a cash crop. The farmer could send his corn and other grains to eastern markets, the rancher could drive his cattle to the railhead and ship them east. The railroad brought coal for fuel and kerosene for the lamps. Becoming part of the national economy, the farmer began to raise grain and cattle to sell, and to buy much of what his family needed. A man no longer tanned leather and made shoes for his family on a last in the barn; he shipped his cattle to the stockyards of Omaha, Sioux City, or Chicago, and bought shoes at the general store in the nearest small town. Gradually, the husband's economic role became centered on production for sale, with maintenance relegated to the winter months.

After the subsistence farm became a cash-crop enterprise, the farm-

9

wife remained a partner. She managed the household, raised her vegetable garden and poultry, and directed the labors of her daughters and (often) a hired girl. She fed the men, including the hired hands. During harvest there might be numerous field laborers whose meals were part of their wage. (The Bureau of Labor Statistics still lists wages for agricultural workers with and without board.) The frugality of the farmwife was important to the successful operation of the farm or ranch. The farm typically operated on a thin margin of profit, yet insufficient or unpalatable food led to disgruntled hands, who might leave during the critical harvest season. The farmwife's ability to feed a dozen or more people well but economically might be a crucial factor in determining whether the farm would turn a profit at the end of the season. Her garden and the rows of preserves and barrels of pickles and corned beef in her cellar were still a part of her productive role.

Thus, even with the shift from subsistence farming to cash crops, the roles of the farmer and the farmwife were still a combination of domestic and productive functions. The family farm continued to be both the center of production and the center of family life. The primacy of the productive function was often evident: the barns were usually more solidly built and better maintained than the house. The farm population was predominantly poor as late as World War II, and in times of depression farmers returned to subsistence farming and barter. In the 1930s, when the price of corn dropped to only a few cents per bushel, some farm families burned corn as fuel, as their grandparents had done in the days of the sod-house frontier. At the depths of the Depression farmers could not sell their corn for enough money to buy coal, and the oily corn burned well. (The unfortunate miners could not eat coal.)

The family farm was the epitome of family-centered production. Farming was not merely an occupation, but a life-style in which working and living were intertwined. There was some useful task to be performed by every member of the family, from the toddler to the aged grandparent, and most tasks were performed within shouting distance of the rest of the family. The typical American family was once such a farm family; that time is gone forever. The proportion of Americans who make a living in agriculture has declined steadily since the early nineteenth century. In 1820 nearly three out of four gainfully employed Americans were engaged in agriculture (72 percent); half a century later, in 1870, over half of the American labor force was still employed in agriculture (53 percent). As the twentieth century began, 37 percent of the American labor force was in agriculture and about one out of every four gainfully employed men was a self-employed farmer (the other agricultural workers were farm hands) (U.S. Bureau of the Census 1960).

By 1940, after decades of mechanization and consolidation of land holdings (the latter accelerated by dust-bowl migration and mortgage foreclosures in the 1930s), only 13 percent of the men in the American labor force were self-employed farmers. By 1974 only 3.1 percent of the

10

Hidalgo, Texas, 1939. By 1940, after decades of mechanization and consolidation of land holdings (the latter accelerated by dustbowl migration and farm foreclosures in the 1930s), only 13 percent of the men in the American labor force were self-employed farmers. Our patterns of work and play and family living have been radically altered since the time when the essence of American life was rural and centered on the family.

men and 0.35 percent of the women in the American labor force were self-employed in agriculture (U.S. Bureau of the Census 1960 and 1975). As the number of farmers has declined, so has the number of farms. The total number of farms in the United States dropped 58.6 percent from 1935 to 1975 (U.S. Bureau of the Census 1975:609). Some farmland has been converted to other uses, from timberland to suburbs. But for the most part, small farms have been consolidated into larger ones. The average American farm contained 155 acres in 1935; in 1975 the average American farm covered 385 acres (U.S. Bureau of the Census 1975:609). There are still many small farms that are operated on a marginal basis, and a small number of large farms that have been called "factories in the field." In 1974, 45.0 percent of total cash receipts for agricultural sales in the United States went to only 4.1 percent of the farms (U.S. Bureau of the Census 1975:621). The family farm is still with us, but it employs only a small fraction of the American labor force and produces a declining part of our food and fiber.

The decline in the number of family farms and of self-employed **11** farmers is more than a trend in patterns of employment, land ownership, and agricultural production. Such statistics are the abstract statement of a change in the life-style of the American people. Our patterns of work, play, and family life have been radically altered—*radically* in its core meaning of "from the root"—from the time when the essence of American life was rural and centered on the family enterprise to an era when our existence is urban and centered on the corporate enterprise.

The unpaid family worker

When most Americans lived on farms, the typical American businessman was a small-town merchant whose livelihood depended on buying farm products for shipment to city markets, or on selling goods and services to farmers from the surrounding countryside. The small-town merchant was often the head of an enterprise owned and operated by the family, and his wife and children were typically unpaid family workers in the creamery, the grain elevator, the general store, the funeral home, or (by the 1920s) the combined filling station and café at the country crossroads. The family lived above the store or the funeral home, or in the rear of the café, or in a small house at the back of the lot where the filling station fronted on the highway. Only if the family enterprise became uncommonly profitable could the family afford to build a house away from its place of business. As recently as the 1930s, much of the lower middle class in America still consisted of small merchants and shopkeepers or craftsmen who lived with their families above or behind their place of business.

In the cities of America as well as the small towns, the household was often a business enterprise. The Mom and Pop grocery could be found every few blocks in residential neighborhoods. The store was a house, undistinguished from other houses on the block except that the "front room" was lined with shelves of canned goods, a counter with a glass front for bakery goods and sweets, and an icebox along the back wall for milk and dairy products. The front porch might have been torn off at some time to make a business entrance, but the store was clearly a residence as well as a place of business. The people behind the cash register and the meat counter were husband and wife, and their children worked in the store after school and on Saturdays (often Sundays and holidays as well). The father was still the head of the household and the proprietor of the business. The line between economic life and family life remained indistinct.

But let there be no nostalgia for the days when every child was a drudge, and so was his mother. As C. Wright Mills observed, "Behind the colorless census category 'unpaid family worker,' there lie much misery and defeat in youth" (1951:31). There was also much misery and defeat for women in that category, women who cooked and cleaned and cared for their children after the shop was closed or after the fields grew dark. For the unpaid family worker, work might be all that life seemed to contain.

For the children there were daydreams of escape to another kind of life; for the women there was a sense of futility, of working harder than anyone else and yet living always with the anxiety that there might not be money enough for the rent on the shop, the mortgage on the farm, or even for food for the family.

The unpaid family worker had to work because there was so little profit from the family enterprise that it was not possible to hire workers. The marginal farm and the small retail business hung on the lip of bankruptcy, and the anxiety that the owner-operator lived with continuously infected the entire family.

Even today, the unpaid family worker has no fringe benefits, no regular schedule of time away from the job. No one goes home from work when home is over the store or shop. Supermarkets may be closed on holidays, but the Mom and Pop store is typically open. A day off means a day that the store is closed and all income ceases. Within the close confines of the family business, husband and wife can keep a constant eye on each other and a tight rein on the children. When economic life overlaps family life, business crises are family crises, and the reverse is also true. As Mills observed:

> Business competition and economic anxiety thus come out in family relations and in the iron discipline required to keep afloat. Since there is little or no outlet for feelings beyond the confines of the shop or farm, members of these families may grow greedy for gain. The whole force of their nature is brought to bear upon trivial affairs which absorb their attention and shape their character. They come to exercise, as Balzac has said, "the power of pettiness, the penetrating force of the grub that brings down the elm tree by tracing a ring under the bark." (Mills 1951:30)

Children who are unpaid family workers have little childhood of the sort that we have come to take for granted; for them there are no carefree hours of playing in the sun or lying on the living room carpet watching television. The child raised on a marginal farm or in a family that is trying to eke out a living from a small retail business has a childhood hedged with endless small chores. He may see this as the tyranny of his parents; he may be able to perceive that behind this is the tyranny of poverty. But perhaps fear as often as affection binds such a family together.

A century ago, most American women and children were unpaid family workers, either on the farm or in small family business. Most aged Americans did not retire, but simply returned to simpler tasks and the status of unpaid family worker in a family business taken over by a son and his family. In 1974 only 1.3 percent of American women and 0.09 percent of American men sixteen years of age and older who were in the labor force were listed as unpaid family workers in nonagricultural enterprise (U.S. Bureau of the Census 1975:360). Unpaid family workers in both agricultural and nonagricultural enterprise constituted only 2.05 percent of women in the labor force, and 0.35 percent of the men. The minute proportion of unpaid family workers in the American labor force today means that most wives are spared the hard labor that left their great-grandmothers faded and misshapen at thirty, and that most children are freed from drudgery during the years of their youth.

The decline of the family firm

Given the grinding poverty and the long hours that were the lot of subsistence farmers and unpaid family workers in the marginal family enterprise, it might be asked why more Americans did not go into business or industry. The answer is that until about 1825 almost all American industry was cottage industry, and almost all business was conducted by small family concerns of the type described above. There was no alternative. When industry began to develop in the nineteenth century, factory workers were expected to work from the predawn twilight until dusk, for a wage that barely sustained life, in dank, unhealthy buildings.

The textile industry, one of the first to use factory labor, began to develop in New England and the middle Atlantic states early in the nineteenth century. Describing American textile mills in the 1830s, Eleanor Flexner wrote: "In Paterson, New Jersey, women and children had to be at work at 4:30 A.M. and work as long as they could see, with time off for breakfast and dinner, until a strike in 1835 cut the working day to 12 hours" (1959:54). Hours and working conditions changed little during the remainder of the nineteenth century. As W. J. Cash described conditions of white workers in the southern textile mills about 1900: "Men and women and children were cooped up for most of their waking lives in the gray light of glazed windows, and in rooms which were never effectively ventilated, since cotton yarns will break in the slightest draft—in rooms which, because of the use of artificial humidification, were hardly less than perpetual steam baths" (1941:204). Cotton fibers in the air combined with poor ventilation and high humidity to produce a high incidence of lung disease among mill workers. Tuberculosis and other diseases of poverty and congestion were endemic. Conditions were worse for the men and boys who worked in the coal mines.

Still, by the latter part of the nineteenth century, the homespun of the frontier was replaced by cheap, factory-woven gingham. The factory system and the machinery developed to provide shoes and uniforms for the Union Army during the Civil War became the basis for the ready-to-wear garment industry. The westward expansion of the railroads meant construction jobs, and the expansion of the steel mills and the coal mines as well. Gradually a growing number of American men, women, and children worked for someone other than the family, someplace other than home.

As production moved from home to factory, people moved from farm to city. Horse-drawn reapers and mowers and steam-driven threshing machines reduced the need for large numbers of farm laborers; even-

14

The Cliff Owen dairy farm, a family operation, served Winchester Kentucky around the turn of the century. This picture was taken in 1905. A few small-town creameries grew into national and even multinational food-processing corporations. But not many survived the 1930s.

tually the tractor and the combine replaced most of the remaining farm hands. Meanwhile, steel mills and factories that produced farm machinery —and trucks and automobiles—needed workers. The farm hand went to the city and became a factory worker.

On the farm, the hired laborers had been attached to the family enterprise almost as if they were distant and poor relatives: typically they had lived in the bunkhouse behind the barns and taken their meals in the family kitchen. The factory worker was no longer part of the household of his employer, although some companies tried to maintain the fiction that their employees constituted a "family." A man who had just arrived in the city found work in a factory or on a loading dock, and lived wherever he could find cheap room and board. An immigrant couple—for people came to American cities from the farms of Ireland, Italy, Greece, and Poland, as well as from the farms of Kansas—might dream of owning their own business someday. Meanwhile, the newly arrived workers were hod carriers on construction projects, wage workers in the factories, or piece workers in the sweatshops, and home was a boardinghouse or a tenement flat. Thus work became separated from family life for a growing number of Americans in the late nineteenth century.

Early in the twentieth century some of the backyard smiths and wheelwrights began making horseless carriages; a few of these family-

15

owned firms survived to become giants of the auto industry. A few small-town creameries grew into national and even multinational food-processing corporations. But most family enterprises were unable to compete with growing corporate industry, and not many weathered the financial crisis of the 1930s. During that decade of depression, chain grocery stores appeared in cities and even small towns, and thousand of Mom and Pop grocery stores went bankrupt. Those that stayed in business did so largely because they were willing to extend credit to their customers, whereas the chain stores were strictly "cash and carry." It was difficult to collect past-due grocery bills owed by the unemployed, and many family-owned stores collapsed under the accumulated bad debts.

Small variety and dry goods stores could not compete with the chain "dime" stores that prospered during the Depression (and have now been revitalized as "discount" stores). The independent, family-owned gas station that never completely closed at night because the owner and his family lived in the house at the back of the lot disappeared. It was replaced by look-alike service stations owned by multinational oil companies and leased to operators who are not allowed to live on the premises.

Men whose family-operated businesses failed in the thirties, or whose farms were foreclosed, eventually found jobs in the war-related industries of the forties. The high failure rate that beset family-owned businesses in the Depression years continued into the decades that followed, and accelerated in the recent severe recession of 1974 and 1975. By 1974, only 6.83 percent of American men and women engaged in nonagricultural pursuits were self-employed (U.S. Bureau of the Census 1975:360). This includes all professionals who are self-employed (doctors, lawyers, accountants, and others), as well as the owners of repair shops, stationery stores, grocery stores, and other small businesses. The largest single group of self-employed Americans were the self-employed retailers, who constituted only 1.4 percent of the white men in the American labor force. Only 0.7 percent of the white women in the labor force were self-employed in retail trade. Percentages were even lower for nonwhites (U.S. Bureau of Labor Statistics 1975:72). Whether a Mom and Pop grocery or an avant-garde boutique, the owner-operated retail store has an uncertain future. Most family operated businesses that remain will probably die with their founders, unless their doors are closed earlier by bankruptcy or urban renewal.

The good provider

The decline of the family farm and the family firm and the transfer of the production of goods away from the home mean that most families no longer work together to make a living. This change has profoundly altered American family life, and reshaped the roles of husband, wife, and child. The separation of family life and economic production created a separation of the domestic and productive roles of the male head of household.

The husband and father ceased to be the head of the family enterprise and became the provider of a cash income, earned away from home.

The separation of the family role and work role of American men began in the latter part of the nineteenth century, in the merchant and professional class of the cities. In 1860, an editorial in the *Monthly Religious Magazine* observed that "the pressure upon a multitude of business and professional men is really frightful; combined with the necessity in many cases of going long distances to their place of duty, it produces little short of an absolute separation from their families" (cited in Bridges 1965:8). The editorial tells us that in 1860 it was remarkable and lamentable that men at work should be separated from their families (something we take for granted today). It also tells us that the new pattern of separation of home and office was emerging. The man who was successful built a home away from his place of business; as a general rule, the greater the man's success, the farther his home was located from the business district. The Victorian mansion on the hill was a symbol. It told the town that the owner's wife and children did not need to work, that the head of the household was able to support them in leisure. But poor families still lived where they worked, or within walking distance of the factory or mine (often in housing built by the company that owned the mill or mine), and women and children still had to work.

Today the wages of a worker are expected to be adequate to support not only the worker, but his family as well. This is a recent expectation. From colonial times until approximately World War I, it was taken for granted that *every* member of a working-class family would work, and wages were expected to cover only the individual worker's living expenses. Describing wages in southern textile mills at the turn of the century, Cash wrote:

> These wages were inevitably such as we mean by the term "family wage." That is, they were on the average just about adequate to the support of a single individual—such wages as required that every member of a family moving from the land into Factory-town, who was not incapacitated by disease or age or infancy, should go into the mills in order that he too might eat. They were such wages as required the labor of the wife and the mother and the woman who was about to become a mother. And—they were such wages as required child labor. In grim truth, one might almost say baby labor. Query any dotard or crone you encounter in a Southern mill town today, and you are likely to hear a tale of their having gone into the mills so young that they had to carry about boxes on which to climb in order to reach the spindles they tended. At six, seven, or eight years, by ten at the latest, the little boys and girls of the mill families went regularly to work. (Cash 1941:203)

Improved machinery and production techniques meant that the productivity of each industrial worker—and of each farmer—steadily increased, so that by the time of World War I, each worker could produce

17

as much as several workers had produced a generation earlier, and one farmer could produce food for a dozen or more persons. It became possible for parents to provide for their children without requiring that the children themselves work. Laws restricting child labor and laws making school attendance compulsory removed most American children from the labor force by 1920. There are still children in the agricultural labor force, children of farm families and children of migrant farm workers, but they are now the exception. We have come far from the late seventeenth century, when John Locke observed that "the children of the poor must begin work for some part of the day when they reach the age of three" (cited in Laslett 1960:607).

By the time most Americans were urban dwellers, productivity had increased to the point that one worker, usually the male head of household, could earn enough to support several other persons: usually his wife and children. The contemporary husband and father who carries out his economic functions away from home can be entirely absent from the family and still fulfill his role as provider, as does the divorced man who makes monthly child-support and alimony payments. But there was once a day when a man could not have supported his family without having them beside him, helping him cut the hay or stock the shelves. From the point of view of the husband and father, the burden of support may seem heavy, especially in view of the rising expectations of the average American family. Expenses that once were borne only by upper-middle-class and upper-class fathers (such as a college education for the children) are now considered necessary expenses in the lower-middle and working classes. In the era when the family lived above the shop or on the farm, the household and the family were the sources of a man's livelihood; now they are a drain on his resources.

For most American husbands, economic life and family life have become separate and unrelated worlds; spheres that once overlapped almost completely have become tangential to each other. The junior executive may take work home, but it is clearly an intrusion on his domestic life. The papers the commuter brings home in his briefcase are only indirectly related to the survival of his family; the skunk Mr. Otis brought home to be rendered for lamp oil had a more immediate relevance to his household. With the separation of domestic and productive functions, the husband has lost most of his domestic responsibilities. The old frontier functions of the man as hewer of wood and drawer of water have been gratefully surrendered to public utilities. What remains of the husband's domestic tasks are vestigial household chores that can wait until the weekend: a screen door that needs repair, a leaky faucet.

One consequence of the separation of domestic and productive functions is the loss of the man's role as task leader for his family. The man whose forebears were patriarchs, directing the family enterprise, now has only the remnants of the task-oriented, action-leader role within his family: attempts to get the children to mow the lawn and clean the garage

18

on the weekend, or to gather firewood on a family camping trip. Even if the father is expected to be the family disciplinarian, his action is usually after the fact, based on what his wife reports to him when he comes home from work.

With a diminished domestic and family role, most men center their self-image and their self-esteem on their occupational role. This is a much narrower definition of self than grandfather had. As head of a household enterprise, a man had an identity with many dimensions. He could take pride in his sons as well as in his land or his business; often, the talent and labor of his sons were reasons for the success of his business. If the family business or farm prospered, he could bask in that success, which was as much a tribute to his family as to his own achievement. But if drought, locusts, and an early frost ruined the crops, or if fire destroyed his sawmill or store, he could still take pride in his ability to cope with disaster and be the strong leader of his family. His role as father was so intertwined with his economic role that he could find many levels of personal fulfillment.

But today, with familial roles and occupational roles sharply differentiated, a man's identity is typically drawn from his occupation. Occupational identity may be a rewarding and sustaining self-image for a man who can think of himself as a surgeon, a trial lawyer, an airline pilot, a research scientist, or some other professional whose work carries prestige, power, and perhaps a certain glamor. But many men have jobs from which they derive little more than their paycheck: the minor bureaucrat in a dead-end job, the legions of men who could easily be replaced by a programmed computer or a coin-operated, self-service center. In a society in which a man's occupation is the core of his identity, these are the hollow men.

Housewife: a pseudo-occupation

As the husband's role has gradually been stripped of most of its domestic functions, so the wife's role has lost its productive aspects. It is cheaper to buy canned goods and ready-to-wear clothing than to produce comparable items at home, and the housewife's productive activities have largely degenerated into hobbies: a few jars of jelly, a hand-hooked rug. She may be able to knit a wool sweater for less than a comparable hand-knit sweater would cost, but a machine-knit acrylic sweater can be purchased at a fraction of the price. The American housewife's needlework has little more economic meaning than the tapestries that medieval ladies worked while their lords were off fighting the infidel. Some of those medieval tapestries hang in art galleries today, and some of the handmade quilts that our great-grandmothers made are beginning to be accorded value as art objects as well as antiques. But as those who are presently trying to make a living through crafts are discovering, the hand-crafted article is often priced out of the market. The question of aesthetics aside, there is

19

This picture was taken sometime between 1910 and 1917, when the housewife still had a productive role that included care of chickens, ducks, and the kitchen garden. Mrs. Jeanette Bernard took this picture in her own backyard, somewhere in the borough of Queens, on New York's Long Island. The house across the street probably had a barn and hen house in the backyard, too, for families living in small towns or in the outlying neighborhoods of large cities still kept poultry, a milk cow, and usually a team of horses to pull the carriage.

little that the contemporary housewife can produce by hand, at home, that cannot be supplied more cheaply for her family at the supermarket or at the discount department store.

With the rising cost of food in the 1970s, many American families have turned part of their yard—sometimes even the front lawn—into a kitchen garden, and some have rented space in a community garden. Some suburban families have begun to raise chickens and rabbits in the backyard to supplement the family diet. Many women have begun to can or freeze their own garden produce and fruit or vegetables bought cheaply in season. Thus to some degree, families have begun to produce their own food again, and the role of the wife as provider is returning. While higher

20

food costs may have been the impetus, gardening yields more than cheaper food. The joy of working together, and of eating the fruits of their labor, has been rediscovered by many American families.

But a garden large enough to provide a significant portion of the family's food requires space (recall that Mrs. Otis gardened ten acres of land). Land is a scarce and valuable commodity in urban and suburban America. The contemporary American house is unlikely to have a cellar. If the family home has a basement, it is likely to be too warm there to store cabbage and potatoes. Even space for fruit shelves may be limited, and few freezers can hold a winter's food supply for a family. City zoning ordinances prevent most families from raising chickens in the backyard and cages of rabbits may be considered a public nuisance, contrary to health and zoning ordinances. Thus few housewives are able to grow and preserve more than a small supplement to the family food supply.

Whatever additions her labors may make to the family larder or wardrobe, the wife has lost her role as a coequal producer unless she leaves the home to work. The domestic reponsibilities of the housewife have been reduced to consumer management and the maintenance of a nonproductive (in the economic sense) household establishment. Much of the housewife's time is spent doing chores that her great-grandmother would have delegated to older daughters or the hired girl. There are hundreds of products sold with the promise that they will enable the housewife to escape or to disguise her role, a fact that in itself suggests that *housewife* has negative connotations. Advertising for detergents suggests that the housewife who uses the right brand will be able to conceal the fact that she has ever had her hands in dishwater. Or, the woman is urged, "Don't be a dishwasher—buy one!"

The American housewife's maintenance burdens are light compared with those carried by her great-grandmother. (To take one specific instance, recall the description above of what wash day entailed on the sod-house frontier, and compare an evening at the laundromat.) Yet for all her comparative comfort and leisure, the housewife is an unpaid family worker still. The services she performs are occasionally tallied and assigned a dollar equivalent (sometimes by an insurance company interested in convincing her husband that it would be costly to hire a cook, chauffeur, baby sitter, and cleaning woman if his wife died or became disabled). Nonetheless, while her work may be of value to her family, the housewife has what Talcott Parsons terms a "pseudo-occupation."

Occupation is a major means of social placement in our society. One of the items invariably included on the forms we fill out for everything from a driver's license to admission to a hospital is a question asking for the occupation of the applicant. For most people, occupation is a source of income, but there are some categories that are not income producing, such as *student, retired,* and *housewife.* All three of these categories are pseudo-occupations. However busy the housewife, or the student, or the

21

retired person may be, he or she has no income derived from the listed occupation.

Various consequences flow from the fact that the housewife is an unpaid family worker with a pseudo-occupation. As an unpaid family worker, the housewife has none of the protection a paid employee receives from various federal laws regarding occupational health and safety hazards, hours, and working conditions. As an unpaid family worker, the housewife is not covered by Social Security. Unless she works at a paid occupation at some time in her life, she will receive Social Security benefits only as her husband's dependent or survivor. (Conversely, if she dies her husband will receive no survivor's benefits, even if he is left with small children.) If she loses her position as a wife (through divorce or the death of her husband), she is not covered by unemployment compensation, and may have no skills for other, paid occupations. (The divorced woman who is back in school learning a skill or preparing for a profession is, in effect, involved in job retraining.)

As an unpaid family worker, the housewife has no income from her major occupation. Unless she has outside employment or some source of independent income, she is her husband's dependent. On the family farm or in the family firm, husband and wife were *mutually* dependent, and often had some individual income from their productive roles (the farmwife had her "butter and egg" money, for example). Having lost the productive aspects of her domestic role, the housewife has also lost her status as a coequal provider. As her husband's dependent, she remains in a childlike status, even after marriage. There is in each of us, male and female, some small residue of the child we once were, a child who longs to be protected, sheltered, pampered, and adored. But a child is also powerless, patronized, and constrained by choices adults make that impinge on him or her.

Because the role of housewife is a pseudo-occupation, it does not place a woman in the social-class structure. While this means that there is a certain equality between all women who are housewives, the fact remains that most Americans are to some degree conscious of status and rank. We typically ask a man we have just met, "What do you do?" It is the single most important thing to know about him, for occupation has become the basis of social placement. But a woman is more likely to be asked, "What does your husband do?" That is the single most important thing to know about her, for even if she has a job, it is her husband's occupation that is the primary basis of the family's position in the community.

Children are asked, "What does your Daddy do?" (Seldom, if ever, are they asked, "What does your Mommy do?") When a boy reaches the point in life when people begin to ask him, "What do you do?" he has come of age as a man. A girl seldom reaches that point. The question "Father's occupation?" will become "Husband's occupation?" when she marries. But whether a woman is trying to open a charge account or enter a hospital, her occupation tends to be secondary; it is assumed that her husband will be financially responsible for her. Her charge cards carry her name

as Mrs. John Jones, not Mary Jones. (Recent changes in some laws, however, have now made it possible for a married woman to establish credit
in her own name.) In our society, a woman is still thought of as the doctor's
wife, the minister's wife, the plumber's wife, and so on. Such a status may
have its own role and responsibilities (as the minister's wife does, for
example), but it is derived from the status of the woman's husband, and
would disappear if she were divorced or widowed—or even if her husband
changed his occupation.

Great-grandmother would have found it no easier to establish credit
in her own name (even if she would have countenanced such a thing as a
revolving charge account). But she had an identity. Throughout the nineteenth century, when more American families lived on farms than anywhere else, the typical American woman was a farmwife—not merely the
farmer's wife. If her husband died, she often kept on running the farm or
ranch, with her eldest son or a hired foreman to take over the man's work.
The difference between the productive role of farmwife and the dependent
role of housewife is the result of the impact of technological change on the
lives of American women.

The employed wife

The transition from subsistence farming and cottage industry to industrial technology and mass market took roughly a century in America. The
separation of the domestic and economic roles of the husband was gradual, and by the time employment of the husband outside the home was the
norm, it also seemed natural. No one worried about the role contradictions of the working father. Over the same period of time, and for the
same reasons, the role of the wife was reduced to a domestic role and this,
too, came to seem natural. In the last thirty years there has been a second
and more abrupt transition for women, as more and more wives have
become employed for wages, outside the home.

In 1890 only 4.5 percent of married American women whose husbands were present in the home were in the labor force as other than
unpaid family workers. In 1940, on the eve of American involvement in
World War II, the proportion of wives in the labor force had grown to 15.4
percent. Over half a century of rapid industrial development and a decade
of depression had not greatly increased the rate of participation of married women in the labor force. But by 1975, 52.4 percent of married
women with children between the ages of six and seventeen and a husband
present in the home were in the labor force (U.S. Bureau of the Census
1975:347).

Much public concern has centered on the "working mother." (The
fact that she has been identified as a "working mother" rather than as an
"employee with children" indicates how her major social role has been
defined.) Questions have been raised about the relative delinquency rates
of children whose mothers did and did not work outside the home (no

23

significant difference was found) and the relative rates of divorce of employed women and housewives (there was no clear relationship demonstrated between employment and marital trouble). Perhaps the employment of women has seemed a problem because there was no parallel development of day-care centers until the present decade. The spate of studies and articles concerned with the employed wife and the working mother seems to have dwindled in the last few years. Perhaps this means that it has now become an accepted and unremarkable fact of American life that mother, as well as father, is likely to go outside the home to support the family.

In the past, there was a certain amount of social stigma placed on the working wife, especially on the working mother. If necessity in the form of an alcoholic or disabled husband compelled her to work outside the home, she could be the object of pity. If her need was less than dire, if her income was spent on luxuries, she could well be the object of scorn. Mrs. Otis and her nineteenth-century contemporaries might work from the predawn twilight until after dusk on the family farm, but they tended to regard a wife who took a job in town as being a woman of dubious character. At the very least, she was reputed to be neglecting her children. The nineteenth-century wife knew her place, and that was in the home as an unpaid family worker.

Not that there were many jobs open to women in the latter part of the nineteenth century. Women could enter domestic service as cooks or maids; women could work for the sweatshops that were the early garment industry, or in the mills; or they could become barmaids or prostitutes. There were few alternatives, and few jobs that a woman would take if she had any other means of subsisting. As industry developed, jobs available to women continued to be those at the lowest levels: factory jobs if manual dexterity was more important than strength, sales work, menial occupations such as charwoman and laundry worker.

In the nineteenth century, most white-collar jobs (clerical, secretarial, teaching, and similar positions) were held by men. However, by 1918 every state had a compulsory school attendance law, and thousands of new teaching positions were created.[1] Many of these new teaching positions were filled by women. In the first decades of the twentieth century, corporate enterprise began to expand rapidly, requiring an increasing number of file clerks, stenographers, secretaries, accountants, and other white-collar personnel, and many of these positions were opened to women. The expansion of governmental bureaucracy also created white-collar jobs, many of them open to women.

The development of clerical, technical, and professional employment opportunities for women after World War I meant that educated, middle-class women could think of a career as an alternative to marriage. Before World War II, most middle-class working women were single.

---

[1]In the 1960s, Virginia, Mississippi, and South Carolina repealed their compulsory school attendance laws, in response to desegregation rulings by federal courts.

Employment, even professional employment, was seen as an alternative of last resort for women unable to make a good marriage. The employment of married women other than those of the most impoverished class was still considered unsuitable.

During the Depression years of the 1930s, most Americans (both men and women) felt that such jobs as were available should go to men with families to support, and that the woman who had a husband should not also seek a job. A working wife was viewed as taking bread from the mouths of others. This was also the ostensible basis for paying men more than women for performing similar tasks: the man was presumed to be the provider for a family; the woman was presumed to be a single individual whose needs would be more modest. That many women were in fact the sole providers for their families was simply not recognized. Those quasi-professional jobs that were open to women (such as elementary school teaching) were often specifically closed to *married* women. In the 1930s, in many American communities any teacher whose name was prefixed with *Mrs.* was a widow. Writing in 1937, Samuel Stouffer and Paul Lazarsfeld reported:

> In the United States the most vocal prejudice against married women finding employment ... has probably been directed against those in white-collar jobs. Did this increase in the depression? Perhaps the most thorough study made prior to the depths of the depression was that of the National Education Association, which found in a study of nearly 1,500 city school systems in 1930–31 that 77 percent refused to hire married women as teachers and 63 percent discharged single women teachers who married.   (Stouffer and Lazarsfeld 1937:55)

During World War II, however, it became not merely acceptable for wives to work outside the home; it became their patriotic duty. There was an acute labor shortage created by demand for both military hardware and consumer goods at a time when several million men were removed from the labor force for military service. Women covered their hair to keep it out of the machinery, and went to work in aircraft plants and shipyards. "Rosie the Riveter" became a national heroine. A flow of paper as well as goods was necessary to the war effort, and white-collar employment of women increased as rapidly as assembly-line employment of women. After the war, there was a period in which the women who had worked while their husbands were overseas continued to work while their husbands went to college on the G.I. bill. These wives were supporting the family while their husbands acquired professional skills, looking foward to the day when they would have a home in the suburbs with a wide expanse of lawn where a bevy of scrubbed and starched children would play. But while they dreamed the conventional dream, they worked.

Before World War II, few mothers were in the labor force unless they were widowed, divorced, or deserted (or unless their husbands were

25

unemployable or in prison). Ivan Nye and Lois Hoffman (1963:12) found that in 1940 the typical employed mother in America was her family's sole support. In 1948, only about one women in ten who had a child under six years of age and a husband present in the home was in the labor force (10.8 percent of the women in this category were employed). By 1973, almost one in three (32.7 percent) of the mothers of children under six years of age were in the labor force, even when their husbands were living in the home (U.S. Bureau of Labor Statistics 1974). Thus among the mothers of preschool children there has been a marked increase in employment even when the husband is present in the home. This suggests that while the absence of any other provider may once have been the reason why the mothers of young children went out of the home to work (still a compelling factor for many employed mothers), other motives are leading growing numbers of married women with preschool children to seek employment.

In 1890, employment outside the home was unthinkable for a woman from a respectable family (that is, a family that had moved above the poverty line); in 1930 a woman took a job until she found a husband; in 1950 a young wife kept her job until she became pregnant; by 1970 a mother often returned to work from her maternity leave. In 1975 a national survey of first-time freshmen conducted by Alexander Astin and cosponsored by the American Council on Education found that only 28.3 percent of the entering freshmen at 366 institutions believed that married women should have lives centered on home and family. In contrast, 47.8 percent of the 1970 entering freshmen had believed that woman's place was in the home. "The changes are just as dramatic for men as for women —from 57 percent in 1970 to 37.4 percent in 1975 for men and from 36.7 percent to 18.1 percent for women," according to Astin (quoted in Watkins 1976:3).

Dual careers and the shared-role marriage

There is some residual feeling among American men that a married woman's employment may reflect unfavorably on her husband's ability to provide for the family. This is a feeling left over from the day when a wife worked outside the home only if she was the family's sole support. However, most husbands are apparently grateful that their wives are willing and able to share the burden of family support, particularly if the husband's occupation carries more prestige and salary than his wife's job, and if his position of dominance in the family is not threatened by his wife's employment. Such conditions are likely to prevail as long as the husband is providing more than half of the family's income. Available statistics indicate that this is still the case in most American families. The Women's Bureau of the U.S. Department of Labor reported in 1974 that wives who work (and approximately half do) contribute, on the average, somewhat more than one fourth of their family's total income (Women's Bureau 1974:7). Among those wives who work full-time for the entire year, the median contribution to the family income is nearly two fifths. (In statistical terminology, the *median* is the middle figure in a series, which is one useful way of describing what is typical of a group.)

Few jobs that have traditionally been labeled "women's work" are likely to pay a woman more than her husband earns or to pose a psychological threat to the husband's sense of competence and dominance. In spite of federal legislation and presidential executive orders regarding equal opportunity, the female executive and the female engineer are still rare. Most working wives are employed at tasks that require more patience than intelligence, more manual dexterity than strength, or in welfare- and health-related services that are supposed to benefit from feminine compassion. In most states, salaries of clerical workers (mostly women) are markedly lower than salaries of gardeners (mostly men). But pressures to adjust such salary differences are growing as clerical workers in and out of government begin to join unions.

It might be noted, moreover, that both the prestige and the salary attached to some traditionally "feminine" occupations has been rising. This is in part a response to, and in part responsible for, greater male participation in such fields. Equal rights legislation cuts both ways, and male stewards, male nurses, and male elementary teachers are appearing in greater numbers, while more women are entering the executive suite. As the line between "man's work" and "woman's work" fades, more men will have to learn to live gracefully with the fact that their wives earn more money than they do, and hold jobs with higher prestige. In 1972 about 2.6 million wives, or some 12 percent of all wives who worked, contributed half or more of the family's income (Women's Bureau 1974:7).

For most families, however, it is still the husband's career that is the most important to the family. It is his occupation, not the wife's, that determines the status placement of the family in the community. If he is transferred, she typically quits her job and looks for another in the new community (part of the reason she may never acquire seniority or tenure in her own job). From the feminist viewpoint, this is grossly unfair. Fair or not, it is at least an advance over the day when the working wife was considered to be of dubious moral character. (And once in a while, one hears of a married couple moving because the wife had a better job opportunity in another city, and the husband was willing to give up his job and move.)

The primacy of the husband's occupation is not merely custom. The family law codes of most states specify that the husband is obligated to support his wife, a burden of support that she is not required to share (although she may choose to do so) unless her husband is incapacitated. In some states, the wife does not have a legal duty to support her husband even if he is an invalid. In return for the support obligation that is placed on the husband, most state codes acknowledge that he is the head of the

27

family, and give him the right to establish domicile (that is, choose the place the family will live). Implicit, and in some state law codes explicit, is the assumption that the man will move to wherever he can find the best employment opportunity and thus fulfill his support obligation. It is the wife's duty to accompany him, whether or not she wants to move away from her job, her friends, or her parents. If she should refuse to move with her husband, in many states she would be guilty of desertion. Such legal constraints and obligations will be considered in greater detail in later chapters. Here, the focus is on marriage with dual careers and the point is simply that the family law codes of most states load the scale so that, on balance, it is the husband's career that carries the most weight.

Most studies of the effects of the wife's employment on the marital relationship have focused on the woman's attitudes, and on what she reports her husband's feelings to be. But granting this limitation, it would appear that there is a growing acceptance by most men of the fact that their wives are employed. During the recession of 1974–75, the employed wife often made the difference between a family that was able to keep on paying the mortgage and a family that was forced to sell its home because the husband and father had been laid off for a long period of time. In low-income, dual-income marriages, the wife's earnings make the difference between "hard times" and "good times." The Women's Bureau of the U.S. Department of Labor reports that "the money contributions of working wives are of crucial importance where they raise family income above the low-income line or from a low to a middle level ... Only 3 percent of all husband-wife families had incomes below $4000 in 1972 when the wife was a worker; 11 percent when she was not" (Women's Bureau 1974:7).

Few working wives are able to afford a paid housekeeper; studies have indicated that the American wife who works outside her home forty hours each week is likely to spend at least another thirty hours each week doing housework and caring for her children. The modern counterparts of Mrs. Otis are to be found working as beauticians or clerks or teachers by day, and at the laundromat doing the family wash by night. For more affluent families, there is the possibility of hiring a cleaning woman, and in all probability mechanical and electronic servants: the stove with self-cleaning oven, the self-defrosting refrigerator, the automatic washer and dryer, the microwave oven that cooks a roast in minutes instead of hours. Much of the wife's income may go to buy these appliances, but this is analogous to the fact that her husband works to pay utility bills instead of hauling water in wooden barrels or cutting firewood for the winter.

The gradual reduction of the work week from more than seventy hours at the turn of the century to forty hours or less, and from six days to five days, and for some workers, to four ten-hour days, has made it possible for men to participate in both productive tasks and household maintenance once again. Perhaps the renewed interest of many husbands in a domestic role ("do it yourself" remodeling projects, backyard cook-

The shared-role marriage. Working four ten-hour days makes it possible for this husband to have three days a week at home, and he is willing to use part of his free Friday to help with household maintenance and care of the children, thus sharing the burden with his working wife.

ing, shopping, even child care) is no more surprising than the desire of many women to recover a productive role.

The major responsibility for household maintenance tasks will probably remain with the wife, however, and this is a point of conflict in many marriages. Yet many couples are learning to cope with dual careers and making cooperative career decisions. It is easier for a married woman to have a career if her husband is willing to participate in what has come to be called a *shared-role marriage*. As John Centra observes, for the shared-role marriage to work, "men must be willing to shoulder more of the child-rearing and home-making responsibilities, and society must become more accepting of people who do so. These major changes in life style will not come easily or quickly, although our survey uncovered signs that they are occurring here and there" (1975:4–5).

The survey to which Centra refers was sponsored by the Graduate Record Examinations Board of the Educational Testing Service (ETS). The ETS surveyed 3,658 people who earned the Ph.D. or the Ed.D degree in 1950, 1960, or 1968. Reporting on the findings, Centra notes that about two thirds of the women, compared with nine tenths of the men, had worked continuously, full-time, since receiving their doctorates. Only between 2 and 3 percent of the women had never worked after receiving the doctorate. The remaining third of the women who had earned the doctorate in the designated years were married and had worked part-time or

29

intermittently since earning the doctorate. Centra notes: "Over half of this group gave reasons for not working that were related to marital and family responsibilities. The most common reasons, in order of frequency, were pregnancy, the lack of suitable jobs in their husband's locales, the anti-nepotism policies of their husbands' employers, the absence of domestic help or day-care facilities, and their husbands' resistance to their working" (1975:1).

Approximately one in ten of the women surveyed by ETS were working part-time, compared with one man in a hundred of those surveyed. Many of these professional women (most of whom were college professors) had chosen to work part-time as a means of coping with family responsibilities. Eleven percent of the women working full-time (and 8 percent of the men) indicated that they would prefer part-time work. Some of these professionals were approaching retirement and wanted to reduce their work load, but others would have preferred part-time employment in order to spend more time with their families. (Part-time workers, even part-time college professors, seldom receive tenure, retirement benefits, health benefits, and other fringe benefits received by full-time workers, so the decision to drop from full-time to part-time employment means giving up much more than a fraction of the full-time salary.)

The ETS survey indicated that married women with the doctorate (whether or not they had children) spent an average of forty-nine hours per week at work and in related professional activities, three hours per week less than the average for single women. Married men with children averaged fifty-two hours per week at work and in professional activities, which was identical with the time invested by single women. Many married women with the doctorate commented on the difficulty in staying in touch with advances in their fields. The demands of a teaching position and those of a family mean that something has to be slighted. Typically, the ETS survey indicates, it is publication that suffers most. Married men surveyed published twice as much as married women: eighteen publications versus nine publications was the average reported for each group. Centra observes: "Our findings for publication rates and time spent isolate a critical difference: Marriage seems to support men in their careers but hamper women. Married men ranked first of the four groups in publication rate and time spent; married women ranked last" (1975:3).

A woman who has both a successful career in science and a happy marriage shared with me a letter she had received from a younger woman, and her response to that letter. The letter was from a young woman who was employed as a technician in a scientific laboratory, but wanted to enroll in graduate school. She was concerned about the effects this might have on her family. Her letter said, in part:

> I enjoyed school tremendously and would love to do more than just be someone's technician. However, my dilemma is that I love spending time with my family—also they take a lot of time. What I

need is someone who can give me good counseling. Medical school would make my family suffer too much. My husband thinks graduate school would also demand most of my time. Is a Master's degree just a cop-out? I'd appreciate any suggestions or advice you could give me and/or someone you know down in L.A. that could give me career counseling.

Sincerely yours,

The reply, from a recognized scientist who is also a loving mother and wife:

Your story and your dilemma are very similar to what I have lived through, so I'll answer in first person. I had our three during graduate student days (the youngest was born just after I got my Ph.D.) and all the way I was bucked by professors who were sure I'd never amount to anything, since I had elected to be a mother. (We had been married at the end of my sophomore year, and I worked five years to put my husband through graduate school, and then got my Master's. By the time the road was clear for me to get an advanced degree, we felt it was unwise to postpone children any longer, so all three were planned and wanted.)

I have done research and other things with almost no interruption since then, and our children, now teenagers, are just fine. I did work only part-time when they were little, but all along have hired at least some household help as well as babysitters ... Housework—cleaning, laundry, etc.—can be done by anyone. Spend your time with your children, not mopping the floor any more than necessary.

Certain priorities must be decided upon, however. In our case, we had always done quite a bit of entertaining and had a lively social life. We decided that it was far more important to spend our non-working hours with our children than with friends, and this we have never regretted. The social life, attendance at concerts, opera, etc., will pick up (and has) when the children leave home—the years really go by very rapidly. I have always tried to maximize my time with the children, and honestly think I spent more time with them than many a "full-time" mother with a busy social life. In addition, my husband, who has always been supportive, had more contact with his children than many men did at that time. His job was demanding, and when it was necessary to do business entertaining, we (or he, or I) took people out to restaurants. I'm sure adjustments would be an individual matter, the important thing is to decide what is most important. My children say they are "certainly glad you work, Mom" and have developed an excellent degree of self-reliance and responsibility.

... Yes, by all means go to graduate school. Medical schools are now at least beginning to recognize the special needs of young women. You might contact the women's group in whatever medical school you're considering, finding out from them what the climate is. Do try to pick an advisor who realizes that women have brains—ask around from his (or her) women students what the attitude is. I did make a bad mistake there, and it added unnecessarily to my burden.

I think child psychologists are finding out that the most important aspect of a mother's influence on her children is really very early, and that short, positive times together are at least as good as long times with less interaction. I'm strictly an amateur there, but my conviction is that children will feel secure with a parent who loves them, even when absences are frequent.

Important also are your husband's attitudes—if he is strongly supportive this will help immeasurably. I had to educate mine to a degree, but he is really wonderful in this respect, thank goodness. This is necessary because his associates and family can certainly throw barbs and you need him to deflect them. There will be other people who wonder what's wrong with you, even in today's climate. There will be subtle implications that you don't really love him, if a career as his wife isn't enough to satisfy you. Cultivate his ego, so he'll be proud of you and understanding when you must be away from him.

Another important thing is to consider your own energy and resilience. If they are high, fine—if not, use all possible ways of conserving them. One more tidbit—cultivate a switch in your mind—when you're at work or study, devote all your attention to it, having made good provisions for your family. The converse is true when you're with your family. This will prevent a lot of inner turmoil.

No, I don't think a Master's is a "cop-out." I think it is wise to get it, even with intentions of going on, because you never know what might interrupt later, and although it won't lift you out of the technician status, it does give you a little leverage. Last, please do join AWIS [American Women in Science]. You will find the contact stimulating, encouraging, and pleasurable. You'll find people who have your bent of mind, and also have children, and the exchange of information is often valuable. There are a lot of us who love being women, with all that goes with it—home, children, domestic activities—but who also relish the life of a scientist. It is not easy to combine them, but it is possible, and very rewarding. Let me know how you fare.

Sincerely,

32   This exchange of letters took place in 1974; the scientist reports that the young woman recently wrote that she had been accepted into a graduate program in the biological sciences.

Marriage as an economic union: a summary

From the landing of the Puritans until the end of the nineteenth century, economic production in America was carried out primarily within the household, as a family enterprise. The basic division of labor was between man's work and woman's work, and the relationship between the spouses was one of mutual dependence and complementary roles. Although many men could cook, and many women could and did drive stagecoaches and plow the back forty, the basic sex-role expectation was mutual dependence between spouses with markedly different skills.

The greater stability of American marriages in the past has been attributed to such factors as religion, morality, and devotion to duty, all of which are supposed to have been stronger in the America we have lost. But whatever the relative virtues of our forebears, it is certain that most marriages were bound together by necessity. Whether on the frontier farm or within the confines of the family enterprise in town, husband and wife were tied together by mutual dependence. However, lest the halo effect that the past generates distort our vision, it should be noted that these two who were tied together by economic necessity might not speak to each other for days at a time, that the husband was often a tyrant, ruling his small world with a heavy fist. The wife might be worked as hard as the mule, with as little reward. Our great-grandmothers kept the Sabbath as a day of rest because they needed it, and they sang hymns in which rest was one of the rewards of Heaven.

Within the last century in America, fundamental changes in marriage and family life have occurred. The watershed—the point from which our life-style flows in a different stream, in a new direction—was the transfer of production from the household to the factory. Today, few Americans live in, over, or behind their place of business. For most of us, home is a dwelling in a strictly zoned residential neighborhood; the man or woman who wants to open a small business must find a location in a part of the city that is zoned for commercial activity, or apply for a zoning variance. This means that even those who are still self-employed typically leave home to work. For the majority of American husbands, domestic and productive functions are now sharply differentiated and physically separated. The only link between the two is the paycheck.

During this transition, the husband's domestic role shrank to a vestige of the old, patriarchal, task-leader role that his forefathers had played; he became the basic provider and his wife and children became his dependents rather than his subordinate coworkers. This transition also meant that the wife lost her economic role as a productive partner in the household enterprise. When domestic and economic function were sepa-

33

rated, the housewife's major role became a service function in the household, with her former productive functions reduced to crafts and hobbies.

Thus what we have come to regard as the "traditional" division of labor, in which the husband is the provider and the wife is the homemaker, is of relatively recent origin. Today, if the wife is gainfully employed, she must work outside the home, for the household has become exclusively a consuming unit for most families. At present, about half of the women who are both wives and mothers are also employees, contributing substantially to the economy and to their family's income. Their husbands may be assuming some domestic responsibilities, but for the most part, the employed wife must also be responsible for the care of her home and children.

If one drives out of the metropolis far enough, and turns off the interstate highway, there are still crossroads cafés where the wife and daughters cook and wait tables while the husband and sons tend the gas pumps and repair tractors; there are still subsistence farms with chickens scratching in the dooryard. And in the rotting core of our cities there are marginal Mom and Pop stores and dingy restaurants where unpaid family workers sweat out their lives in the kitchen. But these are anachronisms in our era of conglomerates and fast-food franchises.

For most American families, home is no longer the place where we earn a living. And because it is not, relationships between husband and wife, and between parent and child, have been profoundly altered. Our ancestors' lives were linked by necessity and bounded by their own fields or small shop; we move between two worlds, the macrocosm where we work and the microcosm where we live. Increasingly, husband and wife are participating in both.

References

Bridges, William E. 1965. "Family Patterns and Social Values in America, 1825–1875." *American Quarterly* 17 (Spring):3–11.

Cash, W. J. 1941. *The Mind of the South.* New York: Alfred A. Knopf.

Centra, John A. 1975. "Women, Marriage, and the Doctorate." *Findings* 2 (no. 4):1–5.

Dick, Everett. 1954. *The Sod-House Frontier, 1854–1890.* Lincoln, Nebr.: Johnsen Publishing Company.

Flexner, Eleanor. 1959. *Century of Struggle.* Cambridge, Mass.: Belknap Press of Harvard University Press.

Laslett, Peter. 1960. "The World We Have Lost: The Sovereignty of the Family." *The Listener* 63 (no. 1619, April 7):607–609.

Mills, C. Wright. 1951. *White Collar: The American Middle Classes.* New York: Oxford University Press.

Nye, F. Ivan, and Lois W. Hoffman. 1963. "The Socio-Cultural Setting." In *The Employed Mother in America*, edited by F. Ivan Nye and Lois W. Hoffman, pp. 3–17. Chicago: Rand McNally & Company.

Stouffer, Samuel A., and Paul F. Lazarsfeld. 1937. *Research Memorandum on the Family in the Depression.* New York: Social Science Research Council.

Tocqueville, Alexis de. 1956. *Democracy in America,* abr. ed., edited by R. D. Heffner, New York: New American Library.

U.S. Bureau of the Census. 1960. *Historical Statistics of the United States: Colonial Times to 1957.* Washington, D.C.: U.S. Government Printing Office.

_____1975. *Statistical Abstract of the United States.* Washington, D.C.: U.S. Government Printing Office.

U.S. Bureau of Labor Statistics. 1975. *Handbook of Labor Statistics.* Washington, D.C.: U.S. Government Printing Office.

Watkins, Beverly T. 1976. "This Year's Freshmen Reflect New Views of Women's Role." *The Chronicle of Higher Education* (January 12):3–4.

Women's Bureau, U.S. Department of Labor. 1974. *Women Workers Today.* Washington, D.C.: U.S. Government Printing Office.

Suggested readings

Kesey, Ken. 1964. *Sometimes a Great Notion.* New York: Viking Press. A lusty novel about a family that owns and operates a small logging company along a river in the coastal mountains of Oregon. The family home is built on the banks of the river, which is the means of transporting their logs. The ungrammatical but uncompromising family credo is "Never Give A Inch": not to big corporations, not to big labor unions, not to the river that is undercutting the bank of which the old house stands.

Lopata, Helene Znaniecki, 1971. *Occupation: Housewife.* New York: Oxford University Press. A study of the way women view and experience their roles as housewives, based on a sample of women in the Chicago area. Social-class differences as well as urban and suburban differences in the role of housewife are examined. Lopata points out that the role of housewife changes with the stages of the life cycle, yet that women who take the traditional view of their role as housewife do so with the assumption that they will be totally involved in it for the rest of their lives.

Mills, C. Wright. 1956. *White Collar: The American Middle Classes.* New York: Oxford University Press. Available in paper. The landmark study of the rise of the white-collar class in the American social structure. The major focus of the book is on the transformation of American society created by the shift from small, family-owned and -operated business enterprise to corporate enterprise, and the problems of mobility between generations in both the old middle class and the new middle class.

McGrady, Mike. 1975 *The Kitchen Sink Papers: My Life as a Househusband.* New York: Doubleday & Company. Mike McGrady traded roles with his wife for one year. She took an office position, he spent the year as an unpaid family worker—a "househusband," as he calls himself. The experiment produced a book filled with humor and insight.

2 Marriage as a search for intimacy

Peer Gynt (to himself): "You absurd old
humbug! I'm going to peel you, however
little you may enjoy it. (Takes an onion and
peels it, layer by layer.) There's the untidy
outer husk; that's the shipwrecked man on
the wreck of the boat; next layer's the
Passenger, thin and skinny—still smacking
of Peer Gynt a little. Next we come to the
golddigger self; the pith of it's
gone—someone's seen to that . . . and here is
the Prophet, fresh and juicy: he stinks, as
the saying goes, of lies enough to bring
water to your eyes. This layer, effeminately
curled, is the man who lived a life of
pleasure. The next looks sickly. It's streaked
with black . . . (Pulls off several layers
together.) There's a most surprising lot of
layers! Are we never coming to the kernel?
(Pulls all that is left to pieces.) There isn't
one! To the innermost bit it's nothing but
layers, smaller and smaller."

Henrik Ibsen, Peer Gynt, act V, scene 5

Like Ibsen's Peer Gynt, those of us who live in a mass society may come to fear that we are nothing more than a laminated set of roles, with no inner core of self. It is an old tradition that behind the comic mask is a sad clown; is the sad face a mask, too? Is the doctor's "bedside manner" as detachable as the surgical mask, and as little a part of the real person? Does the salesgirl's smile come off with her makeup? We may learn to slip easily into (and out of) a variety of roles without feeling that what we say or do behind them reflects our "real" self. We may come to wonder what—if anything—is the core of self within.

Each day of our lives, most of us move through a corridor of strangers or acquaintances with whom we interact not as whole persons but in narrow, fragmentary role relationships. In the great metropolitan warrens where nearly two out of every three Americans live, we are surrounded by people but seldom emotionally close to anyone but our wives or husbands, and perhaps our children.

Alienation in the mass society

The same social and technological changes that removed productive functions from the family have contributed to the rise of what C. Wright Mills called the mass society. Mills was concerned with the processes by which "the classic community of publics is being transformed into a society of masses. This transformation, in fact, is one of the keys to the social and psychological meaning of modern life in America" (1956:300).

In it origins, the United States was close to Mills's definition of an ideal-typical society of publics: "Out of the little circles of people talking with one another, the larger forces of social movements and political parties develop; and the discussion of opinion is the important phase in a total act by which affairs are conducted . . . The public, so conceived, is the loom of classic, eighteenth-century democracy; discussion is at once the threads and the shuttle tying the discussion circles together" (Mills 1956:299).

Mills was looking at the structure of political power, and at the continuum between classic democracy and the totalitarian state that is the extreme form of mass society. But his comments on the nature of communication as a basic factor differentiating the two forms of society are relevant to the present discussion: "At one extreme on the scale of communication, two people talk personally with each other; at the opposite extreme, one spokesman talks impersonally through a network of communications to millions of listeners and viewers" (1956:302).

The difference between communication that flows back and forth between two people talking face to face and the one-way communication that emanates from the television set is parallel to other differences between the small community and the mass society in modes of interaction. People in all societies play roles, but the meaning of role behavior is altered in the mass society.

Even in the simplest societies there are structured roles: repeating patterns of behavior that are expected of people who stand in a particular relation to one another. Mother, father, maternal uncle, husband, wife, shaman: any status that is clearly enough defined to have a set of rights and duties attached to it has a role that can be described and charted by the ethnographer.

In a small, closed community where people have known one another all their lives, roles may be elaborately detailed: a formal etiquette that serves to keep rank and privilege clear in a situation where people live intimately with one another but want to maintain distinctions based on kinship, age, or sex. The younger brother defers to his elder brother; the wife walks behind her husband; a man steps off the path to avoid meeting his mother-in-law face to face. But because in a small, closed system everyone is familiar with the personal quirks and gifts of almost everyone else, the roles played by such people are part of the fabric of intimate relationships. Each person embroiders his roles with unique touches of himself, which others recognize and come to expect.

In contrast, most roles in a mass society are the kinds of patterned behavior that make it possible for strangers to interact and to transact business. People who live in a conglomerate mass must have a set of minimum expectations about the behavior of strangers they encounter, and these expectations must correspond most of the time with what other people actually do. All of us have known the momentary confusion of encountering someone on a sidewalk and sidestepping to the right only to find that he, too, has moved in that direction, then moving to the left simultaneously with his countermove in *that* direction, and finally, in exasperation or laughter, stopping and signaling him to go around one way or the other.

Imagine for a moment what our lives would be if all our encounters with strangers involved unpredictable sidestepping. A situation in which anything could happen would quickly become a situation in which no one could move. The alternative to a minimal set of role expectations shared by all in a mass society would be chaos, and each of us would experience unbearable anxiety about what an unpredictable horde of others might do.

Life in a mass society is made possible by a myriad of standardized expectations, communicated by mass media to millions of people, most of whom have no knowledge of the personal traits of more than a few dozen of the other millions of people. Standardized roles are of necessity impersonal, although many of them involve face to face, reciprocal behavior. Customer-clerk, doctor-patient, lawyer-client, teacher-pupil, landlord-tenant: in the course of a day we move in and out of dozens of role relationships with people we do not encounter in any other context.

Persons who chose a profession because they wanted to work with people often find themselves working with paper. The white-collar worker who moves papers from the in-basket to the out-basket, having made appropriate notations as they passed through his hands, may be making

39

Playing our fragmented roles, we must fit the expectations of strangers encountered in disconnected sequence. Our actions may come to seem reactions: rote responses and patterned gestures. Living among strangers, we may become strangers to ourselves: alienated.

decisions that affect the pensions or health benefits or chances for parole or for admission to college of dozens of other human beings. But he is insulated from the persons whose welfare depends on his notations. Even when he is inteviewing clients, or counseling them, he is eliciting responses to standardized questions. Cases fit into categories more readily than people do. The agency head talks about the "target population" as if it were composed of something other than human beings: the minor functionary talks about his "case load" in similar fashion.

   To some degree, such depersonalization is a necessary part of the bureaucrat's role. Highly personalized treatment of clients could become rank favoritism: special consideration given to some because of their personal attributes, such as beauty, youth, family connections, or race. What in the small community was called "family obligation" may become "nepotism" in the mass society. Justice and welfare, education and medicine, are supposed to be dispensed with an even measure to all, which means without regard to personal characteristics. Justice wears her blindfold so that she may recognize no favorites.

Still, the plaintiff, the client, the defendant, the patient, the case, long to be seen as persons and not merely as file numbers. If the bureaucrat does not often indulge this desire, the retail clerk finds it profitable to do so. Much of what passes for personal interaction in our society is part of a well-patterned transaction that has as much personal meaning as the honeyed voice that tells us, "Thank you for calling. This is a recorded message." The customer is supposed to receive a smile with the service, and the sales manager will see that he does.

Such pseudo-warmth is involved in what David Riesman labeled "false personalization." It is not merely part of the sales pitch to the customer; it is often involved in the interaction between clerk and manager as well. White-collar workers with a monotonous task from which they can derive little creative satisfaction may hope to find some emotional reward from their relationship to the boss. "Where there is apathy about work, the appeal is again to glamor, which depends less on the work itself than on whom one does it for," according to Riesman. "This puts the boss, in effect, in the position of having to satisfy an almost limitless demand for personalization that is partly based on the unsatisfactory nature of the white-collar girl's life outside the office" (1961:266).

There is a kind of Gresham's Law that operates in personal relations: as bad money drives good out of the market, so false personalization may come to dominate our relations with others. People may lose the ability to respond in a genuinely personal manner. As Riesman observes, "the other-directed managers, professionals, and white-collar workers cannot so easily separate coercive friendliness on the job from a spontaneous expression of genuine friendliness off the job" (1961:266).

Playing our fragmented roles, we must fit the expectations of strangers encountered in disconnected sequence. Our actions may come to seem reactions: rote responses and patterned gestures. It may seem that we have lost control over the course of our lives. We may lose awareness that running through our role behaviors is a connective tissue of self, capable of spontaneous response. Living among strangers, we may become strangers to ourselves: alienated.

The term *alienation* is popularly associated with the nonconformist who is hostile to the conventional life-style, or with the revolutionist who is hostile to the power structure of society (as in such phrases as "alienated youth" or "alienated intellectual"). In sociological usage the term is broader. Beginning with Marx's observation that industrial workers are alienated from their labor, the concept of alienation has come to include our estrangement from nature, from other people, and from ourselves.

41

Alienation is more than a problem for the minority who are nonconformist. The person who displays his alienation from the power structure may be no more alienated from himself than is the careful conformist who has modeled his behavior on the expectations of the strangers around him, and in the process has lost awareness of himself. The person, in short, who plays his roles so well that he has forgotten who he is.

The sources of identity: family and community

One of the paradoxes of our time is that the social forces which freed us to be individuals are the same forces which threw us into the limbo of alienation. Less than two hundred years ago, people were neither free nor alienated in significant numbers. People's lives were dictated by necessity and by the accident of birth. Finding or raising food for themselves and their children occupied most of their time and limited their perspective. Only those few who were sure of enough to put in their bellies had leisure and energy to contemplate the stars and the human soul.

Most people were not highly conscious of their individual selves. People defined themselves largely in terms of their kinship group and the place of their birth (as, a generation or two ago, a man from Appalachia might have said, "I am a West Virginia Hatfield"). A man was always seen—and perceived himself—in the context of his kinship: he was the son of old John, the brother of young Jack, the cousin-by-marriage of Henry, the miller. The blood ties were the basic social bonds. A stranger was alien because he was not kin, but if a link of kinship could be discovered—however remote—he was hailed as "cousin" and had an immediate and undisputed claim to the hospitality of his newfound kinsmen.

From the days of Abraham and Isaac to the eve of the American Revolution, the most relevant question to ask any man was, *"Who is your father?"* Today, we ask a stranger, *"What do you do?"* And the expected answer—his occupation—is the most salient thing we can know about him. Between these two questions lies a profound social and technological chasm.

In the past, when a man said, "I am a farmer," or "I am a miner," or "I am a fisherman," he referred to a way of life, not merely to a job category. And he would be likely to say, "*We* are farmers," or "*We* are miners," or "*We* are fishermen," for his occupation was determined by that of his father and of his father's father. His occupation was an *ascribed status:* it followed from the fact of his having been born into a particular family. A boy followed his father into the fields or into the mines or down to the sea because this was what the men of his family and his village had always done. He believed that the soil or the mine or the sea was in his blood, a genetic as much as a social calling. His work role was interwoven with being a son, a father, a brother. His fellow workers were usually his kinsmen, and he understood them by analogy to himself. Making a living was the primary concern of his life, but his occupation was not the source of his identity. Rather, *his identity and his occupation were both derived from the groups into which he was born: family, community, social class.*

Throughout most of human history, men have drawn their identity from the groups into which they were born. A man's belonging did not signify any achievement; it was his birthright. No man was held accountable for his station in life, for this was a matter of the accident of birth and the will of God. If a man's father was a peasant, he was a peasant, too, and the only alternatives were to become a mercenary soldier or to take holy orders. A man who was born poor had no sense of failure if he remained poor all his life: that was the condition to which God or Fate had assigned him, and not the result of his own action. To endure was all that was asked of him, all that he asked of himself. He did not worry about being successful, or even about being adequate. He could simply be.

Each man was linked to his brothers, his uncles, his cousins, and distant kinsmen through an intricate webbing of reciprocal rights and obligations. The most extreme punishment short of death was exile, and exile was a kind of living death. To be cast out of the group from which one drew not only one's subsistence but one's very identity meant the end of all previous existence.

Yet it followed that the man who wanted to be something more than his father had been, or his brothers would be, chose voluntary exile. There were always those who chose to become soldiers of fortune, always the restless or ambitious ones. As soon as the New World was discovered, it attracted thousands of such men—and women—who tore themselves out of the web of kinship.

Generations of Americans have chosen mobility at the cost of their group ties. This is part of our inheritance from the frontier, and as Henry Jackson Turner first pointed out, it was the presence of the frontier that shaped America and Americans. The frontier was a lodestone attracting loosely attached young people from the settled communities of the East. Whether it was gold, furs, or land that drew them, thousands of Americans (and European immigrants) left the small, stable communities of their origin and sought their fortunes in the West.

Mobile, restless, these people were the human edge of the frontier that cut into the wilderness. But in the eighteenth and nineteenth centuries, most settlers went west with other families who were related to them by blood, or were brethren in the same religious sect. The fabric of our society was woven of small, stable groups until at most two generations ago. Brothers helped each other clear the land and build homes. Women helped their sisters, sisters-in-law, and married daughters. What Emile Durkheim termed the *conjugal family*—husband, wife, and their immature children—formed part of a larger family network, even on the frontier. It was not until the end of the nineteenth century that technological changes reduced the American family to its conjugal core. Industrialization and the urbanization it fostered finally ruptured the cord of kinship.

The kinship ties that were essential to survival on the frontier farm were an

43

encumbrance in the city. As the surge toward the frontier ebbed, a counter-current of population began flowing into industrial cities. On the farm, brothers and cousins had needed one another's help in clearing the land and tilling their fields. In the city, brothers and cousins competed with one another for jobs, as they competed with strangers. Two brothers might pool their capital and found a business, but most men who moved to the city had little capital. They might dream of owning their own business someday; meanwhile, most worked for someone else, someone who typically was not their kinsman.

The man who had established himself in the city and started to rise might feel obligated to help his newly arrived brother, but he was also likely to resent the drain on his resources. Such contact as upwardly mobile, urban Americans retained with relatives was often formal and perfunctory: annual visits to the old farmhouse in the polished Packard, laden with Christmas packages for poor relations.

Dropping the burden of kinship on the way to the top is an American tradition. Distance and humor helped ease the sense of guilt. One of the standard comic-strip situations still is the parasitic brother-in-law asleep on the couch (with his shoes on) when the Self-Made Man comes home from the office. The image of a man turning his brother out would make most readers uneasy, so it is his brother-in-law: *her* brother.

It was not mere greed that led men to cut loose from the obligations of kinship. It was also a search for a new identity apart from family belonging. The individual had become the focal point of the value system, and it was in the name of individualism that people exchanged the security of reciprocal kinship obligations for the opportunity to rise. William Bridges observes: "The enemy of mobility is not only a static social structure but also the personal attachments that the individual develops in such a structure. Individualism, in these terms, is not so much an intellectual freedom as it is an emotional disengagement from others" (1965:8).

The man who severed his ties with kinsmen and lived among strangers was whatever his own person could become. When no one knows your father, what he is no longer sets boundaries to your own life. When no one knows you, your dress, manner, and speech become the basis for social placement: graphically speaking, the basis on which the headwaiter shows you a table or shows you out the door. Yet dress, speech, and manner are the outer layers of role that seem so detachable, unrelated to our "real" selves.

Alienation: the dark side of freedom

Those of us who live in the mass society are freer than our agrarian ancestors were to determine the course of our lives. But it is often the freedom of amputation. Cut off from the primary groups that nurtured their forebears and gave them a sense of identity, large numbers of Americans are looking for someone to tell them who they are or who they should be. Depending on their means and level of sophistication, they may enroll in courses that promise to develop "personality" or enter some form of therapy. But most are seeking an acceptable label or the secret to gaining power over others, rather than seeking to know themselves.

The quest for identity is often self-defeating, because what most people search for is a label, rather than a living, developing person. It is this sense of identity as a detachable "thing" that is the crux of alienation from self.

Without falling into a semantic quibble over popular versus technical usage, let us note that in the vernacular personality is referred to as if it were a commodity, not a process of being. Saying that someone has "a lot of personality" is equivalent to saying that he has "a lot of money." Personality is viewed as something he *has* or something he *lacks*, as when it is said of someone that "he has no personality." When personality is viewed as a commodity, the search for self becomes a shopping trip. An advertisement for hair coloring in a national magazine will serve as an example: "Have you found the real you? Some women never do. In fact, many women never make the most exciting discovery of all: they should have been born with blonde hair."[1]

Alienated men and women are voracious consumers, but all the goods they acquire cannot satisfy their hunger for a self. The most that they can accomplish is the enhancement of some facet of the self. This in itself may become a form of alienation, for the person who is preoccupied with perfecting one part of himself is likely to regard that part as if it were detachable, at once something that is his most valuable asset and something that is apart from himself.

The woman who says in jest that she is "putting on her face" says more than she realizes. She is likely to view her beauty as the product of the painstaking application of the contents of bottles, tubes, and aerosol cans. With fine sable brushes and the ball of her little finger she creates her face; it comes off with cold cream before she goes to bed. However vain she may be about her appearance, she does not experience herself as a beautiful woman.

This detachment of some highly valued aspect of the self is a common pattern of alienation among Americans. Beauty, masculinity, old family name: some characteristic is separated from the fluid, changing *I* and regarded as a fixed thing that becomes the support for that person's self-esteem. Such self-esteem is narrowly based—and wobbly. It is threatened always by the possible loss of this "possession" on which it depends. (Thus the discovery of an enlarged pore may send a Hollywood beauty into a suicidal depression.)

Perhaps even more common is the reverse pattern of alienation: some highly regarded characteristic that a person is convinced he *lacks*

---

[1]From an advertisement in *LIFE* magazine, June 23, 1967, quoted by permission of Doyle, Dane, Bernbach, Inc.

becomes the focal point of his concern. Like a six-year-old with his tongue where his front tooth used to be, a person may become preoccupied with a presumed gap in the self. A high school dropout may come to feel that the most significant fact about himself or herself is missing education. When introduced to someone, the dropout may make certain that this lack of formal education is mentioned early in the conversation, believing that the missing education determines forever who and what he is. Another case in point is the woman who worries about not being feminine. She is not simply involved in a debate about the role of woman in our society; she feels that, compared with other women, she *lacks something.* She has a counterpart in the man who worries about whether or not he is really masculine. Like personality, beauty, and education, femininity or masculinity may be regarded as possessions rather than as ways of being.

People who are focused on their presumed lack of some desirable trait may try to buy it. Those who succeed in acquiring their "thing" may be able to prop up their self-esteem with it, but they have achieved only the precarious and still alienated position described above. They become preoccupied with the display and protection of this most valued possession. Wanting others to admire them for what they *have,* they remain fearful that someone may see them for what they *are.*

There are other people who make some presumed shortcoming into a fixed nonthing in which they take a curious comfort. Like the hypochondriac who cherishes poor health, such people cling to a presumed deficiency in themselves. However little they accomplish, they can feel that it is remarkable, considering their handicap. Who could expect much, they seem to say, of a man who has no education? Of a girl who has no charm? And who could blame anyone for being without these things? It is not what they have, but what they lack, that becomes the hollow core of self for such people. Of all the alienated Americans, these may be the loneliest.

The search for self and the intimate other

The way out of the limbo of alienation lies through intimate association with other human beings. To know who and what we are we must experience the self through open, revealing relationships with others. It is in intimate interaction that we are able to discover and to experience most of the qualities that we would like to find in ourselves. Most of the characteristics that we want to believe are part of the inner core of our being involve ways of *being with* someone else. We cannot be loving, amusing, exciting, generous, forgiving, in isolation. Only the potential exists until there is someone present to be loved, to be amused, to be excited, to be grateful, to be forgiven. It is the response that this Intimate Other makes to us that validates our self-image.

Other people are our mirrors. To ask the mirror on the wall what we are, what our innermost self may be, is to ask a question that may be painful, and the answers we give ourselves are likely to swing between our fears and our fantasies. Seeing ourselves through the eyes of another human being is a major means of perceiving what we are. Decades ago, Charles H. Cooley expressed this in his concept of the "looking-glass self."

The picture of ourselves that we see reflected in the eyes of a stranger tells us something, but there is always the question of how accurate this image may be. Does truth lie in the stranger's first impression? Or does he perceive only the carefully prepared surface of ourselves? And even if he clearly admires our public image, there is always the nagging question, "Suppose he *really* knew me—would he still like me?" The suspicion that he might not keeps many people moving from stranger to stranger, fearful of anything but a transitory relationship in which the other can be kept at a safe distance.

Even on those rare occasions when we reveal intimate details of our lives to a stranger, we are conscious at some level that we are presenting our side of the story; he was not there, he did not share the experience, he can judge what happened only through our selective recollections. And which of us does not alter the story a little in the telling, so that we appear cast in the role of the hero? The stranger may applaud, but at some inner level we have an uneasy awareness that the applause is largely for our skill in telling stories.

But someone who was there, someone who experienced a crisis with us, who shared our despair and the bitter moments and witnessed our triumph and is willing to proclaim us a hero—his judgment of the past is one that we trust and his approval of our actions helps us to feel pleased about the kind of person we are and have been for a long time. Old friends spending an evening recalling "the time that we . . ." are reinforcing desired self-images and validating each other's claim to an acceptable self-image, whatever they are doing to the truth.

This is why old friends and close relatives—and especially husbands and wives—are the most significant intimate others in our lives. *It is the continuity as much as the intimacy itself that we require.*

In the small, stable community, continuity in relationships is the norm. Most nineteenth-century Americans—like their ancestors—drew their identity from a closely knit community, from kin relationships that reached far beyond the conjugal family unit. The average American spent his or her entire lifetime in the same small town and had contact with perhaps a few hundred people. The friends of mature years were people who played together as children. They knew each other's parents and remembered their friends' grandparents; they watched their friends' children grow up with their own. They may not have liked all of the persons whose lives were interwoven with their own, but they knew them as we seldom know anyone but the members of our immediate family.

Less than a century ago, the contact most Americans had with all social institutions—economic, governmental, educational, religious—was comparable to their experience with the family. Until well into the twen-

47

tieth century, most Americans lived on farms or in the small towns that existed largely as trade centers and shipping points for the surrounding farms. People knew the owners of most of the business establishments in their town, and they did not buy goods from a *store:* they bought goods from Frank or Charlie. Most businesses were small, locally owned and operated, and their owners were oriented almost entirely to the community where they lived. Their customers were friends, often relatives; in bad times the owner extended credit, and customer loyalty was expected in good times.

Local governments were more autonomous than they are today and (because there was no federal income tax) had relatively greater power over the public purse. Most adult males in the community were on a first-name basis with most local officials, and many of them were involved in local government at some time in their lives, if only as a deputized member of a sheriff's posse.

The school board was a branch of local government. As an educational institution, the school served mainly children. Few Americans were educated beyond the eighth grade until well into the present century. The educational institution thus involved people for much less of their lives than educational institutions do today, for by the age of fourteen or fifteen most people had completed their formal schooling. The schoolhouse was a center of community action, however, often communally built and maintained and as much a meetinghouse for the people of the area as a schoolhouse.

Most towns had several churches, each with a congregation that was small and closely knit, typically dominated by a few extended families. Such churchs were often more responsive to local pressures than to some distant bishop. The lines of cleavage of a community tended to fall along religious lines, not merely Protestant versus Catholic, but often Methodist versus Baptist, or Lutheran versus Congregationalist. Intimacy and continuity did not necessarily lead to harmony.

In any given community, a few families were likely to hold most of the economic and political power and to constitute a local elite. These people encouraged their sons and daughters to marry within this circle of "good families" and thus to perpetuate the local power structure as a kind of kinship structure in which everyone was at least a cousin by marriage to everyone else.

In short, all institutions of our society contained numerous small, locally controlled units, in which most people participated and knew personally everyone around them in a variety of contexts: as coreligionists, neighbors, fellow members of the businessmen's association, or the cattlemen's association, or some combination of these. And running through all local institutions was the thread of kinship.

Urie Bronfenbrenner describes child-rearing patterns in this America that used to be as follows:

48

To begin with, families used to be bigger—not in terms of more children so much as more adults—grandparents, uncles, aunts, cousins. Those relatives who did not live with you lived nearby. You often went to their house. They came as often to yours, and stayed for dinner. You knew them all, the old folks, the middle-aged, the older cousins. And they knew you. This had its good side and its bad side.

On the good side, some of these relatives were interesting people, or so you thought at the time. Uncle Charlie had been to China. Aunt Sue made the best penuche fudge on the block. Cousin Bill could read people's minds (he claimed). And they all gave you Christmas presents.

But there was the other side. You had to give them all Christmas presents. Besides, everybody minded your business. They wanted to know where you had been, where you were going, and why . . .

And it wasn't just your relatives. Everybody in the neighborhood minded your business . . . If you walked on the railroad trestle, the 'phone would ring at your house, and your parents would know what you had done before you got back home. People on the street would tell you to button your jacket, and ask why you were not in church last Sunday. Sometimes you liked it and sometimes you didn't—but at least people *cared.*   (Bronfenbrenner 1970: 23–24)

It is easy to become overly sentimental about the old primary groups in the village or the stable urban neighborhood of the past. Continuity often became rigidity; concern was edged with gossip, privacy was suspect. The local power structure was often a conservative force, politically and intellectually. Many small towns had the stability of a stagnant pond, and the brightest young people often escaped to the city as soon as they were able. Yet limited and limiting as small-town life could be, it did make possible a wide and varied network of continuous and intimate relationships.

Fragmented intimacy: the urban kaleidoscope

Those of us who live in an impacted urban mass live in a kaleidoscope. Our world shifts and pauses and shifts again, and never comes to rest twice in the same pattern. In the course of our lives we are thrown briefly into the company of thousands of others. Our best friends today may have been strangers to us a year ago, and most of our friends are not known to one another. Finding our third-grade class photograph in a pile of mementos in the garage brings a few flickering memories of the boy we liked and the one we fought and the girl we teased—what were their names? And we wonder what they are doing now. As Mills describes the transformation of American life:

What is happening might again be stated in terms of the historic parallel between the economic market and the public of public opinion . . . The small shop serving the neighborhood is replaced by the anonymity of the national corporation: mass advertisement replaces the personal influence of opinion between merchant and customer. The political leader hooks up his speech to a national network and speaks, with appropriate personal touches, to a million people he never saw and never will see. (Mills 1956: 304–305)

The impersonality of our economic and political interaction extends even into our relationships with neighbors. An American couple living in the suburbs may have little in common with their neighbors except the fact that they happened to have purchased houses in the same tract, which indicates that they have roughly the same financial resources and social class aspirations: slender bases for a sense of community.

Most suburbanites are aware that they are likely to be transferred in a few years, or that their neighbor will, and that someone else will buy the house next door. Most of their relations with their neighbors are on levels that make people of their social class interchangeable. The suburban life-style is one in which people get acquainted easily, but at the same time tend to maintain social distance. The suburban couple "know" the people who have lived next to them for a month, and will probably know them no better if they live beside each other for the next five years.

The kind of relationship between neighbors that is customary in a rural or small-town setting involves mutual aid, not merely the loan of a garden tool or a cup of sugar, but assistance at times of family crisis: birth, illness, a death in the family. Such assistance is not merely the token gesture of the city dweller, who is likely to say, "I'm so sorry to hear about your troubles, let me know if there is anything that I can do." In the rural setting the neighbor came in and cooked food, nursed the sick, laid out the dead. To accept such assistance from a neighbor meant the surrender of privacy and the obligation to reciprocate when the neighbor might someday be in need of similar help.

The urban or suburban American cherishes privacy, and would often rather hire the assistance he needs than open his home and family life to the close scrutiny of a neighbor. Rudoff Heberle observes that "the reciprocal obligation between neighbors is a consequence of their proximity and their interdependence. Where interdependence ceases because of the availability of services as in the city, promixity no longer constitutes the basis for a categoric social relationship" (1960:9). Urban and suburban neighbors do, on occasion, become close friends. But proximity can bring conflict as well as intimacy, and people who live in a multiple-family dwelling or in a suburban house that is ten feet from the neighbor's house may fear the potential conflict more than they desire the rewards of intimacy. In the city or suburb, even more than in the country, "Good fences make good neighbors."

Intimacy requires openness with the other, and leaves the open individual vulnerable. The danger is not merely that of possible personal rejection. To take someone into our confidence, to expose personal problems—such as concern about a wandering husband, a drinking wife, or a

50

son with a drug problem—is to give that person the power to destroy our family's good name and perhaps to hurt us economically as well. If we have misjudged our confidant, our most private concerns may become common gossip, and even in the urban setting gossip can be damaging. People have been denied insurance or credit because of what the neighbors have told an investigator; corporate careers have been ruined because word filtered back that so-and-so (or his wife) was of dubious personal reputation. (It does not matter whether or not there is truth behind a rumor; a bad reputation is a "fact" in itself and could damage the corporate image.) And so conversation between suburban neighbors is likely to turn on some topic that counterfeits intimacy without revealing the self. ("Did you see the Johnny Carson show last night?" "Has the fungus infested your bent grass, too?") Such people do not know each other; they are acquainted only with the external layers of self that one chooses to show and the other chooses to see.

These are the Americans for whom marriage has become the most significant intimate relationship. It is the husband or wife to whom they can reveal themselves without fear or pretense, and from whom they seek reassurance that the private, inner self is acceptable.

The conjugal family: our private world

If the people who lived in rural and small-town America were (and often still are) more willing to trust their private affairs to the discretion of their neighbors than contemporary urban Americans are, it was in part because it would have been difficult to keep any real secrets in the small and interconnected world in which they lived. But of even greater significance was the fact that many of their neighbors were also relatives and thus already privy to the family's problems. They were tied to these people doubly, as neighbors and as kin, and the stronger of these bonds was kinship.

At this point a few definitions may be needed for clarity. The terms *conjugal family* and *nuclear family* both refer to the family unit that is formed by a husband and wife and their immature children. For the adults involved, this is the *family of procreation;* for the children, it is the *family of orientation.* Most of us are involved in at least two nuclear or conjugal families in the course of our lives: the one that was our family of orientation and the one that we form as a family of procreation.

More complex family forms arise through the linking of nuclear families by either marital ties or blood ties. Two or more nuclear families may be linked through sharing a common husband (*polygyny*) or a common wife (*polyandry*). When blood ties link two or more families, the extended family structure is referred to as *consanguine.* The consanguine family often includes three or more generations, with several nuclear families included. The possible combinations structured along bloodlines and (or) multiple marital bonds are numerous, and somewhere in the world people

51

are likely to have tried and institutionalized any given combination.

When the group of husband, wife, and immature children appears as an independent family unit, it is referred to either as the *isolated nuclear family* (Talcott Parsons' term) or as the *conjugal family* (Durkheim's term, favored also by William Goode). There has been a good deal of dispute among sociologists about how isolated the "isolated nuclear family" is in our society. Perhaps if the term used had been the *independent* nuclear family there would have been less debate. Meyer Nimkoff and Russell Middleton differentiate between the extended family and the independent family as follows: "A family system is independent if the head of a family of procreation is neither subject to the authority of any of his relatives nor economically dependent upon them" (1960:215).

Probably no one ever intended to suggest that the isolated nuclear family was an island unto itself. However, the term *conjugal family* avoids the unfortunate connotations of both *isolated* and *nuclear*. Moreover, it focuses attention on the relationship between husband and wife as the central axis of the independent family unit. It is the primacy of the conjugal tie, as opposed to kinship ties, that is the salient feature of this kind of family system.

The traditional extended family involved joint economic enterprise and usually a shared household. It has been most commonly associated with settled agriculture, although it has appeared under special circumstances in societies with other economic foundations. Nimkoff and Middleton (1960) found that the extended family was associated with situations in which there was an abundant and stable food supply, in which the family was the basic unit of labor, geographic mobility was not necessary for subsistence, and there was a strongly developed concept of property, but property that was collectively rather than individually owned.

Neither hunting and gathering societies nor industrial societies tend to have extended families (although there are a few instances in which they occur), for one or more of the above conditions are typically absent. Hunting and gathering tribes seldom have a food supply that is abundant or stable enough to support more than the nuclear family, and their livelihood depends in many cases on seasonal migrations over an established hunting territory. In industrial societies, the food supply may be abundant but the family is no longer the basic unit of labor. Moreover, geographic mobility may be required for economic advancement, if not for subsistence. As Nimkoff and Middleton observe, "The hunter is mobile because he pursues the game: the industrial worker, the job" (1960:225).

The American family was never the traditional extended family that characterized the peasants of Poland or Italy. Individual ownership of land rather than family ownership was the pattern in America, and the availability of free land in the West meant that young men did not have to remain on their father's farm as subordinate members of an extended family structure. The availability of land meant that it was possible for even the young and poor to have independent nuclear families; the prevailing value system stressed the desirability of each family having a home of its own. Those who were forced by circumstances to live with relatives were violating the ideal of a separate and independent family existence.

However, to say that these were totally independent families would be to ignore the extensive mutual assistance and the sense of reciprocal obligation that linked most American frontier farm families to their kin. Brothers might own their own farms as individuals, but they were often located just down the section road from one another. To live on adjoining farmsteads was not the same as to live in a single large household, but there was a great deal of labor exchanged and there was mutual dependence. At harvest-time, when a new barn was being built, during periods of illness or other crisis, the related families helped one another.

As indicated above, geographical mobility did not necessarily mean that kin relationships were severed, for in the past kinfolk often moved west together. If some went ahead, they were often able to do so because relatives who stayed behind helped them raise funds to make the journey; it was the obligation of such migrants to establish a place in the new community to which other family members could come later.

Today, as in the nineteenth century, families often move to a place where a brother or cousin has already gone and sent back word of job opportunities. The mobility of blue-collar Americans is often of this kind: they are pulled by the desire to better their own condition and also by the desire to maintain relationships with close relatives. The latter motive may serve to keep working-class families in their old neighborhood, but if a close relative has moved to a distant city, this same family tie may serve as an impetus to migrate. Such moves are made by the older generation as well as by young families; retired persons are free to move to reestablish geographical propinquity with grown children who have settled in another state.

The intense emotional ties that are characteristic of the conjugal family become in time the bonds between related conjugal families. If, after we marry, we do not retain some closeness with our brother's family, our sister's family, our parents, we feel it necessary to offer some explanation. This nexus between families linked by the presence of persons who were once part of the same conjugal family unit does not prove the existence of an extended family structure. It merely proves that people who once lived together over a period of some twenty years share the kind of group loyalty and memories that make intimacy deeply rewarding.

Modern communication and transportation have made it possible for the family to retain across two generations or more the face-to-face contact that is important for the maintenance of primary group ties. To the possibilities of telephone conversation may shortly be added the visual contact that video telephones may make possible. Air travel has made it feasible to render personal assistance in times of family crisis, even if the

53

Modern communication and transportation have made it possible for the family to retain across two generations or more the face-to-face contact that is important for the maintenance of primary group ties. Air travel has made it feasible to render personal assistance in times of family crisis, even if the crisis occurs halfway across the continent. Even if there is no crisis, a family reunion is likely to be an occasion of intense emotion.

crisis occurs halfway across the continent. And in a money economy, the most common assistance that can be offered is cash, which can be provided from any distance.

Family ties tend to be stronger than neighborhood ties among Americans, even when relatives are scattered over half a continent. In our mobile society, where the average family moves once every five years, kinship ties offer much more continuity than ties to neighbors. Those neighbors who do become close friends often find that the friendship is difficult to maintain after one of the families moves away. People may stay overnight with former neighbors when traveling, but the sense of obligation and reciprocity tends to be more tenuous than among relatives. Most former neighbors seem to maintain at best an exchange of Christmas cards, often enclosing a photograph to show how much the children have grown. In contrast, the ties of kinship can more readily transcend distance, for we feel both greater obligation and greater security in making demands on our brother, our sister, our parents.

In the past, social distance as well as physical distance often separated migrants from their relatives "down home." As indicated above, it was social distance that placed the greatest strain on kinship ties. In his research on American kinship, David Schneider (1968) found:

> Distance means three things in American kinship. One meaning is simple physical distance that is, it means living in the same house, or the number of miles between houses, or the hours it takes to travel from one place to another. So one hears it said: "We never see them. They're too far away." "Too far away?" "Yes, it takes almost an hour to get there."
>
> A second meaning of distance is a complex composite of what might be called socio-emotional distance. This in turn can mean anything from a mystical feeling of identity or difference, a feeling of emotional warmth and understanding—or the lack of it—to the fact that certain important prestige symbols are either similar (hence close) or different (hence distant). Thus it may be said, "We never see them. They're pretty far off. That part of town has gone way downhill in the last few years and we don't have much in common with them any more." Another informant put it this way: "... no one has had much to do with them either. It's a matter of the kind of life and education—hardly any of the people in her or Harry's family have been to college and that sort of thing."
>
> The third meaning of distance can be called genealogical distance. This may be roughly measured by how many intervening categories of relatives there are, or how many generations back one must go before a common ancestor is found .... These three different meanings of distance need not all apply in the same way or at the same time. A person who is genealogically close may be physically distant and neutral on the socio-emotional dimension. Or a person may be close socio-emotionally and physically but distant genealogically.   (Schneider 1968:72–73)

The general rise in affluence and education probably means that there is less social distance between relatives than there was half a century ago. But differences in values and life-style that exist between the parental generation and young adult children often cause a deep rift between young couples and their parents. The "generation gap" is a form of social distance in which age level rather than class level separates kin. "Duty visits" may be made across these lines of social cleavage, but intimacy is strained.

For many American families, especially for young couples who have accepted the dominant social values and behavior norms, a modified extended family provides much support, both emotional and financial. For many other couples, however, relations with parents are tenuous, and only in dire emergency would the obligations of kinship be claimed and honored.

Even for those American couples who have maintained intimate ties with relatives, the independence of the conjugal family is valued. According to the U.S. Bureau of the Census, 97.8 percent of American married couples maintain their own households. While some of these couples may live down the street from relatives, most do not; while many of these couples may be on intimate terms with relatives, many are not. Whether

Byron J. Mosier Cigar Store, Stillwater, Minnesota, about 1893. When most Americans lived in small towns, or near them, the post office, the barbershop, the cigar store, the saloon, and the real estate office were centers of male interaction. Every small town had its unofficial center where men came together to express their opinions and reinforce shared biases. The rewards in these discussions were more emotional than intellectual. This was a male world, and its symbol was the brass spittoon.

or not American nuclear families are "isolated," it is apparent that the conjugal relationship is the primary bond.

Intimacy and equality in marriage

If American families are more separated by generational differences today than in the past, they are less separated by sex differences. Until recently, friendship seldom crossed the boundaries of sexual identity. Husband and wife lived in separate worlds; their lives were complementary but not really shared. Among rural and working-class Americans, the old pattern is still common.

In the small towns of America, a man drops by the post office ostensibly to pick up the mail from his box. But the occasion is a social event and, while the mail is being sorted, he talks to other men of politics and fishing and the private affairs of whoever has not yet arrived at the post office. When most Americans lived in small towns, or near them, such patterns of social interaction were the norm. Even more than the post office, the barbershop, the cigar store, the saloon, and the real estate office were centers of male interaction. Every town had its unofficial center where men came together to express their opinions and reinforce one another's biases.

The rewards in these discussions were more emotional than intellectual. When the others were visibly impressed by a man's remarks, he knew that he had been accepted into full adult male status. A man found it easy to accept himself in the company of men he had known and argued with most of his life. Women were not expected to be present, and if a chance errand brought a woman into the room, the conversation stopped until she had gone. This was a male world, and its symbol was the brass spittoon.

The blue-collar worker still expects to find this kind of intimacy and acceptance with male companions (Komarovsky 1967). He often has a circle of men with whom he plays poker, goes hunting, races motorcycles. The women of this class are likely to be closer emotionally to their female relatives than to anyone else, including their husbands. Like their mothers and grandmothers before them, working-class wives confide in their mother, sister, or sister-in-law, telling them things that they would be embarrassed to reveal to their husbands. And even if the wife would like to communicate more openly with her husband, she will probably find it difficult for, as Mirra Komarovsky points out, the men of this class have a "trained incapacity to share" (1967:156). "The ideal of masculinity into which they were socialized inhibits expressiveness both directly, with its emphasis on reserve, and indirectly, by identifying personal interchange with the feminine role" (1967:156).

But if working-class husbands belong to a clique of male friends, the white-collar American is in a situation that often complicates his relationships with other men. The rising young executive or the professional establishing a new practice is often on a first-name basis with dozens of other men, but may have few, if any, intimate friends. His business "friends" are clients or competitors, and he must be continually aware of the impression he is making. His co-workers are the men with whom he competes for promotion, and part of the basis for promotion is how well he gets along with others on the "team". He must not make enemies at the office, but he must also be careful about intimate friendships with men he may be supervising next month or next year. For similar reasons, his wife must be circumspect in her friendships with the wives of her husband's colleagues.

The blue-collar husband, like our agrarian forebears, may not expect to talk to his wife about his hopes and fears; on the contrary, he is likely to want a wife who can cook, handle the children, and hold her tongue. But the white-collar husband turns to his wife for counsel and support, turns to her out of necessity, for his world is a little closed, and out of preference. He wants and needs a different kind of marriage than his grandfather had.

57

On the farms of the past, the man's world and the woman's world were complementary and separate. The tasks, the conversation, the jokes, the ingroup feelings of the men did not include the women, and the latter had their own closed circle. Where the two circles overlapped, the men were dominant, and it is difficult for intimacy to exist in a relationship marked by dominance and submission.

Remnants of this pattern are still found on the American farm and in some working-class families: men and women are voluntarily segregated at family gatherings and a man is more likely to confide in a crony than in his wife. But the urban middle classes have broken with the older pattern. Theirs is a world of couples; even the children are likely to regard their parents as a hyphenated identity, Mother-and-Dad. The tight circle is the conjugal pair.

There is perhaps no better evidence of the intimate nature and relative equality of middle-class American marriages than the common use of terms of endearment as the customary form of address between husband and wife. Forms of address reflect relative position in the power structure of a group: for example, the military insistence on the use of "Sir" when one speaks to a superior. The relative equality between husband and wife in most contemporary American marriages is evident in the customary use of playful and endearing forms of address. We are more concerned with expressing tenderness than deference.

To an urban American there is nothing remarkable about a wife's calling her husband "Honey" in front of strangers. But in many societies a husband so addressed in public would feel the way a ten-year-old American boy does when his mother forgets and calls him "honey-bunch" in front of his playmates. Terms of endearment of the animal, vegetable, saccharine, or "pookum" categories are confined to the bedroom in most preindustrial societies. According to William Stephens (1963:276) "a good many societies do not even permit husband and wife to call each other by name."

In many societies, propriety requires the use of kinship terms between husband and wife. A man will address his wife simply as "Wife" or perhaps by some term such as "Mother-of-my-children," and she will use corresponding kinship terms in speaking to him. The usage is similar to the norm prevailing in our own culture until the recent past that required children to call their parents "Mother" and "Father," or some affectionate diminutive of these terms, rather than by their given names or nicknames. The parents themselves often addressed each other by these role designations, at least in front of the children (a practice that has not disappeared). But with much of our need for warmth and affection and friendly counsel channeled into the marital relationship, there is no place for the stiff formality between husband and wife that prevailed in the past.

"Togetherness" has become so much the norm for middle-class American marriages that it is a cliché, yet for most of the billions of people who live or who have lived as husband and wife in other times and places, the man's world has been largely separate from and superior to the woman's world: when the husband and wife spend most of their lives at pursuits that are separate and unequal there is little possibility for the kind of intimacy between them that most Americans expect in marriage.

What seems to us the "natural" intimacy and togetherness of husband and wife is the exception, rather than the norm. Stephens comments that:

> Marriage in our society, ordinarily involves a certain amount of intimacy and sharing between husband and wife . . . . This degree of togetherness is usually *not* found in other societies . . . . Traditionally barriers frequently stand between husband and wife, curtailing their intimacy, sharing, and togetherness. They usually observe avoidance customs while in public; they may sleep in separate beds, live in separate houses, own separate property, eat separately, go separately to community gatherings, and . . . usually work at separate tasks . . . . In our present-day American society, for some reason, these traditional barriers have largely disappeared.   Stephens (1963:270, 278)

The few other societies that are characterized by intimacy in marriage are, with the exception of Polynesia, urban and industrial societies in many ways like our own. It is probable that the basic reason for the erosion of traditional barriers between husband and wife in our society has less to do with the American ethos than with the circumstances of life in the mass society.

Marriage as a search for intimacy: a summary

In our time, the intimate and stable network of community has been dissolved in the mass society. For most urban and suburban Americans, the relationship with neighbors has become guarded and transitory, and does not contribute much to self-knowledge or self-acceptance. We live among strangers, even if we call them by name.

Most of our institutions—government, business, education, religion—have become sprawling bureaucratic structures, with local control eroded and decisions being made by distant agency directors. But while other institutions have been losing their personal and local quality, the family is the one institution in our society that has become smaller and more decentralized: the only institution to retain human scale.

As our other role relationships have become more narrow and impersonal, our roles as husband or wife, mother or father, have retained the kind of human behavior that transcends the narrow expectations of the marketplace. As other relationships have become transitory, the relationship between husband and wife has taken on added significance. It is our husband or wife with whom we share memories of the past and plans for the future. Ephemeral as the conjugal family may be compared with the ancient extended kinship structure, the family still has more continuity than any other primary group in American society. And in spite of high divorce rates, the average American spends more of his life with one wife

59

or husband than with any other human being. *A primary function of marriage in America is to provide the continuity and intimacy that neither men nor women are likely to find in any other relationship.*

In our mass society, the marital relationship provides a major opportunity for emotional fulfillment. Marriage creates a context of continuous intimacy through which a man and a woman are able to discover and expand the many facets of the self, ways of being that require the response of the Intimate Other. But a marriage that fills this deep emotional need must provide more than sexual opportunity and creature comforts. There must be the kind of response that is possible only between peers. The husband may be "first among equals." But the husband who regards his wife as an inferior—even if he dotes on her as a delightful child—will be a lonely man. Fortunately, the social changes that have placed heavier emotional demands on the marital relationship in our society have also made possible relative equality between the sexes.

Our forebears lived in two complementary worlds: the man's world and the woman's world. We also spend our lives in two worlds: the mass society, where we earn a living and pay taxes, and the private world of the conjugal family, where we love and hate and live. In the first we are identified by code numbers punched into our paychecks, tax forms, and retirement records; our roles are highly specific and involve only specialized facets of our selves. In the second world, the private enclave of our marriage, we are known by a lovingly impudent name, our roles are diffuse, intense, and involve a broad spectrum of human capacities.

Because marriage is now more a matter of emotional than economic necessity, we regard as a failure any marriage that is not marked by a high degree of intimacy and emotional commitment. Goode (1963) describes the emotional demands we place on the conjugal family, especially on the marital relationship, as follows:

> Since the larger kin group can no longer be counted on for emotional sustenance, and since the marriage is based on mutual attraction, the small marital unit is the main place where the emotional input-output balance of the individual husband and wife is maintained, where their psychic wounds can be salved or healed. At least there is no other place where they can go. Thus, the emotions within this unit are likely to be intense, and the relationship between husband and wife may well be intrinsically unstable, depending as it does on affection. Consequently, the divorce rate is likely to be high. Remarriage is likely because there is no larger kin unit to absorb the children and no unit to prevent the spouses from re-entering the free marriage market. (Goode 1963:9)

We Americans have concentrated so much emotional need on the conjugal relationship that we may have overloaded it. As the conjugal family has become more emotionally self-contained, the relation between husband and wife has become correspondingly more intense. Frictions more rapidly reach the flash point; fulfillment is demanded. It may be that the American divorce rate is high not because we think so little of marriage *Marriage as a search for intimacy* but rather because we expect so much of it. There are people who contend that marriage is an anachronism in our time; such people must have chosen to ignore the possibilities that marriage offers for continuity and intimacy in our disjointed and alienated lives.

References

Bridges, William E. 1965. "Family Patterns and Social Values in America, 1825–1875." *American Quarterly* 17 (Spring):3–11.

Bronfenbrenner, Urie. 1970. *Two Worlds of Childhood: U.S. and U.S.S.R.* New York: Russell Sage Foundation.

Goode, William J. 1963. *World Revolution and Family Patterns.* New York: The Free Press.

Heberle, Rudolf. 1960. "The Normative Element in Neighborhood Relations." *Pacific Sociological Review* 3 (Spring):3–11.

Ibsen, Henrik. 1867. *Peer Gynt.*

Komarovsky, Mirra. 1967. *Blue-Collar Marriage.* New York: Random House.

Litwak, Eugene. 1960. "Geographic Mobility and Extended Family Cohesion." *American Sociological Review* 25 (June):385–394.

Mills, C. Wright. 1956. *The Power Elite.* New York: Oxford University Press.

Nimkoff, Meyer F., and Russell Middleton. 1960. "Types of Family and Types of Economy." *American Journal of Sociology* 66 (November):215–225.

Riesman, David, et al. 1961. *The Lonely Crowd,* abr. ed. New Haven, Conn.: Yale University Press.

Schneider, David. 1968. *American Kinship: A Cultural Account.* © 1968, Prentice-Hall, Inc., Englewood Cliffs, N.J.

Stephens, William N. 1963. *The Family in Cross-Cultural Perspective.* New York: Holt, Rinehart and Winston.

Suggested readings

Riesman, David, with Nathan Glazer and Reuel Denney. 1961. *The Lonely Crowd,* abr. ed. New Haven: Yale University Press. Paper. This landmark work on the changing American character is set against the historic background of social change in America. The chapters on false personalization and enforced privatization are particularly appropriate as parallel readings on the conjugal family and intimacy.

Weissman, Myrna M., and Eugene S. Paykel. 1972. "Moving and Depression in Women." *Society* 9 (July-August):24–28. A study of the relationship between moving and the onset of depression in a group of women patients in a psychiatric clinic. The authors found that a high number of clinically depressed women had moved shortly before entering a depressive state, and that this pattern occurred even though the move was voluntary and related to such presumably favorable circumstances as a promotion for the woman's husband.

Young, Leontine. 1973. *The Fractured Family.* New York: McGraw-Hill Book Company. Paper. A thoughtful book that began as research on grandparents in our society, where "the family" is now thought of as the unit comprised of parents and their immature children. The focus broadened, and the research on which Young's book is based covered three generations: grandparents, who now have the "aura of the visitor" as family members; parents, who found it easier to talk about themselves and their children than about themselves and their parents; and the young, who shared "a wistful longing for something they could not name, a feeling of something important missed but still only vaguely sensed and symbolized by family as an ideal, an inchoate dream."

3

Marriage as a monogamous union: the rise and decline of the double standard

... [If] the tokens of virginity be not found for the damsel: Then they shall bring out the damsel to the door of her father's house, and the men of her city shall stone her with stones that she die.

Deuteronomy 22:20

Therefore all ye that be lovers call unto your rememberance the month of May, like as did Queen Guenevere, for whom I make here a little mention, that while she lived she was a true lover, and therefore she had a good end.

Sir Thomas Malory, *Le Morte D'Arthur*

One manifest function of marriage in our society is to channel and contain sexual desire, to be a kind of psychosexual flood control system. The assumption is that sexual activity will be confined within the marital relationship; the marriage vows of most faiths are explicit on the point, and in most states the presumption of marital fidelity is reflected in laws that recognize adultery as a ground for divorce. When it was assumed that the unmarried were chaste, it may not have seemed too restrictive for the married to be limited to one sexual partner. In our era of sexual permissiveness for the single individual, however, the married sometimes chafe under the expectation of sexual fidelity.

Sexual norms are part of the stream of culture that flows down from our past; diverse ethnic, religious, and social class codes have been tributaries to our culture, and to our morality, and some of these currents run counter to others. We have been caught, metaphorically speaking, in the resulting whirlpools. The stronger—if contradictory—currents in our tradition of sexual norms are the patriarchal double standard and religious asceticism, both of which had their origins in Mediterranean cultures. The countercurrent is the more permissive sexual behavior that enters our tradition from northern European customs, which permitted greater sexual freedom for women.

The patriarch and the virgin bride

Few societies have tried to impose a rigid monogamous code on males, but many have insisted on premarital virginity and marital chastity for women. The moral code of a society supports behaviors which that society regards as essential to its continued existence. For most of human history, persons related by blood formed the basic unit of economic production, of defense against maurading bands of aliens, of mutual protection and support in times of flood, drought, famine, and plague. Widows and orphans could claim the shelter of a kinsman's household, and no man was a stranger if he could establish a claim as blood kin. Kinship was the basic structure of society until approximately the end of the seventeenth century; those who had no family ties were outsiders, impoverished physically and emotionally. To be disowned by one's family was to be cut adrift as an outcast whose only future lay in becoming a menial in some other household (like the prodigal son who became a swineherd) or in becoming a mercenary soldier or a beggar.

When kinship was the basis of individual security and of social order, the preservation of a lineage was of utmost social importance. When the preservation of a lineage was a basic social goal, the sexual function of marriage was primarily procreative: the provision of heirs to carry on the family line. Norms regulating sex outside of marriage reflected the social value attached to the line of descent. It was as an attempt to ensure the purity of the *male* line that the double standard originated.

Many preindustrial societies were *patriarchal:* the word derives from two Latin roots, the first meaning *father* and the second meaning *ruler*. Such societies were usually *patrilineal* as well; that is, descent was reckoned through the father's line only. The father was seen as the carrier of the family identity. The mother was viewed as merely a receptive vessel where the male seed developed. Genealogies were reckoned as in the book of Saint Matthew: "Abraham begat Isaac; and Isaac begat Jacob; and Jacob begat Judas . . . " and so on for forty-two generations. In each generation, the mother was ignored. A man had only one significant grandparent: his paternal grandfather. His paternal grandmother, maternal grandmother, and maternal grandfather were not of genealogical import. Of his eight biological great-grandparents, only one—his father's father's father— would be reckoned an ancestor.

When the father was the only significant ancestor in each generation, the highest obligation of a man was to make certain that his line did not die with him. Each man viewed his family line as we view an endangered species of wild life or, rather, as we might view that endangered species if we ourselves were its last representative on earth. A man might be able to recite his lineage backward into the dawn of memory, but he knew that unless he left a son, he would be the last of his line. Each man married as a duty, in order to leave a legitimate male descendant who would bear his family name.

But maternity is more certain than paternity. When the most important question was, "Who is your father?" the chastity of a man's mother had to be above suspicion. Chastity had no comparable social significance for the male, however, as long as he did not have relations with another man's wife and thus cast doubt on the legitimacy of another man's heirs. *Thus the double standard derived logically from a social structure based on patrilineal descent.* When paternity was the basis of social structure and social power, the virgin bride and the faithful wife were valued; the unchaste woman was a threat to the social order.

The specific source of the double standard in Western cultures, including our own, lies in the patrilineal and patriarchal societies that ringed the eastern end of the Mediterranean some four or five thousand years before Christ. "Our own formal attitudes on double standards can be traced back to Southwest Asia as directly as can the oatmeal we have for breakfast," according to Ralph Linton (1955:231). The Semitic herding peoples who lived in the highlands of what we now call the Middle East were united by the mutual obligations of kinsmen. Power and authority flowed along the line of male descent. The chastity of a wife was essential to the preservation of the social structure. Linton states that in this region "premarital sex experimentation was discouraged. Many of the societies which shared this co-tradition placed a high value on virginity at marriage, and all of them enjoyed a double standard of sex behavior, permissive for men and restrictive for women" (1955:231).

When the early Semitic nomads took to their tents, they found it difficult to seclude their women. Unable to lock their wives and daughters behind walls, they imposed swift physical punishment on the unchaste woman. Among the early Hebrews, the bride who was not virginal or the wife who was taken in adultery was stoned or strangled, together with her lover. A betrothed woman was subject to the same harsh penalties, unless she was the victim of rape, in which case the man who had violated her was stoned. Husbands, however, were allowed wide sexual liberty.

Since paramours and rapists were subject to the death penalty, it might seem that it would have been difficult for men to find partners with whom to enjoy their sexual freedom. But the means of preserving the chastity of "good" women without interfering with the sexual liberty of men was found; a special class of "bad" women was created. The Hebrews and other Semitic nomads visited prostitutes in the valley cities: Delilah and her sisters.

The double standard not only reflected the need to keep the male lineage undefiled; but also derived from the dominant status of men. In Semitic cultures a husband had a property right in his wife. If he died, his brother inherited her along with the sheep and goats. A woman who was not virginal when she married was damaged goods and could be rejected, even destroyed. The bride's virginity was often a matter of public record, a tradition that has persisted in parts of the eastern Mediterranean. Linton states that "the exhibition of tokens of virginity is still a part of the regular wedding ceremony in most Islamic countries, and the values which this reflects certainly go back to pre-Islamic times" (1955:287). Tokens of virginity are displayed in some Christian areas of the Mediterranean as well. In remote villages of Sicily, for example, the ancient custom of hanging the bridal sheets on the street wall of the house still exists.

Broodmares and courtesans: the women of the classical age

If the Semitic wife was her husband's property, the Greek wife of the classical period had no higher status. In the dim past of the Homeric heroes, the Greeks may have accorded higher status to women. Maternity at least seems to have been socially significant in that the right to the throne of the ancient Greek cities was apparently transmitted through the maternal line. (This was, perhaps, the reason that King Menelaus was so eager to recapture the fair Helen: his right to the throne may well have been in doubt as long as she was with Paris in Troy.) But by the high point of Greek classical civilization, in the fifth century B.C., Greek sons inherited directly from their fathers, descent was patrilineal, and the family was patriarchal.

According to Aristotle, a proper wife should be as obedient as a slave. The wife of a Greek noble of the classical period would never have met the philandering Paris, much less had an opportunity to run away with him. In the age of Pericles, when Athens was the home of democracy and reason, an Athenian wife could not leave the house without her husband's permission, and if it were granted, she was veiled and escorted by a slave.

It was acceptable for Greek nobles to keep concubines, often women who were captives of war. But concubines could not produce legitimate heirs. A Greek aristocrat of the classical period married as a matter of duty, to keep his house from dying with him. Wives and daughters were confined to the home and, within the house, kept to the women's quarters. While an Athenian woman might join her husband at ordinary meals, she did not attend the banquets he gave.

There were in classical Athens cultivated women who were delightful banquet companions for such men as Sophocles and Aristophanes. They were the *hetaerae:* gracious courtesans. Demosthenes said, "We have hetaerae for pleasure, concubines for our daily needs; and wives to give us legitimate children and take care of the house." Perhaps it is not surprising that the classical Greek men reserved tender, reciprocal emotions for other males. Having sorted all women into broodmares or charming whores, Greek men had no women left to love as equals.

The early Romans were not unlike the Greeks in their attitudes toward women, but they were contemptuous of the homosexuality that had become common in Greek culture. A patrician Roman *paterfamilias* in the days of the Republic was strait-laced, but the double standard was an accepted part of his life. He would have been astounded at the suggestion that he be ashamed of patronizing a prostitute. His wife, however, was not allowed to be unfaithful. A man could divorce his wife for adultery, and if she came from the same social class as her husband, he could banish her from the city, kill her, or sell her into slavery if he chose.

But after the Punic wars, when Carthage had been sown to salt and Rome waxed fat with empire, Roman husbands relinquished both their power and the double standard. The patrician lineage became less significant. In Imperial Rome, power and protection came more from political patronage than from kinship obligations. The preservation of a lineage declined in social significance, and so did the value placed on female chastity. Roman matrons became free to conduct their own affairs, both financial and amorous. If Caesar's wife once had to be beyond reproach, wives of later emperors were not so careful of their reputations. In *The Art of Love,* Ovid suggested that a lover become friendly with the husband of his mistress. Republican Romans had been disgusted by Greek bisexuality. Imperial Romans tolerated homosexual cults. Orgy—Bacchanal—Saturnalia: the prefix *Roman* is not necessary, it is still implied in the words.

Celibacy and Christianity: the denial of the flesh

The decadent days of Rome were the milieu in which Christianity was shaped. A Semitic religion in its origin, filtered through the Greek cities of Ephesus, Corinth, and Athens, Christianity arrived in Rome as an Eastern mystery cult that promised rebirth to the poor and a day of judgment for the rich. Premarital virginity and marital chastity for women had long been part of the Semitic tradition; early Christianity dropped the double standard and made celibacy the most honored state for both sexes.

The early Christian ideal of celibacy was a reaction to the excesses of latter-day Rome. Celibacy was also a corollary to the belief that the Second Coming was at hand. If the end of the world and the day of judgment were imminent, as the early Christians believed, there was no earthly future and thus no need to procreate. It seemed imperative, moreover, that both men and women save their souls by keeping their thoughts on things of the spirit rather than on concerns of the flesh. If procreation was irrelevant and sexual pleasure imperiled the immortal soul, then celibacy was the logical ideal.

The idealization of celibacy was also a reflection of the personality of some early Christian leaders, notably Saint Paul, who said that "it is good for a man not to touch a woman," but conceded that "it is better to marry than burn." Christian hermits went into the desert to live alone and mortify the flesh. Struggling to keep their minds on God, they were tormented with sexual visions. Those who remained in the cities as part of the early Church tried to live celibate lives in the presence of temptation. A saintly married couple might live without carnal knowledge of each other. Occasionally such a husband found the fires of temptation too hot to endure and castrated himself, a practice that was frowned on as being unfair to those who were able to achieve voluntary celibacy (Hays 1964:chap.10). The very word *flesh* took on overtones of sin and death.

Perhaps it is not surprising that men who equated sex with death and celibacy with eternal life should have feared women and blamed them for arousing sexual desire in men. The early Christians regarded women as daughters of Eve, the temptress. The denial of sexuality in marriage waned as Christianity became the established order and procreation once again was deemed godly. But the celibate ideal lingered to touch and chill the ardor of generations of Christians.

The Celtic and Germanic traditions: bilateral kinship and sexual permissiveness

Historically, northern European women were less subordinated to their husbands than were the women of Mediterranean cultures. The greater personal freedom of the northern European women often included greater sexual freedom. A basic reason for this was the system of bilateral kinship reckoning that prevailed in the north. (In a bilateral kinship structure, both maternal and paternal ancestry is recognized.) Bernard Farber (1964:108–113) found that bilateral kinship systems tend to be more permissive sexually than patrilineal systems. The underlying reason is simply that in a bilateral kinship system the chastity of women is of less social import. Lineage may be socially insignificant (usually the case if there is no property to be transmitted through inheritance), or descent through the female line may be as socially significant as through the male line. In

70

either case, there is little reason to restrict the sexual activity of women. (The sexual activity of men is seldom restricted in any social system.)

As anyone who has encountered the anthropological literature on descent systems is aware, the complexities of unilinear, multilinear, and bilateral kinship systems are a maze. But in the simplest terms, because human reproduction is bisexual, the alternatives are these: descent may be reckoned along the father's line only (the *patrilineal* system described above, along with its social and sexual implications); descent may be reckoned along the mother's line only (the *matrilineal* system, fairly common among American Indian tribes but not part of the Western cultural tradition); or descent may be reckoned on both sides (*bilateral kinship*).

People who reckon kinship on one side only—*unilineal* kinship—are not ignorant of the biological function of the other parent; simply, for social purposes, the other parent does not count. In the days when family and clan were the only significant social structures, a period that includes most of human history, a unilineal kinship system meant that power and property could be transmitted along a clear line. When war took the form of family feuds, unilineal kinship determined which group could claim a person's loyalty. The great advantage of unilinear reckoning of descent, whether patrilineal or matrilineal, is that it is clear where one belongs; there are no overlapping group memberships, no conflicting loyalties. Group boundaries are sharply drawn and exclusive.

When descent is reckoned bilaterally, there is no clear group identity established by birth and blood tie. Rather, each individual is related to a large number of persons by some degree of kinship and, except for full siblings, no group of persons exists who share exactly the same kin. Bilateral kinship results in a matrix, not in discrete groupings of persons who either are or are not kindred.

There are advantages in bilateral kinship reckoning, even in societies in which kinship is the basis of social structure. Some of these advantages were apparent in the experience of the ancient Scottish clans, to take one example of a bilateral kinship system. The Scottish clan included all persons who could establish descent from a common ancestor, usually an important chief of the remote past. All who could prove themselves descended from this ancestral chief were clan members, not just those in the direct male line. The hereditary chieftain in any given generation was the man who could claim the most direct descent from the ancestral chief. But if this man died without heirs, there was always *someone* who was then the man who could claim the most direct descent from the honored ancestor. One advantage of this system among small, warring groups was that the clan was in less danger of disappearing than it would otherwise have been. The female descendants of the founding chief could claim membership in the clan, and so could men descended through the female line. If a woman descended from a powerful chieftain married a man whose family was less well-connected, the sons of this union were likely to claim membership in their mother's clan. Conversely, the clan leader who provided best for his

71

clan members was able to recruit young men who were descendants
through a female line to join his retinue, young men who might have
become retainers in the household of their father's clan chieftain.

In general, in a bilateral kinship system maternity is often as socially
important as paternity, and may be of greater social significance if the
maternal line is of higher rank. (People then refer to "collateral branches"
of the powerful family.) There is thus less concern with preserving the
male lineage and typically less concern about premarital virginity and
marital fidelity of women. If a woman's family is more powerful than her
husband's family, the woman may have a good deal of sexual freedom, for
in such a situation maternity is the socially significant fact.

In the north of Europe there were two basic groups of people: the
Celts and the Germans. The Celts included the Gauls, the Scots, the
Welsh, the Irish, and the original Britons, among others. The Germanic
tribes included the Angles, Saxons, Danes, Swedes, and others as well as
ancestors of modern Germans. The Germanic tribes seem to have been
descended from the earlier "cattle people" who came with their herds
from the steppes of southwest Asia in a series of migrations beginning
sometime around 1500 B.C. The cattle people (often referred to as Aryan
from the language they spoke, but the term has been much abused) counted their wealth in cattle and serfs. The serfs were for the most part the
descendants of the neolithic farmers who were raising grain in northern
Europe when the Aryan cattle people came, conquered, and set themselves
up as a ruling class. Linton describes the family structure of the Aryan
people as follows: "Kin ties were reckoned on both sides of the house and
for as long as they could be remembered. This gave poor men and younger sons a wide range of choice among family groups to which they might
attach themselves. The most generous family head naturally drew the most
followers, and stinginess was the most contemptible vice with which an
Aryan noble could be charged" (1955:261).

The basic Aryan pattern, then, was one of bilateral kinship with a
certain amount of individual option in affiliating with a particular kinsman.
Careful preservation of the male lineage was not a factor in the social
structure of the Aryans. The marital patterns of the early Aryans are
described by Linton as follows:

> The early Aryan attitude toward sex and marriage . . . can best be described
> as casual. Although there was no recognized period of premarital ex-
> perimentation, as in Southeast Asia, little value was attached to virginity. An
> exchange of gifts usually accompanied marriage, but there seems to have
> been no formal bride price or dowry during the early period. Lacking such
> economic stabilizers, marriages were brittle. *A woman's ties to her own family
> were always regarded as stronger than her ties to her husband, and in case of a feud she
> was expected to side with them.* Marriage was normally monogamous, as it actual-
> ly is everywhere, but a rich or attractive man might have two or three wives.
> Women often took the initiative in cases of this sort, prefering a share in a

superior man to complete possession of an inferior man. (Linton 1955: 263; italics added)

Among the Aryan peoples, concubinage was an old tradition. Linton says that "concubines, taken from the serf population, were usual. Concubines and wives all lived in the Hall and their children were reared together. A common North European folklore motif of the hero's foster brother who resembles him so much that he can impersonate him is a memory of the days when the foster brother was really a half brother, son of a concubine" (1955:263).

Centuries later, concubinage was still common among both Germanic and Celtic peoples. In pagan Ireland, which Linton believes to have had a family structure similar to that of other Celtic groups, "the concubine relationship was often entered into for a year at a time, usually from May to May, and terminated at the end of the year unless renewed" (1955:360). The occasional modern author who puts forward an innovative plan for a short-term marriage contract with an option to renew might be startled to learn that the concept is as old as the halls of Tara.

The existence of concubinage did not set the sexual norms of northern Europe apart from those of the Mediterranean, where concubines were also common. What did distinguish the sexual norms of northern Europe was the relatively greater sexual freedom granted to women. The basis of this seems to have been the bilateral kinship system. Writing of the Aryan peoples, Linton states: "A woman derived her social position from her own kin group, with the result that wives not infrequently ranked their husbands. Such women not only dominated the household but had as much freedom as men in the distribution of their favors. Although polyandry was rarely institutionalized, a series of lovers do not seem to have been considered to a noblewoman's discredit" (1955:263). Perhaps Queen Guenevere of Camelot should be judged by such standards, and not by values of Semitic origin.

When the last of the Roman legions was pulled back to Gaul, the Celtic tribes of the British Isles retained a life-style that had been only lightly touched by Roman rule. The Germanic peoples on the Continent and in Scandinavia retained their own cultural patterns long after the fall of Rome. As the Church gradually converted these tribes between the fifth and eighth centuries, it discouraged concubinage. However, the northern Europeans retained many of their traditional sexual behaviors long after they had become Christian. Among the nobility, according to Linton, "Sex mores retained the old Aryan casualness. Aristocrats were expected to marry within their own caste to insure the legitimacy of their descendants, but no high degree of chastity was required either before or after marriage and the use of lower-class women in casual liaisons was taken for granted" (1955:265).

The sexual behavior patterns of Europe swung like a pendulum between the relaxed norms that had been traditional among the Celtic and

73

Germanic peoples and the double standard that had prevailed among the patrilineal Mediterranean peoples. Stephens observes: "European sex history seems to follow an uneven course. In some periods and places, restrictions were relaxed and there was a good deal of sexual freedom. This seems to have been true of castle life in the early Middle Ages and, later, of the salon society in renaissance Italy and France" (1963:259).

The aristocracy were prone to extramarital dalliance in part because of traditional northern attitudes, celebrated in epic and ballad, and in part because marriage was usually not to someone of a man's (or woman's) choice. Marriages were contracted by family elders, often when the prospective bride and groom were children. Until the late Middle Ages, marriage was an arrangement between families, a contract sealed by the transfer of lands and money, not by a religious ceremony. When the only institution concerned with marriage was the family, the critical factor in determining whether standards of sexual behavior were restrictive or permissive was the matter of how the preservation of the male lineage was regarded. When the Church became involved, questions of sin and of Church authority were raised as well.

It required several centuries for the Church to establish marriage as a sacrament rather than as a private matter between two families. The transformation of the marriage ceremony from a family feast to a religious ritual occurred gradually over a period of *three hundred years.* William Kephart comments:

> By the tenth century it had become customary for the wedding ceremony to be held at the *entrance* to the church, with the attendance of a member of the clergy required, the normal procedure being for the father of the bride to give her, formally, to the groom, thus signifying the transfer of authority from father to husband. By the thirteenth century the Church's control over marriage was virtually complete, the clergy having assumed the function of performing the ceremony. The father would formally relinquish control of the bride so that the priest could join the couple in marriage, a procedure which now took place *inside* the church.   (Kephart 1961:119)

Although the Church gained control of the power to marry persons, which included the power to determine what factors were impediments to marriage, (degrees of kinship, a prior marriage, and so forth), the family retained the right to arrange betrothals. This power was important to wealthy and powerful families, for marriage was the means of controlling the disposition of titles and lands.

As the feudal system crumbled, the practice of arranged marriage extended to the new merchant class. Parents might barter their daughter and a handsome dowry for a titled son-in-law. The right of the parents to arrange marriages for their children lasted until the late sixteenth century, and the size of the dowry and similar economic considerations were deemed more important than the appearance or even the age of the parties to the marriage. "Smallpox has not improved her looks," was the way a go-between described a prospective noble bride to an English prince anxious to make a political alliance. And a girl of twelve might be betrothed by her father to a wealthy man of sixty. Heirs who were orphaned while still minors were even worse off, for the Crown took them over as wards, and arranged marriages to the highest bidder.

But if young people pledged themselves to each other, such a betrothal was accepted by the Church as indissoluble, provided only that the boy was over fifteen and the girl over twelve. E. S. Turner (1954:43) states that "it was a matter of some chagrin to families angling for rich alliances that a young couple could upset carefully laid plans by betrothing themselves, without benefit of parents or clergy." Although the Church recognized these betrothals, it looked with disfavor on such clandestine agreements. "From time to time through the sixteenth century," according to Turner, "there were ecclesiastical blasts against those 'private and secret contracts' which were designed, in the Church's view, to permit the parties to indulge in 'unclean behavior' " (1954:45).

Some of the secret betrothals were in effect trial marriages. Common, although condemned by the Church, was a form of trial marriage referred to as *hand-fasting*, which may have been of Danish origin. It was also called *hand-in-fist betrothal*, and the name presumably refers to a part of the ritual. Sir Walter Scott described the Scottish version as follows:

> We Border men are more wary than your inland clowns of Fife and Lothian— no jump in the dark for us—no clenching the fetters around our wrists until we know how they will wear upon us—we take our wives, like our horses, upon trial. When we are hand-fasted, as we term it, we are man and wife for a year and a day—that space gone by each may choose another mate, or at their pleasure may call the priest to marry them for life—and this we call hand-fasting. (*The Monastery,* 1820)

The Church had another name for it.

Such customs seem to have persisted over centuries among the Celtic and Germanic peoples. When William the Conqueror came from France in the eleventh century he authorized ecclesiastical courts in England "which showed considerable zeal in arraigning fornicators and other incontinents" (Turner 1954:43). Five hundred years later, in the age of the first Elizabeth, moralists were still deploring the persistence of relaxed sexual norms in England. Thomas Nashe, an Elizabethan dramatist, wrote: "Go where you will in the suburbs and bring me two virgins that have vowed chastity and I'll build a nunnery." His contemporary, Alexander Niccholes, wrote that the "forward virgins of the day" were impatient to be rid of their chastity: "fourteen is the best time if thirteen be not better than that."

But what Church courts had not been able to do from the time of William to the days of the Tudors, the Calvinist Kirk Sessions of Scotland

75

began to accomplish in the late sixteenth century. Fornicators were punished for a first offense by imprisonment in the church steeple; a second offense meant a shaved head and the pillory. And in England, the Puritan tide was rising.

The Puritan code:
whipping and branding for "filthy dalliance"

The morality that we still call Puritan was not generated in the austere New English wilderness. It had its origins in the religious and political movement that was Puritanism in England. Like the early Christians, the Puritans were members of a persecuted sect, and their denial of the flesh was in part a symbol of dedication to the movement.

The Puritans under Oliver Cromwell considered themselves the saints of the seventeenth century, the Elect of God, in whose name they beheaded the king. Like most successful revolutionaries, they were ascetics. They channeled their passion into their love of God and the destruction of His enemies. As the celibacy of the early Christians was in part a response to the excesses of the decaying Roman Empire, so the asceticism of the Puritans was in part a response to the excesses of the decaying feudal order. The Royalists, the aristocratic enemy, indulged in behavior that the Puritans considered vice: gaming, wenching, bullbaiting. The sexual abandon of the royal court was a particular source of outrage for the Puritans. The revolutionary Puritans differentiated themselves from their enemies by cropping their hair and represssing their bodily desires: gluttony as well as fornication was sinful.

Not only were the Puritans a revolutionary religious sect, they were also the archetypes of the rising middle class. A good Puritan conserved his capital by thrift (in contrast to the profligate aristocrat) and he conserved his physical energy by continence. He wasted neither time nor substance on dalliance (in contrast to the aristocrat, for whom leisurely seduction was a way of life).

It was the age of mercantilism, when a London merchant might make a fortune in wool and buy a country estate, thus becoming a member of the landed classes. But the merchant soon found that the lands he had purchased, or the knighthood he had secured, did not open the doors through which titled *heirs* entered. It was the *hereditary* estate, the *hereditary* title, marks of aristocratic or noble lineage, that separated the aristocracy from the newly rich merchant class.

Not surprisingly, the rising merchant class sought to devalue lineage and to exalt the devotion to occupation that might raise a man of humble origins to great wealth. A man's work was his *calling*, as the Calvinists termed it. The Puritans believed that a man was called by God to his particular trade or profession, and devotion to that calling was thus a part of his devotion to God. It followed, then, that godliness could be measured by success in one's calling, and by wealth acquired through the virtues of thrift, diligence, and self-denial. It was at this point in time that occupation rather than lineage began to be the basis for social placement, that the individual rather than the family began to be the focus of concern. This elevation of the individual came to include concern with individual rights and liberties with regard not only to the dictates of the Pope and King, but to those of one's father as well.

Whereas the early Christians had believed that the Second Coming was at hand and had thus been more interested in preserving their souls than in procreating, the Puritans were concerned with the earthly as well as the heavenly future and thus with offspring. They were, however, less concerned with sons who would carry on the family name than with sons who would carry on the family enterprise. The Puritans thus did not advocate celibacy; rather they limited sex to marriage and, within marriage, to procreation. This was a single moral standard. The indulgence of the flesh was unacceptable for either sex.

Although the Puritans considered procreation a proper function of marriage, the conjugal relationship was not supposed to become too sensual, for a man's love for his wife was never to equal his love for God. Edmund Morgan (1958:12) writes: "The possibility of rivalry between these two kinds of love was no mere figure of speech, for the Puritan's religion was no desiccated moralism. The Puritan loved his God with all the sensual abandon he denied himself in dealing with the world." Unlike the early Christians, who often withdrew from the temptations of the city into a desert hermitage, the Puritans did not withdraw from the world. The founding of the New England colonies was not a flight into the wilderness to mortify the flesh. The Puritans had set themselves the more difficult task of living in the world, yet keeping their minds on God.

The Puritans who settled New England were members of a revolutionary religious movement, and their asceticism was central to their lives. John Winthrop, the first governor of the Massachusetts Bay Colony, was an exemplary Puritan. As a young country squire in England, John Winthrop had felt that he was too fond of a good dinner, too fond of taking his fowling piece and walking by the river for a little shooting, too fond of his wife, to please his Puritan conscience. But by the time he was forty, he had learned to contain his enjoyment of the pleasures of this world. His third wife, Margaret, first lady of the colony of Massachusetts, could write that a letter from him was as good as a sermon (Morgan 1958:13). Good Puritan Winthrop regarded a certain amount of affection for his wife as proper, but his passion was reserved for Heaven.

The Puritans believed that morality should be enforced by civil authority. Among the offenses against the public morality that were written into colonial law was kissing one's wife in public. "A classic example," according to Arthur Train, "is that of Captain Kemble, who returning home after a long voyage, kissed his wife on the front steps and was promptly lodged in the stocks" (1931:347). Marital sexuality was to be private, and for procreative purposes only. All extramarital relations were

77

forbidden, and men and women equally were punished for indulging the flesh. In most of the New England colonies, adultery was at one time a capital offense, as were bestiality and sodomy. Few people were executed for adultery; juries proved reluctant to impose the death penalty, perhaps remembering what Jesus had said about casting the first stone at an adultress. By the end of the seventeenth century, the punishment for adultery had been reduced to public whipping, branding on the face, and banishment. The Acts and Laws of the colony of Connecticut read, in part, as follows:

> Whosoever shall commit adultery with a Married Woman or one Betrothed to another Man, both of them shall be severely Punished, by Whipping on the naked Body, and Stigmatized or Burnt on the Forehead with the Letter A, on a hot Iron; and each of them shall wear a Halter about their Necks, on the outside of their Garments, during their Abode in this Colony, so as it may be Visible: And as often as either of them shall be found without their Halters, worn as aforesaid, they shall, upon Information, and Proof of the same, made before an Assistant or Justice of the Peace ... be Whipt, not exceeding Twenty Stripes.   (Quoted in Howard 1904:173)

Incest was punished in the same manner as adultery, except that the offender was branded on the forehead with the letter I instead of the letter A. Somewhat later, the scarlet letter sewn on the clothing was substituted for the letter branded on the face. In most of the New England colonies, fornication was less severely punished than were incest and adultery, especially if fornication occurred between betrothed persons. Even so, both husband and wife could expect a fine and a public whipping if their first child was born too soon. (If we still had the old colonial laws, about one out of every four brides— and her husband—would be publicly whipped.) According to Turner, "in the court records of New Haven, alternating with convictions for dodging military duty ... are listed whippings for 'filthy dalliance' and 'folly' " (1954:73). *Folly* was the euphemism for fornication. Women who were convicted of "unclean carriage" were sentenced to be "severely whipped on the naked body." In a society that forbade theatrical performance, the public whipping of naked women must have been a spectacular happening.

Permissive sexual norms: our eighteenth-century heritage

The Puritan power receded, as was perhaps inevitable. In England, the Puritan tide had ebbed: Cromwell was dead, the Puritans were defeated, and monarchy was restored. With the Restoration came a new wave of sexual permissiveness. The Puritans had closed the theaters—Shakespeare and Marlowe were lewd, in the Puritan view—but with the Restoration the theaters of London reopened with new and ribald vigor. Dalliance returned as the preferred pastime of the court, and all of the lesser social circles that rippled out from it. Restoration England delighted in sensual revels: masked balls, held in houses with secluded rooms where masked strangers could make love without revealing their identity; trysts in labyrinth gardens, designed as maze of high hedges with hidden corners where lovers could be readily concealed.

On the far side of the Atlantic, in the English colonies, puritanical norms relaxed. Only some of the immigrants had been Puritans. Moll Flanders may have been fictional, but she had real-life counterparts. English whores, thieves, debtors, and petty criminals were given the choice of going to the colonies as indentured servants or going to the workhouse. The transportation of prisoners to penal colonies in the New World was practiced for a time. Other immigrants included poor farm boys from Cornwall, Wales, or Ireland who brought old Celtic traditions from the back country. The younger sons of aristocratic families (who were barred from inheritance of family lands) might seek their fortune in the colonies, and they brought the attitudes of the Restoration dandy. Dutch immigrants in New York arrived with their own life-style, including traditional sexual norms.

A century after the Puritans had written their ascetic code into law, the common courtship custom of rural New Englanders was bundling, the practice of courting in bed. Bundling as a courtship custom will be described in a later chapter; the point to be made here is that a more permissive mode of sexual behavior had entered the American heritage. Bundling has been explained by some writers as mere expedience in a time when homes had no parlor or living room and there was almost no place to sit except the bed. It has also been attributed to the harsh New England winter, on the grounds that firewood was dear and the courting couple could keep warm in bed. It is probable, however, that bundling was more than a reaction to the weather or to a shortage of furniture.

It is more likely that bundling was a custom brought to the colonies by immigrants who were familiar with it elsewhere. Bundling was common in Wales; it was also practiced in other parts of the British Isles, especially in rural areas. Some historians credit the Dutch, who settled New York, with introducing bundling, which was similar to the rural courting customs of Holland. Whatever the origin of the custom, by the middle of the eighteenth century, bundling was widespread in God-fearing New England as well as in the middle colonies.

Throughout the frontier, common-law marriage was recognized, in part because there were few ministers in rural areas, and often few authorized judges or justices of the peace. William Kephart comments that "some couples dispensed with all formalities, both social *and* legal. Such marriages were referred to by a variety of terms, such as 'hand-fasting,' 'self-gifta,' or 'clandestine contracts,' and later as 'common-law marriages'" (1961:151). Here were the customs of the rural Celtic peoples— Scots, Welsh, Cornish, Irish—transplanted to America. Itinerant preachers deplored the premarital pregnancy, venereal disease, and general

79

sexual promiscuity of the up-country; their statements sound like the call to repentance with which the rural revival meeting traditionally begins, and these clergymen may not have been the most objective observers. But even if we make due allowance for the fervor of the preachers, it is still clear that sexual norms were permissive along the American frontier.

Indelicacy and the Victorian lady

The literary avant-garde in England had been preparing the mental set we call *Victorian* in the eighteenth century. The novel was a new literary form, and it was an influential medium. As Ian Watt (1957) has pointed out, Richardson's *Pamela* was a novel that created a stereotype. Pamela was a virtuous servant girl who fainted at the suggestion of seduction. After a number of well-timed fainting spells, she married her master (and would-be seducer), Mr. B. Pamela, this servant girl who refused to become her master's concubine and held out for a marriage above her station, became the model for what was called the New Woman.

From Saint Paul to Calvin and Knox, the Christian tradition had stressed the moral frailty of woman, the daughter of Eve. Long before the Christian era, the Greeks had blamed the existence of sin and misery in the world on the easily tempted Pandora. But the New Woman was to become the pillar of morality. If Pamela and her sisters were to tempt the "unregenerate Adam" in Mr. B. and his fellows, yet retain their virginity, women had to be either morally stronger than men or immune to desire. Nineteenth-century English and American women were supposed to be both. The word *indelicacy* was first used in *Pamela;* the novel set the usage for a period in which such words as "propriety, decency, modesty, delicacy, purity, came to have almost exclusively sexual connotation which they have since very largely retained" (Watt 1957:157). Chastity was once one virtue among others, including charity and piety. By the nineteenth century, virtue and chastity were synonyms.

The emergence of the New Woman was more than a response to literary fashion. People seize upon a model offered to them by literature or other media because they are looking for new modes of being, new responses to an altered environment. At the end of the eighteenth century, women needed a new set of norms because two changes had occurred in the social system that fundamentally altered the situation of women. The first was the disappearance of arranged marriage. This meant that a girl was free to accept or to reject a suitor, but it also left her with the necessity of enticing a prospective husband. One of the major reasons that arranged marriage ceased to be the custom was that the expense of a daughter's dowry had become almost ruinous, especially to a man with several daughters. Because the dowry had been a major means of attracting a suitable husband, the girl was left to find her own suitor with nothing but her person to offer. She had only her virginity (and whatever beauty she possessed) to barter for a good marriage.

The second social change that altered the situation of women was the change from a society that placed preservation of the family and lineage above the rights of the individual to a society in which the rights of the individual become the foundation of law and the ultimate social value. Economically, this was the change from feudalism to mercantile capitalism. When preservation of a lineage had been a primary social concern for the landed classes, marriage had been as much a joining of two families as a wedding of two persons. In that earlier era, the marriage of a gentleman to a servant girl would have been unthinkable; the precursors of Pamela could never have hoped to marry a master bent on seduction. A servant girl would have had nothing to offer the family of wealth and privilege in the days when parents chose a bride for their son. The most a beautiful servant could hope for was a stable arrangement as her master's concubine.

Marriage as a monogamous union: the rise and decline of the double standard

But the merchant was free to marry across class lines. The "self-made man" was not bound to the will of his father, for there was no inheritance to be cut off if he married against his family's wishes. Choosing for himself, he was more likely to fancy a beautiful girl. Being upwardly mobile, he had already crossed class lines himself and was likely to perceive the possibility of raising a girl to his station. Since that station depended on his achievement rather than on inherited rank and property, his wife's ancestry was less critical than her demeanor. If she could learn to act like a lady, she would be as socially acceptable as her husband (in those circles where lineage still mattered, her husband was not acceptable either). It was thus possible for a servant girl to aspire to marry her master. All other things being equal, a girl who could bring a dowry was greatly to be preferred. But a girl with nothing to bring to the marriage but her virgin beauty could hope to barter this for a husband.

It was not that the bride's virginity was required to ensure the purity of lineage. Her virginity was valued by the rising merchant more as an exclusive property right. The upwardly mobile merchant or industrialist was highly conscious of property; unable to be proud of his lineage, he was proud of his possessions. The merchant's wife *belonged* to him; her virginity before marriage and her chastity after marriage were marks of his exclusive option on her sexual favors.

Earlier in northern Europe, a woman retained the status of her own family when she married, so that she had rank in her own right, and might even outrank her husband. As noted above, such a woman often enjoyed a good deal of sexual freedom. When lineage declined as the basis of social position, occupation became the basis of social status for men, and a woman's status came to depend on that of her husband. Thus it was not possible for a wife to outrank her husband. The resulting constraints on women were comparable to those placed on women in earlier societies structured by a rigid patrilineal and patriarchal system. If Pamela had been divorced by Mr. B., she would have plummeted back to her former status as a servant.

There was almost no alternative to marriage for a woman. Those occupations open to women in the eighteenth and nineteenth centuries were of the most menial kind. A woman could be a domestic servant in a large household, a textile-mill worker, a coal miner, or a prostitute. The Industrial Revolution occurred in England in the last quarter of the eighteenth century. Textile mills, steel mills, and coal pits offered the first industrial employment. Before that time, women of the English working class were able to earn a living of sorts by spinning in their homes (hence the term *spinster*, although married as well as single women were spinsters in the original sense of the term).

By 1785, however, the development of power looms and spinning mills powered by water or steam marked the end of the cottage textile industry and the beginning of the factory system. Men resisted going into the mills to work. They saw little difference between the factory and the workhouse, which was the most common penal institution of that time. Women and children provided most of the factory labor in the early decades of the Industrial Revolution.

Women went into the mills—and the coal pits—but only out of extreme economic necessity. The conditions of the textile mills were unhealthy. Ceilings were low to conserve space; cotton fluff and moisture filled the air in the unventilated and crowded rooms. Dysentery was common, and the "factory fever" swept through the workers in epidemic form. Tuberculosis and other lung diseases were endemic in the mills and mines. Foremen took sexual advantage of their economic power over young women and little girls who worked in the mills, assuming that females of the working class were debauched and promiscuous, and thus fair game.

If a woman had any choice, she did not go to work in the mills. The coal pits were worse. For most women, marriage represented the best possible situation. For a woman born into a middle-class or upper-class family, there was no occupation (except perhaps governess to the children of an aristocratic family) that would not have caused a precipitous drop in her living standard and social position. The English nunneries had been closed since the Reformation, so this refuge for single women was gone. By the time Victoria took the throne in 1837, the women of the middle and upper classes in England had no economic function and no acceptable alternative to marriage. A marriageable woman was a virgin or a virtuous widow; a married woman did not dare risk her husband's wrath by unchaste behavior.

Prudery and brothels: the double standard in America

Most American men were self-employed in the nineteenth century, and most of their wives were unpaid workers in the family enterprise. Because women in the nineteenth century had few alternatives to marriage, they were in no position to complain about their husband's behavior. The poor man could not afford a mistress, and was more likely to seek diversion in the saloon than the brothel. But even if a man spent the rent money on whiskey and women, his wife had little choice but to stay with him.

American women of the merchant classes in the nineteenth century were absolutely dependent on their husbands, not only for social position but for economic support as well. The husband controlled any property that his wife might inherit, so even wealth inherited from her father seldom meant economic independence for a woman. (Legal reforms in the latter part of the nineteenth century in America finally gave married women control of the property they inherited.) The women of this class had no role in the economy other than the one that Thorstein Veblen termed "vicarious consumption," display of the husband's wealth. But as Veblen pointed out, those who consume vicariously must never be too comfortable. The ladies of the propertied middle and upper classes wore hoops and stays, and were forbidden to indulge themselves; they were to show that they engaged in no productive labor by performing charitable deeds publicly and visibly.

The fact that the wife of a successful American merchant, banker, or mill owner was a lady of leisure did not mean that she was free to indulge in languid dalliance, like the European women of an earlier leisure class. The wealthy American woman in the nineteenth century derived her social status and her economic position from her husband, and she did not dare risk an affair that might end in discovery and divorce; she would have been ruined in every sense of the word. Conversely, the economically dependent wife was in no position to object to her husband's extramarital adventures. The result was prudery—the pretense by proper ladies that sex did not exist.

The age of prudery was an age of elaborate euphemism. A pregnant woman was "in the family way" (if her condition was referred to at all). Undergarments were "unmentionables." When fowl was carved at table, people asked for "white meat" or "dark meat," so that no lady need speak or hear such coarse words as *leg,* or *breast,* or *thigh.* The heavy-legged Victorian tables were decorously draped, lest they remind a man of what might be concealed by a woman's billowing garments. Captain Frederick Marryat, one of the assorted visitors to America who recorded his observations of that era, wrote that even the legs of pianos might be covered with crinoline pantalets, "for decency's sake" (cited in Hays 1964:212).

The wife of the nineteenth-century merchant prince was almost as confined to her Victorian mansion as the classical Greek wife had been to the women's quarters of an Athenian household. Nineteenth-century America was neoclassical in sex as well as in architecture. In the age when banks were built to look like Grecian temples, American women were divided into the same two classes as Greek women of the classical period: "good" women and whores. As wealth came to the American merchant class, the brothels became opulent. Nell Kimball, who came to New Orleans from St. Louis in the 1880s and opened an elegant three-story

83

*New Orleans, 1912. In the age of prudery, American women were divided into two
classes: "good" women and whores. As wealth came to the American merchant class,
the brothels became opulent.*

"sporting house" on Basin Street, wrote in her memoirs: "You can say you
never saw better people in any place in town. I had put in a lot of Venice
glass over the gas jets and drapes of blood-red velvet reaching to the floor
... The silver and the dishes were heavy and good. Wine came in dirty
bottles with the right labels" (quoted in Longstreet 1965:166).

The prudery of the nineteenth century in America was an effort to
reconcile the existence of a *de facto* double standard with the single,
puritanical standard that was the *de jure* sexual code. A *de jure* code is one
that is written law. Adultery was a ground for divorce in every state—the
old Puritan code, mellowed somewhat from the days when adultery was

punished by branding, whipping, or even hanging. But few nineteenth-century American wives exercised their legal right to divorce an adulterous husband. The economic dependency of the wife meant that she had no realistic alternative to an unhappy marriage; legally, she could ask for a divorce if she could prove that her husband kept a mistress, but practically she could not. The social stigma placed on the divorced woman was high, and thus remarriage was unlikely. Even if she had received enough alimony to support herself, she would have forfeited her good name and her social position. Even though she had asked for the divorce and legally was the injured party, socially it would have been whispered that she must not have been all that she should. The woman might win in court, but she lost in the community. On balance, it was the woman who lost most. So the nineteenth-century wife usually preferred to pretend that she knew nothing of her husband's extramarital adventures, while not daring to risk scandal by her own behavior.

Unlike the double standard of antiquity, which rested on the imperatives of the patrilineal kinship system, the double standard of the age of prudery rested on two foundations, one economic and the other psychological: the first was the economic dependency of women on their husbands; the second was the assumption that women had no sexual desire and submitted to their husbands as a matter of duty. The first prop of the double standard meant that women were powerless to protest their husband's behavior; the second made the double standard something that wives could endure emotionally and that the errant husband could rationalize without guilt. If it was assumed that a woman who was a *good* woman was without sexual desire, then she could be expected to look the other way if her husband took a mistress. The wife would have less of the distasteful sexual duty to perform, and it could be assumed that the wife herself would have no interest in a lover.

Prudery was an attempt to reconcile values that were irreconcilable by concealing what everyone knew but did not want to admit. As long as a husband showed his concern for his wife's feelings by being discreet, she could ignore what she was powerless to change, and take what solace she could from the knowledge that many other wives were in the same situation. The double standard and the implicit bargain that supported it could last only as long as there were two kinds of women defined by the social norms, and only as long as the "virtuous" women remained economically dependent and repelled by sex. These circumstances began to change in the early decades of the present century.

The decline of the double standard

As described in an earlier chapter, white-collar employment for women gradually increased after World War I, and such employment opened legitimate alternatives to marriage for women of the middle classes. The White-Collar Girl was the subject of a number of American novels; these

85

Lawyer Albert G. Zimmerman and his secretary, Jennie Nelson, in the Zimmerman law office in Madison, Wisconsin, about 1898. At that time most secretaries were male; Jennie Nelson was a rare exception. By 1920, however, white-collar employment had been opened to women and provided an alternative to marriage for women of the middle classes.

fictional heroines both reflected and shaped the reality of the women who worked in the offices of America. C. Wright Mills analyzed the sociological significance of Booth Tarkington's *Alice Adams* as follows:

> The story of Alice Adams—sociologically the most acute of these novels—is a story of aspirations being whittled down to white-collar size. It opens with Alice going to a party at the home of an upper-class family; it ends with her climbing the darkened stairway of a business college, like a girl taking the nun's veil, after frustration in love and social aspiration. Throughout the book, lurking in the background like a slum by a gold coast, the "begrimed stairway" of the business college is seen by Alice, with a "glance of vague misgiving," as a road to "hideous obscurity." When Alice thinks of it, she thinks of "pretty girls turning into withered creatures as they worked at typing machines"; old maids, "taking dictation" from men with double chins, a dozen different kinds of old maids "taking dictation." The office is a production plant for old maids, a modern nunnery. The contrast is between the business college and the glamorous stage, or the profitable, early, lovely marriage. (Mills 1951:201)

Such novels were in fact cautionary tales; girls were supposed to continue to regard marriage as the first and most desirable choice, and to fear above all else that they might end by becoming an "old maid." Still, the White-Collar Girl was fascinating because she was a *third* kind of woman. By 1920 there were "good" women, "bad" women, and "career" women, and American society made an ambiguous moral judgment of the third group. But if a career for women was perceived as a poor second to a good marriage, it came to be viewed as preferable to a poor marriage. A woman could escape an unhappy marriage without becoming a "fallen woman," and she might choose never to marry at all without having to become a dependent spinster in her father's household. As economic alternatives to marriage increased for women, one of the supports of the double standard—the economic dependence of women on men—began to weaken.

Meanwhile, the norms that tacitly accepted the existence of two kinds of women came under attack. Agitation against the saloon and brothel was a part of the early feminist movement; alcohol and venereal disease became political issues. During World War I, the federal government put pressure on local governments to close brothels within a five-mile radius of any military base. Prostitution did not disappear, but it did become clandestine, and openly elegant houses were closed. Nell Kimball describes the closing of "Storyville" (as the brothel district in New Orleans had been known) in August of 1917. Having given a farewell party for preferred customers, she writes: "Midnight I stood under the big hall chandelier, some of its crystals gone, and we all had the last drink of flat champagne ... One old gentleman at the party, a judge, he began to cry ... and the professor, the real one, gave a long spiel about Rome falling down, which didn't make much sense to me" (quoted in Longstreet 1965: 252–253).

Around the time of World War I, an influential gynecologist of the time wrote: "The majority of women (happily for society) are not very much troubled with sexual feelings of any kind" (quoted in Robinson 1959:10). Such pronouncements reflected the then prevailing assumption that "nice" women found sex a distasteful duty, an assumption that was one of the supporting pillars of the double standard. It was little more than a decade later, however, that the upper-middle-class Americans discovered Freud. What was once called Virtue was renamed Frigidity.

The change in sexual attitudes after World War I reflected the improved education of the upper-middle-class and the upper-class women and their increasing economic independence. But women of this class did not overcome frigidity in defiance of their husbands; for the most part it was their husbands whom they wanted to please. In large part, the change in sexual norms derived from a change in the life-style and composition of the American upper middle class. At the turn of the century, most men of the upper middle class were the *owners* of prosperous businesses and financial enterprises. (The owners of marginal enterprises were, by their

87

very marginality, located farther down the social class scale.) These prosperous merchants and bankers derived their economic and social power
in large measure from their rootedness in a community. People traded or
banked with them because they knew them personally and perhaps had
known their fathers before them. These were men who had close and
continuing relationships with a wide circle of friends and relatives and who
found their deepest belonging in the exclusively masculine fellowship of
a lodge or private club. They were often fond of their wives, but seldom
communicated with them as equals.

In the 1890s, professional men and salaried managers were a small
minority in America. By the 1920s, however, the *salaried* executive (as
contrasted to the *owner*-executive) had become a more familiar figure, and
the number of salaried managers grew rapidly over the next several
decades as small, family-owned companies failed or were merged with
large corporations. The managerial middle class, especially at the upper
levels, was increasingly a salaried class. This "new" middle class had a
mobile existence when contrasted with the geographic stability of the
"old" middle class of entrepreneurs. It tended to be more urban and
suburban than the "old" middle class, which remained embedded in the
small cities it had dominated for a generation or more. The "new" middle
class was marked by the kind of mobile urban existence that disrupts
intimate relationships outside the conjugal family (a point which is developed in some detail in Chapter 2), and the men of this class tended to seek
more emotional satisfaction in their marriages than did men of the "old"
middle class.

Men of the "new" middle class sought to make marriage as rewarding as possible, which meant that as the "new" middle class grew, more
men began to want greater intimacy with their wives, both at the emotional
and the sexual level. They wanted their wives to be sexually responsive.
Husbands who wanted to awaken their wives sexually, wives who wanted
to discover the secret of achieving orgasm, sought assistance from the
sexual encyclopedias that were published in the 1920s. These books were
filled with pedantic detail and cumbersome Latin terms that the reader
might discover (after laborious perusal of the glossary) meant something
like "tickle the armpits." Cross sections of the female anatomy appeared,
with numbered arrows indicating erogenous zones: drawings with the
erotic appeal of a medical textbook crossed with a mail-order catalogue.
There may have been couples who followed the instructions to the last
numbered detail. Such sex must have had the spontaneity of an old-fashioned dancing class with both partners watching their feet while stepping
through the numbered squares. Still, for all the pedantry and self-con-
scious response, the era brought an acceptance of female sexuality. Once
again Pandora had opened the box; Eve had bitten into the apple and
found it tasty.

The women of the upper middle class could afford private gynecologists as well as psychotherapists, and were introduced to new birth control

techniques by the 1930s. Contraception removed the fear of unwanted pregnancy, and wives began to think of sex as an act of mutual passion rather than as a distasteful marital duty. But having been raised by mothers who held nineteenth-century views, many of these women found it difficult to achieve their new ideal of sensuality. No book of instructions can reach the level of the mind where fears and taboos were implanted at the age of two or three years. Changes in the sexual norms of the upper middle class have taken place gradually over a half-century and are not yet complete. The older women of this class tend to be conservative, politically and sexually. Some are still nearly Victorian in their views of sex, especially those living in small towns.

The younger women of the middle classes have come to expect sexual activity to be a pleasurable experience. If it is not, they are beginning to seek professional counseling. There was a time when a woman who found sexual intercourse unpleasant or painful was considered virtuous; a generation ago such a woman was labeled frigid; today she is simply considered preorgastic. With time and counseling, any woman can learn to achieve orgasm.

Women of the "new" middle class tend to be the most liberal in their general world view, and to expect a certain amount of sexual freedom. In a study of upper-middle-class "significant Americans," John Cuber and Peggy Harroff found a tendency for wives to feel like the one who remarked: "I'd say my husband and I love each other—we just don't own each other" (1965:156). The statement is a pithy summary of the emerging norms of this class, which has been moving away from the double standard and toward a single standard of permissiveness. The changes in sexual expectation that occurred within the upper-middle class during the 1920s and 1930s had reached younger members of the working class by the 1950s. The sexual permissiveness that was becoming acceptable in the "new" middle class in the 1960s seems to have filtered throughout the class structure, at least among persons under twenty years of age, by 1975.

The annual survey of attitudes of college freshmen sponsored jointly by the American Council on Education and the University of California at Los Angeles included in the 1975 fall survey entering freshmen at 75 two-year colleges, 247 four-year colleges, and 44 universities throughout the United States. Most of the entering freshmen were recent high school graduates; 73.6 percent were eighteen years old, and 94.1 percent were under twenty years of age. It should be noted that because these were entering freshmen, the attitudes and beliefs they expressed do not reflect the influence of college education, but rather were acquired before they enrolled. Astin, who conducted the survey, reports that there are still differences between men and women in their attitudes toward sexual behavior: nearly two thirds (65.0 percent) of the men but only about one third (33.2 percent) of the women agreed that it is "all right for people who like each other to have sex" (cited in Watkins 1976:3). When asked about their objectives in life, 56.2 percent of the men and 57.1 percent of the women indicated that "raising a family" was "essential" or "very important." At the same time, more than half of the men (53.7 percent) and about two out of five women (41.2 percent) in the freshman class of 1975 agreed with the statement that "couples should live together before marriage" (cited in Watkins 1976:3).

Not all those who agree that a practice is acceptable actually engage in that practice, but it is clear that it is becoming increasingly common for Americans to live together before marriage, and that not all such unions lead to marriage. "Living together" is the common term for what is more formally referred to as a *consensual union:* a phrase that implies that while the two may live as a mated pair, they have not sought formal sanction from state or church.

Most consensual unions are as monogamous as most American marriages. However, a few informal unions involve plural mates. Perhaps the most frequent plural union is the group composed of one man and two bisexual women. (The French have a phrase for it: *ménage à trois.*) Such relationships are sometimes entered with quasi-formal vows and the ceremony and trappings of a wedding. However, group marriage, or any form of polygamy, is illegal in all states. The courts have consistently held that the person who marries more than one spouse (without dissolving the prior marriage) is guilty of bigamy. Robert Drinan, S. J., comments that: "On four occasions in the last century, the Supreme Court of the United States denied every claim of the Mormons to practice polygamy in the name of religion" (1969:51).

If there is no bigamous marriage, but merely an arrangement between the persons and their multiple mates, the group may still be breaking the law. They are living in an adulterous relationship if two of them are legally married but other mates are living with them. If none of them is married, the law may define their living arrangement as lewd cohabitation. But since laws against fornication and adultery are only sporadically enforced, such persons are unlikely to be subject to prosecution. In most states, any children born to women other than the legal wife in such multiple-mate relationships would be illegitimate, although the father would be responsible for their support.

Monogamy and the double standard in America: a summary

There are three sexual traditions that enter the mainstream of American sexual norms: the Puritan code, the more permissive sexual code of northern Europe, and the double standard of morality that characterized Mediterranean cultures. The Puritan code is a slightly modified version of the celibate ideal of the early Christians. This standard is one of abstinence until marriage for *both* sexes, with no extramarital sexuality condoned. Within marriage, sex is expected to be for procreation rather than for pleasure. That is our Puritan heritage. The marriage vows are taken by husband and wife alike: "forsaking all others," they are pledged to life-long monogamy. From the founding of New England to our own time, this has been the recognized sexual standard in America: a single standard of monogamy that prohibits all sexual intercourse except that between husband and wife.

The covert patterns of our culture spring from other sources and run counter to the Puritan tradition of chaste monogamy. The northern European tradition was predominantly one of premarital permissiveness between those who were pledged to marry, and sexual permissiveness for men and for women of high rank. The custom of bundling was part of this tradition, as were various forms of common-law marriage, and these were brought to the colonies shortly after the Puritan code. Such customs fit the conditions of frontier life and the value placed on individualism. Circuit riders and other itinerant ministers admonished, then joined in wedlock, couples who had long been cohabiting. For a man and woman to pledge themselves to each other without benefit of clergy was in accordance with long-standing custom, but because it ran counter to the official moral code, a man might speak of "making an honest woman" of his common-law wife. Because the laws of some states accommodated both traditions, we have today the seeming contradiction of laws that require premarital physical examinations, waiting periods, and marriage licenses, yet recognize common-law marriages that were preceded by none of these.

The third sexual tradition in American culture is the ancient double standard that was derived from the requirements of a patrilineal kinship system; it runs under the surface of our sexual norms, but it has always been a strong current. The nineteenth century brought a new version of patriarchal power, based on property rather than lineage, and a resurgent double standard. The double standard in America never had the legitimate status of the ancient double standard, but it was widespread. The nineteenth-century merchant princes kept mistresses in lavish splendor. But because the official morality was that of the puritanical single standard of repressed sensuality, the wives of such men pretended not to know about their husbands' affairs. It was this conflict between the strict monogamy that was still the recognized sexual code and the *de facto* double standard that created the inner contradictions of prudery. This, and the fact that, with the disappearance of the dowry, all a woman had to offer a husband was the very sex that she was supposed to despise.

Most discussion of the sexual revolution is focused on premarital and extramarital sex. But perhaps one of the most basic changes in the sexual life of Americans is within the marital relationship. As the emotional needs of individuals have become more concentrated on the conjugal relationship, the sexual component of that relationship has changed character. We no longer expect a wife to be dismayed by her husband's advances, or to endure his embraces dutifully; the idea of a mutually rewarding sexual experience has become the accepted norm for a large segment of the middle class and has begun to be accepted by the younger, better-educated members of the working class. Because marriage is no

91

longer an economic necessity for most American women, we are coming to expect marriage to be intrinsically rewarding for both husband and wife. The intimate relationship is one of the principal rewards of marriage for both sexes, and marital intimacy is founded on, although by no means restricted to, a satisfying sexual relationship.

We have reversed the value priorities that the Puritans placed on marital sex. The Puritans believed that the only legitimate function of sex was procreation within marriage, and that it was wrong for a man to be too sensually involved with his wife. Like avarice and gluttony, lust took a man's mind from heaven, even when the lust was for his wife. In our time, the pressures of burgeoning population have led to the widespread conviction that procreation should be limited, that the large family threatens the general welfare and is a personal indulgence that the world can no longer afford. Conversely, the enjoyment of marital sex has come to be regarded as an important part of the emotional bond between husband and wife, and thus as a stabilizing factor in marriage. Because stable marriages are perceived as the foundation of a stable society by most Americans, the belief is growing that satisfying marital sex serves the needs of the individual, of the marriage, and of the society.

References

Cuber, John F., with Peggy B. Harroff. 1965. *The Significant Americans.* New York: Appleton-Century-Crofts.

Drinan, Robert F., S. J. "American Laws Regulating the Formation of the Marriage Contract." *Progress in Family Law: The Annals of the American Academy of Political and Social Science* 383 (May):48–57.

Farber, Bernard. 1964. *Family: Organization and Interaction.* San Francisco: Chandler Publishing Company.

Hays, H. R. 1964. *The Dangerous Sex.* New York: G. P. Putnam's Sons.

Howard, George. 1904. *A History of Matrimonial Institutions,* vol. II. Chicago: University of Chicago Press.

Kephart, William M. 1961. *The Family, Society, and the Individual.* Boston: Houghton Mifflin Company.

Linton, Ralph. 1955. *The Tree of Culture.* New York: Alfred A. Knopf.

Longstreet, Stephen. 1965. *Sportin' House: A History of the New Orleans Sinners and the Birth of Jazz.* Los Angeles: Sherbourne Press.

Mills, C. Wright. 1951. *White Collar: The American Middle Class.* New York: Oxford University Press.

Morgan, Edmund S. 1958. *The Puritan Dilemma: The Story of John Winthrop.* Boston: Little, Brown and Comapany.

Robinson, Marie N. 1959. *The Power of Sexual Surrender.* New York: Doubleday and Company.

Stephens, William N. 1963. *The Family in Cross-Cultural Perspective.* New York: Holt, Rinehart and Winston.

Train, Arthur. 1931. *Puritan's Progress.* New York: Charles Scribner's Sons.

Turner, E. S. 1954. *A History of Courting.* New York: E. P. Dutton & Company.

Watkins, Beverly T. 1976. "This Year's Freshmen Reflect New Views of Women's Role." *The Chronicle of Higher Education* (January 12):3–4.

Watt, Ian. 1957. *The Rise of the Novel.* Berkeley: University of California Press.

Suggested readings

Aiken, Conrad. 1934, 1960. "Thistledown." In *The Collected Short Stories of Conrad Aiken.* New York: Harcourt, Brace Jovanovich. The central theme of this well-crafted short story is derived from the double standard as it existed in America in the early 1930s. The narrator is a middle-aged, upper-middle-class male who becomes obsessed by his feelings—compounded of desire, disgust, and sympathy—for the young woman his wife hires as a secretary. This young woman is the "thistledown" of the story, floating from man to man. The narrator has a brief affair with the young, gray-eyed girl who is less innocent than she seemed, and who refuses to let him make a Great Romance out of their romp. She leaves for New York, where the narrator continues to see her from time to time; casual affairs are depicted as ruining the woman but not demeaning the male narrator. The story was not intended to be sardonic. Times and mores change, and the fact that the moral of this story may seem quaint to a reader in the 1970s is an indication of how far the double standard has declined in America in the last half-century.

Bernard, Jessie. 1972. *The Sex Game.* New York: Atheneum. An influential sociologist (and woman) looks at the myths surrounding sexuality, and discusses a variety of culturally created subsexes, both male and female. Enlightening and provocative.

Longstreet, Stephen. 1965. *Sportin' House: A History of the New Orleans Sinners and the Birth of Jazz.* Los Angeles: Sherbourne Press. A history of both prostitution and jazz in New Orleans, incorporating portions of the memoirs of some famous New Orleans madams. The double standard rested on prudery and prostitution; this is an account of both, filled with historical details such as the origin of the term "hooker."

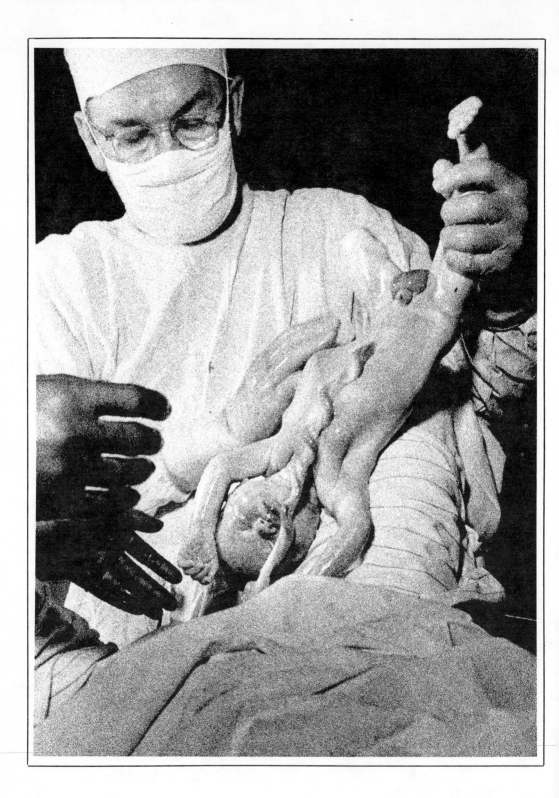

4

Marriage as a procreating union: fertility and family planning

Men and women have always longed for both fertility and sterility, each at its appointed time and in its chosen circumstances. This has been a universal aim, whether people have always been conscious of it or not.

Norman E. Himes (1936)

Children are the future, and in a society structured by kinship, children are the future of one's lineage, not of some vague abstraction called society. In the preindustrial world, children are also the source of the future well-being of their parents. As soon as the children of the rural poor are past the toddler stage, their labor contributes to the family larder. Another mouth to feed is also another pair of hands to help. Once grown, children are expected to provide for their aged parents. In countries such as India, progeny serve in lieu of social security or an old-age pension; a man who has no son cannot even be certain that he will have a proper burial. In such a society a childless marriage is a real disaster, even if the society as a whole is reeling under the burden of overpopulation.

In the last few years, Americans have become aware of the dangers of overpopulation: the press of the people on resources and the probability of world famine if human fecundity is not checked. It is less widely recognized that there can be problems of underpopulation as well, and that societies have often been precariously balanced on the thin line between too many and too few.

Procreation and population: the world before the Pill

When all humanity lived by hunting game and gathering roots and fruit, people lived in small groups; four or five families moved from campsite to campsite on their ancestral hunting territory, finding game and fruit in season. If there were too many people, all became weakened by hunger, and at the end of a hard winter or a long drought only the strongest survived. If there were too few people, disease or an invading enemy could wipe out the entire band.

When game was plentiful, the upper limit of population was about fourteen people per square mile of hunting territory, perhaps two hundred in the band (Linton 1956:150). In a less favorable environment, the maximum group size was probably closer to fifty, including young children, who were the future of the tribe, and old people, whose memories were the only source of information on such vital matters as where water was found in the last great drought or what herbs eased the fever that decimated the group a generation earlier. If the band were to include enough able-bodied hunters and warriors to feed and defend the rest, its numbers could not drop much below the maximum its land could support. Human populations, like the populations of game on which they lived, probably waxed and waned with climatic cycles, but the range between too many and too few was narrow.

When a tribe grew too large for its hunting grounds, a group of young people might split off and go in search of new territory, perhaps returning to the ancestral home for ceremonial occasions. The migrations that peopled the Western Hemisphere, for example, were probably a search for new lands by small bands who had been crowded out at home, bands that moved outward in expanding waves every few generations. But when people ceased to be rare animals, the neighboring territory might already be occupied, and an invasion of hunting grounds was cause for war. The group could not so readily dispose of excess population by sending a group of young people off in search of new hunting grounds.

Nor were improved hunting techniques, new traps or new weapons, the answer. More effective weapons or traps could mean more food for a time; then the herds of game would simply be reduced. Hunters, like all predators, had to live within the balance of nature. If too many animals were killed, the food supply of the hunters was depleted, and shortly the population of hunters declined.

When men hunted, women gathered roots, fruit, and edible plants. It is probable that women developed agriculture, the first great technological revolution. Agriculture meant that an increased amount of food could be obtained from the same territory. Producers could support a larger population than predators, and an agricultural village might have ten times the population of a hunting band. In good years a surplus of grain could be harvested and stored to ease the hunger of the lean years, so the population of agricultural people could be both larger and more stable.

But there was still an upper limit on the number of persons who could be fed by a given area of land tilled by hoes and fertilized by ashes. Surplus sons and daughters might move down the valley or across the river to open new lands to farming, but this came to mean trespassing on the lands of other people, who were likely to regard the immigrants as invaders. With agriculture came war.

The limits of population were somewhat wider for agricultural people than for hunting tribes, but limits there were. Too many people meant that all would be malnourished and that famine would periodically reduce their numbers. Several years of drought or insect plagues could deplete the food reserves of an agricultural village, and if it had grown too large, famine was the inevitable result. Yet if there were too few people, disease or warfare might destroy the entire society. From Easter Island to the English downs, stone monuments stand as silent reminders of people who lost the numbers game.

It was easier for early societies to reduce their population than to increase it. Primitive knowledge of contraceptives was limited by modern standards, but abortion and infanticide were checks to population growth. A mother could not take care of a newborn infant while his brother was still a toddler, clinging to her back as she searched the ravines for edible roots and berries. Many tribes had religious beliefs that made it easier to do what had to be done for the survival of the group. Totemic belief in an endless cycle of life, in which spirits lived alternate lives in human form and as a deer or frog or kangaroo, was common in many primitive tribes. Belief in reincarnation made it possible for a mother to take her newborn, to whom she had not yet become emotionally attached, to a spot sacred to

97

*Known as the Venus of Willendorf and presently reposing in the Naturhistorisches
Museum in Vienna, this fertility figure dates from approximately 15,000 B.C. The
distorted anatomy of the Venus presumably was intended to convey the importance
of female fertility and in some manner to enhance the reproductive power of the
human population and perhaps also that of game animals.*

his totem animal and leave him there to live another life in animal form,
asking him to be born to her again when she could care for him.

But when there were too few children, when women had miscarriage
after miscarriage, when stillbirths and infant mortality claimed a large
number of the children carried full term, people worried about the future.
The continued existence of the tribe and their own old-age security de-

pended on the survival of enough children through the years of high infant mortality to ensure that a sufficient number would live to become the next generation of adults. Thus, in the past, people were more concerned with fecundity than with family planning.

The ancients believed that *all* living things could increase endlessly. Fertility rites were supposed to ensure abundance for all life: plant, animal, and human. The gods who sent mouths would send meat. Contrary to popular modern fantasy, fertility cults did not involve year-round sexual orgies. The primitive belief in sympathetic magic—that is, the belief that what people do in imitation of nature will cause the desired cosmic event—was the basis of fertility rites. The sun was perceived as the male element in nature, the earth as the female. The rhythm of the seasons was repeated in human life. In autumn, when the earth was barren and the generative powers of the sun apparently failing, men were expected to be continent, to conserve their own sexual energies and thus, by sympathetic magic, to conserve the strength of the dying sun. Once safely past the winter solstice, when it was certain that the sun had renewed vigor, men could safely indulge their pent-up passion. By our calendar, this would have been in late December and early January. (A few scattered fertility symbols remain to our contemporary post-solstice holiday season: the druidic mistletoe and the office Christmas party.)

When the spring equinox was past, seed was placed in the earth. The act of planting was regarded as an impregnation of the earth and was repeated in human sexual rites, which were expected by sympathetic magic to ensure the fertility of the earth on whose fecundity all life depended. (Sperm was referred to as "seed" in the Middle East, and children were the "fruit" of their mother's womb.) From the rounded stones set up in the land of Canaan to represent the phallus of the sun-god Baal to the smooth sticks celebrated as the Maypole in northern Europe, phallic symbols were worshipped, not for themselves but for the generative power they represented.

In many cultures, the goddess of fertility has also been the goddess of death: the Hindu Kali, the Greek Persephone, the Sumerian Lilith, goddesses who smiled alike on the creation and on the destruction of life. *They were symbols of a population balance achieved through high fertility countered by high mortality.* Many were born, but few survived to adulthood. The Earth Mother devoured her children and nowhere more greedily than in the cities of ancient civilizations. The ancient city was a population sink that drained the surplus sons and daughters from outlying farming villages. Heaped together inside the walled cities, they died young and few of their children survived. The city was a pesthole; glided temples rose out of streets with open sewers and even the priests had lice.

When human population was sparse, each tribe that survived acquired immunities to the diseases that were endemic in its isolated valley in the mountains or its remote corner of the plain. There were few new sources of infectious disease. But with civilization came trade and warfare,

99

and contact between previously isolated peoples. People from all parts of the known world met in the capitals of ancient empires and traded goods, ideas, genes, and germs. A disease that had been a mild illness in its place of origin often became a raging pestilence as it spread into areas where it had never been known. Epidemics became more virulent as they swept rapidly through crowded, filthy cities, through dense populations with no resistance.

Whereas famine was the regulator of population, plagues depopulated entire regions and sometimes left too few people to sustain a society. Cities were abandoned because of plague; farmland became wasteland. About A.D. 250 one of a series of plagues swept the Roman Empire. Probably a combination of diseases, perhaps meningitis and dysentery, this pestilence spread panic and death from Egypt to Scotland and then doubled back with renewed virulence. Farms as well as cities were abandoned as the living fled the epidemic. Ditches silted up and became stagnant ponds; fertile fields that the ditches had formerly drained became swampy wasteland; mosquitoes thrived and malaria began to take its toll. After this plague, "even in the centre of Italy, large territories became vacant; swamps developed, and rendered unhealthy the formerly wholesome coast lands of Etruria and Latium. Hieronymus writes that the human race had been 'all but destroyed,' and that the earth was returning to a state of desert and forests" (Zinsser 1935:140–141).

The human race was not destroyed by the plague, but the Roman Empire never recovered its vigor. Some three centuries later, the last hope for its restoration was destroyed by the "plague of Justinian." Clearly bubonic plague—the Black Death—the plague of Justinian was said to have come out of Ethiopia in A.D. 540. It arrived at Constantinople, the eastern Roman capital, in the spring of the following year, and hung over the city for four months. The death toll mounted to as many as 5,000 to 10,000 per day, and there were not enough living to bury the dead in Constantinople that terrible summer. The double stone walls of the city were filled with corpses and ships loaded with bodies of plague victims were set adrift at sea. In his classic account of the decline and fall of the Roman Empire, Gibbon wrote "many cities of the East were left vacant, and that in several districts of Italy the harvest and the vintage withered on the ground. The triple scourges of war, pestilence and famine afflicted the subjects of Justinian; and his reign is disgraced by a visible decrease of the human species" (cited in Zinsser 1935:148).

These triple scourges have been linked together through the centuries. Invading armies destroyed crops, looted barnyards, and conscripted farmers; famine followed the troops. When an army laid siege to a walled city, starvation was a tactical weapon and the besieged populace might be starved into surrendering a city that could not be captured. Rats and disease bred on the corpses of men and horses lying outside the city walls; refugees brought pestilence into the crowded city where people were already debilitated by hunger. Yet plague struck both sides, and might save the city by destroying the army at the gate.

Human fertility had to remain as high as nature permits, to replace people lost to war and pestilence and to the starvation that followed after the armies and the fever were gone. The ancient goddess Lilith reappeared in Europe in the Middle Ages as the goddess of sex and death, but only in her dark image: a vampire goddess. Women bore all the children they could carry full term and, worn out with breeding, died young. Life was as Hobbes described it: short, brutish, and nasty.

Fertility and mortality: the balance tilts

The population of Europe grew slowly. Then in the fourteenth century, plague destroyed nearly one person out of every four in all Europe. Bubonic plague was joined by typhus, and as the Black Death and the Red Death the two diseases swept back and forth from the Balkans to the Thames; the virulence slowly subsided, but sporadic outbursts of plague occurred well into the seventeenth century. The last surge of bubonic plague in Europe was an epidemic that reached London in 1664. People fled the city, where even the houses of the rich were marked by the dreaded cross on the door. Looters invaded abandoned houses, fires spread behind the looters, and the great fire that destroyed entire sections of London burned out the slums where the plague-bearing rats had bred. Whether for this reason, or because people gradually became complacent about body vermin, or because the disease had lost its virulence, bubonic plague had subsided in Europe by the middle of the eighteenth century. The European population began to increase rapidly.

In the late eighteenth century, Malthus perceived that human population was balanced with the means of subsistence by inexorable forces. He wrote:

> The vices of mankind are active and able ministers of depopulation. They are the precursors in the great army of destruction; and often finish the dreadful work themselves. But should they fail in this war of extermination, sickly seasons, epidemics, pestilence, and plague advance in terrific array, and sweep off their thousands and ten thousands. Should success be still incomplete, gigantic inevitable famine stalks in the rear, and with one mighty blow, levels the population with the food of the world.

Malthus wrote his famous essay on population in 1798; in the same year that he published the initial draft, Jenner published his paper on smallpox vaccination. Vaccination and the practice of revaccination, introduced in 1832, brought smallpox under control in Europe by the middle of the nineteenth century. Bubonic plague had already receded; typhus appeared only in sporadic outbreaks in Ireland and eastern Europe. The

101

natural checks to population growth that Malthus had written about were no longer functioning with the ruthless efficiency of earlier centuries. The nineteenth century brought significant advances in medicine that further reduced the spread of epidemics. Perhaps the most important was the introduction of antiseptic practices by Lister, which greatly reduced infant and maternal mortality.

The Industrial Revolution began to affect mortality rates, even in crowded cities. The development of iron sewer pipe, to take one example, reduced the spread of disease. (At the beginning of the nineteenth century, even Washington, D.C. had open sewers.) As infant and maternal mortality rates dropped, more mothers survived childbirth to have more babies. More infants were born alive, more lived through the critical first year of life, and then through adolescence to become parents themselves. The birth rate was slowly declining, but the mortality rate was falling more rapidly, and the population of industrial countries began to rise.

The expanding population of Europe found an outlet through migration: Germans, Swedes, Danes, and the Irish came to America by the tens of thousands in the decades preceding and following the Civil War; they were followed by Poles, Russians, Italians, Greeks, Slavs, and other eastern and southern European immigrants who came by the boatload to the United States in the 1890s and in the first two decades of the twentieth century. It was not only the United States that was peopled by the excess population of Europe: Canada, Argentina, Brazil, Australia, and the many European colonial territories also absorbed hundreds of thousands of European immigrants. Most of the host countries had previously been underpopulated, and welcomed the immigrants.

Meanwhile, back in Europe the birth rate began to decline. By the early twentieth century contraceptive techniques had improved, and the birth rate of industrial countries had dropped to a point where a new balance of population was possible. Where once the population had been held relatively stable by a high birth rate balanced by high mortality rates at all ages, the new population balance was made possible by a low birth rate and a low mortality rate. The new balance meant a longer life expectancy for all. In Elizabethan England, the average life expectancy at birth was approximately 27 years; at the time of the American Centennial in 1876, life expectancy for an American at birth was 40 years; by the 1930s, life expectancy at birth in most industrial countries was over 60 years of age and rising. According to the *United Nations Demographic Yearbook* for 1973, the average life expectancy in Britain is 69 years for males and 75 for females; in the United States life expectancy at birth is 67.4 years for males, 75.2 years for females.

Not only did the new balance of low fertility and low mortality rates mean a longer life, it also meant that life was less brutish and nasty. A higher standard of living was both the effect and a contributing cause of the lower birth rate. The more literate and affluent people were able to understand the consequences of high birth rates, and could afford to control births because they did not need child labor. Affluence led to improved diet and medical care, and reduced the causes of early death. As a higher standard of living and the new balance of population spread throughout most of the industrial world, a new era seemed to have begun.

In the 1950s the industrial nations embarked on a campaign to lower the mortality rates of developing nations. Primarily through agencies of the United Nations, effective campaigns were launched against mosquitoes and other insects that carry yellow fever, malaria, dysentery, and other endemic and epidemic disease. The industrial countries set up aid programs to help developing countries halt epidemics, improve water supplies, and lower infant and maternal death rates. But because the birth rates in most of these countries remain as high as they were when a high mortality rate had to be balanced, the result is the sharp increase in population that is leading to famine in many developing countries. There are no more empty continents to absorb immigrants; surplus people must compete for scarce resources. Maximum fertility has ceased to be a necessity and threatens to become a global disaster. The triple scourges—war, disease, and famine—are waiting in the wings.

Family planning and the law in America

At the height of Victorian prudery, agitation by Anthony Comstock, the crusading head of the Society for the Suppression of Vice, led to the passage of the so-called Comstock Law by the U.S. Congress. This law, passed in 1873, made it a federal crime to transport in interstate commerce, to mail, or to import, "any article of medicine for the prevention of conception or for causing abortion." This same law made it equally criminal to import, mail, or transport in interstate commerce "obscene literature." By interpretation, this came to include birth-control information as well as unexpurgated French novels. This law was even applied to medical journals. When Dr. William H. Cary developed a contraceptive jelly in 1918, he found that he could not publish the formula in medical journals. Many states passed legislation similar to the Comstock Law, and gynecologists who gave patients information or devices that could be used for contraception were liable to prison terms, even when the patient had a weak heart or other physical impairment that might cause a pregnancy to be fatal.

Eventually the Comstock Law and the state laws it inspired became as unenforceable as the prohibition of alcohol. The restrictive legislation was gradually worn away, largely through the leadership of Margaret Sanger, a nurse (and the mother of three children) who coined the phrase "birth control." It was a happy choice of words, evoking the old phrase "moral restraint." Although opponents referred to contraception by such pejorative terms as "preventive abortion," it was "birth control" that became general usage. The dedication of Margaret Sanger to the legalization and development of birth control clinics grew out of her experience

103

as a nurse. Working with poor immigrants, she found that self-induced abortion was a major means of controlling family size, and that the subsequent maternal death rate was high.

In her autobiography, Margaret Sanger tells of the experience that shaped her decision to dedicate her life to birth control and family planning (also her term). As a young nurse, she had been called to save the life of an immigrant mother in her twenties who was close to death from hemorrhage and infection following self-induced abortion. The woman survived, but was despondent. When she voiced her fear that another pregnancy would kill her, the doctor's only suggestion was, "Tell Jake to sleep on the roof." A few months later, the woman's husband telephoned Mrs. Sanger with the urgent plea that she come at once; his wife was unconscious from yet another self-induced abortion. The woman died within hours.

That was in 1912, when even a nurse had no practical knowledge of contraception, and it would have been illegal for the doctor to have prescribed contraceptives, even to save the patient's life. Abstinence was all that the doctor could legally suggest. Margaret Sanger devoted the rest of her life to making birth control legal and available to all women, in memory of the young immigrant mother whose death had touched her so deeply.

Gradually, public acceptance of family planning and birth control grew. By the 1930s, the Depression had motivated couples to curtail births; the birth rate in the United States dropped to a minimal replacement level. Withdrawal, use of the condom, use of the diaphragm, and abortion (often illegal) were the means of this decline in the birth rate as documented by the Birth Control Research Bureau in New York (Kopp 1934). A precipitous decline in the marriage rate, to the lowest level ever recorded in the United States, was also a factor in the declining birth rate of the 1930s (Stouffer and Lazarsfeld 1937:122–123).

In most states, laws banning prescription and sale of contraceptives and the dissemination of information concerning them lapsed into unenforced anachronisms. The fiction was maintained that such devices were sold primarily for the control of disease, and it was in this twilight zone of legality that doctors prescribed and patients used contraceptives. By 1960 the era of oral contraceptives had begun. Physicians were freely prescribing contraceptives for their patients, but in some states the old laws were not only still on the books, they were enforced. In an effort to legalize family planning services for all women, those laws were challenged. The crucial legal decision that established the legality of contraception was handed down by the U.S. Supreme Court in June 1965. In the case of *Griswold and Buxton* v. *State of Connecticut,* the Supreme Court held the prescription of contraceptives to be a constitutionally protected right for *both* the physician and the patient.

That decision was based on two sections of the Constitution: The Ninth Amendment and the due process clause of the Fourteenth Amendment. The Ninth Amendment, part of the Bill of Rights, states that "the enumeration in the Constitution of certain rights, shall not be construed to deny or disparage others entertained by the people." In ruling that this amendment ensures the right to marital privacy, the Supreme Court took the position that the individual and the family have rights that may not be preempted by either the state or federal government. This decision could set one of the most important legal precedents of this century. In a concurring statement, three Supreme Court justices stated clearly for the record that any law *requiring* birth control would be as unconstitutional as any law *forbidding* it, since either would violate the right of marital privacy.

Contraceptive devices: out from under the counter

The first condom was devised as a protection against syphilis, which suddenly appeared in Europe in epidemic form in 1495 among soldiers and civilians after a French army had captured Naples. (The French called it "the Neopolitan disease," the Italians called it "the French affliction," but the probability is that the men who sailed with Columbus brought it back from the West Indies [Zinsser 1935:72–73].) In 1564 information was published about Dr. Fallopius's sheath of sheep intestine. By the late seventeenth century, Dr. Fallopius's sheath was in general use by the aristocracy as a protection against syphilis in casual court affairs, but apparently the sheath was not yet used as a contraceptive within marriage (Stone 1960–61:201).

A century later, however, the contraceptive function of the sheath was certainly known. The English called it "the French letter," and Malthus referred to it obliquely in his famous essay, first published in 1798. He regarded its use as a vice, not as a solution to the problem of overpopulation. "To remove the difficulty in this way will, surely, in the opinion of most men, be to destroy that virtue and purity of manners, which the advocates of equality, and of the perfectability of man profess to be the end and object of their views." Considering contraception one of the vices of mankind, the Reverend Mr. Malthus held that the only morally acceptable alternative was delayed marriage, preceded—and followed—by "moral restraint." Ironically, the Victorians used the term "neo-Malthusian" as a euphemism for the advocacy of birth control by mechanical means.

Technological advances of the Industrial Revolution lowered mortality rates and increased life expectancy; toward the end of the nineteenth century other technological developments made it possible to lower the birth rate. When the process of vulcanizing rubber was developed, a new material became available that revolutionized transport: the rubber tire proved to be the biggest improvement on the wheel since spokes. The vulcanization of rubber also brought a revolution in contraception. The condom made of sheep intestine was still preferred by men who could afford it, but the rubber condom was cheap and effective. Like the Model T, it made available to the masses something that had been a rich man's prerogative.

105

The condom was developed to protect against disease, and as a prophylactic it could be manufactured and sold during the period when contraceptives as such were still under a legal cloud. The assumption was that it would protect men from diseased prostitutes, which it did. It also provided contraception within or outside of marriage, a use that was officially ignored for decades. By the 1930s and 1940s, the use of the condom was widespread in America.

During World War II, any young man who had not learned the use of the condom from his high school buddies learned in lectures given during basic military training. The American armed forces began trying to control venereal disease among the troops during World War I by closing brothels around the camps; by World War II it had become customary to instruct military trainees in methods of avoiding venereal disease, including the use of prophylactics.

The condom became part of the paraphernalia of the youth culture of an earlier generation. Adolescent boys learned that rubbers were not merely what one wore on a rainy day. One of the first trials of manhood was working up the courage to ask the druggist for a box, even if the only immediate use the young man had for a condom was to fill it with water and drop it out a window on the head of some unsuspecting rival. For some reason, the service station was a common retail outlet for the condom in that earlier time. Perhaps it was because a gas station attendant seemed less formidable than the small town druggist, who probably knew every local boy's father. (Times and morals change; there are places in the United States today where condoms are sold in vending machines, like cigarettes, with a warning posted as to age restrictions on use.)

The development of rubber made possible not only the modern condom, but also the modern diaphragm. The old technique using a piece of sponge soaked in vinegar was fairly effective, but bulky. About 1880 Wilhelm Mensinga, a German doctor, introduced the modern vaginal diaphragm, a circle of soft rubber with a rubber-covered flexible metal coil forming the outer rim. Properly fitted, it covered the cervix more securely than a sponge, and interfered less with intercourse. When spermicidal jelly was developed in 1918, the combination of diaphragm and jelly provided highly reliable contraception. However, diaphragms were available only on prescription, and, as noted above, in the early decades of this century doctors who prescribed them risked prison and loss of their license to practice. By the 1930s, however, most doctors felt free to fit married patients for a diaphragm, and by the 1940s some were willing to fit unmarried women who were sexually active.

Both the condom and the diaphragm are relatively effective contraceptives. The condom has a failure rate of between three and thirty-six pregnancies per hundred couples using it (computed on the basis of years of "contraceptive exposure," to use the medical terminology). The diaphragm has a failure rate of approximately ten per hundred couples using the device. The diaphragm and spermicidal jelly combination could be almost completely effective if properly inserted before each and every act of intercourse, so the failure rate may reflect less on the effectiveness of the device than on the close relation between time of insertion and sexual activity. Much the same problem exists with the condom. A contraceptive unrelated in time of use to sexual activity is likely to be used more consistently.

One reliable alternative device that has come into extensive use in the last two decades is the intrauterine device, or IUD. The IUD is a simple, effective, and inexpensive device that, like the condom and the diaphragm, was anticipated by ancient devices. Camel drivers of the Sahara reportedly inserted pebbles into the uterus of a female camel to prevent pregnancies during a long journey by caravan. Hippocrates is said to have used a hollow lead tube to insert pessaries into the uterus of female patients, but translators differ on whether or not this was intended to be for contraceptive purposes (Huber et al. 1975:23).

Whatever the ancient antecedents for the device, the modern IUD developed from the cervico-uterine stem pessaries used in Europe in the late nineteenth and early twentieth centuries. Small buttons or caps on a stem that extended into the cervical canal, these devices covered the cervix. Such stem pessaries were in use at least by 1890, but without clear reference to their contraceptive effect (which was surely recognized). "Made from a variety of materials such as ivory, wood, glass, silver, gold, ebony, pewter, and diamond-studded platinum, these pessaries were ostensibly used for many different purposes including support of the uterus, prevention of irregular or delayed menses, and a cure for dysmenorrhea and infertility" (Huber et al. 1975:23). In 1902, a wishbone-shaped device was patented by a German physician, Dr. Carl Hollweg. Hollweg reported (although not in his patent application) that the pessary had been inserted in seven hundred women for the prevention of pregnancy.

Many of these early stem pessaries were used to induce abortion, as well as to prevent conception. The use of such devices to induce abortion sometimes resulted in hemorrhage and pelvic infection. Antibiotics had not yet been developed, and uterine infection was often fatal. The hazards of infection led the medical community to condemn the pessaries, and retarded acceptance of later and safer intrauterine devices. In the late 1920s, a German gynecologist, Dr. Ernst Graefenberg, developed an intrauterine ring, a circle of silver wire that was compressed and inserted into the uterus. It proved to be a highly effective contraceptive. The Graefenberg ring became widely used in Germany, then was adopted elsewhere. In 1934 a Japanese physician, Dr. Tenrei Ota, developed the Ota ring, which has a small disc attached to the outer ring by three spokes. This gold or gold-plated silver ring proved to be even more effective than the Graefenberg ring, of which it was a variant.

But in the 1930s there was renewed protest (sometimes from doctors who had never used the devices) that the intrauterine rings were potentially dangerous. Graefenberg and other German doctors who were pioneers

107

in the field of contraception had to flee Germany during the 1930s. The Nazis encouraged a high German birth rate. Ironically, one of the justifications they gave for the annexation of territories conquered by the Third Reich was that the growing German population needed *Lebensraum*—living space. Research into the contraceptive potential of the IUD stopped for more than a decade, while the world made war.

After World War II, birth rates soared and interest in new contraceptive devices was heightened throughout the world. Both the Graefenberg and the Ota rings were used safely and found to be highly effective. Advancing technology created new biologically inert materials such as nylon filaments and polyethylene. These new materials did for the intrauterine device what rubber had done for the condom and the diaphragm. IUDs now come in a variety of forms: spiral coils with central discs, flattened figure-eight "bows," T-shaped devices, S-shaped devices, some with filament tails for checking placement. The Lippes Loop, a double-S loop with a filament tail, was designed by Dr. Jack Lippes of Buffalo, New York, in the early 1960s and has become the standard IUD in use today in more than seventy countries in North and South America, Asia, Africa, and Europe.

Not one explanation of why the IUD works as a contraceptive has been accepted by medical researchers. Research with animals has indicated that IUDs function differently in different species. In sheep, IUDs seem to function by stimulating the production of uterine secretions that destroy sperm before fertilization can occur. Also in sheep, IUDs reverse the direction of the contractions of the muscle walls of the reproductive tract, thus preventing any surviving sperm from moving toward the egg. In rabbits, IUDs apparently stimulate a higher concentration of a particular hormone that prevents the implantation of fertilized eggs. In the human female, it is probable that the IUD functions primarily to prevent implantation of the egg, but it may also stimulate spermicidal secretions (Huber et al. 1975:25).

Regardless of how the IUD prevents pregnancy, it does so quite effectively. According to Sallie Huber and her associates, "There is no question that the IUDs are more effective in preventing pregnancy than any other nonsurgical method except oral contraceptives. Net pregnancy rates for the devices most commonly used range from 0.0 to 5.6 per 100 women for the first year after insertion compared with rates of 1 to 3 for orals, 3 to 36 for condoms and over 5 for other methods" (1975:33).

The IUD offers contraceptive protection that is highly effective and that requires only one decision by the woman, at a time separated from the act of intercourse; it is long-lasting and inexpensive to manufacture; and its effects are completely reversible: fertility is restored by the act of removing the IUD. Those are the advantages. The drawbacks are the potential side effects. The IUD tends to induce a heavier menstrual flow and, for some women, intermenstrual spotting. During the first few months that the device is in place, there is likely to be severe uterine cramping during the menstrual period. There is some risk of perforation of the uterine wall if the device is improperly inserted, and with some types, there is still some risk of pelvic infection and septic abortion. All of these risks are higher for women who are unable to get adequate medical care. These side effects have been the reason for most recent research into differing shapes and substances used for IUDs.

There is some possibility that the IUD may be expelled without the woman being aware of the fact. The possibility of expulsion, particularly likely for women who have not borne a child, can be minimized by the use of some of the newer shapes. An IUD with a filament tail can be checked by the woman herself to determine whether it is in place. One of the IUDs developed to reduce the risk of expulsion—the Dalkon Shield—has had a higher than expected rate of pelvic infection and septic abortion associated with its use. That is, in those few instances where pregnancy does occur (the risk is greatest in the first month or two that the device is in place, as with all IUDs), there is more likely to be infection and spontaneous abortion with the Dalkon Shield. The complication for the woman can be extremely serious, in a few cases resulting in death. Medical research suggests that the problem may lie with the multiple-filament tail of the Dalkon Shield, which apparently acts as a wick to carry bacteria into the uterus. The firm that had marketed the Dalkon Shield suspended distribution of the device in 1975.

One new IUD that seems to be safe, highly effective, and less likely to be expelled by women who have never had a child is the Copper T. As the name suggests, this is a T shaped device of molded polyethylene with fine copper wire wound around the stem. According to Huber and her associates, "Copper was the first bioactive substance to be added to the conventional polyethylene IUD . . . Copper devices appear to cause less bleeding than inert IUDs and to be better suited for nulliparous women [women who have never borne a child] because of their smaller size and ease of insertion" (Huber et al. 1975:38). However, the copper is exhausted after about two years, and the device must be replaced then because it tends to lose effectiveness.

Much current research in IUDs concerns the addition of bioactive substances to the device. Progesterone, a hormone used as an active ingredient in oral contraceptives, is known to effect the uterine lining. Medical research scientists hypothesized that if such hormones could be placed in direct contact with the uterine lining, the same contraceptive effect could be achieved with much smaller amounts of the hormone and without the systemic effects of oral contraceptives. In addition, progesterone acts as a uterine tranquilizer and may reduce cramping caused by the IUD. One device utilizing progesterone, the Progestasert, was approved by the Food and Drug Administration (FDA) in the spring of 1975. Preliminary tests indicate that the Progestasert has an effectiveness rate of between 98 and 99 percent. The expulsion rate is only about 3 percent in women who have had children, about 7 percent for those who have not.

109

The Progestasert must be replaced once a year, at the time of the annual gynecological examination and Pap test that every sexually active woman should have for basic health protection.

The IUD is not the perfect contraceptive, but its advantages are great, and the undesirable side effects are being reduced by newer shapes and the addition of bioactive substances. For a variety of reasons, the IUD is more effective than the other major contraceptive devices—the condom and the diaphragm—*as a means of contraception*. It should be recalled, however, that the condom (and to a lesser degree, the diaphragm) prevent disease as well as pregnancy.

For the barren and for the prolific: new answers

During the period when research into contraceptive techniques was of borderline legality, there was research into methods of improving fertility. About one couple in every ten have low fertility, or may be sterile. A couple without children face social pressures toward parenthood. If they are not voluntarily childless, they must face the social and psychological implications of sterility. Those who are not voluntarily childless may long for a child, may become obsessed by the child they cannot conceive. Sterility may become a focal point of self-doubt or of bitterness between husband and wife, each blaming the other, wondering if it might be the result of venereal disease contracted in earlier days. If a woman is able to conceive but not to carry a child full term, she may go through a sad cycle of pregnancy and miscarriage, with intense emotional responses of hope, fear, and disappointment experienced over and over again. The ancient stigma that was placed on the barren wife has not been entirely removed.

In the Middle Ages, certain springs and holy places were supposed to have the power to cure infertility; couples made long pilgrimages to such places in the hope of being rewarded with a child. Potions and draughts that were supposed to cure infertility were brewed by old women with a reputation for occult knowledge. By the twentieth century, however, biochemistry had come to the aid of the infertile. In 1904 hormones were discovered. Once their influence on the reproductive system was known, hormones began to be used in an effort to *increase* fertility. Some women are able to conceive but tend to miscarry because of a lack of the hormones that suppress ovulation during pregnancy. It was discovered that hormone injections could be used to help women with a history of miscarriages to carry a child full term.

At first hormones were derived from animal sources, (especially the urine of pregnant mares) and they were expensive. Only the very rich could afford such treatment. Further research led to the discovery that hormonelike substances could be synthesized from a plant substance found in a tuberous root that grows wild in the swamps of Yucatan. Medical researchers noted that the same hormones that suppress ovulation during pregnancy and ease certain types of menstrual disorders could also be used as a means of contraception. In the mid-1950s the late Gregory Pincus of the Worcester Foundation, in collaboration with John Rock and Celso Garcia, demonstrated that a woman's reproductive functions could be controlled by an orally administered combination of hormones. The Pill had been discovered. According to Gerald Oster, by the 1970s some thirty million women throughout the world were taking it daily (1972:42).

This is the age of pills: vitamin pills, pain pills, reducing pills, sleeping pills, pills that stimulate and pills that tranquilize. For one pill to be singled out as The Pill is indicative of the social impact it has had. It is not that the Pill is the first effective contraceptive, for it is not. Rather, it was the first effective contraceptive whose use is completely removed in time and circumstances from the sex act (the IUD, whose insertion is also removed from the sex act, was being reintroduced in its present form at about the time that the Pill was developed; the two techniques actually share this advantage of removal from the coital situation). Oral contraceptives give a woman control of her fertility without in any way interfering with intercourse. The Pill involves no loss of sexual spontaneity, no temptation to do without contraceptives, no interference with sexual pleasure for either partner. Moreover, women who find the diaphragm or a spermicidal foam or suppository objectionable for aesthetic or religious reasons often find the Pill acceptable.

For the vast majority of women, the side effects of the Pill are basically comparable to those of early pregnancy: morning sickness, fluid retention with consequent weight gain, and sometimes mild depression. As in pregnancy, these symptoms are most pronounced in the early months and tend to disappear. Compared with the alternatives, the oral contraceptives seem a reasonable solution for most women. Their effectiveness is extremely high: depending on the type of oral contraceptive, effectiveness varies from 97 percent to 99.9 percent in preventing pregnancy. No other method of contraception currently available is as effective, although the IUD is close.

Recently, however, there has been concern about the safety of oral contraceptives. Extensive research indicates that there are few health hazards for the vast majority of women. The woman with a history of circulatory disorder may be a poor risk, but for the normal woman, especially the younger woman, the risk is slight. The first conclusive studies showing that there is some danger of thromboembolic disease (blood clots) were conducted in Great Britain. These studies indicated that in women between the ages of twenty and thirty-four, the mortality rate from the use of oral contraceptives leading to thromboembolic disease is 1.5 per 100,000 women using oral contraceptives; older women (those between thirty-four and fourty-four) had a somewhat higher mortality rate: 3.9 per 100,000. If we combine these two rates, the British figures indicate a mortality rate of 3 per 100,000 women taking oral contraceptives.

To put such mortality rate into perspective, gynecologist Louis M. Hellman observes that if 100,000 fertile women engage in sexual intercourse without using any form of contraception, within one year 50,000 of these will have babies and 15 of these women will have died in childbirth (calculated on the basis of United States Vital Statistics data on maternal mortality). If 100,000 fertile women engage in sexual intercourse using the diaphragm, within one year, 10,000 of these women will have a baby and 3 will have died in childbirth. But if 100,000 fertile women using oral contraceptives engage in sexual intercourse over the same length of time, there will be no babies born and there may be about 3 deaths that could be attributed to the use of contraceptives (Hellman 1969:40–41).

In short, the chances of death are about the same for users of diaphragms and users of oral contraceptives, but *for women using no form of contraception the chances of death are five times greater.* The only safer course than the use of oral contraceptives is to use the IUD. For all of the potential complications discussed above, the IUD is apparently the safest contraceptive, many times safer than no contraceptive at all. In a report prepared for the FDA, J. Jennings states that "the mortality rate from the intrauterine device is between 1 and 10 deaths per million woman years, while with oral contraceptives it is 22 to 45 per million woman years.[1] The hospitalization rates with intrauterine devices are in the same order of magnitude as with oral contraceptives, .3 to 1.0 per 100 woman years of use" (cited in Huber et al. 1975:36). Compared with the alternatives, the risks from using either oral contraceptives or the IUD do not seem great. Nor do they appear great when compared with other risks that many American women voluntarily take, such as riding in automobiles (the American death rate is 20.8 per 100,000 persons per year) or smoking cigarettes (death rate still in dispute).

Oral contraceptives do pose some additional problems. The use of oral contraceptives must be continuous, with no intervening lapses in taking the Pill except for the brief period each month prescribed by the doctor. Women living in remote areas are more likely to run out of pills than women living a short walk from the drugstore. An even more serious disadvantage is the fact that oral contraceptives tend to suppress lactation (Oster 1972:47). Mother's milk is the most nourishing milk for an infant; it has anti-infective properties that prevent intestinal infections (diarrhea is a common cause of infant death in developing nations). It is less expensive than cow's milk for infant feeding. Not only is mother's milk a valuable food resource in a hungry world, the process of lactation itself has a contraceptive effect, Derrick and E. F. Patrice Jelliffe report that "recent studies indicate that the traditional belief that *unsupplemented* breast feeding has a contraceptive, child-spacing effect is true, and is related to the annovulatory effect of prolactin (and other hormones) secreted by the

---

[1]To compare Jenning's and Hellman's figures, move the decimal point in Jenning's figures one place to the right. Jennings talks about deaths per million woman years, Hellman refers to deaths per 100,000 woman years of use.

anterior pituitary in response to the baby's suckling" (1975:558; emphasis added).

By the time the controversy over the use of the Pill is over, it will probably be obsolete. The long period in which there was little research into contraception has ended. Oral contraceptives for men are being developed, but serious side effects have yet to be overcome. The "morning after" pill for women has been announced, but not perfected. There is some possibility that in the future women may be innoculated against pregnancy for a specific period of time, either with hormonal compounds or with antibodies that destroy sperm.

Research into the reproductive process usually has the dual aims of correcting the sterility of some women and controlling conception in others. Both the barren and the prolific need help. Reports of previously infertile women giving birth to quintuplets or sextuplets have become almost commonplace in the last few years. The newspaper accounts usually note that the mother had been taking a fertility drug, usually FSH (follicle-stimulating hormone). Within the ovary, the initial development of a follicle into an egg is stimulated by a hormone produced by the anterior pituitary gland. This hormonal substance is called FSH, and together with LH, a luteinizing hormone also produced in the anterior pituitary, it is essential to the growth and maturation of a particular follicle. Oster observes that "FSH will induce ovulating in some infertile women. But in half the successful applications of this treatment, there has been an embarrassment of riches and multiple pregnancies (as many as seven) have resulted" (1972:51). Fertility drugs may carry the risk of multiple births, a risk that must be weighed against the desire for a child.

For some women, sterility is an unhappy fact of life. For others, it is a condition deliberately sought: approximately 350,000 American women are sterilized each year. If a couple have all of the children they wish to have, sterilization of either the husband of wife may be the preferred form of contraception. Sterilization is completely effective as a method of contraception, is a low-risk operation and does not impair sexual functioning in either men or women.

Sterilization for women (called *tubal ligation*) involves surgically tying off the Fallopian tubes through which the fertilized egg, or ovum travels. In the past, this operation has required abdominal surgery of about the complexity of an appendectomy. However, new techniques of tubal ligation have been developed that are simpler and involve only the smallest of abdominal incisions. (A hysterectomy—removal of the uterus—will also sterilize a woman, but such surgery is normally performed only out of medical necessity.)

Sterilization for men is a relatively simple operation, called a *vasectomy*, which involves external surgery only and which does not in any way impair sexual function or pleasure; it merely closes the tube through which semen travels. (This accords well with the Hindu belief that retention of semen is highly beneficial to the male, one reason why the government of

113

India has had considerable success in inducing males to come to clinics for sterilization.) After two months, the semen contains no sperm. It is wise for the couple to continue using some other contraceptive measure for at least two months following the husband's vasectomy, unless the doctor indicates that the sperm count has reached zero.

The disadvantge of sterilization is that it is, for all practical purposes, irreversible. Some operations to restore fertility of the male after a vasectomy have been successful, but no one should have the operation with the idea that it can be reversed at some future date. This means that sterilization is useful largely for people who are certain that they do not want more children—or any children at all. However, a growing number of couples are recognizing that sterilization is an effective means of limiting family size without adversely affecting their sexual relationship. Men may experience some psychological trauma with vasectomy, centered on the fear of impaired sexual functioning, but such fears are groundless. For a woman, sterilization can lead to a sense of great freedom, for all concern about pregnancy is lifted from her.

Catholics and contraception: a moral dilemma

While the availability of reliable contraceptives makes it possible for a couple to plan the number of children they want, and to have children when they can care for them, the acceptability of contraception varies between groups within our pluralistic society, as does the desired family size. We are members not only of a family, but also of a church, an ethnic group, a social-class subculture. For some Americans the decisions involved in family planning are primarily personal and economic; for others, such decisions are largely moral and religious.

By the time legal barriers to contraception were removed, religious injunctions against their use had been lifted by all but the Catholic Church. A Catholic doctor, John Rock, played a major role in developing oral contraceptives and wrote a popular book on why the time for their use had come (Rock 1963). Because oral contraceptives function by suppressing ovulation and thus in a sense prolong the "safe" period, many Catholics felt that the use of the Pill was comparable to, but more reliable than, the rhythm method that the Church had approved. In 1966 the Church took the matter under study.

Anticipating that the use of oral contraceptives would be approved, many Catholic women began to use them. In 1965 Charles Westoff and Norman Ryder conducted a national fertility study under a grant from the Public Health Service. They found that in only five years, from 1960 to 1965, the Pill had been so widely adopted by American women of all races and creeds that it had displaced older contraceptive methods: the use of the diaphragm had decreased by 60 percent, the use of the condom by 50 percent, and the use of the rhythm method by 40 percent. Since the rhythm method had seldom been used by non-Catholics because of its lack of reliability, the displacement of the rhythm method by oral contraceptives reflects the changing contraceptive practices of Catholic women. Westoff and Ryder found that by 1965 a majority of Catholic women had used some contraceptive other than the rhythm method (Westoff and Ryder 1969).

But in 1968 the papal encyclical *Humanae Vitae* was issued, which contained a ban against interrupting the "transmission of life." This ban was deeply disturbing to millions of American Catholics, especially to the many Catholic women who had been using oral contraceptives and wished to continue to do so. A young Catholic woman described to me her own moral dilemma and that of the women of her family and their friends:

Before I go on with this I will tell you I am a Roman Catholic. I read the encyclical in the *Catholic Herald*. I heard the first reactions of the priests in my parish and I have heard their most recent comments. I have been to different parishes and heard different priests spend the entire time during their homilies speaking to parishioners on this subject. It is brought up at almost every mass.

The Pope condemned the pill and said no priest could give absolution in confession if the user was going to continue taking it. One priest in my parish told us the following Sunday that he was very sorry but he was under discipline and must abide by this declaration. Dissension arose immediately. My cousin could receive Holy Communion in one church because the priest gave absolution of contraception, but not in another because the priest would not absolve her.

Many Catholics are completely indecisive. Supposedly papal declarations are not binding unless they are spoken from St. Peter's Chair where all that is spoken is dogma and the Pope is said to be infallible. Therefore, a Catholic could rationalize the situation and have a clear conscience concerning the question of birth control. Recently my mother went to confession. She told me that the priest asked her why she should punish herself since the Pope only stated his view. This IS what he did! But he did instruct the clergy that they could not absolve a person practicing birth control. Some of our parish priests say they will not absolve one in the confessional, but they are now saying we should let our consciences be our guides. If something does not appear to be a sin, then don't confess it. But still the Pope's letter is hanging over our heads.

St. Mary's Catholic Church in [the city where she attends college] gives an entirely different opinion. The priests and parishioners are elderly. There are few young people who attend mass alone. The priests are in their seventies or eighties—they have all celebrated their golden jubilees. The parishioners are often elderly or middle-aged with families of four or more. There have been notes in the bulletins frowning on miniskirts and hatless females—as if God cares what one looks like. A recent sermon was on the topic of children. The priest said to create children for the eternal life after this one on earth. He urged people not to worry about the life on earth as the everlasting life is the more important of the two.

I see smaller congregations at mass now, and some of my friends and family are among those who do not attend any more. It is a trying period and a most crucial one for the Church and her people.

Abortion and the law

The controversy over the use of oral contraception has been overshadowed since 1970 by the controversy over abortion. There was no prohibition of abortion in the United States until the middle of the nineteenth century, when the first abortion statutes were enacted. Such laws were primarily intended to protect maternal health. Abortion had often been performed by midwives who had no formal medical training, and in the nineteenth century, even a trained surgeon had no good way to fight the infection that often followed abortion. Self-induced abortion was not uncommon, in spite of the risks it carried. (It might be recalled that it was maternal mortality from self-induced abortion that led Margaret Sanger into her life-long struggle to legalize contraception.)

By the middle of the present century, all states had laws that permitted abortion to save the mother's life. For most states, this was the only ground for a therapeutic (legal) abortion, although one state (Mississippi) also permitted abortion in cases of rape, and seventeen states had laws that permitted abortion either to save the mother's life or to protect her physical or mental health. The mental-health provision meant that therapeutic abortion was relatively easy to obtain in some states, if a woman could find a psychiatrist willing to certify that her mental health had been endangered by her pregnancy. (Often it was certified that she was depressed and potentially suicidal.) In most states, however, it was almost impossible to obtain a therapeutic abortion as recently as the 1960s.

Some women left the United States for abortions. England and Japan were two frequent destinations, for by the 1960s both countries had legal abortion available at the request of the woman. The abortion abroad might not be expensive, but travel was, which meant that only the affluent woman could afford an abortion. Other women sought illegal but comparatively safe abortions in such places as Tijuana, Mexico, where abortion clinics operated almost openly. The alternative for most women who sought abortion was an illicit abortionist closer to home. According to Alfred Kinsey's findings, most of those abortionists were physicians (Kinsey 1966:195). But because of the illicit nature of the operations, they were frequently performed under less than ideal conditions, and women risked not only legal penalties, but life and health.

116

Thus, as Kinsey observed, abortion occurred with surprising frequency. But it was a topic relegated to occasional symposia, not a matter of public discussion (prudery lingered long in America) until the tragic consequences of the tranquilizer Thalidomide suddenly fixed public attention on the need for more liberal abortion laws. Thalidomide had been prescribed in good faith by physicians and taken by pregnant women on doctor's orders (it eased certain side effects of pregnancy, such as nausea). And then it was discovered that there was a high probability that the women who had taken Thalidomide during pregnancy would bear children with extreme birth defects. Suddenly the press was full of pictures of children with flippers where their arms and legs should have been.

The therapeutic abortion laws permitted abortion to save the life, and in some states the health, of the mother, but nothing was said about a deformed fetus. One celebrated case involved a married woman who had taken Thalidomide on her doctor's orders, had subsequently learned about its side effects, had agonized and finally decided that abortion was essential to prevent the birth of her probably defective child. But she could not contend that abortion was necessary to save her life or protect her health, and she was unable to get an abortion in the United States. Not willing to wait for the glacial progress of legislative or judicial change, this woman flew to Sweden for a legal abortion. The Thalidomide crisis focused public concern on abortion reform. Fifteen states altered their statutes to permit abortion to prevent the birth of a physically or mentally defective child, as well as to save the mother's life or health. Some added provisions for abortion in cases of rape or incest as well.

Then in September of 1969, in the case of *People* v. *Belous*, the California Supreme Court declared void a state statute that allowed abortion only to preserve the life and health of the mother on the ground that it was unconstitutionally vague and violated due process of law. Justice Raymond A. Peters wrote in his opinion: "The rights involved in the instant case are the woman's right to life and to choose whether to bear children ... The fundamental right of the woman to choose whether to bear children follows from the Supreme Court's and this court's repeated acknowledgement of a 'right to privacy' or 'liberty' in matters related to marriage, family and sex." This decision liberalized California abortion law late in 1969.

In 1970 the state of New York passed what was at that time the most liberal abortion law in the United States. Unlike other states with permissive abortion laws, such as Alaska and Hawaii, New York did not require a period of residency prior to abortion. Women from other states with more restrictive abortion laws began going to New York for abortion. The New York law had been a matter of intense political controversy before its passage; the controversy did not subside after it went into effect. By the time of the political campaign in 1976, abortion had become a national political issue.

117

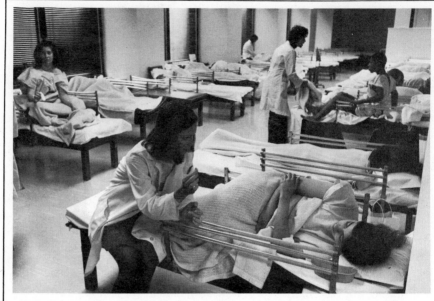

Abortion clinic, New York City.

Surgical techniques in abortion improved dramatically, particularly with the introduction of the vacuum method used during the first twelve weeks of pregnancy (called the first trimester). A study conducted for the Population Council by Christopher Tietze (cited in *Scientific American* 1972:51), covering the period from the middle of 1970 (when the liberal New York abortion law was passed) to the middle of 1971, indicated that the mortality rate for abortions performed during the first trimester was effectively zero, and that even including abortions performed in the second trimester, the mortality rate was only 8.2 per 100,000 therapeutic (legal) abortions. These figures compare favorably to the maternal mortality rate (the number of women who die from pregnancy and childbirth) in the United States of 24.7 per 100,000 births. This study included approximately one seventh of all legal abortions performed during the middle of 1970 to the middle of 1971, and was conducted in sixty teaching hospitals and six clinics in twelve states and the District of Columbia, although a majority of the abortions were performed in New York.

Meanwhile, two cases involving abortions reached the United States Supreme Court. The two women plaintiffs were listed under the aliases of "Jane Roe" and "Mary Doe." "Jane Roe" was single, a waitress in a Texas bar. "Mary Doe" was married, an impoverished housewife from Atlanta. Both were representative of large groups of women who could not afford to go out of their home states for abortion: not to Sweden, Japan, England, not even to New York. They sought relief from the abortion statutes of their home states. The cases were argued during the judicial term of

1971–1972 and again, at the request of the Court, in the autumn of 1972. (There had been two vacant seats on the Court when the cases involving abortion were first heard, and the Court believed that a decision involving so sensitive an issue should be heard by a full nine-justice Court. It was, in the fall of 1972; one of the newly appointed justices voting with the majority, the other with the minority.)

In January of 1973, the Supreme Court announced its verdict: too late to be of benefit to "Jane Roe" and "Mary Doe," but these two women won the legal victory that assured every woman the right to abortion in the first six months of pregnancy. The Court had decided, by a margin of seven to two, that states may not prohibit abortion before a fetus becomes viable: that is, able to sustain life outside the womb. In a highly technical decision written by Justice Harry Blackmun, the majority opinion asserted that that point came somewhere between twenty-four and twenty-eight weeks, that is, during the third trimester of pregnancy. The ruling was based on the right of marital privacy contained in the Ninth Amendment and on the liberty guaranteed by the due-process clause of the Fourteenth Amendment.

Justice Blackmun was legal counsel for the Mayo Clinic from 1950 to 1959, and he returned to the clinic during the Court recess in the summer of 1972 to do background research. The opinion that he drafted for the majority holds that during the first trimester of pregnancy, "the abortion decision and its effectuation must be left to the medical judgment of the pregnant woman's attending physician." After the twelfth week of pregnancy, the increased risks involved make it permissible, the Court held, for the states to "regulate the abortion procedure in ways that are reasonably related to maternal health." (For example, a state statute could require that abortion performed later than the twelfth week of pregnancy must be performed in a hospital rather than in a doctor's office.) However, the Court held that it would be an unconstitutional complication of the abortion procedure for a state to require that a panel of doctors approve an abortion.

In July of 1976 the Court handed down decisions clarifying some remaining legal questions relating to abortion and reinforcing the Court's earlier ruling that first trimester abortions are a matter to be decided by a woman and her doctor. In reviewing a case involving the 1974 Missouri statute on abortion, the Court ruled (by a six to three majority) that a state cannot require a married woman to obtain her husband's consent before terminating a pregnancy. Writing for the majority, Justice Blackmun noted that while the husband has a "deep and proper concern" with his wife's pregnancy, the state may not grant the husband the right to prevent his wife from obtaining an abortion when "the state itself lacks that right."

The Court also ruled (by a narrow margin of five to four) that a state may not grant parents an absolute veto over abortion for unmarried daughters under eighteen years of age. Nearly a third of the 900,000 women undergoing abortions each year are unmarried teenage women,

119

so the issue of parental consent is a sensitive one. The Missouri law that was struck down by the Court in July of 1976 contained a "blanket requirement" of parental consent which could be waived only if the minor's life was endangered by her pregnancy. Justice Blackmun, speaking for the majority, stated that any "independent interest" the parent might have was less important than the privacy right of a minor female "mature enough to have become pregnant."

At the same time the Court unanimously upheld a Missouri statute that defined "viability" as "that stage of fetal development when the life of the unborn child may be continued indefinitely outside the womb by natural or artificial life-supportive systems," and accepted this as the time after which abortion can be prohibited. However, the Court struck down (by a six to three majority) a provision of the Missouri law requiring doctors to take as much care to preserve the life of an aborted fetus as that of a fetus the mother had intended to bear alive.

When the Supreme Court ruled in 1965 on the right of the patient to receive and of the physician to prescribe contraceptives, a clear majority of Americans had already accepted the use of contraceptives and the principle of family planning. But the ruling on abortion came at a point in time when abortion was a matter of intense moral debate. The Court ruling has not ended that debate.

Abortion is still a volatile issue, politically and morally. Groups have rallied to opposing points of view. One of these groups, characterized as the "right to life" movement, has opposed the abortion ruling vigorously, with illustrated lectures and legal actions. The most notable legal action to date was the criminal prosecution of Dr. Kenneth Edelin in Boston, on the grounds that he had caused the death of a fetus he aborted. The trial received national attention, and there were charges of racial bias when the white (and predominantly Catholic) jury convicted the black physician of manslaughter. The proponents of abortion were outraged; the gynecologists and obstetricians of the country were disturbed. The judge, sentenced Dr. Edelin to one year's probation, which in turn outraged the opponents of abortion. The sentence was stayed, pending appeal, and at this writing it is not clear how that appeal will be decided.

There have been some clarifying rulings by the Supreme Court in other cases, however. In February of 1975, the Court let stand a lower-court ruling invalidating a Minnesota law that prohibited abortion after the twentieth week of pregnancy unless needed to preserve the life or health of the mother. It was the twenty-fourth week that had been set by the initial Court ruling as the point at which states could first prohibit abortion, and the lower court had ruled that the Minnesota law and the regulations adopted under it were unconstitutional.

The Supreme Court ruling held that a fetus is not a person under the Constitution and thus has no legal right to life. The Court thus avoided saying at what point life begins, merely stating at what point there is a person with constitutional rights: the point at which the fetus is viable. But

Abortion is still a volatile issue, politically and morally. Groups have rallied to opposing points of view. This is an anti-abortion rally.

medical advances in the care of premature infants may move the point of potential viability to an earlier time in pregnancy. The issue is not closed, although public opinion seems to be moving rapidly toward an acceptance of the right of the woman to control her own fertility, even after conception, provided that abortion occurs early in the pregnancy.

The Supreme Court ruling did not make abortion available on demand; this was made clear in the concurring opinion of Chief Justice Warren Burger, who said specifically that no right to abortion on demand is given. What a woman now has is the right to ask for abortion, and doctors are no longer legally restricted from performing abortion during the first twenty-four weeks. Eventually, a woman should be able to find a doctor willing to perform an abortion, but Justice Burger made it clear that the doctor is not compelled to oblige the woman who asks. Some physicians have chosen not to perform abortions after the first trimester, some on the grounds of conscience and some because of the Edelin verdict.

In the distant dawn of human existence, abortion and infanticide were the major means of population control exercised by human beings. In the United States, abortion is now legal for the first two trimesters of pregnancy, and later if the life or health of the mother is threatened. Infanticide is illegal, and as a concept probably unacceptable to Americans. The moral dilemma that will not soon be resolved turns on the question of whether there is a point of development when abortion becomes infanticide.

Fertility, social class, and feminism

The principle of fertility control had been widely accepted by American families of most ethnic and social-class backgrounds by the 1970s but not all families have the same success in controlling fertility or desire the same number of children. Historically, families that were urban, Protestant, and middle-class, or some combination of these, have been smaller than families that were rural, Catholic, working-class, or some combination of these. And as F. Scott Fitzgerald observed, the very rich are different.

In colonial America, families of ten or twelve children were quite common, and families of twenty children or more were not rare. Benjamin Franklin was one of seventeen children; the Reverend Samuel Willard, the first minister of Groton, Massachusetts, came from a family of seventeen children also, and had twenty children of his own (Bossard and Boll 1966:502). Men frequently outlived a series of wives, who bore children with monotonous regularity and died young. The children often died young, too. The Reverend Cotton Mather had fifteen children, but only two lived to mourn his passing. Someone has said that the twin burdens of the pioneer mother were the bearing and the burying of children. James Bossard and E. W. Boll (1966:502) report the following typical inscription on a family tombstone in an early American churchyard:

In memory of
Mary the Daughter of John
and Effie Lewis who died 9th Nov. 1771
aged 4 years also
seven children of Jno and Elizth Lewis

John Richard died	2nd July 1787	aged 2 months
Elizabeth	16th April 1789	11 months
Richard	25th Feb 1791	7 months
John	17th April 1795	1 year
Eliza	24th July 1797	8 months
Eliza	28th July 1800	3 months
Jessy	3rd April 1805	4 years

Epidemics of diphtheria, scarlet fever, and other diseases to which children are particularly susceptible kept infant mortality high in nineteenth-century America, but there were no great pestilences. Occasional epidemics of yellow fever occurred in New Orleans, Philadelphia, and other coastal cities near mosquito-infested swamps. There were sporadic outbreaks of typhus in seaports (Philadelphia had a typhus epidemic in 1837), but nothing to compare with the plagues that had periodically decimated the population of what had come to be called the Old World. In spite of infant mortality, the American population grew rapidly, both by immigration and by natural increase (the excess of births over deaths). But there was no overpopulation problem, for there was a continent to be filled.

On the subsistence farms of the frontier, children were needed to help in the fields. Before child labor laws were passed in the early years of the present century, the children of poor factory workers might themselves be employed as mill hands by the age of ten. As in the agricultural societies of the preindustrial past, children were their parents' wealth, in the most literal sense as well as in an emotional one. But the upwardly mobile business and professional people of the cities found large families a burden. Like the European aristocracy, they did not wish to divide their property among many sons and reduce the family to a lower class status. A man wanted one or two sons to take over the family business when he retired, but six sons could deplete the family resources.

From the latter part of the nineteenth century until World War II, a small family was considered a sign of middle-class prudence and restraint: one or two sons to carry on the family business, one or two daughters to carry on family traditions, and the desired family size was reached. Families often had one or more children than they had chosen to have, but the urban middle class began to control fertility with some effectiveness by the end of the nineteenth century. Long engagements and deferred marriage, which meant that a decade or more of a woman's fertile years had passed before she began to bear children; periods of abstinence within marriage that may well have characterized the relationship of many middle-class

123

The small coffin was white to symbolize the innocence of a little child. Infant mortality was still high in America when this picture was taken in Wisconsin (sometime between 1911 and 1913). Note how few living children there are among the mourning relatives standing in front of what is presumably a country church.

couples during the age of prudery, particularly after the early years of marriage had passed; the practice of withdrawal and the use of the condom: all were factors that helped the middle class to control fertility in late nineteenth-century America. About 1890, the family size of the urban middle classes began a gradual decline.

When contraceptives became available to the women of the middle and upper classes in the 1920s, fertility declined even more rapidly, especially in the middle classes. During the Depression years of the 1930s, birth rates dropped dramatically for the United States, and were at or below replacement levels. Many couples deferred marriage; there were many families with a single child; others were childless by choice. This was particularly true for the middle classes: fertility patterns of the very rich and the very poor were different.

When Robert and Helen Lynd conducted their classic *Middletown* study, they found that all of the women they interviewed who were members of the upper middle class were familiar with some method of contraception and were in favor of birth control. In contrast, the working-class wives the Lynds interviewed fell into three groups: those ignorant of any form of contraception, those opposed to any form of contraception, and those using ineffective means of contraception (Lynd and Lynd 1929:126–126). The use of the diaphragm was largely restricted to women of the middle and upper classes, who were fitted for a diaphragm by a private physician, often after the birth of their first child. Women who had their babies in charity wards did not receive contraceptive information or devices.

Long after birth control was an accepted practice in the middle classes, contraceptive information and prescription was withheld from patients of public health clinics on the grounds that birth control was a sensitive political issue. It was not until the 1960s that poor women were able to receive birth control information and devices that had long been available on prescription to women who could afford a private physician.

There are several reasons why the poor were the last Americans to control fertility. As has already been mentioned, the health care available to poor women differed from that available to middle-class women until quite recently. But it was not poverty alone that kept many poor women from receiving adequate gynecological care. By the 1960s, public health clinics were offering obstetrical and gynecological services and prescribing contraceptives. With regard to fertility and contraception among the poor in America, Richard Tomasson observed:

> While there is great inability to control family size effectively here, the reasons are now rarely ignorance of techniques. Rather, it is the result of a lack of motivation to exert control and an absence of communication between husband and wife on such subjects rooted in the prudery of the traditional relationship between the sexes. This underdog segment of American society (say, the bottom 15 percent) is the only part of the population where unwanted pregnancies are recurrent.   (Tomasson 1966:332)

The working poor tend to lay great stress on moral values. Working-poor families retained the attitudes of prudery long after sexual norms in the rest of American society became permissive. The working man may object to his wife having a gynecological examination (this is a class that tends to regard doctors with some suspicion), and such an examination is required before contraceptives can be prescribed. Moreover, the husband tends to be dominant in working-class marriages, and part of his dominance may lie in keeping control of fertility. Withdrawal and the use of the condom are techniques that give the man responsibility for and control of contraception; the condom is still a commonly used contraceptive in working-class marriages. In some ethnic subcultures within this class, it is considered a mark of a man's virility to keep his wife with child. (This is the attitude summed up in the country cliché that the way to keep a woman at home is to keep her "barefoot and pregnant.") Contraceptives that enable the wife to control fertility may be regarded as personally threatening by a working-class husband.

The women of the working class, like the women of poverty, tend to have less education than middle-class women. Many are high school dropouts; those from rural areas often have no more than a grade school education. This means they are likely to marry younger and begin child-

125

bearing sooner, which in itself is likely to increase the total number of children they will bear. Lack of education also means that they are more likely to accept the "traditional wisdom" of the older women of their family regarding fertility, conception, and contraception—in short, they are more likely to use ineffective contraceptive techniques. The working man's wife is also likely to be conservative in religious belief, whether she is a Catholic or a fundamentalist Protestant, and to accept religious doctrines that place a high value on fertility. Moreover, the women of this class tend to be reluctant to discuss sexual matters with their husbands (the lingering prudery) and to assume that their husband values high fertility, whether or not this is the case.

Many of the working poor (as well as many of the welfare poor) are relatively recent migrants from rural areas. Whether those rural areas were in the hills of Appalachia, or a farming village in Mexico or Sicily, part of the rural cultural heritage is a high value on fertility. Migrant farm workers find that each additional child means that there will soon be another pair of hands to pick fruit or berries. And playing with small children is often a major pleasure of the father as well as the mother among rural families. For all of these reasons, and possibly yet others, the highest fertility rates in America have been among the poor. It is only within the last decade that the fertility rate of the poor has begun to decline.

For different reasons, the very rich have also tended to have large families. Among the small group of American families who have inherited wealth through several generations, the view of the family is similar to that held by the old European aristocracy: that is, it is considered important to preserve the lineage. The family and family traditions are cherished by this established upper class, where inherited wealth is the basis of prestige and family name and lineage are important concerns. Tomasson (1966:-329) reports data on the fertility patterns of Harvard, Yale, and Princeton graduates that indicate a direct relationship between family income and number of children.

After World War II, there was a prolonged rise in the American birth rate. Demographers had not been surprised that the birth rate went up during the war years; that is a phenomenon that occurs during most wars. But after the war, the "baby boom" continued for more than a decade. Primarily, the increased birth rate represented a rise in the size of the middle-class family. Middle-class women were having more children, not because they lacked contraceptive knowledge or had difficulty obtaining contraceptive devices, but simply because they were choosing to have larger families. Middle-class women were using birth control techniques to space children rather than to postpone childbearing or to remain childless.

American women who were born in the years from 1906 to 1910 had an average of 2.4 children at the end of their childbearing. That was the average; some had larger families, but 40 percent of the white women of this age group had only one child or remained childless. In contrast, the women born in the depression years between 1931 and 1935 had, on the average, 3.3 children when they completed their families. As Tomasson observed:

> A difference between 2.4 and 3.3 children is tremendous in its growth implications. With a continuation of our present high marriage rates and fairly low death rates an average of 2.2 children per couple would insure something close to a stable population. With an average of 2.4 children, the population would grow slowly, by a fraction of one percent a year. With an average of 3.3 children it would double in less than 40 years. At this rate, by the time my young children are in their 90's, there would be a billion of us.   (Tomasson 1966:328)

The question—and it was an important question to those concerned about the growth of the population of the United States—was why a larger family was suddenly desired by middle-class families. There were some who felt that the media had promoted larger families. Tomasson comments that "a generation ago ads with family pictures and movies with 'typical' families almost always had a boy and girl; now they usually show three or four children" (1966:332). It has been suggested by others that children are the symbols of the affluence of their fathers. It is expensive to raise a child in an urban environment, especially if the child is to have braces on his teeth, riding lessons, music lessons, and private school before he is sent to an Ivy League university. The man who can afford to raise three or four children in such fashion shows that he commands a sizable income as surely as the man who maintains a yacht.

But affluence and conspicuous consumption are not themselves a sufficient explanation of the desire to have a large family. As Tomasson observes, "Material well-being and security allow many couples to support adequately three or four children; it does not explain why fewer or more choose to do so in different societies and in different segments of the same society. Why not better vacations or a higher standard of living?" (1966: 330). The answer, he believes, lies in the tendency of the professional and managerial middle classes to seek the "good life" in the home and family.

Gary Becker (1960) notes that in many countries children are "producer durables," valued for the productive services they will render in the home. It was not too long ago that farm children, or the children who were unpaid workers in the family business, were still valued as producers in America. But for almost all American families today, children require the outlay of large amounts of money, and are unlikely even to contribute directly to the parents' support in old age: Social Security, pension benefits, and life insurance annuities provided by the parents themselves are likely to be the major support of older Americans. Why, then, were larger families wanted by middle-class families in the 1950s? Becker contends that children qualify as "consumer durables," valued for the psychic income that they can be expected to yield their parents over many years (Becker 1960). The economist's language seems harsh, but translated into

127

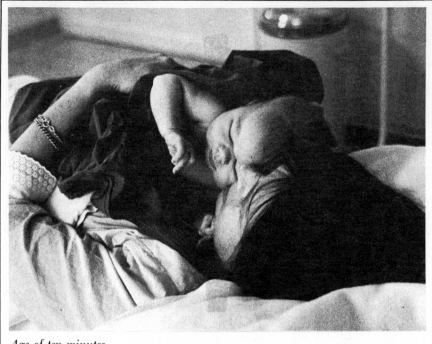

Age of ten minutes.

the statement that parents want children because they are seeking the enduring emotional rewards a child brings, it is a less startling statement.

The large families of recent years were more than status symbols, more than a fad promoted by the women's magazines. The large family was the dream of a generation of little girls who were in their formative years during the most severe depression this country has ever known. The little girl who was an only child often felt deprived of the relationship with the brother or sister she might have had. In the world in which she was raised, small families were considered an economic necessity; that little brother or sister she wanted so much was a luxury the family could not afford. Mother explained that. And the little girl knew that money, or the lack of it, was what her parents quarreled about at night, when the little girl should have been asleep. (America in the 1930s was a world in which welfare payments did not automatically increase if there was another child in the family; even if they had, most Americans of that generation avoided welfare if they could possibly sustain life without it, for to accept it was considered a shameful admission that they had failed to provide for themselves.)

One of the psychic rewards of having children is that they give parents an opportunity to re-create their own childhood, as they would have liked it to be, to experience childhood vicariously through their children.

128

(Whether or not this is a benefit or burden to the child, it is a major motivation of parents, one of the reasons people want to have children, and probably on balance it is functional.) The daughters of the Depression had a dream in which happiness was a large, mother-centered family that never needed to scrimp. The suburban home, with the wide expanse of lawn on which a bevy of little brothers and sisters played happily together, was what they wanted, along with the handsome, successful man who would make it all possible. It was a possible dream, and many women were able to accomplish it in the 1950s. That the shared dream of so many lonely little girls should have become a demographic nightmare of exploding population and expanding suburbs was only one of the ironies of that decade.

However, the crude birth rate began to decline in 1957, and dropped slowly through the 1960s. By 1974, it had dropped to 1.85 per woman of childbearing age, below the replacement level. Growing awareness of the dangers of overpopulation, especially on the part of the young people who are forming the new families of the 1970s, has led to a decline in the desired family size. Many young couples are choosing to have only two children of their own and to adopt others if they want a larger family. Some other young couples are choosing to remain childless. The childless couples often feel defensive, and might be surprised to know that in the generation to which their grandparents belong many other couples chose to be childless.

By 1971 the birth rate in America had dropped to the point of "zero population growth": that is, to the point where the birth rate was in balance with the death rate and the total population is steady, perhaps even slightly declining. The declining fertility reflects the introduction of improved contraceptives. The period of greatest decline in the birth rate coincides with the period in which the Pill was introduced and widely accepted, and with the period in which new, improved IUDs were made available. The drop in the birth rate of the last few years has coincided with the legalization of abortion, which has had a marked effect on fertility, particularly among the very young and the poor, as a last-resort measure when contraception has failed.

The recent decline in the birth rate preceded the severe recession of the middle 1970s, so recession cannot be said to have caused it, although the recession may have contributed to the decision of young couples to continue postponing children. The concern of many young Americans about social ills may be part of the reason for the lower birth rate: unlike pollution, poverty, racism, and war, overpopulation is a problem that the young have the power to control, for most American women concentrate their childbearing between the ages of nineteen and twenty-nine. But there is yet another ideological factor that is perhaps even more important: the rising feminism that has made the dream of the large family in the suburban home seem a snare and a delusion.

Feminism was a factor in the earlier decline in fertility; it does not

129

seem adequate to explain that decline entirely in terms of the business cycle. Those women who had so few children during the 1930s were teenage girls when the first wave of feminism crested in America. They were the "flappers" who dared to break the taboos of prudery; they were the "white-collar girls" who had careers instead of babies. Forty percent of the white women of that generation had only one child or remained childless. Now, a second feminist wave has rolled in, and the number of women who are choosing to postpone marriage, or not to marry at all, is increasing. Some women are choosing motherhood without marriage, although the illegitimacy rate in 1974 decreased for the fourth straight year (U.S. Public Health Service 1976:4). More women are apparently choosing marriage without motherhood, as their great-aunts did some forty years ago.

American women who were between the ages of twenty-five and twenty-nine in 1931 had an average of 2.4 children at the end of their childbearing. This was approximately a replacement rate, and if sustained, would have meant a stable population. But American women who were between the ages of twenty-five and twenty-nine in 1956 had an average of 3.3 children, and the result was the "baby boom." In 1975 the U.S. Bureau of the Census reported that surveys it had conducted indicated that married women twenty-five to twenty-nine years of age had reduced their total childbearing expectations to an average of 2.34 (U.S. Bureau of the Census 1975:table 1).

Birth rates have risen and declined in America in long cycles, cycles that have been influenced by social and economic disruptions, such as war and depression. In turn, cycles in fertility have created some social and economic disruptions. For example, the children of the "baby-boom" of the late 1950s had a great impact on educational institutions, creating a need to divert community resources into building more schools and hiring more teachers. When fertility rates declined, school enrollments declined accordingly, again disrupting educational institutions. Communities had to support and maintain underutilized school facilities, and unemployed teachers sought other work. The high unemployment rates among the young in the early 1970s were caused at least in part by the fact that the children of the "baby boom" years had reached adulthood and the job market could not absorb them all.

It may be that fertility rates in America have now stabilized at approximately a replacement rate. But stability is often an illusion. As June Sklar and Beth Berkov (1975:693) note, during the Depression no one anticipated World War II and the postwar rise in fertility, nor during the "baby boom" years was there any expectation that the birth rate would fall as fast or as far as it has. Sklar and Berkov point out that there is at present a high proportion of young married women who are childless and that there is evidence that many of them do not want to remain childless. They suggest that the decline in fertility rates may have touched its nadir, and that an

130

increase is due in the next few years, as women who postponed children decide that they can wait no longer to become mothers.

References

Becker, Gary S. 1960. "An Economic Analysis of Fertility Behavior." In Universities-National Bureau Conference Series 11, *Demographic and Economic Change in Developed Countries*. Princeton, N.J.: Princeton University Press.

Bossard, James H. S., and E. W. Boll. 1966. *The Sociology of Child Development*, 4th ed. New York: Harper & Row.

Calio, Jim, with Gerald C. Lubenow. 1975. "Abortion and the Law." *Newsweek* 85 (March 3):18–30.

Hellman, Louis M., M.D. 1969. "Oral Contraceptives: Safety and Complications." In *Family Planning Today*, edited by Alan Rubin, M.D., pp. 29–42. Philadelphia: F. A. Davis.

Himes, Norman E. 1936. *Medical History of Contraception*. Baltimore: Williams and Wilkins.

Huber, Sallie C., P. T. Piotrow, F. Barbara Orlans, and Geary Kommer. 1975. "IUDs Reassessed—A Decade of Experience." In *Population Reports*, Series B-2 (January). Washington, D.C.: The George Washington University Medical Center.

Jelliffe, D. B., and E. F. P. Jelliffe. 1975. "Human Milk, Nutrition, and the World Resource Crisis." *Science* 188 (May):557–565.

Kinsey, Alfred C. 1966. "Illegal Abortion in the United States." In *The Unwed Mother*, edited by R. W. Roberts, pp. 191–199. New York: Harper & Row.

Kopp, M. E. 1934. *Birth Control in Practice: Analysis of 10,000 Case Histories of the Birth Control Clinical Research Bureau*. New York: McBrides.

Linton, Ralph. 1956. *The Tree of Culture*. New York: Alfred A. Knopf.

Lynd, Robert S., and Helen Merrell Lynd. 1929. *Middletown*. New York: Harcourt Brace Jovanovich.

Oster, Gerald. 1972. "Conception and Contraception." *Natural History* 81 (August-September):47–53.

Rock, John C., M.D. 1963. *The Time Has Come: A Catholic Doctor's Proposals to End the Battle over Birth Control*. New York: Alfred A. Knopf.

Scientific American. 1972. "Science News." *Scientific American* 227 (July): 51.

Sklar, June, and Beth Berkov. 1975. "Trend of the U.S. Birth Rate." *Science* 190 (29 August):693.

Stone, Lawrence. 1960–61. "Marriage among the English Nobility." *Comparative Studies in Society and History* 3 (November-January):182–206.

Stouffer, Samuel A., and Paul F. Lazarsfeld. 1937. *Research Memorandum on the Family in the Depression*. New York: Social Science Research Council.

Tomasson, Richard F. 1966. "Why Has American Fertility Been So High?" In *Kinship and Family Organization*, edited by Bernard Farber, pp. 327–338. New York: John Wiley & Sons.

U.S. Bureau of the Census. 1975. *Current Population Reports*. Series P-20, no. 277 (February 1975). Washington, D.C.: U.S. Government Printing Office.

U.S. Public Health Service. 1976. "Advance Report Final Natality Statistics, 1974." *Monthly Vital Statistics Report* 24 (February 13):1–5.

131

Westoff, Charles F., and Norman B. Ryder. 1969. "Recent Trends in Attitude toward Fertility Control and in the Practice of Contraception in the United States." In *Fertility and Family Planning: A World View,* edited by S. J. Behrman, Leslie Corsa, Jr., and Ronald Freedman. Ann Arbor: University of Michigan Press.

Zinsser, Hans. 1935. *Rats, Lice and History.* Boston: Little, Brown and Company.

Suggested readings

Brown, Harrison, and Edward Hutchings, Jr., eds. 1970, 1972. *Are Our Descendants Doomed? Technological Change and Population Growth.* New York: Viking Press. Paper. An anthology with topics ranging from "The Changing Balance of Births and Deaths" to "Birth Control after 1984: A Realistic Appraisal of Future Contraceptive Developments." An important book.

Oster, Gerald. 1972. "Conception and Contraception." *Natural History* 81 (August-September):47–53. A description of the process of conception that includes discussion of the role of reproductive hormones; scholarly, yet written for the layman. Illustrated.

Westoff, Leslie Aldridge, and Charles F. Westoff. 1968, 1971. *From Now to Zero: Fertility, Contraception, and Abortion in America.* Boston: Little, Brown and Company. Paper. This book began as an attempt to make the findings of the 1965 National Fertility Study available to a lay audience. It became much more. In addition to the materials drawn from the National Fertility Study, the book includes biological, historical and descriptive information on fertility, reproduction, contraception, and abortion. The section on family planning is precisely that; there are other chapters on contraception.

5 Marriage and legitimacy

Why bastard? Wherefore base? When my dimensions are as well compact, My mind as generous, and my shape as true as honest madam's issue? Why brand they us with base? with baseness? bastardy? ... Now, gods, stand up for bastards!

William Shakespeare,
King Lear act I, scene 2

Marriage represents the attempt by society to control the reproductive behavior of its members. Sex outside of marriage may
be socially condoned, so long as there is no resulting pregnancy.
As Bronislaw Malinowski observed, "Between the freedom of sexual life
and the freedom of becoming a mother, a sharp distinction is drawn in all
human societies including our own" (1930:135). Marriage legitimates.
There is an apocryphal tale that Robert Bierstedt tells to illustrate the
importance of marital status (1970:243):

> It concerns the doctor who, upon completing his examination of a young
> woman, said, "Mrs. Jones, I have very good news for you."
> "My name," the young woman replied, "is Miss Jones, not Mrs. Jones."
> "In that case" said the doctor, "I'm afraid I have very bad news for you."

The use of *Ms.* as a form of social address that eliminates the distinction between *Miss* and *Mrs.* has as one of its effects the blurring of the
distinction between the unwed mother and her married counterpart. This
was in fact a stated objective of some German women a decade or more
ago when a similar blurring of the distinction between *Frau* and *Fraulein*
occurred in West Germany. But while dropping the differentiation in
social address between married and unmarried woman may alleviate some
of the public embarrassment felt by the unwed mother, it does not alter
the legal, social, or economic situation of the illegitimate child.

In the last fifty years, the proportion of illegitimate births in the
United States has risen steadily. In 1925 the illegitimacy ratio (the number
of illegitimate births per 1,000 live births in a given year) was 15.4. By 1940
the ratio was 37.9; in 1950 it was 39.8 (having risen during World War II,
then declined); by 1965 the illegitimacy ratio had reached 77.4 (U.S. Public
Health Service December 1974:8). By 1968 the illegitimacy ratio had
spurted to 96.9 (U.S. Public Health Service August 1974:20). By 1974
there was an illegitimacy ratio of 132.3 illegitimate births per 1,000 total
live births in the United States (U.S. Public Health Service 1976:4). Figures on illegitimate births in the United States are approximations, because some states do not report legitimacy statistics and the figures for
the total United States are estimated from those that do. However approx-
imate the figures, the rise in illegitimate births is indisputable.

The growing proportion of illegitimate births has been cited as one
of the indications that marriage as an institution is collapsing in the United States, particularly among the very poor. In the inner-city populations
of Baltimore, Chicago, Los Angeles, Minneapolis, and New York City, the
proportion of illegitimate births had risen by 1970 to more than 50 percent of all live births (U.S. Public Health Service 1975:31). Illegitimacy has
been linked to poverty and welfare in both a cause and an effect relationship. The solutions suggested by researchers and legislators range from
the preventive (better sex education in the schools, readily available contraceptives and abortion) to the punitive (criminal penalties for the par-

136

ents of illegitimate children). Perhaps the most sweeping solution has been tried by Arizona and Oregon, which have no illegitimacy because these states have elimitated the legal distinction between legitimate and illegitimate birth.

This last solution is stunning in its simplicity. But problems do not disappear because of a change in status definition, however important in itself and as a first step that change may be. For instance, the problems of black Americans did not disappear when slavery was abolished, although abolition of the status of slave was an essential step toward equality. The analogy is appropriate: historically, the illegitimate child has been a second-class citizen.

There are a number of questions that need to be raised: What have been the social goals, historically, of the distinction between the legitimate and the illegitimate child? Are these goals still meaningful in our society? Are there social benefits that would be lost if the distinction between legitimate and illegitimate birth were erased, either by legislative or by judicial action? What would be the effect on marriage as an institution if its function of legitimacy were eliminated? What problems faced by the unwed mother and her child cannot be resolved by defining illegitimacy out of existence? What other solutions to the problem of illegitimacy are there?

Marriage confers legitimacy

To begin with the first question, what have been the social goals, historically, of the distinction between the legitimate and the illegitimate child? It is considered a socially desired goal that children not be born to a woman living without a husband in our society (and in most others), and for reasons that go far deeper than the moral scruples of prudery: the group composed of mother and children is a fragment of a family. Even in cultures that value fecundity more than virginity, the family is considered incomplete unless there is a male willing to assume the role that Malinowski labeled that of the "sociological father" when he formulated his classic *principle of legitimacy:* "The most important moral and legal rule concerning the physiological side of kinship is that no child should be brought into the world without a man—and one man at that—assuming the role of sociological father, that is, guardian and protector, the male link between the child and the rest of the community" (1930:137).

Malinowski's principle of legitimacy was later refined by William Goode, who pointed out that the crux of the matter is not so much the *protection* of the child as the *status placement of the child in society.* "The bastard daughter of a count is still illegitimate even if he 'protects' her," as Goode observes (1960:27). The branding of children born out of wedlock as illegitimate began in an age when rank, property, and authority were inherited; the right to claim membership in a particular family involved too much social and economic power to be left to the vagaries of the sexual

137

impulse. Accordingly, suitable marriages were arranged by family elders, and only the children of a sanctioned marital union were allowed to inherit. The "by-blows" were granted no legal claim to the rank or the property of their father, although he might choose to provide for their care and upbringing, and perhaps even make them his favorites. Thus, in its origins, the concern with legitimate birth was to protect the orderly transfer of the father's power, position, and property, rather than to protect the child.

The status of an illegitimate child in our society is a kind of nonstatus. Like the unwed mother and the nonwhite, the illegitimate child is defined in terms of what he is not. But in some earlier societies, the illegitimate child of a powerful man occupied a specific status, always less privileged than the legitimate child of similar parentage, but with certain prerogatives. In the past, European aristocrats kept concubines openly, kings frequently taking as concubines the daughters of lesser nobles or rich merchants, men who hoped to gain favor at court through a daughter who was the king's favorite. The child of such a union could not succeed to the throne, but did have a recognized status in some societies. This status was often one that entitled an illegitimate son to use the coat-of-arms of the family of his father, but with two parallel lines drawn diagonally across the shield: the "baton sinister," the badge of bastardy.

Because illegitimate sons of kings could not inherit the throne, unlike their legitimate half-brothers they had nothing to gain by deposing their father. On the contrary, their position in society depended on retaining their father's favor and on their father's continued power. Consequently, they were often placed in positions of trust by the king, their father. "Thus the 'Grand Bastard of Burgundy,' a title as specific as that of 'Prince of Wales,' was by custom commander-in-chief of the Burgundian armies" (Linton 1956:266). However, an illegitimate son of nobility could seize some other kingdom, as William the Conqueror did. (In his time, he was called "William the Bastard," which was not a reference to his personal behavior.) Still, the "left-hand" side of the house (so-called because it had been the old Germanic custom for the "bridegroom" to give his left hand in "marriage" when he formally took a concubine) was at a disadvantage. No society is completely closed to people of extraordinary ability, whatever their parentage, but neither is any society completely open; the status to which children are born sets limits to their future.

Status is *not* synonymous with prestige. Prestige is the *esteem* with which one is regarded by others; status is *position* in a social structure. A powerful status is likely to be associated with high prestige, but the two social attributes are distinct. Every social structure is built of interlocking statuses, connected by socially defined roles. Every member of a society occupies some status, usually more than one, but not all have prestige or power. Some statuses have accompanying roles of authority, and the incumbent may be given deferential treatment because of his position, whether or not he enjoys the personal esteem of his fellows.

Social stability requires the orderly replacement of status incumbents: "The King is dead! Long live the King!" Where positions of rank and power are inherited, legitimate birth is the means of orderly replacement, and lineage is the framework on which society is built. This is why such societies try to ensure that the heirs to power have socially approved parentage. Whenever the legitimacy of an heir to the throne has been in doubt, these doubts have led to dispute, and even to civil war, if some other branch of the ruling family claimed the throne: for instance, the contention for the throne of England between Elizabeth I and her cousin Mary, Queen of Scots, which turned on the question of the legitimacy of Elizabeth.

Feudal societies sought to retain large hereditary estates intact, for large holdings were the economic base of the aristocracy. To divide such estates among many heirs would have reduced powerful families to small farmers within a few generations, and destroyed the aristocracy. The heir to both land and title was the first-born son in the legitimate line, or if there were none, the male who was the next of kin in the legitimate line. Legitimacy again was the basis of the orderly transfer of wealth and power.

In our own society, status has both a social and a legal context. Socially, it is not lineage as such but rather the occupation of the male head of household that determines the social placement of the family. Occupation forms the interlocking status structure of our society, and status incumbents are replaced on the basis of education, prior experience, or election. Theoretically, legitimacy should not matter.

But the status placement of the family in which a child is raised determines the economic circumstances of his childhood—the quality of food, housing, and medical care he receives, as well as the class subculture in which he is socialized and the opportunities he will have for a professional or technical education. Thus a child's future is limited, although not determined, by the status of his father; the fatherless child is likely to be both socially and economically disadvantaged.

Except for the occasional American who becomes the president of the firm his father or grandfather founded, there are no inherited *positions* of authority in our society. What is inherited is property, and a parent may leave property to children—legitimate or not—or may decide to leave it to a favorite charity and disinherit all the children. American inheritance tax laws have tended to break up large concentrations of inherited property, indicating that the maintenance of large hereditary estates is not considered a desirable social goal in our society.

If neither the protection of inherited status nor the perpetuation of large property holdings is a major social goal of our society, what then is the presumed social benefit of differentiating between legitimate and illegitimate children? In a case that came before the United States Supreme Court in 1968, the state of Louisiana presented a brief that stated the reasons why that state considered the distinction between legitimate and illegitimate children to be of social value:

139

Louisiana's purposes in this area are positive ones; the *encouragement of marriage* as one of the most important institutions known to law, the preservation of the legitimate family as the preferred environment for socializing the child, and the preservation of the security and certainty of property rights linked with family status.

... Since marriage as an institution is fundamental to our existence as a free nation, it is the duty of the State of Louisiana to encourage it. One method of encouraging marriage is granting greater rights to legitimate offspring than those born of extra-marital unions. Superior rights of legitimate offspring are inducements or incentives to parties to contract marriages, which is preferred by Louisiana as the setting for producing offspring. (Cited in Krause 1969:66)

Louisiana lost the case. However, the argument is instructive, for it indicates the rationale for the maintenance of the distinction between legitimate and illegitimate children. The position assumes that a woman will be so concerned about the legal rights of her future children that she will refrain from extramarital intercourse. With the possible historical exception of Anne Boleyn, it seems doubtful that young women have ever been deterred from sexual intercourse by such legalistic concerns. Fear of pregnancy out of wedlock does inhibit sexual activity, but it is more likely to be fear of the social ostracism that a woman would encounter as an unwed mother than thought of the legal rights of her child to inherit or to sue for wrongful death of a parent (that is, the right to sue someone whose action or negligence caused the death of a parent, the matter at issue in the Louisiana case). Even if such concerns were effective deterrents to extramarital sex, "it would not be permissible to punish an innocent nonparty for someone else's undesirable conduct," as Harry Krause points out (1969:66).

Nonetheless the stigma placed on illegitimacy—especially on the unwed mother and her family—does encourage marriage. According to data collected for the 1964–1966 National Natality Survey, 42 percent of the women fifteen to nineteen years of age for whom the interval from first marriage to legitimate first birth was reported had been married for less than eight months (U.S. Public Health Service 1970). Even if we allow for premature babies, the high proportion of teenage brides who were pregnant before the wedding suggests that the prospect of bearing an illegitimate child is a powerful inducement to marriage.

If the major social goals served by the legal distinction between legitimate and illegitimate children are the encouragement of marriage and the preservation of the family as the preferred environment for socializing the child, as the state of Louisiana argued, then the questions to be asked are whether these are widely held goals in our society and, if the answer is affirmative, whether or not these ends are best served by placing the illegitimate child at serious legal disadvantage. Even the basic social

140

welfare legislation of the United States is inconsistent on this last point.

Legitimacy and the law in the United States

Status has a legal as well as a sociological meaning: those who occupy a certain legal status have certain rights and obligations under the law. For the legitimate child, the *rights* include the right to parental support until the child reaches majority; the right to inherit from either or both parents if they die intestate (without a will); the right to certain benefits provided to the children of veterans; the rights granted survivors under provisions of Social Security and workmen's compensation laws; and so on for a long list, including the right to sue (or for suit to be brought in a minor child's name) in the wrongful death of a parent. The *obligations* of a legitimate child include the right parents have to his labor or wages as long as the child is an unemancipated minor (an obligation that was heavier fifty years ago than it is today) and the obligations that an adult has toward aged and indigent parents.

The illegitimate child, by definition, is not entitled to the rights enjoyed by the legitimate child, nor does he incur the obligations of that status. The laws of most states have long given the illegitimate child the same rights as the legitimate child with regard to the mother, since maternity is usually beyond question. However, it was precisely the right of an illegitimate child to bring suit in the wrongful death of his mother that was the basis for the Louisiana brief cited above. In 1968 the United States Supreme Court ruled, in *Levy* v. *Louisiana,* and *Glona* v. *American Guarantee & Liability Insurance Company,* that the equal protection clause of the Fourteenth Amendment to the Constitution means that illegitimate and legitimate children are equal with regard to their mother. In both cases, a wrongful death claim involving the mother of an illegitimate child was at issue.

If this ruling is extended to include equality of rights regarding the father, there will be in effect no legal distinction left between legitimate and illegitimate children in the United States. The Missouri Supreme Court has so ruled in a case involving an illegitimate child's right to claim the support of his father, citing the 1968 United States Supreme Court decision as the basis. However, the Ohio Supreme Court has denied a similar claim, on the ground that the 1968 ruling applied only to equality of rights with regard to the mother. The Ohio court deferred to the legislature the "dramatic change in social pattern" involved (Krause 1969:67).

Meanwhile, the laws regarding legitimacy are a maze, and vary widely from state to state. According to Krause, "While some general conclusions may be drawn, the range of American states includes those which deny the illegitimate any claim on his father, as well as those that have abolished the concept of illegitimacy" (1969:59). Even federal legislation,

141

such as the Social Security Act, the Copyright Act, the Federal Group Life Insurance Act, the Longshoremen's and Harbor Workers' Compensation Act, and the various statutes involving the rights of dependents and survivors of veterans, are inconsistent in whether or not the benefits provided the children of men covered by these various statutes are available to illegitimate as well as to legitimate children. Krause observes that "more recently, federal welfare laws (especially the Social Security Act) have moved toward eliminating discrimination against the illegitimate, but considerable deference to state policy in the field of family relations remains and this usually spells a disadvantage for the illegitimate" (1969:64–65).

However, there have been numerous recent attempts to alleviate the situation of the illegitimate child by changes in statute law. Under the English common law (the foundation of the American legal system), children born to a marriage that was later annulled were considered illegitimate. Most states now consider such children legitimate, and also the children born of almost any union that resembles a formal marriage. This means that in some states the children of "common-law" marriages (*consensual union* is a more precise term) are considered legitimate. In many states, if a marriage is void because of the failure of the couple to obtain required health examinations, or to obtain parental consent if one of them is a minor, or if the marriage is void because one of the parties was underage, or one was insane, or even if one was a bigamist, any child born to the union is given legitimate status. The newer statute provisions thus reduce illegitimacy by defining legitimacy more broadly. As indicated above, at least two states (Oregon and Arizona) have statutes that eliminate all distinction between legitimate and illegitimate children.

It is assumed by the laws of most states that any child born to a married woman is legitimate, unless there is conclusive evidence to indicate that the mother's husband could not have been the father of the child. However, many states have not yet clarified in statute law the status of the child who is conceived by artificial insemination with semen from an anonymous donor, with the consent of the mother's husband. The matter of the legitimacy of such children has come before the courts in various states, and the case decisions have ranged, according to Krause, "from the sensible holding that the resultant child is legitimate to the remarkable extreme of branding the child a bastard and the mother an adulteress" (1969:61).

If the child is conceived out of wedlock, but the parents marry before his birth, the child is considered legitimate, although some states require the father to acknowledge paternity. In some states the child may be legitimated in this manner even if the parents do not marry until after his birth. In some states, if a father admits his illegitimate child into his family and through this and other acts indicates a voluntary acceptance of the child, the child is legally considered legitimate. The range and variation of state law is wide and confusing; it is an area where a decision by the

United States Supreme Court would bring welcome relief from the present chaos. It is also an area of great moral and political sensitivity and one that has in the past been left to state law.

The unwed mother: who and why

We are all participant observers of our society and inevitably see the world through a cultural prism. The prevailing assumptions regarding right, wrong, and individual responsibility form a social filter through which even the most objective researcher views data. Thus studies conducted in the 1920s concluded that unwed mothers were below normal intelligence, immoral, or both. During the 1930s, researchers focused on the situational influences on the unwed mother's behavior: poverty, lack of education, and in particular the "broken home" syndrome were identified as the causes of illegitimacy. In the 1940s and 1950s, studies indicated either that the unwed mother came from a subculture in which illegitimacy was accepted as a fact of life or else that the unwed mother was acting out deep-seated emotional conflicts with her parents, most frequently a love-hate relationship with a dominant and sadistic mother. Writing in 1960, Blanche Bernstein and Mignon Sauber observed: "The theory of out-of-wedlock pregnancy currently accepted among social workers and members of other helping disciplines is that it is symptomatic and purposeful, an attempt by the personality to ease an unresolved conflict" (1960:22).

To some degree it is impossible to escape the social and intellectual ambience of the 1970s in viewing such a complex issue as illegitimacy. So let it be noted that the prevailing view now, shared by this author, is that it is not sufficient to blame the victim, that solutions without blame need to be found to social problems that touch us all.

Many of the earlier studies of the unwed mother, her characteristics, motives, and choices, were based on data available from homes for unwed mothers and clinics (sometimes psychiatric clinics). These were the populations of unwed mothers that were most readily accessible for research purposes, with minimal invasion of privacy. But these populations were not a random sample of unwed mothers. The women who went to homes for unwed mothers and similar agencies tended to be young (often adolescent), white, and middle-class. They were girls who perceived their pregnancy as a problem, indeed as a severe personal crisis, and who had sufficient education or assistance to obtain professional help with that problem.

The woman who plans to keep her illegitimate child is more likely to stay at home, in familiar surroundings, during her pregnancy; it is the woman who plans to release her child for adoption that is more likely to seek the anonymity of a home for unwed mothers. Until recently, it was difficult to place a nonwhite child for adoption. Thus women from racial minorities and from ethnic groups that frown on adoption tended to be underrepresented among the clients of these charitable organizations.

143

Women who consulted private physicians, and women who found abortion an acceptable alternative and could afford it, were seldom clients in the home for unwed mothers. Thus studies of women in such homes tended to focus on a biased sample of unwed mothers.

Statistical data available on the total population of unwed mothers from the U.S. Public Health Service do not include information on the social class, behavioral characteristics, or personalities of unwed mothers, but do record their age and race (or at least report them as white and "all other"). A special report of the U.S. Public Health Service, published in 1973, deals with the vital statistics of teenagers through 1969, and includes information on illegitimate births across all age groups. These births occurred prior to the recent changes in the abortion laws that have had a major impact on the number of illegitimate births in all age groups and among all races. But at least in the period immediately before the more liberal abortion laws and court rulings, nearly as many illegitimate children were born to adolescent mothers as to all women over twenty years of age. "In 1968, while accounting for 14 percent of legitimate births in the United States, teenage women accounted for 49 percent of illegitimate births. The estimated 165,700 illegitimate births to teenage mothers that year were almost as many as were recorded for all other age groups of women combined" (U.S. Public Health Service August 1974:19–20).

There are two statistical measures of illegitimacy. One, previously mentioned, is the illegitimacy *ratio*, which is the proportion of illegitimate live births to total live births: it compares births. The other is the illegitimacy *rate*, which relates the number of illegitimate live births to the number of unmarried women in a particular group: it tells us how likely a woman was to have an illegitimate child in a given year. In 1968, although nearly as many illegitimate babies were born to teenage mothers as to unmarried women in all age groups over twenty, the illegitimacy *rate* for teenage women was lower than for other age groups of women under forty. The reason for this seeming contradiction is that there are proportionately fewer unmarried women in the older groups, and thus most of the unmarried women who might become unwed mothers are in their teens. On the other hand, older unmarried women were more likely to have babies than were the unmarried teenagers. "In 1968 there were 20 illegitimate births per 1,000 unmarried females at ages 15–19. This rate was scarcely over half the rate for the next age group, 37 per 1,000 for women 20–24 years old" (U.S. Public Health Service, August 1974:21).

To state it simply, most American teenage girls are not married, and most are not pregnant. But of those teenagers who are pregnant, a large proportion are unmarried. The younger the mother, the more likely she is to be unmarried. In 1974, when the mother was under fifteen years of age, 846 of every 1,000 babies born were illegitimate; when the mother was fifteen to nineteen years of age, 354 out of every 1,000 live births were illegitimate; when the mother was twenty to twenty-four years of age, 110 out of every 1,000 live births were illegitimate (U.S. Public Health Service

1976:11). As the U.S. Public Health Service points out, these figures probably understate the number of premarital *conceptions* among teenage women. "Such a count would include conceptions that did not terminate in a live birth (for which no estimates are available) and births that were legitimized by marriage between the time of conception and birth, as well as illegitimate births" (August 1974:18–19).

During the years from 1960 to 1968, illegitimacy *rates* for all women in the United States twenty years of age and older were either stable or declining. However, the illegitimacy rate for women aged fifteen to nineteen increased by nearly 30 percent. The increase in illegitimacy rates for teenage women was high enough to influence the total illegitimacy rate, which climbed steadily from 1962 to 1970 (U.S. Public Health Service 1976:4). Those were the years immediately after the introduction of the Pill, but teenage women were less likely to have access to reliable contraceptives than were older women. Those were also the years of the "flower children," of runaway girls who went to New York's East Village, or to the Haight-Ashbury district of San Francisco. Those were years when it was more painful than usual to be an adolescent girl.

After 1970 the illegitimacy rate turned downward (although the illegitimacy *ratio* continued to increase). In 1974 the U.S. Public Health Service reported the fourth consecutive decline in the illegitimacy rate (1976:4). However, rates of illegitimacy for white women fifteen to nineteen years old increased 4 percent over the preceding year.

The unwed mother is not only likely to be in her early teens, she is also likely to be nonwhite. Although 81.5 percent of the live births in 1974 were to white women, only 40.3 percent of the illegitimate births in 1974 were to white mothers. In contrast, 16.0 percent of all live births were to black women, but 57.1 percent of the illegitimate births in 1974 were to black mothers. (The remaining births were to "other" races.) The illegitimacy rate for black women fifteen to nineteen years of age in 1974 was 95.1 per 1,000 unmarried women in this age and racial group. This was over eight times the rate for white teenage women, which was 11.1 per 1,000 unmarried women in the same age group (U.S. Public Health Service 1976:11).

Finally, the unwed mother is likely to be poor. In poverty areas of New York City in 1974 the illegitimacy ratio for black babies was 512 per 1,000 live births. In nonpoverty areas, the illegitimacy ratio for black babies was 332.7 per 1,000 live births. Among the white population of New York City in 1974, the illegitimacy ratio in poverty areas was 298.8 per 1,000 live births; in nonpoverty areas it was only 56.6 per 1,000 live births. Similar differences were reported between poverty and nonpoverty areas of other large cities in the United States (U.S. Public Health Service November 1975:31).

Although they are by no means the only women who become pregnant out of wedlock, the daughters of the underclass of welfare poor who live in housing projects are more at hazard because of their environment.

They observe coitus from an early age, and are often under peer pressure to participate in sex play. Boone Hammond and Joyce Ladner quote one black mother's comment (1969:43–44):

> These kids grow up fast in this project. These five and six year old heifers [girls] know as much about screwing as I do. My six year old boy has already punched [had intercourse with] two or three of these fast chicks and I'm teaching my four year old boy to be a lady killer too. I can't hide the facts of life from them because they can see them everyday on any stairway, hall or elevator in the project.

What begins as sex play—imitative behavior—at the age of five or six soon becomes an active sex life. Hammond and Ladner quote a thirteen-year-old girl: "When we are hanging around the building and don't have anything to do and boys come around we might start playing with them and before you know it all of us are mellow [having sex]" (1969:50). As another girl explained, "We sometimes do it for kicks, and you don't have to like the boy to do it with him. You do it cause you can be mellow when you don't want to play cards or watch TV" (Hammond and Ladner 1969: 50).

Although certain social situations tend to make illegitimacy commonplace, illegitimacy occurs across class lines and throughout the child-bearing years. But more often than not, the unwed mother is a teenage woman from a deprived family and cultural background, is likely to be a high school dropout, nonwhite, and may be emotionally disturbed. What is cause and what effect may be more difficult to say. There is a cycle of poverty, illegitimacy, depression, dropping out of school, poverty, illegitimacy, and so on, around the closed circle of deprived lives.

Premarital pregnancy: crises and options

Part of the social concern about illegitimacy is concern about the unwed mother, for there are always at least two lives affected by the birth of an illegitimate child. The family of the unwed mother is also directly affected, and premarital or extramarital pregnancy is often a major family crisis. In a peasant village, the illegitimate child of a daughter is often accepted, if not always welcomed, because the child is considered a member of his mother's family, and legitimacy is less important than blood ties: people care for their own. Besides, a child will soon be another pair of hands to help in the fields. The rural poor in America have come close to such an acceptance of illegitimate children; transplanted to the metropolis as the slum poor, they have continued to accept the illegitimate child as part of the mother's family. If the mother is an adolescent, the grandmother will often raise her illegitimate grandchild until the mother herself grows up.

But among the middle classes in America—both white-collar and blue-color—it is another story. An illegitimate grandchild is more than most middle-class matrons in their thirties and forties can bear. He will

146

ruin the family's reputation, and will not even be able to hoe the corn. The teenage daughter who becomes pregnant out of wedlock faces severe emotional crises. The older single or divorced woman who becomes pregnant is more likely to have experience and resources to fall back on, although she, too, may face a severe personal crisis.

The pregnant single girl who is still a dependent in her parent's home has a series of crises to face, at a time when the physiological changes she is experiencing are in themselves likely to have emotional effects. First, there is the emotional crisis that involves recognition of the fact that she is pregnant. Some young women try to hide that fact, and anxiety may enable them to hide it even from themselves. Periodically, there are newspaper accounts of some high school girl, occasionally of a college coed, who gives birth in the dormitory or rest room and claims that until that moment she did not know she was pregnant—whether from ignorance or fear, she may not have known.

Ignorance and fear may keep the very young or poorly educated girl who is sexually active from obtaining prescriptions for contraceptives, and may also keep her from seeking medical attention early in pregnancy. Most teenage girls are timorous about requesting a gynecological examination. A doctor is an adult authority figure and, for a young girl, talking to a doctor about contraceptives, pregnancy, or venereal disease is a terrifying prospect that brings back all the shame and embarrassment of being caught in the play yard without her underwear.

The motives (conscious or suppressed) for the sexual involvement that led to impregnation may also lead her to delay seeking medical attention. She may hope that she is merely experiencing another late menstrual period. But it is imperative that she determine whether or not she is pregnant as soon as possible. Subsequent decisions will be made by default if she delays too long. If she is not pregnant, this knowledge can bring an end to her anxiety and prevent her from making a decision that would needlessly alter the course of her life (such as a hasty marriage or dropping out of school).

If she is pregnant, the certain knowledge of this fact early in the pregnancy leaves her with a wider range of choices. If she is pregnant and decides to have an abortion, early knowledge of the pregnancy is imperative because there is likely to be an interval of time before an abortion can be scheduled, and abortion is safer if performed before the twelfth week of pregnancy (it must be performed before the twenty-fourth week, for both legal and medical reasons). If she is pregnant and decides to bear her child, she needs prenatal care as soon as possible, both for her own health and for that of her child. The infant mortality rate for illegitimate children is markedly higher than that for legitimate children, probably because of the difference in prenatal care received by the mothers.

Turning to someone for help may be in itself an emotional trauma. The girl who thinks she might be pregnant may turn to her sexual partner, who may be supportive or who may reject her and deny paternity. She may turn to her best friend, who is likely to be a girl her own age with little

147

knowledge of where to seek help, who may also reject her. She may turn to her parents, but may be fearful of possible anger and rejection from either or both of them. If she is still in high school, she may turn to her school counselor, who may be able to give her excellent advice and assistance, especially in a school system that provides special services for pregnant students, married or not. (One such school system will be described in detail in a later section of this chapter.) She may contact the public health service of her county or some voluntary agency such as Planned Parenthood. She may even turn to the want ads of the local newspaper, where social welfare agencies often list their telephone number in the personals column.

It may be possible for a pregnant minor to receive medical care related to a possible pregnancy without the knowledge or consent of her parents, depending on the civil code of the state in which she lives. The California Civil Code, for example, states that:

> notwithstanding any other provision of the law, an unmarried pregnant minor may give consent to the furnishing of hospital, medical and surgical care related to her pregnancy, and such consent shall not be subject to disaffirmance because of minority. The consent of the parent or parents of an unmarried, pregnant minor shall not be necessary in order to authorize hospital, medical and surgical care related to her pregnancy.

This provision of the California Civil Code applies to diagnosis, to abortion, and to care during pregnancy and delivery.

Whether she informs her parents, sexual partner, and others before determining that she is in fact pregnant, or after, usually the young woman experiences a secondary crisis in that painful confrontation with these significant others in her life. The school counselor or social worker may be able to help mitigate some of the emotional pain. But the fact of premarital pregnancy may be a major crisis not only for the girl, but also for her family and her sexual partner and his family; the shock waves spread out from her, until they become merely ripples of gossip.

Because both the girl and her family are likely to be distraught, professional help should be sought. Often the girl and her family are too ashamed to ask for the help they need (even though the girl's mother may already have been on the telephone to Aunt Minnie). A family service agency, Planned Parenthood, a public health clinic, sometimes the school district, can help ease both the girl and her family through the crisis. In particular, a professional can help the pregnant woman recognize that pregnancy is not the ultimate disaster but a biologically normal event that she will survive, can help her recognize that she has a future and must make plans and decisions.

The fact that there are choices left to the pregnant single woman is in itself an emotionally significant idea for her to grasp. The first set of choices—and the decisions come in sets of *either-or* choices—is whether to have an abortion or bear the child. This choice has been made by women

The fact that there are choices left to the pregnant single woman is in itself an emotionally significant idea for her to grasp. The first set of choices—and the decisions come in sets of either-or choices—is whether to have an abortion or bear the child.

for decades, but in the past abortion meant either the danger and expense of an illicit operation, the expense of leaving the country for a legal abortion, or the difficult and time-consuming route of finding some medical ground to show that the pregnancy threatened the woman's life or health.

Even when therapeutic (legal) abortions were difficult to obtain and illicit abortions entailed great risks, abortion was the chosen means of dealing with extramarital pregnancy for a large majority of white middle-class single women. Alfred Kinsey reported that among the single white women of his sample (interviewed in 1955) more than one out of every five who had gone to college and more than one out of every four who had not, had become pregnant at least once in their lives. Between 88 and 95 percent of these out-of-wedlock pregnancies had terminated with an abortion (Kinsey 1966:196). The social pressures against bearing children out of wedlock were great enough to override the fear of death, disability, and possible prosecution for the vast majority of single middle-class white women.

Since the United States Supreme Court ruling in 1973, abortion has been both legal and readily available in the United States during the first twenty-four weeks of pregnancy, as has been discussed in some detail in the preceding chapter. New techniques have made abortions comparatively safe: the study made by Tietize and Lewit (cited in *Scientific American* 1972:51) indicated a mortality rate of only 8.2 per 100,000 therapeutic abortions, with most of the deaths occurring when the abortion was not

149

performed until the second trimester of pregnancy (between the twelfth
and the twenty-fourth week). This compares favorably to the maternal
mortality rate in the United States of 24.7 per 100,000 births.

Although there are as yet no precise demographic statistics on who
the women are who have been receiving therapeutic abortions since the
1973 Supreme Court decision, it is apparent that many are young, single,
and poor. Abortions performed in the second trimester, which represent
only approximately 15 percent of all abortions performed (Calio and
Lubenow 1975:23), seem to be performed most often on young, poor,
minority women. One of the plaintiffs in the case involving "Mary Doe"
that was decided in the 1973 Supreme Court case was Dr. James L. Waters,
Jr., of Atlanta. Two years after that Supreme Court decision, Dr. Waters
observed that "college girls come bopping in when they're two weeks late
. . . The fact that a patient gets to eighteen weeks means she has difficulty
making up her mind, she has economic problems, she's not smart enough
to know she's pregnant, and she's scared to death to tell her family" (cited
in Calio and Lubenow 1975:23).

If the unmarried woman decides not to terminate her pregnancy—
perhaps most often for religious reasons—she must decide whether or not
to marry. One of the ways of removing herself from the status of unwed
mother, and of giving her child legitimate status, is to marry. The high
proportion of brides who are pregnant before the ceremony (more than
42 percent of the brides who were under twenty years of age at marriage,
according to the National Natality Survey taken by the U.S. Public Health
Service in 1964–1966) suggests that this option is frequently chosen. The
choice is not a unilateral decision, as some of the other choices open to
the pregnant woman may be. But it is important that the pregnant single
woman decide whether marriage, at this time in her life and to the father
of her child, is what she wants. Too often she may be pressured into
marriage to save face for her family.

If the father of the child is free to marry and is willing or can be
pressured into marrying her, there can still be emotional trauma for the
pregnant woman. There is the woman's fear of rejection by the father of
her child. Even if he agrees to marry her, she may feel that it is only
because of the pressure that her parents and perhaps legal authorities are
applying. (Premarital pregnancy and teenage marriage will be considered
at more length in a later section.)

If marriage is not a choice open to her (the father of the child may
already be married, may be a close relative, or may refuse to marry her),
or if she decides that she does not want to marry this man at this time in
her life, the pregnant single woman still has two remaining options. She
can bear her child and release it for adoption or keep the child and raise
it herself, perhaps with some financial assistance from the father of the
child, perhaps with the support of her own family. This last set of choices
may be delayed until the child is born, and sometimes delayed until the
child is several months old. Giving up her child may be as painful as any

of the emotional traumas the mother experienced in the early weeks of pregnancy, and the pain is probably much greater if she keeps the child for some time after his birth, especially if she nurses the baby.

Homes for unwed mothers and similar agencies used to apply subtle pressures to encourage the pregnant woman to give up her child for adoption, especially if the woman was quite young. (Often, not even the social workers and other staff personnel were aware that they were pressuring the girl.) The pendulum has swung in the past few years to the point where various group therapy programs for pregnant girls may encourage the girl to keep her child. (It may be the only way of remaining in the group, which may have become an important source of social acceptance and self-esteem for a girl who needs such emotional support.)

From the viewpoint of the child's welfare, it is probably best to permit adoptive parents to have the child, and as soon as possible. The child will be legitimated by the process of adoption, and will grow up in a family with two parents who want a child and are able to care for that child. In a social climate in which both white and nonwhite babies are urgently desired by adoptive parents, adoption would seem to be the logical choice. It used to be assumed that releasing the child for adoption was also best for the unwed mother: once she has released her child she is no longer an unwed mother, but returns to her former status as a single woman without children, and can pick up her life where she left it some months before. This assumption has been challenged in the last few years, particularly by feminists who point out that a woman may want to experience motherhood, but may not want to marry in order to do so. For whatever reason or reasons, an increasing number of unwed mothers are opting to keep their babies.

Before the unwed mother makes the final decision on adoption, she must make some other decisions that involve the interim period of the pregnancy itself (and that may in subtle ways support a decision either to release the child for adoption or to keep it). The unmarried woman who has decided to bear her child and to stay single must decide whether to stay in her home town during her pregnancy or to seek the anonymity of a home for unwed mothers in a large and distant city. In the past, many young women chose the latter option (particularly white middle-class women who had decided to bear their children and release them for adoption). Many who choose to leave their home town during pregnancy go to cities in a state that does not require the reporting of legitimacy on birth records.

For the pregnant teenage woman who stays in her home town, there remains the question of whether or not to stay in school. In the past, this was not a choice open to most pregnant schoolgirls, married or single. But this, too, is changing; the situation of the pregnant school girl will be the topic of the following section.

In summary: The single woman who believes that she may be pregnant faces a series of emotional crises, but has more options than she may

151

perceive. Fear and shame may lead the single woman to deny her pregnancy, even to herself, and to postpone painful confrontations and decisions. The result is often that she drifts into the status of unwed mother, without proper medical attention. If she receives medical care early in her pregnancy, she has a number of options. To exercise choice is to be in control of one's life; to recognize what options are open and to choose how she will cope with her pregnancy puts the single woman in control of her own future, and helps her survive the pregnancy with some measure of self-esteem.

The unwed mother and the public school

Before the 1920s, there were many jobs available for unskilled and semi-skilled workers and the schooling of most Americans ended with the eighth grade. Now, the person who is a high school dropout is at a definite disadvantage in the job market throughout adult life. Pregnancy is the single most common reason why girls drop out of high school. Education may not guarantee a job, but the odds are that the unwed mother who is a high school dropout will have little in her future but welfare or marriage.

Until a decade ago, high school girls who became pregnant were expelled, married or not. And in many school districts, girls who married were expelled, pregnant or not. Such expulsion was intended to protect the other girls from contact with those who were sexually active. Many parents assume that, with regard to sex, their daughters are both ignorant and innocent and that the former condition guarantees the latter. It is for this same reason that sex education in the public schools has been a volatile political issue at the local level, even when the rates of pregnancy and veneral disease among adolescents indicate that there is great need for such programs. The contention of many parents is that sex education belongs in the home. Yet mothers seldom impart much useful information about sex to their daughters, beyond an embarrassed and superficial explanation of menstruation. The daughter learns quickly enough not to ask questions that might lead to another painful interview with a tense mother —a situation in which a young girl can find it difficult to breathe. It seems safer (and more exciting) to giggle knowingly with friends over half-understood jokes. From other girls she acquires a hodgepodge of half-truths, made to seem significant by the forbidden aura surrounding garbled stories and illegible notes that the homeroom teacher confiscates.

The whispers about the girl who "had to get married" or "had to drop out of school" are frightening. In the past, the errant classmate seldom reappeared in the high school; her fate was a topic of much speculation. Yet shame and ostracism have never been effective deterrents to sexual activity, not even in the days when the Puritans publicly whipped young women of "unclean carriage." Although pregnancy is still seen by many as a girl's punishment for having fallen from innocence, the father

*Some high schools are creating programs to help the pregnant schoolgirl complete
her education and retain a sense of self-esteem.*

of the child faces no such insistence that he despise himself for the rest
of his life.

Gradually, the attitude toward pregnant school girls is changing. In
the 1950s, students who were married or pregnant, or both, who did not
voluntarily drop out of high school were routinely dismissed. But by the
1960s, some married students had challenged in court the discretionary
power of the school district to expel married students as a class. "The
court decisions were generally favorable to the married student who was
not pregnant and who wanted to stay in school, but tended to give the
school a good deal of discretionary power over the pregnant student,
regardless of her marital status" (Ravacon and Dempsey 1972:5).

In the 1960s, articles in professional education journals began to
focus on the question of whether the schools had the right, legal or moral,
to terminate a student's education because of marriage or pregnancy.
Often implied, although seldom openly stated, was the idea that these
students represented a threat to the school, with the married but not
pregnant students presenting the least threat and the unmarried pregnant
girls the greatest threat. There was a progression of questions raised in
the literature by professional educators, beginning with what legal right
the school had to expel married students, continuing to the question of
the right of married and pregnant girls to remain in high school, and
coming finally to the question of the rights of the pregnant single student
(Ravacon and Dempsey 1972:5). Gradually, the consensus grew that the

153

question of whether the pregnant student had a right to continue her education should be answered in the affirmative.

By the 1970s, school systems in most major cities in the United States had programs designed to meet the needs of pregnant students. In some school districts (New York, Atlanta, Washington, the state of Maryland) pregnant girls are allowed to remain in regular classes (Woodbury 1971). The rationale for this is that there is the least disruption in the girl's life if she is allowed to continue with the courses that she has been taking, with her friends, in her own school. The other viewpoint is that pregnant girls have special needs, which may be met better in a program designed for these girls. Many school districts have special programs for pregnant students. Whether the girls feel ostracized or grateful to be with others who share their situation depends on the way the program is structured.

One successful program for pregnant school girls was created in San Francisco in 1965. It began as a year-long pilot program conducted by the Association of Secondary Assistant Principals of the San Francisco Unified School District. These school administrators had become concerned about the number of girls who became pregnant and dropped out of high school (the number was estimated to be over four hundred girls each year). The program's progress report stated:

> It was recognized that these young girls and their babies were at high risk, both medically and in terms of future social disorder. It was noted that many of them whose attendance was interrupted because of pregnancy did not return to school. Many of them were unaware of such services as maternity homes, foster care or adoption. Their own feelings of self-worth were often debased; their relationships with their families were strained. (Henry and Wolfe 1966:1)

There were thirty-five girls involved in the pilot project, ranging in age from thirteen to sixteen, and in grade in school from the seventh to the eleventh. Thirty-one of the girls were black, four were white. All were from impoverished neighborhoods of San Francisco. A majority of these girls (twenty-six) had been known to the Department of Social Services at some time as children in AFDC families (Aid to Families with Dependent Children.) Twenty-four of the girls came from homes with only one parent, typically the mother. In the families of twenty-two of the girls there were other illegitimacies. Eight of the girls were on probation to the Youth Guidance Center and two were on parole to the California Youth Authority. These were girls caught in the cycle of poverty, illegitimacy, undereducation, and despair; dropping out of school as unwed mothers, they would have perpetuated that cycle; it was hoped that the program would give them a chance to break free of it.

Under the program, the girls received both academic and health education, group counseling, planned recreation, and prenatal, delivery, and postnatal medical care. Social workers were available to counsel the

154

girls, the putative fathers, and other family members. Fathers of thirty of the thirty-five illegitimate infants involved in the pilot program were located, and twenty-eight of them admitted paternity. Seven of them married the mothers of their children, while the girls were still in the program. Two babies were placed for adoption, but the others were kept by their young mothers.

The pilot program was judged successful: the girls received better prenatal and postnatal care than they would have without the program, they attended classes and counseling sessions regularly, gave evidence of an improved sense of personal worth, and most of them continued their high school work to graduation. The following school year (1966–67) the program was made a permanent effort of the San Francisco Unified School District, in cooperation with numerous public and private agencies. A total of seven centers opened over a period of several years, almost all of them in San Francisco hospitals. The program has continued to include work with both the fathers and the grandparents of the infants, as well as the unwed mothers.

The San Francisco program is clearly focused on the needs of girls from impoverished families, although the program is open to any pregnant San Francisco girl who is seventeen years of age or younger, who wishes to continue her high school education, and whose parents request that she be admitted to the program (a married teenager may apply on her own behalf). Middle-class girls may be more likely to seek other solutions to a premarital pregnancy, but the program is available if they want it. In the long run, it should lower both the financial and the human costs of illegitimacy.

The father of the illegitimate child

Since the English Poor Laws first attempted, some centuries ago, to shift support of the illegitimate child from the public purse to his father, there have been laws defining what obligation the father has to his illegitimate offspring. Such statutes vary from state to state. In some, the father has a legal obligation to support his illegitimate child equally with his legitimate children.

Before such laws can be applied in a particular case, however, it is first necessary to establish paternity. In the case of the legitimate child, paternity is established by the legal presumption that the married woman's husband is the father of all her children. All of the other ways (discussed above) in which the child may be legitimated also establish paternity. But in the case of an illegitimate child, establishing paternity can be more difficult. Enforcing laws requiring a father to support his illegitimate child presents a problem parallel to that posed in the old recipe for *hasenpfeffer* that begins, "First, catch and skin a rabbit."

Paternity actions are usually sordid affairs, and sometimes involve wrongful accusation. The paternity action may be a civil case, a criminal case, or a hybrid; it may be held as a jury trial or as a hearing by a judge in a court of competent jurisdiction. It is a situation where the defendant will find himself trying to prove his innocence, even though the presumption of criminal law in the United States is that the prosecution must prove guilt. There is no uniformity from state to state in the matter of what evidence is admissible in a paternity action. As yet, there is no way to prove scientifically that a particular man is the father of a given child, although a blood test may prove that he could *not* be. In some states—but not all—blood tests are admissible if they prove that a man could not have fathered the child. In some states, character witnesses may be called in paternity actions. In most, the statement of the mother of the child carries much weight. In Hawaii, an accusation made by the mother during labor may be entered as evidence to corroborate her testimony, with a logic parallel to the use of the dying declaration in a murder case (both practices seem to have their origins in the medieval belief that Truth will out during torture).

It is most difficult to establish paternity when the child is the product of a casual sexual liaison. The notion that many illegitimate children are conceived by prosmiscuous mothers, to whom the father of the child is a virtual stranger, does not seem to have much basis in fact, however. Studies such as that conducted by Kermit Wiltse and Robert Roberts (1966) indicate that most illegitimate children are born to stable unions, and it is usually not too difficult to establish that such a union did exist during the time that the child was conceived.

In their study of mothers of illegitimate children who were supported by AFDC, Wiltse and Roberts found that approximately half (48.8 percent) of the children of these mothers were conceived in unions that were classified as "long-term stable without cohabitation," and another 13.9 percent were conceived in relationships that were "stable with cohabitation" (that is, "common law" or consensual unions). Only 2.6 percent of the children had been conceived in relationships that were considered "casual" (Wiltse and Roberts 1966:228–229). (The remaining 34.7 percent of the children of these AFDC mothers were legitimate.)

A statement by the father, taken under oath, is usually adequate legal evidence of paternity. That such statement is not too difficult to obtain is indicated by the experience with the San Francisco Teenage Mother Program, described above. During the pilot project alone, fathers were identified for thirty of the thirty-five illegitimate infants involved, and twenty-eight of these men admitted paternity (Henry and Wolfe 1966:3). This program received special commendation from the U.S. Department of Health, Education, and Welfare, for what was then a unique effort to work with the fathers of illegitimate babies.

There is no clear federal statement of the father's responsibility for his children, legitimate or not. However, in 1974 the Congress enacted amendments to the act that created the Aid to Families with Dependent Children program (through which the federal government pays about $8 billion each year to some eleven million poor adults and their children). These amendments require mothers receiving AFDC funds to identify and help locate the fathers of their children. Under implementing regulations developed by the Department of Health, Education, and Welfare, an uncooperative mother could lose support payments; a cooperative mother would be given a cash incentive. It is too soon to know how effective these regulations may be, but they will certainly be more effective in those states that place a legal support obligation on the father, and enforce it through the penal code, than in other states.

A judgment in a paternity suit usually involves a court order for the father to support his child; in some states it may also involve legitimating the child. In a few states a judgment in a paternity suit gives the child equality with the legitimate children of the same father, with regard both to support and to inheritance rights. In other states, only minimal support may be awarded as judgment in a paternity suit, with payments required for a period as short as four years.

If paternity is established, the father incurs some legal obligation to support his child, but unless he legitimates the child, the father has few rights where his child is concerned. In some states, the father who has acknowledged his child or contributed adequately to the child's support may be heard on the matter of adoption. He may be allowed to adopt his illegitimate child under some circumstances. (This is occasionally a solution where the father of the illegitimate child is married to another woman and has other, legitimate, children. Adoption legitimates the child and gives him legal equality with his half-brothers and half-sisters.)

State laws vary widely on what rights, if any, the father of the illegitimate child may have. But in no state does he have the same rights of visitation and custody that the divorced father has with regard to his legitimate children. "In some states, the father is not permitted a right of visitation, even if he supports the child" (Krause 1969:64). This may be incentive to legitimation, if the father is emotionally involved with the child. The most common means that the father may employ to legitimate his child and to have the rights as well as the financial obligations of fatherhood is to marry the child's mother.

Premarital pregnancy and teenage marriage

Marriage is not always the best or even a possible solution to an out-of-wedlock pregnancy. The father of the child may be a married man, or a close relative. If the pregnant single woman is a minor, the father of her child may be a minor as well, unable to support a wife and child. (The fathers contacted during the pilot project in San Francisco described above ranged from fourteen to thirty years of age, but of the thirty fathers identified, twenty-four were still in their teens.) Nonetheless, a large proportion of pregnant single women choose, if the option is open, to marry before giving birth. One of the ways that an unwed mother can escape the

157

stigma of that status is to leave it by ceasing to be a mother (abortion or adoption); the other way that she can escape the stigma is by becoming a married woman. If the pregnant woman marries, her child will be legitimated and she will be a married mother: her maternity will be respected. So the pregnant single woman may choose to marry, having concluded that at the worst she will become a divorced mother instead of an unwed mother, and who knows? the marriage might work out.

Lifting the stigma from both mother and child if the pregnant single woman marries is not mere hypocrisy. If a major reason for maintaining the distinction between legitimate and illegitimate birth is to encourage marriage, then it follows that if marriage occurs, the stigma is lifted. (In some states, as noted above, the husband may be required to acknowledge paternity if the baby is "premature," but if he was willing to marry the mother, he is usually willing to acknowledge the child.)

A study by Samuel Lowrie (1965), in which the level of education of the parents of premaritally pregnant women was reported, revealed something about the family background of women who choose marriage as the solution to premarital pregnancy. Lowrie found that the level of education of the bride, the bridegroom, and the parents of both was significantly lower in marriages that involved a premarital pregnancy than in marriages that did not. Lowrie also found that the parents of premaritally pregnant brides had significantly less education than the bride herself, the bridegroom, or the bridegroom's parents. Premarital pregnancies in Lowrie's sample were heavily concentrated among girls sixteen years of age or younger, which means that most of these girls could not have completed high school at the time of their marriage. If these girls had more education than their parents, the parents of a large proportion of pregnant brides in Lowrie's study had considerably less than a high school education.

Level of education is one of the commonly used indices of class status, for the simple reason that the poorly educated are usually poor. Lowrie's study would support the view that a majority of *premarital pregnancies that lead to marriage* involve girls from poor families. This does not necessarily mean that the daughters of unskilled or semiskilled workers are more likely to become pregnant before marriage than the daughters of more skilled and affluent parents. It may reflect only the fact that the working-class girl is more likely to come from a background where the "shotgun" wedding is preferred to abortion or to bearing a child out of wedlock.

There are probably a number of reasons (in addition to an angry father) why the working-class girl is more likely to choose early marriage as the solution to a premarital pregnancy. The role expectations of the girl of this class typically center on becoming a wife and mother, in that order, and she may see little reason for postponing marriage. In contrast, the middle-class girl may want to complete her education, her parents may want her to complete her education, and both the girl and her parents may hope she will find a more suitable husband later. In any event, the middle-class girl and her family are more likely to have resources, both money and knowledge of where to turn for medical assistance, that are necessary to obtain an abortion. (This was especially likely at the time both the Kinsey and Lowrie studies were made. The 1973 Supreme Court ruling on therapeutic abortion has opened this option to the poor as well as to the affluent.)

According to the U.S. Public Health Service (1970) approximately 42 percent of teenage brides have their first child less than eight months from the date of wedding. A high proportion of teenage brides thus enter marriages that are at least hastened by pregnancy. What the statistics do not indicate is how many of these marriages were motivated by pregnancy and how many of the pregnancies may have been motivated by a desire to marry. If parents have adamantly opposed the marriage of a teenage daughter, she has the ultimate weapon. Pregnancy has made many formerly reluctant parents begin planning the wedding. A girl does not need to admit—even to herself—that the pregnancy was deliberate.

That teenage marriage is closely related to premarital pregnancy is suggested not only by the high percentage of teenage brides who are pregnant, but also by the even higher percentage of teenage bridegrooms who are involved in premarital pregnancy. When the bridegroom was still in high school, Lee Burchinal found that premarital pregnancy was involved in 87 percent of marriages (1960:11). Apparently high school boys in America do not choose to marry—or do not receive parental permission to do so—unless there is a pregnancy involved. Until the recent lowering of the legal age of majority, in all but six states a male required parental permission to marry until he reached the age of twenty-one, although in most states girls were free to marry without parental consent at the age of eighteen or even younger. Thus far, there is no evidence to suggest that lowering the age of majority to eighteen has resulted in any increase in teenage marriages.

There are three closely related phenomena: premarital pregnancy, teenage marriage, and early divorce. Approximately half of the premarital pregnancies in a given year involve a girl in her teens; approximately 42 percent of the teenage brides and perhaps as many as 87 percent of the teenage bridegrooms are involved in a premarital pregnancy; and according to the U.S. Public Health Service, "divorce was twice as likely for early marriages as for those contracted at later ages" (August 1974:18).

Legitimacy and marriage: a summary

Children living with their mother alone have always been at a disadvantage, both socially and economically. There are many parallels between the children whose father is absent because of death, divorce, or desertion, and illegitimate children living with their unwed mother. All such children live in a single-parent family. If their mother remarries, they must learn to coexist with a stepfather, as many illegitimate children must do. All such

159

children are likely to live in reduced economic circumstances; families with a female head of household are predominantly poor.

But the children of divorced parents do see their father on occasion, for he has visiting rights and may have custody of them from time to time. The children of divorced parents are clearly entitled to support by their father. Legitimate children are clearly entitled to a share of their father's estate, even if he dies without a will, and may seek damages in a wrongful death suit if he is killed while they are still his minor dependents. The children whose father has died, or whose parents are divorced, carry no social stigma concerning their origins: they are "lawful issue."

Even if the father of an illegitimate child has been ordered by a court to support his child, this does not in itself give the child equality. As Malinowski pointed out, it is of importance to a child that some man be willing to play the role of sociological father. It is more than a matter of relative income or occupational status; the very presence of the male as head of the household has social meaning for the child. Welfare, day care for the children, and education and job placement for the unwed mothers can improve the children's situation, but there is no social or emotional substitute for the father in the home. The boy raised without a responsible father has no model of adult male responsibility; the girl who is raised as an illegitimate child learns early that she is expected to be "no better than her mother" (a self-image she may acquire from the surrounding community, from disappointed maternal grandparents, or even from her mother). The badge of bastardy is no longer worn visibly on a shield, but it scars the self-image of the fatherless child.

To return to the basic question raised at the beginning of this chapter: One of the historic functions of marriage has been to confer legitimacy on the children born to the union, but are the social ends that once required distinction between legitimate and illegitimate children still social benefits in our society? In its origins, this distinction was the cornerstone of a social structure in which power and wealth were held by aristocratic families, in which the lands and title that made the family powerful were transmitted intact to the eldest legitimate son at the death of his father, and not divided among many heirs; a society in which it was common for the men who were the heads of powerful families to take concubines by whom they had children. This kind of society required that the heir to wealth, title, and power be clearly identified: the first-born male in the legitimate line. The United States of America has never been such a society.

Although there are no great entailed estates in this country, men do leave property. They are free to leave it to all, some, or none of their children, legitimate or not. But when a man dies without a will, as a surprising number do, an illegitimate child may have little claim against the father's estate. Distant but legitimate relatives have a better claim in most state courts. Maintaining this situation would not seem to be an essential social goal. Tocqueville described the meaning of equality in

America in the 1830s: "In aristocratic families, the eldest son, inheriting the greater part of the property, and almost all the rights of the family, becomes the chief, and to a certain extent, the master of his brothers. Greatness and power are for him; for them, mediocrity and dependence . . . Under democratic laws, all the children are perfectly equal, and consequently independent" (1956 ed.:232).

No one has ever stated better what equality meant when this country was founded. All the children of one father are born with equal rights to his support and property—that is, all but the illegitimate children. If the distinction between legitimate and illegitimate children is ruled unconstitutional, as one day it may be, there would still be the problem of establishing paternity. But once paternity is established, every child would have an equal claim on his father, as the United States Supreme Court has now held that the child has on his mother.

A social institution is created to serve social functions. If the functions are transferred to other institutions, or cease to be socially desired ends, the institution may fall into disuse or become largely a ceremonial reminder of a once necessary way of organizing human behavior. One of the major social functions that marriage has served throughout recorded history is the provision of legitimate heirs. As the social reasons for maintaining the distinction between legitimate and illegitimate children have become anachronisms, it is sometimes suggested that the distinction be maintained in order to preserve marriage as an institution. But this is to make children suffer the consequences of the behavior of their parents. Marriage as an institution is undergoing a major crisis of changing function, but it seems likely to survive whether or not children are labeled illegitimate.

Nor is marriage always the best solution to an out-of-wedlock pregnancy. When the bridegroom is not yet twenty, particularly when he and his bride are still in high school and she is pregnant, there is a high probability of marital failure. The marriage of two minors may only create a situation in which two young people are thrust into a marriage for which neither is ready, in order to legitimate a child that neither is capable of supporting. Teenage marriage has too often been a revolving door that leaves bewildered and embittered young mothers divorced and alone—except for the children.

References

Bernstein, Blanche, and Mignon Sauber. 1960. *Deterrents to Early Prenatal Care and Social Services among Women out of Wedlock.* Albany: New York State Department of Social Welfare.

Bierstedt, Robert. 1970. *The Social Order,* 3d ed. New York: McGraw-Hill Book Company.

Burchinal, Lee G. 1960. "Research on Young Marriage: Implications for Family Life Education." *Family Life Coordinator* 9 (September-December):6–21.

Calio, Jim, with Gerald C. Lubenow. 1975. "Abortion and the Law." *Newsweek* 85 (March 3):18–30.

Christensen, Harold T., and Hanna H. Meissner. 1953. "Studies in Child Spacing: III—Premarital Pregnancy as a Factor in Divorce." *American Sociological Review* 18 (December):641–644.

Goode, William J. 1960. "Illegitimacy in the Caribbean Social Structure." *American Sociological Review* 25 (February):21–30.

Hammond, Boone E., and Joyce Ladner. 1969. "Socialization into Sexual Behavior in a Negro Slum Ghetto." In *The Individual, Sex, and Society*, edited by Carlfred B. Broderick and Jessie Bernard, pp. 41–51. Baltimore: Johns Hopkins Press.

Henry, Alice C., and Elaine Wolfe. 1966. "Progress Report: Special Services Centers for Pregnant Girls" (mimeographed). San Francisco: San Francisco Unified School District.

———. 1967. "Special Services Centers for Pregnant Girls" (mimeographed). San Francisco: San Francisco Unified School District.

Kinsey, Alfred C. 1966. "Illegal Abortion in the United States." In *The Unwed Mother*, edited by R. W. Roberts, pp. 191–200. New York: Harper & Row.

Krause, Harry D. 1969. "Why Bastard, Wherefore Base?" *Progress in Family Law. Annals of the American Academy of Political and Social Science* 383 (May):48–70.

Linton, Ralph. 1956. *The Tree of Culture*. New York: Alfred A. Knopf.

Lowrie, Samuel H. 1965. "Early Marriage: Premarital Pregnancy and Associated Factors," *Journal of Marriage and the Family* 27 (February):48–56.

Malinowski, Bronislaw. 1930. "Parenthood—the Basis of Social Structure." In *The New Generation*, edited by V. F. Calverton and S. D. Schmalhausen, pp. 113–168. New York: The Citadel Press.

Ravacon, Patricia B., and John J. Dempsey. 1972. "An Annotated Bibliography on Married and Pregnant Students in Education Journals of the 1960s." *Perspectives in Maternal and Child Health Series A: Adolescent Pregnancy* 4 (January), Baltimore: The Johns Hopkins University.

Scientific American. 1972. "Science News." *Scientific American* 227 (July):51.

Tocqueville, Alexis de. 1956. *Democracy in America*, abr. ed., edited by R. D. Heffner. New York: New American Library.

U.S. Public Health Service, Department of Health, Education, and Welfare. 1970. "Interval Between First Marriage and Legitimate First Birth, United States, 1964–1966." *Monthly Vital Statistics Report* 18 (March):1–7.

———. August 1974. *Teenagers: Marriages, Divorces, Parenthood, and Mortality*. Washington, D.C.: U.S. Government Printing Office.

———. December 1974. *Trends in Illegitimacy: United States, 1940–1965*. Washington, D.C.: U.S. Government Printing Office.

———. 1975. *Selected Vital and Health Statistics in Poverty and Nonpoverty Areas of Nineteen Large Cities: United States, 1969–71*. Washington D.C.: U.S. Government Printing Office.

———. 1976. "Advance Report Final Natality Statistics, 1974." *Monthly Vital Statistics Report* 24 (February 13):1–5.

Wiltse, Kermit T., and Robert W. Roberts. 1966. "Illegitimacy and the AFDC Program." In *The Unwed Mother*, edited by R. W. Roberts. New York: Harper & Row.

Woodbury, Richard. 1971. "Help for High School Mothers." *Life* 70 (April 2):34–41.

Suggested readings

Herzog, Elizabeth. 1967. *About the Poor: Some Facts and Some Fictions.* U.S. Department of Health, Education, and Welfare, Social and Rehabilitation Service, Children's Bureau. Children's Bureau publication no. 451-1967. Washington D.C.: U.S. Government Printing Office. Paper. Approximately half of this insightful monograph deals with the meaning of illegitimacy among the poor. The last section is devoted to a study of unmarried mothers regardless of social class origins. There is an extensive bibliography.

Roberts, Robert W., ed 1966. *The Unwed Mother.* New York: Harper & Row. Paper. An anthology of writings on illegitimacy, including cross-cultural, psychological, sociological, and research perspectives on the unwed mother and the alternative solutions available to her.

6

Marriage as a parental union: sex roles and socialization

Usually fathers care more than mothers that their children learn proper sex role behavior—especially that their sons learn to act like men. The male traits that fathers think their sons should learn are: masculine expressive movements (such as swagger), agressiveness, obstinacy, power, suppression of emotion. Fathers see appropriate girl behavior as including expressive feminine movements, gentleness, sensitivity and emotion, social awareness, coquetry, and affection.

Patricia Cayo Sexton (1969:100)

The socialization of children is one of the basic functions of marriage and the family. Husband and wife are expected to become mother and father in due course, by the society and by most people who enter marriage. In preceding chapters the childbearing function has been examined; socialization is the childrearing function. It is not merely enough to ensure that there will be people in the future; every family and every society wants to ensure that there will be people *like us* in the future. If this desire to replicate ourselves seems egocentric on the part of parents and ethnocentric on the part of society, it is. But it is also the motivation for most of the sacrifices that parents make for their children and that a society makes to care for and educate its young. From the viewpoint of society, aging members of the group must be replaced continuously by younger ones whose skills and values are essentially similar; the only alternative is to recruit and socialize immigrants from another society. This is the social function that Talcott Parsons has termed *pattern maintenance*. Without it, a culture would disappear.

From the viewpoint of parents, children are a form of immortality, an extension of our own flesh. This child who so resembles us gives us an opportunity to relive our own childhood, with improvements. Each of us wants to give our children the kind of childhood we would have liked. This is sometimes baffling to children, who, being adaptable, usually learn to indulge their parents' dreams (at least until adolescence). The fact that many married couples begin to address each other as *Mother* and *Daddy* as soon as they have a child indicates the importance of the childrearing function in the marriage relationship. In some class subcultures, parental roles are the central focus of the marital relationship.

Childrearing provides an opportunity to play roles that each of the parents—particularly the mother—has wanted to play. It is not enough to have borne a child; to be a mother requires that there be a child who is being mothered: it is a reciprocal role. (Which is the reason why a woman feels such a sense of loss when her youngest child leaves home.) It has become fashionable to view the desire to be a mother as something that culture has foisted onto young women. Motherhood is not in itself a sufficient role to occupy a woman's entire adult life. Unless she is exceedingly prolific or dies young, an American woman will outlive her mothering role by more than twenty years, on the average. But to insist that no reasonable woman could find fulfillment in being a mother is to deny the profound sense of well-being that bearing, nursing, and rearing young children can bring. If the rewards are the greatest to the mother when her children are infants or toddlers, as many women believe, there is a certain balance, for that is when the child most needs its mother.

Socialization is the process through which a human infant gradually becomes a human being; a process that requires warm and continuous interaction with other human beings. In an earlier chapter, the discussion of alienation dwelt on the need we have for intimate relationships that endure through time, for such relationships make it possible to develop and maintain a sense of identity and a positive self-image. The infant requires stability and continuity in care if his mental and emotional development is to be normal. The mother or mother-surrogate who provides early care also gives the child his basic feeling toward the world: trust or mistrust, security or anxiety. The developing child acquires his first awareness of self and the early glimmerings of a self-image from the adults who care for him; in our society this has come to mean primarily his mother, secondarily his father. Later in childhood, peers will serve to correct and balance the child's view of himself, and with his peers he develops the capacity for reciprocity and intimacy.

As adults who are isolated from other human beings for extended periods of time tend to degenerate emotionally, so infants who are denied stable, intimate relationships with other human beings fail to develop normally. Children who are raised in an impersonal institutional setting, or who are relegated to an attic or chicken coop by twisted parents or grandparents, usually are severely retarded in mental and emotional development. For the tiny infant, mother's presence is as necessary as mother's milk. Substitutes for both can be found, but stable, nurturing relationships are vital to the development of the child.

Nurturing and nursing: the role of mother

Socialization begins with the earliest interaction between the infant and his mother: nursing. Nursing is the function that all mammals of the earth have in common, the functions that sets us apart from other orders of living creatures. Nursing is a physiological function that developed some two hundred million years ago in egg-laying mammals, and thus even predates childbirth as a physical function. Conditioned by advertising, we Americans tend to think of milk as, well, milk, differing only in whether it comes from a carton, bottle, or can, and in how much fat has been removed. We carefully explain to grade school children that it really comes from a farmer's cow. But all milk does not come from cows, and all milk is not alike. The milk of each species of mammal is highly specific in its biochemical composition. For example, the milk of the blue whale is 40 to 50 percent fat, which meets the high caloric requirements of the whale calf (Jelliffe and Jelliffe 1975:558).

Human milk, specifically formulated by a long evolutionary process to meet the requirements of human infants, has life-enhancing properties. Jelliffe and Jelliffe report that "in the case of human milk, the most significant of the many differences from cow's milk appears to be the abundant supply of nutrients most needed for the rapid growth and development of the central nervous system, including the brain" (1975:558). In the early months of life, the infant is at highest risk; the first year is the period of highest mortality, even in America. Human milk helps human infants to resist disease, according to the Jelliffes: "Much illness in early childhood, especially in developing countries, is related to infection . . . the consider-

167

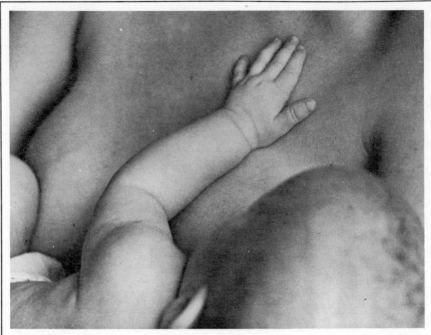

Nursing an infant does more than nourish his body, although it does that superbly. Nursing is also the child's first rewarding interaction with another human being.

able protective effect afforded by breast feeding has been recognized for decades, but has been considered to be related simply to cleanliness and lack of opportunity for contamnination. However, recent work has demonstrated that human milk has anti-infective properties" (1975:558).

The hormones that are essential to lactation are closely tied to the mother's emotional responses, in ways that are just beginning to be understood. The nursing female of most species of mammals is fiercely devoted to her young, and nursing can have a profound effect on a young human mother. As the sex act creates an emotional bond between the husband and wife, so nursing creates an emotional bond between mother and child. Yet the nursing mother in our culture often finds that she is embarrassing people around her if she nurses her child openly; the breast has been so overlaid with sexual meaning in American culture that it has become difficult for people to accept nursing as the simple, primordial, maternal act that it is.

Nursing an infant does more than nourish his body, although it does that superbly. Nursing is also the child's first rewarding interaction with another human being. While nursing, the infant learns to engage in reciprocal behavior with someone else. For the rest of his life, eating will be an activity in which companionship is almost as necessary as food.

The infant is born with a sucking reflex (one of the human being's few instinctive behaviors), but this reflex must be developed into nursing behavior. The infant learns quickly, as he must, or he dies. The nursing infant is dependent on his mother, but not passive. Anyone who believes that an infant need merely open his mouth to receive his mother's milk has never nursed a child, or watched a child nurse. The infant expends a great deal of effort and energy, sometimes even has beads of sweat on his face; it is the mother who learns to relax dreamily during nursing. Sara Winter (1970) gave the Thematic Apperception Test (TAT) to a group of nursing mothers who were asked to respond with stories to a series of pictures; at home, alone with their infants, while nursing they told a tape recorder what the pictures meant to them. The stories told by the mothers while nursing their infants were significantly different from those told by other mothers who had weaned their babies, even though the latter group had their babies playing beside them. The women who told stories while breast-feeding their infants more often told stories with positive emotional content, stories in which pleasure in an activity for its own sake was a recurrent theme, stories with little chronological sequence and much empathic response to the people in the pictures (Winter 1970:32).

The nursing mother finds herself in a warm, empathic mood with little sense that there are other, pressing things to be done, an expansive mood that lends itself to playful gestures and words that develop into the first simple games babies play with their mothers. George Herbert Mead long ago pointed out the importance of games in the developement of social self. Games are not random play; they are organized interaction involving the developement of rules of behavior: you do this when I do that, then we will trade roles, and I will be "it." Learning to make and to follow rules, learning to exchange positions with the other: these are part of learning to play roles in real life, and that is what socialization is all about.

Mead was concerned with the formal games of older children, but babies play games, too. Playmates will be an important part of a child's socialization later, but his first games are played with his mother. Jean Piaget first studied the importance of games in the development of the child's mental processes. Justin Call (1968 and 1970) carried out research on the games that infants play. Call (1970) notes three preconditions for the playing of games by infants. First, the infant must be familiar with the situation; second, the infant must be free from anxiety or any pressing need, yet alert and attentive to external stimulation; third, the infant must have achieved control over the parts of his body being used in the game. Call suggests that all three preconditions for game playing are first fulfilled in nursing: it is a familiar situation; when the infant's hunger has been slaked he is likely to be free of tensions, yet often remains attentive and alert for a time; finally, the infant's mouth is one of the earliest developed of his motor systems and is stimulated by nursing.

When the baby is almost through nursing, he will often let go of the nipple, search for it with his mouth, find it, nurse a moment, let go, and

169

search again. Or his mother may try to determine if he is still hungry by offering him the nipple again. A game often develops that is more random than later games like peekaboo, but it has some of the same elements and is a game that both mother and child delight in playing. Some mothers take nursing very seriously and will not let themselves be drawn into such frivolity; other mothers prefer not to breast-feed their infants for some reason. The children of such mothers will learn to play other games with their mouths, such as suck-the-toe or gum-the-crib, but there is particular pleasure and learning for infants in games involving another human being.

Games played by the baby in the nursing relationship and in other contexts with his mother are an early means by which the infant can begin to distinguish between himself and another person, between people and inanimate objects. Games are an important part of his emerging social nature. The newborn has no sense of self and no awareness of other human beings. He cannot respond to another person as anything more than a series of stimuli: mother is a pattern of soothing sounds, familiar shapes, colors, fragrance, and taste, sensations of warmth and softness. He may smile and make happy noises when his mother enters the room, but in the first weeks he is not yet responding to her as a person. He is anticipating the comforts she brings him, and his response is much like that of the puppy who wiggles and whines with joy while his dish is being filled.

Gradually the baby learns to recognize his mother (at this point he will be suddenly fearful of strangers). Through games, he begins to interact with her. His greatest fear is what has been termed "separation anxiety." This is the fear that his mother, the source of all his need fulfillment, may go away. If the child's mother has become almost exclusively associated with the satisfaction of his needs, if she is the continuous source of his security and fulfillment, it is not surprising that the child's greatest fear is of losing her.

It is some time before an infant reaches a state of mental sophistication that lets him realize that his mother exists when she is not in his presence, that she is simply somewhere else for awhile. In the egocentric universe of the tiny infant, out of sight is out of existence. Separation anxiety seems to be greater in some children than in others, but from the age of a few months (when the baby has learned to recognize his mother) until about the time when true speech develops, or even later, most children are apprehensive when their mother is out of sight for long. When a baby cries and his mother cannot determine what he wants—he has been fed, he is dry, there are no pins sticking him—it may be that he wants to know that she is there. Cultures in which the child is carried on his mother's back for the first year or two seldom have anxious wailing babies. The simplest solution in our culture is for the mother to strap the baby into one of the secure seats for infants (a plastic version of the old Indian cradleboard) and put him where he can watch her cook dinner or fold the laundry.

Games help babies learn to deal with separation anxiety. Almost every infant plays some form of peekaboo game with his mother, usually inventing his version by putting his blanket or his hands over his face and then whisking them away. The baby himself has made mother disappear, then reappear. He is perhaps a little anxious for the instant he has hidden her, and clearly delighted when he peeks at her again. Call points out that this is an example of the way in which playing games teaches the child to create a model situation and deal with it (1970:34). Setting up models and experimenting with them in order to learn about the real world is a mental process that may involve sophisticated and computerized systems analysis; it begins for each human being with peekaboo.

Imitation is the basis of many of the games that infants play with their mothers, and learning to imitate is an important part of the socialization process. Call notes that the "cough game" is a common and early one between mother and child (1970:34). The baby may cough or clear his throat with a sound that his mother finds droll and amusing, so she may imitate the baby's little cough and smile at him; sooner or later he returns the cough, and they have a new game that may be repeated over and over before the baby tires of it. This is the beginning of oral communication, for the baby is learning to imitate sounds and respond to sounds his mother makes. Later on, the baby will make random sounds for the pleasure he finds in making them (as still later he will whistle or sing), but his mother will suddenly recognize in a single syllable one of the words she has been waiting to hear. She is certain that he is saying "ma ma" or "da da" and excitedly repeats the sound, hoping he will make it again. To the infant this is a new variation of his old favorite cough game, and he is likely to repeat the sound after her.

Games between mother and child involve communication: at first it is nonverbal, later it is verbal. Games involve imitation, which is the basis of much early socialization. And games involve interaction, pleasing someone else as well as yourself.

The games babies play with their mothers are as often invented by the baby as by his mother; she does something that he imitates, or he does something that she imitates. Often the game begins by a chance action, and ends with a laugh. It may be repeated and become a favorite. A favorite game becomes more elaborate, with endless variations and developments on the theme. Call observes that new games are constantly being invented from old ones (1970:34).

It is essential that spontaneity and pleasure remain in the game and that the child be involved in inventing it. The overly anxious mother who wants her child to develop as rapidly as possible often buys him educational toys intended for an older child, then hovers over him to see that he plays with them properly. If he takes apart the red and blue plastic clock

171

designed to teach him to tell time (the pieces with the numbers are made so that they will fit only in the proper places) and invents his own game (which has nothing to do with telling time), his mother is likely to put the clock away "for now," because he might lose the pieces. If the child repeats his innovation with the clock the next time his mother gets it out, she may let him know that she is disappointed by what seems to her either his stubbornness or his stupidity. She wants him to be creative, but in ways that she considers appropriate and has structured for him. Such a child may grow up expecting his mother to amuse and entertain him, but not participating much himself. He is the bored child who follows his mother about complaining that there is nothing to do.

The balky child in needless battle

The desire to keep his mother close (the other side of the separation anxiety) motivates the infant to learn to do whatever seems to keep his mother physically present. This may be eating his cereal or playing a game, or it may be screaming and banging his head on the crib. Whatever he has learned will bring his mother to him and keep her in the room will be his repeated technique.

The infant's desire to keep his mother present easily becomes a desire to please her. This desire and the imitation he learns to enjoy through games are the major means of socializing the baby. He learns to eat new food because his mother has a bite to show him it is good. He has a bite too, as if this were a new game. He will get used to the taste of the stuff after awhile if she does not insist that he eat a lot right away. He learns to drink from a cup because he wants to imitate mother and to please her. The easiest way to toilet train the child is to let him perceive that mother and perhaps brothers and sisters use that curious device; a toddler will want to use it, too. He often learns to flush the toilet first. Some children are fearful of the sound and the fact that it makes things disappear; others are fascinated by the fact that they can make things disappear in this fashion, and the plumber may become a familiar figure. But if the mother can relax until her child is about two years old, a child who is learning rapidly by imitation will soon want to use the toilet because the other members of the family do.

The child's desire to imitate and to please his mother are convenient levers by which socialization is accomplished; if used carefully, shame is another means of socializing the child. He is ashamed of an occasional lapse because he does not want to be denied the rewards of his newly developed skills (for example, he may be ashamed of his wet pants because he does not want to be put back into diapers), but shame needs to be used sparingly, for a while a small amount is effective, a large amount simply overwhelms the child.

But the desire to imitate and to please and the fear of displeasing (which shame involves) are not the only motivations the child experiences.

*Marriage as a
parental union:
sex roles and
socialization*

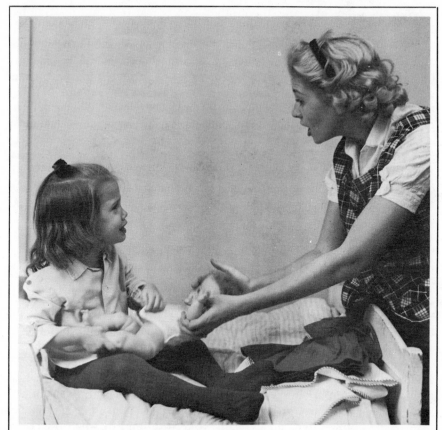

The balky child usually has a mother who hovers too closely, whether she insists on obedience or permits herself to become the child's adoring slave. It is her desire to be a good mother, and fear that she may not be, that leads her to hover.

The mother uses her influence to teach the child *how* to eat, *where* to urinate, *when* to satisfy his needs. But she does not need to urge him to eat, sleep, urinate, or defecate to please her. The child's own inner tensions are stimulus enough. His own hunger, his thirst, his discomfort because he needs to eliminate wastes, his pleasure in dozing off to sleep are all the motivation required. All the mother needs to do is to encourage him to satisfy his needs in the culturally approved manner, and to create a structured and consistent situation in which it is easy for him to form behavior patterns of regular hunger, drowsiness, and elimination. Infants are anxious in unfamiliar situations, and a chaotic day without pattern leaves them fretful and cross. A totally permissive situation is a totally unstructured situation—in effect the mother is leaving the entire responsibility of patterning behavior to the child. Not surprisingly, a child in such a situation is usually anxious and tense, for there is too much expected of him too soon.

173

At the other extreme, the mother who is insistent on asserting her authority may teach the child to satisfy his needs out of fear of the consequences of displeasing his mother. She may usurp his inner motivations and teach him to regard every action as something that was required of him by an external authority. Imagine a baby sitting in his high chair, crumbling a piece of toast and laboriously grasping each crumb between thumb and forefinger, putting it into his mouth. He may be hungry, or he may be engrossed in the game of skill that picking up crumbs can be to an infant. (The development of hand-eye coordination is enhanced by such manipulation of objects.) Suppose his mother takes away the toast and thrusts a spoonful of meat paste into his mouth, scooping it off his chin and back into his mouth as fast as he can spit it out. If this scene is repeated three or more times a day, eating will soon become an unequal contest of wills. If the mother urges, pleads, or scolds until he swallows a given quantity of food, her demand and not his hunger soon will become his reason for eating. He will grow into a child who is not hungry at mealtime, and is able to recognize his own desire to eat only when the ice cream truck goes by.

The desire to please his mother, or the fear of the consequences of her displeasure, may become the only motivation that such a child is able to recognize. The child who has learned to eat to please his mother loses awareness that he is acting on his own need, and may come to feel that the only way he can act for himself is to balk. There is a tendency to regard a balky child as one who needs discipline, and parents are likely to alternate between cajoling and threatening him. This relieves the parent of a sense of responsibility for having created the situation, but it does not resolve the conflict over meals, naps, toilet training, or whatever else it may be across which the balky child and his distraught mother have drawn a battle line.

It is more useful, if one is hoping to avoid or to alter such hostile interaction between mother and child, to regard the situation as one in which the child has been alienated from some of the basic and vital forces within himself. The child who is a "poor eater" is alienated from his hunger. He needs to be allowed to recognize his own inner drives. Sucking, chewing, and tasting were among his earliest pleasures and he will rediscover them if allowed to do so. The balky child has lost awareness even of his desire to please his mother, or perhaps has learned that balking is one way to keep his mother present, if not pleased with him. The parent's impulse to force the child to do something because it is good for him, or because obedience itself is considered a major value (as it tends to be for working-class parents), is likely to reinforce the child's belief that it is someone else's idea and not his own that he should eat, sleep, or defecate.

If the child submits to his mother demands, he will gradually become the "good" child who dutifully satisfies his own physical needs as if they were the needs of someone else. He will go to school and stand in line for a drink and never color outside the line; he will one day become an adult who does things because people insist, or would not like him if he refused. In a totalitarian state, such citizens are highly valued.

If the child persists in balking, perhaps goes on a hunger strike rather than eat the despised oatmeal his mother sets in front of him, sooner or later his mother is likely to give in, let him leave the table or give him something else. The situation will then become a battle for control that was lost by the legitimate authority; repeated with some frequency, the result is a child who grows up with the illusion that he is omnipotent. Some less tender figure of authority may disabuse him of the notion some day; meanwhile he will be a small tyrant.

It is best to avoid the battle for power entirely; second best to disengage from the battle gracefully. This can be done without sacrificing parental authority, for authority does not need to be involved. It may be necessary to use the child's desire to please (and fear of displeasing) in teaching him not to scribbble on the walls or tear up the new magazine, but it is not necessary to invoke parental authority to make him eat his food, go to sleep, urinate, or defecate. Forcing a child to do something that, left alone, he will do anyway is a needless pressure that can only lead to a usurpation of the child's own drives or to a running battle between the generations.

Suppose the baby pushes away the spoon and refuses to eat. The mother can try another kind of food (an infant should have some dignity of refusal allowed to him; most of us permit even the cat to have the brand of food it prefers). Or it may be that the baby seems interested in putting the food in his own mouth, as in the example of the child crumbling his toast. The mother can try giving him other food that he can eat with his fingers, scrambled egg, pieces of banana, cooked peas. Whatever he puts in his mouth is his own idea, and the battle of the spoon is never begun. As long as most of the food is getting into his mouth she can leave it in front of him and go on with dinner preparations; when he starts dropping it on the floor instead of putting it into his mouth she can simply take away the rest without reprimand.

The balky child usually has a mother who hovers too closely, whether she insists on obedience or permits herself to become the child's adoring slave. It is not necessary to impute any evil intentions to the mother, nor to assume that she harbors some deep resentment or other twisted desire to harm or to overwhelm her child; what is most evident in such a mother is anxiety. It is her desire to be a *good* mother, and fear that she may not be, that leads her to hover too closely.

Mothers and mother-surrogates

The role of *mother* carries an enormous amount of emotional freight in our culture, and many women have made it the core of their identity. In the days when an older sister or the hired girl fed the baby while mother cooked for a dozen farmhands, there was less likelihood that the baby would become a "problem eater." Women who have no occupational identity other than "housewife," no other source of pride in creative achievement, may stake their sense of worth entirely on the development of their children. That is a heavy burden for a small child to carry.

Moreover, women who spend most of their day interacting with the baby may come to center their lives on this one role relationship and to expect to share all their experience with the infant. The child may come to represent almost an alter ego, and the mother may try to involve the child in everything she does, gradually excluding the husband and father from the world of mother and child:

> Picture the mother, the child, and the father as they go for a drive in the country. The mother is delighted to get out (hers is a confining life) but from the time the car rolls down the driveway she devotes herself to "making the ride fun for the baby." Her own desires to see and enjoy are projected onto the child, whom she holds up to the window.
>
> Before long the little girl begins to squirm and says "night-night," her signal that she is sleepy. The mother ignores her request (*she* is not tired) and burbles, "See the cow? Isn't that a pretty cow?" The child is not looking. With still greater animation the fond parent tries to rekindle interest. "See the little lamb! What does the lamb say?"
>
> "Go night-night!"
>
> Only when the exhausted baby is tense and fussing does the mother decide to put her on the back seat for a nap. By this time, however, the child is no longer relaxed enough to sleep. The mother struggles to quiet her, but a howling baby, a frantic mother, and a profane father return from the ride. (Putney and Putney 1964:131–132)

In the past, the American mother was by no means the sole agent of early socialization, only the final arbiter. The frontier mother was too caught up in the struggle for subsistence to be a full-time nursemaid to her brood. The eldest daughter was often responsible for younger brothers and sisters, once they were weaned. The same was true for the family that ran the corner grocery or the dairy or the dry-goods store in the small town: the older girls and perhaps a grandmother or the great-aunt were expected to mind the baby. The mother had other, largely economic, responsibilities as the junior partner in the family enterprise.

More affluent families turned child care over to a maid, sometimes beginning with a wet nurse. Everyone who has ever viewed the perennial film *Gone with the Wind* is aware that the white child in the antebellum South was raised by a Mammy. In the North, the immigrant girl served the same function. The bankers, lawyers, and prosperous merchants who made up the Establishment of small-town America expected to hire an Irish, Swedish, German, or other European immigrant girl to do light housework and take care of the children. The extremely wealthy hired a Swiss or a French governess as part of their retinue of servants.

During the 1920s, immigration slowed because of restrictive legislation, and the Mollies, Hildas, and Olgas fresh off the boat became rare jewels available only to the wealthy. In the thirties, the middle class felt the pinch of the Depression and had to cut back expenses. When affluence returned, few American families outside of the South were able to hire a nursemaid for their children. During the same interval of time, the family shrank to its conjugal core. The widowed grandmother, the elderly maiden aunt, the unmarried older sister are no longer common household figures. The dependent female relatives who once served as unpaid nursemaids are now either employed in the labor force or supported in their own homes by Social Security.

Today, older children may be expected to mind the baby, but even the family with four or five children is usually one in which the children are too close in age for the older ones to play an extensive part in the socialization of younger brothers and sisters. Before the widespread use of contraceptives, most women had children for about the first twenty years of married life. High infant mortality kept the total family size down from the maximum of about twenty to the more usual six or so, but these children often ranged in age from two to twenty. High birth rates coupled with high mortality created age gaps between surviving siblings, which meant that the family was an age-graded hierarchy with many age levels represented. There was usually an older sister who could take on much of the socialization of an infant. Now, most American women complete their childbearing during the decade of their twenties and the children are closer in age.

When a majority of Americans lived most of their lives in the same community, grandmother was likely to live within easy walking distance for a child; one or more of his aunts might live close enough that after school he could stop by for a cookie and a glass of milk. For the American working class, this pattern is still a reality; even in the city, working-class families tend to stay in the old neighborhood, close to relatives. In such a setting the parents have primary responsibility for raising children, but grandparents, aunts, uncles, and cousins play a significant part in the socialization of children.

Among the mobile middle and upper middle classes, however, the conjugal unit of father, mother, and young children is often separated by both geographic and social distance from relatives. This tends to place on the parents, especially on the mother, the primary responsibility for the early socialization of the child. Later in childhood, playmates and teachers will play an active role in the child's development, but in the first three to five years his mother is expected to have the basic responsibility for his care and upbringing. This seems natural to us, but it was not always so.

The life-style of the majority can come to seem the only right and natural way of living. And thus Americans have come to take for granted that the right and natural way of bringing up young children is for the mother to do it, for in the last half century this has been the dominant pattern in American culture. Most of the books on child care and even the

177

The day nursery need not be merely a custodial institution.

welfare laws reflect this prevailing assumption (which means that the children of poverty sometimes have *no* close and intimate contact with adult males until well past puberty). Yet there are ample precedents in our own past for someone other than the mother to have the basic responsibility for socializing children.

The need of many mothers for help in the care of their children becomes increasingly evident. If the young woman is to complete her education and become able to earn a living (as many women want to do and most poor women must do), she needs a place where she can leave her tiny children for much of the day. The mother wants and the child needs a situation in which there will be warm, supportive care for the child.

178

The day nursery need not be merely a custodial institution, as the Swedes have long realized and we are beginning to learn. As we debate the merits of the day-care centers for children, it may be useful to bear in mind that the experience of other societies (Sweden and Israel, for example) has demonstrated that the family is not the only group where children can be effectively socialized, and that the mother has not always borne the total burden of socialization in our own society.

Heroes, models and fathers

As American mothers have gradually become more involved in the socialization of their young children, American fathers have become less involved. The basic reason for this is that, in the majority of families, the father goes out of the home to work. As recently as the late nineteenth century, when most of our grandparents were children, this was not so.

When America was a nation of small farmers and shopkeepers, the family was the major producing unit of our economy. As described in detail in Chapter 1 the father in nineteenth-century America was the head of the household enterprise; his relations to his wife and children were at once familial and economic, his dependents were his subordinates on the job, and the child was expected to contribute his labor to the family enterprise as soon as he could walk well enough to pick up chips of wood or perform other simple tasks. The father's role in socializing his children was significantly different than it is in our urban, industrial society, in which the father leaves home to work and the child does not contribute to the family livelihood.

The small child wants to imitate his parents, to do what he sees them doing, but even before the urban American child enters school he has learned that there is little in his parents productive life that he can meaningfully imitate. The tasks that adults and children used to do together are largely gone; only thirty years ago, a small child could work in the garden beside his mother or father, picking peas or strawberries, then sit beside his mother in the shade and shell the peas; when they appeared on his plate at dinner he did not need to be urged to eat them. What he did with his parents was relevant to his existence and to the livelihood of the family. But peas and strawberries come frozen in plastic now, and something is gone from the relation between parent and child.

When the family was the basic economic unit of society, the life of adults was centered on the home. The child grew up aware of what his father's role was in intricate detail; he was thus aware of what his own role would be, and usually learned it from his father. The son imitated his father at first in play, then soon in earnest, much as the little girl still imitates her mother with a toy broom or washing machine, and soon is expected to help wash dishes and dust furniture. It used to be that for a boy, too, growing up meant gradually growing into roles that he had watched his father play.

179

In our agricultural past, most adults of the same sex had basically the same skills, and the transfer of techniques that were crucial to the survival of the society from one generation to the next was accomplished simply by the boy working beside his father, although his older brothers and uncles could be quite as important in teaching him the ways of coaxing a mule to pull a load.

The basic change in socialization in America, that which sets industrial mass society apart from all earlier life-styles, is that the boy raised in America today cannot participate in his father's work, cannot even observe what he does, and has no understanding of it except at the most general level. When someone asks him, "What does your Daddy do?" he has an answer, but it is seldom more than a label. The central focus of an American man's life is typically an occupation carried on outside the home. Few city-bred American boys have ever *watched* their fathers at work; even fewer have *helped* them with their work. This means that except for those few whose families make a living together in a small family enterprise, American boys today cannot learn an occupational role from their fathers.

Being excluded from his father's major activities, a boy does not observe his father's triumph and conflicts. He sees only the effects of prolonged tension on the family while his father battles for promotion. If the promotion is won, the son may perceive only that now the family will have to move, leaving friends and familiar surroundings, for a promotion often involves a transfer. A son may not want to enter his father's line of work for many reasons, but one is likely to be that he has had no opportunity to experience the rewards of the job itself, never having been a participant. He may come to believe that his father's work has no intrinsic meaning, because all he has ever experienced are the extrinsic rewards: the paycheck and the things it will buy.

It is not that the contemporary American father is more preoccupied with his work than his grandfather was; it is rather that the child of today is excluded from his father's productive activities. Fifty years ago a boy was usually an "unpaid family worker" and almost too familiar with what his father (indeed, the entire family) did for a living. A boy raised on the family farm or in a family that ran a small business might long to escape from the confining and demanding family enterprise, but he assuredly had a place in and an involvement with his father's work-related pursuits.

The contemporary American boy tends to be with his father only during the latter's leisure time. Father and son may go camping, fishing, or to the ball game, and if the son grows up to be like his father it is likely to be in leisure pursuits and family activities that have little to do with his occupational role. Many boys do not even participate in recreational activities with their fathers. The boy whose father is absent from the family because of a demanding career or because of death or divorce, may be raised in the world of women and children until he reaches high school. Even then, his mother and women teachers are likely to continue to be dominant adults in his life.

The boy raised in a predominantly female world, where his mother and female teachers are the primary adult models, finds it difficult to define masculinity. Unlike his sister, he is not encouraged to imitate his mother. If his sister gets into mother's cosmetics and tries on lipstick and mascara, she is scolded for violating property rights and for engaging in behavior that is not appropriate to her age. But it will be clear that she is anticipating a role that will be hers one day, and she will probably be made aware subtly that her behavior is considered "cute." In contrast, if a small boy imitates his mother, putting on lipstick and mascara, or playing dress-up in mother's clothing, he will be shamed. He will be made to understand that he has violated sex-role expectations. Thus the boy raised primarily by women tends to define masculinity through a negative process: he is to be nonfeminine. This means that he learns to dissociate feminine qualities from himself and to devalue them. Lacking positive models for masculinity, he has to invent his own images of manhood.

There are few adult males in the family for the child to observe and imitate. Siblings are often close in age and an older brother may be a model for how a big boy acts, but not a model of adult manhood. Contact with uncles is more sporadic than in the days when uncle's farm was about a quarter of a mile down the section road, or when father and uncle ran the grain elevator and feed store together. For most small boys in urban and suburban America, the father is the primary male model, however seldom the boy sees him.

Being a model is more difficult than it seems, and is not at all the same as being admired. There is a difference between an idol and a model: we can worship an idol without emulating his behavior. Before we can take someone as a model for our own behavior, we must be able to imagine becoming a person like him. We must therefore be able to imagine the admired other as having once been like we are now, or it will seem impossible to bridge the gulf between our latent capacities and his developed skills.

To a tiny child, a father can seem all-powerful, able to do things that even mother cannot do, such as open pickle jars and fix broken tricycles, and to know in some mysterious way when the child has broken a switch on the hi-fi set or told a lie. This powerful man seems to his son to have been born ten feet tall. (He will shrink amazingly by the time his son is fifteen.) It is inconceivable to a little boy that his father could once have been a child, weak and powerless like himself, dependent on someone else to manage buttons or zippers when he went to the bathroom.

The father tells stories of his own childhood, but the tales seem to be of daring deeds that the child feels incapable of duplicating. Insofar as he can imagine his father having been a child, the son is likely to picture him as a miniature adult whose life was a series of exploits in a world more exciting than the one the little boy knows. (One of the the important functions of a grandmother is to tell her grandson *her* version of what the father did as a child.)

181

It may be equally difficult for the little boy to recognize his own potential manhood. The characteristics of a baby—being cute, helpless, easily hurt, soft and cuddly—are considered appropriate for a girl in our culture; she can display them all her life and be "feminine." But the father who dotes on such traits in his tiny daughter is irritated by the same characteristics in his small son. As soon as the boy is past the toddler stage, his father chides him with "Don't be such a baby—act like a man!"

The father's sporadic efforts to teach his son to catch a football or to handle tools may be loaded with parental expectations. The son will quickly sense when his father is testing rather than playing. If every time the boy fumbles the ball or strips the threads on a screw he has failed another trial of manhood, the image of failure and incompetence that is mirrored in his father's eyes becomes part of his self-image. If the father insists, "You can do it, if you try," the boy's fear of failure is heightened. At least his father sees him as a boy who could do well if only he would; suppose he were to try and should fail any way? He is afraid that he would be scorned totally by his father. The boy may decide that it is safer to say "I won't" than to risk admitting "I can't."

The small boy projects onto his father the latent capacities that he is unable to recognize in himself. The effect is to heighten the contrast between the father and son in the boy's mind. Having lost contact with his own strength, he has an unmitigated awareness of his weakness. In contast, the father seems a powerful figure and larger than life, for the son has augmented whatever his father's real abilities may be with his own projected potential. Having endowed his father with so much of himself, he craves his father's approval. Yet so long as the boy's perception of himself is focused on weakness, he will discount any approval he receives. When his father admits, "You did that well—for a change," the boy is likely to believe that his achievement was somehow a matter of luck—perhaps even fraud—and he may not want to try again, for fear that it would soon be apparent that he is still a fumbling coward.

Such a child becomes alienated from himself. The pattern of his socialization impedes recognition of his own drives and latent capacities. The self he perceives is a bumbling and inadequate one: unable to feel pride in himself, he craves the approval and love of his parents. If in his early childhood the price of mother's approval was the surrender of most of his drives from hunger to curiosity, acting to satisfy his own needs became an act of submission: mother's approval is antithetical to the aggressive manliness his father requires of him. He would like to please his father, but there is an inherent contradiction in submitting to a demand that he be aggressive.

One of the ways in which the father can avoid this kind of destructive pressure on his son is to begin playing games with him when the boy is an infant. The baby likes to play peekaboo and a variety of other games with his father as well as his mother; as the child learns to enjoy imitating his mother through playing games, so he can learn to enjoy imitating his father through playing games. The child whose father handles him and plays games for their mutual delight will be likely to grow into a boy who feels comfortable with his father, who is predisposed to believe that he can do what he sees his father doing, and wants to learn. An hour or so a day of playing with his father is probably enough to establish such a relationship; even the commuter is likely to have time enough for bedtime games with his children.

Playmates as mirrors and models

The self-awareness of the child emerges slowly, out of a context of group belonging. A father fondles his small daughter and asks, "Whose little girl are you?" and the child learns to say, "I'm Daddy's girl." She has also learned that she is Mommy's darling, and Johnny's little sister, and the little Jones girl when addressed by neighbors down the street. Defining herself thus in terms of relatedness, she tends to think *We* interchangeably with *I*. "I have a new car," she announces proudly to the boy next door, and sometimes it is "We have a new car," and the meaning is the same. Pronouns are confusing to a small child because it is not yet clear where the *We* stops and the *I* begins. Like a figure in bas-relief, the *I* is only partially formed against the background of *We*.

Compared with the giants who surround him—his nose is barely above the level of their knees—a toddler is weak and powerless. But the others who are part of his *We* sustain him with their strength. In a crowd, he clings to his mother's hand or leg. Losing his grip and finding himself surrounded by strangers, he feels exposed and helpless—a lost child who can only cry. If the child is one day to become a functioning adult, he must emerge from the *We* consciousness of early childhood and develop an awareness of himself as a complete person. It is not that he will cease being related to others, but rather that the nature of his relatedness will change. To know the joy of being loving he must have others with whom he can be loving. But so long as he perceives himself as a fragment, requiring the presence of others in order to be whole, he can enjoy neither himself nor other people. He will merely cling to them.

The first sharp break in an American child's socialization comes on the day the child enters the world his parents will know only as visitors, the world of school. Bounded by a Cyclone fence, stratified into an age-graded hierarchy of children, ruled formally by the teachers and the principal and informally by the sixth grade, here is a world where the child is not the privileged character that he is in the world of his family. Here he must learn to compete and to compromise, and to conform to the expectations of his peers or be prepared to defend himself. And here he learns to view himself with a new perspective.

The people who surround the child in his early years give him the first fragmentary glimpses of himself in the epithets they cast at him and in the shining images they sometimes lay on him in benediction. Other

183

people are his mirrors. If the image reflected by parents is grossly distorted (either flattering or repelling), the child will have an unrealistic self-image that he may be unable to live up to, or unable to live down. He needs to turn to a different group of significant others who will reflect a more accurate picture of himself, one that he can live with and like. His age peers serve this function.

If parents have treated a child like visiting royalty, the rest of the third grade will let him know that he is not so special. If he has learned to think of himself as a disappointment to his mother and father, comparison with peers may give him a chance to reevaluate himself. The images of the self that are reflected in the responses of the child's parents may be so different from the images reflected by peers that the boy or girl begins to wonder who the "real me" is. Such existential questions may be painful, but they are part of a growth process.

To correct distortions in the self-image, the child (like an adult) needs to perceive the self through the eyes of another, and to believe that what this significant other sees is real. This means that the child must be open to the significant other, must drop the posturing and bragging that children often exhibit when they are uncertain about themselves. Revealing thoughts and feelings, acting without pretense, entails risks: the risk of being rejected or belittled. No one feels more anxiety about such personal rejection than a child at the threshold of adolescence. Candor and intimacy carry the least risk when the person with whom one is being open is an equal, someone who has about the same level of skill (or lack of skill), someone who has similar fears and shared dreams.

There are always things that a child tries to conceal from mother and father, if only failure to live up to their expectations. Whatever else the parent-child relationship may be, it is one in which power and authority are grossly unequal and thus not a relationship conducive to candid intimacy. The preadolescent child may take an older brother or sister as a model, but the age difference means that they are not quite equals. A younger brother or sister is more often seen as a rival than an equal. Finding a "best friend" of the same age and sex provides an opportunity to see the self through the eyes of someone with whom the child can identify in the most literal sense, someone the child both likes and resembles. Best friends are equals.

Liking the best friend makes it easier to know and like the self. The best friend is both model and mirror. The best friends stand in the same subordinate relation to adult authority, and are equally patronizing to children in the lower grades. Best friends have the same kinds of problems, the same vagrant enthusiasms. The two probably have to contend with the same teacher, the same sixth-grade bully, the same classroom tattle-tale, the same cranky neighbor who thinks azaleas are more important than shortcuts. The response of one sets the response of the other. What one scorns the other will not deign to eat, wear, or play with, however much mother pleads or scolds. (The new doll Aunt Helen brought back from Europe is a "dumb doll" because the best friend said so.)

The best friend relationship serves the same supportive function for both participants, whether they are boys or girls. Learning to know the self and learning to know someone else are reciprocal processes. The child and best friend test themselves, daring each other to try things, venturing, exploring, getting into and out of trouble together, pledging secrecy. Their escapades are part reality, part fantasy, blended in a world they cannot share with grown-ups. The needs of the child and those of the best friend come to be mutual needs. Joint projects are the outward manifestaton of the private world they have created. ("We need some boards and nails for *our* playhouse, Mother.")

Many of the capacities that each is discovering in the self require interaction with a known and trusted other. A boy cannot show off his courage without someone to be his admiring audience; he cannot fight unless he has an adversary. Enemies can serve these functions, but there are some things he cannot be and do without a special friend. A girl cannot share alone. She cannot keep a secret by herself—a confidant who told her the secret must know that she is keeping it, too. The important thing is not the secret, but demonstrating the ability to keep it, discovering that one is loyal and trustworthy by sharing this experience with a friend.

In relations with parents, the preadolescent child is still able only to receive. He may be grateful for the care and pleasures his parents give him, or he may take them for granted like a baby bird with a perpetually open mouth. But when the day comes that a boy or girl can give as well as receive, the child knows a new power and a new source of joy. A small child is told to share his candy and toys with playmates and is reluctant to do so. But the preadolescent child who has a best friend gives that friend half of a candy bar because there would be little pleasure derived from eating it in front of the friend, or from hiding the candy until the friend goes home. Part of having a friend is sharing, and the child knows that he or she will get half of anything the friend has in the future. This is not the same behavior as the attempt by an isolate to buy friendship by distributing goodies on the playground; sharing with a best friend is reciprocal and likely to be confined to this particular friend for a time, this person with whom the child creates a closed group of two.

Best friends have a mutual sharing pact and a mutual admiration pact. The friend with whom the child shares secrets and treasures, whose welfare comes to seem as important as his own, is the first person the child *cares* for in the several senses of the word. Through such a friendship, he learns to recognize the kind of person he is and to be sensitive to the needs of others. The preadolescent who does not experience this kind of friendship, who has playmates but no close friend, will find it difficult to enter into intimate relationships later in life. Sometimes such persons find a best friend belatedly, in adolescence. But the person who never has this

185

Best friends are equals. They test themselves, daring each other to try things, venturing, exploring, sharing. The best friend is the first person the child cares for in the several senses of that word.

experience as a part of growing up will be able to "love" only when someone is giving him things ("But what have you done for me lately?").

Masculine and feminine: sex-role socialization

By adolescence, if the child's development has not been arrested or twisted, he or she begins to want an intimate relationship with someone both like and unlike the self: an age peer, but a member of the opposite sex. The adolescent does not suddenly abandon the best friend of the same sex. On the contrary, the two best friends are likely to experience comparable stresses in their lives, and their closeness helps both make the adolescent transition. Their joint fantasy lives change. Boys stop collecting baseball cards from bubble gum packages and begin collecting back issues of *Playboy.* If either is too shy to approach a girl alone they may descend on girls together, with all the swagger and inept bluster of the junior high school male. (One of my colleagues tells of the day his thirteen-year-old daughter came home bubbling, "He likes me, Daddy, he likes me! I know because he broke all my potato chips in the cafeteria today.")

Adolescent girls share their passionate devotion to a rock musician with their best friend, collecting wall posters picturing their idol, listening together to records featuring his voice, and waiting in line together to see him "live" in concert. Thus they share the early stirrings of sexual feeling, as once they shared a candy bar. They talk about how to interpret the behavior of boys, what to wear, whether a new hair style is becoming, and all the things a girl would rather not discuss with her mother. There is usually a tacit understanding that the two will not compete for the attention of the same boy, and one may even act as a go-between for the other, carrying notes or dropping hints that her friend is interested and interesting.

The need for intimacy is not identical with the sex drive. The quest for intimacy begins earlier as a part of the child's development as a social being, a requirement of the emerging self. The sexual drive is physically based, however subject to social interpretation. The two needs may converge in the same relationship, and presumably it is this fusion that people have in mind when they say that sex is not fully satisfying unless it is an experience of love.

Certainly one of the most difficult transitions in the adolescent period is moving from intimacy based on identity to intimacy with someone who is fundamentally different. It is not difficult to have insight into someone who is like ourselves; comparable experiences enable us to have an empathic grasp of the other's needs and moods. "I know how you feel" is a statement of analogy. But it is inappropriate and often false when the other person has had markedly different life experiences. And even if a boy and girl were raised on the same street by parents who are as interchangeable as the tract houses they own and the late-model sedans they

187

drive, he was raised a boy and she a girl and they have grown up in two different reality systems.

To differences in socialization add differences in body chemistry, and he and she are as unlike as if they had grown up in alien cultures, as in a sense they have. In the grade school world the age-graded hierarchy is cut vertically into Girls and Boys. As in all instances where groups are divided into mutually exclusive factions, "They" are stereotyped. The stereotypes often persist into adult life. When the adolescent boy or the forty-year-old man moans, "I can't understand women!" the odds are that some woman has just behaved in a manner that violated his stereotype. The very use of the generic term *women* indicates that he does prejudge: if not, he would say "I can't understand Mary." The girl who says "All you men are alike" has no better ability to perceive individuals among members of the opposite sex. Her comment reflects the same kind of stereotyping as the racist belief that all Orientals are inscrutable.

An important part of socialization in adolescence is learning how to perceive and interact with persons of the opposite sex, to be intimate with someone who is different. The childhood experience was one of intimacy with someone similar to the self, someone with whom the child could identify. The adolescent learning to be intimate with someone of the opposite sex not surprisingly goes about it by trying to become as much like that person as possible. The result is the "his and her" versions of dress, hairstyle, and personal belongings. Much of what the adult generation dismisses as the appearance of "unisex" has its origins in the adolescent striving for intimacy through identity.

The young seem to sense that true intimacy is possible only between equals. However, people do not need to be identical to be equal; opposites may be equal. The countervailing attraction between the profoundly masculine and the intensely feminine comes later, however, when each is more certain of self and of sexual identity. The adolescent is still searching, and peers of both sexes are essential to the discovery of self.

There is a growing body of psychohormonal research that indicates human behavior may be influenced by sex-linked hormones (see Scarf 1972 for a discussion at length). For example, aggressive behavior seems to be related to levels of testosterone, the male hormone. It should be remembered, however, that while males produce, after puberty, higher amounts of testosterone and females produce, after puberty, higher amounts of estrogen and related hormones, *both* males and females produce similar hormones. The adrenal glands of both sexes produce small amounts of both estrogen and testosterone; *the hormonal difference between men and women is in amount, rather than kind, of hormones produced.*

The channeling and controlling of behavior, whether motivated by hormonal or by learned drives, is a part of the socialization process. The differentiation between masculine and feminine behavior begins with the differing expectations that adults have of young children. The usual question that adult strangers or distant relatives ask a small boy with whom they feel some need to make a conversation is, "What do you want to be when you grow up?" We expect him to answer with an occupational choice. No one expects him to say, "A father." Most boys will grow up to be fathers, and we know that, but this is not a role that is considered to be central to his self-image or social identity.

Adults do not ask little girls what they are going to be when they grow up. We know. They are going to be mommies. Preferably, they will be wives, too. So we simply say to a little girl, " How *pretty* you are," or, if that is patently absurd, "How *big* you are." In other words, while a boy grows up with the expectation that he must decide what he is going to be, that he must choose an identity, a girl learns that she is expected simply to grow into a role. When she is big enough and pretty enough, she will find a husband. Perhaps she will need to prepare for some kind of job as an insurance policy—especially if she is not very pretty—but she has learned that the most important event in her life will be her marriage.

If the most important choice in the girl's life is her choice of a husband, then it follows that the most important competition she enters is with other girls for the most promising young man. A girl is taught—sometimes subtly, sometimes openly—that she should not compete *with* boys. She is supposed to compete *for* boys. A man is the prize, not her competitor. It is other girls who are the competition, and who will remain the competition even after she is married, for there are always going to be prettier girls, and some day there will be younger and prettier girls, and her husband will still be the prize.

The result is that a girl is raised to feel hostile to and competitive with most other women, her immediate family not excluded. Trying to look like one's teenage daughter is, if television commercials are to be believed, a major point of competition for mature American women today. Meanwhile, the woman who wants a career, not just a job, the woman who wants to compete with men and not just for a man, worries about her femininity.

At school, girls learn to please authority, which is not what most boys learn. Boys learn to compete with the other boys, in class or on the playground. The boy's goal is to beat the other player, or the other team, and the boy learns to be a good competitor and a good team player, skills that will be useful in the corporate world later in his life. What girls learn—even girls who are concerned with getting good grades—is to succeed by pleasing authority, in the person of the teacher. Ultimately this skill will transfer into pleasing a man, her husband or her boss. This may make a woman an able administrative assistant, but it hinders her development into an executive with line authority.

The girl who does acquire competitive characteristics is labeled a tomboy—not as derisive a term as may be applied to the boy who learns passive or dependent behaviors, but a term of derision nonetheless. Yet many women who were once "tomboys" have become successful business and professional women. Many successful women were encouraged in "tomboy" behaviors as children, and later encouraged in their career

189

choices, by their fathers. It is often the mother, older sister, grandmother, and aunts who worry about whether that bright, career-oriented girl is going to attract a husband. It is easy to blame chauvinistic males for failing to accept women in the world outside the family, but it is more often women than men who instill childhood expectations that can hobble a girl for life.

Yet there is another side to sex-role socialization. The kind of aggressive, competitive behavior that is supposed to be masculine does not come readily to all boys. The boy who does not achieve as an athlete has a difficult childhood. The man who settles—as most men must—for a job instead of a career, or a career that is truncated at a middling level, may focus his energies and attention on his family. But his upbringing has taught him that this is not enough, that he has ended the career race as an also-ran. Contemporary sex-role socialization may be harmful to boys as well as to girls.

Boys were not always raised and socialized primarily by their mothers and female teachers. In the late nineteenth century, infants and toddlers of both sexes wore dresses and long curls, as a glance through old family photograph albums will indicate. Very young children were raised by the women of the family: mother, older sisters, grandmother, aunts, hired girls. But a boy left the world of women and children when his curls were cut and he put on his first trousers, at about the age of five; at that point in his life he entered the world of boys, which was appended to the world of men. Boys helped with chores on the fringes of man's work. Learning by doing and by watching, a boy worked beside his father, uncles, older brothers, as they harnessed the team or repaired machinery. He hung around the barn, or the smithy, after work and after school. He went to school, but only after the crops were harvested, and he was likely to leave school by the age of fourteen or soon after, when he had become physically strong enough to do a man's work. Two or three generations ago, a boy learned to be a man by participating in the man's world for at least a decade of his childhood. It was not merely work roles that he learned. He smoked behind the barn with his brother or cousin; he tried chewing tobacco, and learned to spit with accurate aim. When he was strong enough to do a man's work in the field, he was considered old enough to be passed the whiskey. A boy entered the world of men as a full participant when he was able to do a man's work all day. Often, this was at puberty.

In contemporary America, boys remain a part of the world of women and children throughout childhood, and often throughout adolescence. This means that a boy must enter the male world and the adult world at the same time. This abrupt transition may come on the first job, or it may come when he enters military service. But it is a difficult transition for most young men. The masculine world is strange to them, and their fear of failure is great.

A decade in limbo:
the dilemma of American youth

For most of human history, childhood ended abruptly at puberty or even before, for in the preindustrial society life is short, the turnover of generations is rapid, and the young must assume adult roles as soon as possible. The American girl of thirteen is a gangling adolescent who papers the walls of her room with color posters of current recording idols; her counterpart in a Latin American mountain village is already a wife with a baby on her back.

In an industrial society such as our own, life expectancy is nearly twice as long as it is in underdeveloped countries, and the turnover of generations is slower. The adolescent does not need to assume a productive role because the proportion of adults in the population is high and because machines do most of the unskilled jobs, tasks that children perform in preindustrial societies. Postponing adult responsibilities and parenthood facilitates the creation of a technically and professionally skilled work force. Yet it also means that childhood is prolonged—or at least the dependent, subordinate, indulged status that children occupy is prolonged—for nearly ten years after the young have reached puberty.

This prolonged dependency of American adolescents and young adults is a radical social change that we have somehow not perceived as the basis of the "generation gap." In the past, only prosperous families could afford a period of dependent adolescence for their children. In poor American families, the labor and wages of adolescent children were an important part of the family livelihood, and the demands of a job kept the young under a certain discipline. While a father could legally demand his minor child's wages (or labor) in return for supporting him or her, a teenage runaway could expect to find work and to become self-supporting. Before World War I, most Americans had no more than an eight-grade or "grammar school" education. High school was for the middle class, although an affluent farmer or rancher might send his favorite son or daughter into town to live with a relative and go to high school. (The children of wealthy families went to private boarding schools.) Most fourteen-year-old boys were in the labor-force, functioning as adult males. The U.S. Bureau of Census listed workers between the ages of ten and fourteen for many decades; it was only in 1940, on the eve of World War II, that workers under the age of fourteen were finally dropped from the labor force statistics.

Girls, as well as boys, entered the labor force at puberty if not before. Before World War I, most American girls were unpaid family workers on the family farm or in the marginal family business until they married; if there were too many daughters at home for the family farm or shop to support, an adolescent girl might find work as a hired girl in a more affluent family. (Room and board was often a part of her pay, as it was for

191

the adolescent boy who was a farm hand.) Most of the poor remained poor, and could survive only by entering the labor force at an early age. There was a certain rigidity to the class structure of America, in spite of the ideal of equality, and most mobility was geographical rather than social. The constricted class structure of eastern cities and towns could be escaped by going west, but only a few made fortunes there. Most were simply poor in a different place.

The disappearance of child labor (except among the migratory field workers) reflects a value change translated into law. Compulsory school attendance laws, laws restricting child labor, welfare laws that permit both impoverished mothers and their children to remain out of the factories and fields, all reflect the belief that it is a greater social good for children to be in school and in the home than in the labor force. The end of child labor reflects not only a value change, but also an underlying technological change. The removal of economic production from the home and the disappearance of the family farm have largely removed the need for "unpaid family workers." Schools still have a long summer vacation, but few children spend it working in the fields or picking fruit. In our factories, unskilled manual labor is rapidly being mechanized and automated. No one would wish our children to return to the labor force. The children who worked in the textile mills and in the coal mines were stunted by their labor and died young.

Whether or not we are more humane than our forebears, it is certainly the case that the untrained hands of children are no longer economically useful in America. Viewed from one perspective, this means that even the children of the poor are freed during childhood and adolescence to acquire the education and skills that well-paid and rewarding occupations require. Viewed from another perspective, this means that the young are kept in an economically dependent and thus powerless state, often until they are in their middle twenties, because there is no place for them in the adult world of work.

Before World War I, only the children of prosperous Americans had an adolescence. Unlike the children of the poor, they did not enter the labor force at puberty. On the contrary, they spent the years between puberty and marriage in a leisure-class status. They were expected to acquire certain skills and an education appropriate to their class, but not to engage in productive labor. Even a middle-class home had servants at the turn of the century, and it would have been unthinkable for the daughters of the family to have worked in the kitchen like the hired girl. The daughter of the merchant or banker was raised to be the wife of a merchant or banker; in the tight family hierarchies of the small towns and cities of America were careful matchmakers. During adolescence, the daughter of a prosperous family learned to be a gracious hostess, to cope with servants, to be concerned with church, charity, and family traditions. The years between puberty and her early twenties were spent in preparing for a suitable marriage and finding a proper husband of her own class; if she could not, she was expected to remain a maiden lady in her father's home. In either event, her socialization was suitable.

The sons of bankers and shipowners and brokers went to college to become educated as befit future bankers and shipowners and brokers. They also enjoyed an indulged, leisure-class life while waiting to enter the family business. They did not have to choose a career; they had been raised knowing they would grow up to take over the family business interests. When they married, the family firm made an appropriate opening for them, with a salary sufficient to maintain them at a "decent" level while they learned the family business. When their father or uncle retired, they were assured a controlling position in the family firm.

Most business was small business until well into the twentieth century in America, and the middle class was primarily composed of the proprietors of family-owned businesses. The middle-class family thus owned income-producing property (the shop, the creamery, the family farm or ranch, the state-chartered but family-owned bank). This property was left to sons (or nephews) who inherited not only wealth, but an occupation and a social class position. Even large corporations were often family firms on a grand scale before World War I, and the sons of such families were raised like young nobles waiting to come into entailed estates. Company stock was closely held by family members, and bequeathed to heirs who learned that the greatest sin of all was touching their capital. Not all sons chose to take over the family business, but they knew the family firm was theirs if they wanted it, provided only that they did not behave too outrageously.

Income and inheritance taxes have altered that pattern irrevocably. The social legislation of the twentieth century, beginning with the constitutional amendment that gave the federal government the power to tax income, has finally opened the class structure and begun to make good on the American promise of equal opportunity to rise above the class of one's birth. The dark side of the promise is the possibility of dropping into a lower class, for the same social and economic transformations that removed the ceiling from social-class status have also undermined the floor.

Corporations today are seldom family controlled; the old patterns of family ownership and inherited position as the president of the family company are disappearing. The middle-class of entrepreneurs has been largely replaced by salaried corporate executives and professionals. Although they have power and high salaries, these men are employees, and they cannot leave the business to their sons. It is not theirs to will. They can see that their sons have an excellent education, but they cannot guarantee that their sons will rise to high executive positions.

The concept of the "self-made man" seems quaint in the middle of the twentieth century; a Horatio Alger hero is as antiquated as a gold toothpick. Yet in a sense, every boy must become a self-made man in contemporary America. There is little to prevent the son of a working-

193

class family from rising into the ranks of the upper middle professional and managerial class, provided that he acquires the requisite education and behavior norms. But at the same time, there is no guarantee that he will not descend into the sump of chronic unemployment. The son of an upper-middle-class family is granted that class status as a birthright only during his childhood; as a young adult he must acquire the education, the technical and professional skills, and the job that will perpetuate his status. If he does not, he will drop out of his class. The children of the very, very rich still inherit enough property to ensure their class status for life. But for most Americans, a childhood of affluence and leisure is no longer the prelude to a life of comfort.

The children of the upper middle class are raised like the sons of the nineteenth-century merchant princes, but unlike earlier children of affluence, they are not necessarily being prepared to live in the class to which they were born. They may inherit some money—life insurance, perhaps a trust fund—but they are unlikely to inherit *income-producing* property. It was the business, or the land, that gave earlier heirs both property and occupation. Such inheritance as contemporary youth may receive is often quickly dissipated, and they may move from the leisured affluence of their youth into chronic unemployment. Perhaps more often they move into the monotone of a lower-middle class, mildly deprived existence. This means that the socialization that the upper-middle-class child receives may not be relevant to his adult life; the adolescent senses this, if his parents do not. Upper-middle-class youth are often, to borrow Frances Cornford's phrase, "magnificently unprepared for the long littleness of life."

Thus partly by design (compulsory school attendance and child labor laws) and partly by the drift of technological change, the years of childhood and adolescence in America have become years of leisure, of waiting and preparing for an adult role that seems remote. Unlike the poor children of an earlier age, today's youth are barred from participation in the labor force; but unlike the children of an earlier affluent class of Americans, they have no guarantee that their decade in the limbo of adolescence will be followed by either leisure or affluence in their adult lives. Adolescence is a period of dependency, the prologue to an uncertain future. These are profound social changes that are fundamentally important in creating the strains placed on contemporary American families and in the rise of a dissident youth culture.

For some thirty years there has been a distinctive youth subculture; Talcott Parsons described it in 1942. The last thirty years have been the period in which more and more young Americans of all social classes have been raised in an enforced leisure in which there is little constructive work for them to do. If the youth culture is absorbing more of the energies of American adolescents, it is basically because the adult world has so little useful place for them. Because the labor of the adolescent is no longer valued, he has no economic function and thus no power. There is nothing productive he can do, and thus nothing productive he can withhold, until he has acquired a high level of technical skill; contemporary American youth is in a human holding pattern, growing restive. (*Restive* does not mean *restless*, although that adjective may also be appropriate for many adolescents. *Restive* means unmanageable, rejecting control.)

The transmission of behavior norms has always led to some friction between the generations, as the old have despaired of teaching the young constraint and the young have resented the rigidity of their elders. But in the past, the basic goals of young and old were fundamentally similar. The young were impatient to have the privileges enjoyed by adults, and their elders were reluctant to let go of their position of dominance. They disagreed on the time when the transfer of property and privilege from old to young should occur, but the generations agreed on what was worth doing and having. In the view of their elders, the young in contemporary America seem to have rejected the prevailing value structure and to have no respect for either authority or property. What is seldom recognized is that the situation of the young with regard to authority and property has been fundamentally altered since the middle of the twentieth century. Simply stated, the children of the upper middle classes can no longer expect to inherit income-producing property, a situation that has altered the attitudes of the young toward property and that has deprived the parental generation of a major basis for authority.

In the past, the son of a prosperous family might grow restive while waiting to take over the family firm (one reason for sending him away for a long, leisurely, college education, followed by a European grand tour), but the ultimate power in the family was held by whoever had the company stock or the deed to the family lands in his or her own name. That economic power kept the younger generation deferential. A wealthy father could keep his son in line by threatening to change his will or to turn the company over to a son-in-law or a nephew. A woman might finally rise to a position of power when she became a wealthy widow, an aging matriarch controlling her grown sons, daughters, nephews, nieces, grandsons, and granddaughters. If the elderly have little power in our society today, it is because they have so little economic control left; their power base vanished with the family firm.

If the young are no longer deferential, it is in part because fathers are increasingly powerless to ensure their sons the means of making a living. Few contemporary parents can either promise or threaten the economic and social future of their children. The most they can do is pay for an education and promise to give—or threaten to withhold—present economic support. All American families are now expected to do what only the wealthy were expected to do in the past: guide and control adolescent children and provide for them during a prolonged period of dependency. The economic burden may be less heavy than the social demand that parents control the behavior of their adolescent children at exactly the time in history that they have lost the major means of doing so: the power to give or to withhold future economic security.

195

In a family with no property, the power of the older generation once resided in the old man's heavy fist; when his son could defeat him, or at least fight him to a draw, the son was free to leave. This pattern is now considered unacceptable in most social classes. The father who beats his children is no longer considered to be within his right to discipline them. On the contrary, he is considered a child abuser. The son who strikes his father and runs away from home may be considered out of control, and a candidate either for juvenile hall or a mental institution, depending on the class level of the family.

Sex roles and socialization: a summary

In most American families in the past, once a child was weaned someone other than his mother was likely to take over his care, to teach him how to blow his nose and tie his shoelaces, and to give him some kind of answer when he asked, "Why?" For most children this mother-surrogate was an older sister or some other female relative who was too young or too old to be more productively employed; for many children it was a nursemaid. Whoever she was, she stood in a relationship to the child that was one of immediate but not ultimate authority. The child could appeal to his parents if his nursemaid's hand became too heavy; the other side of the relationship was that the older sister or nurse might help the child conceal an occasional misdeed from his parents. Between parent and child there was a mediator who never had the same status and authority as the parent.

The most significant changes in the socialization of American children in the last hundred years are the increasing role of the mother and the declining role of the father. As recently as three generations ago, most fathers worked at home and their young sons could learn the skills every male of their class was expected to have by first watching, then helping, their father and older brothers. Men used to teach boys to be men. Today, even if the father has some involvement in the socialization of his son, it is more likely to be participation in leisure pursuits than direct involvement in the serious work of the father. No longer does the boy enter the man's world at the age of six or seven. Most boys are raised today in an environment dominated by women throughout childhood and adolescence.

Girls used to be separated from boys in most childhood activities. Today, they are not. Whether socializing boys and girls together in environments dominated by adult women is good or bad depends on how one regards the consequences. On the one hand, similarities in childhood experience lead to more equality and easier intimacy between the sexes. On the other hand, there is a certain "feminization" of the American male, which is a different way of looking at the same phenomenon.

The family as most Americans know and experience it today functions well in the socialization of small children. But as the locus of socialization and control of adolescents, the family is less satisfactory. Adolescents are not involved in the productive work of society. Having passed the age where they are willing to be considered children in the family, they must remain dependents in their parents' home because there is no place for them anywhere else. Parents are expected to control their physically mature adolescent children, and the only means left to most of them to do so is whatever emotional leverage they may be able to apply.

If the young are comparatively powerless until they have completed a long educational period, parents are also comparatively powerless with regard to their adolescent children. Contemporary American parents and adolescents need to come to personal understanding with each other in a way that earlier generations seldom did. Communication between parents and children was never very good in the past; it did not need to be, for lines of authority and control existed because of the economic power and physical control the older generation could exercise over the younger. Today, each side is aware of its own relative lack of power, and thus of the need to work through problems together. It is a tribute to the strength and resiliency of the American family that so many parents and children do learn to be sensitive to the needs and concerns of each other, and do weather successfully the stormy years when the children are suspended in adolescence.

References

Call, Justin D. 1968. "Lap and Finger Play in Infancy, Implications for Ego Development." *International Journal of Psycho-Analysis* 49 (nos. 2–3):375–378.
_____ 1970. "Games Babies Play." *Psychology Today* 3 (January):34–37, 54.
Jellife, D. B., and E. F. P. Jelliffe. 1975. "Human Milk, Nutrition, and the World Resource Crisis." *Science* 188 (May 9):557–561.
Putney, Snell, and Gail J. Putney (Fullerton). 1964. *Normal Neurosis: The Adjusted American.* New York: Harper & Row.
Scarf, Maggie. 1972. "He and She: The Sex Hormones and Behavior." *The New York Times Magazine* (May 7):30, 101–106.
Sexton, Patricia Cayo. 1969. *The Feminized Male: Classrooms, White Collars, and the Decline of Manliness.* New York: Vintage Books.
Winter, Sara K. 1970. "Fantasies at Breast-Feeding Time." *Psychology Today* 3 (January):30–32, 56.

Suggested readings

Bettelheim, Bruno. 1963 "The Problem of Generations." In *Youth: Change and Challenge,* edited by Erik H. Erikson, New York: Basic Books. Available in paper as an Anchor Book, *The Challenge of Youth.* Bettelheim is concerned here with the problems between the generations created by a society so organized that youth remains dependent on the older generation, and the older generation is neither compelled by the necessity of survival nor psychologically motivated to step aside so that the young can accede to dominance.
Kagan, Jerome. 1969. "Check One: Male, Female." *Psychology Today* 3 (July):39–41. Sex-role identity, and how it is learned, is the focus of this article. A study of

Marriage as a parental union: sex roles and socialization

197

the sex-role responses of two-year-old children is reported, along with a discussion of culturally created sex-role images.

Sexton, Patricia Cayo. 1969. *The Feminized Male: Classrooms, White Collars, and the Decline of Manliness.* New York: Vintage Books. Paper. The author begins by posing such problems as why middle-class white males have the highest suicide rates in the U.S. She relates these problems to the sexual stereotypes that permeate our society. The book describes the process by which women from class and ethnic backgrounds that push women to achieve as individuals *and* to marry and devote themselves to their families are trapped in a double bind, and may wreak a heavy vengenance on their male children. This is not simply another attack on the emasculating mother; it is a thoughtful study of the damage sexual stereotypes can create for both sexes, and is focused primarily on the socialization process in the family and in the school.

Part Two

Marital choice and marital roles

7

Love as myth: the quicksilver foundation

The hero of the modern American movie is always a romantic lover just as the hero of the old Arabic epic is always an epileptic. A cynic might suspect that in any ordinary population the percentage of individuals with a capacity for romantic love of the Hollywood type was about as large as that of persons able to throw genuine epileptic fits. However, given a little social encouragement, either one can be adequately imitated without the performer admitting even to himself that the performance is not genuine.

Ralph Linton (1936:175)

The belief that romantic love is the only acceptable basis for marriage is as entrenched in the American value system as the belief in free enterprise (and the two beliefs have an historic connection). To question the relation between love and marriage is like questioning the connection between motherhood and virtue. Yet love as it is commonly understood and experienced by Americans does not contribute to marital stability or happiness: to build a marriage on a romantic foundation is to build on quicksilver.

Love as ideology: from dalliance to happy ending

Romantic love is surrounded by an elaborate set of expectations: it is supposed to be a sudden, irresistible emotion. A man is smitten and from that moment is in thrall to his beloved. His passion is heightened if the beloved is inaccessible, but an encounter with her—even a brief glimpse as she floats by—leads to a special excitement, a quickened pulse, a flush on the cheek, a glint in the eye. The lover is drained of other desires; he cannot sleep and he loses his appetite. Unrequited love debilitates, leaving the lover pale and wan, pining for his lady. But love that is returned is transformed into a potent force, enabling him to conquer all.

Such beliefs had their origins in the days when troubadours sang of daring deeds done for love, beguiling lonely ladies waiting in cold castles for their lords to come home from the Crusades. But in its origins, the myth of love was not linked to the state of matrimony. The bored lady was not excited by the thought of her crusty old lord, who threw bones to the dogs under the table and smelled of his horse. It was the young squire who cast burning glances at her from the courtyard who brought a flush to her cheek.

When marriages were arranged for reasons of social, economic, and even political convenience, love was a thing apart. As Tocqueville observed: "In aristocratic countries, the object of marriage is rather to unite property than persons; hence the husband is sometimes at school and the wife at nurse when they are betrothed. It cannot be wondered at if the conjugal tie which holds the fortunes of the pair united allows their hearts to rove; this is the result of the nature of the contract" (1956 ed.:239).

In an idealized form, love was woven into the fabric of chivalry, and knights performed feats of courage in the name of a lady they could never touch. In more decadent days, love led to the adulterous adventures that were the sport of a declining aristocracy. But seldom did love lead to marriage. When it did, it was usually in defiance of parental authority. Juliet married secretly and for love, refusing the kinsman of the prince that her father had chosen for her. In an aristocratic society, the consequences of such conduct could only be tragedy.

Yet several centuries later, marriage was invariably the happy ending for romantic novels. Love and marriage were linked by the ascendant merchants and their womenfolk. The rising middle class emulated the

*l'Offrande du Coeur (Offering of the Heart): 15th century Arras tapestry. In an
idealized form, love was woven into the fabric of chivalry.*

aristocracy in many things, including the longing for romance. But the
adulterous context of aristocratic love boggled the bourgeois mind. So
love was made the prelude to marriage, an emotion to be inspired by a
One-and-Only. To choose a mate for love accorded well with the individual freedom prized by the rising middle class. The bride's father was more
likely to give the couple his blessing if the young man had a "suitable
station," but the marriage was supposed to be a love match.

The values of the middle class stressed individual mobility rather
than family connections, equality rather than hereditary privilege. The
right to marry one's love was consistent with these values, just as arranged
marriage had been consistent with earlier values. When Tocqueville visited America in the 1830s, the new middle-class values were just beginning
to displace the older tradition in Europe. But in America, equality was
already assumed to be God-given, and marriage was supposed to be for
love. It was a point on which the usually prophetic Tocqueville was carried
away by enthusiasm:

> . . . the equality of conditions has swept away all the imaginary or the real
> barriers which separated man from woman. No girl then believes that she
> cannot become the wife of the man who loves her; and this renders all

203

breaches of morality before marriage very uncommon: for, whatever be the credulity of the passions, a woman will hardly be able to persuade herself that she is beloved, when her lover is perfectly free to marry her and does not.   (Tocqueville 1956 ed.:239)

If the hope that love would be the underpinning of morality was not borne out by fact, it remained embedded in American mythology: love, if it was true love, led to marriage. If it did not lead to marriage, it was mere infatuation. True love was viewed as a kind of earthly parallel to the Calvinistic state of Grace, to which many are called but few are chosen. Nothing that one could do would guarantee love; some were predestined to find the "right one," the rest condemned to a lifetime of resignation or futile search.

The Victorian girl's romantic dreams were as ornate as the front parlor, but she did not expect to live in either. She dreamed of romance, but she saw marriage as a sober duty. When she married she put her dreams away, tied with a bit of ribbon and hidden at the bottom of an attic trunk. Perhaps it would have been too much to expect the stolid merchant to fall in love and remain in such an unstable mental state for the rest of his life. The image is incongruous, even preposterous, although it was the merchant class that consummated the unlikely merger of love and marriage.

But sometime between Prohibition and the first talking pictures, the mass media began to shape the American images of love and marriage. Sexualized romance became the dominant theme of what was called "the silver screen," and it had only two possible endings: a wedding or a broken heart. The wedding was the happy ending because it was not perceived as the end, but rather as the beginning of an endless romance. The boy-meets-girl plot that ended with wedding bells has gone out of fashion in what we now call "cinema." It appears only as the framework on which to hang a saccharine musical or a racial message. Romance remains, but seldom the sort that might lead to marriage. Today, the plot often centers on romance between balding roué and nymphet, well-preserved matron and college boy, sex-starved spinster and married drifter, or impotent killer and narcissistic gun moll.

Increasingly it is marriage and not romance that is labeled a snare and a delusion, a "wretched institution" (Cadwallader 1966). Perhaps our culture has come full circle, the focus on romance outside of marriage merely another indication of the emergence of leisure-class values in our affluent society. Dalliance has been a traditional pursuit of a bored leisure class. Yet there is also reason to believe that contemporary Americans have a need for stable, intimate marital relationships that the rakes of the Restoration did not.

Many Americans long with their entire being for someone to love them, and go to great expense to appear lovable, without comprehending

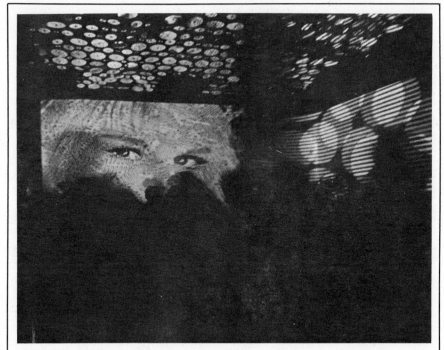

Sexualized romance became the dominant theme of what was called "the silver screen," and it had only two possible endings: a wedding or a broken heart.

how to be loving. Being loving is not at all the same as being in love. The former is a response to another person for whom we care, in every sense of the word. The latter is a mental and emotional state that, as the ancient Greeks perceived, is at best a temporary madness. In English, *love* is an omnibus term that encompasses romantic love, brotherly love, the love of God, the love of Mother, and assorted states of pleasurable excitation. We can say equally, "I love a parade" and "I love you." We mean something quite different by the two statements, but the semantic blurring leads to emotional confusion.

The Greeks, with their customary verbal precision, had several words to cover the assortment of feelings that we blanket by the term *love*. There was a verb, *phileo* ("I love" and related forms), and there were two nouns: *agapè* and *eros*. Greek usage differentiated sharply between the two. *Agapè* meant brotherly love in a broad sense, and combining forms yielded such words as *agapetos*, beloved son, and *agapenor*, loving manliness or simply manly, an epithet used with heroes. *Eros* was used in Homeric writing for sexual passion. *Eromaneo* meant to be mad for love or in love, and had a noun form, *eromania*. Unlike Greek, English does not color the phrase, *to fall in love*, with connotations of madness. But many peoples other than the Greeks have considered this form of love temporary insanity, a kind of

205

manic-depressive state. In some South Sea cultures, erotic behaviors may be the basis of art, dance, and myth, but falling in love is an aberration, comparable to running amok.

Eros was also the Greek god of love, a mischievous scamp who created chaos by shooting darts of desire into the hearts of gods and men. The Romans renamed him Cupid; American culture has reduced him to the silly cherub that decorates heart-shaped boxes of chocolates. We do not fear the sting of his arrow; a classic Greek would conclude either that madness has become normal among Americans or that passion has been reduced to sentiment.

Sexual stereotypes and estrangement from the self

Romantic love is a complex passion, with an admixture of sexual desire that contributes to the racing pulse and the gleam in the eye. But it is more than a glandular response. The lover may believe that he yearns for his beloved, but what he longs to possess are the facets of himself that he experiences vicariously through her. The girl herself is not the object of his adoration; she is only the compliant mannequin on whom he has draped his ideal image. As Erich Fromm has pointed out, romantic love is a form of idolatry (1956:99–100). The self is stripped of vital qualities, which are fashioned into an image and worshipped.

We become estranged from some aspects of ourselves because they seem incongruous in the totality of our self-image. A man may consider tenderness a desirable quality in abstract, but delete it from his self-image because it seems unmanly. The conception of masculinity in our culture is narrow; a man is supposed to be aggressive, competitive, able to seize control of a situation. He should not bully, but he is expected to exhibit a tough practicality and never to betray tender, "womanly" feelings. This is an image compounded of nostalgia for the past and stereotyped heroes of the video screen. Raised in the suburbs, where women abound all day but fathers are seen only in the evenings and on weekends, the middle-class boy lacks male models of his own class, and he is not encouraged to emulate the garbage collector. If he spends hours admiring and identifying with television heroes, his image of masculinity will reflect their aggressive sexuality, churlish independence, and violence. In this conception of masculinity there is little place for gentleness, or for the idea that courage means overcoming fear.

The stereotypes of masculinity and femininity that prevail in our culture do not reflect the natural limitations of men or women. From the broad range of possible human responses, each culture selects certain characteristics that it considers appropriate for men and others that it sets apart for women. The selection is not everywhere the same. In Iran, men are supposed to be intuitive, emotional, and sensitive; women are considered cool and calculating. The Iroquois braves brought prisoners of war home for their women to torture because women were considered more cruel and sadistic than men. To the ancient Athenian, the ideal man was the athlete and soldier who was also a patron of the arts and a lover of beauty.

In each society boys learn to deny facets of themselves that do not correspond to their culture's definition of masculinity. The boy who displays characteristics that do not fit the conception of manhood that pervades American culture is treated with derision by parents and playmates. A man-child in our culture learns not to whimper, not to want mother to comfort him if he has outgrown his tricycle, not to be timid, fastidious, or vain. Directed toward the prevailing conception of masculinity, the boy learns to be ashamed of lingering desires to be cuddled and protected. "Crybaby" is an epithet that makes him cringe (or cry). His feeling for beauty is an embarrassment, to be thrust out of his self-image. The American boy is raised to believe that a man conquers nature, he does not let it engulf him with wonder. Mountain climbing and hunting are "manly," but only a baby would pick wild flowers to take home to mother.

Emotions and responses that the American male does not permit himself are part of his self-potential, nonetheless. Feelings that seem incompatible with manhood well up to embarrass him, so he dissociates them from himself and projects them onto some nearby woman. This is a convenient device for explaining away such responses and at the same time vicariously enjoying them. *Because those alienated facets of the self that a man has been taught to despise both fascinate and disgust him, he will be both drawn to and contemptuous of the women on whom he projects his alienated "feminine" attributes.* Such a man will think women inferior beings because they are fearful and timid, yet at the same time he will find shy women appealing and will enjoy protecting his woman.

Most of the qualities that men learn to despise in themselves and in other males are regarded as properly feminine attributes that make a woman desirable (to men). It would be gross oversimplification to contend that the American ideal of femininity is only a mirror image of the ideal of masculinity. But there are many characteristics that our culture encourages one sex to repress and the other to develop and display. A man who does not permit himself to be impulsive, whimsical, playful, vain, tender, or touched by beauty is likely to project such qualities onto his woman and adore them in her (feeling that they are fitting for a woman, yet also feeling superior to her because she has these qualities).

The cultural stereotype of the ideal woman consists of characteristics that boys typically learn to dissociate from themselves. Because each class has its own variant on the themes of masculinity and femininity, there is a class (and a generational) difference in the image of the ideal mate that leads to selective "falling in love." A young man fills out the culturally defined image of the desirable woman with characteristics borrowed from his mother, or whoever was the prototype of Woman in his boyhood. This is the image he is prepared to adore; he needs only to find a girl willing to become the embodiment of his dream.

207

In similar fashion, a girl develops her conception of the ideal man from attributes she has learned to reject from her self-image, but to admire nonetheless. The culture encourages girls to develop traits that are labeled feminine and subtly discourages the display of "unladylike" or "tomboy" characteristics. Whatever mechanical aptitude a boy may possess, he will be encouraged to maximize. Mother buys him educational toys put together with big wooden screws; in a few years father gives him an Erector set. Older boys tinker with their bicycles and motorcycles and the little boy imitates them. But his sister is not expected (and often, not permitted) to have comparable mechanical aptitude, and nothing in her upbringing leads her to develop it. She is given baking sets and bride dolls for playthings. If she hangs around the garage while her father repairs the car, he is likely to ignore her or tell her to go inside where it is safe; if she comes into the house with grease in her hair, her mother will certainly not register approval. It is not "feminine" for a girl to tinker with machinery, so the culture directs her away from mechanical skills.

These lines are blurring; it is becoming more acceptable for girls to tinker with sports cars and for men to do needlepoint. But the basic pattern of sex-role differentiation in socialization lingers. The little girl learns that it is not acceptable to tear her shirt while playing ball, or to fight, not even if the other child hit her first. Raised to reject aggressive qualities from her self-image, she goes through a stage of scorning boys for being rough and loud. (The boys reciprocate and form a club with "No Girls Allowed.") But by the time a girl reaches puberty, she finds boys the most exciting creatures in the world (that is, they are allowed to do things forbidden to her). A teenage girl thinks anything a boy does is marvelous; she even titters when he emits a loud belch.

The delicate, fainting lady of the Victorian era is no longer the model, but the girl who is considered the most feminine is still one who has dependent, childlike qualities. The use of "baby" as a term of endearment is revealing. The girl who is self-reliant, ambitious, and capable is often uneasy about her femininity. The American girl still learns that she is expected to be emotional but not rational, intuitive rather than analytic. The qualities that she learns to dissociate from herself (for fear that men will not find her appealing) are precisely those that would have made it possible for her to function as an independent human being. Her ideal mate is a masterful man.

Low self-esteem and the romantic ideal

Although many of the alienated facets of self that form a girl's romantic ideal are qualities she has been taught are incompatible with feminity, others are qualities that are considered appropriate for either sex but that she lost from her self-image in childhood. The gangling girl who hardly knows where to put her size-nine feet may very well grow into a poised and regal woman. But the awkward years of rapid growth are also critical years in the formation of her self-image. Misplaced humor or well-intentioned

nagging directed at poor posture and stumbling feet may convince her
that she has, as one young woman ruefully put it, "All the grace of a
club-footed elephant going downstairs backward." Her ideal man will be
a smoothly coordinated athlete who is a marvelous dancer.

Thus a girl's image of the man she hopes to marry is formed of all
the qualities she has never been allowed to develop in herself. And she
rounds out this image with details drawn from her father's personality, for
he was her first model of manhood and her first love. A father may be
incensed by the suggestion that there is any resemblance between himself
and the long-haired adolescent who parks out front and imperiously blows
the horn. The similarity lies in the characteristics his daughter projects
onto both.

When a boy and girl fall in love, they hang on each other the ideal
image each is already prepared to adore. Their eyes meet across a crowded room and, in the words of the comics, "Pow!" She fits some part of his
preconceived image, so he assumes that the rest fits, too. That initial
glimpse may be the only view they have of each other for a long time, for
from the moment they choose each other as the beloved, they will see only
what filters through the overlay of projections. As the old adage has it,
Love is blind.

The "irresistible force" that draws them together is a desire to possess and enjoy (at least vicariously) the alienated facets of themselves that
each has built into an ideal and now projects onto the beloved. Wanting
these longed-for parts of themselves back, they want each other. When
they are apart he feels restless and she mopes. The lovers would deny with
heat and indignation any suggestion that they are attracted to anything but
the beloved. But notice that they can fall in love and out again without
having changed. The girl who charmed him yesterday may be an embarrassment to him today; yet she is the same girl. He may say that she has
changed; his friends will assure him that he is finally seeing her as she is.

Reflections in a loving eye

One of the things romance promises is a new and glamorous self. The
desire to escape a dull, despised self fuels the romantic dream. The couple
who have fallen in love play the starring roles they have watched on the
television or movie screen: knowing the lines, they pick up cues from each
other, stage dramatic entrances and passionate fade-outs. Hollywood B—
featuring the exciting new face of Me!

The image of the self that we carry around in our heads is seldom
so beautiful and shiny as when we are involved in a romance. Most of us
have a self-image that is wavering and unclear, a reflection in a flawed and
fly-specked glass. The need to recognize who we are and to feel pleased
to be ourselves is a basic human need. The most flattering mirror is held
up by someone who says, "I love you." Lovers gazing soulfully into each
other's eyes are looking at the beautiful reflection of themselves.

It is impossible to know ourselves if we are isolated from other **209** people, screened by conventional roles and social distance; a close and honest scrutiny by someone whose judgment we respect is one of the most reliable sources of self-knowledge. But a romance is seldom a candid relationship, not even when he and she are telling each other the story of their lives. That story is usually selective; each is really saying to the other, "This is the sort of person I am, admire and love me, please." The gilded image of the self that each presents to the other is further embellished by the beloved. We want to believe that our partner in romance is a very special person. There is little ego gratification in being loved by an ugly wretch.

If there is sufficient correspondence between the real person and the loved image, the romance may develop to the stage of self-discovery. A couple involved in a romance begin to perceive all manner of exciting possibilities in themselves, for which each gives the other credit. Because he finds her exciting, she is able to think of herself as the desirable woman she has longed to be. He says, "Baby, you're beautiful!" And she says, "Who, me?" But only to herself. Because she wants him to keep on saying it, she devotes even more time to her grooming and is likely to make the most of her natural charms. The excitement of being in love gives her a sparkle that transforms even a plain girl. She is delighted with herself. But she needs his assurance that she is attractive; she spends the afternoon setting her hair, painting her eyes, shaping her mouth, looking long and fretfully into the mirror. But the question, "How do I look?" will not be answered until he comes to the door. He is the mirror that matters.

Because she expects him to be dominant and gallant, he finds himself opening car doors and carrying her over puddles. If he had had doubts about his manliness, he finds it exhilarating to have someone certain that he is a masterful male. She hangs on his words and believes every opinion he voices (she has been raised to deprecate her own ideas and to expect men to be authoritative). He is enchanted to find someone who considers him an oracle. The image of himself that he sees reflected in her eyes is one that he wants to believe, and he finds it easier to like himself in her worshipful presence.

In the excitement of being together, they laugh at minor mishaps that either would have grumbled about before (being caught in the rain is a lark, not an annoyance). Mundane events assume new significance: an aura of joy hangs over them that neither has known before (or has experienced since the last romance). Each has the illusion of having become a new person, gay and witty and sexually exciting, but believes that this state of being can exist only when the beloved is present.

He has made it easier for her to explore and develop attributes that she has longed to possess. But she does not perceive that she can be this exciting new self always and with anyone. She thinks it is a special self, elicited by her lover. Like Cinderella, she feels that she is only temporarily transformed. A man in love is equally unlikely to recognize the development of facets of himself. She is the catalyst for changes that have occurred within him, but he may find it difficult to incorporate the newly discovered potential into his self-image. He is more likely to believe that his girl's presence is essential to the continued existence of the dynamic male he has so lately become. Their dependence on each other grows; their love deepens.

The great romance

Eromania involves sexual desire, and a couple just discovering sex are likely to credit each other with the excitement exuding from their glands. Their physical responses are heightened by the state of being "in love," which generates a desire to unite in order to possess alienated facets of the self. For each, the beloved is the epicenter of a soul-shaking passion. The myth is that true love will last forever. The reality is that those who fall in love sooner or later fall out. Whether he leaves her or marries her, the romance will end; the only uncertainty is whether it will be an abrupt or a lingering process.

Suppose the romance is a summer love that waxes during sunny days of driving to the beach and through long warm evenings of dancing to a beat that matches the pulse. In the ecstasy of love, time becomes elastic and one exciting day flows into another. The girl has a sense of having been born the day she met her lover; in a sense she was, for her self-image is transformed as new and exciting possibilities in her self unfold. Then September comes. He goes away and she feels the incomparable loss that overwhelms a young girl at the end of her first Great Romance. It is loss of self that leaves the void. The gay, exquisite woman who existed briefly is gone, and she is once again the colorless, uncertain girl she has known all her life. She feels like a butterfly stuffed back into the old cocoon, or worse, turned back into an ugly, crawling caterpillar. She loses her appetite, turns pale and listless, wanders about the house aimlessly. Her mother nags her about eating, teachers wonder why her grades have suddenly dropped.

The girl finds a bittersweet pleasure in immersing herself in sorrow; others, the ones who have never been touched by love, may chatter and laugh, plan for the weekend with some stupid dolt, but she has known Great Passion and would rather stay home with her memories. It is difficult for an adult to take seriously the heartbreak of adolescence, but it is real. The lonely girl retreats into the recesses of her mind and tries to make the summer live again. She calls up an evening and relives each moment; with practice she can almost hallucinate the presence of her lover, feel the pressure of his hand, smell the aftershave lotion he used. Fragments of conversation return, subtly rearranged to suit her need to have the affair seem perfect. The one interest she finds in the world outside herself is in watching the mail to see if there is a letter from him. There is none today, there was none yesterday, but perhaps tomorrow—and waiting for the mail becomes a ritual. Then one day there is a postcard and she is briefly animated. The card has a picture of a ski resort on the back and says, "Hi, how are you? This is quite a place." To her the words are fraught with meaning. She carries the card in her purse as a token, a talisman, and for awhile it feeds her dreams.

The girl believes her lover made her happy and that she cannot recapture joy until he returns. But happiness is not something that people can give us, like candy. Happiness is generated by actively *being* the person we want to be. This requires involvement with someone else, for many of the qualities that we want to find and enjoy in ourselves have to be bounced off another person to be realized. A girl cannot be exciting unless someone is excited by her, cannot be amusing without someone to amuse. Memory is at best a reminder of what we once were.

There are probably several million young men with whom the lonely girl could rediscover the lost potential in herself, and several dozen may live within a few blocks of her. But because she assumes that her summer ecstasy was caused by some magic in a particular boy, she sits and waits for him to return and make her happy again. Being young, the girl will eventually find a new love, and old memories will lose their poignancy. This cycle of ecstasy and misery is one to which women are prone (they expect it to end with marriage, but it seldom does).

A man longing for an absent sweetheart is perhaps less likely to lapse into prolonged melancholy, more likely to try to recapture remembered joy by dating girls who resemble the one he has lost. The resemblance is often startling; in part, he is trying to replace the girl he loved with a close facsimile, and in part the close resemblance reflects the fact that both girls are a reasonable fit for his projected ideal image. But men, too, are vulnerable to the aching emptiness that is left when romance is gone. *What seems a broken heart is the shattered image of the self that existed during the love affair.* Particularly if the girl has left him for another man, the tenuous self-acceptance that he felt during the romance may vanish with her, leaving him feeling inadequate and unwanted. A man is expected to conceal his hurt, but he feels it all the same.

Unrequited love follows much the same course, except that it never involves the initial romance, only the period of melancholy longing. One loves, the other does not; they live in two different worlds, bounded by two different realities. The two meet—apparently by chance—and to the one who loves it is the emotional crest of the week. His heartbeat is suddenly erratic, sweat beads his temples and trickles into his armpits, speech stops short in his constricted throat. And she who loves not has felt mild amusement or a vague embarrassment, but preens a bit, for her vanity is touched. The exaggeration of her walk will be built into hours of his daydreams. The lonely lover may be a gangling adolescent or a man in his sixties; the same torment can afflict any man.

The misery of the spurned lover has been the recurrent theme of poetry and song: less remarked is the predicament of the beloved who does not feel the stirrings of desire. "Hard-hearted Barbara Allen" is the

*By the artificial light of romance, a man in love perceives only what he wants to
see. But under the gossamer projection is a woman with human failings.*

legendary prototype, although love—or at least remorse—did come to her belatedly, and she followed her stricken lover to their rendezvous in the graveyard. In real life, the person who is the object of a grand passion is likely to experience a variety of feelings, if he or she does not return the love. There is annoyance at the attentions of a person one finds unlovable, if not worse. Love may be blind, but the unsmitten is acutely aware of the wart on her suitor's nose, or the hair on his ear lobes. There is a heady sense of power, for the happiness of another human being hangs on whether or not one smiles. There is pity mixed with contempt. And there is embarrassment at being the object of what seems an overdrawn, cloyed emotion. It is a rather sticky business. Perhaps it is better to love than to be loved. The lover at least feels that he is experiencing a great and noble passion.

The Great Romance that culminates in marriage is equally doomed. Romance happens in a space of time apart: an ecstatic pause in which no alarm clocks ring. It cannot long survive the routine demands of daily life. In the early months of marriage there is still an aura of enchantment; painting and furnishing the first apartment is nest building in which newlyweds delight. They are creating a private world and feel like children who have built a treehouse high up where no parents can climb. But the outside world reaches them; the dream world is slowly permeated by reality. Their life together is structured by bus schedules and circumscribed by bills. A

213

marriage is saddled with responsibilities that never impinge on a romance. The casual, carefree manner that he found charming in his beloved may become his wife's exasperating inability to keep the check stubs balanced. The idealized image begins to peel.

Eromania cannot endure because it is not founded in affection for another human being, but only in a wistful searching for lost facets of the self and in sexual deprivation. A man in love sees his girl as an angel, a creature from a different world. By the artificial light of romance he can perceive only what he wants to see in her. But under the gossamer projection is a girl with human failings. When they were lovers, one of the bonds between them was the flattering image each held up to the other. After a year or two of marriage each is quite aware that the other no longer thinks he or she is perfect. The idealized images fade under constant exposure to the unflattering light of daily intimacy. Each begins to perceive less than ideal qualities in the other.

Romantic love as a barrier to intimacy

It is quite possible to love someone without knowing him (he is the passive porter of our projections) and thus equally possible to marry someone without liking him. Quite apart from the romantic projections that blur the perception of lovers, there are other aspects of American courtship that tend to limit the couple's knowledge of each other. A typical American boy and girl on a date play culturally patterned roles; from the opening gambit to the last feint at her door when they say good-night, each knows the basic maneuvers. "False personalization" is as common between boy and girl as it is between salesperson and customer in an exclusive dress shop (and terms of endearment are likely to be used in the same manipulative fashion).

Mass entertainment elicits standardized responses; the fact that he and she both laugh at the same things means only that they respond to the same cultural cues. A good dancer is interchangeable with any other good dancer, and the same is true of a skillful sexual partner. Conversation conducted in the limited clichés that are the current in-group jargon reveals nothing of the self. The initial shock of marriage is the discovery that one has married a stranger.

If marriage is corrosive to romantic love, the corollary is that a rewarding marriage cannot be built on the quicksilver foundation of romance. Marriage offers one of the few opportunities in our mass society for the intimate and continuous association that human beings require. But such a mutually fulfilling relationship requires an awareness of who we are and a roughly accurate perception of our partner. A marriage based on romantic love is unlikely to be such a relationship. The ideal image that the lover cherishes so dearly is fabricated from alienated facets of the self: its very existence indicates a lack of self-knowledge.

When a man hangs this ideal image on a woman it becomes a barrier between them, a curtain of illusion. So long as he sees her only through this romantic filter, he cannot know her. He may cling to her as the embodiment of lost and loved fragments of himself, but she will not exist as a person for him. She will be an extension of himself. It is probable that she will have some qualities that resemble those he projects onto her; he probably would not have married her unless there had been some correspondence between the real woman and the ideal image he carried around in his head. But if many of his projections are appropriate, they are still projections. When she acts in ways that reveal capacities his mental image does not encompass, he has an opportunity to begin to know her. But if he is trying to believe that there is a perfect correspondence between the real woman and the ideal, he will be angry and bewildered by any glimpse of his wife as she is.

If her behavior is at variance with his expectations, he shakes his head and mutters about the vagaries of woman. Suppose that a husband loves and indulges childlike qualities that he has projected onto his childlike wife. He plans a surprise that would please the child in himself (whose existence he cannot admit). He anticipates her response, running over in his mind what she will say and do, the joy that will bubble over to gratify him. But what would delight the childlike side of the man may bore his wife, even embarrass her. If her response to his surprise is polite and perfunctory, he is likely to feel personally rejected. She is likely to feel resentful that she had to feign delight, and complain about lack of communication.

As the ideal images on which love was based begin to fade, it becomes possible for husband and wife to perceive each other, to learn to respond to the other person rather than to the projection. When the tissue of delightful lies is torn away, the reality that is revealed may be unexpected and fulfilling. Marriage offers an opportunity to develop what Tocqueville said our forebears sought in a mate: "that sort of deep, regular, and quiet affection, which constitutes the charm and safeguard of life" (1956 ed.:241–242). But the contemporary couple are more likely to mourn the passing of romance than to seize the opportunity to build a marriage. Either or both may begin covertly looking for a new romance. Or they may settle resignedly into a joyless existence because they do not know how to reach—or even to see—each other.

Spun-sugar dreams and the romantic appetite

Happy marriages there are, but they are not endless romances. It is the nature of romance, not the potentialities of marriage, that creates the inner contradiction in the myth. The essence of romance is longing, and only when we long for the unattainable can romance endure through time (a principle well recognized in the Middle Ages). Romance is the whetted appetite. Marriage offers a maximum opportunity for satisfaction: unimpeded access to one's mate, unlimited time to indulge in all the

215

A wife may define herself as the woman her husband believes her to be, the creation of his love. Before this man loved her, she was just another body in the crowd, jostled by others but insulated from meaningful human contact by the cushions of indifference with which each person surrounds the self.

games that young lovers can devise. It is this very possibility for limitless satisfaction in marriage that dulls the edge of romantic desire. Imagine a small boy standing in front of a candy counter, with his nose to the glass and two pennies in his fist. Give him the candy store and lock the door behind him, but stay around: he will be pounding on the door before long. Like a sweet tooth, romantic craving leads away from more basic needs, and overindulgence spoils the appetite without contributing to growth.

Women often cling to the last thin illusion of romantic love out of fear: fear that their husbands will leave them, fear that they will cease to be vital people if they are no longer loved. There is an old song that runs, "You're nobody until somebody loves you." It expresses a widespread feeling among women. A wife may define herself as the woman her husband believes her to be, the creation of his love. Before this man loved her, she was just another body in the crowd, jostled by others but insulated from meaningful human contact by the cushions of indifference with which each person surrounds the self. But this man singled her out; he said, "You are special, you are delightful, I love you." Being loved, she found it easier to believe she was a lovable, even an exciting woman. She basked in his adoration. But unless she has learned to know and to accept herself, she will require constant reaffirmation of his love in order to believe that

216

the woman he adores exists. When it becomes apparent that her marriage is not a life-long romance, she begins to feel cheated, resentful, afraid.

Romance is more important in the lives of women than men. Boys grow up dreaming of conquest and adventure, but little girls are raised on romantic fantasies. The daydreams of a young girl center on the lover who will one day transport her out of her dull existence. What will his initials be? Will he be rich or merely handsome? Her hopes for the future lie not in doing exciting things, but in having a man who does exciting things love her. It is the function of love to sweeten the subordinate role women play. But the spun-sugar dreams have no substance. The disappointed housewife, past the age when she can dream of the future, fills her days with television's instant romance. If her physical charms remain, or can be retouched, she may pursue the fantasy of love from marriage to marriage.

And lost in the labyrinth of corporate structure or governmental bureaucracy, there are men for whom the only remaining dream of conquest is in the realm of sex. In this fantasy world jaded men and fading women pursue love, hoping always that this time it will not elude them. Like the rainbow that appears to touch the hillside just beyond, romance hovers ahead, shimmering perfection that can never be grasped.

There are signs that romantic love may be obsolescent. The word *love* has become a shibboleth of the youth culture, but the usage is more in the sense of *agapè* than of *eros*. In its ideal form, it means feeling at all seasons the glow that most Americans expect to share only at Christmas. And although the myths of romantic love are still expressed in popular songs, the lyrics are changing. There is a notable departure from lacy sentiment in American courting behavior. But if the young are beginning to put aside antiquated conceptions of the One-and-Only Love, it is not yet clear what may replace it as the American way of choosing a mate.

References

Cadwallader, Mervyn. 1966. "Marriage as a Wretched Institution." *Atlantic Monthly* 218 (November):62–65.

Fromm, Erich. 1956. *The Art of Loving.* New York: Harper & Row.

Linton, Ralph. 1936. *The Study of Man.* New York: Appleton-Century-Crofts.

Tocqueville, Alexis de. 1956. *Democracy in America*, abr. ed., edited by R. D. Heffner. New York: New American Library.

Suggested readings

Casler, Lawrence. 1969. "This Thing Called Love is Pathological." *Psychology Today* 3 (December):18–20, 74–76. Casler observes that while love has many determinants, instinct is not one of them. He goes on to describe the emotional needs that are the causes of love and the emotional complications that are caused by love (fear of loss of the beloved or fear of loss of self-respect, leading to jealousy, anger, etc.).

Fromm, Erich. 1956. *The Art of Loving.* New York: Harper & Row. Available in paper as a Bantam Book. Fromm describes the pathological forms that love has taken in Western society, from "falling in love" (which he considers a form of idolatry) to symbiotic attachment (which he considers "an enlarged egotism"). He then describes in detail the art of loving, which requires discipline, concentration, patience, and concern.

Maugham, W. Somerset. 1921. "Red." In *The Trembling of a Leaf.* New York: George H. Doran Company. (Also available in various anthologies.) A master storyteller writes of love and romance in the South Seas. "Red" was a lithe, red-haired Apollo, a young sailor who jumped ship to remain with an exquisite Polynesian girl in her island paradise. Their love was the kind of which legends are created. For twenty-five years another man lived on that legend, a sickly Swede who came to the islands to die, but fell in love with the girl after her lover had been kidnapped by a passing ship in need of crew. The story contains the essense of romance, and the irony.

8 Premarital bargaining and the sexual revolution

It is obvious that today's mate-selection is no longer a period of determining the best bargain and sealing that bargain in marriage. Rather, today this "courtship" period is one of training in bargaining. In other words, "courtship" teaches the individual how to bargain—how to form, maintain, and leave relationships. The emphasis in modern life is on keeping up one's bargaining skills, for one never entirely leaves the market.

Michal M. McCall (1966:197)

Courtship behaviors—to use a term that can apply across time and species—focus on male display and other attempts to attract the female and establish the intentions of the potential mate. In recent years, some observers of the American scene have lamented that courtship seems to be becoming an end in itself, rather than a prelude to marriage. This is in fact what courtship has been throughout most of Western history; human beings are not innately monogamous, like loons or bowerbirds. For most of Western history, courtship has led to seduction more often than it has led to marriage.

Premarital bargaining and arranged marriage

In the days before Henry VIII restructured English religion, there was an English saint named Uncumber, to whom young girls prayed to be rid of unwanted suitors (in a church in London there is reportedly a representation of St. Uncumber that escaped the destruction of the 1530s). Marriages were arranged by the families concerned, and such courtship as there might be between husband and wife tended to occur after marriage. A girl might be allowed to reject a suitor, but her family usually prevailed. Sometimes a persistent suitor resorted to kidnapping his bride. The daughter of Baudoin, Count of Flanders, refused to marry William the Conqueror because he was a bastard. (It was his family origins, not his personality, to which the lady objected, although she may have been dismayed by the latter as well.) William lay in wait at the door of the church where the lady regularly attended mass, seized her when she came out, and beat her until she agreed to marry him (Hays 1964:104). William may have loved the lady less than the extensive estates that were her dowry; in any event, courtly love had not come into fashion, and a certain amount of beating was thought to soften a woman's innate shyness.

When marriages were arranged, an aristocrat found that the marriage of a daughter was an expensive occasion. The father of the bride was required to provide the trousseau and the wedding feast, which might go on for days and require feeding a small army of relatives and newly acquired in-laws. These are expenses that sound familiar to a contemporary American father of the bride. But in earlier times, the bride's father also had to make a cash settlement with the bridegroom's family, which was called the daughter's marriage portion, or dowry.

The beauty and disposition of a woman had rather little to do with attracting a husband, although a man might be willing to settle for a smaller marriage portion if the girl were beautiful and docile than if she were ugly and ill-tempered. In Sheridan's *The Rivals*, a late seventeenth-century comedy that satirized the manners and courtship of the English upper classes, a young man worries that the heiress his father has chosen for him to marry may not be comely. His father, Sir Anthony Absolute, replies: "Odds life, Sir! If you have the estate you must take it with the livestock on it, as it stands!" Although this was a lampoon of arranged marriage, which was already beginning to decline as a custom, the truth was not far different.

In return for what was almost the outright sale of his son and heir to acquire immediate cash or land, the father of the bridegroom promised to provide for the bride during her future widowhood: this arrangement was called a jointure, an annual allowance from the family estate for as long as the widow might live. Because there was a good chance that the bride might die in childbirth early in her married life, the odds favored the family of the bridegroom in this financial bargain. Life insurance, annuities, and Social Security have replaced the jointure in contemporary society, but there was a day when a young girl's wedding arrangements had to provide for her years as a widow.

There was little that an unmarried woman could do but remain in her father's home. No acceptable occupations were open to upper-class women, and Henry VIII had closed the nunneries, which had been used by the aristocracy as "convenient stowage for withered daughters," to borrow Milton's acid phrase. The aging spinster daughter became a common figure in upper-class families. The sex ratio was unfavorable to girls in marriage bargaining. Younger sons of a landed, aristocratic family seldom had more than a limited inheritance. After provision had been made for the marriage portion of his sisters, the eldest son inherited all the lands; younger sons had to take a small cash settlement and go to the colonies, or into the military, or the church. Younger sons were thus not desirable husbands, for they had no prospect of inheriting the title or the lands of their family unless their elder brother should die without a male heir.

The number of eligible males (by the standards of the time) was thus reduced to far fewer than the number of sons born to the landed classes, while the number of eligible females was augmented by the inclusion of the daughters of wealthy and ambitious merchants in the pool of eligibles. Given the unequal sex ratios, the marriage portions of girls had to be exceedingly large. According to Lawrence Stone (1960–1961), by the early seventeenth century most fathers of the merchant and landed classes of England were offering no less than the equivalent of a full year's income as marriage portions for their daughters.

Ultimately, the "Age of Enlightenment" (as the eighteenth century came to be called) brought an end to arranged marriage. The real reason was that fathers could no longer afford the inflated marriage portions for their daughters. There were other reasons, as well. There was much moral indignation aroused by the flagrant abuses of the Court of Wards, which sometimes sold orphaned heirs into marriage to the highest bidder, while the heirs were still minors and unable to refuse. Moreover, this was an age when individualism was fostered by religious and political movements. Both Calvinism and Puritanism stressed individual choice. John Locke, the philosopher who was the most influential voice of the new democratic political ideology of the seventeenth century, opposed all forms of paternalism. As soon as the son was able to be self-supporting, Locke declared that the "bonds of subjection" to the father should "drop quite off, and leave a man at his own free disposal." Among other freedoms, this meant freedom to contract his own marriage.

Marriage to a wealthy widow or an heiress, whose father was able and still willing to provide a handsome dowry, was one of the few ways a man of good family but poor financial prospects could become a landed gentleman. Making an advantageous marriage became a major goal for a bachelor, but he had to woo and win the wealthy woman for himself. Mastering the art of courtship was a means to wealth through marriage by the seventeenth century. Writing of Restoration England (that is, England after the monarchy was restored in the seventeenth century) E. S. Turner notes: "Courtship was a counter in a game in which the prizes were titles and lands and fortunes" (1954:70).

Courtship in colonial America: from inveigling to bundling

Arranged marriage was still practiced in England when the Puritans settled New England, and some of the Puritan fathers had entered arranged marriages in their youth. John Winthrop, the English Puritan who became the first governor of the Massachusetts Bay Colony, entered an arranged marriage at the age of seventeen. His grandfather, Adam Winthrop, was a London textile merchant who purchased part of a confiscated monastery in Suffolk and became a landed gentleman. John's father, the second Adam Winthrop, was a lawyer who devoted himself to his estate when he inherited the land, and made it return a good living despite fixed rents for his tenants and rising prices. When young John Winthrop returned home after two unhappy years at Trinity College, Cambridge, his father arranged a marriage for the seventeen-year-old John with the daughter of a gentleman in the next county. The marital bargain was favorable for the Winthrop family; according to Edmund Morgan (1958:7), it included "large quantities of land."

John Winthrop's first wife died some ten years later, having borne him six children. Six months later, Winthrop married again, this time apparently making his own arrangements, which again included a dowry of land. His second wife died a year later, and a year or so after that, Winthrop married again. His third wife was the woman who was later to join him in Massachusetts as the first governor's lady of the Puritan colony. Her name was Margaret, she was the daughter of Sir John Tyndal of Much Maplestead in Essex, England, and, Morgan comments, "as usual, John seems to have received a substantial dowry" (1958:13). This was what marrying well meant in the seventeenth century.

Viewed against the background of arranged marriage, the fact that the American Puritan father insisted only on prior approval of his daughter's suitor seems almost permissive. The Puritan father believed that he had a God-given duty to see that his daughters were properly disposed of in marriage. No young man could court a girl until he had asked for—and received—her father's permission. If the girl's father approved his courtship, the suitor had then to win her affection.

Unauthorized courtship was called *inveigling*, and it was listed as an offense on the statute books of several colonies. As Turner observes, "Since a father was carrying out God's will in disposing of his daughter in marriage, it followed that any unauthorized young man who sought to engage the girl's affections was frustrating the intentions of God and man" (1954:61). In Massachusetts, a 1647 statute declared that "it is common practice in diverse places for young men irregularly and disorderly to watch all advantage for their evil purposes, to insinuate into the affections of young maidens by going to them in places and seasons unknown to their parents for such ends, whereby much evil hath grown among us, to the dishonor of God and damage of parties." The penalty for such conduct was five pounds for a first offense, ten pounds for the second, and prison for a third offense (cited in Turner 1954:61).

Inveigling was not a euphemism for fornication. Fornication was punished by more severe penalties, as described in an earlier chapter. The offense of inveigling was quite literally courting without the permission of the girl's father. There are cases on the old court records of men who were fined for inveigling, most often for courting the daughter of a powerful man without first obtaining his permission. However, the law did recognize that the individual had rights. If parents refused to grant their daughter permission to marry, the law provided that the parents could be required to show cause. If the court decided that the cause was insufficient, the parent could be overruled by the court.

Considering that the young were tempted to inveigle and to engage in other and more lusty behavior, the Puritans encouraged early marriage. Bachelors were taxed and harassed in a variety of ways and by a number of laws, including ordinances that required unattached young men to live in lodgings that were approved by the town council (Turner 1954:60). In the colonial era, according to William Kephart, "People were expected to marry, and they normally did so at a young age, girls often in their early teens and boys frequently before they were twenty . . . if a girl reached her twenties without being married, she was likely to be referred to as an 'antient' (ancient) or 'old' maid" (1961:148).

The Puritan influence waned, and courtship customs from Wales, Scotland, Cornwall, and Holland spread through the colonies. By the eighteenth century, bundling was the customary mode of courtship in New England. *Bundling*, or *tarrying*, as it was sometimes called, was the practice of courting in bed. (Those old folk songs that implore the true love to "tarry awhile with me" may have been suggesting something more sensual than lingering at the garden gate.) There were means of minimizing temptation, however, the simplest being a bolster to separate the couple. The same purpose was served more effectively by the bundling board, which dropped into slots in the headboard and footboard of the bed. Sometimes

225

the girl's mother insisted that she wear a bundling bag, or she might tie her daughter's ankles together, or sew up her clothing at strategic places. Then, again, some parents tucked the young couple in and retired. However permissive the parents, bundling seems to have occurred always at the girl's home and to have been part of courtship with marriage in view, not merely a casual encounter.

In that era when overland travel was slow and hazardous, and inland from the port cities there were few inns, travelers often spent the night with a farm family. Beds were scarce, and the bundling board might be used to create accommodations for a passing stranger. This was a convenience for the traveler and a source of occasional cash income for the subsistence farmer (Turner 1954:107). This custom was apparently the original source of "the traveling salesman and the farmer's daughter" stories, which seem to have endured for nearly two hundred years.

Bundling seems to have been most common during the quarter century preceding the Revolutionary War, although it is reported as early as 1636. The clergy opposed the practice. In 1735, Jonathan Edwards deplored the fact that people were "ready to laugh at its being condemned" (Morris 1955:27). But if the clergy influenced their town congregations, they had little effect in the rural areas. New England farmwives defended bundling (most of them having been courted in similar fashion) and told the visiting ministers that an "honest bundling board" was less likely to debauch their daughters than the French sofa, which had just been introduced into the parlors of the townspeople.

What preaching could not do, ridicule accomplished. The very acceptability of bundling in the outlying rural areas meant that it came to be identified as the courting practice of the sort of country bumpkin who was lampooned in "Yankee Doodle." No one wants to be thought a backcountry lout, and the day came when New England farmhouses had a front parlor—and a sofa—and travelers who spent the night no longer slept with any member of the family. Courtship moved to the sofa, and became as stiff and formal as the parlor itself.

Along the southern frontier there were few such refinements as the bundling board. In general, courtship customs of the rural areas of the central and southern frontier seem to have been somewhat casual. Richard Morris (1955:27) describes a document, duly attested, that has survived in the Columbia, South Carolina, archives: "a document of wife sale bearing the date of 1781 in which one William Colling, who signed his name with a mark, sold his wife to Thomas Schooler for two dollars and a half a dozen bottles of grog."

Marital bargaining in the age of prudery

Alexis de Tocqueville, observing America in the 1830s, was interested in the effect on morality as well as in the effect on government of a value system in which equality was fundamental. The Americans had created the first society in which hereditary titles were forbidden and all people were commoners. Tocqueville observed that because there were no hereditary class distinctions and no arranged marriage, no girl could be persuaded that a man who professed to love her could not be free to marry her. Tocqueville believed that this would be conducive to marital stability, or at least that it would eliminate exploitive seductions. He believed that the absence of hereditary class distinction would make for a more virtuous people and happier marriages. The usually prophetic Tocqueville seems to have been wrong.

There were no explicit class barriers to marriage, and mate choice was based to a considerable degree on affection. But, gradually, the merchants and shipowners of the port cities of New England came to form an elite, as did the owners of large plantations in the tidelands South. Daughters of these families began to find that there were few young men whom father considered suitable. It was acceptable for a girl to marry someone from a higher social position than her father occupied, but not for her to marry "beneath her station." The daughters of the "first families" of New England and the tidewater South had to compete with the daughters of successful tradesmen for young men of the upper class.

The result was a surplus of females in the upper social strata, a pattern that spread from the Atlantic coast westward. Every small town in America had its local elite, and the daughters of the "best families" had what is often referred to as the "Brahmin problem": because they belonged to the highest class, there were few young men they could consider eligible prospects for a husband, and they had to compete for them with pretty girls from farther down in the class structure. The ideology of free mate choice made the competition all the more difficult for the daughters of the elite. Once a woman had passed the marriageable age, she was relegated to an obscure position in the household where her wants would be few, but where she would not have to do any labor that would be unsuitable to her station. (Every American household of middle class and above had at least one servant in the nineteenth century.) The maiden daughter, gradually fading into spinsterhood and ending her days as the eccentric maiden aunt, has long been a familiar figure in the American upper classes.

The "nice" American girl in the nineteenth century ("nice" was one of the many words that had acquired a sexual connotation in the age of prudery) had a problem that girls of an earlier era never faced. The American father kept a veto over his daughter's marriage plans, but he did not find a husband for her. Nor did he offer a formal dowry. A young man might marry the boss's daughter with hopes of profiting thereby, but it was not an open agreement, or at least was not supposed to be. Marrying for money had been the accepted pattern earlier, but by the nineteenth century, a man was supposed to marry for love. The "nice" American girl in

227

In the first decade of the twentieth century, a chaperone was still required when an unmarried couple went for a walk in the woods. Carving their names in the bark of a living tree was considered a romantic gesture, a kind of public record of the courtship that would endure and grow with the tree. This picture was composed by the chaperone, amateur photographer Mrs. Jeanette Bernard, who would probably have agreed with Henry Seidel Canby's observation that "romance suffused the American nineties, and romance was incompatible with our quite realistic knowledge of sex. A thrilling imagination sometimes suggested the possibility of joining the two, but that was to be later. The girl must be won first, and won romantically." (1934:428).

the age of prudery thus had to attract a husband by displaying her charms, but without losing her reputation. (For a woman, *reputation* had only a sexual meaning.)

The behavior that had characterized English girls since *Pamela* became the pattern for the "ladylike" behavior of American girls. The "good" girl tempted her suitor with sexual charms that she withheld until she was safely married. A girl had to learn to flirt without seeming to suggest anything indelicate, to draw attention to her body without seeming to display it. Her clothing was cut to draw attention to precisely that which it seemed to conceal. Such props as an ornate fan, properly employed, could work marvels in the hands of an accomplished young woman. Seeming to cover a modest blush, a fan could draw attention to the eyes. Fluttered softly and with no obvious intent but to create a gentle breeze, it could draw a suitor's eyes to her cleavage.

Proper young ladies became blushing, fainting Victorians, quick to put a sexual construction on a remark—and to condemn it. Respectable dowagers of Boston and Philadelphia and Charleston kept their daughters in ignorant innocence, while making them highly aware of a catalogue of immodest behaviors that called for blushes. A woman did not have legs, she had "limbs," and these disappeared beneath multiple layers of padded clothing. The girl who learned to walk "like a lady," with mincing steps, could glide about as if there were no substance beneath her hoop skirts, as if the hoops alone supported her. The merest suggestion of an ankle as she descended the stairs could make a man giddy. A long stairway into the room where her suitor waited was almost as important to a successful courtship as an artfully handled fan.

The double standard was the basis for the courtship bargaining of the age of prudery. A virtuous man was one who had never seduced a girl of his own class. In the view of the middle and upper classes, the lower-class girls were already debauched and were therefore fair game. (For all the ideals of equality, a class structure had formed in America, and the old pattern of sexual exploitation of the servant girl was common.) An exceptional beauty could still hope to barter her looks and virginity for an upwardly mobile marriage, but most girls found it safer to smile on a promising young man of their own social class. There was less danger of an exploitive seduction.

As long as American women had no status-conferring economic functions, they had to barter sex for security, but in a manner that kept them in the category of *good* and thus marriageable women. The process of bargaining was romanticized to conceal the rather crude nature of the bargain: this, too, was part of prudery.

The idea of exchange as an analytic approach to human behavior has been developed by several theorists, notably Claude Levi-Strauss and Peter Blau. Michal McCall (1966) has applied the concept specifically to the courtship exchange. The concept of social exchange as developed by Blau (1964) is, in essence, that people choose relationships that involve reward-

229

ing reactions and continue in these relationships only so long as they continue to be rewarding. Each party to the relationship provides rewards to the other in exchange for those he receives. The exchange process may be conscious, or it may be so embedded in cultural traditions that it is not evident. When the process is conscious, the parties to the exchange are aware of striking a bargain.

In the days when kin groups arranged marriages, the premarital bargaining was overt and shrewdly calculated. When the parties to a marriage arrive at an understanding by themselves, romantic myths tend to conceal the bargaining process. But whether the marital bargain was consciously struck or not, nineteenth-century marriage in the American middle and upper classes involved an implicit exchange: the woman traded her virginity and marital sex (in which she was presumed to have no interest herself) for economic security; the man traded economic support for exclusive sexual rights. To some degree, this bargain characterized the working class and farm folk as well, although there the woman was expected to have useful skills and be willing to work as well as to be virginal.

Thus an eligible bachelor was a man with a good income and good financial prospects, and an eligible girl was an attractive virgin with the manners appropriate to her class. A man who could not support a wife was not supposed to marry until his circumstances had improved; a woman who was no longer virginal had dropped out of the marriageable category and was a "fallen woman."

In the age of prudery, the male was in the superior bargaining position (as he probably has been in most times and cultures). For the prosperous, "self-made man," marriage was a luxury, and a symbol of his status: he had arrived at a point in his career where he could afford an elegant home and an elegant wife. For a girl of the upper and upper middle classes, a good marriage (that is, to a prosperous man) was the means of subsistence, the basis of social placement, the point toward which her whole life had been directed. It was the woman who was most interested in marriage, the man who bargained from the position of power. As Lord Byron, writing in the nineteenth century, put it: "Man's love is of man's life a thing apart, 'Tis woman's whole existence."

This marital bargain—sex for economic support—contributed to the dominant position of the husband. McCall points out that "to the extent an individual has no viable alternatives to the present relationship as a source of other rewards, the person is said to possess *power* over him. This other person, being less dependent upon the relationship as a source of rewards is the person who . . . is 'least interested' in the continuation of the relationship" (1966:191). The nineteenth-century American husband was able to exercise the power of the "least interested." As long as his wife was the sexual partner he most desired, she might have some power over him, but he had ready alternatives if she locked her door too often, and she had almost no alternative means of support.

Time heightened the already unequal balance of power; as the wife's physical charms faded, the husband was more likely to seek other sexual alternatives. The wife could take comfort in the knowledge, however, that her position as legal wife and mistress of the household was secure, that none of her husband's mistresses were women he would consider suitable for marriage. In the nineteenth century, a man of wealth and position did not *marry* "that sort of woman."

The "ever-narrowing field" model of courtship

"*All* courtship systems are market or exchange systems," William Goode observes. "They differ from one another with respect to *who* does the buying and selling, which characteristics are more or less valuable in that market, and how open or explicit the bargaining is" (1970:8). The actual premarital bargaining in America has always been carried out by the potential mates rather than by the kin group. The pattern of courtship and the process of premarital bargaining that emerged in the eighteenth and nineteenth centuries in America fits the analytical model that Goode has labeled the "ever-narrowing field." The young woman is courted by several eligible young men; she attempts to keep alternatives available while arriving at a marital bargain with her preferred suitor. There are no exclusive rights on either side until an engagement is announced, when all bargaining with others is expected to cease. This was the meaning of engagement.

The ever-narrowing field was the pattern of American courtship until the middle of the twentieth century. As McCall describes the process: "Individuals did not form exclusive attachments (at least until the latest stages of the courtship process), but rather bargained with several others and narrowed the field of suitors by successively dropping the least favorable bargains ... The point was to keep several alters as bargaining partners and to allocate and reallocate commitments among them through bargaining" (1966:195). It was a highly competitive bargaining process, cloaked by romantic intrigue.

The nineteenth-century belle, surrounded by fawning suitors, was epitomized by Scarlet O'Hara in *Gone with the Wind.* The young met and courted at formal, chaperoned parties. The kin group issued the invitations, thus sorting out the most suitable marital partners; the kin group paid for the entertainment, and chaperoned the young during the courting process.

During the age of prudery, premarital bargaining was focused on obtaining the most desirable marital partner, not on the amount of premarital sexual intimacy that a girl would permit. It was assumed that a marriageable girl would permit *no* sexual liberties. Her escort did not feel cheated that he was allowed to kiss her hand and little else, for that was the way any girl he would want to *marry* was supposed to behave. And it was taken for granted that a man courted a girl of his own class only with the intent of marriage. (If he did not, he was a cad, sir.) Henry S. Canby, writing of the sexual norms of Ivy League college students in the last decade of the nineteenth century, commented: "We were familiar with the

231

sexual in every sense, yet did not think in these terms of the girls of our own class for a simple reason—we did not want to" (1934:428).

The internal barriers generated by the double standard seemed adequate to enforce the sexual code of the 1890s, and it seemed safe enough to let the system of chaperonage slowly disappear. That exciting new invention of the late nineteenth century, the bicycle, put the young couple on wheels and the chaperone could not have kept up in any event.

The courtship of the technical virgin

Not many societies have tried to insist on both deferred marriage and premarital chastity for both sexes. The Puritans tried to ensure the latter by encouraging early marriage. But for reasons discussed above, by the nineteenth century a young man was expected to defer marriage until he was able to support his bride at the level of living deemed minimally acceptable for her class. Deferred marriage raises the question of premarital sexuality. During the age of prudery, this problem was resolved by negative sexual conditioning of "nice" girls, by the double standard that permitted young men to find sexual release with prostitutes, and by the sexual exploitation of lower-class girls. To some degree, this pattern of a double standard during courtship still holds for the working class. For the middle and upper middle classes, however, moving away from the double standard meant that premarital sexual intimacy became a point of bargaining and anxiety.

World War I, Prohibition, and the automobile (not necessarily in that order) altered courtship dramatically. In the ambient excitement of 1918 —young men on the eve of battle, the sense of a new age being born from the ruins of the old—conventions began to shatter. For too many reasons to detail here, World War I was the end of an era, in Europe and in the United States. Speaking of America in the summer of 1919, Sherwood Anderson observed that "these are gaudy days." The recession that followed World War I was hardly noticed by the upper classes in America, and the prosperity that followed in the 1920s meant sudden financial success for many men. Marital bargaining among "old" families was thrown into confusion by the rise of so many young men to new wealth. Moreover, the impact of Prohibition was hardly what its backers had intended. Suddenly, young men were taking *girls of their own class* to "speakeasies."

Flappers were "nice" girls who scoffed at convention by bobbing their hair, raising their hemlines, smoking, drinking, and dancing in what their elders considered a lewd manner. Yet these girls did not relinquish their eligibility as brides for the young men of their class. Only a minority of girls were flappers in the 1920s, but they pushed back the limits of what a respectable girl could do. These Flaming Youth, as F. Scott Fitzgerald called them, are now grandmothers in their seventies, but it was they who began the "sexual revolution."

232

In earlier chapters we have seen how the white-collar girl acquired acceptable alternatives to marriage in the early part of the present century, and how women of the upper middle and upper classes acquired a growing awareness of their own sexual nature. Both changes eroded the double standard, and one of the consequences was that premarital sexual norms gradually became more permissive.

The setting of courtship changed. Parties chaperoned by parents were still held, and young people still met at choir practice, but for many young people, courtship moved out of the parlor, off the porch swing, and into the automobile. The automobile provided a rolling parlor with comparative privacy, especially in a day when most roads were back roads and any tree-lined country road could become a lovers' lane. By the 1930s, the motion picture theater provided a courtship setting for those too poor or too young to have access to an automobile. Thus courtship was removed from parental supervision. Parents still laid down rules, but enforcing them was difficult. *Gradually the function of establishing and enforcing sexual norms passed from parents to peers.*

As the old proverb has it, "He who pays the piper calls the tune." Once parents had paid for parties at which young people met and courted (whether the church social or the presentation ball). Now the young man financed the "date" and thus acquired a subtle dominance of the situation. The chaperon was gone, and with her went the physical presence of the parental generation in the courtship situation. It was now the girl herself who was supposed to have internalized the parental sexual code, and who became the arbiter of sexual intimacy.

The sexual code that emerged in American courtship in the second quarter of the twentieth century was established by the participants and enforced by the girl's fear of losing her reputation (the meaning was still sexual for a girl). The "ever-narrowing field" model of courtship still was the norm, which meant that a girl wanted to keep each of her suitors interested enough to retain him as an alternative. At the same time, she could not seem to offer her sexual favors too freely. Each suitor assumed that what he was allowed to caress and enjoy would also be carressed and enjoyed by his rivals, and a girl had to guard her reputation among potential husbands.

A young man was likely to press for more liberties than he expected would be allowed: behavior that he could rationalize by saying that he was testing her. (In the 1890s, he would have been called a cad.) The girl knew, however, that if she submitted sexually she might lose him as a potential husband and lose her reputation with others as well, for young men tend to boast of their sexual exploits. The word *cheap* acquired a sexual meaning: applied to a girl it meant that she had parted too cheaply with the one thing she had to barter for a husband. Marriage was supposed to be her price, and the "good" girl held out for it.

The sexual norms that evolved among American middle-class youth in the period from 1930 to 1950 were basically as follows: A "good" girl

233

Courtship moved out of the parlor, off the porch swing, and into the automobile. The automobile provided a rolling parlor with comparative privacy, especially in a day when most roads were back roads and any tree-lined country road could become a lover's lane. Thus courtship was removed from parental supervision.

(one who was considered marriageable) did not kiss on the first date and did not have sexual intercourse before marriage. Between these two events there was a period of gradually increasing sexual intimacy. The behavior considered permissible on the second date and on the third was a matter of much dormitory discussion on college campuses. Some sororities insisted that *their* girls were not to kiss before the third date, and "double dating" was much encouraged so that the girls could function in a limited way as chaperones for each other. The definition of what constituted a date became important, for if a certain degree of intimacy was permissible only after a given number of dates, it was necessary to know what counted as a date. Was a "coffee date" equal to a dinner date? The careful tabulation and calculation seem absurd in the 1970s; they were completely earnest in the 1940s and 1950s.

Not until the field of eligibles had been narrowed to one, and there was at least a private understanding that the couple would marry, could a "good" girl safely permit intimate caresses, and even then she was expected to draw the line short of intercourse. There emerged a pattern of highly elaborated sex play in which the girl remained technically a virgin, yet participated in a good deal of oral eroticism and other sexual practices that the Puritan fathers would have dubbed "filthy dalliance." In a sense, however, this pattern represented a turn back toward the more permissive norms that had characterized America before the Revolutionary War. Like bundling in the 1750s, "heavy petting" in the 1950s involved premarital intimacy *between those who were planning to marry.* It was not an abandonment of standards, but rather a shift from the double standard of prudery toward a single standard of permissiveness between those who were pledged to each other.

The distinction between "good" girls and "cheap" girls blurred over the decades, but one essential difference remained: a "good" girl was supposed to be a virgin for her future husband. Like all other codes, this one was violated, but it was nonetheless a functioning code. The girl did not cease to be marriageable if she submitted, provided that she did not have other suitors. Gradually, *exclusive commitment* came to replace the earlier requirement of virginity until marriage.

The pattern of courtship that was characterized by "technical virginity" was characterized by role strain and anxiety, however. The intimacies permitted by the girl were supposed to be in response to a commitment to marry, yet this commitment was not always honored. Pressured for complete sexual surrender by her "intended," the girl might fear losing him if she refused, yet fear also that she might be rejected as a potential wife if she permitted intercourse. And such rejection did occur, for there was a lingering remnant of prudery, and many young men still expressed a desire to marry a virgin. Girls were caught in a double bind.

Premarital intimacy had a tendency to escalate. As sex play became more intimate on successive dates, guilt often entered the relationship—an emotion hardly compatible with the romantic dream of young love. American girls were—and often still are—raised with highly ambivalent feelings about sex. As it gradually became more acceptable (in the peer group code) to have intercourse with one's intended husband, it became emotionally necessary for a girl to believe that the first man with whom she had intercourse was the One-and-Only Love she had dreamed of marrying. The alternative was to accept a negative self-image, and regard herself as promiscuous and "cheap." Thus guilt might conclude the marital bargaining as often as love.

Shame tended to hasten the commitment to marry on both sides. Whereas in the 1890s a man who seduced a virgin of his own class was a cad, by the 1930s he was a cad only if he did not ultimately marry her. Thus seduction came to imply a commitment to marriage. It was not always clear who had seduced whom, but the male usually assumed that he was the seducer and often felt obligated to marry the girl.

John Cuber and Peggy Harroff quote a career diplomat, in his early fifties at the time of the interview and therefore probably married in the 1930s:

In a very real sense I knew before I married her that I shouldn't. In some ways she was completely satisfying—like in bed. But in other ways I knew we were strangers and I knew it would get worse—but I had made a commitment —and besides she was a virgin when I first met her—and then there was

235

that dammed betrothal announcement in the *New York Times* and the whole social superstructure that would have collapsed if we had broken up. All this was something at twenty-one I didn't have the guts to face. Now I'm facing a lot worse—but now I'm not a kid. But what can you do about it—*now* that is? (Cuber and Harroff 1965:65)

Theoretically, the "ever-narrowing field" model of courtship was a process of mate selection that should have led to perfect marriages. But there were many who felt that they had made a bad bargain, and spent the rest of their lives regretting it.

The "series of commitments" model of courtship

As exclusive commitment gradually became the basis on which "good" girls might permit premarital intercourse, the courtship pattern began to undergo another qualitative change. If the commitment to marry was not honored, *both* the woman and the man could enter new relationships without prejudice. There was a day when a jilted girl—or her father—might file a breach of promise suit if her suitor broke the engagement. The legal presumption was that the girl had suffered damage to her reputation that impaired her future prospects of marriage. But by 1950 a jilted girl suffered little social disadvantage. If she had been seduced by a man she loved and seriously intended to marry, she did not have to think of herself as a "fallen woman." A girl could continue to dress, speak, and act "like a lady," even if she were no longer virginal. If she had been reasonably discreet about her romantic adventure, her reputation did not suffer. And when she finally married, she would probably wear white.

The norms gradually shifted until a young man felt a moral imperative to marry a girl only if he had impregnated her. Sexual relations were no longer restricted to marriage, but parenthood was. What was evolving among the young was a standard that permitted intercourse, provided there was affection, commitment, and contraception. Ira Reiss carried out extensive research into the attitudes toward premarital sexual behavior expressed by high school and college students in the latter part of the 1960s. He found evidence of a range of premarital norms, which he grouped as follows (1967:25): *abstinence* (definition of abstinence varied widely, and responses ranged from those few who still believed that there should not be kissing without affection to those who regarded "heavy petting" as a form of abstinence); *the double standard* (Reiss differentiates between the "orthodox" double standard, which accepts premarital coitus for males but not for females, and a "transitional" double standard, which permits greater sexual freedom to *engaged* girls); *permissiveness with affection* (a standard that permits intercourse in any relationship in which there is strong affection, apparently differentiated from the "transitional" double standard by the lack of insistence that the couple be engaged); and *permissiveness without affection* (essentially, promiscuity).

236

The proportion of respondents who accepted each of these standards varied widely with such factors as region and ethnic subculture. Reiss found the most marked difference between the students in a predominantly white high school in Virginia, where 65 percent accepted some form of abstinence as the standard in premarital behavior, and the students in a predominantly white New York college, where only 19 percent expressed some form of abstinence as the ideal code of premarital behavior. Reiss found that the high-permissive groups were characterized by: urban residence, low church attendance, a cultural tradition of high sexual permissiveness, and a generally liberal viewpoint (1967:177). Reiss comments: "The newer sexual codes reflect the new courtship context. In place of the ancient double standard and abstinence classifications, the permissiveness-with-affection standard is increasingly found ... Equalitarianism is more likely to be a factor today, together with much greater emphasis on affection, rather than the older male emphasis on pleasure" (1967:176).

Equalitarianism and affection: these are the foundations of the emerging sexual code. For the young, especially the young who are urban, liberal, and middle class, the commitment to marry (which in the transitional double standard is the point at which intercourse is considered acceptable) is increasingly becoming the valued, essential quality of the relationship.

In the ever-narrowing field mode of courtship, commitment came *after* the bargaining had narrowed the field to one suitor; the fact that the commitment was not always honored led gradually to a modification of the pattern: bargaining was followed by exclusive commitment, but a broken commitment released both man and woman to begin bargaining with others, leading to new commitments. As prior commitments gradually ceased to have adverse affect on future commitments, a new pattern of courtship began to emerge.

The emerging pattern tends to take the form of a *series of commitments* in which at any given time the individual is involved with only one member of the opposite sex. Instead of narrowing the field before commitment, there is a series of commitments, one of which ultimately leads to marriage. This pattern begins in the early teens with "going steady." The parental generation tends to regard going steady as too much, too soon; the young regard the situation differently. "Going steady" implies an exclusive commitment for as long as both parties are willing to maintain the relationship, which may be a matter of days or most of the school term. "Going steady" by no means implies a final and irrevocable commitment between childhood sweethearts who will one day marry, nor does it necessarily mean that the girl will have intercourse with her first, or even her tenth "steady."

In the series of commitments model of courtship, each relationship is a self-contained episode. Prior commitments may enhance rather than detract from future commitments, for as the boy or girl becomes more

237

skillful in developing and maintaining relationships with the other sex, he or she becomes a more able partner, and is in a better bargaining position in the sense of having more highly developed interpersonal skills. The bargaining itself is quite different from the bargaining in the ever-narrowing field mode. As McCall observes: "That which the individuals are bargaining about is still commitment to the role relationship and to the mate, but an individual is expected to become committed each time he becomes involved. The emphasis is upon intimacy or exclusiveness of involvement at any time" (1966:197).

In the emerging series of commitments mode of courtship, marriage is a more formal and enduring commitment, but not necessarily the final commitment. Courtship in America is no longer a time of seeking the best marital bargain and sealing that bargain in marriage. Courtship has become a learning situation. What the individual learns is how to give without resentment, how to strike a compromise when goals conflict, how to find fulfillment of self through interaction with the intimate other. Or, as McCall puts it: "In other words, 'courtship' teaches the individual *how to bargain—how to form, maintain, and leave relationships*" (1966:197; emphasis added).

Learning how to form an intimate rather than an exploitive relationship, learning how to maintain a relationship despite conflicts, learning how to leave a relationship with self-esteem enhanced rather than shattered: if the series of commitments pattern can in fact help young—and not so young—people to develop these skills, it will prove to be a more helpful prelude to marriage than the ever-narrowing field model ever was. In effect, the series of commitments may be participant training in intimate response. There is less bargaining about how much sexual intimacy a woman will allow on the first date or the third, for sex is no longer her only counter in the bargaining process. There is more concern about communication, involvement, and commitment. *In a society in which intimacy is an increasingly important function of marriage, it may be that this experience in responsive commitment is of vital importance in the courtship process.*

The old morality and the new

As courtship has come to be run by participants, with rules established by the peer group rather than by the kin group, the norms of the youth culture have come to determine premarital sexual behavior. These norms have become increasingly permissive, particularly if marriage is deferred until after the young have established residence apart from the parental household: in college dormitories, in singles apartments, in communes, or in other settings dominated by the young. The emancipated young may not live in the state of endless orgy that some members of the parental generation imagine, but a desire to escape constant conflict with parents over dating behavior is among the reasons why the young choose to live apart from their elders.

238

It is in the relatively low value placed on premarital virginity that the sexual code of the young most strikingly conflicts with that of the older generation. Those who defend the old morality are predominantly (but not exclusively) people past forty: people who courted and married in the time when the ever-narrowing field mode of courtship was the pattern, and premarital virginity for females was an accepted moral standard. Not all women who are now middle aged were virginal when they married; Kinsey's figures on the large proportion who were not came as a social shock in the late 1950s. But these older women were often propelled into marriage by a sense of guilt or shame over their sexual involvement; their husbands may have married them out of a sense of obligation to the fallen virgin they had seduced. The older generation may feel that they can understand why the young are tempted, but not why the young apparently feel so little guilt. Behavior that the young regard as blameless their elders consider shameless.

For their part, the young tend to feel that the old moral code has become encrusted with hypocrisy, that the double standard reflects male chauvinism, and that "technical virginity" borders on deceit. Their concern is with honesty and commitment, rather than virginity. It is not surprising that those who are not married should be more approving of premarital permissiveness than those who are married, for the latter are not expected to be abstinent, only monogamous.

Age and marital status are not the only dividing lines on the issue of sexual morality. There are demographic characteristics that tend to set those who hold to the old morality apart from those who have embraced the new. Small-town and rural traditions are still strongly those of premarital abstinence and tacit acceptance of the double standard as a means to ensure the chastity of "good" girls. Country folk have long regarded the city as a center of depravity; city dwellers have historically prided themselves on being more sophisticated and liberated than their country cousins. Reiss found that young people who were raised in urban settings tended to be more permissive in their views of premarital sexual behavior than other young people (1967:177). Viewed from this perspective, the sexual revolution is a part of the rapid urbanization of our society, a process that has rendered many old rural norms obsolete.

It is predominantly the group of age peers, rather than social-class peers, that influences the values of young Americans. A report of a survey taken by Daniel Yankelovich, Inc., in the late spring of 1973 states:

What we find today is an astonishingly swift transmission of values formerly confined to a minority of college youth and now spread throughout the generation. This is not to say that noncollege youth have arrived at precisely the same value orientation as their peers. What the research does show, to an almost uncanny degree, is that noncollege youth today are just about where the college population was in 1969. (Cited in Skinner 1974:6)

239

The Yankelovich survey found in 1973 that only one third of the noncollege youth believed premarital sex is morally wrong, while two thirds felt it was acceptable, and that only 48 percent believed that abortion is morally wrong. In the spring of 1970, a Gallup poll that included interviews with 1,114 students on 55 college campuses across the United States, found that nearly 3 out of 4 of these students did not believe it was important whether the person they married was virginal (reported in Swift 1970:7). In contrast, a similar Gallup poll taken a few months earlier (in the fall of 1969) had indicated that a representative sample of American adults had a firm conviction that it was important for a girl to be virginal when she married: some 68 percent believed that premarital sex was wrong (reported in Swift 1970:7).

The value of virginity will not, however, be established by a vote of the entire adult population. Increasingly, the parental generation is losing its power to enforce its beliefs about premarital behavior, for it is no longer the custom for girls to live in their parents' home until the day they marry. It comes as a surprise to many eighteen-year-old girls today to learn that as recently as the 1950s, most girls lived with their parents until they were twenty-one or older, often leaving home for the first time on the day of their wedding. Those who went away to school lived in women's dormitories or sororities or other university-approved housing, where a housemother watched over their dating behavior, and locked the door at midnight. Girls signed out, giving their destination and expected time of return, and signed in again, noting the exact time. Violations of the sign-out rules could lead to university disciplinary action. But by the late 1960s, American colleges and universities had largely given up the attempt to supervise dating behavior, having more pressing problems than the dormitory sign-out sheet. The advent of the coed dormitory is an indication of the rapid change in sexual norms on campus.

The shift in values that made intercourse with the girl's intended husband permissible has culminated in living arrangements off campus. The couples who participate in such arrangements are a minority, but their behavior is not censured by many of their peers. The problems most often voiced by unmarried student couples seem to be largely questions of how to spare their parents' feelings: whose name goes on the mailbox, how should the telephone be listed, what about unexpected weekend visits from parents? The parents may threaten to cut off financial support, but this is an age when the young are beginning to cut financial ties with their families, and most manage to survive, even to stay in school, without parental assistance. The strongest hold the parents have over the behavior of their daughters is an emotional one, a hold that is often stronger than either parent or daughter realizes.

Girls raised in working-class homes tend to marry earlier than the daughters of the middle class who anticipate college before marriage. But the working-class girls who do not marry immediately after high school graduation are less likely to remain under the parental roof than they

240

would have been only a decade or two ago. As recently as the 1950s, it was the custom for a girl from a working-class family to take a job and begin paying room and board at home when she left school. Today, there is little likelihood that a working girl will be content to live in her parents' home (perhaps sharing her room with younger sisters) and pay for her keep.

Once a girl leaves home and becomes financially independent, her parents are in no position to control her sexual behavior. It is this sense of being powerless to control the premarital sexual behavior of their children, and especially of their daughters, that is so frightening to many parents. The young may have little economic or political power in our society, but they do have the power to determine the norms of premarital sexual behavior; it is a power that they are not likely to give back to an older generation.

The youth culture is not without a sexual code; it is rather that the young have a different code. It stresses a sense of involvement and commitment, of sensitivity to the needs of the other; it is moving rapidly toward the "permissiveness-with-affection" norm that Reiss describes. It is a code that values commitment to one individual for as long as the relationship continues to be mutually rewarding. Gradually, it is becoming less important in the youth code that the commitment be to a person of the opposite sex. The stress is on *now*, rather than *forever*. This is what makes it so appealing to those who value individual freedom and what makes it so threatening to those who value social stability.

It is clear that the youth culture, or the "new culture" as Philip Slater terms it, is fundamentally different in its view of sex and sensuality from what Slater calls the "old culture." As he observes (1970:105), the old-culture Americans are afraid of arousal, especially of sexual arousal. This fear of sensuality has its origins in the guilt, anxiety, and fear of being sexually exploited that characterized the courtship bargaining of most people over forty and many who are younger; that anxiety in turn was rooted in the negative attitudes toward sex that mothers carefully cultivated in their daughters and in the attitudes toward virginity prevalent in a society still characterized by the double standard and imperfect contraceptives.

Having moved past the anxieties of the dating period (it was supposed to be the happiest time in a person's life), the old-culture married couples presumably have a permanent contract that precludes any further cross-sex bargaining. Yet because the old culture is more permissive for males than for females, the wife is fearful of the sensual because she does not want her husband to be exposed to needless temptations. One of the consequences of increasing sexual permissiveness is that the difference between "nice" girls and those who would once have been called "cheap" has become a matter of degree. If a girl does not take money for sex, she can remain in the pool of eligible marital partners. Class differences in attitude remain, but one of the fundamental changes brought about by the sexual revolution is that many men are now willing to marry a girl who has

241

been their mistress. There was a time when the "other woman" could never hope to replace the wife. Now, many a second wife was once the man's mistress, and wives are fearful of the sensuality of the youth culture because they see sensual young girls as potential rivals.

Yet, paradoxically, the taboos surrounding premarital and extramarital sex in the old culture served less to prevent illicit behavior than to enhance it. The most ordinary action is exciting when viewed through a peephole. A tingle of guilt adds to excitement, an excess of guilt leads to madness: somewhere between lie the sexual anxieties that characterize the old-culture Americans.

In contrast, as Slater observes, the new-culture adherents have embraced the sensual openly, yet "seem in general to be more certain that desire can be gratified than that it can be aroused" (1970:105). These are the youth who were raised in a setting of unprecedented affluence in which all their needs and most of their whims were readily gratified. Sometimes, as Slater notes, they were offered a choice of gratifications before they were fully aware of wanting anything. They were bored children surrounded by expensive playthings, children who complained that there was nothing to do, while their mothers sought new ways of entertaining them.

As young adults, these sons and daughters of the middle and upper classes have tended to turn away from things, and to seek experience instead. Sensual experience of one form or another is the hallmark of the youth culture. But a surfeit of anything leads to a jaded appetite, and thus either to apathy or to a search for something still forbidden or scarce. The excesses of the more exotic fringes of the youth culture may lead to self-destructive behaviors; perhaps they will lead full circle to a new asceticism; perhaps this is what the "Jesus People" and the new mystic religions are all about.

Politics and the sexual revolution

If the phrase *the sexual revolution* has more than allegorical meaning, it is in the sense that the phrase *the industrial revolution* has meaning: it describes a technological change, accompanied by a value change, leading to a restructuring of some fundamental social institutions. The sexual revolution was made possible by the technological advances of modern medical science that led to reliable contraception. These advances in contraception are discussed in some detail in an earlier chapter; here let it simply be noted that without these new contraceptives, the series of commitments mode of courtship would be cut short by pregnancy. It is reliable contraception that makes it possible to defer marriage without requiring sexual abstinence for women.

The value change that has accompanied this technological change is the decline in the value placed on premarital virginity and the corresponding erosion of the double standard. The restructuring of fundamental institutions is evident in the changes that have come to courtship, marriage, and the family. Among the many imponderables in our future is whether permissive sexual behavior will become a broadly accepted norm for both men and women, in and out of marriage, or whether the pendulum will swing back toward a more ascetic code (as it did after the American Revolution).

Political ideology is one of the factors that will determine the direction of American sexual norms in the future. The Gallup data (reported in Swift 1970:7) indicated that students who were more liberal in their social and political philosphy tended to be more sexually permissive than those who were conservative in politcal philosophy. The Gallup poll found that 79 percent of those who identified themselves as "liberals" felt that it was *not* important to marry a virgin. Of those students who considered themselves conservative, 58 percent felt that virginity *was* important. (The students who described themselves as liberals outnumbered the avowed conservatives two to one.) Reiss found a similar relationship between political ideology and sexual norms, especially in the higher status groups (1967:65).

The women's movement, a growing political force in the 1970s, has taken some stands which might seem to indicate a turn toward asceticism: the protest of the use of women as sex symbols and of the exploitation of women by pornographers. However, the women's movement has also taken a strong stand for legal abortion, and in general has promoted the demise of the double standard.

Conservative groups are also increasingly evident on the political scene, forming less around political parties or candidates than around specific issues. One of these issues, busing of school children, has only an implied sexual concern. But other issues that have become the focal point of conservative political groups are specifically sexual: sex education in the schools and abortion. The anti-abortion groups are becoming well organized and politically sophisticated; abortion will be a central political issue for the rest of this decade.

Groups on the far Right have tended to link the chastity of women to patriotism. In an article entitled "For Our Sons: On How to Choose a Wife," which appeared in *American Opinion,* a monthly review edited and published by Robert Welch, founder of the John Birch Society, E. Merrill Root counsels young men: "avoid any woman whose heresies deny her destiny—her home, her children, her country, her traditions, her eternal and absolute values—avoid her, distrust her, shun her, for no true man should mate with one of the deracinated of earth" (1967:37). Root also urges, in a manner that echoes the Puritan view of conjugal sex, that marriage "be based on more than biological affinity, or pride of the eye and lust of the flesh; it must be a marriage of true minds. Much of the lie of marriage today comes from the sex habits of the 'Liberal' hour, of which a decent rabbit would be ashamed" (Root 1967:32).

It is not only extreme conservatives who extol asceticism. On the Left there are militant black groups who defend the chastity of black women and express the belief that liberalized abortion laws are a form of genocide against blacks. We live in times rife with talk of revolution, and every real revolution has produced its ascetic radicals. Radicals are not merely liberals who have moved farther left on the political spectrum. Radicals passionately believe that the existing order must be destroyed before a new and better society can be created. Typically, one of the charges radicals make is that the existing society is decadent and corrupt. (One of the first things that successful revolutionaries tend to do is close the brothels and the casinos.)

Members of a radical political party tend to be ascetic: it is part of the discipline required of the revolutionary. The success of the revolutionary movement depends on a core band of revolutionaries with one single passion: the movement, personified in the leader. Lust, greed, avarice, and all other passions can only corrupt and lead people to betray the movement. At best, other passions will drain energies that the movement needs. People who are incapable of focusing all their desires into one consuming passion seldom remain in such a movement for long. It is the pinpointed intensity of energy and desire that makes the fanatic.

Unless some sweeping political revolution—from either Right or Left—should overtake the sexual revolution, however, it seems probable that the sexual norm of the American future will be a single, permissive standard for both sexes.

Premarital bargaining and the sexual revolution: a summary

The sexual revolution in American is above all a revolution against the double standard that characterized the age of prudery. It is a rejection of the hypocrisy of the double standard; it is an acceptance of female sexuality; it is a trend toward greater sexual permissiveness in premarital bargaining. Comparing the ever-narrowing field mode of courtship that prevailed in America until recently with the emerging series of commitments mode, McCall observes: "Today, sexual intimacy need not imply pregnancy, and herein lies the difference between the two patterns. Today sexual behavior is only an involvement; children constitute (marriage) commitment. In fact, an individual may decide not to have children with a specific marital partner, often giving as a reason the fact that the marriage is unstable or that he or she is not fully committed" (1966:199–200).

What is disturbing to those who value the earlier courtship norms is the number of sexual involvements that may precede marriage today, and that in the emerging mode of courtship, marriage is not necessarily the final commitment. There are some who fear that courtship may become little more than a pattern of dalliance, an end in itself and not a prelude to marriage. There are historical precedents for this. But dalliance focuses on conquest, not commitment: dalliance is exploitive. If the series of commitments is precisely that, the emerging pattern of courtship can lead to personal growth, not to exploitive promiscuity. And in the long run, it may lead to more stable and rewarding marriages.

References

Blau, Peter M. 1964. *Exchange and Power in Social Life*. New York: John Wiley & Sons.

Canby, Henry S. 1934. "Sex and Marriage in the 'Nineties.'" *Harper's Magazine* 169 (September):427–436.

Cuber, John F., with Peggy B. Harroff. 1965. *The Significant Americans*. New York: Appleton-Century-Crofts.

Goode, William J. 1970. *World Revolution and Family Patterns*. New York: The Free Press.

Hays, H. R. 1964. *The Dangerous Sex*. New York: G. P. Putnam's Sons.

Kephart, William M. 1961. *The Family, Society, and the Individual*. Boston: Houghton Mifflin Company.

McCall, Michal M. 1966. "Courtship as Social Exchange: Some Historical Comparisons." In *Kinship and Family Organization*, edited by Bernard Farber, pp. 190–200. New York: John Wiley & Sons.

Morgan, Edmund S. 1958. *The Puritan Dilemma: The Story of John Winthrop*. Boston: Little, Brown and Company.

Morris, Richard B. 1955. "Three Hundred Years Too Soon for Kinsey." *The Pocketbook Magazine* 1 (September):19–37.

Reiss, Ira L. 1967. *The Social Context of Premarital Sexual Permissiveness*. New York: Holt, Rinehart and Winston.

Root, E. Merrill. 1967. "For Our Sons: On How to Choose a Wife." *American Opinion* 10 (October):31–40.

Skinner, Frank. 1974. "College, Noncollege Youth Views Compared." *Higher Education and National Affairs* 23 (May 31):6.

Slater, Philip E. 1970. *The Pursuit of Loneliness: American Culture at the Breaking Point*. Boston: Beacon Press.

Stone, Lawrence. 1960–1961. "Marriage among the English Nobility." *Comparative Studies in Society and History* 3 (November-January):182–206.

Swift, Pamela. 1970. "Youth Notes." *Parade* (July 5):7.

Turner, E. S. 1954. *A History of Courting*. New York: E. P. Dutton & Company.

Suggested readings

Bermant, Gordon. 1969. "Never Mind the Birds and Bees; Regard the Praying Mantis." *Psychology Today* 3 (July):28–31. In many species, the participants in sexual behavior are vulnerable during intercourse. In some species, the threat comes from predators and it is thus important to mate quickly, to minimize the period of risk. In other species, it is the mate who poses the threat, and it becomes more important to establish the intentions of the potential mate than to mate quickly. Such species employ courtship behaviors; a sequence of actions that assure the potential mate of benign intent. The human species and human courtship behaviors are among those described in this article on the sociobiological basis of courtship.

Reiss, Ira L. 1967. *The Social Context of Premarital Sexual Permissiveness*. New York:

245

Holt, Rinehart and Winston. A sociological inquiry into changing norms regulating premarital sex. Guttman scales were constructed for this study to measure premarital sexual permissiveness. Students at five selected schools (two high schools, three colleges) were interviewed. Differences in standards of premarital sexual permissiveness are noted across social-class and racial lines, as well as regional and political differences.

Simon, William. 1969. "Sex." *Psychology Today* 3 (July):23–27. Observing that it makes as little sense to talk about sexual revolution in exclusively sexual terms as to talk about political revolution only in political terms, the author describes changes in public and private attitudes toward, acceptance of, and concerns about sexual behavior in America.

Turner, E. S. 1954. *A History of Courting.* New York: E. P. Dutton & Company. Available in paper as a Ballentine Book. A delightful sampler of styles of courtship, from castle dalliance in the twelfth century, through Elizabethan romps, Puritan restraint, Restoration masquerade, Victorian intrigue, and Edwardian elegance to romance American style.

9 Marital choice: the pool of eligibles

Deny thy father and refuse thy name;
Or, if thou wilt not, be but sworn my love,
And I'll no longer be a Capulet.

William Shakespeare, *Romeo and Juliet*

Romeo and Juliet were of the same race, the same religion, the same elite class, and were raised in the same city in Italy. But he was a Montague and she a Capulet. The relevant question is not how similar two lovers are in background or personality profile, but whether the groups that claim their loyalty are willing to be linked by marriage.

In-groups, out-groups, and marital choice

The pool of eligibles in which young people are expected to catch a mate is determined in every society by the groups that are there regarded as socially significant; in contemporary America, race, religion, ethnicity, and generation form the nucleus of group identities. Other times have stressed other allegiances. But the underlying reason why such groups are determinants of marital choice is that *marriage creates the assumption of equality and alliance between the family of the bride and the family of the bridegroom, and some alliances are unwanted and embarrassing to both sides.*

An American couple may attend the same university, be activists in the same political movement, come from similar suburban homes. But if he was raised in a group with a strong sense of identity, bolstered by a traditional enmity toward a group to which she belongs, the two will find that parents, friends, and the community will create obstacles to their marriage.

The in-group always cherishes a sense of "We few, *we* happy few": *we*, the chosen people of our God, *we* who suffered together, *we* who make things happen around here. *They* are sometimes only a residual category: all outsiders. But sometimes *they* are a particular group, the once and present enemy. An intense feeling of group belonging is often accompanied by antipathy toward an out-group. Feelings of loyalty and loathing reinforce each other, and form the emotional substructure of racism, nationalism, parochialism, sectionalism, and all of the other forms of group pride and group hatred that lead to holy wars, pogroms, and lynchings. And *they* are certainly not considered eligible mates for our sons and daughters. When *they* live an ocean away, the question of marriage is not likely to come up often, perhaps only after a war when our occupying troops begin to fraternize with their daughters. The question of who is in the pool of eligible mates and who is excluded from it is more continuously an issue when *we* and *they* live in stratified layers of the same society.

Marriage is important not only to the individuals who are being married, but also to their families and the larger social groups that claim them, for marriage is the means by which the group perpetuates itself. Marriage involves the pairing of fertile members of the group to produce the next generation and thus ensure the group's future, and marriage also creates alliances that strengthen the group in the present.

Marriage between members of the in-group tighten the structure of that group. People who are already friends, neighbors, members of the same church, members of the club, become more closely bound as in-laws.

The grandchildren are linked by blood ties to both families, and the existing ties of class, religion, or ethnicity are strengthened by the bonds of kinship. A requirement that marriage be within a particular class, race, religion, or ethnic group is called a *rule of endogamy:* marriage within the group.

But a marriage may also be the means of creating an alliance across group lines. Alliances between nations used to be sealed by the marriage of a ruling prince to a princess from the allied (or conquered) country. Most primitive societies required their young men to seek a bride from outside their kinship group, and sometimes required them to choose a bride from a particular neighboring tribe, a practice intended to ensure that the tribe on their border remained a friend and ally. A requirement that people marry outside of their own group is called a *rule of exogamy.* The prohibition of incestuous marriages is the most common example.

In every society, the pool of eligibles is bounded on one side by the rules of endogamy and on the other by the rules of exogamy. A marriage that connects groups that do not wish to be allied or that consider each implacable enemies is considered a misalliance. In the days when parents arranged marriages, there were few misalliances. The parents were concerned with questions of rank and wealth when they arranged marriages for their nubile offspring; these were matters about which bargaining took place. Racial and religious endogamy were not open to bargaining; some groups were separated by social chasms that marriage could not bridge. The young couple whose marriage had been arranged with a suitable concern for the rules of endogamy and exogamy were expected to become fond of each other in time. If they did not, the marriage was not considered a failure, for it had in fact united powerful families, consolidated fortunes, solidified the in-group, and, if there were children, ensured the future of the in-group.

In America, the value system has stressed the individual rather than the group from colonial times forward, and free choice of mate is one of our fundamental freedoms. But just as arranged marriage was tempered by the right of the individual to refuse to marry the person chosen by the parent, so free mate choice in our society has been limited to some degree by the requirement of parental consent. Parental consent is still required in most states before minors can marry. Typically, parents have granted or withheld their consent on the basis of whether or not the match followed those rules of endogamy that the parents believed important: social class, religion, age, race, or ethnic origins.

Marital choice and social class

In societies where rank is hereditary, family connections are the only basis for class membership. One must either be born into a class or contrive to marry into it; there is no other valid admission. But because hereditary rank is not formally structured into our society, the determinants of social-

251

class status are multiple and overlapping: family lineage, wealth, occupation, and education. The scion of a prominent "old" family, wealthy both by inheritance and in his own right as a ranking executive of a large corporation, who holds a law degree from Harvard or Yale, would epitomize the established upper-class male in America (and a most eligible bachelor).

Because, in America, the criteria of class membership are additive, a given individual may rank high on one and lower on the other, and two persons may arrive at the same general social status by various combinations of wealth, family prestige, education, and occupation. It may be difficult to determine whether a marriage is between social peers or between two people who have similar class status acquired in different ways. There are still people in America to whom such distinctions are important, especially when they are meeting their daughter's fiancé for the first time.

Because the Constitution of the United States forbids hereditary titles (that is what the principle of equality originally meant in America), the major determinant of class position in our society has been wealth rather than lineage. Yet until the recent past, when inheritance, gift, and income taxes began to erode the great family fortunes, wealth could be linked to a particular family through inheritance, and thus lineage came into our class structure by an indirect route. (In the 1890s, the U.S. Bureau of the Census estimated that 9 percent of the families in the United States owned 71 percent of the wealth.) Wealth may be the single most important determinant of class position in America, but all money is not equal. The patina of "old" money gives it the most status value: "old" money has been in the family long enough for time and philanthropy to have obscured any irregularities in the way the family fortune was amassed. Moreover, "old" money is likely to be represented by controlling interests in corporations that have grown to be immense and powerful. Few fortunes accumulated in the present are likely to be tied so closely to power.

But if wealth alone does not always ensure class status, neither does an old family name. Lineage may be considered apart from present family wealth. If the family was once extremely wealthy and powerful, the prestige may linger for awhile. If the family loses all its resources, however, it will be quietly forgotten. In the years following the Civil War, the scion of an impoverished "old" southern family might have to barter the prestige of his name and lineage for a marriage to new wealth, especially if the new millowner had a daughter with a pretty face and the father was anxious for the local prestige of a tie with "quality." (Such marriages have kept the class structure open to new and upwardly mobile groups, and are a means of preventing the establishment of a new closed caste system.)

But outside of the tidewater South and New England, family names are important in America today only in two circles: the small group of extremely wealthy, established families and the many tiny social circles found in stable—or moribund—small cities. In many small cities and towns, people still remember who the families were that homesteaded the land in the last century, built the first sawmill, incorporated the town, chartered the bank, and made a small fortune by selling the county the land where the courthouse stands. The elderly matrons of such families are still the social arbiters of their communities and pass judgment on the suitability of marriages in their small world; for those who dwell in such towns, that world matters very much.

Class standing based on the prestige of one's family of origin is largely a localized phenomenon, and in our increasingly mobile society it has eroded rapidly. Wealth is easier to measure than family prestige, and does not require a significant group of people with long memories to validate the status claim. The decline of small-town class hierarchies and the rise of mass society have swept away the lesser establishment, the upper class of the small cities. In the large metropolitan centers, family name no longer matters except to the few dozen families at the very pinnacle of the class structure.

For most of the several millions of people in a given urban metropolitan cluster, occupation and not family lineage has become the basis of social placement. The meaning of class endogamy has shifted from marriage within a small group of families with similar resources and life-style to the marriage of persons with similar social and occupational achievements. Family background has meaning largely in terms of the social skills and opportunities a person enjoyed as a child and as a dependent youth.

The eclipse of the local status hierarchy has had a subtle effect on mate selection in America. Only a generation ago, a "good marriage" for a girl was a marriage into a family that was established in a higher social stratum than her own. In the past, such a marriage was a virtual guarantee of the future social status of the young woman and her children, and entailed less risk than marriage to a promising young man of her own class who might or might not rise. A women had little means of upward mobility outside of marraige, so a "good" marriage was her one great opportunity, and thus the focal point of her own and her family's concern.

Today, the family-owned banks and small industries on which the class structure of American cities was once built are disappearing, through acquisition, merger, or public sale of stock if the business is profitable, through closure or foreclosure if it is not. Even if the son and heir is willing to take over the family business, he may no longer have that choice. Short of marrying the heir to a fabled fortune, there is little guarantee today that marriage into an affluent family will ensure a girl's future class status.

Nor is the tradition of marrying the boss's daughter any longer a certain path to higher class status. This particular violation of class endogamy was condoned in the past if the young man showed ambition, dedication to his job, and other characteristics that were conducive to upward mobility (and if the prospective father-in-law had no son, or only an errant son, and was hoping for a son-in-law who could carry on the

253

family business.) This was the upward path of the fictional Horatio Alger heroes; upward mobility enhanced by marriage to a woman from an established family was the path chosen by some real-life heroes as well, such as Abraham Lincoln (see Baltzel 1964: chap. 1 for an analysis of the rise of Lincoln and the Lincoln family). But the new class of executives are managers, not owners, and they may not be able to do much for a son-in-law except provide him with the right introductions. For the rising young man, a wife who has the social graces of the class to which he aspires can be a real asset, and a girl's family background may thus be a matter of some import still—but marriage to the daughter of a wealthy family is not the alliance it would have been only a quarter of a century ago.

Marital choice and education

The young women who are still interested in a "good match"—and there are some—are more likely to be concerned with the occupation and professional education of a prospective husband than with the level of affluence of his family of origin. A young man who has, or is preparing for, a profession is considered highly eligible by prospective brides and their parents, whatever his family origins, for his profession is the best contemporary guarantee of future affluence and upper-middle-class status. Education is important as a prerequisite for a highly paid and prestigious occupation and as a symbol of class status (few members of the upper classes are uneducated), but beyond the campus, education is not particularly valued for itself.

Education has a strangely equivocal influence on both class status and occupational opportunity. Education enhances class status if it is associated with an occupation of high prestige and income. But it may have a negative status value if the educated person is poor (unless he or she is still a student, or has gone into a profession such as the clergy, where it is expected that the professional will be both well educated and ill paid). If a man cannot find employment in his field of specialization, or if he has an education other than one that led to a technical or professional degree, he may be denied even routine, semiskilled jobs because he is "overeducated." (Women are probably even more frequent victims of this kind of job discrimination.) If education is not commensurate with other elements of the individual's class status (such as occupation and income), it may be taken as a mark of personal instability or even of failure.

Still, education remains an important element of class status; if not all highly educated persons enjoy upper- or upper-middle-class status, most persons of upper-class status are highly educated. Thus as a symbol of class belonging, and as the prerequisite for an occupation of high prestige and income, education is a significant factor in mate selection in America. It is what makes a promising young man promising.

Education may be replacing the status of the family of origin as a dominant factor in determining the pool of eligibles. According to the

U.S. Bureau of the Census (1972:270) persons who married in the decade between 1950 and 1959 and who have been married only once report a close correspondence between the education of the husband and wife, with the husband having a few more months of formal education, on the average. The women who had completed only the eighth grade had husbands with a median of 9.2 years of formal education; the women who had completed high school had husbands with a median of 12.5 years of formal education; the women who had completed 4 years of college (16 years of education) had husbands with a median of 16.7 years of education. Finally, the women with 5 years of college or more (some graduate work, perhaps a graduate or professional degree) had husbands with a median of 17.2 years of formal education. For the couples who were married during the decade between 1960 and 1970, the median years of schooling for husband and wife differed from those of couples married during the 1950s by only one tenth of a year of education or less.

These are median years of education and there are, of course, some exceptions. It is not considered a problem if the husband has more education than his wife, provided the discrepancy is not so wide that the wife is a social embarassment to her husband. Of the couples married between 1950 and 1959, only 7 men in 1000 who had five years of college or more had wives with an eighth-grade education or less, but 257 men in 1000 who had five years of college or more had a wife with a high school education. Both of these figures declined for persons married in the next decade. Of those married in the 1960s, only 5 men in 1000 who had five years of college or more were married to women with an eighth-grade education or less, and 181 men in 1000 with five years of college or more had a wife with only a high school education (U.S. Bureau of Census 1972:269–270).

Violations of educational endogamy, like most other violations of status endogamy, are considered more socially acceptable if a woman marries "up" than "down." But the women who has markedly more education than her husband is supposed to have demeaned herself by the marriage, rather like the heiress who marries the gardener. Quite apart from the marital problems created by social pressures (most likely created by her family), such a couple may have marital difficulties arising from discrepancies in self-image and self-esteem. Yet among persons married in the 1950s, 23 women in 1000 who had five years of college or more were married to men with an eighth-grade education or less, a figure that declined to 10 women in 1000 with five years of college or more who married a man with an eighth-grade education or less in the 1960s (U.S. Bureau of the Census 1972:270).

A man and woman who have a marked difference in educational level when they marry may not always have a "mixed marriage" in this respect. The one with less education is often encouraged by the other to return to school, especially if it is the husband who has less education. A more educated wife is likely to use her education and skills to support her husband while he is completing some technical or professional degree

255

program. Unlike many other attributes that limit the pool of eligibles, education is entirely an acquired characteristic. One is born into an "old" family, born into a particular religious or ethnic community, born into a given generation or race, but no one is born with an education.

Marital choice and religious belief

To a lesser degree, what is true of educational endogamy is also true of religious endogamy. It is simpler to alter religious affiliation than to change family, generation, or race. There are many people for whom membership in a particular church was simply part of being raised in a given neighborhood and family. It is something that they accepted as given, something that under normal circumstances they might not change. But if forced to choose between religious affiliation and the person he or she wants to marry, some persons may find it not too difficult to alter their faith.

Like education, religion has a tangential association with social-class status. In certain sections of the country, certain denominations were once synonymous with the established elite (Congregationalists in Massachusetts, Episcopalians in the tidelands South). Partly because of such historical associations and partly for reasons of class-associated values, certain churches are still likely to have a membership that is predominantly drawn from a particular social class. In general, the more fundamentalist the religion, the more likely it is to have a working-class membership.

Particularly for Protestants, moving from rural areas to the city and rising in the social-class structure have often meant a change in religious affiliation. Few people would care to admit that they altered their beliefs to fit their new class status, and the change in religious affiliation usually has an easy rationalization. Moving up economically typically means moving out residentially, and in the new suburban community it is easy to justify affiliating with the "neighborhood" church, which is one that reflects the class level of the area. Ostensibly this makes it easier to attend Sunday service, but for people who will drive twenty miles to see the motion picture of their choice, this hardly seems reason enough to change what are presumably core beliefs.

For such people, a difference in the religious affiliation of husband and wife presents no particular problem; they alter their religious beliefs more readily than their dietary habits. (There are, in fact, many couples who maintain the dietary taboos of a religion they no longer practice in any other way.) If the couple are withdrawing from former group memberships and seeking new affiliations in other areas of their lives, religious endogamy can be created after marriage through a change in the church affiliation of either or both.

But there are other Americans who identify deeply with the church in which they were raised. The child who learns to think "I am a Catholic" or "I am a Jew" or "I am a Mormon," as he learns to think "I am an American" and "I am a boy," grows up with religious belonging a structural part of his self-image. His religion is something he *is*, not something he consciously chooses to believe.

Only slowly does such a child grasp what the label means, and what it might be like to be a member of some other faith remains one of the mysteries of his childhood. ("I wonder what They do in There?" is the half-curious, half-fearful question that floats through his mind when he passes the temple of another faith.) Such a child becomes an adult for whom a religious community is a highly significant in-group; all outsiders are different in a way that is somehow sinister. Such people find it difficult to live in emotional comfort with a husband or wife of a different religious faith. For them, religious endogamy is probably a prerequisite for marital happiness.

If they do violate religious endogamy, conflict may be buried early in the marriage, but as soon as there are children, the latent religious conflict is likely to emerge and may become divisive. The mother is traditionally expected to oversee the religious training of the children, just as she is expected to be responsible for most aspects of their early socialization. Yet the modified patriarchy that still prevails in our society decrees that the father's views are to be the official family position. Marital conflict arising from a violation of religious endogamy is thus likely to center on the religious education of the children (with grandparents often contributing to an issue that to them involves no less than their grandchildren's immortal souls).

As Glenn Vernon (1960) has pointed out, however, there has been a tendency for the amount of conflict generated by religious difference to be exaggerated, even in articles written for professional journals. He notes that it is customary to quote statistics in such a way that they suggest much greater risk than is actually involved. One widely quoted study (Landis 1949) presents the divorce rates when both partners are Catholic as 4.4 percent, when both are Protestant as 6.9 percent, and for mixed Catholic-Protestant marriages as 14.1 percent. This suggests that there are 200 to 300 percent more divorces when religious endogamy is violated than when it is observed and that interfaith marriage is a bad risk. As Vernon observes, it would seem quite different to the reader if the figures were quoted the other way around: if the authors had noted that when both partners are Catholic, 95.6 percent kept out of the divorce courts, compared with 93.1 percent when both were Protestant, and that by the same criterion, 85.9 percent of the interfaith marriages were successful (Vernon 1960).

It should also be noted that comparative divorce statistics are difficult to obtain with accuracy (the state does not inquire into the religion of persons filing for divorce). Moreover, it makes a great deal of difference, as Hyman Rodman (1965:53) has pointed out, whether the statistics are shown as a percentage of *all marriages* involving Catholics (or Protestants, or Jews) or as a percentage of *all Catholics* (or Protestants, or Jews) who enter marriage.

Statistical considerations aside, to the persons who are wondering whether or not a difference in religion will make their own marriage more difficult, the answer, of course, is yes. The very fact that a person has asked the question means that religious belonging is important to either the prospective bride or bridegroom in a way that will make a difference. (The people for whom religious endogamy is not important seldom raise the question.) How much difficulty a religious difference will make in a marriage depends on how deeply either or both identify with their church, and to what extent their religious affiliation represents loyalty to a significant in-group.

To some degree, religious endogamy overlaps ethnic endogamy. In the case of the Jews, this is particularly evident, although it exists as well in the Irish-Catholic, Italian-Catholic, Greek Orthodox, and other ethnic-religious communities. Being Italian and being Catholic, to take one example, are so entwined in the self-image of a small child growing up in an Italian-Catholic neighborhood that it will never be entirely possible for that person to separate these two group affiliations, or these two core aspects of the self. When an Italian-American man marries, he is likely to marry not only a good Italian girl, but in all probability a good Italian-Catholic girl. The ethnic neighborhoods of eastern cities in the United States tend to promote such endogamy.

Marital choice and age-group boundaries

If the ecumenical spirit of our time has made religious endogamy less rigid than it once was, age endogamy seems to have become more closely observed. Considering those couples who were married at the time of the 1970 census, and for whom the marriage was the first for both husband and wife, both the median difference in age between husband and wife and the proportion of marriages in which the husband is older decline steadily by age group. Since these are first marriages, the pattern of age difference between husband and wife reflects the norms of mate selection in America at the time the couple were married.

Among couples in which the marriage was the first for both husband and wife, and the husband was 70 years of age and older, there was a median age difference of 3.8 years, and in 80.4 percent of the marriages, the husband was older than his wife. When the husband was between 65 and 69 years of age, the median difference in age was 3.4 years, and in 79 percent of the marriages, the husband was older. Among couples in which the husband was between 35 and 54 years of age, the median age difference was 2.4 years, and in 75.7 percent of the marriages the husband was older. Finally, in those marriages in which the husband was under 35 years of age, the median age difference was only 1.7 years, and the husband was older in 71.7 percent of the marriages (U.S. Bureau of the Census 1972: 256).

Among persons who have been married more than once, the patterns of age endogamy are somewhat different, although the general tendency for those couples who are younger to be closer in age still holds. When a woman marrying for the second time marries a man who has not been married previously, the couple are likely to be closer in age than couples in which there has been only one marriage for both. When the husband was between 35 and 54, and it was his first marriage but his wife had been married more than once, the husband was older in only slightly more than half of the marriages (52.1 percent), and the median age difference between husband and wife was only 0.7 years. When the husband was under 35 and it was his first marriage but his wife had been married previously, the husband was older in less than half (44.6 percent) of the marriages and the median age difference was 0.0 years (U.S. Bureau of Census 1972:256).

In contrast, men who have been married more than once, but whose wives have not been married before, tend to marry younger women more often than do any other group of men. Among husbands between 35 and 54 who had been married before, but whose present wife had been married only once, 85.1 percent were older than their wives, and the median age difference was 6.2 years. When the husband was under 35, if he had been married before and his wife had not, the median age difference was 3.9 years, and the husband was older in 84.2 percent of the marriages.

When both husband and wife had been married before, the age difference tended to be similar to that of persons marrying for the first time. Apparently when both husband and wife have been married more than once, the tendency of a previously married woman to marry a man close to her own age, or slightly younger, and the tendency of a previously married man to marry a woman some years younger than himself cancel out.

The tendency of men who have been married before to seek a younger wife can be explained simply by noting that the standards of beauty of our culture are centered on the young woman of twenty or so. An older man who has economic resources (in spite of alimony and child-support payments) that enable him to support a second family is likely to be a successful and established adult male, quite able to compete with younger men for the most desirable sexual partners. The age difference may in fact be an attraction to some young women, who may have despaired of the apparent irresponsibility and lack of resources of men their own age, and who find the security of a relationship with a mature and successful man a compelling point in marital bargaining. This is a pattern of many centuries' standing.

When men outlived a series of wives, who died young because of excessive childbearing under unhygenic conditions, there was likely to be an increasing age gap between the husband and each successive wife. A

259

young woman was willing to marry a widower twenty years or more her senior if he offered security, particularly if most men of her own age had gone west to seek their fortunes. Such age differences are infrequent today. When a marriage between a man of forty-five and a girl of twenty occurs—as it occasionally does—more eyebrows are raised than would have been at the height of Victorian prudery.

Older women must compete for men of their own age group with younger, and thus usually more physically attractive women, and older divorced women and widows find remarriage difficult. (Most divorced women remarry, but this is because the highest rate of divorce comes during the first years of marriage, and most divorced women are thus still in their twenties and able to compete successfully with other young women for husbands.) But the increasing economic opportunities for women not only give women alternatives to marriage, they may also make older women better able to compete for husbands. A man who is burdened with alimony and child-support payments from a former marriage may be pleased to find a woman who is established in business or a profession, and thus able to share the financial burdens of marriage. This may in fact be the only way in which a second marriage is financially possible for many divorced men.

Age-group stratification is one of the few areas of social stratification that seem to be increasing in America, and age-group endogamy is likely to become even more narrowly restricted than it is at present. American adolescents are particularly conscious of age differences. "What grade are you in?" is one of the first questions that one junior high school student asks another. In high school, a freshman girl who dates senior boys is likely to be considered sexually permissive if not promiscuous; the high school girl who dates college men or working men is even more likely to be viewed as promiscuous and may be ostracized by her age peers. ("Why else," the gossip runs, "would those *older* boys be interested in her?")

The college student is less sensitized to age and year in school, but is likely to identify strongly with the youth culture, and suspicion of people over thirty extends to a distrust of their motives for interest in a younger sexual partner. Any liaison, including marriage, that crosses the line between generations is viewed by the young as involving a "dirty old man." Except for their professors, moreover, college students are not likely to be in close contact with older persons who are seeking marriage partners, and they are immersed in a large pool of eligibles of their own generation.

People who are marrying or remarrying in their thirties or forties may feel that "our generation" includes persons who are as much as ten years older or younger than themselves. Still, questions of age are raised. There was the perhaps typical experience of a woman in her late thirties who telephoned her mother, halfway across the continent, to tell her that she was marrying again. The mother's first question was, "How *old* is he, dear?" The second question was, "What does he do" and the third was, "Have you met his family?"

*There is a tendency for people to choose mates who are like themselves in both social
and physical attributes, including stature. But a short woman and a tall man may
not find their difference in height an insurmountable barrier to romance.*

The man of sixty-odd who marries a woman in her thirties or forties
is regarded as a bit of a rake (especially if he has recently divorced a wife
his own age). And a woman of sixty who marries a man of thirty or even
forty creates a scandal. It is widely assumed that he must be demented, or
she must be terribly rich. ("Why else," the gossip runs, "would that *younger*
man be interested in her?")

Stratification by age group is a form of social stratification that is
increasing in America: housing developments may be restricted to persons over forty-five years of age; recreational facilities may specialize in
activities that appeal to young adults rather than to families; a heightened
sense of generational belonging forms the basis of most voluntary as-

261

sociation. People who marry must first meet, and age-segregated activities (including education) contribute to narrowing the average age difference between husband and wife.

This trend toward age-group endogamy is compatible with the trend toward greater equality in marriage. In the past it was assumed that the older person in a relationship should take responsibility for the younger: parent for child, older brother (or older sister) for the younger brother (or sister). The older person was assumed to have wisdom that came with years and greater experience, and the younger person was expected to show deference. When the husband was typically some years older than his wife, she was expected to defer to him both because he was a man and because he was older. The young are less inclined to defer to their elders today, and this change in attitude, together with the tendency for husband and wife to be approximately the same age, has helped create greater equality between husband and wife in American marriages.

Marital choice and racial barriers

All norms of endogamy other than racial barriers have been merely custom; if the price for violating these norms was sometimes ostracism from family and former in-groups, there was no legal penalty. But until the last decade, many states made it a crime to violate racial endogamy. The miscegenation statutes, as they were known, forbade individuals belonging to certain racial groups to marry persons from certain other racial groups, and sometimes specified a particular degree of nonwhite ancestry that would render a person ineligible to marry a white person. (Often the prohibition was one quarter or more ancestry in another race, but in some states it was even less.)

It was not only the South that banned interracial marriages. One of the first laws that Nebraska passed after it was granted statehood was a law that prohibited interracial marriage. (The Nebraska statute, like the laws of many other western states, was intended to prevent marriage between white and Indian.) The question of statehood for Hawaii languished for years because of mainland suspicions about "miscegenation" in Hawaii. When World War II ended, interracial marriage was illegal in thirty of the forty-eight states.[1]

But World War II was one of the great watersheds in American social history; our cultural currents ran in new directions after the war. One of its ideological legacies was a spreading belief among white Americans that racism was wrong. In the name of Nordic supremacy and racial purity, the

---

[1] States in which interracial marriage was still prohibited by law in 1945 are (* indicates that the state eliminated its miscegenation statute by court ruling or by legislative action prior to the U.S. Supreme Court ruling): Alabama, Arizona*, Arkansas, California*, Colorado*, Delaware*, Florida, Georgia, Indiana*, Idaho*, Kentucky, Louisiana, Maryland*, Mississippi, Missouri, Montana*, Nebraska*, Nevada*, North Carolina, North Dakota*, Oklahoma, Oregon*, South Carolina, South Dakota*, Tennessee, Texas, Utah*, Virginia, and Wyoming.

Nazis had committed atrocities against the Jews that had horrified the world. The American troops who fought to liberate Europe believed that they were fighting for the basic American ideals of equality and human dignity—and it became difficult to justify fighting in segregated units and even harder to justify the fact that Americans of Japanese descent were interned back in the United States for no reason other than their racial ancestry.

After the war, there was a period of high hope and idealism, during which the United Nations was founded. There were many American soldiers on occupation duty in Japan who wanted to bring Japanese brides home. It was in this ideological climate that challenge to the laws forbidding racial intermarriage first succeeded in court. In 1948, Sylvester S. Davis, a black graduate of Los Angeles City College, challenged the California statute under which he had been denied a license to marry his white fiancée, Andrea Perez. Both were Catholics, and one of the grounds on which these two young people brought suit (with the aid of the Catholic Inter-Racial Council of Los Angeles) was that the California statute interfered with their religious freedom, for it denied them one of the sacraments of their faith, the sacrament of marriage.

It was, however, on the broader grounds of the equal protection clause of the Fourteenth Amendment to the Constitution that the California Supreme Court found the entire series of California miscegenation statutes unconstitutional. Justice Roger Traynor, speaking for the majority, said that "marriage is something more than a civil contract, subject to regulation by the state. It is a fundamental right of free men."

Over the next two decades, thirteen other states dropped their miscegenation statutes, some through court action, some by legislative action. The first case bearing directly on miscegenation laws that was decided by the United States Supreme Court was one involving a Florida law that made it a criminal offense for interracial couples "not married to each other" to habitually live in and occupy "in the night-time the same room." Because Florida also had a statute forbidding interracial marriage, the defendants could not plead that they had a common-law marriage. The Supreme Court declared this cohabitation statute unconstitutional in a unanimous decision in December of 1964. Justice Potter Stewart wrote in a concurring opinion: "I cannot conceive of a valid legislative purpose under our Constitution for a state law which makes the color of a person's skin the test of whether his conduct is a criminal offense." But the Court noted that this unanimous opinion did not express "any views about the state's prohibition of interracial marriage."

North of Richmond, Virginia, in secluded pockets in the hills of Caroline County, whites and blacks (some with an Indian ancestor) have lived in comfortable tolerance of one another for generations. So there was no local scandal when Richard Loving (white) was courting Mildred (black, with an Indian ancestor). They knew that the state of Virginia would not issue them a marriage license, so in 1958 they traveled to Washington, D.C., to be married. They went home to Caroline County as man and wife.

Five weeks later, the Lovings were routed out of bed at two in the morning by a knock on the door. The county sheriff was there with a warrant for their arrest. The Lovings were charged with being married.

Judge Leon M. Brazile sentenced each of them to a year in the county jail, but suspended sentence on the condition that the Lovings leave the state of Virginia immediately and not return for twenty-five years. People raised in the city are mobile and can move from one city to another, one state to another, one coast to another, without feeling more than an occasional twinge of nostalgia for the place of their birth. But the Lovings were hill people and their roots were deep. Exile was a bitter sentence.

The Lovings lived in exile in Washington, D.C., for five years: lonely, frightened, insecure financially. But Mildred wanted to visit her family and they slipped back into Virginia—as visitors, not residents. They were arrested. Relased on bail, they wrote a letter to then Attorney General Robert Kennedy seeking help. The letter ultimately reached the American Civil Liberties Union, which offered them legal assistance. The Lovings decided to stay home in Virginia (free on bond) and fight for their right to be married.

When the case appeared before the United States Supreme Court in 1967, the state of Virginia referred to an 1883 Supreme Court ruling that if both white and negro were equally punished, there was no discrimination. Chief Justice Earl Warren, in presenting the unanimous opinion of the Court, declared, however, that "there can be no question but that Virginia's miscegenation statutes rest solely upon distinctions drawn according to race. We have consistently denied the constitutionality of measures which restrict the rights of citizens on account of race."

The decision did not have much immediate effect on the amount of interracial marriage that actually occurred. Of the couples married in the decade between 1950 and 1959, approximately 1.0 percent were interracial. The decade between 1960 and 1970 was the highwater mark of the civil rights movement in America, a decade marked by white student interest in eliminating racism. Of the couples married during the 1960s, however, only 2.0 percent were interracial (U.S. Bureau of the Census 1972:283). Racial endogamy is deeply rooted in custom. But whatever the trend of custom, the law is now clear. Marriage is a fundamental right of free people. By the delightful chance of the defendants' surname, this landmark Court decision will go down in history as *Loving v. Virginia*.

The forbidden mates: legal barriers to marriage

The civil code of each state defines who may marry. There are still some rules of endogamy, and some of exogamy, that are written into law, although the *Loving* decision means that all of these are under a legal cloud: if marriage is a fundamental civil right, then any restriction on the right of an individual to marry will eventually come under judicial scrutiny.

264   To turn first to the laws requiring endogamy, the civil codes of most states permit only persons who are within certain groups to marry. These are groups determined by medical or legal status, and are seldom groups with organization or group identity, but these are rules of endogamy, nonetheless. State codes vary, but many refuse marriage licenses to persons who are mentally ill, mentally retarded, suffering from venereal disease, drug addiction, or alcoholism. Several states have had laws forbidding the marriage of persons with epilepsy or tuberculosis, but these laws either have been repealed or are no longer enforced, presumably because medical ability to control these conditions has reached a point where it can be assumed that if afflicted persons marry, they will be able to bear healthy children and care for them adequately. Eugenic concern is the primary reason for the laws requiring that those who marry must be free of certain medical conditions. Persons having a disease that is communicable to the unborn child (congenital syphilis, for example) or a medical condition that might make them unable to function adequately as a parent (such as insanity) have been defined by the laws of many states as outside the group of marriageable persons.

If laws restricting marriage to persons who are free of certain medical disorders have a eugenic basis, however, there are other laws restricting marriage that are based on social norms of what the family should be. Such laws are those having to do with the age and marital status of persons permitted to marry. Those who are already married are forbidden to marry without first becoming legally divorced, and even then, most states require the divorced person to wait from six months to a year before the decree is final and he or she is free to marry someone other than the original spouse. (Such laws are intended to promote reconciliation between the divorcing spouses; whether they will ever be held to violate the civil rights of the individuals involved remains to be seen.) Laws forbidding bigamy are in force in every state. The ease with which the married person can become divorced in many states now means that this is essentially a requirement that a person have only one spouse at any given time. Group marriages or any form of polygamy are illegal, for such marriages violate the laws prohibiting bigamy.

Minors are the other category of persons who are restricted in their right to marry because of legal status. Robert F. Drinan observes that:

> These laws often seem to have been written to protect parents rather than their children. The law does not provide, for example, for a hearing to be granted to a minor whose parents object to his marriage. The law somehow assumes that an "unemancipated" youth (that is, one under twenty-one or eighteen who lives at home and is financially dependent on his parents) has no right to be heard when his desire to marry is contrary to the wishes of his parents. Similarly, those states which permit parents to prevent the marriage of their underage children grant no right to be heard to a pregnant underaged daughter who desires to marry in order to legitimize her future child. (Drinan 1969:55)

265

Until the recent past, most states required parental consent for the marriage of a male under the age of twenty-one, but permitted females to marry without parental consent at the age of eighteen. (Thus for eighteen-year-old women, marriage was often a means of escape from parental control, escape that would not otherwise have come until the women reached the age of twenty-one.) When the Twenty-Sixth Amendment to the Constitution was adopted in July 1971, guaranteeing the right to vote to citizens eighteen years of age or older, many states changed the age of majority to eighteen for both sexes.

In forty-five states eighteen is now the age at which both men and women may marry without parental consent (as well as the age at which both men and women become eligible to enter other contracts besides marriage, and become financially responsible). Alaska, Nebraska, and Wyoming have revised their marriage laws to permit both men and women to marry without parental consent at the age of nineteen. Mississippi and the Commonwealth of Puerto Rico require that both men and women under the age of twenty-one have parental consent to marry (twenty-one has remained the age of legal majority in these two jurisdictions). Alabama and the District of Columbia have retained a difference between men and women in the age at which they may marry without parental consent: eighteen for females, and twenty-one for males. (Women's Bureau, U.S. Department of Labor 1976:373–374)

In most states, the age for males to marry with parental permission used to be eighteen years, and recent changes in laws relating to majority have not included changes in the age at which marriage is permitted with parental consent. In these states, eighteen is the minimum legal age for males (and sometimes for females) to marry, and parental permission has become meaningless as a legal requirement for marriage. In other states, males and females may marry under the age of majority provided they have parental consent. State laws vary widely. Perhaps the youngest statutory age for marriage with parental consent is in New Hampshire, where males may marry at the age of fourteen and females at the age of thirteen, provided that they have both parental consent and a court order (Women's Bureau, U.S. Department of Labor 1976:374–375).

There are other state laws that require exogamy—marriage outside the group. Every state has laws prohibiting incestuous marriage. The origins of the incest taboo lie in the remote past, when no one had the slightest understanding of recessive genes or why it was dangerous to breed within a small population. The social definition of kinship often did not coincide with biological kinship. Distant cousins who were reckoned as belonging to the same lineage might be considered brothers and sisters, subject to the incest taboo. Conversely, close cousins who were members of different lineage groups sometimes constituted the only acceptable pool of eligible mates. It cannot be assumed that the recognized function of early incest taboos was the prevention of birth defects.

266   There have been a variety of explanations offered for the incest taboo, the most common rule of exogamy. Among the more plausible is that in a society structured by kinship, it must have been easier to keep the hierarchy intact if the relationships between persons were not tangled by incest. For example, if a man was supposed to have a specific kind of relationship with his paternal uncle, what would happen to that relationship if the man's uncle were also his half-brother and younger than he was?

Claude Levi-Straus has explained the incest taboo as an extension of trade relationships, and says that marriage may be the most profound trade relation. In formulating his *principle of reciprocity*, Levi-Strauss observes that the function of exchange in primitive societies "encompasses at the same time material objects, social values, and women" (1957:92). He points to the example of tribes who moved from hostile relations to trading relations and ultimately to the exchange of brides as well as goods: "the exchange of betrothed women is merely the termination of an uninterrupted process of reciprocal gifts, which brings about the transition from hostility to alliance, from anxiety to confidence and from fear to friendship" (1957:94).

According to Levi-Strauss: "The prohibition of incest is a rule of reciprocity: It means: I will give up my daughter or my sister if my neighbor will give up his also ... The fact that I can obtain a wife is, in the last analysis, the consequence of the fact that a brother or a father has given up a woman" (1957:9). Even the contemporary weddng rituals of most religious faiths contain some form of the question: "Who gives this woman?" and the father or father-surrogate affirms that he does.

The incest taboo was once singled out by scholars as the only universal behavior norm in a world of contradictory moral codes. But Russell Middleton has found ample evidence that brother-sister marriage was not only permitted, but frequently practiced, by the ancient Egyptians, and by commoners as well as by kings. According to Middleton: "The most plausible explanation that has been advanced for the marriage of brothers and sisters in Egypt is that it served to maintain the property of the family intact and to prevent the splintering of the estate through the operation of the laws of inheritance" (1962:610). (Middleton has indicated in a private communication that further research had led him to question whether this explantion for brother-sister marriage in Egypt is valid.)

Whether or not the consolidation of property was the motive for incestuous marriage in the ancient civilizations, it was clearly a motive in the common practice of marriage between close cousins among the established upper-class American families in the nineteenth century (a custom that has not entirely disappeared). Both southern planters and northern bankers encouraged their offspring to marry cousins, and the effect was to consolidate great family fortunes and to keep the controlling interest of large enterprises in the hands of a kin-related elite.

The definition of incest in contemporary America varies from state to state, but all states have laws that forbid men to marry their sister, mother, daughter, aunt, niece, grandmother, or granddaughter, and that

267

forbid women to marry the corresponding male relatives. A majority of states forbid marriage to half-siblings and first cousins, but about twenty states do not. About half of the states make marriage between stepfather and stepdaughter, or stepmother and stepson, illegal. Almost as many prohibit marriage between a man and his father's former wife, or his son's former wife, or his former wife's mother. A few even forbid marriage between a man and his former wife's grandmother! The fear of defective offspring is clearly not the only motivation behind laws defining incest, even in our time.

In fact, eugenics has had little to do with the formulation of American laws defining incest. The degrees of relationship within which marriage is prohibited in most of the United States of America is drawn closely from Leviticus: the law is slow to change in some areas. As Drinan notes:

> Although reliable predictions about defective offspring from marriages between an uncle and his niece, or between first cousins, are difficult if not impossible to obtain, laws forbidding such unions, presumably based on accurate information, hardly ever become a public issue. Nor is there ever any controversy about other restrictions on marriages between persons related by consanguinity. . . . Impediments based on affinity—that is, on legal relationships arising solely from marriage—seem to be indefensible. These restrictions, which exist in twenty states and the District of Columbia, are in the laws of states almost exclusively in the northeastern and southern parts of the nation.

There is a second rule of exogamy that most of us take for granted: the laws requiring that we marry someone of the opposite sex. This rule of exogamy ensures that the most basic and stable primary group in our social structure will be composed of an adult male and an adult female; perhaps it, too, is a rule of reciprocity and the basis of an alliance between the two most fundamental in-groups in the human race.

This rule of exogamy had survival value for society when reproduction had to be maximal to compensate for high infant mortality. It has not necessarily coincided with moral disapproval of homosexuality. The classic Greek culture had a high regard for homosexual relationships, but required men to marry women because of the importance of perpetuating the family line. If the basic functions of marriage in a society are procreation and socialization of children, the homosexual union could never fulfill marital functions. In our era of low infant mortality, of burgeoning population, and of ephemeral conjugal families, rather than enduring consanguine families, the procreative function of marriage can probably be performed adequately by those persons—still the large majority—who are heterosexual. It may be that sexual exogamy has less social urgency in our time.

There are still, however, two basic rules of exogamy in our culture, and these are both written into the laws of every state: we must marry outside our family circle (how far outside depends on the civil code of the state in which we marry) and we must marry someone of the opposite sex. Both rules require that we go outside highly significant in-groups when we choose a spouse.

Pride and prejudice: the built-in bias in mate selection

In the laws governing marriage, the interests of the group and the interests of the individual are balanced. In the past the balance was tilted in favor of the group; at present it is tilted in favor of the individual. We Americans are highly conscious of the civil rights of the individual. We are less aware of, or sympathetic toward, the right that groups may have to perpetuate themselves, although the growing pressures for bilingual-bicultural education may indicate a new consciousness that groups, too, have a right to continue to exist.

When society was structured by lineage, the preservation of a kinship group was socially valued; this is a point made in several previous chapters. But with the declining importance of kinship groups, other kinds of groups have become more important elements of social structure. From the time that people created cities, groups larger than kinship units have existed: groups that promoted peace by making it possible for those who were not kindred to have common bonds; groups that made it possible for a society to grow beyond tribal organization.

These were groups united by religion or by citizenship in the city state, which ultimately became nationality. The bonds between these people who were not kin were ties of belief, of language, of common history, of shared nationality: these are the elements of *ethnicity*. Often, these bonds were regarded as analogous to kinship ties. Coreligionists became "brothers" and "sisters" by being "reborn" in the faith. When a particular piece of earth was regarded as the people's mother, not its property, there was a sense of familial identity among those who were born in a particular place: *we* who sprang from the same soil.

Those who speak the same language have an affinity as strong as the way of viewing the world implicit in the verbal abstractions that are a given language (in English, we say "John is dying," a statement in which the person is the actor, and dying is the action; in the Navajo language, the sentence would translate roughly as "Dying is taking place with John," a statement in which the person is experiencing a process). "He speaks my language" is a strong statement of a common bond, going back to a time when the people of every village spoke a different dialect and sometimes an entirely different language, from that of the tribe across the river.

Just as marriage to provide heirs so that the family line would not disappear forever was once a person's most compelling duty, so marriage to preserve the group composed of the faithful, or the group with common ethnic or racial ties, has been a goal of many people. Groups resist absorption, for absorption means the disappearance of the group. Yet to per-

269

petuate a people's existence requires that the young marry within the group and produce children who are replicas of themselves. If the value placed on the preservation of an ethnic or religious group comes into conflict with the value placed on free marital choice, both American tradition and the American Constitution insist that the civil rights of the individual take precedence.

But the group may seek to perpetuate itself by encouraging its youth to make their "free" mate choice within the group. This can be done without interfering with the rights of individuals if the young can be taught to identify strongly with their own group, and to regard the attributes of persons who are group members as being the most desirable of all human attributes: such an attitude is called *ethnocentrism.* Whatever the negative impact of ethnocentrism on relations between groups, it functions to promote endogamy. The person considered most desirable as a mate will be likely to be a member of the same ethnic group, if ethnocentrism has been encouraged in group members.

Group pride is built into the child's developing self-image. The image of *we* that the child incorporates into his self-image in his formative years begins with his family, and extends out to include racial, religious, and ethnic groups to which his family belongs. The child who does not acquire such consciousness of group identity from his parents is likely to acquire it from his peers. If the other children in the third grade are talking about religion, or race, or politics with the self-assured ignorance that third-grade children often possess, the child who has not been raised to a strong in-group image will come home and ask, "Mother, what are *we?*" And the child wants a label, not a statement of philosophy.

Children learn—from peers, if not from parents—to regard people who are unlike *us* as ugly, bad-smelling, deceitful, and probably damned. Such prejudices are the dark side of group pride. They are also a fundamental means of encouraging endogamy. If members of the out-group are considered physically repulsive, few of *us* will want to marry one of *them.* On the other hand, group pride builds a preference that probably accounts for a great deal of marital choice. Clothing, haircut, manner of speech, even the way a person holds his head and moves his body—*style,* in the most inclusive sense of that word—separates one class and one ethnic group from another. Style also separates one generation from another. That which makes a man or woman attractive to age, class, and ethnic peers makes him (or her) ludicrous and repulsive to those who are in another pool of eligibles. ("Some of those girls might be attractive if you washed them.")

Sometimes the appeal of the forbidden and the thrill of repulsion make the rebellious son or daughter of one group seek out members of the most forbidden out-group for sexual adventure. But marriage is another matter. The image of a suitable husband or wife (as opposed to the image of an exciting lover) that is firmly focused in the minds of most people is still typically that of their own class and ethnic group.

270

Not content to trust the selective responses, the pride and prejudice, they have built into their children, however, many parents try to encourage endogamy by restricting their nubile offspring's contacts. American parents no longer have a formal veto over the marital choice of their children, once the latter are of legal age. Most debt-ridden middle-class parents can threaten to cut a rebellious child out of their will, but the threat is empty without property to bequeathe. So parents try to create a situation that will enhance the chance that their children will make a "suitable match." These are situations that sort the young by social class, by religious faith, or by other factors (such as ethnicity and race) that the parental generation hopes to control. Parents know that propinquity is a large part of love, or at least of marriage: it is impossible to marry someone you have never met.

At the upper-class level, the summer colony at the shore or in the mountains or at the lake is more than a place for summer vacations; the summer colony is a place where the young people meet their class peers every summer from childhood through adolescence. The presentation ball at which the debutantes of the season "come out" to meet eligible young men of their class, and only such young men, is another device to promote class endogamy. (The presentation ball and the debutantes' season seem to be fading customs. Perhaps the end of an era was marked when, according to newspaper reports, some daughters of prominent families in New York and San Francisco who were scheduled to be debutantes in the 1970 season indicated that they were too involved with their own activities to participate, and some declined to participate on political grounds.)

Most American parents are eager for their children to marry well, which means at their own class level or higher. But not too much higher, for if the social distance between in-laws is too wide, parents sense that they will not be able to cross it, even if their child does. They try, therefore, to restrict their children's contacts to others of approximately the same or a slightly higher class status. The stratified suburbs and their schools have been a major means of doing precisely that.

Where a family lives is a fairly reliable index of the class status of the family. When only the wealthy lived on estates in the hills beyond the city, living in the "country club district" was evidence of upper-class status. Racial and religious restrictions that once applied to such neighborhoods have been removed by law, but the economic restriction is still in effect: the amount of the down payment, the amount of the mortgage, and the annual income required by the lender for a mortgage of a particular amount act as class barriers. Subdivisions with houses priced in a narrow range and designed to appeal to a given age and income group provide a finely graded series of screens that sort people into the substrata of class as efficiently as the screens used for grading fruits and nuts.

Most people who claim that they have moved to a "good neighborhood" for the sake of their children have in mind the class level of their

271

If, underneath, the old pattern of endogamy meant an inherent class, racial, and ethnic snobbery, on the surface it was as innocent as marrying the girl next door.

children's playmates as much as the fresh air. Living in a setting where one's children will be surrounded by others of their own class is one of the ways that the people have tried to provide approved models for their children and ultimately to encourage class endogamy. The suburban high school is likely to be attended only by children whose parents can afford a comparable house and the life-style to go with it. The economic screening of suburban neighborhoods has often functioned secondarily as racial or ethnic screening as well. While many white middle-class families were drawn to the suburbs by the life-style there, many others fled to the suburbs to escape busing ordered to integrate city schools.

The working-class neighborhood, with its strong ethnic identity, is also a neighborhood where endogamy is encouraged. Class identity is less valued in such a neighborhood than ethnic identity, which often includes a strong religious component. Within these stable ethnic enclaves, persons of similar origins and beliefs grow up together, go to school together, meet and marry. This is part of the reason why court-decreed busing of school children—including high school students who form the immediate pool of eligibles—has been so volatile an issue in cities such as Boston.

Upper-class families use private schools to accomplish the goal of sequestering their young with a pool of approved eligibles during their adolescent years. The private boarding school, like the parochial school, is seldom coeducational, but there is usually a "sister" school for the opposite sex located nearby.

One of the latent functions of the college or university is to provide a pool of eligibles. In the large, state-supported universities and in the community colleges, the classes now mingle, and only age and educational endogamy are promoted. The basic reason for the survival of many small, denominational colleges is the hope of parents that such schools will immerse their sons and daughters in a pool of potential mates of the same general class background, the same religion, the same ethnic group, and of marriageable age. Any alliances established there are likely to meet with full parental approval.

Endogamy in America was once a matter of choosing a mate from among the people with whom one was raised, of the marriage of childhood sweethearts whose parents belonged to the same club, the same lodge, the same church, and other groups that symbolized class status and ethnic belonging but, more than that, were groups with a sense of identity and group pride. If, underneath, the old pattern of endogamy meant an inherent class, racial, and ethnic snobbery, on the surface it was as innocent as marrying the girl next door.

Mate choice in the schismatic society

When there are numerous in-groups in a society, even if the lines between them are sharp and drawn with hostility, endogamy may not be feasible for all group members. There simply may not be enough potential mates in the small pool of eligibles. The person who cannot find a mate within the in-group has the alternatives of remaining single or marrying an outsider. Given the choice, young people seem to prefer the latter alternative. This is illustrated by the significantly greater tendency for Jews to marry outside their faith when there are only a small percentage of Jews in a community (Rodman 1965). With the rise of mobile, pluralistic metropolitan populations, endogamy has become almost unenforceable in America.

Every religious schism, every fragmenting of society along lines of ethnic origin or class envy, has created more in-groups, yet at the same

273

time has made it more difficult for members of these groups to practice endogamy. Endogamy is more easily enforced when lines between the in-group and the out-group are clearly drawn and when certain characteristics almost invariably coincide with membership in a particular class or race or ethnic group. Where this occurs, the cleavages in society are deep and often bitter. But in a pluralistic society such as our own, most individuals belong to numerous and overlapping groups. A marriage that unites coreligionists who share a common ethnic ancestry (two Irish Catholics, for instance) may also be a marriage that crosses class lines or educational boundaries, or both.

The results of our overlapping group affiliations is that a large proportion of American marriages violate *some* rule of endogamy. Conversely, this means that most people in our society can be considered to be in the same broad pool of eligible mates, provided that they are over the minimal age to marry, of opposite sex, and not closely related. It is no longer even required by custom (as opposed to law) that both be single; that can be arranged. Bernard Farber has developed a conceptual model of the contemporary American pattern of mate selection that he calls *universal, permanent availability:* "Each adult individual, regardless of his current marital status, is available as a potential mate to any other cross-sex individual at any time" (1964:109). Farber finds support for his theoretical model in the decline of premarital chastity, the declining age at first marriage, the increasing rates of divorce and remarriage, the growing proportion of divorces that involve children, and the increase in extramarital sexual relations.

But if theoretically all adult Americans comprise a vast pool of eligibles, clearly there are some who are considered more eligible than others, especially for marriage. The basis for mate selection in contemporary America seems to be a sorting and balancing of the similarities and differences between individuals, a process that often reflects the built-in biases of the groups in which each of us was raised.

In choosing a mate, part of the problem is determining what each of us as an individual is seeking from marriage. Before it can be determined what makes a good marital choice, the question must be asked, good in terms of what goal? The ability to produce and raise healthy children? This seems to be the social goal implicit in most of the state laws restricting marital choice (for example, the prohibitions against the marriage of persons who are insane, mentally retarded, syphilitic, or suffering from various other diseases). Or is a good marital choice one that will make it possible to raise our children in a given religious or ethnic tradition, so that the group of which we feel ourselves a part may survive? Many religious and parental pressures are directed toward this goal. Or is a good marital choice one that will unite and solidify relationships between families who already share common social-class interests? Is a good marital choice one that will guarantee economic security for one or both partners? These used to be significant criteria when marriages were arranged. Or

is a good marital choice one that is likely to make the spouses happy, or
at least not end in divorce? It is easier to say that a particular marriage will
establish a family of a given ethnic, religious, class, or racial group than
that a particular marriage will make two persons happy; easier to determine whether or not the marriage ended in divorce than whether or not
it was fulfilling for either partner.

Marriage is the longest personal commitment that any of us makes.
Even with the high divorce rates, marriage is still a lifetime commitment
for a majority of Americans. For most people, marriage is a commitment
not only to a shared life with the spouse, but also to parenthood. When
choosing a husband or wife, we are also choosing the father or mother of
our children. The question of how to choose, and whether or not the
choice we are about to make is a good one, is of deep personal importance.

There have been a number of testing instruments devised to predict
marital happiness—or at least to predict which marriages are least likely
to end in divorce. Some of these have been used, in modified form, for
over thirty years, which means that such tests can be checked against the
failure rate of real marriages. The most famous of these is the predictive
instrument designed by Ernest Burgess and Leonard Cottrell, which was
first constructed in the 1930s (it was an outgrowth of Burgess's instrument
for predicting success in parole, which may or may not have any significance). But such predictive instruments do not seem to have much reliability. Goode observes that: "Successive studies have confirmed the
relevance of only a few items: for example, most show that if the couple's
parents' marriages were happy, if the couple have been acquainted for a
long time, and if the engagement was long, there is a greater chance for
marital success; but most other items are not confirmed by various re-
searches" (1962:509).

If there is a useful rule of marital choice that emerges from these
studies, it would seem to be to look for a spouse whose parents are happily
married (there is not much we can do about the marriage of our own
parents). And when we find such a person, to have a long and close
relationship before marrying. Most of us acquire our basic mental image
of what it means to be a husband and father, or a wife and mother, by
watching the day-to-day (and sometimes the blow-by-blow) interaction of
our parents. Someone whose parents are happily married is likely to have
been raised with functional role models; he or she has watched while
marital difficulties were resolved successfully, and expects to be able to do
at least as well. (We are all certain that we will be a better wife and mother,
or a better husband and father, than our own parents were, since most of
us fancy that we are more enlightened than our parents.)

It is not enough to *ask* a prospective mate whether or not his parents
or her parents are happily married: the question might be misinterpreted,
and, in any event, happiness is such a subjective category that the answer
might be given in very different terms than we intended the question.
Better to visit the family, as frequently as distance makes possible. To

275

observe someone interacting with his mother, or with her father, is as instructive as watching how that person's father and mother interact. It may seem old-fashioned to visit your lover's parents over a holiday, but there is no better place to learn what he or she is like at home.

It is less important to marry someone with whom you are in love than it is to marry someone with whom you feel comfortable, under a wide variety of situations. (This point was discussed at length in an earlier chapter.) Someone who has a sense of who he or she is, and wants to be, and is comfortable with this self-image, will be a more rewarding spouse than someone who is still trying to define himself. (There are some people over thirty who are still trying to decide what they want to be when they grow up.) Be sure that you can accept this person as he or she is, not hoping that he or she will grow out of some traits, or grow into others. It is certain that he or she will change (we all do), but not at all certain that a spouse can direct that change.

Avoid marrying someone who seems to need you desperately. It is flattering to be needed, and some of us want to be needed, or believe that we do. It is easy to believe that such deep need is great love. But desperate need indicates that, sooner or later, you will be smothered by a relationship with a possessive and jealous spouse.

For the rest, two people who share basic beliefs and values will have fewer conflicts than two people who have different values and beliefs. If religious beliefs are important to you, but not to the person you are thinking about marrying, explore how far apart your beliefs may be. If political activism is important to you, but not to the person you are thinking about marrying, explore that difference as well. Marriage is not a state of bliss, but a series of hard choices, and without some base of shared values and life goals, there will be no common ground on which to make those choices.

References

Baltzell, E. Digby. 1964. *The Protestant Establishment: Aristocracy and Caste in America.* New York: Random House.

Drinan, Robert F., S.J. 1969. "American Laws Regulating the Formation of the Marriage Contract." *Progress in Family Law: The Annals of the American Academy of Political and Social Science* 383 (May):48–57.

Farber, Bernard. 1964. *Family: Organization and Interaction.* San Francisco: Chandler Publishing Company.

Goode, William J. 1962. "Marital Satisfaction and Instability: A Cross-Cultural Class Analysis of Divorce Rates." *International Social Science Journal* 14 (no. 3): 507–526.

Landis, J. T. 1949. "Marriage of Mixed and Non-Mixed Religious Faiths." *American Sociological Review* 14 (June):401–407.

Levi-Strauss, Claude. 1957. "The Principle of Reciprocity." In *Sociological Theory,* edited by Lewis A. Coser and Bernard Rosenberg, pp. 84–94. New York: The Macmillan Company.

Lowrie, Samuel H. 1965. "Early Marriage: Premarital Pregnancy and Associated Factors." *Journal of Marriage and the Family* 27 (February):48–56.

Middleton, Russell. 1962. "A Deviant Case: Brother-Sister and Father-Daughter Marriage in Ancient Egypt." *American Sociological Review* 27 (October): 603–611.

Rodman, Hyman. 1965. "Mate Selection: Incest Taboos, Homogamy, and Mixed Marriage." In *Marriage, Family and Society: A Reader*, edited by Hyman Rodman, pp. 48–64. New York: Random House.

U.S. Bureau of the Census. 1972. *Census of Population: 1970 Marital Status*. Final Report PC(2)-4C. Washington, D.C.: U.S. Government Printing Office.

Vernon, Glenn M. 1960. "Bias in Professional Publications Concerning Inter-Faith Marriages." *Religious Education* 55 (July-August):261–264.

Women's Bureau, U.S. Department of Labor. 1976. *1975 Handbook on Women Workers*. Bulletin 297. Washington, D.C.: U.S. Government Printing Office.

Suggested readings

Marquand, John P. 1949. *Point of No Return.* Boston: Little, Brown and Company. Available in paper as a Bantam Book. The protagonist of this best-selling novel is a successful banker who has a marriage as secure as his career, but who remembers with wistful longing the girl he almost married in his youth. Business takes him back to the New England town where he was raised—on the right side of the tracks, but not in the highest stratum of a sharply stratified community. His lost love was the daughter of a family that was one of the oldest and proudest (although no longer the wealthiest) families in town. This novel utilizes the pattern of social stratification described in W. Lloyd Warner's landmark *Yankee City* studies. Courtship occurs across class lines, but marriage across class lines does not happen in this New England town.

Rodman, Hyman. 1965. "Mate Selection: Incest Taboos, Homogamy, and Mixed Marriages." In *Marriage, Family, and Society*, edited by Hyman Rodman. New York: Random House. Paper. Rodman's article summarizes a number of research studies of mixed marriages, primarily studies of interfaith marriages. The concept that social characteristics (such as social-class status, religious faith, etc.) function as "filtering factors" in mate selection is presented.

Starr, Joyce R., and Donald E. Carns. 1972. "Singles in the City." *Society* 9 (February):43–48. A report of a study based on interviews with never-married college graduates of both sexes, in their early or mid-twenties, who were employed in the Chicago area and living in Chicago's North Side singles community. Includes data regarding how often these young college graduates frequented singles bars and alternative situations in which they found dating partners.

10 The metamorphosis of a lover: marital roles and role images

The early months of marriage are usually characterized by a high degree of euphoria . . . when the whole of life is suffused with erotic pleasure . . . during this time of exploration . . . the habit systems of the two individuals must adjust to new situations arising out of the fact that they are now a dyad.

Willard Waller and Reuben Hill (1951)

Certain functions of marriage in our society are what Robert Merton (1967) has termed *manifest functions;* others fit Merton's definition of *latent functions.* Merton uses as an example the Hopi rain dance, nothing that whether or not this activity fulfills its manifest function of rainmaking seems doubtful, and in any event is a matter for the meteorologist to determine. However, he notes, the ceremonial does fulfill its latent functions, which are to build group solidarity by providing an occasion for the gathering of scattered members of the clan and to reinforce group identity in the process.

A wedding serves similar latent functions in our society. The manifest function of the wedding ceremony in American culture may be to initiate a lifetime romance for the young couple (an outcome that probably occurs less often than rain follows the Hopi rain dance.) But there are latent functions of the wedding. As in Merton's example, these include building group solidarity by providing an occasion for the gathering of scattered members of the clan and reinforcing group identity, particularly between the young couple and their families.

The wedding as a rite of passage

There is an additional and important latent function of the wedding and the events that lead up to it: the wedding is a rite of passage. Most primitive tribes have secrets that a child may not know until he has gone through a puberty initiation ceremony, or rite of passage. These secrets are the prerogatives of the adult members of the tribe, and until one has been granted adult status, he is kept in the ignorance of childhood. In primitive tribes such secrets usually involve religious mysteries. In our society, the secrets that adults try to keep from children are largely sexual, indicating where our society lays its emphasis. Moreover, most primitive tribes have both a puberty initiation and a marriage ceremony, but our soceity is poor in ritual. We have no puberty initiation ceremony (unless we count the examination for the first driver's license, with its tests and trials). So, except for some ethnic groups (such as the Jewish community with its bar mitzvah), the wedding has to do double duty. The married are admitted to the secrets of the tribe, including techniques of contraception. Considering the proportion of brides who are already pregnant, this is a little late to let them in on the secrets.

The wedding is our rite of passage from youth to adulthood. Marriage is regarded by the parental generation as the ultimate solution to the "youth problem," for it is assumed that when the young marry, they will "settle down." Streetcorner gangs break up as members marry; obstreperous students are transformed after marriage into management trainees making payments on the mortgage. The adult generation regards marriage as the means of channeling and controlling sexual behavior and procreation, and indirectly as a means of controlling other behavior as well. Romance is a central theme of the youth culture; responsibility is a dominant theme of the adult world. Reaching from romance to responsibility, marriage is the bridge that spans the generation gap.

It is the romantic involvement leading to marriage that draws the young out of the group scene of the youth culture. Lovers withdraw into a closed world for two. While the romance lasts, other people are at best a nuisance, at worst, rivals. Even friendships of long standing seem suddenly superfluous during the early, intense days of a romance. The two exist only for each other; even when they are not together they remain inaccessible to other people, withdrawn and dreamy. The peer group is likely to resent this; friends feel left out and may tease or apply subtle pressure to reduce the exclusiveness of the romantic couple. A male gang that seeks to retain its cohesiveness may relegate girls to a depersonalized fringe group used by the brotherhood for sexual purposes only; a communal living group may stress the value of keeping on intimate terms with everyone in the group and avoiding exclusive pair relationships. The interest of the youth culture may be in keeping young persons from forming exclusive relationships and withdrawing from the peer group; the interest of the larger society lies not in dividing the couple but rather in keeping the pair from withdrawing too far.

It is the pressure on the individual to conform to group expectations or face expulsion that is the fundamental basis of social control in every society. There could never be enough police, not even in a complete police state, to control the daily activities of all the citizens of a modern nation. A mass society is controlled in much the same way that a crowd is kept orderly, and that is by the continuous awareness of each individual that the significant others in this life are passing judgment on his actions. Every crowd is made up of many small groups: families or friends who came to the fair, the football game, the rock festival, the protest demonstration. A kind of informal order prevails as long as people stay in these small groups, for each person is being observed by people who matter to him.

The continued good opinion of the significant others in our lives is a strong motive for keeping our behavior within group expectations. But if someone yells "Fire!" or does anything that starts people milling or running—and thus separates each person from the people he knows and whose good opinion he values—the orderly crowd may become a rioting mob. If each person finds himself surrounded by strangers who form a surging mass that he must move with or be trampled under, if no one knows him, will remember him, or notice him, if everyone else is screaming, shoving, or looting, he is likely to scream, shove, or loot, too. His only alternative is to escape, which may be more difficult. Once the small group structure is shattered, control is gone. The only way to restore control and dispel panic is to make it possible for the mob to disperse; shortly people will find their friends and family, and the small groups that create and sustain social order will form again.

In a less spectacular way, the small, intimate groups formed by conjugal families are the basis of our social order in daily life. Other groups

281

(lineages, religious brotherhoods) have been the structural elements of past social orders; still other groups (perhaps generational groupings) may be the basic units of our society in the future. But since the founding of America, the conjugal family has been the basic structural element in our society. In contemporary America, marriage creates the thousands of small, relatively stable family units that are the foundation of our social order.

Conversely, the reason that deviant subcultures are so threatening to social order is precisely that they, too, contain structured groups with a deviant value system that they are able to enforce. The same kinds of group pressures can be applied to the individual by the deviant group as by the culturally approved group: conform to group norms or risk expulsion. Anyone who has already been expelled by the larger society, or who has chosen to drop out of it, is particularly vulnerable to the pressures applied by a deviant group, for he has no place left to go. The protection and acceptance that the deviant group offers may seem worth whatever demands it places on him. The means by which a given individual can be removed from a deviant subculture is to incorporate him into another group with norms closer to those of the larger society; this will be effective, however, only if he values the new group more than the old.

To some degree, the youth subculture is usually deviant—if not always in the extreme sense of the groups centered on drug use or political terrorism, at least in the sense that the distinctive youth culture is basically a leisure culture in a world in which adults must perform productive functions. There comes a point at which society hopes to draw the older youth out of the youth culture and into the adult community. The inclination of a man and woman to form an exclusive group of two is a natural lever that pries many young men and women out of the youth culture. Society thus has an interest in the pairing of its young, and it is not only that of procreating and rearing yet another generation.

From the viewpoint of the parental generation, the tendency of the romantic couple to create a world apart is functional in that it pulls the young out of the peer group; it is dysfunctional, however, if the couple remains isolated from society. The society needs to draw the young couple into the larger social structure, to make it a subunit of society.

Society copes with the romantic couple's withdrawal by pressures toward marriage. Marriage might seem to legitimize the closed world of the lovers, but *marriage is in reality the means by which the couple are tied back into the social structure.* Because a married couple (unlike lovers) expect to have children, the society assumes that marriage will shortly change the group of two to a group of three or more and will thus transform the withdrawn lovers into a conjugal family that will fit into the system of conjugal families that forms our social structure.

The wedding itself is a means of invading the private world of the lovers. It reestablishes links of reciprocal obligation between the bride and groom and their families and guests, who symbolize the entire community. Parents on both sides become involved in planning the wedding and all of the secondary rituals leading up to it, often to such an extent that the bride, and especially the bridegroom, may feel that they have lost all control over the event. The couple usually defer to the wishes of the bride's parents in making wedding plans, for her parents customarily pay the bills.

During the period immediately before the wedding the bride may be so busy with wedding preparations that she has little time to be alone with her future husband. The married friends who give her "showers" make her feel both grateful (that is, obligated to the family and friends present) and highly aware that she is joining the group of young matrons. Relatives she has not seen in years arrive from out of state for the ceremony, and she has a heightened sense of belonging to a kin group. The groom has a growing awareness of the assortment of relatives who now claim him as "one of the family." The traditional bachelor dinner is supposedly his last fling; it, too, underscores the fact that the wedding is a rite of passage.

If the wedding is a religious ceremony, the ritual itself and the less formal words of advice from the minister, priest, or rabbi emphasize the involvement of the entire religious community in the marriage of the couple. Philip Slater comments that "in many denominations it is explicitly stated that marriage is a contract involving three parties—husband, wife, and God, and that He is always 'present' so long as the marriage lasts. It would be difficult to find a more vivid symbol of the institutionalization of the dyad than this, nor a more clear illustration of the Durkheimian equation of God and society" (1963:354). (A *dyad* is what a sociologist calls a couple.)

The couple who elope escape the rituals by which their families and the community would tie them back into the social structure. This is the reason that elopement is always regarded with suspicion by family and community, even when it turns out that the bride was not pregnant. In fact, the prevailing assumption that the teenage bride who elopes is probably pregnant seems unwarranted. In his study of young marriages, Lee Burchinal found that "premaritally pregnant brides more frequently had conventional weddings than other brides" (1960:10).

Even more than the couple who elope, the pair who choose to live in a consensual union are frowned on because, not having asked permission from society to live together, they are more likely to withdraw into a private world. Slater comments that "marriage in our society resembles the ritual of the parent who discovers a child eating candy, and says 'I didn't hear you ask for that,' whereupon the child says, 'May I?' and the parent says, 'Yes, you may' " (1963:355).

The honeymoon is an interval of privacy, a respite from the intrusion of outsiders. But note that it is traditional for the bride and groom to try to keep their destination secret, and for the best man and ushers to decorate the "get-away" car to make it conspicuous. Custom makes it clear that the privacy granted the newly wed couple is temporary and grudged.

283

After the wedding trip is over, the pair are expected to reenter the society as full adult participants, with new roles and new group memberships.

Marital transformations: new roles for old

However the relationship was structured during the romance, the first weeks of marriage set patterns that can be altered only with difficulty. We are creatures of habit, however much we may talk about the joys of spontaneity and the freshness of change. The chair we chance to sit in when eating the first meal at the table in our new home is the chair we are likely to sit in for the second meal, and soon it is no longer merely a chair but has become "my place at the table." If someone else happens to sit there, we have an emotional response that is oddly strong—someone is sitting in *my place.* Wherever we happen to hang our toothbrush the first time we brush our teeth in a particular bathroom is the place where we expect to find it the next day; by the end of a week that is the place we expect to find it until the day we move. If someone straightens the cabinet and moves that toothbrush, we feel a vague sense of outrage.

In similar fashion, patterns of expectation and response are quickly established between people who live together; the first few months of marriage determine the broad outlines of the relationship. Never again will either be so open and flexible in relation to the other, or so motivated to learn new roles and alter old habits.

In sociological usage, a *role* is a pattern of behavior that members of a group expect from another group member. Some roles are the formal duties and perquisites that go with a given position or *status* in the group and are formally defined in its charter or bylaws. Other roles are informal, personal, and idiosyncratic: "Charlie is a real clown." No one assigns the role of clown to Charlie (unless he is a clown by profession). He adopts it in social situations because he finds it a rewarding role to play; friends value him because he is amusing, although they would never think of asking him for advice, for that would be out of character. That is, it would be inconsistent with his chosen role, which by now is an expected role.

Whether formal or informal, all roles are defined and elaborated within the context of some group. Marital roles have formal aspects, certain rights and responsibilities that are defined by the statutes of each state. The husband is responsible for supporting his wife, for example, and has the right to determine the place of residence. Few newly married couples are concerned with the formal, legal aspects of their marital roles, however. The period of marital adjustment is one of working out informal role expectations, of adjusting the role images each has of what it means to be a husband, what it means to be a wife.

The self-image is a group portrait. The focus is on the self, for inevitably each of us stands at the center of the world as we experience it. But although the images of the others are less sharply focused, they must be there. A woman cannot think of herself as a wife without having a mental image of *my husband;* if he were not there, she could not be a wife. Conversely, a man's image of himself as a husband implies a mental picture of *my wife,* and a set of expectations about what *my wife* will be and do.

Our basic role images are acquired in childhood, from the examples of husband and wife that we observe at close range: parents, aunts and uncles, the parents of friends. Inevitably, this means that the particular class, ethnic, and religious subcultures in which we were raised have formed the broad outline of the role images we carry into marriage, and the way our parents played their roles has filled in much of the detail. Within a given subculture, there are many common elements in the role of husband and the role of wife. Andy Capp (lower-class British husband) and Dagwood Bumstead (white-collar, middle-class American husband) are familiar figures, evoking a sense of recognition even across national boundaries (which is why they are funny). Mass media also contribute elements to our role images, and they may tend to make marital expectations somewhat more homogeneous. But there is still the probability that the newly wed couple will have some contradictory role expectations derived from differing role images.

Both the bride and the new husband enter marriage with a mental image of how marital roles ought to be played. A couple who share a common class, ethnic, or religious subculture will have roughly comparable expectations and will be able to stretch or to reshape their mental images to coincide with the other's idea of what a wife and husband should be. But a couple who come from grossly disparate backgrounds will have such a discrepancy in their understanding of marital roles that they will be caught up in continual, bewildering conflict. Imagine Andy Capp married to Blondie.

The couple may agree that part of the role of wife is being a good cook, but if her image is that of the gourmet cook who can prepare an exquisite French omelet, and his idea of a good cook is someone who can make dumplings like those his mother used to make and turn out a good pan of gravy, they are likely to experience what can only be considered culture shock. (She retreats to the locked security of the bathroom to sob, for she spent all day shopping and cooking "just for him" and feels unappreciated when he asks if that was all there was for dinner. In truth, her forays into the specialty shops in search of an imported copper omelet pan and her culinary adventures were quite as much for herself as for him, part of her exploration and enjoyment of a role she has long wanted to play. But because she assumed that he would share her expectations—and tastes—she was able to convince herself that she was laboring to please him, not recognizing the degree to which she was acting to please herself. He stands in front of the locked door listening to her cry, and wondering why she attaches so much importance to a few scrambled eggs.)

Gradually, a married couple come to know what to expect of each other, and there is less conflict because of divergent role expectations.

Role structures are built on basic values, however, and there may be some differences in role perception that reflect deeper differences between husband and wife. The matter of marital dominance, for example, may be more difficult to resolve than differences in tastes. In the past, there was no question about who should be the dominant member of the family. In the patriarchal societies that have characterized Western cultures, it has long been given that the status of husband carried with it the power of command. Dominance was attributed to the husband because he was male. He did not have to achieve supremacy in the relationship or demonstrate ability to lead or make decisions; he was the man of the house and that was enough to establish his supremacy. Like a hereditary noble, he might on occasion have to quell a minor uprising, but this was a matter of asserting his rightful authority. His belief (and his wife's) that it was proper, God-given authority gave weight to his claim. His belief (and hers) that it was improper, even sinful, for a wife to disobey her husband made it easier for him to maintain his dominant position.

The emancipation of American wives that began in the nineteenth century with bloomers and bicycles and the wife's right to own property in her own name has culminated in the relative freedom granted by economic independence and the Pill. This emancipation of women has eroded the *ascribed* foundations of male dominance. There remains a residual cultural belief in the natural superiority of men, however. Although the ideal of equality runs deep in America, the notion that the husband should be at least "first among equals" runs even deeper. A man who allows his wife to make most family decisions of consequence will be considered something less than a man by the neighbors, by himself, and by his wife. A wife who is docile and submissive will be considered "sweet." There is no feminine counterpart to the stereotype of the "henpecked husband." Thus a wife is often in the ambiguous position of testing her husband, perhaps wanting him to be the stronger (the latent role images she learned in childhood include that of the dominant husband), yet insisting that he demonstrate and not merely claim superiority. The husband is increasingly called on either to admit his wife to an equal partnership or to prove that he is stronger than his woman. Because most class subcultures (and the law) prohibit wife beating, a husband is expected to dominate by means other than physical force. If a power struggle becomes the focus of the relationship, the marriage may not survive.

Thus in the first months of marriage, the couple define and establish marital roles and patterns of marital interaction, from the basic structure of dominance or equality to the many small adaptations each makes to the other, so that patterns of expectation and response, of give and take, fit their lives together. Marital roles are played at many levels. Some roles are consciously learned, some are subliminal. The bride is aware of learning to cook to her husband's taste and manage the budget, but there are other, less obvious, behaviors to be learned by the newlyweds, such as how to share a bed.

286

Whatever premarital sexual experience the couple may have had, unless they have actually lived together they will have to learn to sleep comfortably in the same bed. The middle-class American child is raised sleeping alone. He does not sleep with his mother in infancy (as is common in many other cultures). He does not sleep with his siblings in childhood (as is common in American families who live in poverty). The middle-class American ideal is for each child to have his own room; if that is impossible, each shall at least have his own bed. A triple-deck bunk bed in a room shared by three brothers is marginally acceptable, but to put all three in one big bed would be to drop to lower-class living arrangements and would violate the touching taboo that is one of the deep-seated phobias of American middle-class culture. So the typical American boy grows up sleeping with a pile of stuffed animals and the family dog, but not with his brother. And certainly not with his sister. He has to learn to sleep with his wife.

The first several months of marriage are likely to be a period of pulling and tugging at the bedclothes and competing for space. But he will gradually learn not to sleep diagonally across the bed, and she will learn not to roll up in all the blankets. Each will reach the point of being able to sleep well only on "my side of the bed." Eventually, they will be able to roll over at the same time without rousing, and when they are separated for any reason—travel, illness, divorce, or death—the empty side of the bed will be one of the most poignant reminders of the absent husband or wife. The sense of loss will by no means be entirely sexual.

The bride's new identity: "what's in a name?"

The initial period of marriage involves more than accommodating to the presence and habits of another person. For those who are young, especially for the bride who lived with her parents until the day of the wedding, the first year of marriage is a period of socialization as an adult. A basic part of the socialization of a small child is the development of his self-image; in a parallel manner, marital socialization involves developing a new self-image.

The bride is aware of having become someone new, because she has a new name. Mrs. John Smith (née Elizabeth Jane Jones) has only a developmental connection with Liz Jones, who was derived in turn from a little girl with fat, dimpled knees called Betty Jane. She may have written "Mrs. John Smith" and "John and Liz Smith" over and over in the front of her history notebook to see how the names would look together, and whispered them under her breath to hear how they would sound, but the first time someone addresses her as "Mrs. Smith," she is likely to turn around to see if her husband's mother is standing behind her (that being the only Mrs. Smith she knows). By the time she is through writing "thank-you" notes for the wedding presents, she is accustomed to the name.

287

The new name and the new status it symbolizes are the core around which she builds her adult self-image. As Betty Jane in grade school and Liz Jones in high school and college, she was a daughter in her most stable primary-group relationship. But as Mrs. John Smith, she is first of all a wife. She is a daughter still, but that is secondary now; she will probably be a mother someday. Until then, being a wife is the central focus of her new identity.

For most girls, the years between the role of daughter-in-family and the role of wife are spent in the limbo of the youth culture. There is an abrupt break between the role of the single girl and the role of the housewife. It is the difference between "What shall I wear tonight?" and "Will the grocery money last all month?" It is the difference between mercurial involvement in the present and a life in which the present is the prologue to "some day." Waiting for the first of the month when there will be another pay envelope in her husband's hand; waiting for the promotion that will make it possible to buy a house; waiting out the months until the baby is born, the wife does things that are there to be done meanwhile. In the routine bleakness of today she finds it hard to believe that in a few years she will recall this ancient stove, this dark hallway, this narrow room, with a nostalgic sigh.

If a cramped and chilly apartment evokes warm memories, it is because of the tender moments and the funny incidents that she and her husband shared there. The first apartment is always a joy, for it is the physical space that encompasses the world of the newlyweds; the dank kitchen undergoes a transformation when the bride and her new husband begin to paint and put up curtains. If the husband's role is predominantly that of the provider of material goods, the wife's role is that of provider of emotional substance for the marriage: to create the mood of warmth and laughter that transforms three small rooms and a bath into a place with ambient magic.

Girls are raised to expect to play the role of wife; much of the play activity of a small girl involves what is known as anticipatory role behavior: playing at a role she assumes will be hers someday. If "playing house" foreshadows her future motherhood more than a future role as wife, it is in part because it is easier to find other little girls to take the roles of baby, little girl, and teenage daughter than it is to find small boys willing to play husband or father. Boys spend little time anticipating the role of husband, and a young man is often startled to find himself cast in that role.

It might help the new husband to make the transition to his new marital status if he, too, took a new name at the time of the wedding to symbolize his new status and role identity. Among the plains Indians in the old days, when a young man reached puberty he went alone into the wilderness and could not return until he had seen a vision. From that vision he took his adult name, and from that time forward he was no longer known by the name he had been called during childhood. It was a part of the rite of passage to manhood. If our customs included a change of name for both husband and wife at marriage, the wedding would be even more clearly a rite of passage for both.

Some married women are choosing to retain their maiden name, or *birth name,* to use the new term. Some couples are choosing to hyphenate their names at marriage. Perhaps it should be noted that taking the husband's name is a common law *right* of the wife, not a legal requirement in most states. Only the state of Hawaii has had a statute requiring a woman to adopt her husband's name as a family name. This law was replaced by a new statute, effective January 1, 1976, that permits a newly married couple to choose among the following alternatives: 1) both may take the husband's name; 2) both may take the wife's name; 3) both may take a hyphenated name composed of his name and her name, in either order. Further, the Hawaiian law permits either to elect any of the above choices regardless of the spouse's choice of name. The federal government of the United States will issue passports to married women in their birth name. However, many states do not permit married women to use their birth name either in voting or in obtaining a driver's license. Women who desire to use their birth name after marriage or couples who want to use a hyphenated name should obtain legal advice.

From young lover to responsible husband

A love affair and a marriage are distinct social situations. The indulgent lover who caters to his beloved's every whim may define his role quite differently once he has the status of husband. The role of husband is not merely a legally sanctioned version of the role of lover. The two roles are distinct, and one is not merely an extension or elaboration of the other. The change from lover to husband is a metamorphosis.

The role of lover is essentially one of playful, direct, and expressive behaviors. The things two lovers do together, whether playful or passionate, are intended to evoke pleasure here and now; there seems to have been no other time. Last week is remote and unreal to two people who became lovers yesterday; the future will take care of itself. In contrast, the role of husband has a large component of task-oriented behavior in which the future is an ever-present concern.

The married man is expected to provide for the present needs and the future well-being of his wife and children, a responsibility that usually ties him to a job. The role of husband assumes occupational stability; the man who drifts from job to job is seldom a "good provider," which is part of the role expectation of a husband in both the working class and the middle class. If a man's occupation is one that he feels pleased about, it will be both a means of achieving other goals and a source of direct satisfaction. If he *likes* being an engineer, a doctor, a museum curator, a trucker, or whatever he *does* and therefore *is,* the fact that his job makes it possible for him to support his family will seem almost a bonus. All this and a paycheck, too.

289

If, however, his occupation is one he chanced into, a job found after marking well-thumbed want ads, riding endless elevators to waiting rooms, undergoing interviews as a caterpillar suffers critical scrutiny by a small boy, he may feel trapped in a job he would not have chosen but for the necessity of paying the rent and buying food. The burden of supporting the household may seem heavy. The husband who feels that all *he* receives from his labors is an occasional symbolic cigar will become resentful, however much he may love his wife and children.

Many of the demands on him, however, such as taxes and payments into the retirement fund, have little or nothing to do with his role as a husband, but are derived from his parallel role as an adult male in our society. It is easy to confuse the two roles, because they are often acquired at the same time. But the fact that the two roles were acquired together does not mean that they can be shed together. When the weight of adult male responsibilities seems too heavy, it may appear that the answer is to leave the marriage. But although divorce may end the marriage, it does not return a man to the status of carefree adolescent. Divorce may remove him from the role of husband and alter his role as father, but child-support payments and the property settlement may actually increase his responsibilities as an adult male. The only way he can withdraw from these responsibilities is to abandon his status as an adult male and become a derelict: Skid Row and its drug world counterpart are peopled by men who have opted out of adult male roles.

The role of husband is complementary to other roles of the adult male in our society. If the occupational role is specialized, goal-oriented, and requires impersonal (that is, impartial) treatment of others, the role of husband is diffuse, people-oriented, and highly personal. The adult male in our society has a set of roles, most of which complement one another. His roles as husband and father are the counterpoise to his occupational role, and each set of behaviors enhance the others to some degree. Role conflicts do occur, and have been commented on at length by many critics of the contemporary social order. What is not always so apparent is the complementary nature of a man's occupational and familial roles.

As the role of husband is part of the usual cluster of adult male roles, so the role of lover fits well with membership in the youth culture. There is a period of withdrawal from the group during romance, but there is a strong probability that if the romance runs its course without leading to marriage the young man and woman will return to the group involvement of the youth culture. The basic values and life-style of the lover are compatible with those of the youth culture: present-time oriented and pleasure oriented, with little responsibility for others.

Some men make the transition to adult male roles before they marry (this used to be the prevailing pattern: a man "established" himself *before* he married). Some men who marry while still in their teens may fail to make the transition to either marital or adult role requirements. Some of those who do not make the transition in role behavior abandon the marriage. Others try to live as a married couple in the life-style of the youth culture. But for most young men, marriage is the point at which they expect to assume adult male roles.

The euphoria of the first months of marriage often makes the transition from youth to adult roles more inviting. But even so, marriage is often burdened with the difficulties of the transition from the youth culture to the adult world: this is truly a metamorphosis.

Emerging marital solidarity

In the early months of marriage, the emergence of group solidarity between husband and wife is essential. The sense of being a family cannot wait until there are children; parenthood adds many dimensions to a marriage, but it must build on the solidarity formed before the husband is also a father, the wife also a mother—before the dyad becomes a triad.

Other people who once claimed a man's loyalty—parents, brothers, friends—are expected to relinquish or at least to reduce their claims when he marries, for the primary solidarity of the husband is with his wife. The bride is expected to leave family and friends and go wherever her husband goes; her loyalty to her husband is expected to be so deep that the law no more compels her to testify against him than against herself. The primacy of the conjugal tie is not universal; there are societies in which a man's first loyalty is to his father, others in which a man's brother rather than his widow inherits his goods. But in our society the conjugal tie is considered deeper than the blood tie. Husband and wife are expected to be loyal first to each other and only secondly to parents, brothers, sisters, old friends. Part of the strain of marital adjustment is caused by the gradual severing of emotional ties to parents and former friends.

The "silver cord" that ties a son to his overly protective, covertly seductive mother is a frequent theme in literature and drama, but the more common pattern in real life is the married daughter who remains emotionally dependent on her mother. The bride who has lived with her parents until her wedding day and then moves away from her home town may become as homesick as the freshman girl pining for familiar faces in the college dormitory. The bride's identity may still be deeply rooted in her "family of orientation," the family in which she was raised. In the course of marital adjustment, she must transplant her identity to the "family of procreation" that she and her husband have formed.

Parents often urge greater independence on their son than on their daughter, encouraging him to take a paper route or a summer job, granting him greater freedom of friends and movement. The classic exchange between parent and child, "Where are you going?" "Out," may be accepted from a son, but seldom from a daughter. The same parents who try to make their son an independent person try to shield their daughter from the world beyond the family. The greater sheltering of the girl tends to create dependency on her parents, a dependency that may make it

291

difficult for her to develop into an independent adult, and that may also make it difficult for her to shift her primary loyalty to the family she will create with her husband.

Some daughters are subjected to such tight supervision (and an inquisition regarding their sexual behavior) that the result is rebellious flight, perhaps to the anonymity of the street world of Berkeley or to a canyon below Big Sur. Often, such a girl flees into marriage for the haven it offers from parental authority. Yet rebellion is often merely the inverse measure of the girl's emotional dependence on her parents. Once married, even these brides often remain closely identified with their parents and younger siblings. The wedding itself, or the announcement of pregnancy, is likely to be an occasion of reconciliation and renewed emotional bonds.

A young married couple whose origins are in the less affluent reaches of the working class may experience conflict arising from the wife's desire to give financial assistance or a haven to a younger brother or sister. The bride who worked before marriage and contributed a large part of her earnings to her family of orientation may feel a continued obligation to help her parents. She may feel emotionally torn when savings that have been intended for new furniture or the down payment on a home are requested as a "loan" by an ailing parent or by a sister wanting to go to college. The inner struggle may become a conflict with her husband. It will seem to be a fight over money but, underneath, it will be unresolved conflict between two competing loyalties. In the long run, unless there is some dire emergency in her family of orientation, American values give priority to the claims of her husband.

A newly married couple with more affluent parents and in-laws may have difficulty because of a flow of money from the opposite direction. If the parents of one (or both) are able and eager to "help the children," there may be a certain expectation that control still rests in the hand that holds the purse. Again, ambivalence felt by both the bride and her husband may become conflict between them. One may suppress uneasiness about the possible loss of independence and see the gift or loan as a generous gesture, a proof of love and acceptance; the other may insist that the money is a substitute umbilical cord, threatening their autonomy as a family unit. As in the former case, such a conflict only seems to be about money; it is in reality another struggle to establish the autonomy and solidarity of the conjugal unit.

Another group loyalty that may compete with marital solidarity is a tie to old friends. The recently married blue-collar worker may cling to the male clique to which he belonged as a single young man. If he is the first of his friends to marry, they will expect his continued loyalty and participation in group activities (drinking bouts and the like) where his wife would be out of place. His bride may find it hard to compete for her husband's time and attention, although the husband may not regard his behavior as in any way disloyal to his wife.

292

Mirra Komarovsky reports the complaint of one such bride that shortly after marriage her husband "started going out with his four buddies almost every evening just as if he was still single. Sometimes if he drank too much he would go to his mother's house to sleep it off and not even come home at all" (1967:30). This young husband ultimately severed his ties with his friends after his wife had a child and he found a steady job. The loyalty that once tied men in friendship is preempted by the marriage of any or all members of the group. Within the context of American culture, the husband is expected to recognize the primacy of the conjugal tie and to relegate friendship to a secondary place.

Particularly within the middle classes, many newly married couples resolve the problem of old loyalties impinging on the new conjugal solidarity by gradually replacing "your friends" and "my friends" with "our friends." The last are often new friends, other young married couples who happen to live nearby. From this point on, most married middle-class Americans participate in social activities with other married couples; single friends are vaguely threatening. Thus shift in the network of friendships is functionally a part of marital adjustment, for the group of married friends supports the norm of primary solidarity between the conjugal pair and adds to their sense of group identity by responding to them as a hyphenated identity ("John-and-Liz").

Marriage and the first person plural

Developing a sense of marital solidarity and learning to play marital roles are an interwoven process; learning to play a role and gradually identifying with the role lead to a sense of belonging to the group where the role is played. The special group of two formed by lovers is transformed by marriage into a new kind of group. As George Simmel pointed out, there is a sense that the marriage itself constitutes a third element in the relationship (1950 trans.: 129). *Our marriage* becomes an entity to be preserved in and for itself; there is a sense of the family as a superpersonal entity even before there are children.

Other groups of two—two friends, two lovers—do not have this quality; they contain one relationship only. The group of two is a special kind of group, as anyone who has ever been a best friend or a lover knows. The *group of two* has just one relationship within it: the one between *you* and *me*. If either one drops out, that one relationship is severed and the group falls apart. *I* am indispensable, and so are *you*. This usually means that each is willing to make allowances for the other, to extend himself to preserve the single relationship that holds the group together.

The *couple relationship* is at once fragile and resilient. Typically one person has more at stake than the other; the one who feels that he has fewer alternatives to the existing relationship will be willing to give more to preserve it. If *I* feel that our relationship is unique, that no one could replace *you*, then *I* am willing to make many more concessions than if it

293

seemed that numerous other persons could offer as rewarding a relationship as the one *we* have. If *I* find our relationship very special, then *I* must make certain that *you* feel the same. Your wish is thus likely to be my command. However, *you* must meet my needs, or *I* will soon begin to feel that this is not such a special relationship after all. There is a built-in reciprocity in the group of two: the wishes and needs of both members receive considerable attention, for unless both want the relationship to continue it will dissolve.

In any *group of three people*, there are always alternatives available. The *number of possible relationships within the group* has increased from one to three: the relationship between *you* and *me*, the one between *you* and *him*, and the one between *him* and *me*. Suddenly there is a triangle, and the very word suggests jealousy. *You* may dominate *him* and *me*; he may persuade *me* to join *him* in defying *you*; *you* may pressure *him* into betraying *me*; he and *I* may become rivals for your love and approval. The possibilities for intrigue in a group of three people is familiar to anyone who has ever tried to have two "best friends" at once in childhood.

Yet a group of three or more people has an essential quality that the couple relationship lacks: as soon as the group is larger than two, the group has an existence apart from any single member. One could be expelled—any one—and the group would still exist. This means that the possibility of expulsion can always be held over the head of each member. The group of three or more is in a position to outvote any individual member and to pressure him into accepting and acting on a group decision that he did not favor. If he cannot make his views prevail, his alternatives are to accept the group decision or to leave, voluntarily or by expulsion. The important sociological characteristic of groups of two is that they lack the sense of the group as a superpersonal entity that all groups of three have. In a group of three or more persons, the group is an entity that confronts each individual member. Groups of two do not have this possibility; there are only two individuals confronting each other.

But a married couple not only expect certain rewards and assume certain obligations toward each other; they also have expectations about what they will receive from and what they owe to *our marriage*. Part of the reason for this superpersonal nature of the marital relationship may be religious: the sense that God is also a party to the marriage. For those who are not particularly religious, there is still a sense that tradition is present, that *you* and *I* as individuals are reenacting roles that run back into the morning of time. Even though the way in which contemporary Americans define and play their marital roles is in fact quite different from the way in which our great-grandparents played marital roles, this sense of being the bearer of tradition is still commonly felt. The wedding ceremony reinforces it, and so do all of the rituals leading up to the wedding.

This is a primary reason why a couple who have lived together before marriage typically find that marriage alters their relationship. Two lovers living together share a world that is personal and remote because it is to some degree clandestine. That world is altered by marriage. The relationship is now socially sanctioned and the sense of permanence is added. For some people this is a welcome public recognition of their union, and a security they have not known before pervades the relationship. For others, marriage may be something they drifted into without quite knowing when they made the decision to marry, and once married, such persons may feel trapped. What was an adventure has become a fixed situation from which there is no easy exit.

To some degree, both feelings are likely to be present in everyone who marries. All who marry have been lovers who shared a voluntary relationship (whether or not it was consummated sexually), and now this is a permanent union that it would be difficult to leave. Being human, we are ambivalent about our relationships, and some sense of regret at having married is almost inevitably mingled with some sense of security created by the fact of marriage. But the mixture of feelings is not equal, and often one spouse is more aware of feeling secure and the other more conscious of feeling trapped.

This, too, is a critical point in marital adjustment. Both must come to feel more secure than trapped in the marriage, or it will disintegrate. The turning point comes when each begins to define himself or herself in terms of the conjugal role and the marriage from which it derives: to think *We* rather than *I*, and thus be unable to imagine himself or herself without the relationship to the other.

A woman is not a wife in abstract. To say that she is a wife implies that she is some man's wife and that the two form a conjugal unit. To think of herself as a wife she must think of herself within a group context. As the role of wife becomes an integral part of her self-image, so does the sense of group identity.

As a small child draws much of his awareness of self from his consciousness of belonging in a particular family and sharing all the things that *We* do and like and believe, so that bride derives much of her new identity from the awareness of having become cofounder of a new family and of developing new traditions with her husband. She may say, "At home, we used to . . ." but always in the past tense. And soon *home* is where her husband is, and her solidarity is with her husband.

Both the lover and the husband play roles in which there is a major focus on the collectivity. The lover is so oriented toward his beloved that he may neglect things he would normally do for himself: eating his breakfast, picking out two matching socks from the drawer. But whereas the lover concentrates on things he does *with* his beloved, the husband is often preoccupied with things which he does *for* his wife (and, later, his children as well) but in which she does not participate.

The lover becomes a husband who must turn much of his attention and energy outward, but as the representative of that private world to

295

which he returns at night. It is for the welfare of the family that he labors, the group that includes himself and his wife and ultimately their children, but that transcends the individual entities who constitute it. If he can avoid the psychic trap of surrendering his own identity, he will find in this group intimate association through which he can extend himself, discovering potentialities that no other situation evokes. His sense of *commitment*—not just to his wife but to the group, even when it contains only the two of them—is the basis for the stability of the marriage and often an anchor for his own self-image as well. In any society home is the one place, the family is the one group, a man will always defend. And he does not fight for a woman or a house or a child, but for that group identity that attaches to home, woman, and child but is more than their sum.

From love to empathy

The role of the lover is presumed to be one of intense commitment to the beloved. But as romantic affairs become more patterned, brief, and casual, each affair part of a series of romantic involvements, the role of lover becomes more universalistic. This is especially true for the man who has made the role of the playboy bachelor central to his self-image and has evolved a standardized set of seductive behaviors in which his partner is essentially interchangeable with any other who falls into the general category of "attractive female." If Farber's conceptual model of American mating behavior is apt, and "universal permanent availability" is becoming the norm (Farber 1964:109ff.), then the role of lover is becoming as universalistic and impersonal as the role of realtor.

Conjugal roles, in contrast, are still highly particularistic. The expectation is that the husband will respond to his wife in ways that he does not respond to any other woman, and that she will play a similarly unique role with him. It is the feeling that the relationship is special and unique that makes marriage rewarding; it is also this expectation that makes marriage vulnerable. We expect marriage to be a profound relationship, and if it does not develop depth and unique meaning it may seem a superficial and disappointing union. Simmel's penetrating analysis of this expectation of uniqueness is to the point:

> For only where there is a claim on the irreplaceable individuality of appearance or performance, does its failure to materialize produce a feeling of triviality. We have hardly paid sufficient attention to the way in which relationships of like content take on a different color, according to whether their members think that there are many, or only very few, similar ones. And it is by no means only erotic relations which attain a special, significant timbre, beyond their describable content and value, through the notion that an experience like theirs has never existed before . . . in dyadic relations—love, marriage, friendship—and in larger groupings . . . the tone of triviality frequently becomes desperate and fatal.   (Simmel 1950 trans.:125–126)

*The
metamorphosis of
a lover: marital
roles and role
images*

*It is the feeling that the relationship is unique that makes marriage rewarding; it
is also this expectation that makes marriage vulnerable. We expect marriage to be
a profound relationship, and if it does not develop unique meaning it may seem a
superficial and disappointing union. If a marriage is to avoid the pitfall of becoming
trivial, the relationship must pass beyond love to empathy.*

If either one of the spouses comes to regard the marital relationship
as trivial, and readily interchangeable with a variety of other relationships
(real or potential), the marriage is probably doomed. Any minor crisis can
shatter it. In contrast, the marital relationship that seems unique and
irreplaceable is strengthened by crisis.

If a marriage is to avoid the pitfall of becoming trivial, the relationship must pass beyond love to empathy. As indicated in an earlier chapter,
love is generated within the lover, and any of a large number of love
objects will serve equally well as a repository for this emotion. We can fall
into—and out of—love without ever perceiving the unique characteristics
of the other, the person we thought was the cause of our passionate
attraction. Love, in the usual meaning of romantic love in our culture,
requires a little distance, so that the aura of perfection that surrounds the
beloved may not be marred by some flaw in his or her person or character.
Love needs to be blind, or at least myopic.

Marriage is a setting in which it is difficult to sustain love, but possible to develop empathy. Empathy requires that we perceive the intimate
other as he or she really is, and develop the kind of acceptance for the
other's faults that we have for our own shortcomings, which we always
manage to view somewhat fondly. The lover is egocentric, pursuing his
own projected potential, which he hopes to find embodied in an angel of

297

the opposite sex. In contrast, the empathic husband or wife perceives the many facets of the spouse and finds each facet endearing. It is this final metamorphosis, from egocentric lover to empathic husband or wife, that saves a marriage from the danger of triviality, that makes the relationship unique.

Marital roles and role images: a summary

Almost all of us were raised in a family, and we carry into marriage latent role images fixed in our minds by the collective imprint of childhood memories. The way father treated mother, or uncles treated aunts, formed a montage of impressions of how husbands treat wives. Unless we examine carefully our expectations of marriage and of marital roles, we are likely to do one of two things: try to act out the role images we acquired in childhood—and expect our husband or wife to fit our preconceived images—or rebel and try to live in a mirror image of the roles our parents played. Either way, we will be caught up in behaviors that may not be appropriate to the relationship we would like to have with the person we married. The remaining alternative is to seek out more contemporary role images to replace those we formed from our childhood experience, and create our own variations on new themes.

In rural America and in the urban working-class family, the roles of husband and wife tend to be highly segregated. A sharp line is drawn between man's work and woman's work, as described in some detail in Chapter 1 of this book. In middle-class families of the city and suburb, marital roles are more often shared. Not every bride wants to share the financial burdens of her family; not every husband is willing to share in the domestic tasks of the household. But for those who seek greater equality between husband and wife, a shared-role marriage offers a liberating alternative.

In a shared-role marriage, husband and wife carry out some tasks together, some interchangeably, depending on which one has time and energy for the task at that moment. A shared-role marriage is one in which the husband shares in creating the ambient magic of home. This is no longer a world she creates for him, but a world they create together and give to each other: a fine and private place. In a shared-role marriage, the wife shares the responsibility and burden of providing financially for the family. This means not only that she relieves her husband of part of the heavy burden of support, but that she is removed from the childlike status of dependent, and her participation in the marriage—like his—is by choice, not out of economic necessity. As equally participating members of a shared existence, husband and wife create reciprocal roles. The image they form of "our marriage" is that of a unique relationship; such a marriage is unlikely to seem trivial or easily replaced.

*The
metamorphosis of
a lover: marital
roles and role
images*

References

Burchinal, Lee G. 1960. "Research on Young Marriage: Implications for Family Life Education." *Family Life Coordinator* 9 (September–December):6–21.

Farber, Bernard. 1964. *Family: Organization and Interaction.* San Francisco: Chandler Publishing Company.

Komarovsky, Mirra. 1967. *Blue-Collar Marriage.* New York: Random House.

Merton, Robert K. 1967. *On Theoretical Sociology.* New York: The Free Press.

Simmel, George. 1950. *The Sociology of Georg Simmel,* translated and edited by Kurt H. Wolff. New York: The Free Press.

Slater, Philip E. 1963. "On Social Regression." *American Sociological Review* 28 (June):339–364.

Waller, Willard, and Reuben Hill. 1951. *The Family: A Dynamic Interpretation.* New York: Holt, Rinehart and Winston.

Women's Bureau, U.S. Department of Labor. 1976. *1975 Handbook on Women Workers.* Bulletin 297. Washington, D.C.: U.S. Government Printing Office.

Suggested readings

Lindbergh, Anne Morrow. 1965. *Gift from the Sea.* New York: Pantheon Books, a division of Random House. Passages of this work describe the marital relationship with beauty and insight. See especially Lindbergh's description of the double sunrise sea shell as a metaphor for the marital relationship. In another passage she describes the oyster shell and the struggle of the oyster to cling to its place on the rock of the oyster bed, and sees in them analogies to the struggle of the married couple to achieve a place in the world, this common struggle forming a bond between the husband and wife.

Rossi, Alice S. 1968. "Transition to Parenthood." *Journal of Marriage and the Family* 30 (February):26–39. Although the central focus of this article is on the transition to parental roles, the analysis of role-cycle stages includes discussion of the transition to marital roles. Moreover, for those young couples who have their first child within the first year of marriage, the transition to parental roles may have a major impact on the developing marital relationship. Rossi points out that the conventional view of parenthood as a step in the maturation of the adult does not allow for negative outcomes of parenthood. She observes that many women who have been able to combine successfully the roles of wife and of worker find that the addition of the maternal role leads to fundamental and undesired changes in both prior sets of role relationships. Some other women who have been functioning with minimal adequacy as adults, and might have continued to do so if they had not become parents, suffer personality deterioration with pregnancy and child bearing.

11 Sex and the conjugal bed

When you came, you were like red wine and honey,
And the taste of you burnt my mouth with its sweetness.
Now you are like morning bread,
Smooth and pleasant.
I hardly taste you at all for I know your savour,
But I am completely nourished.

Amy Lowell, *A Decade*

One of the common—and mistaken—assumptions about human sexual behavior is that people instinctively know how to engage in the sex act. We are endowed with sexual impulses but not with innate patterns of sexual behavior: as children must learn how to walk, so adults must learn how to copulate. The honeymoon may be the most delightful period in a marriage, but for some couples it is a bitter disappointment. Perhaps at no other time is there so much expectation and so much anxiety in the sexual relation of a married couple.

Sexual communication and inhibition

Premarital intimacy may have prepared the couple for their honeymoon. Often, however, the circumstances under which any premarital sexual experience occurred may have been less than ideal. If the tradition is that all the world loves a lover, the reality is that there are few places where two lovers can find privacy for an extended interval of time. Unless the couple have in fact lived together, typically there has been no fine and private place for them to be undisturbed through long sexual idylls. The usual consequence is that such sexual encounters as they may have had before marriage were probably hurried and burdened with the fear of possible intrusion. Under such circumstances, the tendency is for foreplay to be prolonged but for actual coital connection (which is the more compromising situation) to be brief and male-oriented.

One of the delights of the honeymoon is the sense of unlimited time and privacy in which to enjoy the physical pleasures of marriage. But the husband may not be sure how to approach his bride to make the most of this new set of circumstances. Prior experience oriented to hasty orgasm may have set a pattern of brief coital connection that he may find difficult to alter. With the exception of the most Victorian fringes of the working class, or the most exploitive males of any class, most men want to please their brides sexually, at least on the honeymoon. But the typically male-oriented premarital experience may have left the new husband uncertain how to please a woman. And his bride typically expects him to know what to do and is reluctant to try to tell him what she would enjoy. If she comes from a class, ethnic, or religious background in which ignorance, as well as virginity, is expected of a bride, she may not know what would give her pleasure, and may be more ready to admit feeling pain than excitation.

Communication between the bride and her husband is imperative, but words are seldom a satisfactory medium. She may be reluctant to speak up and inarticulate about expressing sexual requests. She may have no words to describe a particular act or a specific genital area. This may be true even for those girls who have adopted a four-letter vocabulary more suited to a logger than a lady. Such words tend to be used to shock, rather than to communicate (that is the function of an obscenity). However effective she may have found such words for irritating parents, or even for

302

punctuating sentences, she may not find them useful in articulating her feelings about specific sexual behavior.

Nor would a precise vocabulary of Latinized anatomical terms be the solution. When two bodies are finely attuned to each other, words can only intrude into that more exquisite communication. Words pull the mind back from sensory to cognitive levels. Thinking is a barrier to feeling. Sexual interaction is a situation in which nonverbal communication, especially communication by touch, is infinitely more direct and unobtrusive. A hand placed lightly on the hand of the lover can communicate volumes, can guide and direct.

The anatomy of sex: the female

Lack of anatomical knowledge impedes more than verbal communication; a woman's external genitals are a mystery to most men, and even to some women. Ignorance of one's own body and misperception of the anatomy of the opposite sex are the sources of a great deal of sexual difficulty, and not only for newly wed couples. The external sexual organs of the female are referred to collectively as the *pudendum,* which is a word derived from Latin, meaning "that of which one ought to be ashamed." Nothing could indicate better why until very recently most women had so little knowledge of their own bodies. *Vulva* (from a Latin word meaning *covering*) is an alternative term for the external female genitals, regarded collectively, and this is the word that will be used in the following discussion.

The vulva includes the *mons veneris* (mount of Venus) which is also called the *mons pubis* (pubic mount). This is the pad of fatty tissue over the pubic bone. The mons veneris has nerve endings that are stimulated by weight or pressure. During puberty, hair covers the mons veneris, which is the most visible part of the female genitalia.

Also part of the vulva are the major and minor lips, the *labia majora* and the *labia minora.* The major lips are two long folds of skin that begin at the mons veneris and flatten out toward the anus, merging with other tissues. The major lips are covered with pubic hair on their outer surfaces, but the inner surfaces are hairless. The major lips vary widely from woman to woman, in some women almost concealed by thick pubic hair, in other women a prominent anatomical feature. Usually they are set close together and give the female genitals a closed appearance.

The minor lips (labia minora) are hairless folds of skin set inside the major lips and merging with them at the back. The skin of the minor lips is well endowed with blood vessels and nerve endings. The minor lips do not contain erectile tissue, but during sexual excitement they do change in form and color, becoming engorged with blood and flaring out.

The upper part of the minor lips forms a fold of skin over the *clitoris.* The clitoris is a small cylindrical structure that is the homologue of the penis, but not the analogue. Biologically, one organ is the homologue of

303

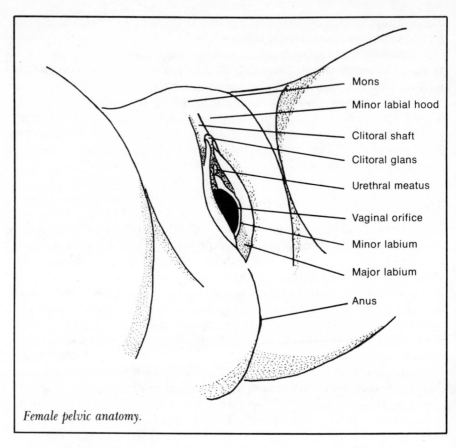

Mons
Minor labial hood
Clitoral shaft
Clitoral glans
Urethral meatus
Vaginal orifice
Minor labium
Major labium
Anus

Female pelvic anatomy.

another if the two organs evolved from the same or a corresponding organ. In contrast, one organ is the analogue of another if the two serve the same function. In the human fetus, the same type of tissue that becomes the penis of the male becomes the clitoris in a female. Thus one organ is the homologue of the other. But the two do not serve the same function. The clitoris has no function either in urination or impregnation, as does the penis. The clitoris is a center of sensory excitation, and has no function other than in sexual stimulation and orgasm.

The clitoris is normally about one inch or less in length, but when stimulated it enlarges to about twice its normal size, with much of the enlargement being in the diameter of the shaft. The clitoris is formed of two stalks that rise from the pubic bone and are fused to form the shaft. The shaft is covered by the upper folds of the minor lips, which form a hood over the clitoris. Only the *glans,* the bulbous tip, is exposed. The glans of the clitoris is abundantly supplied with nerve endings, and is the most sexually sensitive area of a woman's body.

304 Within the minor lips of the vaginal vestibule are both the vaginal and the urethral openings. The urethral orifice (opening) is above the vagina and below the clitoris. It is much smaller than the vaginal opening and cannot be confused with it. The urethral orifice is the urinary outlet, and is not connected in any way to the reproductive organs. The vaginal orifice lies within the minor lips, below the urethral orifice.

The *hymen* partially covers the vaginal orifice of a virgin. This particular membrane has probably been the object of more social myth and personal misery than any other single piece of bodily tissue. The hymen has no known physiological function, and may take one of several forms. It may form a ring around the vaginal orifice, but be perforated like a sieve. Or the hymen may form a bridge across the vaginal orifice, dividing it into two smaller openings. There has to be some opening, or normal menstruation would not be possible. (Depending on the type of hymen a woman has, she may be able to use sanitary tampons without tearing the hymen). Some women with a very flexible hymen are able to have intercourse without damaging that bit of membrane. On the other hand, a virgin may have a torn hymen because of some accident or as a result of strenuous physical activity. (The possibility of such an accident used to be an argument against the participation of young girls in active sports.)

Thus the state of the hymen is no certain indication of the virginity of the woman. Nor is the state of the hymen any longer a matter of life and death for a bride. However, there was once a time when the bride who was found not to have an intact hymen could be cast aside by her new husband, even publicly stoned to death. The ancient custom of hanging the blood-stained sheets of the bridal night (which indicated a torn hymen and thus a virginal bride) on the street wall of the house, or of parading them before the wedding guests, was never brought to America from the Mediterranean. But even here the condition of the bride's hymen has been a matter of concern.

Deflowering a virgin (tearing the hymen) has been a matter of almost mystical import in times past, often accompanied by some sort of public ritual, and the act still has emotional significance for many men. (It may well be that the old custom regarding the bloody sheets was as much homage to the demonstrated potency of the man as proof of the virginity of the bride.) Fear of the pain involved in the tearing of the hymen is often a source of anxiety on the part of the virginal bride. But Herant Katchadourian and Donald Lunde comment that "under ordinary circumstances it is an untraumatic event. In the heat of sexual excitement the woman feels minimal pain. Bleeding is generally also slight" (1975:35).

The internal sexual organs of the female include the ovaries, the Fallopian tubes, the uterus, and the vagina. The *ovaries* produce both hormones and ova (eggs). The ovaries are almond-shaped, small (about an inch to an inch and a half long), and are located vertically above the uterus and attached to it by ligaments. The ripened egg, or ovum, leaves the ovary by rupturing the ovarian wall, which ultimately becomes pocked and scarred in the process. The ripened ovum is attracted to the fringed

305

opening of the *Fallopian tube,* by some process yet to be understood. Once within the Fallopian tube, the ovum is moved by rhythmic contractions of the muscle wall of the tube, down toward the uterus. Conception normally occurs during this passage of several days, so it is the Fallopian tube that is the usual site of conception.

The Fallopian tubes (sometimes called the uterine tubes) enter the *uterus* at the top. The uterus, or womb, is a pear-shaped, muscular organ. The fertilized ovum, an embryo by the time it reaches the uterus, is implanted in the uterine lining and develops there during pregnancy. The smooth muscle fibers of the uterine wall have both unusual strength and elasticity, for they must be able to expand to many times their original size and still be strong enough to propel the child during childbirth, by means of powerful contractions.

The *cervix* is the mouth of the uterus, opening into the vagina and permitting the passage of sperm and also the passage of the child during childbirth. The cervix, like the uterus itself, must be able to expand many times its original size. The cervix has so few nerve endings that it is possible to cauterize it (to heal erosion caused by childbirth) without any anesthesia. (It is this paucity of nerve endings in the cervix, and in the vagina, that makes childbirth a comparatively painless process, unless anxiety has heightened tension.)

The *vagina* is a muscular tube, which William Masters and Virginia Johnson call a "potential, rather than an actual space" (1970:336), for the walls of the vagina are normally collapsed together. The muscle walls of the vagina have few nerve endings, but sexual stimulation produces a "sweating" effect of the inner lining of the vagina, which serves as a natural lubricant during intercourse. Although the vagina itself is not well endowed with nerves, and thus not highly sensitive, the ring of muscle at the vaginal opening is. This opening, the *introitus,* contains erectile tissue, which has a significant role in orgasm. The size of the vagina is another subject of speculation and myth. Katchadourian and Lunde observe that:

> Functionally, it is more meaningful to consider the introitus separately from the rest, for in many ways it differs from the remainder of the organ as much as the glans of the penis differs from its body.
>
> The vagina beyond the introitus is a soft and highly distensible organ. Although it looks like a flat tube, it actually functions more as a balloon. Thus there is, first of all, no such thing as a vagina that is permanently "too tight" or "too small." Properly stimulated, any adult vagina can, in principle, accommodate the largest penis. After all, no penis is as large as a normal infant's head, and even that passes through the vagina ... The introitus is another matter. First, it is highly sensitive. Both pain and pleasure are intensely felt there. Second, the arrangement of the erectile tissue of the bulb of the vestibule and, more important, the presence of the muscular ring of the bulbocavern around it make a great deal of difference in how relaxed or tight it will be. It must be emphasized that these muscles permit a significant degree of voluntary control over the size of the opening. A woman can relax or tighten the vaginal opening as she can relax or tighten the anal sphincter

... Furthermore, in common with all other muscles of the body, those around the introitus can be developed by exercise. Katchadourian and Lunde (1975:40)

The exercise mentioned above can be described simply by indicating that the same set of muscles are involved in controlling urination (although the vaginal orifice and the urethral orifice are distinct, the muscular control involves both). A woman can identify them by voluntarily interrupting urination several times. Having identified these muscles and their control, she can strengthen them by contracting and slowly relaxing the muscles (the slow relaxing is the more difficult at first) then repeating this exercise several times each day. (It is not an exercise that is in any way apparent to those around her, and so can be carried out while waiting for a traffic light to change, or while talking on the telephone, or waiting in any line.) Such exercise strengthens the muscles of the introitus (particularly important after childbirth) and improves voluntary control, both of which add immeasurably to sexual pleasure for both partners during intercourse.

This same set of muscles of the introitus may be subject to muscular spasms (known as vaginismus) in women who are anxious and fearful about sexual intercourse, and the spasms may be so intense that intercourse is impossible. This condition sometimes persists for months, even years, and therapy is required to alleviate it. (One couple who were ultimately divorced because vaginismus had prevented consummation of the marriage for over five years involved a Jewish wife and a Protestant husband. When the woman later remarried—this time, a Jewish husband—she had no trouble with vaginismus, which indicates the extreme role that psychological factors can play in intercourse. Endogamy may indeed be an internalized norm!)

The anatomy of sex: the male

The external male organs consist of the *penis* and the *scrotum*. The scrotum is a pouch of loose skin with two separate compartments, each of which contains one testicle and its spermatic cord. The testicles develop within the abdominal cavity of the male fetus (like the ovaries, to which they correspond). Just before birth, or shortly after, the testicles descend into the scrotum. This protected location outside of the abdominal cavity enables the testicles to remain at the lower temperatures necessary for the production of sperm.

The testicles have two major functions: the production of sperm and the production of such male hormones as testosterone. The hormones enter the blood stream directly, and need no ducts. The sperm are produced within a network of vessels in the testicle, and after about six weeks of maturation are transported through the ducts of the spermatic cord. The spermatic cord contains a pair of ducts. The first of these is the *epidiymis*, which is about twenty feet long, but so convoluted that it appears

307

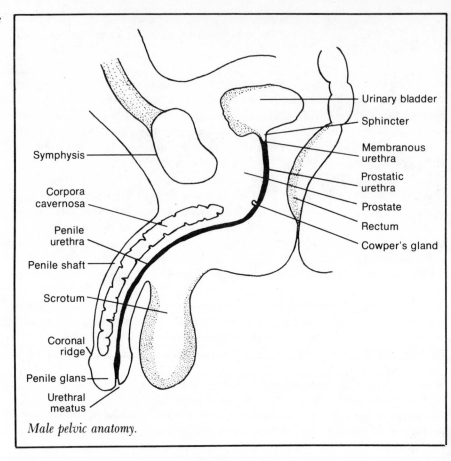

Symphysis

Corpora cavernosa

Penile urethra

Penile shaft

Scrotum

Coronal ridge

Penile glans

Urethral meatus

Urinary bladder

Sphincter

Membranous urethra

Prostatic urethra

Prostate

Rectum

Cowper's gland

Male pelvic anatomy.

to be about the size of the testicle. It forms a C-shaped tube above the testicle. The second duct, the *vas deferens,* carries the sperm from the scrotum into the abdominal cavity. (It is this duct that can be felt as a prominent cord in the scrotum. The vas deferens is cut in the operation called a vasectomy, which is the simple sterilization operation for men.) The vas deferens enters the abdominal cavity, passes behind the bladder, then narrows and joins the *seminal vesicle,* one of a pair of saclike structures located behind the bladder, near the prostate gland. Here, the vas deferens joins the duct of the seminal vesicle to form the *ejaculatory duct.* This runs through the prostate gland and into the urethra.

Although sperm are produced in the testicles, it is the prostate gland that produces most of the ejaculate. According to James McCary:

> That part of the prostatic secretion discharged at the time of ejaculation is a highly alkaline, thin, milky fluid that contains many substances including proteins, calcium, citric acid, cholesterol, and various enzymes and acids . . . The alkalinity of the secretion apparently serves to allow the sperm to move

through acid areas at a rapid pace, since, for example, acid in the vaginal fluid will easily destroy them if left in contact even for a short time. (McCary 1973:64)

Located slightly below the prostate gland are the Cowper's glands. These small glands (about the size of a pea) secrete an alkaline fluid during sexual excitation of the male, before ejaculation. The amount of fluid secreted is usually not sufficient to act as a coital lubricant, but this does not seem to be its major purpose. The alkaline fluid secreted by the Cowper's glands neutralizes the acidity of the urethra (which may have acidic residue left from urine that could kill sperm). Although this fluid is not part of the ejaculate, it may contain some sperm (one of the reasons why *coitus interruptus* is not a reliable contraceptive technique).

Below the Cowper's glands is the base of the penis. The *penis* is a cylindrical organ containing three parallel cylindrical bodies, two of which are cavernous; the third is spongy. The urethra runs from the bladder through the prostate to the spongy cylinder of the penis, and terminates at the tip of the glans in the urethral opening. In the male the urethra has a dual function, carrying both semen and urine. There is an internal sphincter, however, that inhibits the passage of urine during ejaculation.

Throughout the mass of the penis are large arteries that feed blood to the spongy tissue. During sexual excitation, the cavities and spaces fill with blood, and the penis becomes stiff and erect. There is also a network of veins in the penis, and erection is lost when the blood leaves the veins more rapidly that it is supplied by the arteries. The *glans* of the penis (the name is derived from the Latin for acorn, which describes the general shape of the glans) is the smooth, conical head of the penis and is the most sexually sensitive part of the male body. The corona, or ridge, at the back edge of the glans is particularly sensitive. The entire surface of the glans is covered with nerve endings, but the shaft of the penis (like the interior of the vagina) has relatively few nerve endings.

The penis is hairless, and the skin is loose, permitting expansion during erection. At birth, some of the skin of the penis is folded over part of the glans: this is the *foreskin*. Under the foreskin are glands that produce smegma, a cheesy substance that has no known function and that can cause sanitary problems. In most men, the foreskin can be readily pulled back. In a few it cannot, and circumcision is a medical necessity. Circumcision involves the surgical removal of the foreskin; it is a simple operation, and if performed under sanitary conditions, the wound heals quickly and leaves only the smallest scar. Most male infants born in American hospitals are circumcised a short time after birth. (Some research has indicated higher genital cancer rates in uncircumcised men—and in their wives, as well.)

During puberty, the male hormone testosterone makes the penis grow larger (as, during puberty, female hormones make a girl's breasts and vulva develop). Many adolescent boys are concerned about the size of

309

their penis, and for some men this continues to be a matter of concern. However, the size of the penis is unrelated to potency or fertility. When flaccid the penis is normally between 2.5 and 4.0 inches long and a little more than an inch in diameter. When tumescent (in the state of erection), the average penis is between 5.5 and 6.5 inches in length, and approximately 1.5 inches in diameter.

There is a persistent myth that the penis can become trapped in the vagina during copulation, as sometimes happens to dogs. Such tales are usually told as the true experience of a friend of a friend, but for human beings, this predicament is anatomically impossible (McCary 1973:68). Dogs, like other carnivores, have a bone in the penis, but the human penis has no bone. In its flaccid state it can be withdrawn from even the smallest vagina. The difficulty that human beings sometimes experience is the converse situation, in which *penetration* is difficult because of vaginismus in the woman, or some condition (such as a tendency to premature ejaculation) that makes it difficult for the man to maintain an erection.

Procreation: the process of conception

Certain bodily functions, such as the process of digestion, are basically similar in all higher animals, but the system of reproduction varies from species to species. Thus research on animal reproduction is of limited applicability to knowledge of human reproduction. Partly for this reason, and partly because of the cultural and religious pressures against research into human reproduction, the knowledge that we have of the process of conception in human beings is surprisingly recent. Gerald Oster, a research professor of obstetrics and gynecology at the Mount Sinai School of Medicine, says that "at the present time more is known of the reproductive functioning of the sow, for example, than of women" (1972:48).

In some animal species, for example, the dog, the female has a bloody vaginal discharge at the time of ovulation. For centuries this was confused with menstruation in the human female, an error that led to the mistaken notion that the time of greatest fertility in women was during the menstrual period. It was not until the early 1930s that K. Ogino and H. Knaus, who developed the rhythm method of birth control, established that women are fertile at the midpoint of the menstrual cycle. About five days after the onset of menstruation, the number of cells in the uterine lining, called the *endometrium,* begins to increase rapidly. In about two days the damage from menstruation is repaired, and by the time of ovulation the uterine lining will have thickened nearly fivefold. For the next two weeks the endometrium becomes increasingly convoluted and spongy, ready for the implantation of a fertilized egg. But if a fertilized egg is not implanted within approximately one week after ovulation, the endometrium breaks down in the process of menstruation.

What the physiological function of menstruation may be is still unclear. Oster says that the classic statement of C. W. Corner, written some

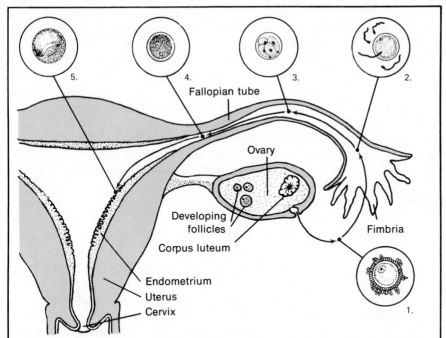

The egg discharged from an ovary on day 14 (1) awaits the arrival of sperm (2), which has passed up the Fallopian tube via the cervix and the uterus. The egg's actual size is about one-hundredth of an inch. The fertilized egg undergoes several cleavages without changing its size (3 and 4) and passes down the Fallopian tube. The blastocyst (5) is implanted in the uterine wall. The whole process, from ovulation to implantation, takes about one week. (Oster 1972:53)

thirty years ago, still applies today: "Menstruation, then, is still a paradox and a puzzle—a normal function that displays itself by destruction of tissues; a phenomenon, seemingly useless and even retrogressive, that exists only in the higher animals; an unexplained turmoil in the otherwise serenely coordinated process of uterine function" (cited in Oster 1972:-48). Oster adds, "Certainly menstruation is not a detoxification process, as was once commonly thought, due, perhaps, to the constant references to it in chapter 15 of Leviticus as being 'unclean'" (1972:48).

The process of human reproduction begins within the ovary, with the development of a follicle into an egg. Why one follicle rather than another develops is one of the unanswered questions, but the process is known to be stimulated by hormones secreted by the pituitary gland, at the base of the brain. At the appropriate time in mid-cycle, the ripened egg passes through the ovary wall and down the Fallopian tube, moved along by the beating of cilia (hairlike appendages) and by rhythmic, undulating contractions (*peristaltic action*) of the muscle wall of the tube itself. This is the most propitious time for fertilization.

311

Sperm move through the vagina and into the mouth of the uterus, the *cervix*. This movement is so rapid that some studies have shown sperm present in the cervix one minute after intercourse (the reason why a douche following intercourse is a futile contraceptive technique). Research has also shown that sperm reach the site of fertilization in the Fallopian tube within fifteen minutes after intercourse. This rapid movement is not due primarily to the ability of the sperm to propel themselves; in fact, test particles of carbon granules are propelled at the same speed as sperm through the female reproductive system (Oster 1972:52). It is the peristaltic action of the muscle wall of the female reproductive tract that is apparently responsible for the rapid movement of sperm.

Why one sperm and not another is accepted by the ripened egg is another of the unanswered questions. For whatever reason, only one sperm is accepted. The ovum has become a fertilized egg, a single cell that multiplies by cleavage into two cells, then four cells, and so on, in geometric progression. The fertilized egg is about one hundredth of an inch in diameter, and the first several cleavages occur without any increase in the overall size of the fertilized egg. After that, as cells multiply, the embryonic human being grows rapidly. The initial cleavages occur while the egg is moving down the Fallopian tubes toward the uterus. If it has developed sufficiently to be acceptable to the uterus, and if the endometrium is ready to receive the fertilized egg, the egg—at this stage of development known as a *blastocyst*—is implanted in the uterine wall. The process from ovulation to implantation of the blastocyst takes about one week.

The ovaries produce estrogens, hormones that stimulate the repair and development of the endometrium. The *corpus luteum*, a short-lived organ, develops in the ovary immediately after the release of a ripened egg. The corpus luteum produces progesterone, a hormone that is essential to the preparation of the uterus for the implantation of the fertilized egg. If implantation does occur, the estrogens and progesterone act together to maintain the implanted blastocyst. If no pregnancy occurs, the corpus luteum degenerates and forms a connective tissue scar. If no fertilized egg is implanted in the uterus, there is a sudden drop in hormone level followed by menstruation. And the cycle begins again.

Unless impregnation occurs, this cycle repeats about every twenty-eight days (although some women are on a cycle of different length, and some are on an irregular cycle). It continues for approximately thirty years of a woman's life, from the menarche (the onset of menstruation) to the menopause. The average age at the menarche seems to have dropped in most Western countries from approximately seventeen (which it was a century ago) to approximately thirteen today. The reasons are not clearly understood, although it has been suggested that diet may be a factor. At the same time, the average age for the onset of the menopause has been steadily rising, until today it occurs at about fifty years of age for most women. This lengthened period of fertility is of real significance to those who are concerned with the growth of populations: maximum fertility for a woman used to be between twenty and thirty children, it may now be between twenty-five and thirty-five children.

If conception occurs, it will be some weeks before the impregnated woman knows for sure that she has conceived. The most obvious symptom is that she will stop menstruating. But there are reasons other than pregnancy that may cause her to miss a menstrual period, ranging from physical illness to emotional trauma. The fear of pregnancy may be sufficient to delay menstruation. And even without any symptoms of illness or anxiety, women still in their teens and women over forty often miss a menstrual period for no obvious reason. A woman who is nursing her infant may not menstruate for five or six months after her child is born. The hormones that stimulate the mammary glands also inhibit menstruation, and sometimes ovulation. Nursing thus has a contraceptive effect (Jelliffe and Jelliffe 1975:558). However, the nursing woman cannot assume that because she is not menstruating she cannot conceive (she need not menstruate to be fertile; ovulation is all that is required). By the same token, the nursing mother cannot assume that because she is not menstruating she is pregnant again.

For all of these reasons, missing a menstrual period is not in itself a sure symptom of pregnancy. On the other hand, a woman who is pregnant may have some menstrual bleeding during the early months of pregnancy, which is of shorter duration than her normal period and smaller in quantity of flow. (This bleeding is technically not a menstrual period, but "spotting," which can sometimes be a warning sign of impending miscarriage, but may also be a normal occurrence, particularly if the woman has had children before.)

There are other early symptoms of pregnancy. The hormones that are activated by conception stimulate the mammary glands, and the woman becomes aware of tingling in her breasts and a feeling of fullness. Her breasts enlarge and become quite tender, with the nipples becoming particularly sensitive. (Oral contraceptives sometimes have similar side effects.) Also in early pregnancy, a woman has a sudden change in bladder function, finding that she needs to urinate more frequently. This is related to pressure on the bladder from the increased size of the uterus, and is a symptom that decreases later in pregnancy as the uterus rises in the abdomen. In the last weeks of pregnancy, the need to urinate more frequently returns, as once again there is pressure on the bladder.

A generally recognized symptom of early pregnancy is "morning sickness." The pregnant woman often has a queasy stomach on rising, is nauseated by the smell of food, and sometimes vomits. However, some pregnant women have these symptoms in the evening, and about one in four never experiences "morning sickness" at all. Sudden fatigue and an unreasonable need for sleep are for many women one of the most sudden and dramatic symptoms of pregnancy. The newly pregnant woman may experience sudden, overpowering drowsiness and drop off to sleep in the middle of a conversation.

313

Any one of these symptoms may have some cause other than pregnancy, but if a sexually active woman experiences two or more of them, the odds increase that they are symptoms of pregnancy. It will be about the sixth week of pregnancy (that is, about the time she is aware that she has missed a second menstrual period) before a physician can determine with any certainty that she is pregnant. "By this time certain changes in the cervix and uterus are apparent upon pelvic examination . . . Various laboratory tests may also be performed in the sixth week, and if properly administered, they are 95–98 percent accurate" (Katchadourian and Lunde 1975:124).

The response of the woman and her husband to pregnancy may vary from joy to panic. Given the reliability of oral contraception and the IUD (discussed at length in Chapter 4), there is less probability today than at any time in the past that an unplanned pregnancy will throw a marriage into turmoil. But people do not always respond to pregnancy and impending parenthood as they had expected. Pregnancy as an element in marital conflict will be discussed in the following chapter.

Pregnancy is the biological reason for the elaborate human reproductive system, but the advent of reliable contraception has meant that sexual relations can be separated from the reproductive process. The sexual relationship creates an emotional bond between husband and wife, and the capacity of each to arouse and to satisfy the other sexually is basic to a mutually satisfying marriage.

Sexual arousal

The capacity to respond to erotic stimulation is culturally conditioned, and reflects the individual's unique experience, but it is a capacity shared by all human beings. All of the senses—vision, hearing, smell, taste, and especially touch—are involved in sexual arousal. Certain objects are endowed by cultural tradition with erotic meaning: the cherry is a symbol of the virgin hymen in the West, the peach is a symbol of the testicles in the art of the East. But even the flesh in the garden of earthly delights is subject to cultural interpretation.

The sight of a beautiful woman, particularly if she is nude, is a universal erotic stimulus for men, but culture defines beauty. There have been times and places in which men considered women to be voluptuous who in other times and places would have been considered gross. Women have padded or starved themselves accordingly. A woman's hair is considered one of her major physical attractions: that is, the hair on her head. "Fain would I kiss my Julia's dainty leg, Which is as white and hairless as an egg," Herrick wrote in the seventeenth century. The erotic stimulus of a hairless female body seems to have persisted in Western culture to the present. Men are apparently more responsive to visual stimulation than women, but whether this is an innate or a culturally conditioned response is not clear.

The erotic effect of sound is learned and culturally conditioned. A soft, modulated voice can be sexually stimulating; a strident voice can cool ardor. Music can arouse human emotion as almost no other art form can, and music that has a rhythm to match the heartbeat is often an accompaniment to erotic dance. Certain perfumes are supposed to be sexually stimulating, although they may function more as a signal of sexual availability than as a direct erotic stimulus. The secretions of a healthy human body are potentially erotic if fresh, but stale body odors are repellent. The manufacturers of soap, deodorants, and toothpaste have grossed millions of dollars because of this, and their advertising has contributed to the distaste in American culture for all body odors.

The sense of taste is little developed among Americans as a means of erotic arousal, but the stimulation of the mouth, one of the most highly sensitive areas of the human body, involves taste as well as touch. Never has this been more beatifully described than in the Song of Solomon: "Thy lips, O my spouse, drop as the honeycomb: honey and milk are under thy tongue."

Erotic stimulation through vision, hearing, smell, and taste are learned, but touch is both conditioned and reflexive in its capacity to arouse the human body. Katchadourian and Lunde observe that:

> In man, though other modalities are also important, touch remains the predominant mode of erotic stimulation. It is, in fact, the only type of stimulation to which the body can respond reflexively and independently of higher psychic centers. Even a man who is unconscious or whose spinal cord is injured at a point that prevents impulses from reaching the brain (but leaves sexual coordinating centers in the lower spinal cord intact) can still have an erection when his genitals or inner thighs are caressed. Katchadourian and Lunde (1975:52)

Touching—and being touched—are subject to psychological as well as physiological response: the same touch may stimulate erotically or be experienced as a tickle (it is the potentially erotic nature of tickling that makes it an element of play and occasionally of torment). Some areas of the skin are particularly sensitive receptors of stimuli, because they are richly endowed with nerve endings; other areas of the body have comparatively few nerve endings. (For example, the fingertips and the palm of the hand are highly sensitive, the back of the hand less so. Most of the back is comparatively insensitive, for there are few nerve endings, but the buttocks are quite sensitive.)

The awareness of erogenous zones was established in American culture by the sex manuals of the 1920s, with their clusters of arrows pointing to various parts of the anatomy in drawings of fully clothed females. Although the form in which they were once presented is hilarious by today's standards of candor, the concept of erogenous zones is quite

315

valid. For the female, such zones include the clitoris, the minor lips of the vulva, and the vaginal orifice (introitus), but not the vagina itself. The breasts, especially the nipples (which are sensitive in *both* sexes), are another major erogenous zone. The mouth (both the lips and the interior of the mouth), the earlobes, buttocks, and inner thighs are sensitive in both men and women. The most highly sensitive area of a man's body is the glans penis (but not the shaft of the penis).

Other areas of the body that are highly endowed with nerve endings may also acquire erotic sensitivity through experience and association with pleasure. Such areas include the soles of the feet, the fingertips, and the palms of the hands. To kiss lightly a woman's fingertips and the palms of her hands as a prelude to making love may sound like a 1950s perfume commercial, but for some women it can be electrifying. The nape of the neck and the throat are particularly sensitive in some women. It is probably the case that more of a woman's body than a man's is sensitized to erotic stimulation, but it is also the case that there has traditionally been less attention paid by women than men to arousing their sexual partner.

It should also be noted that an area that is highly sensitive for one person may not be for another, and that the amount of pressure that is pleasurable to one person may be intensely painful to another. In general, a light touch is enjoyed most until the person is thoroughly aroused. Masters and Johnson found that lubrication—a simple hand lotion is quite adequate—makes most tactile stimulation more enjoyable, and they have used it successfully in working with couples who have come seeking clinical help for sexual inadequacy in marriage (Masters and Johnson 1970:79–82).

There are two basic bodily processes that underlie the physical response to sexual stimulation: *myotonia* and *vasocongestion*. Myotonia is an increase in muscle tension. From the normal "muscle tone," or firmness, that a person's body maintains, there is an increase in muscular tension in both the voluntary and involuntary muscles. Sexual excitement in both men and women involves increasing muscle tension, which builds until orgasmic release.

Vasocongestion is, as the word itself suggests, a collecting of blood in the blood vessels and certain tissues. As Katchadourian and Lunde describe the process:

> Ordinarily the flow of blood through the arteries into various organs is matched by the outflow through the veins, so that a fluctuating balance is maintained. Under various conditions blood flow into a region will exceed the capacity of the veins to drain the area, and vasocongestion will result .... Congested tissue, because of its excess blood content, becomes swollen, red, and warm. Sexual excitement is accompanied by widespread vasocongestion involving superficial and deep tissues. Its most dramatic manifestation is the erection of the penis. Erection has been called the "blushing of the penis." Katchadourian and Lunde (1975:68–69)

316

The most obvious sign of male sexual arousal is the erection of the penis. (It should be noted, however, that erection can occur under other than sexual circumstances, and that even infant males can have erections.) Erection in mature males under forty years of age typically occurs in about ten seconds from the onset of sexual arousal. There are other, less apparent, signs of sexual excitation in a man, including increased sensitivity (and often erection) of the nipples, general muscular tension (myotonia), and an increase in pulse rate and blood pressure. The scrotum undergoes vasocongestion, the smooth muscles of the scrotum contract, and the testicles are elevated.

The excitation of the male may be more obvious than that of the female, but the sexually aroused woman undergoes a number of physical changes, most of which are readily apparent. The woman's nipples become erect, although this can occur without sexual excitation. As McCary observes, the same effect can be produced by "cold water, cold baths, and removal of an excessively binding brassiere" (1973:198). The throat, breasts, and stomach of a sexually excited woman often become flushed. (This flush occurs with some women, some of the time, not with all women in all instances of sexual arousal.) Her pulse and blood pressure rise, the muscles of her entire body exhibit tension, and she moves restlessly and forcefully. In more specifically genital response, both the major and minor lips of the vulva become engorged through vasocongestion, and flare outward. The clitoris becomes tumescent (although this change is not visible in a majority of women until a later stage of sexual response). McCary points out that "direct manipulation of the clitoral region will produce more rapid and greater enlargement of the clitoral glans than will less direct stimulation (such as fantasy, breast manipulation, or sexual intercourse)" (1973:199).

The most certain sign that a woman is sexually aroused, however, is vaginal moistening. As a woman becomes sexually excited, a clear fluid begins to collect on the vaginal walls, which lubricates the vagina. This fluid is not secreted by a gland, but by the tissue of the vaginal wall itself, and may be an effect of vasocongestion. According to Masters and Johnson, "With the onset of any form of effective sexual stimulation, the first definitive physiological evidence of female responsivity is the production of vaginal lubrication. In the younger woman, lubrication is naturally evident within 15 to 30 seconds of initiation of the excitement phase of the sexual response cycle" (1970:336).

Coitus: variations on a theme

To describe in words any sequence of physical actions (a dance step or a tennis serve, for example) is almost inevitably to make what are simple and spontaneous movements (once the rudiments are mastered) seem complicated and mechanical. The difficulty is compounded when the actions

317

being described are sexual, and thus the words must carry the additional emotional freight of a culture that is still uncertain where to draw the line of good taste. The result often reads like instructions that come with a kit to be assembled: "Insert Tab A into Slot B." There is, nonetheless, a useful purpose to be served. As Balzac observed: "Marriage must continually vanquish a monster that devours everything: the monster of habit." One of the ways to combat the monster of habit is variety in coital positions.

Although sexual activity between two persons may involve various combinations of oral and genital contact, "*coitus* is heterosexual intercourse involving vaginal penetration by the penis" (Katchadourian and Lunde 1975:200). Some coital positions are more likely to result in pregnancy than others (conception is possible in any position, but knowing which positions enhance impregnation is useful to those couples who may have a problem with infertility or who simply want to accelerate a desired pregnancy). Some positions are more comfortable than others during pregnancy. Some require less strenuous activity than others, and may be preferable if either partner has been ill and has not recovered full strength or agility. And some are more stimulating than others to man, to woman, or to both.

For all the many variations on the coital theme that are enumerated in such classic erotic works as the *Kama Sutra*, there are essentially two anatomically possible approaches: either the couple are face to face, or the man is positioned behind the woman. The couple who are face to face may be standing, sitting, kneeling, lying down, or somewhere on a continuum between these planes. If they are lying down, the man may be in the superior position, the woman may be in the superior position, or they may be lying side by side. Similar variations are possible when the man is behind the woman.

There are some states that restrict by statute the positions that a married couple may legally take in intercourse. The U.S. Supreme Court ruling that laws prohibiting the sale and use of contraceptives violate the right to marital privacy, which the Court ruled was protected by both the Ninth and Fourteenth Amendments, may some day be applied to laws restricting marital sexuality. It is more likely that such laws, which are seldom enforced, will simply lapse into unenforced anachronisms.

The most common coital position among Americans, and the one that some states legally prescribe, involves lying down, face to face, with the man above. Kinsey found that about 70 percent of his male respondents indicated that they had never copulated in any other position. But this is by no means the only "natural" position, nor is it an instinctive one. There are cultures in which this is called the "missionary position," indicating that it was not common among these peoples until they came into contact with the manners and morals of the West. There are a number of variations on this position, largely in the placement of the woman's legs, which may be open, closed, locked around her husband's body, or pulled to her shoulders. Such variety is facilitated, along with the woman's comfort, if the man supports much of his weight on his elbows.

The fact that the man is in the superior position and the woman supine may have some psychological significance to one partner, or to both. But if the conjugal bed becomes a battleground for marital dominance, the sex will be less than satisfactory, however the battle goes. Psychological implications aside, this coital position has some advantages and some disadvantages. Among the advantages are that the woman is likely to be relaxed, which may be important if she is anxious or fearful about intercourse. Entry is easy, especially if the woman's knees are raised. Also, the woman can readily tighten the vaginal opening by closing her legs after entry, which increases the pressure on the base of the penis and may help her husband maintain an erection. This is a position conducive to impregnation, because the woman can raise her knees after her husband's ejaculation to retain semen, and penetration is deep.

The disadvantages of this common coital position are that the woman may be too restricted in her movements to achieve orgasm. Penetration may be too deep for her comfort (especially if she is pregnant). If her husband is heavier than average, she may be uncomfortable even if she is not pregnant. For the man, the very fact that this is an exciting position, one in which he does almost all the pelvic thrusting, may be a disadvantage in that he is likely to reach his climax too quickly, for either his own pleasure or that of his wife.

The face-to-face position with both partners lying on their sides is a comfortable one for both husband and wife. The woman crosses her upper leg over her husband to permit penetration, and there are then a number of minor variations of position possible. There is a great deal of freedom of movement for both husband and wife, and hands are free to caress. If the legs are in an interlocking position, there is stimulating contact between the man's body and the most sensitive areas of the woman's vulva, including the clitoris. This position is useful if either has been in ill health and has not fully recovered strength and stamina, for neither is under physical strain. Intercourse in this lateral position is likely to be prolonged, somewhat leisurely, and mutually rewarding. According to Masters and Johnson, the lateral coital position is reported to be "the most effective coital position available to man and woman, presuming there is an established marital-unit interest in mutual effectiveness of sexual performance" (1970:310).

The face-to-face position with the woman astride is the second most commonly used by Americans (a somewhat distant second, except among the college-educated). This position is depicted in murals dating from as early as 3200 B.C. (McCary 1973:180). The wife may be prone, the husband supine, or the wife may be in a sitting position with the husband supine. The husband may draw up his knees to support his seated wife's back. While the husband is supine, he need not be passive; his hands are free to caress his wife, and pelvic movement of the supine male is highly

319

effective in bringing his wife to orgasm. A Dutch physician, T. H. Van de Velde, states that coitus with the woman astride "affords the summit in excitement and response, the acme of specific physical sexual pleasure, to both man and woman" (cited in McCary 1973:184).

The advantages of this position are that the woman has freedom to express her sexuality and maximum control of movement and thus of her own orgasm. The most sensitive areas of her genitals—clitoris, major and minor lips, and the entire vaginal vestibule—are in contact with her husband's body, and the position is thus highly stimulating to her. Because the man is supine, his hands are free; he can be more relaxed and thus more free to indulge in erotic fantasy. Because he is somewhat more passive in this position, he may be able to sustain an erection longer. For these reasons, Masters and Johnson (1970:307) recommend this position, in one of its variations, to couples seeking to overcome problems of sexual inadequacy (especially when the wife has had difficulty in achieving orgasm, or the husband has a tendency to premature ejaculation, or both).

There are some disadvantages, primarily for the husband; these are largely a matter of cultural imprinting. As McCary notes: "The man's freedom of movement and pelvic thrust may be too restricted for his tastes, or the sacrifice of his 'male-superior' position may cause him to lose his erection, sexual drive, or even interest" (1973:184). Conversely, the woman may be psychologically uncomfortable about the more active sexual role she must take in this position. Finally, this is not a good position for impregnation, and is not comfortable in the later months of pregnancy.

A variation on the face-to-face positions is for the partner who is above to be kneeling. When the woman in the astride position is kneeling, she has maximum control of pelvic thrusts, and can use the strength of her thighs. This is a position that provides a high degree of stimulation to the woman and has the advantage, mentioned above, that the man's hands are free to caress his partner. The disadvantages are the same, although most of the male reluctance to take the more passive position is culturally induced, and not a matter of reduced physical stimulation to the man. This position was a favorite with the Romans of the Classical period, and is one of the most rewarding for the woman.

When the husband is in the kneeling position, it is preferable for him to kneel on the floor beside the bed, with his wife lying on the bed supine, feet placed on the floor, legs open. According to Katchadourian and Lunde, "The kneeling position is often recommended for a woman's first coitus. The superior control of the man, the angle of penetration, and the exposed position of the woman in combination are said to make the rupture of the hymen least painful for her and easier for him" (1975:301). This position gives the man excellent leverage and control. Because his weight is on his knees, rather than on his elbows or his partner, both husband and wife may find it more enjoyable than the "missionary position," although it retains the elements of masculine control and superior position that many men (and some women) prefer.

A less common variant of this position is one in which the husband is standing and his wife is lying back on a higher object than a bed, such as a table. This has the same basic advantages as the kneeling position, but bedroom furnishings may limit its usefulness.

When both partners are standing, penetration may be more difficult, but it is possible. The woman's legs may be closed, and her feet on the floor, or her legs may be open and locked around her husband's waist, while his hands are under her buttocks. (This last position, called "climbing the tree" by the ancients, places a considerable strain on the husband's back.) The advantage is largely a matter of variety. If both partners have their feet on the floor, it is adapted to the shower—making love while bathing together is a sensual luxury enjoyed by many couples. The disadvantages to the standing position are the potential back strain for the husband, especially if he is supporting his wife's weight, and the fact that in some of its variations, this position is limited by the physical strength and agility of both partners (it requires excellent balance).

A less athletic variation of the face-to-face position is to have the husband sit on a chair without arms or on the edge of the bed (the chair provides support for his back, which can be important). The woman sits on his lap, lowering herself onto his penis. If her feet are on the floor or if she is kneeling on the bed, she is in full control of her pelvic movements. If she places her feet on the bed behind him, and he puts his hands under her buttocks to provide support and control, the husband becomes as active as the wife in this coital position. This position has the advantages and disadvantages of the woman-astride positions described above. In addition, it has the advantage of variety, and may be possible in some situations where prone positions are difficult to assume (for example, it is one of the few positions possible in an automobile, as more than one generation of American youth has discovered).

All of the coital positions described to this point have been face to face. The other major approach is for the man to be behind the woman, a position that is less common in large part because it may seem too strongly to suggest the animal. This is an unfortunate cultural bias. Another objection has sometimes been lack of clitoral stimulation. Katchadourian and Lunde comment that "it was generally maintained until recently that the rear-entry approach bypassed the clitoris and left it unstimulated by the penis. Direct observations have now shown that the movements of the clitoral hood during coitus stimulate the clitoris, no matter what the direction of entry" (1975:301).

When the couple are lying side by side (preferably on their left sides), rear entry begins with a close snuggle that is possible in almost no other coital position. The man's hands are entirely free to caress his wife. Penetration is easier if the woman's upper leg is bent toward her chest (penetration is possible even if the man has only a partial erection). The husband assumes control of pelvic thrusting, but the wife is free to move as well, and the movement of her buttocks against her husband's thighs is highly stimulating to him. This coital position is one of the few that are

321

comfortable for a woman during pregnancy. There are no disadvantages for either partner in this position.

Rear entry in the sitting position is a variation in which the husband sits on the edge of the bed, or on a chair without arms, and pulls his wife into his lap; she should use her hands to guide herself down onto his penis. This position involves deep penetration, which is enjoyed by some women, but may be painful to others. Both partners have freedom of movement, particularly if both have their feet on the floor, a position that provides excellent leverage for pelvic thrusts. The man's hands are free to caress his wife, including manual manipulation of her genitals. The deep penetration in this sitting position makes it unsuitable for the later months of pregnancy, however.

There are numerous variations of the rear-entry approach, including kneeling positions, in which the man is astride his wife's buttocks. She may kneel beside the bed, with the bed supporting her torso and her husband kneeling behind her. Or she may be on hands and knees, with her head down ("knee-chest position"), a position in which penetration is easy for her husband, who is positioned behind and over her. This is an exhilarating position for some couples; others may object to its similarity to animal coitus.

The standing rear-entry approach permits easier penetration than the standing face-to-face coital position, provided that the woman bends forward. Variants of this standing position include one that is described in ancient erotic literature as "the wheelbarrow," in which the woman first assumes the knee-chest position, while her husband effects intromission from a standing position. Then, while her hands remain on the floor, he picks up her legs and proceeds with intercourse. This coital position gives almost all control to the man, and like the face-to-face standing positions, requires a certain agility, but it can be a stimulating variant, especially if that "monster of habit" Balzac warned about has overtaken the marriage.

During an episode of love making, husband and wife may begin in one position (often one that affords maximum stimulation of the wife) and then move to another (often concluding with one that affords maximum stimulation to the husband). As Katchadourian and Lunde observe:

> To speak of coital positions is thus misleading, for we are actually dealing with general approaches rather than specific postures. During face-to-face intercourse, for instance, a woman lying on her back will stretch her legs out, then pull them up halfway or bring her knees close to her chest for a while, then stretch them out again, and so on. Even when more marked shifts in posture occur, one position flows into another, and sexual activity never loses its fluid quality.   Katchadourian and Lunde (1975:298)

Finally, it might be noted that while older sex manuals tended to stress the importance of positions in which the woman's clitoris would be in continuous contact with her husband's penis, such concern is mis-

322

placed. Contact between the penis and the clitoris is rather awkward to achieve in coitus, and is not necessary for clitoral stimulation. The hood of the clitoris is formed by the upper part of the minor lips of the vaginal orifice, and the pelvic thrusts of coitus pull the hood of the clitoris rhythmically, furnishing quite adequate clitoral stimulation (Katchadourian and Lunde 1975:294). In some coital positions (especially rear-entry positions), the husband is able to stimulate his wife's clitoris manually. Most of the positions in which the woman is astride her partner provide maximum contact of the entire vulva with the male body, and thus stimulate not only the clitoris, but the major lips, the minor lips, and other highly sensitive tissues of the external female genitals.

Orgasm: climax and myth

"Ladies don't move" was the sexual dictum of the age of prudery, and no victorian lady was concerned about why she had not experienced an orgasm. She knew that sex was a man's pleasure and a wife's duty. By the 1920s, however, the educated women of the upper middle classes in America had heard of Freud, and learned about frigidity. Educated, upper-middle-class men began to measure their sexual performance in terms of the orgasmic pleasure they were able to give their wives.

A man who wanted to be able to think of himself as a sensitive, skillful lover tried to delay his own orgasm by thinking about something nonsensual (such as the office) and meanwhile watched his wife closely for signs of impending orgasm. She watched him watching her, and might finally fake orgasmic response to end the tension. The sexual relationship of many married couples became a pursuit of that elusive female orgasm, with feelings of sexual inadequacy compounded for both if an epochal orgasm continued to elude the wife, like the Blue Bird of Happiness (which, by the way, is a sexual allegory).

But female orgasm is not a physical state that can be turned on automatically if the man has rubbed the right genital nerve endings. The passivity of the woman that was instilled by prudery (and that still lingers in American sexual attitudes) inhibits female orgasm. The woman who learns to participate actively in coitus is not likely to be deprived of orgasmic response.

The time required for a woman to reach orgasm is somewhat longer than the time required by a man, but it is still surprisingly short. Katchadourian and Lunde note that:

> The average female, for example, takes somewhat less than four minutes to reach orgasm during masturbation, whereas the average male needs between two and four minutes. Some women may achieve climax, however, in as little as fifteen to thirty seconds. The disparity between the sexes in achieving coital orgasm is therefore related not to fundamental physiologi-

323

cal differences but to the mechanical and psychological components of sexual intercourse. (Katchadourian and Lunde (1975:58)

Sexual response, in both men and women, occurs as a cycle with four identifiable stages: excitement, plauteau, orgasm, and resolution (Masters and Johnson 1966:5). The excitation phase has been described above. The first and most apparent symptom of male sexual excitation is the erection of the penis. The man may move quickly to the plateau phase, or remain for some time in the excitement phase. If the excitation phase is protracted, "the varying firmness of erection reflects the waxing and waning of sexual excitement and desire. During this period a man is quite vulnerable to loss of erection. Even if sexual stimulation continues uninterrupted, distraction that alarms can cause partial or total detumescence" (Katchadourian and Lunde 1975:69). When a man enters the plateau phase, the corona (ridge) of the glans of the penis becomes further engorged, making the erection more stable. On occasion, vasocongestion turns the glans of the penis red.

Changes in the scrotum and the testicles during the excitement phase were described above. The scrotum responds to sexual excitement in a manner similar to its response to cold, fear, and anger: the scrotal skin contracts and thickens (in cold, fear, and anger, this seems to function to protect the vulnerable testicles). There are no further changes in the scrotum during the plateau or orgasmic phases of sexual response; in the resolution phase there is a rapid return to the normal thickness of the scrotal skin.

The testicles are subject to vasocongestion, and increase in size (typically by about half) during the excitement phase. The testicles are lifted within the scrotum during the excitement phase as the scrotum contracts and the spermatic cords shorten. The testicles are elevated further during the plateau phase, until they are pressed against the body. Orgasm does not occur until the testicles are fully elevated. During the resolution phase, the testicles return to their normal position and to their normal size.

During orgasm, there are rhythmic contractions that begin in the prostate and seminal ducts, but quickly move to the penis. These muscle spasms initially occur at intervals of about eight tenths of a second, then progressively become weaker and more irregular. Ejaculation, which accompanies these contractions, occurs in two stages. First, the prostate, the seminal vesicles, and the vas deferens empty their varying fluids, which together form semen, into the urethral bulb. The man is aware of this process, which he recognizes as the signal of impending ejaculation. (If he is practicing coitus interruptus as a means of birth control, he withdraws at this time.) The second stage is the actual ejaculation of semen, which may be propelled vigorously at first, then in slower spurts. Katchadourian and Lunde comment:

324

The amount of fluid and the force with which it is ejaculated are popularly associated with strength of desire, potency, fertility, and so on. These beliefs are difficult to substantiate, however. There is also a popular notion that semen is generated entirely by the testes, for during prolonged abstinence the testes may feel tense and full. This feeling, which may be uncomfortable, is relieved by ejaculation. Nevertheless, the contribution of the testes to semen is restricted to sperm and the minimal fluid that carries them. The pelvic sensation of fullness before orgasm results from vasocongestion and sustained muscular tensions. Women have similar experiences. Katchadourian and Lunde (1975:70–71)

For the adult male, the physical sensations of orgasm are linked to ejaculation: "First, there is a sense that ejaculation is imminent, or 'coming,' and that one can do nothing to stop it. Second, there is a distinct awareness of the contracting urethra, followed by fluid moving out under pressure" (Katchadourian and Lunde 1975:59). Although ejaculation occurs as a manifestation of orgasm, it is not entirely synonymous with orgasm in the male. As Katchadourian and Lunde differentiate the two processes:

Ejaculation and orgasm are two separate processes. Orgasm can be experienced by both sexes and probably at all ages. It consists of the neuromuscular discharge of accumulated sexual tensions. Ejaculation on the other hand is experienced only by males following puberty, when the prostate and accessory glands become functional. Females do not ejaculate. The fluid that lubricates the vagina is produced during arousal and does not correspond to the male semen. Katchadourian and Lunde (1975:59)

The physiological changes of the female genitals during the sexual response cycle are in many respects parallel to those of the male. During the excitement phase, both the glans and the shaft of the clitoris become tumescent. In the plateau phase, however, the entire clitoris (including the glans) retracts under the clitoral hood and almost disappears from sight; it does not emerge until excitement abates. If the plauteau phase is prolonged, the clitoris may retract and emerge several times, an occurrence that, as Katchadourian and Lunde point out, "may confuse the uninformed male who is attempting to stimulate his partner's clitoris" (1975:75). During orgasm, the clitoris is retracted under the clitoral hood, but it emerges within ten seconds after orgasm.

The response pattern of the labia of women who have borne a child differs somewhat from that of women who have not. During the excitement phase, the major lips of the woman who has not given birth become more flattened and thin, separating farther to expose the vaginal vestibule. Her major lips do not change further during the plateau phase or during orgasm. In the resolution phase, they decongest rather quickly and return to their former size and shape. The major lips of the woman who has given

325

birth are larger and more pendulous and become markedly engorged rather than flattened during sexual arousal. Although they do not flatten, they do expose the vaginal orifice. They do not change in the plateau or orgasmic phases, and may be slow to decongest during resolution.

The minor lips become markedly engorged whether or not the woman has given birth. The tumescent lips, which may be two or three times their normal size, project between the major lips. Vasocongestion also causes the vulval heat of sexual excitement. During the plateau phase, the minor lips become pink, then progressively brighter red. If the woman has given birth, the minor lips become a deeper, wine red. Masters and Johnson refer to the skin of the minor lips as the "sex skin" of the excited woman (1966:41). According to Katchadourian and Lunde: "Orgasm does not occur unless labial congestion first reaches this peak" (1975:76). During the resolution phase following orgasm, the minor lips lose their color as the blood that has caused tumescence recedes.

The first obvious symptom of the woman's sexual excitation, mentioned earlier, is the "sweating" of the vaginal walls that lubricates the vagina during intercourse. (This clear, slightly alkaline fluid may also help protect sperm from the normal acidity of the vagina.) A second vaginal change during the excitement phase is the expansion of the interior vaginal walls. Normally, these walls touch each other, like a collapsed balloon. With sexual excitation, the inner two thirds of the vagina expands, in what has been described as a "tenting effect." In the plateau phase, the outer third of the vagina becomes tumescent. It is this congested outer vaginal wall that forms the *orgasmic platform.* During orgasm, this orgasmic platform contracts, rapidly and rhythmically.

The uterus is subject to vasocongestion, and increases in size during the excitement phase, returning to normal size during the resolution phase. Myotonia occurs, the muscle tension lifting the uterus from its normal position and thus to the tenting effect within the vagina. During orgasm, there are contractions of the uterus, ranging from weak and sporadic to strong and intense.

The nature of female orgasm has been (and continues to be) a matter of debate. In 1933, Freud differentiated between *clitoral orgasm,* which he indicated was experienced by young girls (as a result of masturbation), and *vaginal orgasm,* which he considered possible only for a mature woman who had made a successful transfer of her dominant orgasmic zone from the clitoris to the vagina. In a strict Freudian interpretation, a woman is considered frigid if she is able to achieve a clitoral orgasm, but unable to reach orgasm vaginally (that is, if she is able to achieve orgasm after masturbation or clitoral stimulation by her sex partner, but unable to achieve orgasm through coitus).

Masters and Johnson found no such dichotomy in female orgasm, but reported only one type of orgasm experienced by the subjects in their

326

extensive research program. They reported that both clitoris and vagina responded identically, regardless of which one was stimulated. Although the "single orgasm" finding of Masters and Johnson has been accepted by many research scientists as definitive, there have been other physiologists—especially women—who have insisted that there is a qualitatively different orgasm that can occur only as the result of coitus.

I. Singer and J. Singer (1972) identified three types of orgasm in women: First, there is the *vulval orgasm*, which may be the effect of coitus or of stimulation of the clitoris only, and which is characterized by involuntary, rhythmic contractions of the orgasmic platform. According to the Singers, this is the type of orgasm that was observed by Masters and Johnson. Second, the Singers identify the *uterine orgasm*, which is induced only by coitus, and which involves involuntary contractions of the uterus. (Masters and Johnson also noted uterine contractions, but did not accord them the same significance.) The third type of orgasm defined by the Singers is the *blended orgasm*, which contains elements of both the first two types, thus involving muscle spasms of both the orgasmic platform and the uterus.

Two other physiologists, C. A. Fox and Beatrice Fox (1969), report orgasmic contractions in both the vagina and uterus immediately following the male's ejaculation. Other research has indicated that hormones present in a high concentration of semen (the prostaglandins) cause smooth muscles to contract. It is possible that semen may be a factor in uterine contractions of female orgasm, which may indicate why studies that involve mechanical devices rather than actual coitus have not produced uterine orgasm in female subjects. (It would also explain the long tradition that simultaneous orgasm is more intense.)

The resolution phase is significantly different in men and in women, in that the man, but not the woman, goes through a *refractory period* in which he is temporarily resistant to sexual stimulation. Nothing can arouse him sexually, and he may in fact have a negative reaction to what earlier was a positive sexual stimulus. During this phase, the penis loses erection, at first going quickly to a semierect state, then shrinking more gradually to its unstimulated normal state. (In an older man, the loss of erection occurs rapidly.) If the penis remains in the vagina, it tends to remain tumescent longer, but if the man withdraws, is distracted, and especially if he attempts to urinate, detumescence occurs rapidly. According to Katchadourian and Lunde: "A man actually cannot urinate with a fully erect penis because the internal urinary sphincter closes reflexively during full erection to prevent intermingling of urine and semen" (1975:71).

Women do not enter a refractory period during the resolution phase. They remain capable of repeating the cycle of sexual response, and may experience one or several more orgasms. This capacity of women to experience multiple orgasms is not shared by men, who at most are able to return to sexual excitation after the passage of an interval of time that may last from a few minutes to several hours.

327

To give is to receive: sexual reciprocity

Probably in no other form of human interaction is reciprocity as rewarding as in the sex act. To give pleasure is to receive stimulation, and this is true for both the woman and the man. Moreover, to be focused on the pleasure one is giving removes a common barrier to full sexual involvement: the barrier that arises from a sense of detachment, of being at once a spectator and a participant.

Pride in sexual performance is a strong element in a male's self-esteem, and fear of sexual failure is one of the deepest male fears. Men who are anxious about how well they are performing sexually are likely to become critical observers of their own performance. The result is a formidable barrier to their own pleasure and, in extreme cases, the very failure that they fear. As Masters and Johnson observe:

> Through their fears of performance (the fear of failing sexually), their emotional and mental involvement in the sexual activity they share with their partner is essentially nonexistent. The thought (an awareness of personally valued sexual stimuli) and the action are totally disassociated by reason of the individual's involuntary assumption of a spectator's role during active sexual participation.   (Masters and Johnson 1970:10–11)

Typically, young women have the erroneous notion that male potency is automatic. Never having thought about it, the wife is not prepared for the possibility of any sexual incapacity on her husband's part, and is likely to consider it a personal rejection if suddenly he is unable to develop or maintain an erection, or has ejaculatory failure. Her sense of rejection is likely to lead to a hostile response, which only adds to the anxiety he feels.

A woman may also develop a sense of being a spectator as well as a participant, which may not render her incapable of the sex act but which can inhibit the full flood of sensory stimulation. If she finds the sense of being a participant distasteful because of prior negative conditioning, she may become more the detached spectator; if she finds even the sense of being a spectator distasteful, she may avert her eyes and awareness from the sexual encounter altogether, and become focused on some extraneous detail of her surroundings. There is an old joke about this sort of wife: the wife who comments, "Honey, the ceiling needs painting."

Both husband and wife can dispel the illusion of being a detached spectator, and the sexual malfunction to which it often contributes, by keeping their attention focused on the pleasure they are giving their partner. To give of oneself sexually is to lose the hyperawareness of self that underlies performance anxiety and the spectator illusion. To put it simply, *I* can stop watching and criticizing *me* by becoming involved in giving pleasure to *you*. As Masters and Johnson describe the exchange:

In a natural cycle of sexual response there is input in any sexually involved individual from two sources. As an example, presume an interested husband approaching his receptive wife. There are two principal sources of his sexual excitation. The first is developed as the husband approaches his wife sexually, stimulating her to high levels of sexual tension. Her biophysical response to his stimulative approach (the pleasure factor), usually expressed by means of nonverbal communication, is highly exciting to the male partner. While pleasing his wife and noting the signs of her physical excitation (increased muscle tone, rapid breathing, flushed face, abundance of vaginal lubrication) he usually develops an erection and does so without any physical approach from his wife. In this situation he is giving of himself to his wife and getting a high level of sexual excitation from her in return.

The second source of male stimulation develops as the wife approaches her husband with direct physical contact. Regardless of the technique employed, his wife's direct approach to his body generally, and the pelvic area specifically, is sexually exciting and usually productive of an erection. When stimuli from both sources are combined by mutuality of sexual play, the natural effect is rapid elevation of sexual tension resulting in a full, demanding erection . . .

[A] man should never attempt to give pleasure to his wife with only the concept of receiving pleasurable stimuli from her in return. He must give of himself to his wife primarily for her pleasure, and then must allow himself to be lost in the warmth and depths of her response, and in so doing divest himself of his impersonal spectator's role. *In brief, if a man is to get the essence of a woman's sensual warmth, he must give of himself to her. This concept has been dubbed the "give-to-get" principle.*   (Masters and Johnson 1970:197–198)

Sexual intercourse is not done *to* someone or *for* someone; it is an act we engage in *with* someone.

The element of play in sex

The bed is often the reef on which a marriage breaks, whether the cause is sexual or whether sexual difficulties are only the symptoms of deeper conflict. Yet sex is also the means of making peace between husband and wife, the one way they can touch when angry words have blocked all other communication. People may think of sex as a goal. But sex may also be a powerful means to a variety of other interpersonal goals: the sex act may express love or aggression, fear or joy. For some, it may simply be a means of proving that they are still alive.

If the sexual relation between husband and wife becomes a means of acting out hostility or a dutiful act, sensuality is lost from marriage. The sexual relationship cannot be taken for granted, or it will become as routine as a commuter's schedule. Marital sexuality must be endlessly creative, without becoming contrived. No book of sexual technique can teach what is fundamentally a matter of empathy, communication, and shared passion. Concentrating on whether one is experiencing the appropriate sensations during intercourse can destroy sexual passion more effectively than a cold shower.

It is the element of play that makes sex a delight, that can remove it from the routine, or keep it from becoming a serious, even anxious, performance. Maintaining an atmosphere of play in sex (*foreplay* should be precisely that) also keeps the female role from becoming too aggressive. Much of what we consider "masculine" or "feminine" is cultural in origin, but there are some differences that seem to be inherent in the male or female of the species. Male sexual aggressiveness seems to be such a trait. Women sometimes equate being uninhibited with being aggressive; some women may be able to find a husband who enjoys being pursued by his wife, but the results are usually disappointing sexually, however much a man may enjoy the fantasy of being pursued by beautiful women.

The wife who consistently takes the sexual initiative may seem to her husband to be demanding that he perform his sexual function. Anyone who has ever commanded a person (or even a pet) to perform an action he was not in the mood to perform has encountered difficulty. And even though a child may be bullied into eating, drinking, or eliminating, even though a woman may be bullied into a sexual encounter that she is not eager for at the moment, no man can be bullied into an erection. The wife who is sexually demanding may find that her husband gradually loses both his ardor and his potency.

If the woman happens to be sexually interested at a time when her husband is not, a playful approach can avoid the appearance of sexual aggressiveness. If her husband does not want to play, this will be quickly apparent, and she can drop the matter gracefully with no one's ego bruised. Moreover, if the playfulness involves an invitation to male pursuit, she will have tapped a rich sexual vein. The excitement of pursuit—whatever the quarry—is a keenly felt male pleasure. Chase and capture, satyr and nymph: our fantasy lives abound with scenes that might have been depicted on the walls of a Roman villa. Playful sexual encounter and pursuit need not disappear after marriage if the wife can master the art of inviting, then retreating, without seeming to reject her husband's advances.

References

Fox, C. A., and Beatrice Fox. 1969. "Blood Pressure and Respiratory Patterns during Human Coitus." *Journal of Reproduction and Fertility* 19 (August):405–415.

Jelliffe, D. B., and E. F. P. Jelliffe. 1975. "Human Milk, Nutrition, and the World Resource Crisis." *Science* 188 (May 9):557–561.

Katchadourian, Herant A., and Donald T. Lunde. 1975. *Fundamentals of Human Sexuality*, 2nd ed. New York: Holt, Rinehart and Winston.

Masters, William H., and Virginia E. Johnson. 1966. *Human Sexual Response*. Boston: Little, Brown and Company.

_____. 1970. *Human Sexual Inadequacy.* Boston: Little, Brown and Company.

McCary, James Leslie. 1973. *Human Sexuality: Physiological, Psychological, and Sociological Factors,* 2nd ed. New York: Van Nostrand Reinhold Company.

Oster, Gerald. 1972. "Conception and Contraception." *Natural History* 81 (August-September):47–53

Singer, I., and J. Singer. 1972. "Types of Female Orgasm." *Journal of Sex Research* 8 (November):225–267.

Suggested readings

Hariton, E. Barbara. 1973. "The Sexual Fantasies of Women." *Psychology Today* 6 (March):39–44. Research involving 141 women subjects indicates that nearly two thirds of the women fantasized during intercourse with their husbands. The nature of these fantasies, and their normalcy, are the focus of this article. Illustrated.

Katchadourian, Herant A., M.D., and Donald T. Lunde, M.D. 1975. *Biological Aspects of Human Sexuality.* New York: Holt, Rinehart and Winston. Paper. Part of a more comprehensive work by the same authors, this book focuses on the anatomy of the sex organs, the physiology of sexual functions, sex hormones and the reproductive period, conception, pregnancy, childbirth, contraception, and sexual disorders. Illustrated.

Scarf, Maggie. 1972. "He and She: The Sex Hormones and Behavior." *The New York Times Magazine* (May 7):30, 101–107. A detailed discussion of the influence of male and female hormones on sexual drive, sexual preference, and aggressiveness in the individual. Research reported in scientific journals is described here in language for the nonscientist. Illustrated.

12 Marriage and money

Life is not a having and getting, but a being and a becoming.

Matthew Arnold

W e Americans are as ambivalent about money as we are about sex. We tend to regard money at once as the measure of all things, and as the root of all evil. The classic marital bargain of the age of prudery was a balance struck between money and sex: the wife was to render sexual services in return for financial support provided by the husband. A hundred years later, this bargain is still implicit in the marital roles that most of us expect to play and in the marriage contract as defined by law.

The ability to manage money is a skill that borders on being an art, but when resentment and marital conflict enter into the way we handle money, spending patterns are likely to become irrational. We may buy something we cannot afford as a peace offering, or buy something we cannot afford out of spite. We may spend to prove our love for someone, or try to buy someone's love with an extravagant gift. We may withhold money as a display of power, or out of pique. It is not surprising that money or, rather, the misuse of money is a catalyst in marital failure, although the money problems created in a troubled marriage do not go away with divorce.

The financial burden of the young husband, the management of family financial resources, including credit, the legal support obligations and property rights of spouses, all will be the concerns of the present chapter, which explores the relationship of money to marriage.

The financial burden of the young husband

A nineteen-year-old husband and father told me: "One thing I've been thinking about, made aware of, is that I have a family now and that I'm going to have to offer some means of support for them. And I don't mind shoveling fish, really, but it's just that there possibly might be some more interesting things to do."

Having a wife, and perhaps soon a child, places a heavy burden on a young husband. He must be concerned about keeping a job, and cautious about offending those who could deprive him of the means of supporting his family. He may feel constrained to modify his behavior and his appearance—from the length of his hair to the cut of his clothing and the color of his political views—to protect his livelihood and that of his family. The financial burden of marriage may thus be the catalyst for the process by which a dependent adolescent becomes an independent young adult.

But if marriage comes too soon, it may actually impede the transition to adult status and independence. Sometimes a teenage married couple, with the encouragement and even the financial assistance of their parents, try to adopt a life-style that they cannot afford, and for which they must pay too dearly. This is particularly likely to happen to those who marry while still in high school, when neither partner has yet emerged from the dependent subculture of youth.

How young is too young to marry is a relative matter. There are societies (the Indian cultures of Latin America, for example) in which brides of twelve are common, for a twelve-year-old girl is able to function adequately as a wife. (The fact that she is likely to live with, or close to, her mother or her mother-in-law means that she can turn to an older woman of her family for help when she needs it.) However, even in such societies, young men are normally expected to postpone marriage until they are able to perform a man's work, and have a plot of land large enough to support a family. This means that most men are past twenty years of age when they marry, and a decade's difference in the age of spouses is usual in these agricultural village settings.

In the United States, a man is also expected to postpone marriage until he has the means of supporting a wife and family in the manner that his class considers "decent." In the nineteenth and early twentieth centuries, this meant waiting to marry until the young man had established himself in a business or profession or on a farm that could support a family. A farm youth had to work as someone's hired hand until he acquired land. As long as the frontier was open, particularly during the years of the Homestead Act, land was not difficult to acquire if a man was willing and able to clear it and build some rudimentary shelter for his bride. In the town, an enterprising young man might be able to secure a position as office boy and clerk with an attorney, and "read for the law" with his employer. Americans who owned family businesses large enough to support more than one family often made it possible for a son to marry by offering him a partnership in his father's firm as a wedding gift. This practice enabled a young man to marry sooner than if he had to build a career outside the family business; it also gave his parents a strong voice in his choice of a bride.

But today there is no cheap land in the West, and few young men come from families that operate a business large enough to support two or three generations. This means that most young men must postpone marriage until they have completed their technical or professional education. Since World War II, there has been an alternative pattern widely accepted: the couple can marry if the *bride* has a job that will enable them to survive while the husband completes his education. This pattern requires that the couple postpone children until the wife no longer needs to be the major breadwinner.

The parents of either the husband or wife may be able to assist, but may not be able to do much more than let the young couple live with them. Or they may provide considerable financial assistance, with the understanding that it will cease when the husband has completed his education. But as William Goode notes, "the growing power of decision in the hands of young people and the relative instability of marriage mean that the elder generation is unwilling to make a substantial investment in the marriage" (1970:34).

Although there was a gradual decline in the age at first marriage among Americans from the late nineteenth century until approximately

335

1960, since then the age at first marriage has stabilized and begun to rise. The rising age at first marriage is in part a function of improved contraceptives, and in part reflects the fact that the age at which the young are able to enter the adult world of work is moving up steadily. The girl of sixteen or seventeen may be able to function as a housewife, and even as a mother, but the boy of the same age is unlikely to be able to find other than low-paid, dead-end jobs. Even a married man of eighteen or nineteen may find it difficult to get other than menial work, especially during a period of recession when the jobless rate for the young is several times that for older, experienced men. The nineteen-year-old husband and father quoted above (the one who recognized his responsibility, but hoped there might be something more interesting to do in life than shovel fish) described his experience as provider for his family as follows:

> We lived for about six months behind Jennie's folks. They had a little adobe house that her father built. And I worked in a cemetery. I would start the day—I had an eight-hour day—and I would set up sprinklers the first hour and I would turn them all on the first hour and then just keep walking around the premises changing them for eight hours. And occasionally I would dig a grave . . . I'm working for the fish company over on Washington Avenue now, shoveling fish. They bring the catch in about four o'clock in the morning and I go to work from about eight in the morning until noon. What I do actually is take it with a net out of bathtubs full of formaldehyde and fish and put it up on a table where ladies sort it and do other things with it and then I take trays and stack them in buggies and wheel the buggies around. It's used for bait—herring.

This young couple were divorced a short time after that interview; the financial struggle had been too much, and had overwhelmed them. The marriage had been precipitated by a teenage pregnancy, and the young divorced mother returned to live with her affluent parents, to take part once again in the activities of single young people, while her mother assumed most of the care of the baby.

The teenage married couple may cling to their marriage but abandon the life-style that their parents and in-laws expect. The youth culture accepts poverty as the price of independence. There are a growing number of young couples who have turned away from the acquisitive life-style and who take a certain pride in coping with the struggle for subsistence and a simple life.

Family financial planning

Most married couples have a strong desire to have a home of their own, whether a cramped city apartment or an old farmhouse. The pattern of American marriage from earliest colonial times has been one of *neolocality*,

336

which is the sociological term indicating that the newly married couple are expected to establish an independent household, rather than move into an extended household with the parental generation. Sometimes necessity compels a young married couple to live with his parents (perhaps more often with hers), but this is regarded as an expediency, which all concerned hope will be temporary. The expectation that the newly married couple will create an independent household is implicit in federal tax laws, as well as in the family law code of most states. According to the U.S. Bureau of the Census, 97.8 percent of American married couples maintain their own households.

For a majority of young married couples, the household created by marriage is their first independent household. The initial months of marriage are a time of nest building, when painting the old kitchen cabinets in a drab apartment some outrageous color becomes an act of mutual commitment. He and she are creating *our place,* and buying or making or scrounging furniture is pure adventure. This is the time, and it should come sooner rather than later, to work out the rudiments of financial management of the household. Having pooled their resources, they should manage their finances jointly. If one of them assumes total responsibility for earning money and paying the bills, the other is encouraged to continue living like a dependent child, with outstretched hand.

During the early weeks of marriage, while mutual habits (including habits of consumption) are being set, the couple need to sit down together and review their financial situation. The first step is to determine their combined net worth: that is, what they have, less what they may owe. First, the list of assets. Does either of them own a car? If so, what is its current market value? If each of them owns a car, they may want to consider whether they can afford the luxury of being a two-car family at this point in their married life. (Giving up an automobile, especially if it was your first, can be a little painful. The spouse who is not giving up his or her car needs to give dignity to the other's disappointment and sense of loss; the one who is parting with the car might remember that affection is more likely to be returned if it is bestowed on persons, rather than machines.)

What cash assets do either of them have in the bank? Does either of them have a life insurance policy? If so, what is its cash value? (The insurance company will know what the cash value—which differs from the face value—of the policy is at any given time.) What other negotiable assets do they have, such as rings, cameras, household furnishings, and so on? The total of their assets may not be much when they are first married, but it is probably more than they thought they had, and it is both useful and encouraging to know what assets their new family has.

The next step in establishing the family financial baseline is to compile a list of liabilities. What does either of them owe, to whom, as they enter marriage? Perhaps there is a student loan that must be repaid. Perhaps one of them is making payments on an automobile. Perhaps there is a loan from his parents or her parents; if it was a loan, rather than a gift,

337

it should be repaid as if it were a loan from a bank, or there will be lingering ill-will in the family that no one will be able to live with comfortably. The list of liabilities will not be long for most newly married couples, but debts incurred before marriage must be paid, and taking them into account is part of knowing where they are starting from financially at the time of their marriage.

The third step is to determine what their total family income will be during the first year of marriage. If both are working, their combined wages will constitute most of their annual family income, although they may also have some income from interest on savings accounts or dividends on stocks or mutual funds. Most young married couples have a modest income. The U.S. Bureau of the Census (1972) reports that at the time of the 1970 census, men (all races) between the ages of fourteen and twenty-four who were married, with the spouse present in the home, reported a mean annual income of $5,389 and a median (middle-case) annual income of $5,344. Some income was reported by 97 percent of all men in this age and marital category. About 65 percent of the women between the ages of fourteen and twenty-four who were married, with the spouse present in the home, reported income of their own. The mean annual income for this group of women was $2,747, and the median was somewhat lower, $2,527. Wages have risen since the last census, but so has unemployment. For illustrative purposes, the typical young married couple (both husband and wife under twenty-four years of age) can probably be considered to be one in which both husband and wife have income, with a combined annual family income between $7,500 and $8,000.

Having estimated what annual income they can anticipate in their first year of marriage, the couple need a plan to guide them in using their income to meet their mutual needs. How they spend their money can be as important as how much money they have to spend. The word *budget*, like the work *diet*, has negative overtones of constraint and denial for most of us. This is underscored by firms that advertise products "for families on a budget." *All* families should be on a budget; that is sound fiscal planning. A budget is simply a plan to manage family financial resources, and agreement between husband and wife on the priorities of spending is an essential foundation for a successful marriage.

Planning is easier when it is based on past experience; it is difficult for the newly married couple to develop an initial estimate of what they will need in various categories of consumption. Living costs vary by region, by rural or urban location, by such factors as distance between home and place of work, by the life-style expected of persons with a particular social class or ethnic background. However, a general guide for a young couple's initial budget can be drawn from the cost-of-living estimates of the U.S. Bureau of Labor Statistics. At periodic intervals, the U.S. Bureau of Labor Statistics calculates what it considers the necessary expenditure for a nonfarm family of four to live at lower, intermediate, and higher levels. (The lower level of living is an adequate but minimal living standard; below that would be a substandard level of living, with less than adequate diet, housing, clothing, and so forth). These budgets are expressed in dollar amounts, as a measure of the cost of living at a particular time. For present purposes, a more useful and less dated planning tool can be derived by expressing these dollar amounts as percentages.

The total family budget required at the lower level of living in the 1974 edition of the *Handbook of Labor Statistics* was $7,386. This is close to the annual income for young married couples estimated above from the U.S. Bureau of Census figures. For families at this level of living, the annual consumption budget is distributed by the U.S. Bureau of Labor Statistics (1974:Table 147) as follows (percentages are shown as well as the dollar amounts that appear in the *Handbook*):

Annual Consumption Budget: Lower Level of Living

$2058 (27.9%) Food
 1205 (16.3%) Renter costs
  349 (04.7%) Household furnishings and operation
  546 (07.4%) Transportation
  669 (09.1%) Clothing
  195 (02.6%) Personal care
  629 (08.5%) Medical care
  378 (05.1%) Other family consumption
$6029 (81.6%) Total family consumption
 1357 (18.4%) Other costs
$7386 (100%) Total family budget

The "other costs" that are shown separately from the family consumption budget include personal income taxes, Social Security and disability payments, life insurance, gifts and contributions. Most of these "other costs" are deducted from wages by employers. (The law requires that federal, and sometimes state, income taxes and Social Security payments be deducted; life insurance may be deducted if the employee belongs to a group plan where he or she works; many employers also make arrangements to deduct United Fund or Community Chest contributions.) This means that most "take-home" pay is available for the family consumption budget.

Recognizing that every family has its own unique patterns of living and consuming, the newly married couple can use the above percentages as guidelines for constructing their initial annual family consumption budget. Since the U.S. Bureau of Labor Statistics was assuming a family of four, the newly married couple will be able to adjust some percentages to their smaller family size, probably reducing the percentage of the budget that is allocated for food, and perhaps adding to the household furnishings category, or to the "other family consumption" category, which includes items such as education and recreation, likely to be major expenditures for a young married couple.

339

Preparing the annual budget requires identifying both those expenses that occur monthly and those that occur only once or twice each year (insurance premiums, tuition, automobile registration fees, and so on). The expenses that occur only sporadically are of two kinds: those that are predictable (for example, insurance premiums) and those that are unknown but likely to occur and for which some emergency reserve is needed (major automobile repairs or medical expenses, for instance). Such expenses should be estimated on an annual basis, and included in the appropriate category of consumption.

To take the "household furnishings and operation" category as an example, the subcategories in the annual budget would probably include the following: (1) a monthly expenditure for any utilities not included in the rent (such as the telephone); (2) a monthly amount budgeted for expendable household items (such as soap, toilet paper, small utensils); (3) semiannual payment of premiums for fire and theft insurance on clothing, furnishings, and personal belongings (even a newly married couple should have insurance protection for their belongings, regarding it as a reserve for disasters they could not afford to cover from their own savings); (4) an amount, however small, to acquire more durable household furnishings. This last amount can be a monthly allotment to be used for bargain hunting in thrift stores, or a monthly payment on some item purchased on the installment plan, or it can be an amount put into a savings account toward the future purchase of some major item of household furnishing.

After the annual budget is constructed, each category is divided by twelve to create the monthly budget. The monthly budget will contain some dollars allocated for monthly expenses and some dollars that represent that month's share of annual expenses and reserves. The money intended for annual expenses and emergency reserves should be put into a savings account on the first of the month, or the money will disappear, budget or no. Some savings institutions encourage their clients to open several accounts: one for vacations, one for the new automobile you are saving to buy, one for Christmas gifts, and so on. This can be a useful way of managing savings. No omnibus item marked simply "savings" has been proposed for the family budget, because most of us are more likely to save if we are saving *for something*.

Once the budget is established, the next essential step is to start a system of record keeping. Every office supply store has ledgers for keeping track of household expenses. Look for one that meets your particular needs, and then bring it up to date with regularity the first of each month. Have some system for filing receipts and other records of financial transactions. (An expanding file is an inexpensive way of keeping receipts sorted by category of expenditure.) These records and receipts are proof you paid a bill; they are useful for determining how your budget is working; they are essential for tax purposes.

340

It is not necessary for either husband or wife to be an accountant, although a course in bookkeeping could well be a high school graduation requirement. One young couple, married while both were still in their teens, was about to succumb to financial difficulty, neither of them seemingly able to balance a checkbook or plan beyond the end of the week, or resist spending whatever was in his pocket or her purse. But a marriage counselor was able to help them learn to manage their family finances by what may seem a childishly simple process. Having worked out a budget with the marriage counselor, the couple sat down together on the first of the month (payday) and put their money, in cash, into envelopes labeled *Food, Rent, Transportation,* and so forth.

During the month, they took money out of the rent envelope, paid the landlord, and put the receipt into the envelope. They took money out of the food envelope when they went to the grocery store, and put any change back into the envelope instead of into their pockets. During the month, if they ran out of money in one envelope, they had to borrow from another, but they put into the envelope a slip that said something like "the food kitty owes the clothing kitty $10."

This simplistic arrangement worked. They were highly conscious of using their money for the planned purpose, and impulse spending stopped. When spending in a particular category was too much for their limited resources, that fact was apparent from the empty envelope at mid-month. They had to decide, and quickly, how to reduce the expense of that particular category. (The most painful decision was selling their car and using public transportation and a bicycle for a year or two.) Over a period of time, they learned to adjust both expenditures and the distribution of funds. The process meant that instead of quarreling with each other about where their money had gone, at the first of each month they decided together where it ought to go. They were vulnerable to theft, but were fortunate in living in an area where theft was not a major problem. After a year or so, both of them learned to balance a checkbook, and their patterns of spending, consuming, and joint financial planning were well set.

Most married couples will find it more satisfactory to pay bills by check than in cash and to plan their budget on paper instead of by putting dollar bills into envelopes. But however they do it, a couple need to learn to manage resources well, in a manner they have planned together, with mutual agreement on priorities. It gives a couple a sense of unity, and of having control over their lives. It is part of the security they find with each other.

At the end of the first year of marriage, or at some other transition point, a couple should sit down together and prepare a new "net worth" statement and review the past year's expenditures. Perhaps this is best done at the beginning of the calendar year: marking the New Year by taking stock of their joint lives and fortunes. This is also a useful time to compile income and expenses for income tax returns, and one balancing of the family accounts can serve both purposes. Husband and wife should

341

work out their family balance sheet together, and prepare tax returns jointly. If only one assumes financial responsibility, there is likely to be a sense that one is making the money and the other is spending it. If he does all the earning and bookkeeping, she will be his sheltered child bride, which has some serious implications (if she is widowed, she will be completely vulnerable).

The use and misuse of credit

For many American families, credit is a way of life. For some, credit purchases are an expensive form of indebtedness that they never seem to master, while other families use credit in ways that enable them to make maximum use of their financial resources. There are countless businesses —banks, credit card companies, furniture stores, department stores, oil companies—that seek credit transactions because they are highly profitable; and the newly married couple will receive a barrage of advertising urging them to buy now, with little or nothing down, and pay only a few dollars a month for years to come. Most of these businesses are reputable, but the young couple need to learn when it is advisable to borrow, how to shop for credit, and how to avoid the burden of debt that may drag them under financially.

There are circumstances in which borrowing is necessary, some in which it may be advisable, and some in which it should be avoided. (Credit purchases are one form of loan, however they are presented.) Sooner or later, every family experiences some crisis, such as serious illness, accident, or fire, and the family's savings may be insufficient to cover the costs. Insurance taken out before disaster strikes is the best way to protect yourself and your family from the financial effects of such crises. But even a family with insurance and a reasonable savings account may find that a serious illness, accident, or natural disaster exceeds their resources and leaves them with unpaid bills. Borrowing may be a necessity under such circumstances.

There are other circumstances in which borrowing may be advisable, although not necessary, such as an opportunity to purchase a home, or some major item of household equipment, or an automobile, at a favorable price. Both husband and wife should decide, together, whether the family will derive sufficient benefits from the purchase to offset costs, including credit costs and maintenance. After they have weighed the benefits of having the item versus the costs of acquiring and maintaining it, and on balance have agreed to make the purchase, there remains the question of whether it is better to save money to pay cash for the item at some future date, or to buy on credit now. If they save money for a future purchase, the money will be earning interest while they are pursuing their savings program, and this potential interest should be added into the balance sheet as one of the benefits of postponing the purchase.

If they buy on credit now, they will be paying interest on their purchase, and this interest must be computed as part of the credit price of the item. The added cost of the interest may be offset, however, by a lower price on the item if they buy now (during a special year-end clearance sale, for instance), and the family will have the benefits of the use of the item while it is being paid for on the installment plan. (The consumer should decide whether the sale price is really a saving by doing some comparative shopping to determine the standard retail price of this or a comparable item.) If having the item now will make possible some other family goal, the potential benefits of purchasing now may be enhanced. For example, buying an automobile now may make it possible for the husband to take a better job in an area where no public transportation is available.

Once a couple has decided to make a purchase, there is a strong impulse to buy now, simply because it has been agreed that the family will want to make such a purchase at some time. There is likely to be a feeling that this particular car, or house, or piece of land is perfect, and there might not be one as desirable as this available later. (Such feelings are fanned by the dealer or the realtor, whose job it is to sell.) The emotional component of buying a car, a house, or five acres in the mountains is akin to falling in love: the husband or wife or both are imagining themselves as the owners of the property, seeing it as an extension of, an enhancement of, the self. Like Cinderella, each may believe that he or she could be transformed by the possession of the modern equivalent of a coach and four, or the palace itself. All reason may be overwhelmed by the compelling dream of owning that car, or that house, or that view of the valley.

Impulse spending is always questionable from a financial viewpoint, although buying a new spring outfit may be a tonic that lifts us out of a period of mild depression. But a major purchase, such as a new automobile, a home, or several acres of land is nothing to buy on emotional impulse. Forget the view, and check to determine whether there is a year-round water supply and an access road (or whatever may be the equivalent information needed to make a wise investment). Above all, do not sign anything, not even an option, until you have had days, not hours, to make the decision.

Sometimes borrowing enables a family to purchase property that is in reality an investment. Perhaps the best example is the purchase of a house on a twenty- or thirty-year mortgage. The family has a place to live, and the interest on the mortgage may be more than recovered by inflation over the twenty- or thirty-year period. The house is likely to maintain its value, even allowing for inflation, and may increase in value considerably. It should be remembered, however, that houses (like cars) do eventually deteriorate and that depreciation can occur if something you have not foreseen happens, such as a freeway right-of-way being cut through the neighborhood.

Buying a home with a low downpayment and long mortgage has become so basic to American family life (and to the construction industry

343

and the financial institutions involved in housing) that it may seem the way families have always acquired homes. Only fifty years ago, however, it was customary for a downpayment of 50 percent to be required on a house, and five-year mortgages were common. This meant that only the comparatively wealthy could afford to buy a custom-built house, or even an older home. Before World War II, many families who owned their own homes built them, acquiring a piece of land and putting up some kind of temporary housing while they built their home as time and money for materials permitted. Often the basement (necessarily the first part of the house to be constructed) was roofed and used as the family dwelling while money and materials to complete the house were accumulated. In the future, housing may become so expensive that most families may be unable to afford either the required downpayment or the monthly mortgage payments, and there may be a return to the older pattern of the family building a home for itself (some signs of this are already evident, especially in rural areas, where a pre-cut "shell" may be put up and completed by the family).

Not every purchase can be considered an investment; most items we buy become "used goods" with reduced value as soon as they leave the dealer's showroom. Goods and services that are consumed even before the bill comes in are the most dubious of credit purchases. Unless such bills are paid regularly with other monthly accounts, credit purchases of such items as food and gasoline can become a gradually accumulated debt and a heavy financial burden. A good general rule is never to buy on credit (unless you are able to pay in full at the end of the thirty-day period) any goods or services that will be consumed before they can be paid for in full.

Finally, there is borrowing to consolidate outstanding bills. If a couple have not managed their finances well, and have accumulated monthly bills that they cannot pay, a consolidation loan gives them money to pay outstanding debts, and the loan can then be repaid in a single monthly payment over a longer period of time. This will cost more in interest in the long run in most cases, but it may be the only way out of a situation created by poor management or by some unforeseen disaster.

If it is established that there is good reason to borrow money, the next question is where to borrow. There are a variety of financial institutions, most serving particular needs. A savings and loan association is restricted by regulation from lending money for any purpose except mortgages on real estate. A commercial bank makes loans for a variety of purposes (real estate, automobile, personal), but is required by regulatory agencies to keep risks minimal and thus must ask for collateral, or evidence of ability to repay the loan. If either husband or wife has a life insurance policy with cash value, it is possible to borrow against the cash value of the policy, usually at the lowest rates of interest available. Life insurance companies are not in the business of making loans, as banks and other financial institutions are, but do permit policy holders to borrow against their own accumulated funds.

If either husband or wife is eligible to join a credit union, it may be possible to borrow the money needed from the credit union at a favorable interest rate. The credit union is a membership cooperative, serving only its members. For a credit union to be granted a charter, the members must have something in common. Usually the members of a credit union work for the same employer, or belong to the same labor union or to the same profession (such as the public school teachers of a given county). But credit unions can be formed by people who belong to the same fraternal order, church, or other groups. (There are a growing number of feminist credit unions.)

A credit union is owned and operated by its members. The expense of operation is low because there are no advertising costs, because board members (and sometimes other workers) are volunteers, and because the office usually is in modest quarters (compared with those of banks, savings and loan associations, and other commercial financial institutions). Because overhead is low and the credit union is a nonprofit organization, loans usually are available to members at lower interest rates than at other financial institutions (only the loan against a life insurance policy is likely to carry lower interest rates). If the credit union members work for the same employer (state government employees, for example), there may be a requirement that payment of a loan be deducted from a member's paycheck, along with taxes and other deductions. This can be a convenience, however, and it may mean that all you need to get a credit union loan is to be an employee in good standing where you work, a good credit rating, and your signature.

Whether from a bank or credit union, signature loans are limited in amount (seldom more than $1,000). Any amount borrowed beyond that limit must be secured by collateral. The collateral is required by credit unions for the same reason that a bank must require it: to reduce the risk factor to their investors. If a couple is borrowing money to purchase an automobile or a major appliance, the article they are buying may serve as collateral to secure the loan, provided there has been an adequate downpayment. If they need money for some other purpose (to pay medical bills, for example), some collateral or a cosigner will be needed. The parents of a young married couple may be willing to cosign a note, but it should be recognized that a cosigner is responsible for repayment in case the young couple default on the loan.

The consumer finance company is permitted by federal and state regulatory agencies to charge higher interest rates than commercial banks, and is expected to handle high-risk clients. If a couple cannot qualify for a loan from a bank or credit union, the consumer finance company may be their best alternative. The consumer finance company will also require collateral for most kinds of loans, however, the most common being a second mortgage on the family home.

Many retail stores handle their own financing, and some offer revolving charge accounts that, in effect, open a "line of credit" for purchases

345

that is repaid at a fixed amount per month. These charge accounts, like bank credit card accounts, can be used as thirty-day accounts, without interest. Or they can be treated as an installment loan with, typically, an 18 percent interest charge, considerably higher than either a bank or credit union charges for a loan. (Even though the same bank may handle both credit card purchases and other kinds of loans, the credit card purchase carries a higher rate of interest.) The "revolving credit" plan is tempting, as is the more widely accepted credit card, but either may lead the consuming family into paying a high rate of interest, month after month, with the debt never being cleared or even reduced substantially because of continuing purchases. The credit card is a convenience, but it can be an expensive way to borrow money.

The married couple who find themselves so deeply in debt that no financial agency is willing to lend them any more money may be tempted to deal with a loan shark. The loan shark runs an illegal operation, charges usurious rates of interest, much higher than the law allows, and may use violent means of collecting an unpaid debt. Rather than be entrapped by such an operator, the couple who are in financial difficulty should seek counseling.

Many credit unions offer family budget and financial counseling to members, often as a free service. Since 1955, free community family financial counseling centers have operated in many American cities, supported by credit agencies (banks, savings and loans, and so on), but offering free service to families. Some families need only counseling: help in constructing a budget or in identifying assets they were unaware they owned. Other families may need the assistance of the counseling center in getting payments spread over a longer period of time, at reduced rates. The counseling center must have the signed authorization of the client to discuss the family's problems with creditors, and may require that the family seek no more credit during the time in which the bills are being paid at the reduced rate. But for families in financial difficulty, this kind of free counseling can be a turning point. These service agencies cannot offer legal assistance, but they will usually make referrals to an agency that can or to a lawyer's referral service that can usually help a client obtain thirty minutes of legal advice for a small fee.

Money and marital conflict

A family in financial difficulty is frequently a family having marital problems as well. The marital conflict may focus on money, particularly if the family's finances have been badly managed. However, money is often the apparent rather than the real issue. A pattern of cross projection is often concealed by the conflict over money. Imagine a married couple who have a running battle over money. The husband resents his wife's expensive tastes, and she resents his tight-fisted, penurious attitude. The family quarrels are apparently about money. But threading through the accusations regarding the use and misuse of family funds are fears, anxieties, and projected desires.

The man may be afraid that if he denies his wife the luxuries she demands, she might leave him. His fear is derived from the poor opinion he has of himself apart from his role as a provider. Moreover, having been raised in a family in which being a good provider was the mark of being an adequate husband and father, he measures his personal worth against a monetary standard. Low self-esteem makes adequacy as a provider assume exaggerated importance in his eyes. He would like to be able to indulge her slightest whim, to play the Good Provider in a grand manner. Yet he has a deep fear of bankruptcy, which to him would mean admission that he was a failure as a man. Thus the desire to spend money impulsively seems an unreasonable desire, a threatening desire, and he cannot think it could be his own. So he projects his spendthrift inclinations onto his wife, where they seem to fit. That she does spend money recklessly does not alter the fact that his own ambivalent feelings lead him alternately to spend and to withhold money.

Projecting his own desire to be extravagant onto his wife, he has a distorted view of her. He sees her as his dear but exasperating Child Bride (which may be his pet name for her). Believing her to be irresponsible where money is concerned, he gives her a household allowance (which she consistently overspends), does all of the family bookkeeping, and conceals from her the state of the family finances.

For her part, not knowing what resources the family has or what her husband's financial prospects may be, the wife is inclined to believe that her husband has the first dollar he ever earned put away somewhere. She resents being treated as his Child Bride, and yet adopts the role to wheedle her husband into buying expensive things for her or for the children. Because he "shelters" her (his term) from knowledge of the family's financial situation, she believes that it is not as bad as he frequently claims, and that he gives or withholds money more as an exercise of power than as a matter of financial necessity. To some degree, this may be an accurate perception. The power of the purse is obviously a power that her husband is unwilling to share. Never having been encouraged to assume financial responsibility or to develop skills in money management, the wife accepts the role of demanding dependent that her husband expects her to play. In turn, she projects onto him any inclination she may have to worry about money, a projection encouraged by her husband's secretiveness about family finances.

This is not the only pattern that may underlie marital conflicts over money. Sometimes the roles are reversed and it is the husband who spends extravagantly, the wife who is the worried planner. Sometimes there are patterns that border on mental illness, such as compulsive spending or gambling. But the pattern described above is a common one. Underlying it are some traditional expectations about the support obligation of the husband, his dominance in family financial matters, and the dependent role of the wife. These traditional expectations have their origins in the common law.

The legal support obligation of the husband

Under the common law, the basis for family law codes of most of these United States, the husband has a duty to support his wife. Blackstone, the eighteenth-century English jurist whose *Commentaries on the Law of England* became the legal foundation of both English and American law, observed that under the common law: "The husband is bound to provide his wife with necessaries by law, as much as himself; and if she contracts debts for them, he is obliged to pay them" (Blackstone 1765–1769:442). Two centuries later, state laws still reflect this common law obligation. For example, the state of California, which revised its family law code extensively in 1969, still retains a statute that states: "If the husband neglects to make adequate provision for the support of his wife . . . any other person may in good faith, supply her with articles necessary for her support, and recover the reasonable value thereof from the husband" (Section 5130, Title 8, Part 3, Division 1, of the Civil Code of the State of California).

In the nineteenth century, under the impetus of an earlier feminist movement, many states modified laws regarding the status of married women. However, the laws regarding the duty of the husband to support his wife remained on the books. Writing in the *Virginia Law Review*, Robert C. Brown states:

> No part of the law has been more completely transformed in the past century than that relating to husband and wife . . . But certain phases of even this branch of law remain substantially unchanged, and of these one of the most conspicuous examples is that relating to the duty of the husband to support the wife. It is entirely clear that the married women's acts in the various states have not substantially affected the binding force of this obligation. (cited in Kanowitz 1969:271–272)

The Task Force on Family Law and Policy to the Citizen's Advisory Council on the Status of Women stated in its *Report* (1968) that *all* states have statutes that make "a husband liable for the support of his wife, but without regard to the ability of the wife to support herself."

In contrast, nineteen states do *not* require the wife to support her husband under any circumstances, and the other thirty-one states impose an obligation on the wife to support her husband only if he is unable to support himself.[1] Monrad G. Paulsen found that state statutes regarding

---

[1]At the time of the Task Force *Report*, the following states did not impose an obligation on the wife to support her husband if he was unable to support himself: Alabama, Colorado, Florida, Georgia, Hawaii, Indiana, Iowa, Kentucky, Maryland, Massachusetts, Mississippi, Missouri, Rhode Island, South Carolina, Tennessee, Texas, Virginia, Washington, and Wyoming.

support obligations of the wife fall into three categories (with some states including more than one in their family law codes): "(1) Those that provide that husband and wife contract toward each other obligations of mutual respect, fidelity and support; (2) those which provide that the wife shall support her husband if he is unable because of infirmity to do so; and (3) those which require a wife to support a husband who is likely to become a public charge" (cited in Kanowitz 1969:271). Observing that the first set of statutes create "a moral duty only," Paulsen notes that "the creation of a duty in the wife only when disaster strikes the husband falls a good deal short of treating the sexes equally" (cited in Kanowitz 1969:271).

The proposed Equal Rights Amendment bears directly on the matter of the support obligations of husband and wife. It declares the sexes equal under the law, and there is at present a glaring inequality between the sexes in laws requiring the husband to support his wife, regardless of her ability to support herself, but requiring the wife to support her husband only if he is disabled, and not even under that circumstance in some states.

In state laws and in controversy regarding such laws, there are two contradictory philosophies regarding the nature of women. The older view is that of the childlike woman, who remains the dependent of a man all her life. The contrasting view is that of the independent woman, who is capable of assuming responsibility for herself as an adult. These two contrasting views are written into present law, the newer view being wrapped around a legal core of the old, common-law viewpoint. It is the older view, for example, that made a widow with dependent children eligible for Social Security survivor's benefits, but not a widower with dependent children. Recent suits have resulted in court rulings that such laws are unconstitutional and discriminatory, and widowers with dependent children are now entitled to the survivor's benefits earned by the deceased wife while she was alive and employed. Such court rulings reflect the newer view of the wife as an equal partner with her husband.

The two contradictory views of the wife also appear in the reports of various presidential commissions and task force groups that have recommended changes in the law in the last decade or so. In 1963, the President's Commission on the Status of Women stated in its *Report* that "in view of the child-bearing and home-making functions of the wife ... the husband should continue to have primary responsibility for support of his wife and minor children" (1963:48). Commenting on this report, Nancy Reeves observes that:

> Any self-respecting feminist of the past would have been really aroused by this relegation of the wife with minor children, as an equivalent albatross on the husband's shoulders ... Second, this proposal makes no distinction between childbearing wives and other wives, between wives reponsible for the rearing of minor children and wives whose children are grown. Finally, the proposal does not differentiate between the Judy O'Gradys who do, in fact, manage a household in the most direct sense, doing the scrubbing and

349

the washing, the cooking and the tending, and the Colonel's ladies whose home-making consists of symbolic courtesies. According to this definition, "a wife's a wife for a' that." (Reeves 1971:40)

On the other side of the philosophical fence, that same report of the President's Commission on the Status of Women asserts: "However, in line with the partnership view of marriage . . . the wife should be given some legal responsibility for sharing in her own support and that of her children to the extent she has sufficient means to do so" (1963:48). Reeve's comment on this statement is: "Of course this does not require a woman to find 'sufficient means to do so.' It is only suggested that if she happens to have funds she should be required to share them. The parasitic woman remains the legal prototype" (1971:40).

In 1968, the Task Force on Family Law and Policy to the Citizen's Advisory Council on the Status of Women made another set of suggestions on how state laws should define the economic status of the married woman, but like the earlier group, the Task Force was divided between persons holding contradictory philosophies. Its report ended in an awkward straddle of the two positions. Some members of the Task Force believed that the husband should be legally responsible for the support of his wife only if she were physically handicapped, while others believed that the general inequalities for women in our society are such that factors in addition to physical handicaps need to be considered. There was apparently consensus on the position that the wife should be responsible for providing for a handicapped husband. There was also agreement on the general principle that marriage is a partnership in which each spouse should be responsible for the other, in accordance with need and ability to provide support, and that this principle should be reflected in state laws.

However, translating a moral obligation of mutual support, in accordance with need and ability, into a legal obligation would be extremely difficult. Moral obligations can be worked out between husband and wife with the unique circumstances of each marriage taken into account. But legal obligations must be spelled out, for everyone, in enforceable detail (if not, the law may be challenged in court and found unconstitutionally vague). Would the wife be legally required to seek gainful employment? Under what circumstances? How would her fair share of the legal responsibility for support of the family be determined? Who would determine need and ability to provide support? Would the state make provision for child care if women were required by law to provide some portion of the family's support? Would a dollar equivalent be placed on the household and child-care services of the wife? If so, would these services be subject to social security and survivor's benefits taxes, in a manner similar to that in which self-employed persons are now required to pay social security taxes at the time they pay income taxes? Sometimes a moral obligation that is clear and simple becomes a legal monstrosity, whatever the good intentions of those who write the law. The issue of the support obligation of the wife will be a legal thicket for years to come.

It has been argued persuasively by Leo Kanowitz that if the law gave *Marriage and* the wife equal responsibility with the husband for family support and *money* family debts, the major beneficiary would be the family's creditors. According to Kanowitz:

> It is the rare marriage in which a wife uses her separate earnings for purposes entirely unrelated to family needs. If adopted, therefore, the rule's major effect would be to create an additional fund to which family creditors could look for satisfaction of outstanding obligations.
>
> That creditors may need such assistance is not unlikely. Though in a few states, family expense statutes render a wife liable for certain family items furnished on credit, in most states it is the husband alone who is liable. (Kanowitz 1969:74)

The duty of the husband to provide financial support is not necessarily as great a benefit to the wife as it might seem. It has as its corollary the duty of the wife to provide services to the husband. In a *Virginia Law Review* article entitled "A Reconsideration of Husband's Duty To Support and Wife's Duty To Render Services," Paul Sayre makes the point that the common-law duty of the husband to support his wife has as its counterpart the common-law duty of the wife to render services to her husband (including sexual services). Sayre comments that these respective common-law duties have remained "fantastically unchanged, through succeeding generations, when the nature of the family and the other rights and duties of husbands and wives apart from their families have clearly changed" (cited in Kanowitz 1969:272).

If it is the legal obligation of the husband to support his wife, it follows that legally she is his dependent. The status of a dependent is, like that of a child, a sheltered but powerless status. Moreover, having laid upon the husband the duty of financial support, state laws recognize him as the head of the family and grant him certain rights, including the right to establish domicile: that is, the right to choose where the family will live. The legal presumption is that if he is to support the family he must live where he can make a living, in a house that he can afford, and that it is the duty of the wife to accompany him to the place he chooses or be guilty of desertion. For example, the California civil code states: "The husband is the head of the family. He may choose any reasonable place or mode of living, and the wife must conform thereto." (That provision remained in the California family law code after its revision in 1969.)

Moreover, the right of the wife to be supported by her husband is one of those rights that, if enforced through legal channels, is likely to destroy the marriage. Few wives seek a court judgment of nonsupport against their husbands unless the husband has deserted or the wife is seeking a divorce. While the couple are living together, it is only the family's creditors who normally seek to enforce the husband's obligation to pay his wife's debts. (Contrary to popular opinion, the husband cannot escape his

351

The duty of the husband to provide financial support is not necessarily as great a benefit to the wife as it might seem. Having laid upon the husband the duty of financial support, state laws recognize him as the head of the family and grant him certain rights. Few wives seek a court judgment of nonsupport against their husbands unless the husband has deserted or the wife is seeking a divorce.

obligation by publishing a statement in the newspaper saying that he will no longer be responsible for his wife's debts.)

Typically, it is only when a marriage is being dissolved that the state, through the court of competent jurisdiction, defines in precise dollar amounts the support obligation of the husband—by this point, the support obligation of the former husband to his former wife. If the wife should lose her legal right to be supported by her husband through the adoption of the Equal Rights Amendment, she may not, in truth, lose much and she will at last emerge from a legal state of dependency that has kept her in perpetual childhood in the eyes of the law. At present, as Reeves observes, "we have the curious legal situation that children over 21 [now, in most states, children over 18] are assigned greater financial burdens and greater financial autonomy than a wife. No matter what her age, she is classed with juveniles" (1971:40).

The marriage contract: ownership and management of property

Under the common law, husband and wife were one person, and that person was the husband. As Blackstone made clear:

The very being or legal existence of the woman is suspended during the marriage, or at least is incorporated and consolidated into that of the husband; under whose wing, protection, and cover she performs everything; and is therefore called in our law a *femme couverte*. Upon this principle of a union of person in husband and wife, depend all the legal rights, duties, and disabilities that either of them acquire by marriage. (Blackstone 1765–1769:442)

Between 1849 and 1950, state laws were passed that collectively are referred to as the "Married Women's Acts." These acts amended the existing civil code in the various states to give married women the right to hold property in their own names and various contractual rights that made a married woman a legal person, empowered to act in her own behalf.

The definition of the property rights of husband and wife are an important part of the marriage contract in every state. This is a contract that is entered by persons who marry in that state, although few couples are aware of the terms of the marital contract. Regardless of where a couple were married, they become subject to the laws of the state where they establish legal residence. Although laws defining marital rights and obligations vary in detail from state to state, the laws determining the property rights of spouses fall into two basic categories: those that are based on the common law, and those that recognize community property (the former stem from the English common law; the latter derive from the Napoleonic code or Mexican law). In the community property states, income and property acquired by each spouse before marriage or by inheritance after marriage is separate property, but income or other property acquired (other than by inheritance) by either husband or wife during the marriage is owned in common by both. There are eight community property states: Arizona, California, Idaho, Louisiana, New Mexico, Nevada, Texas, and Washington. The other forty-two states are common law states, in the sense that their civil codes define the property rights of spouses in a manner derived from the Engish common law: all income or other property acquired by either spouse before or during marriage is the separate and sole property of the spouse who acquires it.

From the wife's point of view, there are advantages and disadvantages in each system of laws. The community property laws recognize that even if the wife works only within the home, as a housewife and mother, she contributes to the family livelihood and to the ability of the husband to be outside the home earning a living. In those states that have community property laws, the wife has an equal interest with the husband in all income and property acquired from the date of their marriage until the date that marriage is ended by death or dissolution. In California, for example, the family law code provides that at the dissolution of a marriage, all community property is to be divided equally between husband and wife, regardless of whether the wife had any earned income during the marriage.

353

However, the community property laws have some disadvantages for working wives. Typically, community property laws give the right to manage and control community property to the husband. This means that he has the right to encumber the community property, often without his wife's written consent. As the Task Force on Family Law and Policy to the Citizen's Advisory Council on the Status of Women observed: "The income of a working wife as well as that of the husband becomes part of the community property and, under the traditional community property system is managed by the husband, with the wife having no say in how her income is to be spent" (1968:3).

Some states have amended their community property laws to correct this inequity to working wives. California gives the husband the right to manage community property, but grants the wife the right to manage and control any community personal property earned by herself that has not been commingled with other community property. (For example, if she puts her earnings in a bank account in her own name, such earnings are community property that she has the right to manage; if she puts her earnings in a joint account with her husband, they become community property that he legally controls.) Also, California law provides that whether or not the wife has earned income of her own, her written consent is required before the husband can mortgage or sell such community property as household furnishings or her clothing.

Texas has amended its community property laws to provide that "each spouse shall have sole management, control and disposition of that community property which he or she would have owned if a single person." Texas also provides that when property is commingled with that of the other spouse (as, for example, in joint accounts or real property owned as joint tenants) such property is subject to joint management unless the spouses agree otherwise.

In the forty-two common-law states, there is separate ownership and thus separate management of all property. Husband and wife may acquire property jointly; for example, they may become joint tenants in real estate. But all other property is separately owned, and each spouse manages his or her own income and property. On its face, this is an equitable arrangement. But the wife may not have much opportunity to acquire property of her own during the years when the children are young and her major energies are devoted to the care of the home and to childrearing. Although most women are gainfully employed at some time during their marriage, the average earnings of women, both monthly and over their working lives, are demonstrably lower than those of men.

The President's Commission on the Status of Women included the following recommendation in its report:

> Marriage as a partnership in which each spouse makes a different but equally important contribution is increasingly recognized as a reality in this country and is already reflected in the laws of some other countries. During mar-

riage, each spouse should have a legally defined substantial right in the earnings of the other, in the real and personal property acquired through those earnings, and in their management. Such a right should be legally recognized as surviving the marriage in the event of its termination by divorce, annulment, or death. Appropriate legislation should safeguard either spouse and protect the surviving spouse against improper alienation of property by the other. Surviving children as well as the surviving spouse should be protected from disinheritance. (President's Commission on the Status of Women 1969:47)

Property rights in marriage are as closely related to the definition of marital roles as is the support obligation of the husband, and any redefinition of either set of rights and obligations must be accompanied by a restructuring of the entire marriage contract. There are no simple solutions, but the present mosaic of laws is anachronistic at best.

Marriage and money: a summary

The newly married couple are typically unconcerned about the legal nuances of what property is his and what is hers, or what is commingled. They have committed their lives and fortunes to each other, and are blissfully occupied with creating a world in which they regard everything they acquire as *ours.* Early in marriage, while marital roles are still flexible and patterns of living—including patterns of spending—are being established, husband and wife need to sit down together, review their combined assets, and work out a budget.

The word *budget* has negative overtones, suggesting pleasures denied and evoking images of shoddy merchandise sold "for families on a budget." But a budget is simply the way a particular family has assigned priorities: What money must be spent for necessities, and how much remains as discretionary income? And what are necessities? What do the couple really want to own? Do they want a summer vacation enough to cut back on some other expenditures? The couple who do not plan their expenditures are likely to pay too much for things that they neither need nor want. A system of keeping financial records is also essential. A monthly review of actual expenditures will help both husband and wife to know whether their budget is a workable plan. If not, their record of income and expenditures will help them see what changes need to be made, *before* they are in financial difficulty. A budget is a pattern of choices. Without a budget and supporting financial records, a couple are likely to have little choice but to respond to their most pressing creditors.

Credit can be a useful means of expanding a family's financial resources. It is purchasing power borrowed against future income, however, and if used to provide for current living expenses, credit purchases can encumber future earnings too heavily. "Easy" payments can mask a

355

A budget is simply the way a particular family has assigned priorities. What money must be spent for necessities and how much remains as discretionary income? And what are necessities? Is a handmade quilt that will give warmth and beauty to the married couple every night of their lives a luxury, a necessity, or an investment?

precarious financial situation, leaving the family vulnerable to a period of illness or unemployment. Learning when and where to borrow is an important part of learning how to manage the family financial resources.

The married couple who are still in their teens are sometimes pulled abruptly out of the youth culture by the financial responsibilities of marriage. When a man marries, both custom and the law define him as an adult male, regardless of his age; with marriage he becomes the head of the household, a status that symbolizes his emergence from the subordinate and dependent roles of childhood and adolescence. (This function of marriage as a rite of passage was explored in some detail in Chapter 10.) The support obligations of the husband have remained essentially unchanged from those based in the common law.

The obligation to support wife and children is the basis for the dominant position that society has given to the husband as head of the household. The wife who would have a more equal marital relationship may have to relinquish her right to be supported, and accept a mutual support obligation. Historically, women were not permitted to own income-producing property. Since the nineteenth century, however, most states have permitted married women to own and control property and to enter into contracts. Community property laws in some states have both advantages and disadvantages for the wife, and both parties to a marriage have a clear interest in learning how the laws of the state in which they live define the rights of husband and wife to joint and personal property. Too often, property is not a matter of concern to either husband or wife until one of them is faced with the problems of probating an estate, or until they are reaching a divorce settlement. Financial difficulties may overwhelm a married couple and be a contributing factor in divorce. But often a quarrel over money is a symbolic battle, masking a deeper and less obvious marital conflict.

References

Blackstone, William. 1765–1769. *Commentaries on the Law of England,* vol. I.

Goode, William J. 1970. *World Revolution and Family Patterns.* New York: The Free Press.

Kanowitz, Leo. 1969. *Women and the Law: The Unfinished Revolution.* Albuquerque: University of New Mexico Press.

President's Commission on the Status of Women. 1964. *Report: American Women.* Washington, D.C.: U.S. Government Printing Office.

Reeves, Nancy. 1971. *Womankind: Beyond the Stereotypes.* Chicago: Aldine-Atherton.

Task Force on Family Law and Policy. 1968. *Report to the Citizen's Advisory Council on the Status of Women.* Washington, D.C.: U.S. Government Printing Office.

Tocqueville, Alexis de. 1956 ed. *Democracy in America,* abr. ed., edited by R. D. Heffner. New York: New American Library.

U.S. Bureau of the Census. 1972. *Census of Population: 1970 Marital Status, Final Report.* Washington, D.C.: U.S. Government Printing Office.

U.S. Bureau of Labor Statistics. 1974. *Handbook of Labor Statistics.* Washington, D.C.: U.S. Government Printing Office.

Suggested readings

Credit Union National Association. 1966. *Using Credit Wisely.* CUNA International, Box 431, Madison, Wisconsin 53701. Simple direct language and clear information on the uses and management of consumer credit. Includes discussion of "truth in lending" laws, loan sources, types of charge accounts, credit cards, and the cost of installment sales credit. A booklet intended for classroom use, it has discussion questions and similar aids.

Consumer Reports. 1975. "How to Shop for Credit." *Consumer Reports* 40 (March): 171–178. A comprehensive review of all forms of consumer credit, how to obtain it, how to use it, how to compare costs of borrowing from different sources. Credit cards, their uses, cost, and potential problems are discussed, as is the Fair Credit Billing Act, discrimination in credit, and how to handle repayment problems.

Marital choice and marital roles

O'Henry. 1906. "The Gift of the Magi." In *The Four Million.* New York: Doubleday and Company. (Also available in various anthologies.) This poignant tale of an impoverished young couple who learn that to love means to give the most precious thing one has is an American classic. It bears O'Henry's trademark, the ironic ending.

Neisser, Edith. 1960. "Emotional and Social Values Attached to Money." *Marriage and Family Living* 22 (May):132–138. This article begins with a discussion of the origins (both historic and psychoanalytic) of the emotions that most of us experience with regard to money. Neisser then goes on to describe the impact of money on marriage, including some research results indicating that financial difficulties rank second only to sexual dysfunction as a source of marital problems, and concludes with a discussion of working wives.

Part Three

Marital conflict and marital dissolution

13 Marital conflict: hostility in intimacy

The "conflicts" of most people are actually attempts to avoid the real conflicts. They are disagreements on minor or superficial matters which by their very nature do not lend themselves to clarification or solution. Real conflicts between two people, those which do not serve to cover up or to project, but which are experienced on the deep level of inner reality to which they belong, are not destructive. They lead to clarification, they produce a catharsis from which both persons emerge with more knowledge and more strength.

Erich Fromm (1956:104)

It is part of the conventional wisdom of American culture that a good marriage is one in which there is no conflict, only minor differences that can be talked out in an earnest manner. The happy marriage is assumed to be one of eternal tranquility (as befitting a marriage made in heaven). Yet a close relationship inevitably generates both positive and negative emotions: where there is contact, there is friction.

Living with someone means living with the whole person, faults as well as virtues, under the best and worst of circumstances. This was recognized in the traditional marriage vows: "I take thee, for better or for worse." Often, that which we enjoy most in the intimate other is inseparable from a quality we find most irritating: creativity, for example, seldom coexists with predictability and order. To live with and enjoy a highly creative person may mean learning to coexist with a certain chaos. To live with anyone requires rubbing against the rough edges of his or her personality on occasion. There is an inescapable ambivalence in all intimate relationships.

Thus even the most loving husband and wife generate some hostile feelings toward each other. If we believe that *any* hostility felt by either is a symptom of impending marital failure, we may try to deny that any negative feelings exist in our marriage. But tension and hostility are one part (often the smaller part) of an inevitable ambivalence. If not allowed to surface, anger will turn inward. Some people say that they choke back anger, others say they swallow it. These common metaphors suggest what is often the outcome of suppressed conflict: asthma, ulcers, or other bodily damage from accumulated tension. In the long run, pent-up hostility bursts through the barriers of civility that have contained it, and the marriage may be destroyed.

The ability to express, channel, and discharge tensions in a marriage is as important as the ability to express affection. Because this has not yet been accepted as part of the conventional wisdom about marriage, let us first examine the myth that a marriage without overt conflict is the "perfect marriage."

Suppressed conflict: life behind the "rubber fence"

Most newly married couples withdraw from the larger world to some extent and create a private world with its own boundaries. But sometimes husband and wife act as if their interlocking conjugal roles formed a closed system. The marriage becomes a self-sustaining world protected from the outer (presumed hostile) environment by a continuous boundary with no outlets. This boundary of relationship stretches to include all those behaviors that can be interpreted as complementary, but compresses to squeeze out all behaviors that are not shared. This elastic boundary has been called a "rubber fence."

362 Limited and limiting though such a "rubber-fence" marriage may be, it offers the security of the known and completely predictable. A person with low self-esteem is often eager to retreat behind the "rubber fence," into a carefully defined role structure. Any situation that has not been previously structured calls for imagination and spontaneity. Novelty is threatening to people who have a nebulous or negative self-image, because novelty demands that the *person* choose, act, participate, there being no clear precedent for what *wife* or *husband* is expected to do in the circumstances. Someone who is certain that he or she has no imagination, no sense of humor, has to live "by the book," and is uncomfortable unless there is a detailed set of instructions. Early in marriage, such people settle on the details of the marital role each will play, and both hope there will be no surprises in life.

This rigid patterning of marital roles contributes to a preoccupation with making two lives dovetail that is characteristic of a "rubber-fence" marriage. People caught up in such a marriage exert a good deal of energy in an effort to mesh the behavior and expectations of one with the behavior and expectations of the other. Any personal characteristic of one that does not have a counterpart in the other is stripped away, so that there will be nothing to mar the smooth fit of their lives.

This is an abnormal preoccupation with an element found in most enduring relationships. All relationships that persist have some complementary aspects. If there were no fit between people's lives, they would not stay together long. However, in a "rubber-fence" marriage, there is an insistence on fitting together at the expense of the identity and growth of the persons involved in the relationship. Other people say, "You two have so much in common," and the husband and wife feel pleased. But there may be flickering memories of interests put away early in the marriage because they were not shared: his old motorcycle helmet collects dust on top of a pile of yellowed issues of *Variety*, all that remains of her fascination with the theater. Any new interest that one may toy with is quickly dropped if the other is not inclined to share it. The result is that both are fenced in by the relationship. Growth is ruled out in order to maintain the sense of fitting together perfectly, the illusion that each is able to fulfill the other completely. If expectations are sufficiently limited, the illusion may be preserved.

Few new interests will be cultivated by either husband or wife caught behind a "rubber-fence" marriage, for any new interest that one partner might develop would require a corresponding development in the other if their lives are to remain perfectly meshed. Altering the fixed paths of their lives to accommodate something new seems to threaten the role structure of the marriage. If one partner should challenge existing role expectations, the other will make efforts to quash the challenge and to restore the previous role structure.

Two common responses to a threatening situation are to ignore it (in the hope that it will go away) or to attempt to neutralize it. Such responses are frequently used to maintain a kind of ultra-stability in the

363

role system of a "rubber-fence" marriage. The husband or wife may brush aside incidents of conflict as if they had never occurred ("We won't mention it again"), in the hope that ignoring the incident will mean that nothing has changed. Behavior that conflicts with existing role expectations may be repeated, however, especially if one of the spouses is trying to escape the confining role structure and develop as a person. If it becomes clear that the divergent behavior will not cease, that ignoring it was ineffective, the disapproving (and threatened) spouse may try to neutralize the behavior.

The most frequent technique used to neutralize a new pattern of behavior is to extend role expectations to include it without altering the basic role structure. The rubber fence expands to include the new behavior. The new behavior is "accepted," while at the same time it is made clear that this new behavior will not be allowed to change the existing set of roles. Thus the new behavior is not allowed to be a wedge to open up new modes of being; it is dismissed as "just a phase."

Consider, for example, the woman who returns to college after years of keeping house and rearing children. She begins to broaden her perception of the world and to acquire new perspectives on her self. She may also encounter passive resistance, disguised as a bland acceptance, from her husband. Outwardly accepting his wife's new status as a student, he may suddenly find activities to fill each weekend, activities that require her presence and that take her away from her books or mean that it will not be possible for her to go to the library. He may suddenly undertake projects around the house, perhaps projects that she has long wanted him to do, certainly projects that will require her assistance. The weekend before her major term paper is due, he may suddenly plan a trip to the national park with the children. She would feel guilty if she did not go, especially since the children and their father have "surprised" her by packing the lunch.

Thus pressures are applied to bring the innovating wife back into line. These pressures include the maintenance of prior expectations (in the name of "family tradition"), shaming ("the children will be so disappointed, what kind of mother are you?"), and a refusal to admit that any accommodations in the existing role structure might be made to allow for growth. There are repetitive discussions in which the meaning of the innovative behavior is interpreted and reinterpreted (sometimes discussions involving other members of the family: her mother or mother-in-law). Finally, the wife who has been trying to break through the constricting boundaries begins to regard the innovative behavior as negative and deviant, and recants. Alternatively, her husband may continue to refuse to discuss the situation, tacitly insisting that it does not exist, until she begins to believe that it is all a grotesque illusion. Either way, the "rubber fence" retains its elasticity; what cannot be squeezed out will be surrounded and contained.

A common characteristic of a "rubber-fence" marriage is that both husband and wife are more concerned with maintaining a *sense* of related- ness than with relating to each other. When persons of low self-esteem marry, each brings into the marriage an urgent desire to maintain a sense of relation. Each clings to the other out of fear that if this wife, or this husband, were lost, no one else would ever want to marry him or her. Often such persons bear the emotional scars of early, painful love affairs. Perhaps they were isolates nobody wanted to play with in the sixth grade; perhaps a parent left or threatened to leave them in childhood, and dimly remembered separation anxiety shadows the back of their minds. For whatever reason, such men and women are anxious about the possibility that the significant others in their lives may leave them suddenly, inexplicably.

Persons who have a negative view of themselves are certain that no one else would find them attractive either. The person with a negative self-image often tries to fabricate a more appealing pubic image: a false front to conceal the self. The public image is intended for other people to believe and admire; the person behind the image is painfully aware that it is a sham. However well the public image is presented, the person hiding behind it is fearful that someone may see through it. Intimacy seems a threatening situation to such a person, who believes that anyone coming too close would perceive the truth and go away in disgust.

Yet the man or woman behind the mask is lonely. A person with low self-esteem and a carefully maintained public image longs to be loved, but is certain that he or she is unlovable. Such a person is astonished to find that someone has fallen in love with him or her. A girl with an ill-defined or negative self-image may believe that she has somehow tricked her man into thinking of her as pretty and charming, and hope to be safely married before his illusions are dispelled. Once married, a woman of low self-esteem is likely to idolize her husband, projecting onto him the attributes she would like to possess but cannot recognize are potentially within herself.

If the husband is also a person of low self-esteem, he is pleased by his wife's idealization of him, comes to expect it from her, and at the same time to discount it. The man she seems to see bears slight resemblance to his self-image. But, like a carefully posed and retouched photograph, the picture of himself that he sees reflected in his wife's eyes is a flattering likeness that it pleases him to keep in view.

Intimacy is one of the major functions of marriage in our society. But a "rubber-fence" marriage is not an intimate situation: rigidly structured roles are barriers to intimacy. Nor can a "rubber-fence" marriage provide the candor that intimacy requires. The rewards of intimacy flow from the knowledge that the significant other knows me, knows some things about me that I may not be aware of in myself, and still accepts me as I am, "warts and all." In a "rubber-fence" marriage, each spouse is afraid to let the other get too close a look at the "real" self, certain that it would repel him or her.

365

The angry, melancholy "perfect wife"

The man who has a nebulous self-image and little self-esteem may seek a strong woman to marry, sometimes an older woman who may assume a nurturing, motherly role as his wife. But often a man with low self-esteem and a negative self-image marries a girl even more anxious and passive than himself. Her submissiveness gives him an opportunity to play the role of dominant male, a role he has coveted since he was a small boy deferring to his father and the neighborhood bully. The girl who feels that she is no one at all until she becomes some man's wife will not object to domination. Like a younger child allowed to tag along behind admired older children, she is delighted that he deigned to notice her and asked her to come with him.

The woman involved in a "rubber-fence" marriage is usually the spouse with the most at stake. She tends to model her behavior on the expectations of her husband as she perceives them (which may be pure projection of her own expectations). The woman who is convinced that she must live up to her husband's expectations in order to be loved by him is a woman who believes that her husband is the source of all rewards in her life, and she is anxious to please, fearful that if he does not love her he will leave her. Her fears are parallel to the separation anxiety of childhood: the all-powerful parent figure from whom life support flows must be pleased and kept from going away.

Consider, for example, the basically attractive woman in her late twenties who told me that she longed for: "genuine acceptance, love, and concern for my individuality. I had all this as a child. My mother fulfilled all these needs until I was thirteen. She died then. However, I do not have this relationship, nor have I since then, with anyone. I feel if I'm good and the perfect wife, I will be loved. And if I were myself, my husband would not love me. I must keep improving myself." Notice that this woman is saying, in effect, "Mother loved me, but she died." The only person who ever loved her went away. She fears that her husband may go away, that she must be the perfect wife or he will not love her. And she believes that she is not lovable. From someone (perhaps her mother?) she acquired the belief that she is a person only a mother could love. Her low self-esteem is both the reason she craves to be loved and in itself a barrier to intimacy in her marriage. Having a negative self-image, she hides behind a carefully maintained role that she cannot imagine reflects her "real" self. She plays at being the perfect wife, but does not think she is one, for she says, "I must keep improving myself."

Because this woman is certain that her "real" self is unlovable, she feels compelled to conceal it behind the "perfect wife" mask. She never risks the revealing intimacy that might make it possible for her husband to see her as she is, and give her the acceptance and approval she craves: acceptance and love that she claims to want very much. She has in fact prejudged the outcome of any open, intimate encounter: "If I were myself, my husband would not love me."

Playing the role of the perfect wife—clearly a limited and carefully defined role in her "rubber-fence" marriage—is the means by which this woman hopes to hold her husband. *By controlling her own behavior, she hopes to manipulate him.* "I feel if I'm good and the perfect wife, I will be loved." There is neither much happiness nor overt conflict in this marriage— there is too much anxiety, at least in the wife, to permit either. However, if her anxiety reaches a critical level, she is likely either to explode in fury over some minor incident or turn her anger back on herself in debilitating depression.

Imagine the "perfect wife" on a rainy Saturday with the children at home, errands to run, the kitchen to clean, and a sense of being left out when her husband telephones to say that the client he is playing golf with has not signed the contract yet, so he is taking the client out to dinner. When her husband arrives home at 10:30, after wining and dining his client, the children are in bed but she is still waxing the kitchen floor. He greets her with, "Haven't you finished the cleaning *yet?*" and she bursts into tears. She might have thrown the wet sponge at his head. Or she might have guessed that the business deal had fallen through and mixed him a drink. Why does the "perfect wife" cry?

Having cast herself in the role of "perfect wife," she spends a great deal of time cleaning and polishing the house to a level of cleanliness her mother would have applauded. She feels ambivalent about the housework and the children (her expectations for both are perfection, which does place heavy demands on her—and on them). This day she has been more aware of resenting her work than of enjoying herself in a role that she has created. Resentment makes the children seem beastly and the housework seem endless. As her work drags on, she begins to suspect that it is because she is dragging her heels. She could accept this feeling as self-criticism (which it is) and use it as an admonishment to herself to dispatch her work quickly. She could set as an incentive for herself the idea of finishing her work in time to bathe, change, and apply her new perfume before her husband comes home (a part of her chosen role of "perfect wife" that she enjoys more than scrubbing the kitchen floor). She does neither. Instead, she imagines what her husband would say if he arrived home to find her still in her splattered jeans, grubby and sweaty, still cleaning the kitchen.

Now her self-criticism is transformed into an unfair criticism that her husband would voice, if he were only there to voice it. (It is a safe rule that whatever criticism one imagines someone else *might* make is self-criticism.) This woman has an inner conflict between her desire to be the "perfect wife" and her desire to toss away the mop and go indulge herself in that long, hot bath. The more she thinks about what her husband might say, however, the less she is able to recognize her own ambivalence. The

367

criticism seems unfair, coming from him. She needs to feel that she is an acceptable person; she believes that she is not. She believes that only her husband can assure her that she is acceptable, and that he will do this only if she is able to play the role of "perfect wife" convincingly. She has created this circular trap for herself, and she is caught in it.

Feeling tense and needful, she retreats from her own resentment (anger and resentment seem dangerous emotions to this woman, who lives by her husband's approval). She turns the anger inward, retreating into feelings of melancholy and fatigue. She drifts slowly through the rest of the day, barely noticing the children. Her projected self-criticism becomes prophecy. She is still cleaning the kitchen when her husband comes in and speaks the lines she has imagined. Her inner conflict teeters on the edge of a quarrel with her husband. Wanting to avert the quarrel (and perhaps to shame her husband), she turns her anger into tears.

Anger that is turned inward is destructive. Over time it takes its toll in elevated blood pressure, ulcers, asthma, or other bodily damage induced by tension. The psyche is affected as well. Anger contained becomes melancholy. The depression experienced by the woman trying to be the perfect wife begins as anger she is afraid to express. Screaming would not resolve her problem; it would only provide a temporary release of accumulated tension. Her anger is symptomatic of the tension of unfilled needs, and the need she feels most desperately is to be able to regard herself as an acceptable person. Neither the criticism nor the praise she receives from her husband is the real issue. She needs to learn to evaluate her own actions and efforts, to set standards for herself that she recognizes as her own, to act in ways that will meet her self-expectations, and thus to find herself an acceptable (if imperfect) person.

But a woman with low self-esteem tends to surrender self-evaluation and to project onto her husband both her expectations and her self-criticism. She is likely to have been a child who never learned to judge the worth of her own actions and endeavors. In all probability she was an obedient little girl who ate her vegetables to please her mother, and sought praise for each crayon creation. Never having learned to evaluate her actions and thus to accept herself, she lives on the praise of others: first her mother and father, later her husband. Acceptance by the significant others in her life seems always to be conditional on whether or not she is behaving properly: "If I'm good and the perfect wife, I will be loved." Because she has never developed the capacity to evaluate herself, she solicits her husband's praise and shrinks from his criticism. But even praise is unlikely to improve her poor opinion of herself, for such a woman tends to believe that she is only being praised for performance in a role.

This woman of low self-esteem frequently places self-criticism in her husband's mouth. The role of "perfect wife" that she is struggling to play may or may not correspond to *his* image of the perfect wife. But even if they have coauthored the script, her role is one that she has created. Projecting the role she has chosen for herself so that it seems to be one demanded by her husband, she can see that the role expectation is unreasonable. How could he expect anyone to be perfect, especially someone as flawed as she believes herself to be? The "perfect wife" is a difficult role, and she resents playing it. However, feeling that she must play the role in order to be loved, or at least not deserted, believing it better to play the part than to be replaced by an understudy, she turns her anger and resentment back on herself as moping melancholy.

Jealousy and the "perfect wife"

The identity of a woman is often derived from the significant men in her life: her father, husband, son. Children view themselves within the context of their family roles. Parents have a way of insisting that their sons become independent and purposeful, but of asking that their daughters be loving and good. "Daddy's little girl" may become some man's "child bride" without ever becoming a person. The development of a sharply defined identity has not been encouraged for girls in our culture (although this attitude is now changing). It has been assumed that a girl will simply grow into the most important of her social roles. As teeth erupt in childhood and breasts develop at puberty, sex-role behaviors are expected to emerge with marriage and maternity.

In the interval between being a child and becoming a wife, the American girl lives in a limbo in which she has little means of defining herself except in terms of her attractiveness to men. Throughout adolescence, a girl is likely to remain more concerned about the development of her breasts ("Is one growing faster than the other?") and the clarity of her skin than with the clarity of her career goals. Her femininity seems validated when a man notices that she is a woman. As a small girl, she felt invisible. Not even the clerk at the grocery counter seemed able to see her standing there with her soft drink and after-school cupcakes. Suddenly the pubescent girl discovers that she has become highly visible, and is waited on with solicitude and suggestion by the most arrogant male clerks. It is a metamorphosis.

A girl typically grows up finding herself acceptable because a man finds her desirable. If the man who has chosen her suddenly seems interested in another woman, one of the major props of her self-esteem is threatened. To say that she is jealous does not convey the depth of her feeling. She feels betrayed, empty, worthless. Her first reaction may be to find another man who will desire her.

The girl who has never considered herself attractive, but who finds a husband nonetheless, tends to be the kind of woman described above, the "perfect wife." Such a woman is prone to debilitating jealousy. When she became this man's wife, she projected onto him the strength and purpose she never developed within herself, and she feels inept and vulnerable in his absence. If she has projected onto him her own creativity and initiative, she will feel it necessary to consult with him on the most

369

minute details of domestic life (which also serves to get his attention for a time). In short, she does everything she can to monopolize his time and attention, for she needs to have him present to experience the alienated self-potential she has projected onto him. Having endowed him with the better part of herself, she is depleted when he is away from her.

A woman who enjoys her own latent capacities only by finding them in her husband tends to become her husband's satellite. She comes to believe that she can enjoy herself only when her husband is there to shine upon her. When he is not present, she may carry on a continuing inner dialogue with him, imagining what he would say and do if he *were* there. His preferences and expectations are a continual frame of reference for her. If she should lose him, she would feel herself a fragment of a person. Such a woman is likely to be painfully jealous not only of any woman her husband talks to (or about) but also of his male friends, and the amount of time and attention his career demands. She may even be jealous of the pet on which he lavishes affection.

The jealous wife may find her husband's male companions a source of unwelcome competition for his attention. They may seem a threat in themselves, for he may prefer their company to hers. And they also pose a symbolic threat: suppose, she asks herself, those rascals lead him to Other Women? Imagine an evening on which such a woman's husband brings home a buddy from his Marine Corps days, or from some period of his wild, "hippie" youth, for dinner and an evening of recalling old times. Pleased to meet the friend her husband has talked so much about, or believing that the "perfect wife" would be so pleased, she is at the same time aware of a pang of jealousy. As the two men recall adventures they shared in former times, she begins to feel herself an outsider, and is jealous after the fact for being left out of exciting escapades these two have shared. She begins to hate this stranger who is her husband's friend. She may begin to discern flaws in his character and to pick subtly at these. Or if she is fearful of angering her husband by a display of hostility toward his friend, she may cover her jealousy with the composed face of the perfect hostess and make it clear that her husband's friend is a welcome *guest* (a guest is always an outsider) who must come back—sometime. If all else fails, she may try flirting with the man in the hope that her husband will become jealous, knowing full well that jealousy would destroy the masculine camaraderie that she finds so threatening.

A woman who believes that she is a dull and unattractive creature and that the only joy in her life is that which her husband sometimes gives her will be frantic if forced to share her husband with anyone. Always afraid that he will find others more stimulating companions than herself, believing that he will see through her "perfect wife" disguise and leave her if she has anyone else with whom to compare her, she is concerned with trying to keep him from close association with others. Any woman with whom her husband has more than the most brief and impersonal contact will immediately become an object of hatred for such a wife. She will be filled with suspicion and the agony of wondering what more there may be between them. She is often afraid to pry too closely into what may be there, fearful of what she may discover.

The jealous wife may be too fearful of losing her husband to risk openly confronting him with possible infidelity (believing it is better not to know than to ask and be told a lie, or than to be told the truth and perhaps divorced). Unchecked imagination feeds her jealousy. Finding a book of matches bearing the name of an expensive restaurant in his shirt pocket may fire her suspicions for days. Sooner or later, her jealousy will burst through her tight restraint, and the resulting explosion may be literally murderous.

Once she has given vent to jealous rage, she will find it easier to rage again. But the ensuing conflict cannot be resolved by any action of her husband. The jealous wife believes that her anger is caused by her husband's behavior. It is not. Her emotion is derived from her fear of being abandoned, aggravated by suspicion, emotions generated entirely within herself. Jealousy cannot be dispelled by any change in her husband's behavior, for her fears are independent of anything that he may do or refrain from doing. He may be innocent: trying to prove one's innocence is almost impossible, as our judicial system has recognized for centuries. What can a faithful husband say when his jealous wife demands: "Answer me, yes or no, have you stopped seeing your mistress?"

Her fears, not his behavior, form the basis of her jealousy. And her fears will remain as long as she is certain that she is unlovable. One proof that a woman's jealousy has little to do with the behavior of her husband is the fact that the most burning jealousy may be focused on the dead. A woman may be certain that she could never live up to her husband's dead wife, and try to eradicate all traces of her departed rival. Because jealousy is generated by inner fears and self-doubts, not by anything her husband has done, there is nothing her husband could do to allay her fears or satisfy her jealous demands that he demonstrate his love for her. Meanwhile, her jealousy may bring about the very abandonment that she fears. Few men find it rewarding to live with a suspicious, possessive woman, however ingratiating she may try to be at times.

Jealousy: the dark side of a husband's love

Men, too, are prone to jealousy, especially the man who has a low opinion of himself and fears that he may not be man enough (usually in a sexual sense) to hold the complete attention and devotion of his woman. Two people involved in a love affair are likely to have projected onto each other the idealized image each has created out of alienated (but desired) self-potential. This is a point developed at some length in an earlier chapter, but it is essential to an understanding of jealousy. Romantic love includes a mutual admiration pact: the two have a tacit agreement that each will see reflected in the other's eyes the image that he or she would like to believe. A man with low self-esteem who dreams of being strong, masterful, exciting, audacious, the embodiment of the American male myth, may be startled to discover that this woman believes him to be all these things. In trying to live up to her expectations, he manages to give a convincing performance, and is able to enjoy the role immensely. It may be difficult for him to believe that such potential could be a permanent part of himself (although if he can play the role, he has demonstrated that he has this capacity). He credits her with making it possible for him to feel good about himself. And he would like to have her there all the time, so that he could feel this way about himself all the time.

If his woman is beautiful and sensual, he will display her proudly to other men: possessing her gives him visible proof of masculinity. If he snaps his fingers and she comes running, he has demonstrated something to himself and to any other men in the room. But if her adoration is the major prop for his self-esteem, he will be possessive and jealous. If the day comes when she does not come running, but remains talking to some other man, he will be furious, feel betrayed, and either sulk or fight.

Even couples who have agreed to grant each other sexual freedom can be plagued by jealousy. Such jealousy is compounded by the fact that there is no hidden behavior (so infidelity cannot be ignored) and that there has been prior consent to the extramarital affair. The jealous husband may try to suppress the fear and anxiety. Not being able to feel self-righteous about his jealousy, he finds it even more painful. A pattern of stormy scenes alternating with tearful reconciliations is likely to develop.

The man who has established a "rubber-fence" marriage will feel threatened by *any* third party who intrudes into the couple's closely meshed lives. Such a husband is likely to be jealous of the people his wife works beside, especially any male who is her coworker or boss. If she talks about the job at home, as most people do, he will make derogatory remarks about her coworkers. If his jealousy mounts, he will begin to make derogatory remarks about her job and the presumed neglect of the children and housework. The couple will believe that they are fighting over whether or not it is necessary for the wife to work outside the home. But at its core, such conflict is based on the husband's fear that his wife may leave him if she does not leave her job. ("Why would a woman who could support herself want to stay with a failure like me?" is his unvoiced fear.)

A man with low self-esteem, who felt like a nobody until his wife told him he was wonderful, may come to depend on having her complete attention. During the early months or years of marriage she may be his constant companion. If he has a project, she runs and fetches for him, working beside him like an eager apprentice. Her adoring presence makes him feel complete and strong. He is a possessive husband because he requires her admiration in order to feel himself a man. Such a husband will consider his wife's first pregnancy a disaster.

The insecure and jealous husband may try to ignore the unborn child. He may be solicitous, as tender with his wife as if her pregnancy were a terminal illness, but he will have no interest in decorating the nursery or in choosing a name for the child. To him (and perhaps to her) the baby

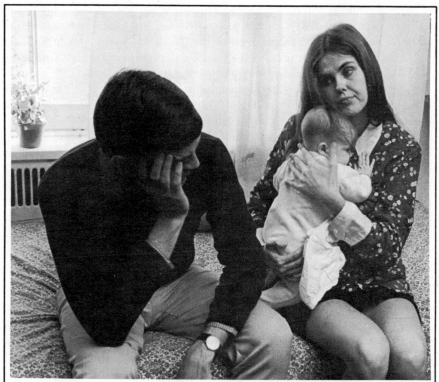

*A man with low self esteem may come to depend on having his wife's complete
attention. He is a possessive husband because he requires her adoring presence in
order to feel himself a man. Such a husband will consider his wife's first pregnancy
a disaster. After the child is born, the possessive husband may view the infant as
a rival for the affection and attention of his wife, who is now a mother.*

seems an interloper who will alter the interlocking roles that structure
their lives. He may urge his wife to get an abortion. After the child is born,
the possessive husband may view the infant as a rival for the affection and
attention of his wife, who is now a mother.

The possessive husband who is jealous of his own child can put
intolerable pressure on his wife. She feels bewildered. It is not as if she
had taken a lover, or as if this were not her husband's child. She may refuse
to feel guilty about the affection and attention she gives her infant. Yet her
husband may act as if she had betrayed him, in darker moments hinting
that perhaps the child is not his after all. Conflict over the first-born can
rip a marriage apart. The wife can try to include the husband in the circle
of mother and child; she cannot ignore the pressing needs of the infant.
Such marital conflict may require professional counseling.

Often a man is ashamed to admit feeling jealous of his child and may
express his feelings in covert fashion. He may, for example, persuade his
wife that breast-feeding will ruin her figure and interfere with their lives.

373

(Breast-feeding is often a focal point of the father's jealousy of his child.) The father may express willingness to bottle-feed the baby. Bottle-feeding might seem an obvious way to include the father in a parental role and ease his jealousy. But a baby that is bottle-fed at all is soon bottle-fed completely. Breast-feeding provides very real physical advantages to the infant in the early months of life (these advantages were discussed in some detail in Chapter 6.) Thus to some degree, bottle-feeding is a compromise that deprives the child of potential health benefits.

There is really no compromise that will satisfy a man who is jealous of his child. Like the jealous wife, the jealous husband is tormented by inner fears and self-doubts. It is his own low self-esteem that leaves him unable to feel whole unless his woman is present and attentive to him. This negative self-image creates his need for her full attention and is the basis for his possessive love for her and his inability to share her with anyone else, even their child.

Self-discovery: beyond jealousy

The jealous person, man or woman, is a person with low self-esteem, a person able to feel adequate and whole only when the loved one is present and attentive. It is this psychological dependence on the continuous approval of the loved one that creates the possessive attachment, the unwillingness to share the beloved. As noted above, there is nothing that the spouse of the jealous person can do or refrain from doing that will ease the fears of the jealous person. Resolution of the conflicts created by jealousy requires that the jealous spouse arrive at a better opinion of himself or herself.

The person with a limited or negative self-image can develop latent capacities, can become self-accepting and thus a whole person with no fears leading to jealous attachments. Self-discovery is a slow but rewarding process. One obvious example is the jealous wife whose fear of losing her husband arises from the shame she feels about being fat, and whose fat increases because food is her solace (and her revenge against her husband). It is a vicious circle of self-destructive eating and jealous fear. She may try to hide her volume under tentlike dresses; indeed, she may have no other choice in clothes. Ashamed to have her husband see her naked body, she avoids sex and then becomes convinced that he is avoiding her. She is jealous of every slender woman her husband knows, or might want to know. If she believes that she is dieting to please her husband, she is likely to hide food (as an alcoholic hides a bottle) and stuff it down hurriedly on the sly. If she can recognize that it is for herself that she is trying to reduce her bulk, she is likely to succeed. Like a junkie or an alcoholic, she cannot be helped until she looks in the mirror one day and decides that *she* can no longer live with herself as she is. But she will have to admit to herself that she will always have a problem with compulsive eating; she can take fat off and keep it off only by changing her eating habits for the rest of her life.

If this compulsive eater is convinced that under her too solid flesh is hidden a slim woman, she can eventually become the person she wants to be. It is a matter of hundreds of small choices: to eat this candy bar, or to abstain. No one choice is critical, but each time she succumbs to the small temptation, she is likely to spend the rest of the day gorging on forbidden foods (having fallen off the wagon, so to speak, she goes on a binge). Conversely, each time she refuses the candy bar or forgoes the second helping, she strengthens a pattern of response, alters her image of herself, and gradually changes her eating habits. As the pounds disappear, she has less need to seek solace from food and more pride in herself.

Similarly, the development of desired personality traits is a process involving a series of minor choices and actions, each building on prior choices and actions. A painfully shy person who clings jealously to husband or wife because this person seems the only friend he or she has ever had or is likely to have, can become outgoing and confident. The process is similar to that described for the fat wife trying to become slender. Consider the shy husband. In his case, the process is a matter of accepting an invitation, or if none are forthcoming, of extending an invitation to someone he would like to know better, to engage in some activity that he already understands and enjoys. The major pitfall for the shy husband is that once he makes a friend, he may not venture after other friendships. Exclusivity breeds jealousy. He is in danger of becoming possessive of his newfound friend, crediting that person with suddenly making his life exciting. It is the process of self-discovery that is changing his life, something he is more likely to recognize if he urges his shy self forward into a variety of new friendships. Instead of clinging jealously to his outgoing wife, the shy man can become a warm, friendly person, comfortable with himself in social situations and thus comfortable with others.

One choice at a time, one action at a time, latent potential is gradually built into a prominent feature of the self, and sustained by a new and positively valued self-image. What we have done once, we feel less fearful about trying again. What we have done many times, we are confident we can do again. We are the summation of the actions of our lifetime; each of us is the person we have chosen to become. A person who has developed latent capacities and learned to value and accept himself or herself is unlikely to experience more than an occasional twinge of jealousy.

Even that occasional twinge can be used to further self-discovery. The jealous pang suddenly felt is evidence that we are trying to experience through another person some latent capacity we want to develop within our self. Instead of reaching possessively for that other person, we can use the moment to reach for insight into ourselves. Asking first what it is that we so value in this person that we want to have it for our own, we can gain a useful glimpse of the person we can potentially become. This is an initial step toward a new self-image. The next step is to recognize that this quality

375

or way of being is one that we can add to the inventory of our expanding self: it is a matter of choice, and a series of conscious choices. Finally, taking others as our models, not claiming them for possessions, has the rewarding effect of making them our friends.

Nonrealistic conflict: the family scapegoat

The low self-esteem and unfilled needs of a husband or wife are the source of most tension within the family. If the energy and sense of urgency that tension generates are turned into action, and if that action is directed toward need fulfillment, the tension has served as a stimulus to appropriate behavior. The pattern of personal growth described above is motivated by some unfilled need, experienced as tension. The action toward satisfaction of need may sometimes lead to conflict with another member of the family. The example used above of the woman who returned to college and encountered resistance from her husband is a case in point. But as long as the behavior remains goal-oriented, the conflict is realistic and some form of compromise and accommodation is possible.

But when the barrier to need satisfaction is, or appears to be, the husband or wife, direct confrontation may seem to carry too high a risk. The tense, needful spouse may turn the accumulated tension of unsatisfied needs into free-floating anger and vent his or her fury on some less threatening target. Such attacks do not remove the source of the tension, which is the unfilled need of the attacker. But beating someone physically or verbally at least serves to drain off excess energy and to dispel anger. Beating the family scapegoat thus serves some function for the attacker, but it is at best a temporary discharge of emotion.

Attacking the family scapegoat is a form of *nonrealistic conflict. Nonrealistic conflict* functions only as a release of aggressive tension. In contrast, *realistic conflict* is goal-oriented, and is directed toward the object or person impeding progress toward that goal. Because it is goal-oriented, realistic conflict involves a choice of means, and openly hostile actions are not the only alternative. Persuasion, arbitration, and compromise are usually preferred means of overcoming obstacles to reaching the goal. Aggressive actions will usually be the last resort.

In nonrealistic conflict there is a choice of issues or antagonists, but not a choice of means. It is hostile action itself that is wanted. Conflict is not a means to a goal; the battle is both means and end. As Lewis Coser defines it: "Nonrealistic conflicts . . . although still involving interaction between two or more persons, are not occasioned by the rival ends of the antagonists, but by the need for tension release of at least one of them" (1956: 49). Because in nonrealistic conflict there is no choice of means, but only a choice of victim, the person on whom hostility is vented is simply a convenient target. The victim is someone who seems vulnerable to attack, not someone who is between the attacker and his goal. The person being attacked is a scapegoat.

The origin of the term *scapegoat* suggests the nature of nonrealistic conflict. In the Middle East of antiquity, the herding tribes had a ritual that was supposed to rid the people of accumulated sins. From time to time the priest would call the people together and cast sin out of them and into a goat. Then the people beat the goat or stoned it, and drove it into the wilderness. This was the original scapegoat; today, the target for our accumulated inner demons is a person, or a group of persons, and we are less likely to perceive that it is our own projected evil that we are attacking. The scapegoat must be a plausible target and can usually be made to provoke the wrath of the attacker. But if the scapegoat is driven away or destroyed, he will soon be replaced by another, for the source of the anger is untouched.

The scapegoat, however, is injured—how badly depends both on the intensity and the duration of the attack, and on how close to the attacker the scapegoat must live. A person who is only tangentially involved in the life of the attacker may be only marginally affected by the role of scapegoat and rarely present for abuse. The outraged wife who confronts her husband's mistress, the outraged husband who pummels his wife's lover, have only a brief, if violent, encounter with their victim. The victim can probably avoid further contact with the enraged attacker. The mother-in-law who is the object of a tirade is probably not living with the couple and, if she is, will probably move out if the scapegoat role becomes intolerable to her.

The child who becomes the family scapegoat is, unfortunately, less able to remove himself physically from the situation in which he is the target of choice. (The ranks of runaway children are swelling, however, and although not all of them are family scapegoats, it is probable that many are.) The child who is the family scapegoat may be a physically battered child. If he comes under verbal and psychological attack only, he may become an emotional cripple. Ezra Vogel and Norman Bell (1968) studied a group of families, each of which had an emotionally disturbed child, and compared them with a group of families in which none of the children was disturbed in any clinical sense. In all of the families with emotionally disturbed children, families that Vogel and Bell referred to as "disturbed families," there was one particular child who had been caught up in the tensions of the parents. That was the emotionally disturbed child, who had been made the family scapegoat.

The child is a convenient scapegoat for a number of reasons. He is physically present on a continuous basis, so that he is available for scapegoating whenever the tensions of his parents reach a point where some outlet is required. He is in a subordinate, relatively powerless position, so that he can be attacked with impunity (one requirement of a functioning scapegoat). And because the child is malleable, he can be formed into an effective scapegoat. That is, he can be encouraged to develop the characteristics that his parents deplore in him, which are the characteristics they dislike in themselves.

American adults, especially those who grew up in the middle classes, have learned that to be acceptable they must be hard-working, ambitious, self-controlled, self-sacrificing, law-abiding, honest, courteous, clean, and chaste. They are likely to have defined their self-image to exclude the converse characteristics: tendencies to be lazy, indolent, undisciplined, self-indulgent, defiant of the law, dishonest, insolent, unwashed, and promiscuous. Yet each of us is capable of such behaviors; we choose not to act in ways that we consider unacceptable. If we are aware that such latent capacities are an inevitable part of the self, that to be capable of doing good means knowing that we are capable of doing evil, these latent capacities need not be a problem. They are simply there, and we choose not to let them become an active part of the self.

But there are people who have difficulty finding themselves acceptable, people who believe that they should *never* have certain feelings, or even wish to indulge in certain behaviors. The child may have learned to believe that mother and father could not love a child who *ever* told a lie, hit the baby, masturbated, or even wanted to do any number of wicked things. Yet that child knows he is capable of such unacceptable thoughts and actions, because he learned that they were unacceptable when he was punished for doing or saying something forbidden. He may well have sought to escape punishment by saying that the misdeed was really his brother's idea. Such a child is likely to grow into an adult who is troubled by the forbidden thoughts, feelings, and desires that float up into consciousness on occasion. Aware that *someone* is having such unworthy impulses, and uncomfortable about acknowledging that they could be his own, he looks around for someone who could be feeling or thinking or acting on these rejected feelings of his own. There stands the scapegoat, ready to become the porter of sinful desires and thoughts and other alienated and despised aspects of the self. Perhaps the scapegoat is someone outside the family, perhaps it is a member of some minority group that has become a conventional scapegoat. Perhaps the scapegoat is one of his own children.

When conflict between spouses is suppressed, as it is in a "rubber-fence" marriage, there is no accepted way for either of the spouses to deal with hostility generated in marital interaction. Criticism that one would like to make of the other, but does not dare to voice, may be bounced off one of the children who happens to be a plausible target. Sometimes this is a conscious effort to draw attention to the objectionable pattern of behavior, in the hope that the offending spouse will recognize it as similar to his or her own behavior, and realize that it is offensive. Such a ploy is seldom successful, since behavior that we may agree is reprehensible in others is seldom perceived as something that we would do ourselves. ("He is a glutton, but I am a gourmand.")

Thus a woman who regards her husband as a liar and a cheat because of his extramarital escapades may be afraid to confront him about his behavior, but instead points out to him what a despicable liar and cheat their son has become. The husband and father, not wanting to recognize such tendencies in himself, may find the son a convenient repository for these aspects of himself that he refuses to recognize as his own. He may then punish the boy for lying about where he has been and what he has been doing. The husband's shame becomes transformed into self-righteous parental wrath. The boy, having encountered disbelief even when he told the truth (for it is now important to his father to believe the boy a liar) soon becomes a consummate liar. Such a pattern of projection and punishment makes him a plausible target for parental hostility. He becomes the problem child of the family.

The deflection of criticism from the spouse to the scapegoat-child may initially be a conscious transfer, but in order for an attack on one's child to seem justified, the child must be seen as the disgusting culprit. The parents reinforce the scapegoat role of the child (which has become an important element in maintaining marital stability) by rewarding and thus reinforcing the problem behavior. This is seldom done overtly, and seldom consciously. But they reward his problem behavior in indirect and subtle ways.

Parents do not directly or consciously encourage a child to wet his bed, shoplift, start fires, or take drugs. But by threatening punishment that is never carried out, by appearing indifferent to, or blandly accepting of, the child's behavior, and by giving him special attention because he has a problem, the parents encourage the very behavior they deplore.

Such parents are often highly ambivalent about certain social norms, perhaps those relating to achievement or to constraint. They may have shaped a child to carry out their own suppressed desires to flout convention or the law, much as other parents may try to achieve vicariously through their children. Sometimes one parent may be covertly encouraging the child to act out the hostility that parent feels toward outside authority, and the other parent may criticize in the child behavior that he or she is reluctant to criticize in the spouse. A woman who is concerned about her husband's ability to provide adequately for the family may be fearful about criticizing his adequacy as a breadwinner openly, but may focus instead on their son's performance at school, on his lack of motivation and drive. The husband may recognize that by joining with his wife in criticizing their son he is able to keep critical attention away from himself and to deal with the boy's problems instead of his own.

Usually only one child in the family is the scapegoat. Once he or she becomes a clearly defined victim—and disturbed—the family role system is stabilized. More often than not, it is the eldest child who becomes the family scapegoat, although the second child has the role in some disturbed families. Sometimes when the child who was the scapegoat escapes from the family, another child is singled out for the role.

When the latent conflicts between husband and wife are deflected onto one of their children, the marriage may acquire stability at the price of the emotional stability of the child. Such parents think their problem is the child, and certainly they expend a great deal of their time, energy,

379

and resources in dealing with the disturbed child's behavior. The underlying marital conflicts can thus be disguised and ignored. But the price of marital stability achieved by scapegoating a child can be high, for the child and for the parents.

Open conflict: heat and light

Suppressed conflict does not dissipate. As preceding sections of this chapter have shown, suppressed marital conflicts tend to surface as depression, jealousy, psychosomatic disorders, scapegoating, and other forms of human misery. Conflict, like a festering sore, heals best when it is opened.

However, some apparently open conflicts are symptomatic of more serious differences. They may generate considerable heat, but little light. A married couple may bicker continually over money, or the lack of it, and believe that if only the husband could get a better job, or a promotion, their problems would be solved. It seldom works out that way; several promotions later the couple are likely to be still quarreling about money.

Imagine a family in which the monthly ordeal of paying bills ends in a predictable quarrel. The husband blames his wife for the heavy installment debt and the credit card charges that have run over the maximum credit limit—again. He blames her for high utility bills ("Do all the lights and every appliance have to run all the time?"). He accuses her of running to the doctor with the children every time one of them has a runny nose. After the bills are paid, there is barely enough money to buy groceries for the month, and he feels physically, emotionally, and financially drained. There must be more money put into savings, he insists, and their insurance is inadequate. "Quit spending all our money!"

Her response is: "Same side of the record again, scratch, scratch, scratch." She is defensive about the household expenditures, quick to seize on the matter of the children's visits to the pediatrician—doesn't he care about the health of the children? She insists that she manages as well as she can, considering the inadequate household allowance he gives her. Behind the blaming—an ineffective tactic, which will be discussed later— lies a deeper conflict over basic goals and role images. Money is the weapon, but not the issue.

In the preceding chapter, a similar scenario was described for the man whose self-image is focused on being a good provider, and who regards his wife as his extravagant child bride. Underneath the pattern of projected role images lies a power struggle. He holds the purse strings, including control of the bank accounts, investments, and so on, as a means of dominance. The power of the purse is his. She spends on credit defiantly, squandering his resources and thus eroding his power. The couple may bicker continuously about money, without ever addressing the question of marital dominance.

380 The Good Provider has a desire—probably not a conscious desire—

The husband who has adopted the role of Good Provider regards his wife as an extravagant Child Bride and blames her for their heavy installment debt and the credit card charges that have run over the credit limit—again. Behind the blaming lies a deeper conflict over basic goals and role images. Money is the weapon, but not the issue.

to keep his Child Bride irresponsible. This keeps her clearly his dependent and his subordinate. If straightening out the family finances were his real concern, he could accomplish this in a variety of ways, such as closing the charge accounts, tearing up credit cards, and taking over the grocery shopping. Such measures would undoubtedly cause a major fight with his wife, but another quarrel over money would be nothing new. That he permits his Child Bride to have credit cards and other means of tapping his bank account indicates that he does choose to let her spend recklessly. This fits his latent desire to be a generous provider, and at the same time permits him to keep his image of her as an irresponsible Child Bride intact. He makes it possible for her to fit the image he projects onto her.

For her part, she is aware of her husband's expectation of her, and

381

she chooses to play the role. She could escape the dependent financial status that she complains about so bitterly by taking a job. If the children are small, it might have to be a part-time job, but even so, she could have income of her own if she chose. That she does not seek paid employment is an indication that she accepts the role of Child Bride, much as her husband has prepared the script. The extent to which she is permitted to indulge her expensive tastes is greater than she admits. And she enjoys wheedling extra money from her husband. This is a skill that she has developed over the years, and it gives her a sense of manipulating him. Because the underlying conflict has to do with dominance and power, manipulative skills seem important to her.

The quarrels over money are thus a symptom of a more complex marital conflict. But the conflict is realistic in that it is goal-oriented, and not merely a discharge of hostility or an end in itself. The man's goals include providing more insurance, including annuities, for his family, making long-term investments for future security, and advancing in the company where he holds job tenure and has a stake in the pension plan. All of these specific goals contribute to his major goal, financial security for his family, including money for the children's college education. His self-image as a Good Provider is consistent with this goal. His chosen means to reach this goal is careful money management: what used to be thought of as Yankee thrift. He considers himself frugal. His wife has another word for him.

This woman has a primary goal: being a Good Mother. More specifically, she wants to be a better mother than her own mother was. She wants to give the children the best medical care, the best schools, the best piano teacher, the best corrective shoes to straighten out their daughter's pigeon-toed walk. She expects her husband's income to rise over the years and does not understand why he is so insistent on putting money away for the future. She wants to use their cash—and credit—to have the good life, as she defines it, while their children are home to enjoy it. She does not want to scrimp and limit their childhood in order to provide for retirement for the two of them in a luxurious empty nest (as she saw her parents do). She wants a comfortable home in a pleasant neighborhood with good schools, and she wants it now, while the children are growing up. She wants to take family vacations while the children are young enough to enjoy going somewhere with their parents. Her tastes are expensive, and her goals are fostered by a culture oriented to consumption, but she does have a deep desire to provide for her children the kind of childhood she would have liked: a goal that seems to her to be worthy and maternal.

If at some point in time there is an intense confrontation between this husband and wife over money—perhaps when some account goes to a collection agency, perhaps when he decides to refuse the offer of a new job that might have meant a higher salary—this conflict could become the catalyst for marital growth. Sitting down together (with professional counseling if they are unable to make progress by themselves), each needs to

list the personal and family goals that are important to him and to her.
Comparing their diverse goals, they will note that there is at least one
major goal that both share: concern about providing adequately for their
children. (That he considers her one of the children is a point that will have
to be raised and recognized.) The difference in their goals is one of time
perspective: she is focused on the present, where the children are living
and growing; he is concerned for the future well-being of his family. But
both share a desire to provide well for the children.

With this point where their goals converge made apparent, the two
may be able to reach some compromise on the means of attaining their
shared goal. She may be less resentful of having a share of their current
income put into insurance and savings when it becomes apparent to her
that some of the insurance is to provide for a college education for the
children. And she may perceive that her husband's present job may be a
more certain if somewhat slower means of arriving at the desired level of
living she wants to share with the children. The risks of changing jobs may
not previously have been clear to her, or the financial and emotional costs
of moving. For his part, he may quit blaming her for high medical bills and
find a group health plan that would provide both for his concern for
long-term security and for her worry about this week's virus infection.

Having found some common ground, the two can concentrate on
achieving what have become revealed as shared goals, family goals. The
process can contribute to family solidarity. He will have to become less
secretive about family finances, and she will have to become more skillful
in money management. He will have to share control of the family income
with her, and thus to some degree he will have to give up dominance over
her. If he is unwilling to consider the possibility of their marriage evolving
into an equal partnership, he will at least have to recognize that the price
of continued dominance is likely to be continued financial difficulty and
deepening resentment on both sides.

Realistic conflict can lead to insight that clarifies personal and family
goals, insight that makes it possible to accommodate differences and even
sometimes to redefine marital roles. This man may be surprised at how
quickly his child bride grows up, given some financial responsibility and
a more equal role in making family decisions. Open, realistic conflict can
offer an opportunity to see beyond role images and through projections
to the spouse as a human being of many dimensions.

Conflict resolution: complaining without blaming

Open, realistic conflict can be resolved, and the process is a means to
personal and marital growth. If conflict is to be constructive, there must
be mutual awareness of the point at which one might go too far and a sense
of fair play on both sides. There must be some rules that each will honor,
even in the heat of argument.

One important rule of marital conflict is that either must have the right to register a complaint. Of equal importance is the rule that neither should place blame. There is a difference between complaining and blaming that determines the entire tone of a marital confrontation. When we blame, we are denying our own responsibility for creating the situation. In all probability, when we blame we are projecting our own faults onto our spouse, where we find them disgusting. Blaming invites a defensive response, often in the form of a counterattack. Finally, blaming seldom produces any positive change in the behavior of the other. If the aim is to give vent to frustration, a scream will do. If the goal is to change the behavior of our spouse, a specific complaint, registered at the time of the action, will be much more effective.

Accumulated resentments over actions that no longer matter to either partner are best forgotten. Grievances sour with time, and should not be thrown at our partners in the heat of argument. These are the bitter words we regret later. When we find ourselves berating someone about something that happened more than a few days ago, the odds are that we are blaming. The time to register a complaint is the moment the offending action occurs. If neither the time nor the place is appropriate for an extended hearing of the issues, simply lodge a protest and request a hearing at the earliest possible time.

The next rule is that a complaint deserves a hearing. This is a reciprocal understanding that can be made to work, especially if the complaint is made at the appropriate time. The hearing of a marital grievance should be held when there will be time to reach some resolution of the issues. A conflict that begins at the breakfast table, when one or both are rushing to work, cannot be resolved at that time. An unresolved conflict is a poor way to begin the day; it creates a dangerous state of mind in anyone driving an automobile, and it leads to stress on the job. A quarrel that begins at bedtime takes place when either or both are tired, and may serve only to disrupt sleep. The timing of a hearing for a marital complaint is thus a delicate matter. It should follow closely the action to which we are taking exception, but it should also come at a time that allows for a full hearing of the issues and a consideration of alternatives.

The place in which we confront our spouse with a complaint, and particularly the place where we agree to hold the hearing, should be a neutral corner. Usually each spouse has some territory in the home that is his or her ground: for the wife, this is usually the kitchen; for the husband, it is typically the garage, workshop, or den. Avoid giving the advantage of the setting to either party; this is an extraneous factor that should not enter into the conflict. Find a place that is clearly common ground. At the same time, it is best not to take a quarrel into the bedroom. The possibility that a marital conflict will take on sexual overtones is greater if the fight takes place in the bedroom.

The manner in which we register a complaint is an important factor in resolving marital conflicts. We should learn to listen to our own voice when registering a complaint. The words we use may not matter if we are shouting or if there is a strident edge to our voice. Children respond more to the tone of voice than to the words; so do husbands and wives. And if there is a whine in our voice, we are blaming. The whine gives us away.

To agree that each has the right to make a complaint, and that a complaint deserves a hearing, means that we have agreed to hear out our spouse. Reciprocity is a necessary foundation for marriage. We have agreed to listen, to bite our tongue if necessary until the full complaint is made. Listening to the words, listening to what is said between the words, and watching the face, the body, the gestures, of our spouse, we have an opportunity to understand and resolve conflicts that have been submerged.

These are revealing moments in which it is possible to see through the role images we have long projected onto our spouse. If the complaint is surprising, if we had no idea that our husband or wife had any objections to certain behavior, or resented doing things we assumed he or she enjoyed, there is a high probability that someone is projecting. Perhaps we have been projecting our own expectations onto our partner. Perhaps he or she has been projecting expected role images onto us. Perhaps both of us have been projecting. One of the functions of marital conflict is insight. Another function of marital conflict is stripping away inappropriate role images, bringing home our projected desires. It is not a pleasant process, but it can be a cleansing one.

Marital conflict: a summary

A marriage without conflict is not necessarily a happy marriage. A couple who are preoccupied with maintaining harmony and consensus may in fact have a "rubber-fence" marriage. When persons with low self-esteem marry, the marriage may be more a flight from the self than a fulfillment. It may be an attempt to merge two people who are convinced of their individual inadequacy into one synthetic superperson in the hope that this hyphenated identity (John-and-Mary) will be able to function, or at least to cope. Thus each has a heavy emotional investment in the marriage, and seeks to maintain it by creating a "rubber fence" to hold the other in the relationship.

For all their clinging together, the husband and wife with a "rubber-fence" marriage do not enjoy each other. There is little overt conflict in the marriage, but then there is little intense emotion of any nature expressed. There is above all no humor, no zest in their life together. Perhaps neither expected to find joy in marriage, perhaps all either sought was an ally.

In a "rubber-fence" marriage, both spouses tend to be more concerned with maintaining an illusion of relatedness than with relating to each other. Open efforts to relate to the other may seem to carry a risk of rejection, a risk of exposing the defects that each is trying to conceal. Husband and wife may play marital roles as if they were trying to hide

385

behind them. Few new interests will be cultivated by either, if both insist
that their lives remain perfectly meshed. Any deviance from expected
marital roles seems threatening. They have coauthored the script, and
each can cue the other.

One mark of a "rubber-fence" marriage is a preoccupation with
harmony. Conflict is seen as likely to precipitate disaster. Ritualized role
playing is supposed to propitiate the family monster: something that lurks
within some member of the family and may be called forth by any deviation
from rigid role behaviors. Perhaps this monster is the legendary rage of
husband or wife ("Don't do anything to upset your father, you know how
he can get.") Sometimes the "monster" is an illness that hangs over the
family, an illness that family legend says will be brought on by a breakdown
of the existing family role structure. Even a minor protest against the
family *status quo* may be seen as provoking a heart attack, a stroke, an
asthmatic seizure. One of the family rituals may involve the husband
bringing the children to kiss their mother goodby (again) while she gasps
for breath and sympathy, and all promise to be good if only she will get
well.

Within the tyranny of the "rubber-fence" marriage, any complaint
seems provocation, and all differences are stifled. A couple with such a
marriage have a desperate preoccupation with unanimity and harmony,
and conformity to role images is seen as an end in itself. If one partner
should challenge existing role expectations, the other will make efforts to
discourage the challenge. Failing that, there will be efforts to accommodate to change in ways that will restore the previous role structure, the
"rubber fence" stretching to contain the new behavior, contracting to
squeeze it out.

As a last resort, husband and wife may exchange roles. For example,
if a dependent spouse becomes independent, the formerly "strong" partner may assume the helpless role. (That impending heart attack may
occur.) This is a pattern sometimes seen in a marriage where one partner
is an alcoholic and the other has had to be the strong and stable member
of the family. If the alcoholic spouse finally is able to achieve control of
his or her illness and becomes able to function, hold a job, and take
responsibility, the other spouse may develop some debilitating disorder.
Dramatis personae may change, but the family role system tends to stay
intact.

The "rubber-fence" marriage is a form of relationship that closes off
the outside world, a marriage in which the relationship between husband
and wife becomes stagnant, like a pond with no stream running through
it. A marriage in which there is no overt conflict is likely to be a marriage
in which there is no personal growth. It is also likely to be a marriage in
which one spouse or the other is depressed (the unexpressed anger turned
inward) and a marriage marked by intense jealousy. Unless there are ways
in which anger may be expressed, one spouse or the other may feel

386

crushed, and react by withdrawing physically (desertion, divorce) or by withdrawing into depression.

In such a marriage, one partner, or both, may be too fearful of losing the relationship to risk any expression of resentment or hostility. This partner is perhaps most often the wife. Because the husband is typically the member of the family who encounters and copes daily with the outside world, he tends to develop some degree of autonomy from the relationship and is usually the least dependent on it. This fact gives him a dominant position within the marriage. As the one with the least to lose, he can exert maximum pressure on his wife to conform to marital role expectations. He may be oblivious to facets of her personality that do not complement his self-image. After a period of time she may conform to his persistent pressures—like a comfortable old shoes that has been pushed out of shape.

The husband described in an earlier section of this chapter who tried to ignore the fact that his wife had returned to college and had new roles to play was communicating through actions louder than words: "What you are doing is so insignificant that I have not even noticed it." It is not that there was no conflict, but rather that it had taken the form of metacommunication (*meta* is a Greek prefix, meaning *over*, or *beyond*.) This kind of attack is difficult to counter with reason. It creates a defense that is almost impenetrable. If there is to be room for marital change and personal growth, room for reasonable compromise, the first move is to make the conflict open. This means talking about conflicting goals, making change a recognized issue, insisting that a complaint be heard. Learning to register a complaint is the first step toward resolution of conflicts, even those hidden behind the "rubber fence."

Some overt marital conflict is nonrealistic in that it has no aim or goal, except the release of tension. The apparent cause of the trouble, the target of hostility, may be only a scapegoat (often, one of the children). But realistic conflict is goal-oriented. In realistic conflict there is a choice of means. An angry confrontation should be the last resort, not the first attempt to alter a behavior pattern. Joking may be an effective way to call attention to a conflict in role images or marital role expectations. It may be possible to make a request at an appropriate time, instead of waiting to express a grievance after the fact. A direct, specific request is likely to produce the desired response; waiting for our wife or husband to second-guess what we would like is an invitation to projection.

Thus realistic conflict may be resolved through humor, through persuasion, or by seeking an arbitrator in the form of a marriage counselor for the deeper conflicts. But it should be recognized that realistic conflict is a means of opening up a marriage to change. Realistic conflict can lead to clarification of family goals, to accommodation of differences in personal goals, and sometimes to redefinition of marital roles. Hearing a complaint can make both husband and wife more aware of what they share

387

and where they differ. Conflict keeps each aware of the boundary between Me and Thee, and sharpens recognition of the spouse as an individual with desires and dreams that must be given dignity.

References

Coser, Lewis. 1956. *The Functions of Social Conflict.* New York: The Free Press.

Fromm, Erich. 1956. *The Art of Loving.* New York: Harper & Row.

Vogel, Ezra F., and Norman W. Bell. 1968. "The Emotionally Disturbed Child as the Family Scapegoat." In *A Modern Introduction to the Family*, rev. ed., edited by Norman W. Bell and Ezra F. Vogel, pp. 412–427. New York: The Free Press.

Suggested readings

Porter, Katherine Ann. 1967. "The Downward Path to Wisdom." In *The Leaning Tower and Other Stories.* New York: Harcourt, Brace Jovanovich.

"Mama was being cross with Papa again. He could tell by the sound . . . Papa was being cross, too, much crosser than Mama this time. He grew cold and disturbed and sat very still, wanting to go to the bathroom . . . He slid off the bench. His mother's voice rose in a terrible scream, screaming something he could not understand, but she was furious; he had seen her clenching her fists and stamping in one spot, screaming with her eyes shut; he knew how she looked . . . He stood still, doubled over, and all his his body seemed to dissolve, sickly, from the pit of his stomach." Caught up in the conflict between his parents, perceived by his grandmother and maternal uncle as being a liar and a thief, "like his father," the small boy who is the protagonist of this short story is gradually becoming the family scapegoat.

Young, Leontine. 1964 *Wednesday's Children.* New York: McGraw-Hill Book Company. Available in paper. This is a penetrating study of child neglect and abuse, and of the patterns of family conflict involved. Writing of the parents in such families, Young states: "Most of them played out a strange drama of aggressor and victim in relation to each other as well as in their behavior toward the children. The aggressor might be mother or father; there was no indication that either sex had a monopoly on that role. Whether the aggressive parent selected as his primary victim the other parent, one child or all the children, the passive parent tended to defend him, to deny the realities of the family situation, and to cling to the family situation and to the abusing partner."

14 Divorce: legal fictions and social realities

The law should make it possible to dissolve the legal tie once that has become irretrievably broken in fact. If the marriage is dead, the object of the law should be to afford it a decent burial.

Great Britain Law Commission (1966)

"I'm getting married tomorrow, and I'm scared. I hear a great steel door sliding shut behind me." The uncertain bride was a beautiful woman, a sensitive and intelligent woman of twenty-two. She obviously liked the young man she was about to marry: she had been living with him for nearly two years. But tomorrow the vault door of marriage would close behind her, and she was in a state of intense anxiety. Her own parents were divorced, so she was quite aware that there was a legal exit, but this thought did not give her ease. The door she heard was in her head. She was leaving a casual living arrangement for something she wanted to believe was a lifetime commitment. Yet she was terrified by the thought that she was about to make an irrevocable promise. No one watching her the next day, as she walked down the aisle looking like Nefertiti reborn, would have guessed her inner qualms. Less than two years later, she was a divorcée.

Clifford Kirkpatrick observes that "husband and wives locked by social pressure in the close bonds of marriage may react like cats in a sack and scratch and tear at each other in sheer panic of confinement" (1963: 576). The heaviest pressures on marriage are the inner ones: if marriage is experienced as a commitment, divorce is a broken promise; if marriage is considered a sacrament, divorce is a sin.

Church, state, and divorce: a brief history

The feelings toward marriage and divorce that each of us has are deeply rooted in childhood experience: the teachings of whatever church we knelt in at the age of five or six; memories of the first wedding we ever saw, of the chance comment we overheard about a divorced woman who lived up the street and was reportedly no better than she should have been. The cumulative effect of experience is different for each person, but for a given social class, ethnic group, and generation there tends to be a consensus, reflecting common childhood situations. Attitudes toward marriage and divorce reflect tradition as well as individual experience, but "tradition" is often a deceptive label. Our view of the past is always foreshortened—like those first photographs we took on our Brownie camera at summer camp, those shots of friends sitting on the grass with their legs extended toward the camera, friends who seem to have huge feet and pinheads. *Whatever is close to us in time seems to dwarf the major body of tradition.*

Thus the concept of marriage as a sacrament and an indissoluble union may seem to have existed from the dawn of time, or at least of the Christian era. But in fact, it was not developed until the middle of the sixteenth century. The longer tradition, of several thousand years standing, held that marriage and divorce are private, family matters. The early Hebrews permitted a husband to dissolve the marriage bond by preparing a writ of divorcement or merely by pronouncing, "I thee divorce," or its counterpart. Things have become rather more complicated in the twenty-five centuries since. But throughout most of Western history, for the ancient Greeks, Romans, and Teutons as well as for the Hebrews, divorce —like marriage—was a private matter. It was settled by the parties concerned and their relatives.

Historically, especially in the Mediterranean societies from which our Judeo-Christian tradition springs, divorce was the husband's prerogative. It could not be initiated by the wife for any reason. In a patriarchal and patrilineal society, marriage was contracted for the dual purposes of creating family alliances and of perpetuating the family line. A barren wife could be "put away," for she had failed in her most important duty. Divorce was the least of the punishments meted out to an adulterous wife, who might be stoned for her sin, sold into slavery, or banished. Because marriage was not expected to be an emotionally intimate relationship, however, such grounds for divorce as incompatibility and cruelty were not even imaginable. A chaste wife who had borne sons was assured of continuous status as wife.

In some early societies, a bride-price functioned as a bond posted by the husband. If a man divorced his wife for any reason other than infertility or adultery, he had to forfeit the bride-price he had paid to her family. Among some Germanic tribes, part of the bride-price was given to the bride herself, and she kept this when she returned to her own family after divorce (Nash 1955). The engagement ring may be the last vestige of the "bride-price" given to the bride. In societies with a dower system, wealth flowed the other way at the time of marriage. But again, the effect was to enhance marital stability. The husband might have to return the lands and cattle his wife had brought into the marriage if he divorced her without cause. There was no court to compel him to return the property with the woman, but the wife's brothers and cousins could be expected to mount an expedition to recover the family property. Thus for all the ease with which a man could divorce his wife in most early Western societies, pressures applied by kin groups and the property settlements that accompanied marriage kept divorce an uncommon occurrence. (However, a second wife or a concubine was commonly permitted to men with the resources to support more than one family.)

In Western societies, there were no grounds on which a woman could divorce her husband until Roman women gained the right to divorce in the days of the Empire. Marriage—and divorce—were private matters in Rome; no court had jurisdiction. In the days of the Republic, the Roman *pater familias* was the law in his own household. But women acquired more rights during the days of the Empire. Imperial Romans married more for personal reasons (including the acquisition of wealth and power) than as a matter of family alliance. If the fortunes of a spouse took a turn for the worse—favorites of Caesar had a way of falling out of favor—the wealthy Roman matron might break her marital bonds as lightly as she had contracted them. If Juvenal is to be believed (and he may have been a misogy-

393

nist as well as a satirist), Roman ladies of leisure were prone to leaving their husbands to run after gladiators. Seneca made the bitter comment that Roman women "counted the years by husbands."

The reaction to excess is often extremism in the opposite direction. The early Christians reacted to the dissolute Romans of their day by elevating celibacy, rather than marriage, as the supreme human state. Those who did marry were expected to remain faithful to the spouse and to leave marriage only for the celibate state. Throughout the early Middle Ages, however, as William Kephart observes, "there were limits to the Christian influence on marriage and divorce ... since these were still regarded largely as private matters rather than as affairs of State or Church" (1961:112). The canon law of the Church regarding marriage and divorce was formulated slowly. According to Kirkpatrick: "For many centuries Christianity had waged war against the relatively free divorce practices of Romans and Germans. Yet divorce did occur. Divorce apparently was allowed for adultery and for other grounds, with remarriage possible after the divorce" (1963:113).

At the Council of Trent, which met from 1545 to 1563, the canon law regarding marriage and divorce was clarified. The bonds of marriage were declared indissoluble, but legal separations *a mensa et thoro* (with bed and board) were granted for cause. The "bed-and-board" legal separation did not terminate marriage, and thus did not free the parties to remarry. Legal separations were permitted on grounds of adultery, spiritual adultery (heresy), and cruelty. Another provision made it possible to dissolve marriage by papal dispensation if a Christian spouse were abandoned by an infidel spouse. And marriage could be nullified because of the existence of some impediment, such as the fact that one of the spouses was under age when the marriage was contracted, or because of incest, bigamy, or a variety of other factors *existing prior to the marriage*. If an impediment to the marriage were found by an ecclesiastical court, then a valid marriage had never existed and both parties were declared free to marry someone else.

Annulment thus was the means of bypassing the indissoluble marriage that existed from the time of the Council of Trent, for *some* impediment could usually be discovered if sufficient pressure were exerted on the ecclesiastical court. Among the inbred nobility and aristocracy of Europe, it was usually possible to establish some degree of consanguinity that would nullify a marriage, if that were desired. According to Kirkpatrick, annulment could even be procured because of the "impediment that a husband had stood godfather to the cousin of his wife" (1963:113–114).

The Protestant Reformation brought a value crisis in which divorce was one of the points of contention. The desire of Henry VIII to divorce and remarry was the precipitating factor in the schism between England and Rome. (Actually, Henry VIII wanted an annulment, for that would have made his daughter Mary illegitimate issue, and cleared the right of succession for the legitimate sons he hoped to have by a subsequent marriage.)

The Protestants took a somewhat more liberal position on the question of divorce, permitting absolute divorce from a valid marriage. Luther seems to have believed that only adultery and desertion were adequate grounds for divorce (Kirkpatrick 1963:116). However, in addition to adultery and desertion, cruelty and "refusal of conjugal duty" (which meant refusal of sexual intercourse) were also considered grounds for divorce by most Protestant churches. There was a tendency for the Protestants to favor full divorce rather than the "bed-and-board" legal separation that the Catholic canon law provided as the only relief from a valid marriage.

Milton, the great Protestant epic poet, wrote a series of pamphlets in favor of divorce in the years between 1643 and 1645. "His ostensible purpose," H. R. Hays observes, "was to free mankind from irksome fetters and his real purpose was to express his desire to get rid of his wife" (1964:171). Milton had married the sixteen-year-old daughter of a Royalist family, a girl accustomed to fun and games at the fringes of the Stuart court, who must have been as bored with the scholarly poet as he was with her. In any event, Milton comments ruefully, "Is is not strange how many who have spent their life chastely, are in some things not so quicksighted, while they haste too eagerly to light the nuptial torch." In spite of Milton's pamphleteering, an Englishman seeking a divorce had to receive a decree from a ecclesiastical court and then arrange for a private bill to be passed by Parliament granting the divorce. Except for a brief period under Cromwell, the Puritan revolutionary, it was not until 1857 that judicial divorce (that is, divorce granted by a court of law rather than by an act of Parliament) became available in England.

"Dead chickens in my teapot": three centuries of divorce in America

The Puritans were convinced that the state, rather than the church, should regulate moral behavior. Thus there were no ecclesiastical courts established in the colonies of New England and American colonial assemblies granted divorce without the prior ruling of an ecclesiastical court. When the United States became independent, state legislatures took over the power to grant divorce by special bill (corresponding to the power of the English Parliament). There was, for example, the divorce that the Connecticut legislature granted to Mrs. Polly White, who charged that her husband "went to bed with his boots on to annoy me and put dead chickens in my teapot." Although this divorce was granted on grounds that would today be called "mental cruelty" or "indignities," most divorces in early America were granted on grounds of adultery or desertion.

State legislators often combined divorce petitions into an omnibus bill. Thus Nelson Blake (1962:55–56) describes a bill that was passed by the Missouri state legislature in the 1830s that divorced thirty-seven couples; at another session the Missouri legislature divorced forty-nine couples. But the practice was open to abuse, and there was the problem that

395

the specifics of a given divorce settlement could not be dealt with properly when thirty or forty other marriages might be sundered by the same legislative act. Moreover, only the wealthy were able to press effectively for a special act of the state legislature. In 1846 New York passed an amendment of the state constitution that abolished legislative divorce. Other states followed a similar course and passed constitutional amendments barring legislative divorce.

Judicial divorce had existed concurrently with legislative divorce in the early decades of U.S. legal history. In 1777 the Maryland legislature empowered the judiciary to grant divorce to petitioners who could prove the spouse adulterous. In 1786 the legislature of Massachusetts passed similar legislation. In 1787 Alexander Hamilton, lobbying on behalf of a cuckolded client, persuaded the New York legislature to make adultery a ground for judicial divorce. Until the state constitution was amended in 1846, the New York *legislature* continued to grant divorce by special act on a variety of grounds, ranging from desertion and drunkenness to "leaving the family to join the Shakers." But it did not amend the statute empowering the *judiciary* of New York to grant divorce until 1966; for nearly two hundred years adultery was the only ground on which divorce could be obtained in a court of the state of New York.

By the middle of the nineteenth century, it had become apparent that the citizens of states with strict divorce laws (such as New York) were going to other, more lenient states for divorce. In the recent past Nevada was the state best known as a "divorce mill." But before that other states had encouraged migratory divorce, including, at one time or another, Vermont, Pennsylvania, Indiana, Illinois, South Dakota, and Wyoming. In the 1850s legal scholars had drawn on some court decisions and writings in the field of family law, and had constructed the theory of divorce jurisdiction known as *marital res.* According to Doris Freed and Henry Foster, Jr.: "Under that theory, marriage was regarded as a legal status, or *res*, and the only proper court to grant divorce was that of the domicile of the parties. The theory was refined so as to permit a deserted wife to acquire a domicile of her own, independent of that of her husband, and contrary to English law, the rule became that the domicile of either had jurisdiction to grant a divorce" (1969:74).

There was another position, however, which held that only if both parties had submitted themselves to the jurisdiction of a court for the settlement of the dispute could the decree be valid (this is known as a *bilateral* divorce decree), and that a divorce granted under such circumstances was valid without regard to domicile. This position was adopted by New York, Pennsylvania, and North and South Carolina. Freed and Foster comment that "the clash between the majority and minority positions led to several of the most famous Supreme Court decisions with regard to the full faith and credit obligation to recognize sister-state divorce decrees, and today federal law in this regard is an illogical but practical compromise between the two theories" (1969:74).

By the end of the nineteenth century, the broad outline of divorce law had been worked out in the United States. Divorce is a matter of state, not federal, law. The Protestant position that absolute divorce should be granted for cause was accepted in all states (except South Carolina, which repealed all laws pertaining to divorce in 1878 and did not grant divorce again until 1949). Legislative divorce had been banned, and the courts given the power to grant divorce by judicial decree, on grounds established by the legislature of each state. Most states had agreed that only a state that was the domicile of at least one spouse had jurisdiction to grant divorce. "In order to guard against frivolous divorce, affirmative defenses were set up as a bar, and corroboration of the plaintiff's complaint might be required . . . The premise was that only an innocent and injured spouse was entitled to a divorce, which must be obtained at home, on the ground of a serious marital transgression" (Freed and Foster 1969:75).

Although the political philosophy that was the foundation of American democracy embodied the ideals of individualism, including the right to the "pursuit of happiness," and American marriages were supposedly love matches based on free, individual choice of mate, there was no return to the ancient concept of marriage and divorce as private, family matters. Grudgingly, some states recognized common-law marriage. But there was no such thing as common-law divorce. Desertion did not free either party to remarry, although desertion was an accepted ground for divorce in most states.

Divorce is not regarded as a private matter in any state; on the contrary, the state perceives itself as an interested third party. The position of the state is explained by the fact that an abandoned wife and minor children often become public charges. In the ancient civilizations and in medieval Europe, the extended family assumed the care of abandoned wives and children, along with widows and orphans. Today, the state is in many respects a surrogate for the kinship network of ancient societies. As pressures from kinfolk once operated to keep marriages together, so the state has tended to exert pressures to keep marriages intact, or at least has tended to make divorce difficult to obtain. The state has an interest in keeping families together, and it is more than a financial interest. Most state codes implicitly (sometimes explicitly) recognize the family as the basic unit of social structure and as a primary source of social stability. Marriage is a contract between two persons, but the state must give its permission for the contract to be valid. A divorce suit is a civil action brought by one person against another, but it is not an ordinary breach-of-contract suit or suit for damages. There is a plaintiff and a defendant, but the state forms a third side in the hearing.

Unfortunately, crowded court dockets make most divorce hearings perfunctory. Family matters (including, but not limited to, divorce actions) constitute more than 50 percent of all civil litigation (Foster 1969:133). The great crisis in the lives of a man and a woman is a routine matter for the court. The average time for a divorce hearing in California before its family law code was reformed in 1969 was seven minutes, and this, according to Aidan Gough, only "if counsel strives to speak the litany

397

clearly and not run his words together" (1970:19). One recent divorcée—not yet able to think of herself as belonging in that category—voiced a sense of bewildered disappointment felt by many women: "I thought there would be more to it than that. My attorney just asked a few questions and the judge asked something without even looking up from the papers in front of him, and then my attorney indicated that I should step down. It couldn't have taken five minutes and my marriage had lasted five years. I still feel married."

Divorce bargaining: alimony, property, custody

Part of the reason that divorce actions often seem perfunctory is that most are uncontested. According to the U.S. Public Health Service (1973:10), the proportion of divorce cases that are contested has always been low. In the years between 1887 and 1906, only 15.4 percent of divorce actions were contested. According to Foster: "The routine issuance of divorce decrees in uncontested cases increased to the point that, by the 1950's, over 90 percent of American divorces were uncontested" (1969:130). It is not that there are no battles, but rather that they are usually won or lost before the plaintiff appears in court. If one wants the divorce and the other does not, it may be more effective to use such weapons as money and children in a battle out of court to block the divorce than to contest the divorce in court. The spouse who wants his or her freedom may become persuaded that the cost of that freedom would be too high.

The issues on which divorce bargaining centers are money, property, custody of children, and the divorce itself. The custody of children of "tender years" (by which a court usually means children under the age of fourteen) is almost always awarded to the mother, unless she is found by the court to be an unfit parent. Usually most of the property is in the name of the husband. Thus she goes into the bargaining session with the children as counters, and he holds the property. This leaves the matter of which one is most eager to have his or her freedom. Usually one wants the divorce more urgently than the other, and the bargaining may thus turn on what will be the price of freedom.

A husband who wants to block a divorce may threaten to challenge the mother's fitness for custody. Each may sincerely believe that the other (and perhaps the prospective stepfather or stepmother waiting in the wings) would be a bad influence on the child or children, so custody may be the real focus of the battle and not merely a means of blocking the divorce. Or the husband may use his control of property and income as an attempt to prevent the divorce. A woman who wants out of her marriage may have to settle for a small amount of property and no alimony as the price of freedom, if her husband wants either to block the divorce or to punish her for leaving him.

Conversely, a rejected wife may demand a generous (or punitive) property settlement and alimony as the price of freedom for her husband.

398

She may hope either to hold him by the threat of impoverishment or at least to make it difficult for him to marry the "other woman." Even if the settlement is a fair one, few men have resources adequate to maintain two households on the same level of living that they formerly maintained one. Even if both spouses are agreed that they want to dissolve the marriage, the division of money and property can turn what might have been an amicable separation into a bitter struggle. It is not merely a matter of greed. Morris Ploscowe observes that:

> When a husband comes into a lawyer's office and confidently asserts that, despite the breakup of the marriage, he would like to maintain his family at the standard of living that they are now enjoying, simple arithmetic may give him a rude shock . . . . Wives sometimes leave a lawyer's office in an unbelieving daze, when they are brought to realize that a dissolution of the marriage necessarily requires a cut in their standard of living or additional income, which may require them to go to work—which they may be unable to do because of children or lack of skills. (Ploscowe 1969:14–15)

If one of the spouses wants out badly enough to pay the price, the two will arrive at a settlement. Bargaining is usually conducted through attorneys, and ultimately results in an agreement on division of property, alimony, child support, custody, and visitation rights. This usually takes the form of a separation agreement. If the separation is followed by a divorce, the provisions of the separation agreement are usually incorporated into the divorce decree (Ploscowe 1969:15). However, the court may render its own judgment on an equitable settlement, and is likely to be most sensitive on the issues of custody of the children and the amount of child support awarded. Children over the age of fourteen may sometimes be questioned by the judge in chambers as to their preference in the matter of custody, but typically children have no opportunity to speak for themselves in court.

Child support should not be confused with alimony. If there are children, child support is awarded, for a father's obligation to support his children does not end with divorce. In most states, the mother also has a legal responsibility to support her child. The obligation of the parent does not cease until the child is of legal age (in most states, this now means the age of eighteen). Child support is in addition to any alimony that may be awarded. The court retains jurisdiction, and may order changes in the amount of child support at a later time, if the child's needs become greater (for example, because of medical expense or the expense of education).

Alimony is derived from the marital support obligations that were discussed in the chapter on money and marriage. Historically, alimony was support for the wife who was granted a "bed-and-board" separation from her husband by an English ecclesiastical court. Alimony was not awarded in the case of an absolute divorce under English law (Ploscowe 1969:16). Thus in its origins, alimony was paid by a man to support a

399

woman who was still his wife, although she had won the right to live separately and to be exempted from her marital duties. Such an award was not as unfair to the husband as it might seem, for under English common law, the husband came into control at marriage of any property his wife owned, and had the income or rents from that property at his disposal. Along with control of his wife's property went the obligation to support her; if she won a legal separation, he retained control of her property (he was still her husband) and he was still responsible for her support. Even if a particular wife had never owned property, the principle was still observed. There was also a punitive element in the award of alimony. According to Ploscowe, if "the parties were legally separated because the husband was guilty of cruelty or adultery, then the husband could be required to provide alimony and support for the wife when she was authorized by a court to live separate and apart from him" (1969:16).

In the United States, statutes regarding the property of married women were amended in most states during the nineteenth century. These amendments, known collectively as the Married Women's Property Acts, gave a married woman the right to hold property in her own name and to control any property that she acquired. (In the nineteenth century, women were most likely to acquire property through inheritance, from either father or husband.) Giving the married woman control of her own property removed the original basis for the support obligation of the husband and also the original legal basis for alimony. However, the obligation of the husband to support his wife remained in state statutes. The divorce laws that were promulgated by most states (also in the nineteenth century) made absolute divorce possible and extended the support obligation of the husband to his former wife (in contrast to English law, which did not provide alimony in cases of absolute divorce).

But the man's support obligation is to a wife or to a former wife. This means that if the marriage is annulled, there will be no alimony. If no valid marriage has ever existed, if the woman has never been the man's wife, he has no obligation to support her. Ploscowe observes: "If there is no legal marriage there is no basis for alimony. The woman was never a wife. Nevertheless, legal logic has yielded in some states to realities . . . Thus, in some states like New York, alimony may be granted to women who seek to annul their marriage and who, in effect, are stating that there never was a marriage from the beginning" (1969:17). In most states, however, there must have been a valid marriage before a court will award alimony. Thus the decision of whether to seek divorce or annulment of marriage may be shaped in part by the issue of alimony.

If a woman leaves her husband without cause, specifically without a cause that is a recognized ground for divorce in the state in which the couple reside, he is not obligated to support her. He has the legal right to establish domicile, and she has deserted him. If the wife is guilty of any legal ground for divorce—desertion, adultery, cruelty—alimony will not be awarded to her. And even if she has not been found guilty of any action that is a ground for divorce, she must establish that her husband is guilty of some marital offense before she can be awarded alimony in most states (Ploscowe 1969:17). Alimony has survived as a punitive award.

In most states, alimony is granted to the wife on the basis of a successful divorce suit against her husband, and with some consideration of the husband's means. The legal tradition, which in some states is explicit in the law, is that alimony will be no more than one third of the former husband's income. The amount is often agreed on when the attorneys for the husband and wife draw up a separation agreement. If not, the court will set the amount of alimony, if any, and will take into consideration such factors as how long the couple have been married, whether there are children (who would make it more difficult for the wife to work outside the home), whether she is able to earn a living, what assets the wife has, what the husband's income and assets may be, and how much the wife may have contributed to her husband's career and acquisition of assets.

Alimony is not a fixed amount in most cases, but can be modified if the circumstances of either party change. If even a token amount of alimony is included in the divorce decree, the award of alimony is established and the amount can be open to further court hearings. Ploscowe comments: "Thus long after a divorce has been granted and the parties have lived separate and apart for years, the battle for alimony may still be carried on between the former spouses" (1969:20). If the husband refuses to pay alimony, there are a number of legal pressures that can be placed on him, the most severe being imprisonment. In most states, alimony is granted only to the former wife. But in some states[1] alimony may be awarded to a former husband, if he is unable to support himself and likely to become a public charge. Alimony for a former husband is more likely to be awarded on a welfare basis than a punitive basis.

The payment of some form of financial penalty at the time of divorce is an ancient custom, whether it consisted of the return of the dowry the woman brought to the marriage or of forfeiting the bride-price the man had paid for her. Such financial penalties were considered means of strengthening the bonds of matrimony. Financial penalties may still serve this function today, for many couples discover that divorce is a luxury they cannot afford. But the punitive use of alimony is an archaic custom, surviving from a time when women were considered incapable of providing for themselves or managing their own property, and were thus of necessity the dependent of some male. Bride-price, another archaic custom, is now regarded as immoral in our culture (and wife sale is illegal); alimony may some day be viewed in the same light.

---

[1]States that permit alimony to be awarded to husbands include Alaska, California, Illinois, Iowa, Maine, Massachusetts, Nebraska, New Hampshire, North Dakota, Ohio, Oklahoma, Utah, Vermont, Virginia, West Virginia, Wisconsin, and Washington (Foster 1969:130).

Grounds for divorce and other legal fictions

There are two quite different legal ways in which a marriage can be dissolved: annulment and divorce. *Annulment is the finding of a court that there was some cause that existed prior to the marriage that makes the marriage null and void: no valid marriage ever existed.* (Technically, any children born to the couple become illegitimate, but most states have laws that provide that any children of an annulled marriage will continue to be considered legitimate.) In contrast, *divorce refers to the dissolution of a valid marriage for a cause that occurred after the marriage was contracted. Grounds for divorce are thus actions that have occurred subsequent to a valid marriage.*

Divorce law developed in the form of an adversary action (in contrast to annulment, in which there is no fault, merely some prior condition that makes the marriage void.) In a divorce action, the plaintiff brings charges of severe marital misconduct against the spouse. If the spouse does not contest the charges and a witness corroborates them, the divorce is usually granted. Not only are most divorces uncontested, most divorce hearings are default procedures. The defendant must be notified as to the time and place of the hearing, and his absence from the court creates the legal presumption that he has no desire to defend himself against the charges. This is a default hearing. The majority of divorces in the United States are default procedures, and, not surprisingly, about three fourths of all applications for divorce decrees are granted.

There are a series of legal assumptions in this process. It is assumed that the plaintiff appears before the court as an aggrieved and innocent party. It is assumed that if the defendant does not appear in court, he (or she) has no desire to contest the divorce or to defend himself against the charges. It is assumed that the marriage has failed because of the action of the defendant, which is the basis for the divorce suit. There are a number of difficulties inherent in these assumptions, not the least of which is the matter of the grounds on which the divorce is sought. Instead of being able to present to the court reasons why the marriage has failed, the plaintiff must find some ground on which divorce can legally be granted in the state where the divorce action is heard, and try to prove the spouse guilty of that behavior. For example, until 1967 adultery was the *only* ground on which divorce could be granted in the state of New York. A New York woman who had been deserted, neglected, or routinely beaten by her husband could not be granted a divorce on any of these grounds.

At present, all states in the United States permit absolute divorce from a valid marriage, and all insist that divorce not be on frivolous grounds. Beyond these two points, state laws regarding divorce vary widely. Beginning with the middle of the 1960s, there have been sweeping changes in the divorce statutes of many states. However, to understand reform it is necessary first to understand the conditions that are being reformed. Moreover, there are still a significant number of states that have not changed their divorce laws substantially in the last half-century or more.

Most states initially adopted as grounds for divorce the old ecclesiastical grounds for "bed-and-board" separation. The most common grounds were adultery, cruelty, desertion, or abandonment. In a comparison of marriage and divorce statistics for the United States in selected years from 1867 through 1967, the U.S. Public Health Service (December 1973:49) noted the frequency with which certain grounds were cited. In the years from 1867 to 1887, the most frequently cited ground for divorce was desertion or abandonment (44.1 percent of divorces were granted on this ground). The second most common ground for divorce in 1867–1886 was adultery (24.6 percent), then cruelty (16.3 percent), drunkenness (7.8 percent), and neglect or nonsupport (4.6 percent). All other grounds for divorce (bigamy and fraud, conviction of a crime, incompatibility, and "other grounds") totaled only 2.6 percent of all divorces granted in the years between 1867 and 1886.

The U.S. Public Health Service (December 1973:49) indicates that of all divorces granted in the United States in 1965, the largest percentage (41.7 percent) was on grounds of cruelty (physical and mental); the second most common ground was neglect or nonsupport (18.0 percent); the third most common was "indignities" (15.5 percent); the fourth was desertion or abandonment (13.8 percent); the fifth was "other grounds" (4.1 percent); followed by separation or absence (3.5 percent), adultery (1.4 percent), incompatibility (0.7 percent), conviction of a crime (0.5 percent), bigamy and fraud (0.5 percent), and drunkenness (0.3 percent).

If we compare divorce statistics over nearly a century of court records, we find what appear to be some marked changes in marital behavior (or misbehavior) in the United States. Two grounds, desertion and adultery, accounted for well over half of all divorces granted (68.7 percent) in the years between 1867 and 1886. In 1965, two grounds again accounted for well over half of all divorces granted (59.7 percent), but by this time the two grounds were cruelty and neglect (or nonsupport). If "indignities" are included with cruelty (as they were in most prior years), the percentage of divorces granted on the grounds of cruelty (physical and mental, including indignities) and neglect or nonsupport rises to 75.2 percent of all divorces granted in 1965. Desertion or abandonment dropped from the most common ground for divorce in 1867–1886 (44.1 percent of all divorces granted) to the fourth most common ground for divorce in 1965 (only 13.8 percent of divorces granted). Adultery dropped from the second most common ground for divorce in 1867–1886 and 24.6 percent of all divorces granted to only 1.4 percent of divorces granted in 1965, ranking behind cruelty, neglect or nonsupport, indignities, desertion or abandonment, "other grounds," and separation or absence. Drunkenness dropped from the fourth most frequently cited ground for divorce in 1867–1886 (7.8 percent of all divorces granted) to the least frequently cited ground for divorce in 1965 (0.3 percent of divorces granted).

But these changes can hardly be construed as proof of a decline in adultery or problem drinking or in the damaging effects of such behavior on a marriage. Rather, these changes seem likely to have been the result

403

of changing judicial interpretations of divorce statutes, interpretations that have made it easier to obtain a divorce on such grounds as mental cruelty. People tend to seek a divorce on whatever ground will be least painful to air in public, provided that it is sufficient to obtain a divorce under the laws of the state where the divorce is sought. That this is the case is indicated by the fact that in some states the vast majority of divorce decrees are granted on one single ground: whatever is the least damaging ground that is sufficient to obtain a divorce in that particular state. Thus cruelty is the ground for more than 90 percent of the divorces granted in Idaho, Iowa, Michigan, Nebraska, Oregon, Utah, and Wisconsin. Desertion is the ground for 90 percent or more of the divorces granted in Virginia; incompatibility is the ground almost always given in Alaska; and "indignities" is the ground on which an overwhelming majority of divorces are granted in Wyoming (U.S. Public Health Service 1967:36).

Cruelty, both physical and mental, accounts for the largest proportion of divorces in America. If "indignities" are added, the total in the late 1960s was nearly 60 percent of all divorce actions. Twenty-six states include "mental suffering" as a part of the cruelty statute. Of the forty-six states in which cruelty is a ground for divorce, only South Carolina requires a finding that there was actual physical violence (Freed and Foster 1969:85). Physical cruelty typically takes the form of wife beating, and a neighbor or relative is usually able to testify as a witness who has seen bruises, if not the actual blows. Mental cruelty is more nebulous and, depending on the custom of the court, may be broadly interpreted. Repeated humiliation of the spouse in front of others, attested to by a witness, is one of the most common mental cruelty charges.

Neglect or nonsupport, the second most common ground for divorce, is also not too difficult to prove in court. (Some state codes use the term *neglect,* others use the term *nonsupport,* but the behavior referred to is essentially the same. In the collection of statistics on divorce, the two categories are combined.) Because most states make support an obligation of the husband, but not of the wife, a divorce on the grounds of neglect or nonsupport is almost always granted to the wife.

Desertion or abandonment (again, the same basic behaviors, so the two categories are combined when statistics are compiled) is a less frequently cited ground for divorce than cruelty or nonsupport. Desertion must be for a specific period of time. In some states, it may be necessary to establish that the deserting spouse has been *continuously* absent for two or even three years. It is possible to establish neglect or nonsupport in a much shorter time, and the element of continuity is less important.

However, the wife as well as the husband may be charged with desertion. If a man moves to another city to take a job and his wife refuses to accompany him, it is the wife who is guilty of desertion. In the eyes of the law, the right to establish domicile belongs to the husband. In some states, a spouse who orders the other to leave can be guilty of desertion. If the spouse who deserted had some compelling reason, if the "desertion" was in fact a flight from cruelty, for example, the spouse who drove the other out may be denied the divorce because he or she was equally at fault.

If a divorce is contested, there are a number of legal defenses, and the suit is likely to become protracted and bitter. The law assumes that the plaintiff is innocent and did not provoke the injury suffered. The plaintiff must come before the court with clean hands, metaphorically speaking. If both parties are at fault, the divorce will be denied. If the defendant wants to contest the divorce, one effective way is to prove the plaintiff guilty of some behavior that is a ground for divorce in the state where the suit is being heard. This is called *recrimination,* and will usually mean that neither party will be granted a divorce. It is not a matter of relative injury or guilt. If the plaintiff can be shown to be guilty of *any* action that is a ground for divorce in that state, a divorce can usually be blocked. The legal concept of recrimination in divorce cases is a direct transfer from the ecclesiastical courts that used the concept when hearing suits for "bed-and-board" legal separation. Ecclesiastical courts usually refused the request for separate maintenance if both were guilty of offenses (Freed and Foster 1969:73). The spouses were, in effect, sentenced to live together as a kind of penance.

Another form of defense that can be used effectively to block a divorce is proof that the "innocent" spouse has condoned the behavior that is being used as grounds for divorce. *The injury must be unprovoked and unforgiven.* Because forgiveness is difficult to prove in a court of law, the legal assumption is that if the spouses have had sexual relations after the guilty one's behavior became known, the offended spouse has forgiven— condoned—the behavior that is being used as grounds for divorce. "In most divorce suits, therefore," Kephart observes, "one question is almost certain to be asked by the court: When did you last have sex relations with your spouse?" (1961:575).

Both recrimination and condonation are effective defenses in contested divorce suits. Two other legal grounds on which a suit for divorce may be denied are seldom used to contest a divorce, although they represent actions that occur with unquestionable frequency. These are *fraud* and *collusion*. Legally, collusion means any subverting of a legal contest. Our legal system is founded on the assumption that there is a contest between plaintiff and defendant, and that in the course of each pursuing his own interest, opposed to the interest of the other, the truth will become apparent. But usually both husband and wife have agreed that they want out of the marriage. This may be the only thing they can agree on anymore, but toward this common goal they are willing to cooperate. Cooperation is no more legally permissible than forgiveness. The defendant who suppresses evidence that would be a defense and agrees not to contest the divorce may technically be guilty of collusion.

Sometimes the couple deliberately fabricate some innocuous ground for divorce. This is both fraud and collusion, and the suit will be thrown out of court if it is discovered, but it seldom is, for if both parties want

405

a divorce their attorneys are usually able to present the case effectively. As a case in point, there is the divorcée who said (in confidence, not in court):

> Rodney and I had never really exchanged a cross word. I guess you might say the problem was we had not exchanged many words of any kind for years. We were not really hostile, just killing each other with boredom. I had found a new man, but Rodney was too much of a gentleman to bring that up in court, and I have a notion that he may have found some sweet little thing to play games with—I hope he did—but it wouldn't have been fair for me to have dug that out. The lawyer said we'd need some kind of cruelty, did he leave me alone all the time to play golf, or something like that. Rodney never had the drive to do anything but sit in front of the television set and that didn't count because he did that at home. So he learned to play billiards and dutifully went out to a pool hall every night for a few weeks so I could complain about that, how he left me all alone and miserable to frequent a pool hall. After all, it had to be true, and with a witness.

The divorce was granted to this wife, on the ground of extreme mental cruelty. This particular case was heard in California in the early 1960s. It was the kind of divorce action that the members of the California Governor's Commission had in mind when they reported in 1966 that 96 percent of California divorce actions were brought on the ground of extreme cruelty, that 94 percent were uncontested, and that the system "lends itself to a form of sham inquiry."

The changing law: "no-fault" divorce

The California Governor's Commission recommended in 1966 that fault issues be abandoned in the divorce statutes, pointing out that the traditional grounds were merely symptoms that the marriage was troubled. The principle of fault as applied to divorce suits is legally parallel to fault in a damage suit. If both drivers involved in an automobile accident are found to have been guilty of some infraction of the traffic code, neither will be awarded damages. The inequities that this legal requirement has caused to persons injured in an accident led to the development of "no-fault" automobile insurance, and a number of states have amended their statutes to reflect the "no-fault" concept with regard to automobile accidents. The need for "no-fault" divorce is at least as great.

Pitting husband and wife against each other in an adversary action tends to polarize couples rather than to draw them back together. Moreover, the adversary action tears deeper the divided loyalties of children, who may feel that they must take sides and place blame (on occasion, a child may be called as a witness against one of the parents). The legal requirement that the divorce suit be a contest in which one party comes before the court as an injured innocent and must prove that the other is guilty and unprovoked is likely to be contrary to reality, and invites fraud and collusion.

The alternative to sordid entrapment by detectives, or hypocritical collusion and a staged incident that can be used in court, is to go to a state where divorce is easier to obtain and the residency requirement is short. By the 1950s, many Americans (especially from New York and California) were going to Nevada (some even to Mexico) for divorce. Freed and Foster point out that "for the less affluent, however, migratory divorce, entailing a prolonged stay at the divorce forum, was impractical or too expensive . . . Thus, the form and substance of divorce law and its application worked a discrimination between economic classes and created a dichotomy between broken marriages in which only one party wanted a divorce and those in which both parties wanted one" (1969:75).

As mentioned earlier, divorce law, like other law pertaining to the family, is enacted by state legislatures. There are no federal statutes pertaining to family law, although occasionally some state statute may be held to violate the federal Constitution and thus come under the jurisdiction of the federal courts. Those United States Supreme Court rulings that have pertained to family law have declared some state laws unconstitutional violations of individual rights. (The *Loving* decision, which struck down the miscegenation statutes, is an outstanding example.) Such decisions protect individual civil rights and civil liberties from state laws, but the right to legislate in the area of the family, including marriage and divorce law, has thus far remained within the domain of the states. Beginning in 1884, bills that would regulate divorce, especially migratory divorce, have been introduced periodically into sessions of the Congress, but none has been enacted. In the opinion of W. J. Brockelbank, "Under the United States Constitution, Congress has no power to legislate on family law. To turn the problem over to Congress would require a constitutional amendment" (1969:28).

In the last decade, a number of states have amended their family law codes to make divorce a more simple and honest proceeding. There are basically two ways in which reform of divorce laws can be accomplished. One is to recodify divorce law: to replace old statutes and provisions with new ones. The other way is to amend the existing statutes by adding nonfault grounds. Piecemeal reform has the disadvantage of leaving the old adversary system (and its mythology) intact, but it has the advantage of being politically possible in states where a sweeping recodification of family law would be unacceptable to powerful groups in and out of the legislature. Divorce reform in the two most populous states—California and New York—will serve to illustrate the two approaches. Both states established study commissions in the 1960s, both commissions made their reports in 1966, both reports ultimately led to legislative reform of divorce statutes.

New York had a divorce law that was essentially unchanged from the

407

time it was first proposed by Alexander Hamilton until 1967. During almost two centuries, adultery was the only ground for judicial divorce in New York. A pattern of accommodation was built by the courts and by custom to this narrow and stringent requirement. Annulment became a practical alternative to divorce in New York, because that state (unlike many other states) permitted alimony in cases of annulment and because the legitimacy of children was not adversely affected by annulment. Moreover, as noted above, New York was one of the few states that recognized a divorce granted in another state regardless of residence, provided that both parties had submitted themselves to the jurisdiction of the court. This meant that migratory divorce was a common solution for affluent New York residents, but that desertion (and subsequent extralegal cohabitation) was the common pattern for the poor, who could not afford divorce as it had evolved in the state of New York. For the rest, those who could establish reason for an annulment chose that route, and there was also an ugly pattern of motel entrapment and collusion to produce evidence to sustain a charge of adultery in New York courts.

A bill to reform divorce in New York was passed in 1967 after an intense political battle. This bill added a number of new grounds for divorce to the New York statutes and, perhaps more important, deliberately ommitted any defenses to those new grounds. "The new grounds were cruel and inhuman treatment endangering 'the physical or mental well being' of the plaintiff so as to make further cohabitation unsafe or improper; abandonment for two or more years; imprisonment for three or more years; and living separate and apart for two or more years pursuant to a decree of separation or a written separation agreement filed with the court" (Foster 1969:134). The political price of the law was the addition of a requirement for a mandatory stay of divorce proceedings for 120 days while a Conciliation Bureau determined whether there was hope for a reconciliation, and limitations on the validity of migratory divorce.

Most of the new grounds added to the New York divorce law are fault grounds that have long been recognized by the statutes of other states: cruelty, abandonment, and imprisonment. But the separation provision added a nonfault ground. The spouses must sign a separation agreement (including support and property settlement) and file this agreement with the county clerk within thirty days; if they wish to keep the terms of the agreement confidential, they may file a memorandum of agreement with the county clerk. Either party may then file for divorce if the agreement is "substantially" complied with for at least two years. The other route to divorce on the ground of separation is to obtain a separation decree (the old "bed-and-board" judicial separation) and to observe it for at least two years. This may seem a more cumbersome route, but it has been held by the New York Supreme Court to apply to judicial separation decrees granted prior to 1967 when the divorce reform law was passed in New York. This has meant that persons who have been living with a legal separation for many years have been able to obtain a divorce and become free to remarry, for *either* the plaintiff or the defendant in the original suit may request the divorce if the terms of the legal separation have been complied with for at least two years. As Foster observes, separation as a ground for divorce "is not related to fault but is based upon the assumption that under such circumstances the marriage is dead and that the public interest is best served by making it possible to legally terminate dead marriages" (1970:16–17).

The California Governor's Commission found that the system of adversary pleading was a barrier to the reconciliation of the spouses, and recommended that all fault issues be abandoned. The commission recommended further that the requirement of divorce be simply a finding that the marriage had "irreparably failed" and that conciliation and counseling be urged. After lengthy legislative hearings, the California legislature passed in 1969 the Family Law Act, which changed an action for divorce to a proceeding for dissolution of marriage. The change of wording may seem insignificant, but it is a part of the change in approach: no longer does one spouse divorce the other, now it is simply that the marriage is dissolved.

One of the innovative features of the California Family Law Act is that it eliminates the assumption of guilt and innocence. Neither party is plaintiff or defendant. Fault is not—and may not be—established. Since January 1, 1970, only two grounds have existed for dissolution of marriage in California: incurable insanity and irreconcilable differences that have caused irremediable breakdown of the marriage. Both are nonfault grounds, because even the rarely used insanity ground is not considered willful behavior. The concept of irreconcilable differences removes the fiction that one and only one spouse is at fault: it takes two to differ. Incurable insanity must be established by competent medical authority. Irreconcilable differences are established by evidence that there are substantial reasons for not continuing the marriage; the hearing is more an inquest than a trial. As a practical matter, either spouse may obtain a dissolution by asserting that irreconcilable differences exist, regardless of objections of the other spouse. Acts of misconduct may not be admitted into evidence, and no corroborating witness is required, unless custody of a child is at issue.

To obtain a dissolution of marriage in California, it is necessary for the spouse who is filing to have been a resident of California for six months and a resident of the county in which the proceeding is heard for three months. (It is not necessary for the other spouse to be a resident of California.) The interlocutory period has been reduced from one year to six months, which means that the dissolution of marriage is final six months after the decree, provided that one of the spouses (usually through an attorney) indicates to the court that he or she still wishes to have the marriage dissolved.

409

In parallel legislation, California has made it more difficult for minors to marry. In 1970 the age of consent was lowered from twenty-one to eighteen for males (eighteen had been and remains the age of consent for females in California). Persons under eighteen years of age may contract a valid marriage only after obtaining the written consent of one or both parents, or a guardian, *and* a Superior Court order granting permission to the minor to marry. Both of these documents must be filed with the county clerk before a marriage license can be issued. The court may require the minor to have premarital counseling before permission to marry is granted. The California legislature had come to the conclusion that the old system, which had made it easy for minors to marry and difficult (in theory) to obtain a divorce, had only led to a cycle of early marriage and early divorce, not to family stability. It is hoped that the new laws that make it more difficult for minors to marry and easier to dissolve marriage without bitterness will serve the public interest better than the old laws. The removal of fault grounds and adversary action from divorce may mean less bitterness and enhance the possibility of reconciliation. The California reform has removed the motive for collusion and fraud that was too often involved in the old "extreme mental cruelty" fault ground for divorce.

By 1975 twelve other states[2] had followed the pattern set by California and had adopted irretrievable breakdown of the marriage as the *sole* ground for divorce. In these states the concept of fault and of adversary action in divorce has been eliminated. In an additional thirty-two states, some nonfault ground has been added to the existing statutes. In 1975 only five states—Illinois, Massachusetts, Mississippi, Pennsylvania, and South Dakota—had not yet adopted some form of nonfault divorce.

In the states with both fault and nonfault grounds for divorce, the nonfault grounds added were irretrievable breakdown of the marriage (eleven states), incompatibility (seven states), and separation or absence for a specified period of time (twenty states, the District of Columbia, and Puerto Rico). Separation is not a euphemism for desertion. Desertion is a fault ground for divorce in most states. Separation is a nonfault ground that means that the couple have been living apart by mutual agreement, for a specified period of time. The time required to establish separation as a ground for divorce varies from two to seven years, depending on the state statute. Separation is clearly not a ground for quick divorce, but rather a means by which a marriage that is dead can be legally buried, with as little bitterness as possible. According to Donald Cantor, "No defenses exist, except to deny the fact of the separation for the requisite period,

---

[2]The states in which irretrievable breakdown of the marriage is the *sole* ground for divorce were, in 1975: Arizona, California, Colorado, Delaware, Florida, Iowa, Kentucky, Michigan, Minnesota, Missouri, Nebraska, Oregon, and Washington.

misbehavior of the plaintiff and the opposition of the defendant to the separation being irrelevant" (1970:11).

The addition of such nonfault grounds as incompatibility and irretrievable breakdown of the marriage make it more likely that the suit will be brought on a ground that is honest, and cause the least possible emotional damage to the family involved in divorce. Cantor observes that "these three innovations—incompatibility, separation, and irreconcilable differences—are all basically of the same philosophy. Each forms an inquiry into the viability of the marriage. The wording is different and the approach is different, but each forswears the concept of fault for an examination into the health of the relationship" (1970:11).

When divorce or dissolution of marriage can be obtained on nonfault grounds, either spouse is able to obtain the divorce and there are no effective defenses. This means that bargaining leverage is reduced for the spouse least interested in obtaining divorce; he or she can no longer hold out for a favorable settlement as the price of divorce. However, divorce reform needs to make some provision in the law for an equitable financial settlement. The ownership and control of property by husband and wife was discussed earlier, in Chapter 12. A brief review may be useful here. In the forty-two states where the statutes regarding marital rights and property are based on the English common law, only the property that is actually in the woman's name is clearly hers, and she has no claim to the property that is in her husband's name. Any property that the couple hold as joint tenants (typically, real estate) is property in which each holds an equal interest, although the husband has the right to control such property in most states.

In the eight states with community property laws (Arizona, California, Idaho, Louisiana, New Mexico, Nevada, Texas, and Washington), the husband and wife have an equal interest in all property acquired by either during marriage. However, property that either of them received through inheritance or owned before the marriage is individual property. In such states the wife and husband are likely to divide the community property equally in a divorce settlement, unless a punitive judgment is made by the court (often on the basis of an agreement arrived at through bargaining between attorneys). The reform of divorce law in California included a provision that the community property and quasi-community property[3] be divided equally when the marriage is dissolved, although if the court determines that one of the spouses has deliberately misappropriated community property or if economic circumstances warrant, the property

---

[3]*Quasi-community property* is defined in California law as "all personal property wherever situated and all real property situated in this state" that was acquired: (1) by either spouse while a resident of some other state and that would have been community property had that spouse been a California resident; or (2) in *exchange* for real or personal property acquired other than by gift or inheritance by either spouse during the marriage, while residents of some state other than California.

may be divided by the court on some other basis. Most California dissolutions of marriage involve an equal division of the community property.

With regard to alimony, California law provides that upon the dissolution of marriage the court may order one party (either the husband or the wife, depending upon the circumstances) to pay for the support of the other party an amount for a period of time that the court "may deem just and reasonable, having regard for the circumstances of the respective parties, including the duration of the marriage, and the ability of the supported spouse to engage in gainful employment without interfering with the interests of the children of the parties in the custody of such spouse." To cite one specific case: A couple had been married for five years, during which the wife worked in a clerical position to support the family while her husband completed a Ph.D. The marriage was dissolved shortly after the degree was conferred. There were no children, and the husband was currently employed as a college professor. The court decreed that the former husband support his former wife while she completed an advanced degree in her own field, setting both the amount of support and a reasonable time limit for the woman to complete her education.

The equal division of community property when a marriage is dissolved in California is a more equitable distribution than sometimes occurs in the forty-two states with a common-law basis for the ownership of marital property. In the latter states, the enactment of nonfault grounds for divorce has reduced the bargaining leverage of the wife. Some changes in the basis of property settlement may be a necessary addition to divorce reform in states with a common-law basis for the ownership and control of marital property. A woman who has contributed to her husband's business or occupational success for many years may be cut off without an equitable property settlement in a nonfault divorce action. Only such property as may have been in the wife's name, or her interest in property held in joint tenancy, is clearly hers.

Henry H. Foster, Jr., chairman of the research committee on family law of the American Bar Association, has drawn a bill that could serve as a model for property settlement in all common-law states. This bill would be called the Marital Property Act, and would provide for equal division of assets acquired during the marriage, regardless of which spouse acquired them or in whose name they are held (inherited property excepted.) Alimony would be based on one spouse's need and the other's ability to pay, without regard to sex. Child support would be mutually shared, and based on the actual income and earning ability of each parent.

The critics of divorce reform fear that the result will be a soaring divorce rate and ultimately the destruction of marriage and the family. But Foster, writing of the New York divorce reform, observes: "Unquestionably, the price will be an increase in the incidence of divorce accompanied by a reduction in perjury, fraud, insult, and disrespect for the administration of justice. A modern and humane public policy should be more concerned with the quality of marriage than the quantity of divorce" (1970:17).

Estrangement as process

Finding the reason why a marriage comes apart is like finding the cause of a war. Strained relations and growing expectations of hostility build a situation in which both sides are in a perpetually defensive mood, and any small incident can trigger open aggression. Perhaps a civil war that turns brother against brother is the closest analogy, for the remembered intimacy gives an extra edge of bitterness. When your enemy is someone you once loved dearly, there are no simple solutions.

There is no point at which a marriage suddenly turns sour. There may be a sudden *recognition* that something is terribly wrong, but it is usually an awareness that has been suppressed for a long time. Husband and wife can create a surface of the kind they want the world (and the children) to see, and may come to believe that it is real. But suddenly the point may be reached when at least one of the spouses can no longer pretend to live in the best of all possible marriages. The recognition may be held off until a marriage has reached the point of no return. Counseling helps, but it needs to come while there is still a possibility for each to put some trust in the other's good will.

Some marriages are failures from the outset. The transition from the role of lover to the role of husband or wife is never accomplished. The expectations of one may be too different from the expectations of the other; one or both may be unwilling to put away the role behaviors of the single individual and act married—whatever that means in terms of the social class and generational subculture to which the couple belong. There must be a minimum reciprocity in role behavior for a marriage to survive, and one or both may have been unwilling to adapt to the role behaviors required by marriage.

Data gathered by the U.S. Public Health Service (1973:23) indicate that in 1969 "The modal duration of marriage to separation was less than 1 year." *Modal* is statistical terminology for the largest category; in this instance it means that although the average (mean or median) duration of marriage was longer than a year, there were more separations leading to divorce within the first year of marriage than in any subsequent year. The duration of marriage to the point of the final separation is a more informative statistic than the duration of marriage to the time of the divorce decree, because of the time lag between the decision to divorce and the court hearing (which may be several months) and because of variations in state law. The fact that the modal duration of marriage to separation was less than one year means that a large proportion of divorces represent an early recognition that the marriage was a mistake. Some of these marriages involve people who had misgivings before the ceremony, but felt

413

compelled by social pressures to go on with the wedding (like the bride quoted in the opening paragraph of this chapter).

Teenage marriage is related to unusually high divorce rates, although only a small number of divorces are granted to teenagers. The reason for this apparent paradox is the length of time that it takes to get a divorce. If either husband or wife is eighteen when they marry, the slowness of the legal process means that even if the couple separate within the year, either or both are likely to have reached the age of twenty before the divorce decree is granted. The more significant statistic is thus not how many divorces are granted to persons under twenty years of age, but how many divorces are granted to persons who were under twenty when they married.

Only a small proportion of American men marry before the age of twenty: according to the U.S. Public Health Service (April 1973:2) only 14 percent of the men who married during 1969 were teenagers. However, 19 percent of the men who received divorces in that year were married in their teens. In that same year, about one third of the women who married were fifteen to nineteen years of age, and about 46 percent of the women granted divorces had been teenage brides. (During the preceding decade, when most of those getting divorced in 1969 had married, the age at first marriage had slowly risen for women, and declined slightly for men.)

Early divorce may be precipitated by a pregnancy that comes early in the marriage. A premarital pregnancy may leave husband or wife, or both, feeling trapped. Testimony before the California Assembly Interim Committee on Judiciary indicates that the court may be a factor: "the tendency of some judges to make very strong suggestions to a defendant male that if he didn't want to serve a term for statutory rape, he had better get married occasions a good number of paper marriages which then turn up as paper divorces" (1965:15). (Statutory rape involves sexual relations with a minor female; even though the girl may be willing to engage in sexual activity, if she is under the legal age of consent the act is statutory rape—in contrast to forcible rape.)

The sense of entrapment that the man who has been pressured into marriage often feels is at least one factor underlying the high divorce rate among couples involved in premarital pregnancy. Christensen and Meissner matched a sample of couples on such factors as the husband's occupation, the age of the wife at marriage, residence, type of wedding (church, civil, elopement) and so forth. Matching is a research technique designed to neutralize the influence of certain factors (those on which the subjects are matched) in order to isolate and study the influence of yet another factor. In this instance, the factor being studied was the relation of premarital pregnancy to divorce. Harold Christensen and Hanna Meissner found that when other factors were matched, the couples who had had a premarital pregnancy had divorce rates more than twice as high as those who delayed pregnancy until after marriage. The lowest divorce rates were among couples who waited several years to have children. Christensen and Meissner concluded that "though the disproportionately high divorce rate is to be partially explained by the presence there of other divorce favoring factors [such as teenage marriage] a large part may also be accounted for by the fact of premarital pregnancy itself" (1953:643).

Whether premarital or not, a pregnancy that comes early in the marriage means that before the couple have had much opportunity to develop marital roles, they are forced to add the complexity of parental roles. The dyad is suddenly a triad, with all the social and emotional differences between a group of two and a group of three. Moreover, that third person is a dependent infant. The social and recreational life of the couple will suddenly be cut off, for the expense of a sitter is likely to be prohibitive, and there are not many places that it is possible (or desirable) to take an infant. The wife may increasingly see herself as *mother;* if the husband is not prepared to take on the sociological role of *father,* the first child is an emotional crisis as well as an economic burden. If the husband has made an emotional dichotomy between sexy women and mothers, he may find that he has difficulty responding sexually to his wife, who is now engrossed in the role of mother.

Elopement also seems to be a factor in early divorce. Samuel Lowrie (1965) found that of the minor brides he studied who had married outside their home county (presumptive elopements), between one third and two thirds were involved in divorce actions within five years. (Such inferential data are about all that can be gathered on elopement). There is a common presumption that if teenagers elope, the bride must be pregnant. However, Lee Burchinal (1960:10) found data to indicate that pregnant teenage brides more frequently had conventional weddings than teenage brides who were not pregnant. (Perhaps the pregnant brides found it easier to convince their parents that the wedding was a good idea.) Whatever their motives for eloping, apparently the young couple whose marriage is clandestine find it more difficult to build a stable and rewarding marriage. The pull of conflicting loyalties may be felt after the fires of defiance that led to elopement have burned out. It is possible that some early marriages fail because they are subjected to parental sabotage: the parent who did not want this teenage son or daughter to marry may try subtle ways and not always consciously to create a situation in which the parent can say, "I told you so."

Lack of supportive relationships with friends as well as family may be a factor in early divorce. The teenage bride and bridegroom, for whom marriage is a rite of passage to adulthood, may find the transition to adult roles difficult. If they are the first in their group of age peers to marry, they may also find that this is a transition they have to make alone. A young woman who lives with her parents until the day of her wedding is highly aware that she is leaving home; she sheds a ritual tear with her mother, but is prepared to make the transition away from her family. (Leaving home may be one of her motives for getting married.) But she is unlikely to anticipate that she may also be leaving her friends.

It is emotionally painful to be wrenched out of the group of close friends that has sustained one in adolescence. Often it is the young hus-

415

"I think the marriage might have lasted longer if I hadn't been cut off by my friends. I felt so alone. And perhaps seventeen was too young."

band who is not ready to give up being "one of the boys." But sometimes a young bride finds that she is cut off from her friends who are single, and that she is not yet ready to identify with the married women who are older than herself. This was the experience of one young woman who had been married and divorced before she was twenty. At the age of seventeen, while still in high school, she married her high school sweetheart (who had graduated the preceding spring). She was not pregnant, nor did she elope. The couple had a church wedding, with family and friends present from the entire rural community in which they lived. But the marriage lasted less than a year. As she related her experience:

> All my close girl friends talked about how exciting it was that I was getting married, and how wonderful it was that he was from such a good family, big ranchers and all. And we had all talked a lot about sex and what it would be like, and I thought I could tell them all about what it was really like when I got back from my honeymoon. But somehow, when I got back, they didn't want to talk to me about it, they didn't even seem to want to see me much anymore. I was different, somehow, and out of their world. I think the marriage might have lasted longer if I hadn't been cut off by my friends. I felt so alone. And perhaps seventeen was too young. But what else was there to do in Montana?

Middle age and marital disenchantment

Marriages that survive the initial period of socialization evolve an interlocking role structure with a certain resiliency; every year that passes means that the chances of the marriage ending in divorce are reduced. The fact that half of all divorces occur after the seventh wedding anniversary (U.S. Public Health Service April 1973:49) does not mean that there is a "seven-year itch." The data indicate that after the initial peak of divorce, occurring in the first year of marriage, the number of divorces occurring in each year of marriage thereafter falls off on a long, declining curve. Whether this means that the length of marriage is correlated with happiness or habit, it is the case that the proportion of divorces on the long tail of the curve does not add up to any more than occur in the first seven years of marriage. However, one of the trends in American divorce in the last two decades has been for more divorces to occur later in marriage, after fifteen years or more of married life.

Peter Pineo (1961) reported the results of a third interview of couples who had been involved in a longitudinal study of marital adjustment carried out by Ernest W. Burgess and associates over a fifteen-year period. These data were not gathered on divorcing couples, it should be noted, but rather on couples who had initially participated in a study that began with the engagement period and extended over fifteen years of marriage. Pineo observes that although it might seem reasonable to expect that about as many marriages would show an increase of marital happiness and intimacy over the years as would show a decline, the data collected for this long-term study indicate that almost all the indices of marital adjustment, consensus, satisfaction, and affection dropped, several of them significantly. According to Pineo, this may be inevitable:

> In any situation, such as marriage, in which individuals have made a major, irreversible decision to accept a long-term commitment and where the data upon which they decide are not or cannot be perfect, some process of disenchantment is to be expected. When fit and satisfaction are maximized at the point of accepting the commitment, they must, on the average, subsequently reduce.   (Pineo 1961:7)

The late-divorcing couples who were included in this sample (that is, couples who had participated at engagement in the original study by Burgess and associates and in a second interview after the early years of marriage, but were divorced by the third interview date) displayed significant differences between men and women. According to Pineo, the late-divorcing men had initially high marital adjustment scores. "They are typified by a great drop rather than by an initially low score. Among these late divorces it is the magnitude and speed of their disenchantment which most fully characterize the husbands" (1961:11).

417

The women involved in late divorce displayed a different pattern. Pineo states that:

> The divorced women begin with below-average adjustment and although their losses are greater than the married women their initially low adjustment is also a factor in divorce. One of the clear elements contributing to the divorce in this panel is that the women tended to have definite doubts during the engagement period but did not act upon these doubts until after the marriage had occurred. The men, more typically, broke the engagement if they had doubts. In the few cases where men married despite severe doubts they did not frequently divorce.   (Pineo 1961:11)

Pineo summarizes the pattern of late divorce that emerges in the study as follows: "The later divorces in this panel typically occurred when the wife experienced aggravation of doubts which she had held for some time while the man suddenly lost his above-average degree of contentment" (1961:11).

Marriages that have survived the early critical period of disenchantment, that have been able to withstand the jolt of the first child, that have been going concerns for years, may begin to come apart under the strains of middle age. The man who has reached an age when he can no longer regard himself as a "promising young man" and who has yet to make his mark may begin to feel desperate. The mental image that comes first to mind is the rising executive or professional man who has the sudden realization that he has hit the ceiling of his career. But the blue-collar worker may have a comparable jolt when he realizes that he has gone as far as he will ever go, that his dreams of owning his own tractor truck or repair business will probably never be realized, that he is past his prime in terms of age and energy. For the working man, that feeling may come at the age of thirty: twelve years after leaving high school. He has the growing realization that he will never be more than he is now, that life goes downhill for him from this point onward. For the professional man or the executive, the sense of being youthful and rising may last until he reaches forty; that birthday is an unwelcomed reminder that youth is gone, and there is so much unaccomplished that he had wanted to do.

His wife is not to blame—and yet, if she had managed better, been able to help him more, if there had not been so many children: the wife, in short, is a convenient scapegoat, the more so because there is likely to be enough truth in his feelings to make them plausible. And the wife may be making it clear that she is disappointed in the station in life where the couple have stalled, that she had hoped for more. She may not say much, she may feel compassion for her discouraged husband and assure him that she is content with their home and the security he provides. But in a moment of anger—which she is likely to feel if he airs his feeling that it is her fault they are trapped—she may well let her disappointment show. Lack of achievement is likely to be his weak point, and who among us has never thrust at the soft underbelly during a quarrel?

418

One such quarrel, or a dozen, does not necessarily mean that the couple are on the way to a divorce. But failure in role expectations—*shared* role expectations—leads frequently to unrealistic conflict. A man who is afraid that his youth and drive are gone quickly begins to wonder about his sexual potency and attractiveness; a younger woman may make him feel young again, and he wants the feeling. A younger woman will not remind him of the past promise that has gone glimmering—she will suggest that he is already Somebody and could still go Somewhere.

Because the wife is likely to be feeling the loss of her youthful figure and freshness, she is easily threatened by her husband's flirtations. A woman usually has more to lose by divorce than a man does. Her emotional security, economic security, and security in class status depend on the marriage. Because they have so much to lose, many women pull back from the brink of divorce and negotiate some sort of uneasy truce. They may disengage from their husband's lives without divorce, turning most of their time and emotional involvement toward the children. Minimal contact brings a reduction of friction. They may agree, openly or tacitly, to the sort of double-standard arrangement that prevailed in great-grandmother's day.

But although women have more to lose by divorce, it is not great-grandmother's day, and there are alternatives to an unhappy marriage. It is usually the American wife who brings suit. Divorce was a husband's prerogative in the past, but in our society it is the wife who files in about three fourths of all divorce cases. This statistic reflects a widespread feeling that it is less damaging to the wife in the eyes of family and friends if she files and that the husband will be a gentleman about it. Also, it probably reflects the recognition by most couples that the court is more likely to be sympathetic to the woman and to grant a divorce on what might seem thin grounds if the husband were the plaintiff.

However, William Goode observes that it is probably more often the husband who first wants to escape the marriage, even if it is usually the wife who brings suit. And, he adds, it is "the husband more often than the wife who is able to adopt a strategy of divorce which forces the other spouse to ask first for the divorce" (1956:154). The husband may or may not be aware that he is manipulating his wife into a position where she will want the marriage to terminate. But usually involvement with the "other woman" and similar provocative behavior come after the husband is disenchanted with his marriage, and is more effect than cause of the deterioration of the marital relationship.

Some couples avoid conflict by avoiding each other. They simply become strangers by imperceptible degrees. Finding less and less to say to each other, wanting to say less and less to each other, they drift while the gulf between them widens until they can barely shout across it. But more often, there is a progressive estrangement that proceeds like a spinning Yo-Yo: flung away from each other by a quarrel, each suddenly feels the distance and fears the potential loss of the mate with whom he has had the most intimate relationship of his life. In the clutching mood

419

induced by separation anxiety, they pull back toward each other. Feeling closer than before the quarrel, for grievances have been aired and hostility discharged, they feel that everything is going to be all right, that their relationship is stronger than before.

It may be. But often, conflicts are not brought to resolution, for fear leads either or both to repress hostility. Theirs is now a tenuous relationship, and conflict seems to threaten its recently mended fabric. Things that have been said in anger are more often brooded on than acted on, and lie at the back of consciousness. One or the other begins to pick at old wounds, and sooner or later they begin to fester. Unrealistic promises made in fear rather than understanding are soon broken. Pride is bruised and does not recover; lowered self-esteem leads to greater jealousy. The next quarrel is likely to find each pulling back farther, longer, and less willing to return to the old closeness for fear of further hurt.

When the spouse begins to seem the enemy, a period of alternating gestures may begin. Where once both rushed back after a quarrel, now one may be willing to bend, to forgive, to reach out, while the other is nursing a grudge, savoring the sense of being in control and wanting to make the most of the spouse's apparent willingness to negotiate. The rebuffed spouse then pulls back to nurse wounded pride, and roles reverse. As one disgruntled man warned his mate, "Baby, you are going to stretch my psyche until it loses its elasticity."

Trends in divorce in the United States

The number of both divorces and marriages has risen in the United States with the increase in total population. However, the U.S. Public Health Service (December 1973:6) compared data for 1867 with that for 1967 and found that while there were 5.4 times as many marriages in 1967 as there had been a century earlier, there were more than 50 times the number of divorces. The crude divorce rate states the number of divorces for every 1,000 persons in the total population. That rate rose steadily for nearly eighty years from 1867 to 1946. There were only minor fluctuations from the trendline, and these were related to depression or war. Fewer divorces occurred during the early 1930s. (There were fewer marriages, as well.) The impulsive marriages of the early 1940s, the years of World War II, were followed by a soaring divorce rate when the troops came home.

After 1946, there was a decline in divorce in America, which was not merely a correction from the upsurge after the war, but became a pronounced drop from the previous upward trendline. During the decade of the 1950s, there were markedly fewer divorces in America than would have been expected. In 1946 the crude divorce rate had reached 4.3 per 1,000 population. By 1958 the crude divorce rate was only 2.1 per 1,000, about half what it had been in 1946. The upward trend resumed in 1963, however, and accelerated throughout the remaining years of that decade. By

1975, the divorce rate in America had reached 4.8 per 1,000 persons in the population. This is double the divorce rate of 1964, and the highest ever recorded for the United States (U.S. Public Health Service March 1976:3).

The crude divorce rate is based on the ratio of divorces in a year to the total population. However, the total American population is not at risk of divorce, only the population of those who are married. The crude rate may be affected by the proportion of children in the population who are not of marriageable age and by the proportion of single persons in the adult population, which may in turn be affected by the ratio of men to women. In 1910, there were slightly more than 115 men for every 100 women in the United States, the imbalance being the result of the heavy immigration of unmarried men to the United States in the years between the Civil War and World War I. But by 1960, as a consequence of legislation limiting immigration, the number of men killed in wars, and other selective factors, there were only approximately 83 men for each 100 women in the United States (U.S. Public Health Service December 1973: 8). The sex ratios influence the number of possible marriages, and because only the married can be divorced, the sex ratios also influence the number of possible divorces. A measure of the divorce rate that avoids the distorting influence of all such factors is the adjusted divorce rate, which compares the number of divorces in a given year to each 1,000 married women.

By 1890 there were 3.0 divorces for every 1,000 married women in the United States. By 1910, there were 4.7 divorces for every 1,000 married women; by 1920 the rate had climbed to 8.0. In 1930 the rate declined slightly to 7.5 (reflecting the Depression), but by 1940 it reached 8.8 per 1,000 married women. In 1946 the rate soared to 17.9 divorces for every 1,000 married women. Then the divorce rate in the United States declined throughout the decade of the 1950s, and in 1958 reached a low for the decade of 8.9 per 1,000 married women. This adjusted divorce rate has been rising steadily since 1963, and by 1967 was 11.2 per 1,000 women (U.S. Public Health Service December 1973:24). By 1974 the rate had reached 19.3 divorces for every 1,000 married women, and provisional figures indicate that it is still rising rapidly (U.S. Public Health Service April 1976:1).

If we consider the entire period since 1867, the duration of marriage until divorce has been surprisingly stable in the United States. The median duration of marriage to divorce in 1867 was 7.4 years; in 1967 it was 7.2 years. There was, however, a marked increase in the proportion of couples with a marriage that lasted less than 2 years: in the late nineteenth century only 5 percent of divorces were granted to couples with marriages of less than 2 years' duration, and this proportion increased to 15 percent in the 1960s (U.S. Public Health Service December 1973:15). This increase may be due in part to changing divorce statutes and to changing methods of collecting and computing vital statistics. The modal duration of marriage

421

to *separation* (rather than the duration of marriage to divorce was less than 1 year in 1867, and again in 1967 the modal duration of marriage to separation was under 1 year.

A rise in the divorce rate does not necessarily mean that there is a higher proportion of unhappy marriages than there used to be. It may simply indicate that more people are able to afford divorce and that more people are choosing to dissolve an unhappy marriage than previously. The myth that obscures the past makes it seem that all was joy around that great iron kitchen stove. But in the Victorian era, when nice women did not divorce their husbands, ulcers were so common among women that they were considered a "female disorder." Moreover, it is impossible to say to what extent the increase in divorce represents an increase in the proportion of broken marriages and to what extent the increase in divorce reflects fewer desertions. There are no adequate figures on desertion available. Certainly in the distant past, when it took a special act of a state legislature to obtain a divorce, only the well-to-do and the well-connected ever got divorced. The poor person had only the alternatives of remaining in an unhappy marriage or deserting. There was a day when the frontier was an alternative to divorce.

It is easier to get a divorce today, and cheaper. Conversely, it is more difficult to desert. Employment records, unemployment records, tax records, bank accounts, reciprocal agreements between states for the enforcement of child-support decrees, and other aspects of our computerized and numbered existence make it difficult for a man to evade the law that says he must support his family, whether or not he lives with them.

The changing grounds for divorce are a reflection of the changing functions of marriage. In antiquity, when a man could set aside his wife for being barren or unchaste, and there were no grounds on which a woman might divorce her husband, divorce norms reflected a social structure in which the preservation of the male lineage was the primary function of marriage. In our time, such grounds for divorce as mental cruelty, incompatibility, and irreconcilable differences reflect a social structure in which the emotional functions of marriage for the individual have become paramount. The preservation of any particular lineage has ceased to be a matter of great social concern; unlimited procreation has become a threat to the social order rather than a social and economic necessity; economic functions were severed from domestic functions a century ago; socialization of children is increasingly accomplished by educational institutions, by the media, and even by the children's peers. As long as young children are in the custody of their mother, the state assumes that socialization will be accomplished adequately. But the emotional functions of marriage are increasing in importance. Marriage offers one of the rare situations in our mass society in which continuity and intimacy are combined, and thus any marriage that has become, in Goode's descriptive phrase, an "empty shell" has failed.

422

References

Blake, Nelson Manfred. 1962. *The Road to Reno.* New York: The Macmillan Company.

Brocklebank, W. J. 1969. "The Family Desertion Problem across State Lines." *Progress in Family Law. Annals of the American Academy of Political and Social Science* (May):23–33.

Burchinal, Lee G. 1960. "Research on Young Marriage: Implications for Family Life Education." *Family Life Coordinator* (September-December):6–21.

California Assembly Interim Committee on Judiciary. 1965. *Final Report on Domestic Relations (Executive Session Working Papers). Part II: Youthful Marriage and Parenthood as Affecting Family Stability.* Sacramento: State Printing Office.

California Governor's Commission. 1966. *Report.* Sacramento: State Printing Office.

Cantor, Donald J. 1970. "A Matter of Right." *The Humanist* (May-June):10–12.

Christensen, Harold T., and Hanna H. Meissner. 1953. "Studies in Child Spacing: III Premarital Pregnancy as a Factor in Divorce." *American Sociological Review* 18 (December):641–644.

Foster, Henry H., Jr. 1969. "The Future of Family Law." *Progress in Family Law. Annals of the American Academy of Political and Social Science* (May):129–144.

–––––– 1970. "Reforming a Divorce Law." *The Humanist* (May-June):16–17.

Freed, Doris J., and Henry H. Foster, Jr. 1969. "Divorce American Style." *Progress in Family Law. Annals of the American Academy of Political and Social Science* (May): 71–88.

Goode, William J. 1956. *After Divorce.* New York: The Free Press.

Gough, Aidan R. 1970. "Divorce without Squalor: California Shows How." *The Nation* (January 12):17–20.

Great Britain Law Commission. 1966. *Reform of the Grounds of Divorce: The Field of Choice.* CMND No. 3123. London.

Hays, H. R. 1964. *The Dangerous Sex: The Myth of Feminine Evil.* New York: G. P. Putnam's Sons.

Kephart, William M. 1961. *The Family, Society, and the Individual.* Boston: Houghton Mifflin Company.

Kirkpatrick, Clifford. 1963. *The Family: As Process and Institution,* 2nd ed. Copyright © 1963. New York: The Ronald Press Company; quoted by permission.

Lowrie, Samuel H. 1965. "Early Marriage: Premarital Pregnancy and Associated Factors." *Journal of Marriage and the Family* (February):48–56.

Nash, Arnold S. 1955. "Ancient Past and Living Present." In *Family, Marriage and Parenthood,* edited by H. Becker and R. Hill, pp. 84–103. Boston: D. C. Heath and Company.

Pineo, Peter C. 1961. "Disenchantment in the Later Years of Marriage." *Journal of Marriage and the Family* (February):9–11.

Ploscowe, Morris. 1969. "Alimony." In *Progress in Family Law. Annals of The American Academy of Political and Social Science* (May):13–22.

U.S. Public Health Service. 1967. *Divorce Statistics Analyses, United States: 1963.* Washington, D.C.: U.S. Government Printing Office.

–––––– 1970. *Children of Divorced Couples: United States, Selected Years.* Washington, D.C.: U.S. Government Printing Office.

‑‑‑‑‑ April 1973. *Divorces: Analysis of Changes in the United States, 1969.* Washington, D.C.: U.S. Government Printing Office.

‑‑‑‑‑ December 1973. *One Hundred Years of Marriage and Divorce Statistics: United States, 1867–1967.* Washington, D.C.: U.S. Government Printing Office.

‑‑‑‑‑ March 1976. "Births, Marriages, Divorces, and Deaths for 1975." *Monthly Vital Statistics Report* (March 4):1–8.

‑‑‑‑‑ April 1976. "Final Divorce Statistics, 1974" *Monthly Vital Statistics Report* (April 14):1–4.

Suggested readings

Cantor, David J. 1970. "A Matter of Right." *The Humanist* (May/June):10–12. An attorney discusses the adversary system and fault concept in divorce law, the bargaining process involved, and the traumatic effects of these on the husband, wife, and their children. Cantor suggests that divorce should not be considered the consequence of fault, but rather a right available to either spouse.

Despert, J. Louise, M.D. 1953. *Children of Divorce.* Garden City, N.Y.: Dolphin Books, Doubleday & Company. Paper. Written by a psychiatrist, this insightful book focuses on the impact divorce has on children. The author analyzes case materials and suggests what parents can do to ease the pain their children feel during and after divorce.

Goldstein, Joseph, and Max Gitter. 1970. "Divorce without Blame." *The Humanist* (May/June):12–15. Two lawyers propose a model divorce statute that would abolish the fault system.

Sheresky, Norman, and Marya Mannes. 1972. *Uncoupling: The Art of Coming Apart.* New York: Viking Press. Primarily concerned with the art of leaving a relationship, this book also contains a suggested *premarital* contract that would make a divorce later less traumatic (and also less probable). This legal memorandum of understanding and intent includes statements concerning any hereditary diseases, any prior marriages, children by any prior marriages, willingness to have children, and other representations of each party to the other. It also includes a statement of intent with regard to future ownership and division of property, matters of estate, and arbitration.

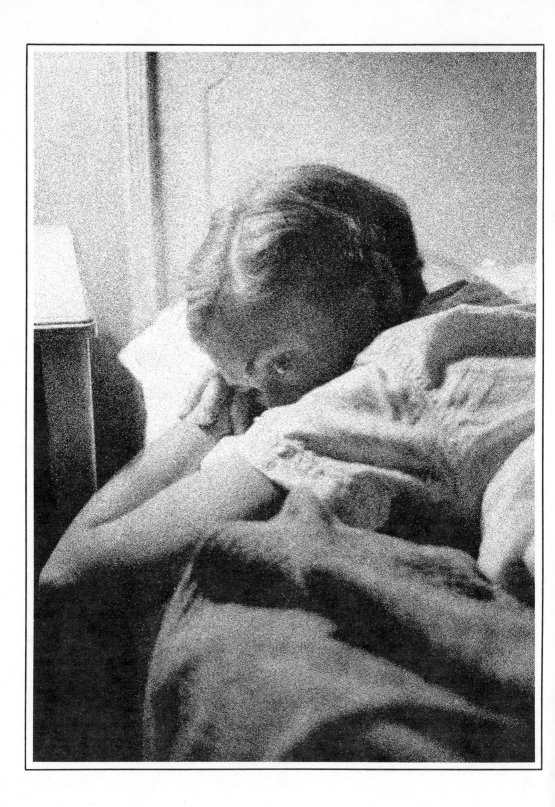

15 Bereavement: the widow's role

And we forget because we must
And not because we will.

Matthew Arnold, *Absence*

"The first thing people thought of was, 'What about money?' That says a lot about us, doesn't it? And several people commented in the first week about how lonely I would be in the middle of the night in bed alone, and what was I going to do for sex. And these were the types of relationships where you don't talk about money or sex. But I was vulnerable and nobody thought a thing about mentioning it to me."

The widow was not yet thirty. Her long blonde hair fell nearly to the waist of her maternity smock; her eyes were red and swollen: the eyes of a woman who has wept, and not just for a little while. Yet she was composed, controlled, and the control was a victory she cherished.

Mortality and marriage: "till death do us part"

Most American marriages do last so long as both still live; in the last years of life millions of Americans whose marriages have survived the vicissitudes of forty years and more are widowed. Because women tend to live longer than men and to marry men older than themselves, more women than men survive the spouse. In 1970 only 8.8 percent of American men between the ages of sixty-five and sixty-nine were widowers, but 36.5 percent of the women in this age group were widows. For those Americans between the ages of seventy and seventy-four, 13.8 percent of the men but 49.0 percent of the women were widowed (U.S. Bureau of Census 1972:3–5). Perhaps a woman can expect to lose her husband at an age when the biblical allotment of three score years and ten has been exhausted, but death always comes a little soon. We are never quite ready for death or for widowhood. Not this week. Not today.

And when death comes to people still in their twenties, it seems to have cheated cruelly. Time was when women could expect to be widowed young and when a vigorous man might bury three wives or more. A century ago, life expectancy in the United States was little longer than it is in India today. But if the ravages of disease and childbirth do not sunder marriage as frequently as they once did, death still comes early to some, early and often violently: on the battlefield, on the freeway, from homicide and suicide—ugly words that are not usually brought up in the same breath as marriage. It is customary to pretend that such things cannot touch the sanctity of the home. But in 1970, for every four divorcées in their late twenties, there was one widow.

This widow with the dry red eyes and hurt smile had been the wife of a young design engineer. He was killed on the freeway in the early dawn of a Sunday morning in September. It was about two months later that she graciously consented to a lengthy interview. She is a brave and insightful woman; in our age of violent death these seem to be the core requirements of the widow's role.

Death is like a sudden storm that leaves people stranded together, when perfect strangers will talk to each other as they would never have talked in twenty years of commuting side-by-side. Yet unlike the natural catastrophe that touches alike everyone who is caught in it, the death of a man leaves his widow in an isolated prominence, at once the target of sympathy, and well-intended familiarity and morbid curiosity.

Right away that Sunday morning—I was notified at three in the morning—people started coming in, about eight or nine. And I felt naked. I said things that I would never normally say, like—I thought at the time I might be pregnant, and I just blurted all this out to everybody. Strangers, you know, and I guess that lasted a couple of weeks. There was nothing sacred or private.

The new vice-president of the division came by Sunday morning and I just opened right up. And people ask questions they would otherwise never ask. They asked about—it really shocked me because that was the last thing I wanted to think about Sunday morning—what my finances were going to be. I didn't know and I didn't really care right then.

The role of the bereaved

It is a truism in our culture that we have traditional ways of dealing with widowhood, but lack comparable institutionalized means of responding to the divorced. When asked if the customs surrounding death and widowhood in American culture seemed adequate to her, this young widow replied, "No, and they don't seem very clear-cut, either."

Oh, the traditions were gone through. People brought food in, which really surprised me. But people had no qualms about putting me down. I had a closed-casket funeral, and nobody viewed the body beforehand. And people that I had only passed on the street—neighbors way up the block that I had not even passed the time of day with—came and put me down for it. The landlord was really vehement. And the landlord let me know that cremation—you know, he wasn't going to get to heaven, by God! And having the closed casket —that really surprised me, because with an auto accident, you know, I should think it would be perfectly understandable to anybody. He was not banged up, but that is beside the point. Nobody else knew that. These were people who had never spoken to Bill.

This young widow had violated the ritual aspects of her role; society, in the person of her neighbors, reprimanded her for it. Others were intent, however, on playing their roles in the situation: friend of the bereaved or relative of the bereaved. These roles require the *bereaved* to act according to role expectation.

People wanted to take over immediately, the whole household. My | **429** mother came up to stay for a week—either that or take me "home" as she put it. She had never thought of me as having a home any place else. And other people wanted to come in and take over or to take me away. I allowed this just for eating. I found that the hardest thing for me to do was to cook dinner for just Diana and myself, but I stayed home alone at night from the very beginning. I never went anyplace else or had anybody come in. I felt I had to have control of something, and keeping control of the house helped me keep control of myself, and I still have that feeling.

One fellow from Bill's design group—who was not a close friend but we had associated with him and his wife a little bit—ran around immediately without telling me and found out about Social Security and veteran's benefits and arranged for the life insurance—just everything, which bothered me a little. I was very grateful, but it bothered me. It was taking control away from me, which I had to maintain. I had to control things to control myself.

For relatives and friends, sudden death is a crisis to be met; they are filled with the urge to do something. The network of relationship that ties people into groups has been torn, and they want to mend it rapidly; like busy brown spiders, they dash out to repair the web.

Everybody wanted to do something; the men, Bill's colleagues, boxed up his books and drawing equipment at the office. They had this to do, and they donated money. They are making a fund at the company, and they could do this, but for the women there wasn't much they could do, physically do, and I think this was why they all wanted to play the role of comforter, and I couldn't accept it. A lot of them said, "But what can we DO?" So I made up little projects for everybody to do and they went home happy.

Sudden death has a different meaning to the bereaved spouse than it has even for close relatives and friends; for the latter, it is a cutting off of one of numerous relationships; for the bereaved spouse, it is a tearing apart of the entire fabric of life. Like all shock, sudden death is experienced first as numbness, a lack of feeling; it takes a little while for the survivor to admit the enormity of the injury and pain.

I started the tests to find out whether I was pregnant about two days after the funeral, and I really couldn't cope with it or think about it too clearly then. After I found out for sure, I had been through a period of blocking everything out, and it just broke me down for a couple of days. I really thought I was going to lose control, because it brought all these memories back, right in my face, and I couldn't block them out. And realizing how lonely it was going to be this time, how much Bill had meant to Diana, and, you know, being around that and the new baby never knowing it and the closeness we had all through that time—all of that.

The functions of anger

Some of the overwhelming emotion can be discharged as anger. Harry Stack Sullivan points out that "anger blunts the feeling of personal insecurity" (1956:96). And almost always there is someone who makes a convenient target for the anger of the bereaved: a hospital staff that does not seem to have done all that might have been done to save the patient; a callous relative who is visibly impatient to have the will read; the driver of the other car.

I had a real thing happen that took this function. A funeral director, who was also a city councilman, by devious means came to find out about the death and came to notify me about three o'clock in the morning and brought two city cops with him, which he could do because he was a city councilman. And left his business card and asked me about five times if he could bring the body over, which is soliciting business, which you are not allowed to do in a situation like this. So I was able—immediately, I had this other thing to think about and I knew I had to write down what was said and what went on in order to prosecute and I knew that I wanted to. I was told directly that they can get away with this because most people don't want to prosecute, they don't want to think about it. I am following through on it, but I am going to have to find some way to finance taking it to court.

It was an emotional release, though, something to be furious about. And then at the funeral there were two bad errors. One was my fault, I was terribly angry at myself. They asked me did I want classical or religious music, and I was thinking of great classical music, you know, Vivaldi or something like that, and they put on this maudlin, horrible funeral music and that made me mad. It was just one of those things I didn't think of, and they had an error in that little program they give you, so I had this immediately when I walked into the funeral, to take my mind off it.

Anger directed against whoever makes a plausible object; anger turned back on the self for some mild sin of omission—such anger drains off the emotion that seems about to burst the psyche; it also diverts attention from anger at the dead. The child that lives in the recesses of every adult consciousness feels bewildered, rejected, left alone for no reason. Yet the adult that must be in control during this interlude of shock and sorrow knows that the dead did not die willfully, and anger at him seems unthinkable.

I don't think I felt any anger at Bill. A few other people did. His friend

431

Dick came over and said, "You know, I just want to go and see his body and hit him, for allowing this to happen." Obviously, Bill had been drinking; what else he had been doing, I don't know. But I talked to him on the phone at seven in the evening, and he was drunk. So Dick was angry at him for making this thing possible. I didn't feel that way. That was the kind of life we lived. We just knew this kind of thing was possible. I had thought of the possibility before and there was just nothing to do about it. And so I—I didn't feel anger.

But I think it was this thing with the funeral director, something else to talk about. You know, here are all these people sitting around for hours, what do you say? Here was something convenient to talk about. And then after the funeral, talking about the funeral itself. That was something everybody could talk about for weeks. What do you say when people come to see you? Everybody expected me to fall into their arms and cry, which I couldn't do. I couldn't lose that control again. So here was something to talk about. And the funeral was almost a happy thing to talk about, because everybody was so amazed at what a great funeral it was. It came off so well, considering.

I didn't believe it, and yet I did, that this was the last thing I could do for him, give him a decent funeral, and the kind we believed in. Even though I knew he didn't believe in funerals, as such, but to give him something—it was the last thing I could do for him.

Something to do—for him—something to talk about—besides him—something to be angry about, to cauterize the wounded psyche.

The dead are always heroes

Part of the anguish is a sense of failure: "I should have made his life happier; I could have done more; if only I had known." And this is often, perhaps always, accompanied by the placing of a halo over the memory of the dead—the funeral eulogy, the recollections of friends who come to pay respects and stay to gild the memory, above all the tendency to remember only the good things in the past. He is not merely a dead human being; he is suddenly a dead hero, quite possibly a saint.

Everyone does this and with me it was even stronger, and I am sure all wives think—all the things I should have done for him. That was one of the first things I felt; that our life could have been happier, I could have bent more, had I known. And this especially happens because people—and everybody does this—all of the friends did this—have a tendency to make a hero out of him immediately. He had done no wrong. I did it and everybody I know did it. And that made my role look even worse.

432   The idealization is in many ways similar to the romantic ideal, which is draped, however poorly it may fit, on the person with whom we "fall in love." Marriage dispels many of the romantic illusions, but some cling, and these are blended with the good memories that every husband or wife has into a larger-than-life image, and there is no longer any reality to compare with the illusion. Sullivan comments:

> Even two or three years of intimate life as husband and wife may leave relatively untouched a large body of illusion in each person as to the character of the mate. Very real and objectively demonstrable interaction has been unable to brush aside this great body of illusion about the other person —of what we ordinarily flippantly call wish-fulfilling fantasies. Surely, then, you can see what I mean when I speak of the danger that the death of either person in this situation will deliver the other over to life with a fantastic illusion of the person who is gone.   (Sullivan 1956:107)

To break from this morbid idealization of the past, which can make any future relationship with a living and thus fallible human being seem pallid and unsatisfactory by contrast, it is necessary to reach back to recall the man before he becomes a myth.

I did go through this horrible failure and guilt thing. And then I had to realize, No, Bill was human. He had some faults and we were not living in terms of somebody dying. I could have made life easier, but I would have been false to myself if I had put him on a pedestal while he was alive. I shocked several people by saying that. But, you know, it should be said. You're being truer to his memory. But they thought I was pretty crass and crude, hard. They all think I'm hard because I have held onto myself so tight. I didn't fall into everybody's arms like they wanted me to do.

When two people have lived as closely as husband and wife do, especially in the middle class, the sudden death of one leaves the other with most of his or her interaction patterns ruptured, except for the memory of how it was. Recalling intimate, tender, funny moments, calling to mind the familiar touch, the repeated gesture, perhaps even the irritating habit, can become a vivid reexperience: the fragrance of lilacs where no lilacs bloom, when something reminds us of the dead whom we once embraced in a garden in the spring. The widow remembers so much, so vividly: the warmth, the touch, the laugh, the animal smell of her man.

The sudden and poignant memory hurts less if it is allowed to expand to fantasy; the danger lies in a deep retreat into a fantasy life that blocks new relationships. One who clings to a memory avoids real experience. Memory is a fragile thing, and new experience seems to threaten to block its return, to make it harder to summon the past. Anyone who has ever tried to hang onto memories of a romance of summer through a winter of slush and dreary dates with stolid, dependable people has had

433

a foretaste of the conflict between fantasy and reality that confronts the widow. (Or the widower; the lost Annabel Lee has a deep fascination for men.)

Sullivan observes: "When we are deprived of a valuable relationship, by accident or design, we are in great danger of translating a more or less real intimacy into a wholly fantastic intimacy" (1956:106–107). And there is always the desire to bring back the dead, to reunite the self with the lost other. Such fantasies ease the pain for awhile; like dreams where the dead return, the daydream becomes a temporary relief from sorrow, and this is what makes it tempting. Probably everyone who experiences such a loss does indulge in a fantasy in which the dead person is miraculously restored. If fantasy can be put away when it has served its purpose, there is no reason to believe that sanity is in danger.

> I guess I have done what everybody has done, I hope everybody does this. You know, the fantasy every so often that I let creep in—that there was an error, that he is in the hospital with amnesia, that it was somebody else—and it hasn't hurt to put the fantasy down, afterwards. The first time that I started thinking this way I was driving home at night on a long drive, and I thought, good grief, I've got to stop this, this is really going to make it bad. But it never did. It eased it a little bit, somehow. And so, since this I've been—you know, at night—and I guess I'm quite conscious of what I'm doing, too—which makes it even sicker, I guess [*nervous laugh*]. I'm allowing myself to have a fantasy which is—hard to cope with. But it works. What else can you do?
>
> The reason I was able to use this fantasy was that no one that knew Bill ever saw the body. I didn't and nobody else did, and so, you know, that made it—"maybe it's real." Oh, and the way it started, when they came to inform me they asked if there was anybody else in the car. Which after I started thinking about it—it was almost a month later that I started doing this—it was that remark that started it.
>
> It was a few minutes of peace. And it went to great extremes of bringing him home and reuniting him with Diana—it got quite involved. Yet I could stop it when it had gone far enough.

The functions of grief

The great utility of grief is that it saves the surviving spouse from becoming enmeshed in a fantasy life with the dead. Its function is to extinguish a response. Like the electric shock that discourages the laboratory rat from making certain responses, the sudden realization that "he is gone" makes the survivor pull back from behavior that can offer only illusory fulfillment. It is the pain that brings us back to reality, and back to life. As Sullivan describes the process: "The first day after the loss, since

intimacies interpenetrate so much of life, it is almost impossible not to be
reminded of the loss by any little thing—even the position of the saltcellar
on the table, for instance" (1956:108). The saltcellar was always between
"my place" and "his place," which was so much more than a space of table
top and a chair. Even if it is possible to avoid looking at the empty chair,
carefully putting the salt back halfway can bring a twinge.

"But each time this happens," Sullivan observes, "the power of that
particular association to evoke the illusion of the absent one is lessened"
(1956:108). Gradually, the response is extinguished, and after a bit, a
saltcellar on the table is only a saltcellar. *Grief is an erasing process.*

I think this was what I did with blocking it out, and then letting just
a little float up. I think this is what I was doing when I stayed home—
stayed home and kept control. I was afraid then that it would be too
hard to come back if I left it. I couldn't have gone with my mother.
For the first couple of weeks, Diana and I went out to a friend's house
for dinner each night, and the first time I cooked dinner and shopped
for just the two of us was terribly painful. And it is funny that that
should be the worst thing, but I think it was because I put it off for
so long. I had been cooking breakfast and lunch for us, but not
dinner. And dinnertime was the big time for the three of us.

Now, shopping will hit me every so often, but not like before. I
think about it later when I'm home. I put the lid on and bring it back
when it's convenient. The half-completed projects were pretty hard
to look at, the reports hadn't been written up yet, and getting those
taken care of and to the proper people, that was—it wasn't the getting
rid of them, it was the half-done feeling of it.

When I started to get his clothes ready and things, that hurt awful
bad. But after I adjusted to it and started doing it, this was blocking
out again. I was able to complete it without trouble. I had them in the
trunk of my car for a couple of weeks before I got down here, and
then finally giving them away—I cried, but it was really—it was more
of a release. That's done, and I just fell apart for a minute.

And I realized that I had done all my Christmas shopping but I had
not bought anything for Diana. And all of sudden it dawned on me,
this is the thing Bill and I did together and I was just avoiding it
without knowing it.

Grief allows us to bring up one association at a time, one action that used
to be a joint action, and carry it out alone, or with someone else, and
thereby remove it from the grip of the past. But sometimes the healing
function of grief is not allowed to operate. Sometimes, as Sullivan observes, "instead of progressively losing its power to evoke tragic recollections, the saltcellar is now surrounded by a very elegant doily" (1956:110).
Morbid grief is as truly a perversion of a life-giving function as any perversion of the sexual drive. An article that once belonged to the dead **435**

"When I started to get his clothes ready and things, that hurt awful bad . . . I had them in the trunk of my car for a couple of weeks before I got down here, and then finally giving them away—I cried, but it was really—it was more of a release. That's done, and I just fell apart for a minute."

becomes a fetish capable of evoking his presence, and the survivor feels that the deceased spouse is still there in spirit.

The man or woman who used to carry on conversations with the absent spouse on the way home from work, or while scouring the sink, may carry on elaborate conversations with the dead spouse. It may seem almost a palpable presence that is spoken to, appealed to, asked forgiveness. This perversion of grief tends to occur most frequently when the surviving spouse is a person who married a "magic helper," in Erich Fromm's phrase. Fromm (1941) describes the pattern of dependency in which persons who feel unable to cope with life seek the protection of a power outside themselves, a power that they may personify as some specific individual (father, mother, husband, wife, even dictator of the nation). Or

436

they may structure the "magic helper" as an intangible, mystic force that protects and guides them. As Fromm describes this pattern:

> The intensity of the relatedness to the magic helper is in reverse proportion to the ability to express spontaneously one's own intellectual, emotional, and sensuous potentialities. In other words, one hopes to get everything one expects from life from the magic helper, instead of by one's own actions. The more this is the case, the more is the center of life shifted from one's own person to the magic helper and his personifications. The question is then no longer how to live oneself, but how to manipulate "him" in order not to lose him and how to make him do what one wants, even to make him responsible for what one is responsible for oneself.   (Fromm 1941:176)

The person who has made a living spouse a "magic helper" tends to feel like an extension of the husband or wife, rather than experiencing himself as an integral being with a sharply individuated identity. The man or woman (perhaps more often a woman) who has experienced life largely as an extension of the spouse will have a particularly difficult time handling bereavement. If the spouse personified the "magic helper" in life, in death he may be structured as a shadowy "other" that can still protect. A pair of shoes, a half-filled pipe, a battered hat, can suggest a sudden presence.

This is not to say, however, that all things that were once used by the dead should be destroyed, or that it is necessary to flee from the home that was shared. On the contrary, a period of grieving in the midst of these familiar things can be useful in the erasing process: picking up the "salt-cellar" and letting the old associations come, more faintly each time, until they have lost their power.

I made a big point of staying home nights, and about a week after the accident I told a friend that the house didn't bother me, and his things around didn't bother me—it was my house! It's just as simple as that, it was my home! I was told I was making a mausoleum out of it. You know, it was some sort of sickness on my part to stay there. Friends let me know I should move out of there within the month, at least. It was almost like the cultures in which they burn the house down when someone dies! I gave away his clothing and, oh, a lot of his books and things that I would never have any use for—but a lot of things I kept, too, because they were mine. And this they thought was very sick.

The person who is able to surmount the death of a spouse, to use grief to wipe away the associations that could block future intimacy, is the person who has always had a sense of self that is complete and, on the whole, adequate. When I asked this young widow, "To what extent did you experience a crisis in your identity when you were no longer Mrs. Bill

437

Leonard?" she answered, with dignity, "I've always been Virginia Leonard." (Which, of course, is not her real name.)

There are cultures in which a widow removes the white clay of mourning after a certain time has passed; removes it in a special ceremony in which she dances on the grave of her husband. This is not a desecration of the dead, but rather the return of the living. There is so little ceremony in American culture that each widow or widower has to find a point where life takes precedence over the dead past. Intimate relationships often are renewed first with the children, whose needs cannot be met by memories.

I never let them take Diana away so that I wouldn't have the responsibility, because I needed responsibility. It was only for the funeral that I left her. But I found out—just in the last week—that I haven't really been relating to Diana. That I haven't really related closely to anybody since it happened—I've just been drawn up tight. And it dawned on me that I was really doing this poor little child harm, because I wasn't close to her. Oh, I'd play with her, but not in the normal way. And so I started then, relating to her, playing with her in the bathtub, this sort of thing. It really hurt for awhile.

Bill and Diana were very close, not like any other father and daughter that I have ever seen. And I guess that was why I just rejected her—that is what it was, I was rejecting her—we slept together and that sort of thing, but it wasn't a closeness. And it was just last week that it dawned on me what I was doing. She was beginning to throw temper tantrums, and really rebelling, and all a sudden it dawned on me—no wonder, the poor little kid hasn't had anybody. I'd been taking her out to lunch, things like that, but with Bill away I'd go into a restaurant and sit down and tell her to eat and shut up and sit down myself and that was it, you know, going out together.

I was doing all these things that are considered nice, but with no feeling. I think part of it may be controlling myself, not showing warmth or real feeling because then other feelings might come out. Perhaps it was, "If I don't feel anything, then I won't hurt."

I bought her a lot of things, a lot of new things. It wasn't with the idea that it would take the place of affection, but—she just needed something extra. It was the only thing I could do for her, really. I set aside this money and everything was Money—Give—Buy. Which I had never done before. I used to like to get her things, but it was never such a vehement thing, so constant. It was over two months that I did that without knowing it. That is what surprised me.

The widowed mother: "a housewife who isn't a wife"

Everybody thought I should abort the baby. Except for the family, the family all thinks it's great, and their reaction is that it is a little bit of

Bill growing inside me, sort of "Doesn't God work in strange and mysterious ways," and all of this. I don't see Bill in Diana, or that sort of thing, so I don't think of it that way. But I was glad. It was something we were planning to do together, which will be done. And all of the reasons we wanted the baby—mainly for Diana, two seems like a nice number—all of the reasons were still there.

And the next question was financial. This was the first reason they wanted me to abort. You know, how am I going to afford it, it's going to tie me down more, I won't be able to work—but that is no problem. I get more money from the benefits I have with a baby, so that is no problem. There was just no reason to do it.

Friends thought money was the reason I should abort the baby, and that it would tie me down. I think they meant that it would keep me from getting another husband in a hurry—money and sex again —although that was never stated. It's hard enough to find a man when you have one kid, and think what it is going to be like with two. That has been a very carefully guarded subject—whether I am going to marry again, or not. Broached all around and then finally pecked at a little bit, never directly said. It's "Of course, you don't want to think about that now, Dear."

And of course I need to think about it. I've got the rest of my life and that has got to be part of it. Yet they ask me how I am handling my sex life. Now, how do you explain that one? It was a colleague's wife that was the main one in asking about my sex life—several others did, too—and then Tom, the one that got everything arranged, there was a jealousy thing with his wife, right away, which surprised me. But here I was, a female alone, and that's pretty scary to wives.

I wanted to leave Vine Hill as soon as I could, in spite of my feelings for my home, because of the expectations of the people there. They wouldn't let me live a normal life. My first reaction was to come back to the valley. And then I found out with my income I couldn't afford the rents down here. And I wanted to get into school by February. I figured I would have to start doing something. I couldn't sit around and be a housewife who wasn't a wife.

I'm going back to school. I've got to plan to make a living. I figure I can live on my income about three or four years before inflation takes over on me and the new baby starts costing more. In the first year or so, it's not going to cost much. So I have to think in terms of earning money when I get out. What field, I don't really know yet.

And Diana isn't enough for me. She's been a great help, but you can't rely on a two-and-a-half-year-old for your life. I wanted to get into school by February, so I figured I wanted to move by the end of November, to get her settled down so I could leave her with a baby-sitter before I left her regularly. I wanted to be sure she was going to be used to it. This was going to be a big shock to her to be left a good part of the day, on a regular basis, so I wanted to ease her into it. So I was in a hurry to move for that reason—but I would have preferred to stay and move the last minute.

Even in a basically satisfying marriage, there are some facets of either husband or wife that are not involved in the relationship and that often are allowed to fall into disuse because they do not fit the pattern of life evolved in the marriage. In the latter stages of mourning, as the process of grief gradually extinguishes the pain, these formerly submerged aspects of the surviving spouse begin to emerge. In part because these are aspects of the self that do *not* carry memories of the lost husband or wife, and in part because these aspects of the self can surface now, these long dormant abilities and interests are reactivated. There can be a sense of rediscovery of the self.

Sullivan says: "Thus at the same time that grief in the self is making tedious the once-valuable associations and so releasing one from persistent preoccupation with the object of one's loss, the rest of the personality is, so to speak, renewing its youth, looking with new hope at possibilities for the future" (1956:109).

> Friends suggested I move to Monterey, near them. They said there would be a great social life and everything for me. But then I decided —or felt—I was just being pulled, and this is the first time in my life that I have ever been free of a leader-type, so this was my time to see what I was going to do with my own life. To see how I'm going to develop as a person. You know, in the wife's role no matter how sophisticated we are, the wife still follows, so this was my chance to do what I wanted to do, free from all influence. And so, I thought rather than to go into a set scene that was already going, I'd just go off someplace new. And so I decided on Portland because I do have one brother-in-law there, and other than that it's all new.
>
> I haven't been there long enough to establish any kind of relation with anybody. One person has questioned how long ago my husband died—since I'm obviously pregnant. They're trying to figure that one out. Well, I guess that's to be expected. I hope the baby's a girl. Mainly because I don't know when I'll marry and my mother raised both my brother and me alone and it was much harder on him than it was on me, and I think it would be easier to raise a girl alone than a boy. So for that reason I hope it's a girl, but it doesn't matter. But I know the family is hoping for a boy.
>
> I think I will get married—when it occurs, you know. I like to be around people now. As far as Bill's and my feeling went, this would not violate anything sacred.

Perhaps the hardest thing for the widowed mother is to explain to the children why their father is gone and that he will not be back. The younger the child, the greater the difficulty in making it clear without frightening

440

*"I can't tell her he's dead, she wouldn't understand it. I've tried to make it fairly
clear to her that he is gone for good, but I can't tell her that, either, she has no
way of understanding it. She still reacts like he is just gone for the day. She expects
him home."*

the child. The explanation that the missing parent is "asleep" is a risky
euphemism, for a young child can become fearful of ever again falling
asleep. But even the most emotionally neutral explanation is still fraught
with hurt and bewilderment and a sense of rejection for a small child.

Diana was twenty-six months old when he died. I just said he's "bye-
bye." I can't tell her he's dead, she wouldn't understand it. I've tried
to make it fairly clear to her that he is gone for good, but I can't tell
her that either, she has no way of understanding it. She still reacts
like he is just gone for the day. She expects him home.

Last June he hurt his back, was in the hospital—had to go off in
the ambulance, couldn't get out of bed for a week. And she turned

441

against him, "He's not going to hold me." She just clung to me and would not let me out of her sight for about a month. We'd go to a friend's house and she'd stay right in the room with me. And then she slowly got over that and realized that he wasn't rejecting her and learned to play games with him without hurting his back, but she really felt rejected at that time.

She still talks to him on her toy phone and writes him letters. While we were still living in Vine Hill, she wanted me to take her and go pick him up after work. Now that we are in Portland she doesn't ask that anymore but still—two or three letters she writes him, every day, and talks to him on her phone. And if we are going to do something —like we're off on this trip—she told him all about it and where we were going to be. And she has wanted to know if he can find the new house. And—what can you say?

References

Fromm, Erich. 1941. *Escape from Freedom.* New York: Holt, Rinehart and Winston.

Sullivan, Harry Stack, M.D. 1956. *Clinical Studies in Psychiatry.* New York: W. W. Norton & Company.

U.S. Bureau of the Census. 1972. *Census of Population: 1970 Marital Status, Final Report.* Washington, D.C.: U.S. Government Printing Office.

Suggested readings

Agee, James. 1967. *A Death in the Family.* New York: Grosset & Dunlap. Available in paper as a Bantam Book. A Pulitzer Prize–winning novel by one of the most sensitive American authors of our century. The novel is focused on the responses of a family to the anticipated death of an aging father and to the sudden, accidental death of his middle-aged son. Although written as a novel, the focus of the book is on the emotional interaction and role expectations of family members as they gather at the bedside of the old man who is dying, and as they gather to console the widow of the younger man.

Berardo, Felix M. 1968. "Widowhood Status in the United States: Perspective on a Neglected Aspect of the Family Life-Cycle." *The Family Coordinator* 17 (July):191–203. This article focuses on the widow in American society, but also touches on the widower and the orphan. Berardo includes some statistical profiles, some discussion of the widow's economic problems, and some discussion of her social isolation and mental health (for example, the social isolation of the aged widow who is "marooned" in a society in which couples are the basic unit of social interaction).

Lopata, Helena Znaniecki. 1972. *Widowhood in an American City.* Cambridge, Mass.: Schenkman Publishing Company. Available in paper. The sociologist who wrote *Occupation: Housewife* turns her analytic skills and research capability to the problems of being a widow in urban America.

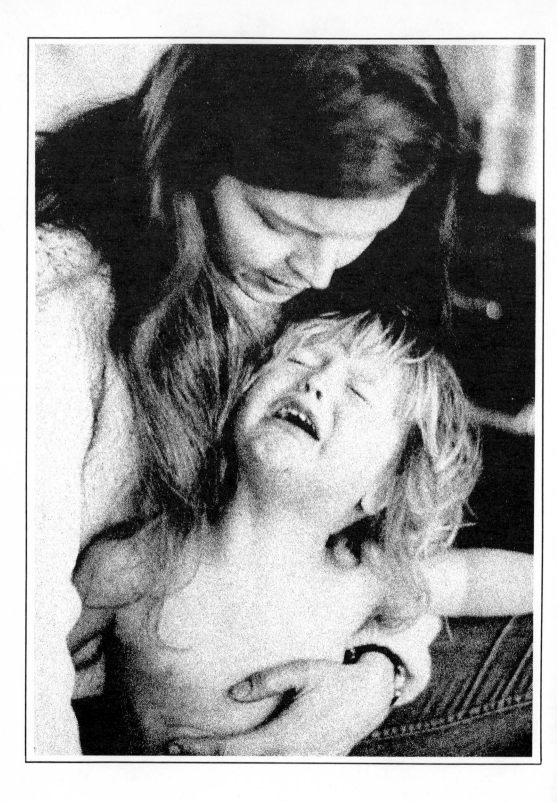

16 Postmarital roles

You think about what you're getting out of, that divorce will be the end of something that has become intolerable. What you don't know is that you are getting into another way of life that can be just as painful, that divorce is only the beginning.

A lonely divorcée

The rueful comment quoted above was made by a divorcée in her late thirties, a woman who had not remarried in the four years since her divorce. But even for the divorced who remarry soon, divorce brings a time apart from the even flow of their lives, an interval comparable to a severe illness with a long recovery: a period of pain but also of pain overcome, a period of being alone with the self, a turning point in life.

Separation: the empty hand

The widow is expected to grieve. The divorcée is not sure whether she is expected to grieve or to celebrate, to feel ashamed or relieved, and her behavior is likely to involve erratic swings as one set of emotions temporarily dominates another. Like the widow, the divorcée has to face the poignant awareness that "he is gone." But unlike the widow, who may have had to cope with the sudden and unexpected loss of her husband, the divorcée has usually gone through a period in which she has had a growing expectation of divorce. From being an unthinkable possibility, divorce has gradually come to seem an inevitability, as certain as the conclusion of a Greek tragedy. This sense of inability to control one's life, inability to slow the onward rush of events, is a common experience of people who are divorcing. It is part of their sense of vulnerability.

The period of greatest trauma tends to come at the time of final separation, rather than at the time of the divorce itself. The final separation may occur before the decision to divorce or after, before filing the suit or after, and some couples do not separate until the decree is granted. However, most divorcing couples are separated before filing suit, and the period of anxiety and loneliness is thus likely to begin while the couple are still legally married.

Even though there has been long and bitter conflict, nonrealistic conflict that served little purpose except the release of hostility, the final separation is bewildering. It is like pushing against a door that suddenly gives way. Sometimes the man—or woman—who has established separate residence finds himself sitting in front of food that he cannot eat, looking around at a furnished apartment where everything has the stale smell of use by strangers, and a feeling washes over him, leaving an emptiness where questions echo: "What am I doing here? I ought to go home—I want to go home." And sometimes he rushes home, an action that sometimes is the beginning of reconciliation. But often the timing is wrong; the spouse who was left may not be in the mood for reconciliation at the moment the doorbell rings. Perhaps yesterday, perhaps next week, but today her hair is a mess and she has on her old robe and looks a fright and why didn't he call first? And so, afraid that she will botch the opportunity, she does.

The couple who are divorcing or who have just divorced may find as many excuses to arrange meetings as a young couple in love. And there are good excuses: the children, property to divide, all of the business arrangements that must be carried out between them, including the arranging of the divorce itself. But often one or both may cherish the hope that such meetings will not be merely business; there is often a high sense of encounter, an anticipation in meeting that has not been felt between them in years. "When people walk hand in hand there's neither overtaking nor meeting," in Congreve's phrase. The couple who are divorcing discover again the joy of meeting, the excitement of overtaking, but they have an aching awareness of that empty hand.

And so he invites her out to lunch to talk business: lunch at an expensive restaurant where the drinks come in frosted glasses and the candles are lit even though it is early afternoon. The meeting at the restaurant begins with the warm glow of nostalgia and the glimmer of hope, but the bitter past sits at the table, too, and before lunch is over the hope of reconciliation may have faded. Whatever led to the separation is still there, and the emotional cost of separation may have been so high that one (or both) cannot risk the possibility of going through it again.

The latter stages of the divorce process may be marked not by an escalation of conflict, but rather by a strong wish to escape a situation that has become intolerable. The high level of emotional energy required to break free from a marriage cannot be sustained indefinitely. A person who has wrenched free from a destructive marriage may be emotionally exhausted, a survivor who feels perilously close to sliding back over the edge.

The temporary separation often begins as a search for peace, a peace so desperately needed that there may never come a point when both husband and wife are willing at the same moment to venture another attempt at their marriage. The "temporary" separation gradually becomes the final separation. The separation trauma is marked by one or more of the following symptoms: declining physical health, disturbed sleep, a drop in work efficiency, lapses of memory. The trauma gradually eases during the separation, and for some people is never too intense.

Mourning for the living

The separation trauma is similar to the widow's grief in that it is punctuated by sudden reminders of a relationship that is no more. There are things to dispose of, but this disposition is not quite the same as the widow's disposition of the personal possessions of the dead. It is rather a sorting out of things that were acquired as *ours* into piles labeled *yours* and *mine*. Old record albums or even a set of cracked dishes can evoke nostalgia with a bitter aftertaste. Perhaps to hold back memories that are too painful, there is likely to be petty possessiveness, alternating with grudging gestures. Does a toaster equal an electric blanket?

The parallel of morbid grief is the state of mourning for the living, once known as "carrying a torch." Some divorced men and women keep

447

alive the fantasies of reconciliation long after any reasonable possibility of restoring the relationship has faded. These are people who heap blame on themselves, who say, "If only I could have done things differently." As Harry Stack Sullivan says of those who fall into morbid grief: "Presently one of two things befalls these people. Either they cross the line into the, to my way of thinking, very dangerous condition of depression, or they become unhappy wreckages of life by the slow deterioration process of the fantastic life with the lost alleged love-object" (1956:112). It is not so obviously a fantasy involvement with the missing spouse, for he is not dead, only estranged, and thoughts of possible reconciliation can ease the hurt without seeming to be a morbid flight from reality. The divorce suit can be withdrawn—many are. Even after the hearing, if there is an inter-locutory decree there is still the possibility of reconciliation, and some plaintiffs never ask for the final decree. So the possibility of reconciliation is real, which gives a certain plausibility to the fantasy life of the divorcée.

Sometimes there is a recognized element of unreality, which may take the form of imagining that an unlikely event makes it possible to "start over" without bitterness, such as both suffering from an attack of amnesia. In such a fantasy, the two may meet accidentally, after the amnesia, and seeing each other with fresh eyes, fall in love again. Such a fantasy may become elaborate and detailed, carefully evoked in the middle of a sleepless night and filled with such comforting trivia as the details of the dress that she will be wearing, and what he will say, and go on to the manner in which they discover that they were once married. It is not surprising that many divorced persons seek counseling.

Recovery from the trauma of divorce is not a matter of wiping out all feeling for the former husband or wife, although the divorced person has as much need to extinguish painful associations as the widow or widower. Neither people who nurse old hatreds toward their former spouse nor people who cling to the fantasy of a romantic reconciliation are able to free themselves from the past. The woman who is preoccupied with how shamefully her former husband treated her, how miserable her life was and is, does not make an interesting companion. The man who asks her out, only to be regaled with tales of bitter recollection of another man, is not likely to ask her out again. Similarly, the woman who is still waiting for her former husband to phone is unable to build a new life. If the old responses are not erased, it will be difficult for the divorced person to enter any meaningful new relationship.

The process that seems to enable people to build a satisfying new life involves gradually letting go: letting go of feelings of possessive love, of punitive hate, of jealousy, and then becoming friends with the former spouse. Nothing dispels fantasy more quickly than an encounter with reality. When each of the former spouses has begun to build a new life and to develop new roles, it will be possible for them to transact the inevitable business they still have with each other in an atmosphere of detached friendliness.

Less than two generations ago (1928), Emily Post wrote that "con- ventions are shocked" if divorced spouses became friends. But there is a growing expectation, at least in the upper middle class, that people ought to be able to be friends even if they are divorced. And it is probable that friendship between persons whose lives will never be disentangled is the only solution that can free both spouses and their children to create rewarding new lives.

Children and divorce

There is a persistent belief that children bind a couple together and that a large family will contribute to great marital stability. Data gathered by the U.S. Public Health Service indicate that it is in fact the case that couples who have no children under eighteen have a higher divorce rate than do couples with minor children: 18.7 per 1,000 for childless couples, compared to 8.9 per 1,000 for couples with minor children (April 1973:16–17). Moreover, divorce rates decline as the number of children in a family increases (U.S. Public Health Service 1970:3–4). But divorce rates also decline as husband and wife grow older, and as the number of years they have been married increases. There are thus four variables interacting: age of husband, age of wife, duration of marriage, and number of children. The longer a couple have been married, the older they are, the less likely they are to divorce, and the more likely they are to have a large family. It is probably impossible to separate the impact of children on family stability from other related factors, but the presence of children is clearly one of several elements that combine in such a manner that each heightens the stabilizing effect of the others.

In the last two decades, however, the number of children in families broken by divorce has been sharply increasing. There were 398,000 American children whose parents divorced during 1958; 840,000 children were involved in divorces in 1969. The divorce rate is often expressed in terms of the number of divorces in a year per 1,000 total population (the crude rate) or per 1,000 married women (the adjusted rate). It can also be expressed in terms of the number of divorces per 1,000 children under eighteen years of age; the divorce rate so computed was 6.5 per 1,000 children in 1958, and 11.9 per 1,000 children in 1969 (U.S. Public Health Service April 1973:18–21).

Having a child in the hope of holding a faltering marriage together is a dubious decision. Conversely, marrying in order to legitimatize a child already conceived will accomplish that objective, but the child is no guarantee that such a marriage will endure. Particularly if the pregnant bride is still in her teens, the marriage carries a high risk of divorce. The age of a woman at marriage is inversely related to marital stability, whether she is pregnant or not. The U.S. Public Health Service reports that in its sampling, 40.6 percent of all divorced women reported no children, but only 25.6 percent of divorcing women who had married in their teens were

449

childless (1970:9). Or, to put it the other way around, nearly three out of four of the women who married in their teens and were subsequently divorced had children. In an earlier chapter, the impact of premarital pregnancy and early pregnancy on marriage was considered. Here, the focus is on the impact of divorce on the children.

If the widow finds it difficult to explain death to a small child, at least she can convey the certainty that the father will not return, and reassure the child that the father loved him or her and did not want to leave. The woman whose husband has left her finds it more difficult to explain to the children, because of the high level of uncertainty in the situation. The children will see the father again, in all probability, but perhaps never live with him again. The most difficult period for the children is often the interval of separation, when it is not yet certain that the separation is final. Father has probably packed a bag and left home before on a trip; the children want to know when he will be back from this one. At the outset, the mother may assure the children that he will be back, because she hopes he will. And perhaps he will return. But if the father does not come back, or if he returns only to take more of his belongings, the children begin to question anxiously. If the children do not feel secure enough in the relation with their mother to ask openly, they will display anxiety through behavior that is often exasperating to an already emotionally drained mother.

The children may wonder what they did to make their father go away; this may seem preposterous to an adult, but each of us believes that our actions are important, even when we are only five or six years old. The children may think that they are to blame for the parent's departure, but whether or not the children feel guilty, they will feel rejected. If the parent who remains with them is preoccupied with marital troubles, the children may feel rejected by both parents.

The children may become an instrument through which one parent tries to manipulate the other: a complex range of emotions can be evoked in the spouse through the child or children (on the average, when there are *any* children involved in a divorce, there is more than one child). Parental roles are difficult to play from a distance, and most parents feel deeply guilty about the effects of divorce on their children. It is not surprising that many divorce suits are withdrawn, and interlocutory decrees may be allowed to lapse, because of concern about the children. If the marriage can be rebuilt into a rewarding relationship, there is no question that the children, as well as the parents, will be happier.

However, as William Goode observes, "It seems likely that role failure within the home has a more destructive impact on children than the withdrawal of one spouse" (1964:102). The marriage may be stabilized, "for the sake of the children," but such stability is likely to be tenuous. If marital stability is achieved by making the children scapegoats (as described above in Chapter 13), the cost will be high to the children. In the long run, children are probably more emotionally secure in a tranquil home, where they have a warm relationship with a single parent, than in a home where two hostile parents tolerate—for the children's sake—a relationship that becomes daily more embittered. It is impossible to keep children from knowing that there is conflict between their parents. Even if the parents are careful not to quarrel in front of their children, the children sense anxiety, anger, and fear, and respond in kind. The pajama-clad child huddled at the top of the stair listening to quarreling parents is hardly experiencing a happy childhood. When a marriage is emotionally shattered, the children grow up in what Goode has called an "empty shell" family.

J. Louise Despert, a child psychiatrist, comments: "Divorce is not the beginning of a child's troubles. Divorce is the end result of a conflict which has already engulfed the whole family" (1953:167). She advises parents that they should "look to their children not the day after the decree is granted, nor even the day before, but at the moment when they begin to be aware of trouble between themselves ... A marriage can be saved at too great a cost, especially to the children" (1953:10–11).

"He who pays the piper": the role of the former husband

The saddest men are these: they are neither young nor old, but somewhere in between; they sit on the rock by the pond at the Children's Zoo in Central Park on Sundays and watch their daughters play.

They take their sons to see the Knicks, and their daughters to the movies, and after they have taken the children home to their ex-wives they go to the hotels, the furnished rooms, the borrowed apartments, the places where they live, and brood about the children, and wonder what to do that night.

They never go to the singles' bars on Third Avenue, and they know that if they did they would only feel foolish. They never go to group therapy, an encounter group, sensitivity training, or to the workshops in Greenwich Village that are run by men with beards and women in smocks.

They are too old or too skeptical for all that. Instead, they poke at their dead marriages, they drink, they watch television, they read, they have affairs.

Some of them are always having affairs. It is a risk, when already they are bruised by the failed marriage; someday they may have that one affair, that love affair, which will also fail, and from which they will never recover.

Still, New York is a big city, and there is always someone else to meet at a party, at the office, at a bar, or perhaps through the friend of a friend. It will not help, but it will be something.

It is the way things are in the city, and all over town there are divorced men who move into women's apartments, and who for years never get all their own possessions under one roof.

Their ex-wives have long since packed their stuff in boxes and put them in the basement. Old girlfriends have some of their things, and friends have, too, and they have forgotten themselves what happened to the books, the records, and everything else that once meant something special.

If New York were less expensive, perhaps it would be different for them.

451

They never seem to have any money, or at least not enough of it, and they remember when they first heard that the husband is supposed to pay for the attorneys who battle over the terms of the settlement. At the very least, they were told, it would cost $2500. They have been suspicious of lawyers ever since.

These are the men who are in Central Park and Prospect Park and at all the museums on Saturdays and Sundays. When their children are very young they hold their hands too tightly, and when they see another man with his children they can tell if he is separated or divorced, too.

He will also be gripping the children too tightly by the hand, or else he will be too solicitous to them, or else there will be hanging over the man and his children the same look of sadness and strain.

These are the men who bring a magazine or a book with them when they go into a restaurant. These are the men who dread Christmas, who work overtime at the office because they have nothing else to do, and who never know what to do about their laundry.

These are the men who get the early editions of the Sunday papers on Saturday nights, who stop in at a bar after work for a couple of quick ones, and who, when they talk about their ex-wives, are always wondering why those ex-wives are so bitter about them.

These are the men who want a home, who are desperate for a home, who will do anything for a home. These are the men who will get married again. (Corry 1973:21)

The childless couple who are divorced may soon have scant reason for seeing each other, and the former husband may have almost no continuing social role to play *vis-à-vis* his former wife. They are likely to have been married only briefly: the median duration of marriage to divorce decree for childless couples was only 3.8 years in 1969 (U.S. Public Health Service April 1973:17). If they are both in reasonably good health and able to be self-supporting, no alimony is likely to be awarded. Both are likely to remarry within a short period of time.

But when there are children, divorce is different. Over 60 percent of divorces now involve minor children, and in each such divorce, the man must learn to combine the role of former husband with the continuing role of father. Usually it is the husband who moves out during the period of separation, particularly when there are children in school. There seems to be less disruption of life for the children if he is the one to go, and it seems the thing for a gentleman to do. (There is a social-class difference here, however: the workingman's wife often goes "home to mother" and takes the children with her.)

The former husband is likely to feel like an intruder when he visits what was once his home. If he comes often to see the children, he may be accused of "hanging around too much." If he does not visit often, he may be accused of rejecting the children. If he buys them too many presents, he is charged with spoiling them and trying to purchase their affection; if he does not buy things for them, he is accused of being miserly. His

former wife and relatives may make the overt judgments, but he is likely
to have ambivalent feelings of his own that are easily confused with other
people's attitudes during a period of his life that is likely to be emotionally
charged.

Because the ex-wife is likely to be given custody of the children, the
former husband who is a father finds that he has the legal responsibility
for supporting his children, yet is denied most of the customary role of
a father in our culture. He has visiting rights, but finds that his role with
the children is more like that played by the favorite uncle than like the role
of father. He is the man who comes to see them sometimes, who takes
them to the movies or the circus or the zoo or wherever else a grown man
can imagine small children would like to go on a Saturday afternoon—
something not many fathers do in the course of normal family life. He
usually ends by buying them a little too much that is sweet, or toys that
are fragile and expensive, when they need a sensible sweater.

The former husband is likely to be afraid to discipline his children,
for he feels that he has only a tenuous hold on their affection. (What has
their mother told them about why he went away? Do they think he does not
love them anymore?) He may feel that his sons need the firmer hand of
a man and a man as a model; a growing boy should have more to listen
to at the dinner table than talk about how to take the spots out of a skirt.
Yet the father may be reluctant to think about the possibility that his
former wife may marry again, and be annoyed with himself for his feelings.

His relationship with his children may have deteriorated during the
months of conflict before the final separation. Even very young children
are aware of a troubled relationship between their parents. Because adults
think that communication requires words, they are careful about what they
say in front of the children, forgetting that stiffened shoulders, a fixed
smile, a vacant look, cold hands, the smell of fear, tell even a toddler that
there is reason to be anxious. Anxiety is a highly communicable state.

Feeling the anguish of separation, the divorcing father may not be
able to give his children much of himself, so he is likely to try giving them
things; he feels he has to give them something. (The father who deserts
may be an exception, but often the reason he deserts is that he is without
resources to give his children even necessities.)

A man's relation to his children and to his former wife is likely to be
complicated by the presence of a new wife. If he left the old marriage for
what seemed a more meaningful alternative, he may find that the children
resent the presence of his girlfriend or new wife. They may want their
father to themselves when they see him; the small daughter who felt guilty
about her desire to compete with her mother for Daddy's attention and
affection can feel righteously indignant about the presence of the "other
woman"—a feeling her mother is likely to encourage whether she means
to or not.

When the divorce is final, the former husband finds that his role as
a father is often reduced to purely financial terms, with visits becoming

453

The former husband who is a father finds that he has the legal responsibility for supporting his children, yet is denied most of the customary role of a father. He is the man who comes to see them sometimes, who takes them to the movies or the circus or the zoo, or wherever a grown man can imagine small children would like to go on a Saturday afternoon. He usually ends by buying them a little too much that is sweet, or toys that are fragile and expensive, when they need a sensible sweater.

less frequent as he feels less welcome. (This is especially likely if his former wife remarries.) Legally, the father has the right to participate in major decisions affecting the children, but practically, he may have little means of implementing this right without a court battle, which may be harder on the children than on anyone else; gradually his role as father may dwindle to the single act of mailing a monthly check.

Child support is set by the court and continues until the children are eighteen or sometimes until they are twenty-one. It may be changed, by the mother's application to the court, to reflect changing needs of the child. If the father does not send the money, he is liable to fine and even imprisonment for being in contempt of a court order. Usually, if he makes the back payments, the court will not send him to prison, for the courts regard a man who is free to work as more able to support his family than one who is in jail. Still, the threat of prison is the ultimate source of the state's power to make him continue to support children with whom he is no longer allowed to live.

Alimony ceases when the former wife remarries, but child-support payments continue until the child is of age, whether or not the former wife remarries. If the former husband remarries, neither alimony nor support payments cease, although he may petition the court for a reduction. (The former wife may petition the court for an increase in payments, based on increased expense.) It may not be the case that two can live as cheaply as one, but it is undoubtedly true that two households are more expensive to maintain than one. One of the effects of divorce is that, except for the wealthy, the living standard of both divorced spouses is likely to drop. The former husband may find that he cannot afford a second wife and a second family. The real and symbolic power of money being what it is in our culture, a man may come to regard his former wife as a drain on his financial resources and, symbolically, a drain on his virility. It is not surprising if he begins to see her as a "bloodsucker," as one divorced man described his former wife.

Yet the reality seems to be that the average absentee father pays little child support. In California, a state task force estimated in 1971 that less than 15 percent of the divorced or separated fathers of children in welfare families in that state contributed anything to their children's support. In Santa Clara County, where the distict attorney's office has one of California's highest rates of recovery of child-support payments (wages are attached for the purpose), officials estimate that the average absentee father of children on welfare contributes only $6 per child per month, and that divorced or separated fathers in that county whose children are not receiving welfare contribute only an average of $10 per child per month (Harris 1971). Welfare and working mothers must assume the major part of child support in most fatherless families in California, and the situation in other states seems little different.

A federal law that became effective in July of 1975 involves the federal government in the search for deserting fathers and in the collection of child support. The new law established a parent locator service, which will function under the direction of the Department of Health, Education, and Welfare. There will be financial bonuses—and penalties—for states, depending on the success of their efforts in locating deserting fathers. The new law opens such federal files as Social Security records and Treasury records to the parent locator service. And when the deserting parent is found (in most cases it will be the father, but it could be the mother), the Internal Revenue Service will be the agency of last resort for the collection of support money. It will use the same methods that it uses to collect taxes, which means that it will be backed by the federal courts. Not even a declaration of bankruptcy will exempt a father from support obligations. There is a provision that requires the welfare mother to name the father of her children (whether or not they are legitimate) or risk losing welfare support. This service is intended to reduce the federal expenditure for Aid to Dependent Children (which had reached $7.5 billion in 1975), but the service will also be available (for a fee) to families who are not on welfare but need to prod a reluctant parent into paying child support.

Divorce is only the beginning: the role of the former wife

If he controls the money, she controls the children. These are the counters in a game that may be played in bitter animosity. "If he sends the money, she will let him him see the kids, and if she lets him see the kids, he will send the money," is the way one divorcée put it. The role of the former wife and the role of mother often collide and leave a woman immobilized.

As one divorcée describes her inner conflict: "When their father comes to take the kids somewhere I'm afraid they *won't* have a good time, and they have been looking forward to it so. And I'm afraid they *will* have a good time, that he will spoil them and bring them home discontented with anything I can offer. And when they get home I can't even *ask*, 'Did you have a good time?' because the kids are likely to say, 'What's it to you?'"

As another divorced mother tells her experience: "I've just cooked dinner and we are about to sit down to the table, when *he* drives up and toots the horn and the kids run out—and I sit there feeling as unwanted and left over as the cold pork chops sitting on the table. Yet I hate to have to cover for him when he doesn't come. My little girl—ten years old—told me 'quit making excuses for Dad.'"

If learning marital roles is difficult, learning postmarital roles is painful. There are no clear guidelines in our culture, although as divorce becomes more common there are patterns evolving. There was a day when the role of the divorced woman was to withdraw from society and hide her shame. The alternative was to live as a "fallen woman." The divorcée is no longer shunned by former friends and spoken of in hushed whispers by her relatives. She is treated in many ways like the widow. There is a tendency for her family and close friends to "rally round" her during the

period of separation. Sometimes her husband's family may approve of the Postmarital roles
divorce, and may even express solidarity with her.

After the crisis of the separation period is past, the woman must adjust to the role of former wife. She must accept the fact that she can no longer simply ask her husband for money. He is now her former husband, and his financial responsibility is stated in detail in the divorce decree. Unless some real emergency occurs that affects the children, she must manage to live within her newly reduced means. If she kept the house when the property was divided, she is likely to be able to maintain her old circle of friends and so are the children. But on her child support and alimony (if any), it may be difficult to maintain the house and the standard of living that the neighborhood implies. Typically, she must either move to less expensive quarters or find a job, sometimes both.

The divorced mother may have worked before marriage, but that is likely to have been seven or eight years earlier, and her skills are as dated as the clothes she used to wear to the office. If she goes back to school to acquire new skills or to refurbish old ones, she must make arrangements for the children, manage the house, and still compete with younger students who have not been out of school for the better part of a decade.

Once she finds a job, her income is likely to be modest. At the time of the 1970 census of the United States, divorced women (all races) between the ages of twenty-five and thirty-four reported annual incomes that averaged $4,532 (the mean). Divorced women between the ages of thirty-five and forty-four reported slightly higher incomes, an average of $5,163. This was income from all sources, including employment, alimony (if any), and child support. (In contrast, divorced men who had not remarried reported, at the time of the 1970 census, average annual incomes of $7,160 for those between twenty-five and thirty-four, and $8,110 for those between thirty-five and forty-four years of age.) Only 2.8 percent of divorced women between the ages of twenty-five and thirty-four reported annual earnings between $10,000 and $14,999, and less than 1.0 percent earned $15,000 or more (U.S. Bureau of the Census 1972:181).

In 1970 only 14.6 percent of white divorced women between the ages of thirty-five and forty-four were employed as professional, technical, and kindred workers (most of those were teachers, nurses, or health technicians). This age group (thirty-five through forty-four) reported the highest average income of all white divorced women, and even so, only 1.6 percent had incomes of $15,000 or more. The largest group (38.9 percent of white, divorced women between the ages of thirty-five and forty-four) were employed as clerical workers (secretaries, bookkeepers). The next largest groups were service workers (waitresses, kitchen workers, charwomen, beauticians) at 15.8 percent and operatives (sewers and stitchers in the garment industry, laundry workers, factory workers) at 14.7 percent. The remainder were self-employed, except for a few who were workers in private households or on farms (U.S. Bureau of the Census 1972:176).

Black divorced women between the ages of thirty-five and forty-four included about the same percentage of professional and technical workers (14.7 percent) as white divorced women of the same age (14.6 percent). The largest group of employed black divorced women were service workers (28.8 percent), and the second largest group were clerical workers (21.0 percent). Operatives (sewers, laundry workers, factory workers) accounted for 15.6 percent, and private household workers were the smallest group (11.6 percent) except for the farm laborers (0.6 percent) (U.S. Bureau of the Census 1972:176).

The average divorced woman will *not* be able to find a challenging job with a high salary, whatever her fantasies before divorce. A drop in income and a lower prestige occupation than her husband is likely to have had impel the divorced woman downward in class status. As the doctor's wife or the plumber's wife, her status was clear; as the doctor's widow or the plumber's widow, her income is lower but her status still derives from her dead husband's occupation. But the doctor's ex-wife has a vague and ill-defined social status. The divorced woman is no longer a social pariah, but she typically is downwardly mobile for economic reasons. The fear of this downward mobility, and its potential effects on the children as well as herself, holds many women in unhappy marriages. The experience of downward mobility as a divorced woman may be a major factor in her decision to remarry soon, as most divorced women do. Meanwhile, if she was once the doctor's wife and is now a divorced medical secretary, she is downwardly mobile. The child support she receives and her alimony (if any) do not fill the dollar or the status gap.

But like the widow, the divorcée may find the period of living alone, or alone with her children, a time of self-discovery. She may have a heady sense of freedom to choose her own life, of being an adult at last. *She* is head of the household, something she never was before, regardless of class level. She has certain legal rights she never had while married, such as the right to establish domicile (translated out of legal jargon, this means if she wants to move to San Francisco, she can). She can open charge accounts in her own name, rather than as Mrs. John Jones. Unlike the never-married single woman, who often has a lingering sense of dependence on her parents, the former wife has a sense of being her own woman. Personal characteristics that were muted during marriage may become dominant themes in her new life. Because these were the aspects of herself that she did not share with her husband, they will be the least painful to experience in the period of separation trauma. From least painful experience, these may develop into most delightful. Simply stated, she may find that she likes "the new me," and her self-esteem may begin to rise.

Interests that lay dormant during the years of marriage can be developed if the divorced woman chooses. The key to her new life is precisely that: she chooses. Some of her new interests may involve group activities: political groups, consumer groups, women's groups, church groups, little theater groups, wherever her interests lie. (Parents without Partners is an

Like the widow, the divorcee may find the period of living alone, or alone with her children, a time of self-discovery.

association specifically organized to meet the needs of widowed or divorced women and men who have children and who are experiencing the special problems of single-parent families.) In any group activity she will meet people and make new friends. This is a time in her life when she needs to meet new people, needs to go out to satisfy needs that can no longer be met at home.

One of the myths that clings to the divorced woman in American culture is that she is promiscuous; some are. Behavior that would not have been expected of her before marriage is expected of her after divorce, by both men and women, whether she likes the idea or not. Perhaps this cultural expectation—one of the few concerning her role as a divorcée—allows her to feel a certain license. Perhaps the divorcée feels a desperate need to prove that she is a desirable woman still; perhaps she just wants the sexual freedom that a male head of household enjoys. Sometimes a high-pitched gaiety, a determined frolic, is the manic peak of a manic-depressive rollercoaster that may gradually level out as her emotional trauma eases. But many divorced women behave as circumspectly as Emily Post could have wished, forty years ago.

The pressures to remarry

There is no institutionalized pattern in American culture for dealing with divorce. Yet in one sense we do have a solution that is remarkably uniform: **459** remarriage. Except for the rare woman who builds an exciting career and prefers not to submerge her new identity in another marriage, most divorced women want to remarry, and do. Most women feel more uncomfortable about answering "divorced" to questions of marital status than about answering "housewife" to questions of occupational status. (They can hardly answer "single" if they have children.) The drop in living standard, the loss of class status, the social pressures, the pressures of their children, who may urge them to find a "new Daddy," perhaps the simple fact that they have been accustomed to marriage and miss it: for whatever combination of reasons, divorced women have the highest marriage rate of any group of women in the United States.

According to the U.S. Public Health Service (December 1973:6), in 1969 the remarriage rate for women in the age group between fourteen and twenty-four was 433 per 1,000: this means that of every 1,000 formerly married women in that age group, 433 married again during the year. The remarriage rate for women between fourteen and twenty-four years of age was more than four times higher than the marriage rate for women of the same age who were marrying for the first time. The marriage rates for women decline as women grow older, but in every age group the divorced women have the highest marriage rates, followed by widows, with single women having the lowest marriage rates at all ages.

The divorced woman used to be a rarity and a pariah. Now the very fact that there are so many women who have been divorced makes their presence an unwelcome reminder to their married friends that even "our kind of people" can and do divorce. Women who claim to be the divorcée's friends will be protective of their husbands when she is around. If they invite her to dinner, it will be to meet some nice man. They may not ostracize her, but they will feel more comfortable when she is married again. As Goode observes: "The unmarried, whether divorced or single, are viewed by spouses as potential threats. The divorced particularly represent *symbolic* threats, in that their existence demonstrates the possibility of ending existing marriages. They represent an *actual* threat to the extent that they are a potential *alternate* spouse for someone already married" (1956:212–213).

One divorced woman in four who remarries does so within four or five months after her divorce. Half of those who remarry do so within approximately one year, and three out of four divorced women who remarry do so within about three years of the divorce (U.S. Public Health Service, December 1973:13). There are some women who have a new spouse in mind before the divorce. This does not necessarily mean that the affair was the reason the first marriage disintegrated. It may have been only the catalyst in a marital situation that had been in an unstable, deteriorated state for years. John Cuber and Peggy Harroff quote a psychiatrist who observed: "Almost all divorcees are belatedly getting out of a situation which has long been psychologically detrimental. They seem to wait and wait until someone takes them by the hand and leads them out" *Postmarital roles* (1965:94).

There are pressures on divorced men to remarry, as well as on divorced women. Many men have occupations that involve a certain amount of entertaining and of being entertained; most of this required social contact is structured for couples—married couples. The divorced junior executive feels pressure to remarry. If he hopes to be promoted, remarriage may be considered evidence of his "stability." But for men as well as for women, many of the pressures to remarry are internal. Divorce always leaves the question of personal failure. Unlike the widowed, who can attribute the end of their marriage to an act of God, the divorced must always wonder if their marriage collapsed because of some inadequacy in themselves. Sometimes a man marries again to prove to himself that he is capable of a successful marriage. (Women may remarry for the same reason, of course.) Or a man may remarry simply because he has been accustomed to the comforts of a home and misses them, even if he was not always happy in his previous marriage.

Whatever their motives for marriage, men have remarriage rates that are more than three times those for women (U.S. Public Health Service December 1973:1). The U.S. Public Health Service reports that "the remarriage rate for men fourteen to twenty-four years of age was 521 and the rate for men twenty-four to twenty-nine was 524" (December 1973:6). This remarriage rate for men would indicate that for every two widowed and divorced men in the population, one remarried during the year. Divorced men have the highest marriage rate of any group of American men. Remarriage rates in reporting states increased sharply between 1960 and 1969, largely because of an increase in remarriage among the divorced men.

Widows and widowers also tend to remarry at rates higher than those for single persons, but the rate did not change significantly during the decade of the 1960s. For all age groups, the remarriage rates for widows and widowers are lower than remarriage rates for the divorced, but higher than marriage rates for single individuals. Those who are widowed at a relatively young age have higher rates of remarriage than do older widows and widowers; in the later years of life, remarriage rates decline steadily, especially for widows.

There is a strong tendency for people to marry someone with similar marital status. Thus, single people choose each other more often than they choose to marry divorced or widowed persons; divorced persons show a strong tendency to marry other divorced persons rather than single or widowed persons; widowed persons tend to choose another widowed person when they remarry. The U.S. Public Health Service (December 1973: 10) reports that in 1969 more than 90 percent of men marrying for the first time chose brides who had never been married before, and vice versa. Approximately 54 percent of the divorced men who remarried chose a

461

divorced woman, and 57 percent of the divorced women who remarried chose a divorced man. Of the widowers who remarried, 54 percent selected widows, but only 46 percent of the widows who remarried chose a widower. (This last statistic may be due to the fact that older widows greatly outnumber the widowers in their age group.)

Commenting on the data indicating that divorced men and women who remarried tended to choose divorced partners, the U.S. Public Health Service states:

> This fact takes on greater significance when it is realized that single persons comprised the largest proportion of eligibles in the age group 20–64, the group containing most of the divorced persons who remarried. For both men and women, over 50 percent of the remarriages of the divorced were to divorced partners while less than 20 percent of the unmarried population ages 20–64 was divorced. Thus for divorced men and women there did appear to be a selection in favor of a divorced person rather than a single or widowed person.   (December 1973:10–11)

Widows who remarry do so within a median time period of 3.6 years after the death of their husband. Widowers remarry sooner, the median time from the death of the wife to remarriage being 1.9 years. Divorced persons tend to remarry soon after the dissolution of their previous marriages. The median length of time between divorce decree and remarriage was 1.2 years for divorced women and exactly 1 year for divorced men. In the states for which such figures were available, 25 percent of divorced men and women remarried in approximately four to five months after the divorce (U.S. Public Health Service December 1973:13).

Although remarriages constituted, on the average, 25 percent of all marriages in reporting states, the highest remarriage rates were reported by those states with liberal divorce laws combined with a short residency requirement and no required interval of time between divorce decree and remarriage. In Idaho, 42 percent of all marriages in 1969 were remarriages of the bride. Idaho grants divorce on the nonfault ground of separation, has a six-week residency requirement, and no waiting period for remarriage. In the same year, Wyoming reported that 38 percent of all marriages in that state were remarriages for the bride. Most divorces in Wyoming are granted on the fault ground of "indignities"; there is only a two-month residency requirement and no waiting period for remarriage. The U.S. Public Health Service (December 1973:5) indicates that of all reporting states, the ten with the highest percentage of remarriages have no waiting period between the divorce decree and remarriage.

Strains on second marriages: on becoming a stepparent

There are a number of strains on second marriages that are seldom present, or if present are less intense, in first marriages. People are older

when they marry for a second time. According to the U.S. Public Health *Postmarital roles*
Service, brides who have been previously married are, on the average,
about thirteen years older than brides entering their first marriage. The
average age of men who are remarrying is approximately sixteen years
older than the average age of men who are marrying for the first time. For
women, the median age for remarriage falls in the middle thirties; for men
the median age for remarriage falls in the late thirties (U.S. Public Health
Service December 1973:6). People over thirty usually are not as flexible as
people in their twenties, and their habits are harder to change. Or, to say
the same thing with the value emphasis turned the other way, the bride of
nineteen may be more malleable because she is still immature. The woman
who has been married before does not need to learn to cook and manage
the household, but her new husband may have to adapt his taste to her
cuisine.

If remarriage comes before feelings of love for the former spouse
are turned into simple friendship, or before grief for a dead spouse has
completed its erasing function, there may be additional strain on the
second marriage. Mourning for the lost love cannot be shared with the
new. It is likely to trigger anxiety or jealousy if it is too apparent, for it is
hard to compete with the dead. And even if the former spouse is alive and
well in Kansas City, the slip of the tongue that equates the new husband
with the old can chill the honeymoon.

Remarriage frequently involves children, so the period of marital
adjustment is frequently one of adjusting to stepchildren. Both husband
and wife may have been parents in a previous marriage, but the role
expectations may well have been different. In any event, the role of stepfather or stepmother is more difficult than the role of natural parent. Social
norms make it difficult for stepparents to assume parental roles completely. The stepparent must always consider the rights of the biological parent
of the same sex, whether that parent is living or dead. This is most apparent when the child's natural parents are divorced, but a dead parent leaves
a legacy: perhaps a religious faith, certainly a memory, probably family
ties.

Fast and Cain (1966:490) suggest that the stepparent family should
be seen as a variant of the conjugal family, with a distinct role structure.
The role of stepparent is poorly defined and implies that the person can
function as parent, as stepparent, or as nonparent. He can try to be a "real
daddy," she can try to be a "real mommy." Or either can adopt the
depriving stepparent role that is developed in the folk tradition. The
remaining alternative is for the stepparent to adopt a nonparent role in
some variation, ranging from holding aloof from the child to being a
friend, but not a parent to the child. In folklore, the stepmother has an
even worse reputation than the mother-in-law. The stepmother in folklore
is a witch: from Snow White to Cinderella, stepchildren suffer from the
wicked stepmother who wants to destroy or at least to demean them. And
if the stepchildren see the stepmother as responsible for luring their   **463**

father away from the real mother, they may well pour onto her all the resentment that they do not want to feel for the father. If the role of mother is a valued and desired role, the role of stepmother is a suspect and difficult one.

The stepfather may have fewer problems with the children simply because he is out of the home working. But there are still complexities in the role. If the natural father is often seen by children as a rival for mother's affection and attention, a stepfather can seem even more a rival, for he may be viewed as an interloper. The same children who urged their mother to remarry (having in mind that it would be nice to have a *daddy* in the house again) may become resentful of mother's new *husband*. Mother is a bride again, bestowing attention on her new mate that the children have been used to receiving during the interval between their mother's marriages. The children of a former marriage are often a disruptive influence on a second marriage. The pull of divided loyalties may prove to be too great.

The ambiguity of the role of the stepparent is described by I. Fast and A. C. Cain (1966) on the basis of a study of agency case records on fifty families. Fast and Cain found that families in which there were stepparents had difficulties focused on discipline of the children and on the financial responsibilities of the stepfather for the children. The children tended to express dislike of the stepparent in ways that were disruptive to the family, which led parents to blame the children for marital difficulties. Even a natural parent sometimes makes his child a scapegoat, and it is perhaps not surprising that stepparents would have a tendency to do so, particularly if the stepchild seems to invite the projection of hostility and blame.

An alternate outcome is that the stepparent may become the scapegoat. Given the fact that divorce more often than death breaks the family in which there are young children, and given further the tendency of courts to award custody of the children of "tender years" to their mother, the most frequent family structure involving a stepparent is that of stepfather, stepchildren, and the children's natural mother. During the years in which the mother struggled as a single parent to raise her children, she may have had fantasies in which a new, strong husband appeared on the scene and took care of her and the children, filling all their emotional and financial needs and providing the discipline that the children needed. But a real husband (who has the limitation of being human) can seldom live up to the fantasy image. The children may begin to act out their anger at the man who has become the rival for their mother's attention. They may openly resent the efforts of their stepfather to discipline them. If he tries to impose rules that they did not have to obey in the days before their mother remarried, they may disobey the new rules to test him. The mother who struggled to control her children while she was a single parent may find to her dismay that the children are behaving worse than before she remarried. Marian Mowatt observes: "Since most of the child problems were first noticed after the remarriage, it was easy for the mothers to

project blame on their husbands ... Coming in as an outsider with an
unclear role, the stepfather was particularly vulnerable to being cast as the
scapegoat, which of course escalated the problems of limit-setting"
(1972:330).

Mowatt worked with families in group therapy. This group was composed of stepfathers, mothers, and adolescent children, and these families
had sought help because of behavior problems of the children. Most of
these couples had been married for five years or more, yet the stepfathers
were still uncertain about the extent to which they could or should take
over the role of father. They were not certain how much affection to give
to their stepchildren, or how to show it, particularly with their stepdaugh-
ters. But discipline was perceived as an even greater problem. The
mothers were defensive about their children, often making excuses for
them and protecting them from the stepfather's discipline. It was apparent
that these women felt personally attacked and accused of inadequacy when
their husbands criticized their children. The stepfathers felt that their
wives did not support them when they tried to set rules for the children.
These men resented having responsibility without authority. They felt
superfluous in the family: outsiders.

Yet, Mowatt observes, the stepfathers "seemed more concerned and
willing to involve themselves in the children's improvement than many of
the natural fathers seen at the clinic, possibly feeling less threatened (but
no less annoyed) by the misbehavior of stepchildren than of 'flesh and
blood' offspring" (1972:329). Group therapy seems to have eased the
problems in these families. Mowatt reports: "Gradually the mothers
become aware that their criticism only drove the stepfathers further away
from the children. As they listened to the other women revealing themselves as complaining martyrs, they could begin to see these traits in
themselves. Over the weeks the members gained some acceptance of their
strong dependency wishes, and became more objective about their disappointed hopes" (1972:330).

The second spring

Remarriage has a dubious reputation. A remarried couple are considered
marital retreads, and people rather expect that the marriage will not last.
In part, this attitude reflects the lingering bias against the divorced: they
may no longer be expected to retreat from public view, but they are not
supposed to find real happiness. Data on previous divorces are not well
reported on divorce records, but on the basis of available information, the
U.S. Public Health Service observed that between 1963 and 1969 there was
a marked rise in the divorce rate, with the greatest increase occurring
among persons who had been married only once. By 1973 the U.S. Public
Health Service reported: "Divorces of husbands and wives who had married only once increased from 1963 to 1969 at a higher proportion than
those of persons married twice, while divorces of persons marrying three
times or more were affected least by the increase" (April 1973:13). As

465

remarriage becomes more common, it may also be growing more stable. (It may also be the case that few people can afford to divorce and remarry more than once.)

Whether or not second marriages are as stable and rewarding as first marriages *in general*, the man or woman who marries for the second time is comparing that marriage to another very specific one: his or her *own first marriage*. For those who divorce and remarry, the second marriage is always compared to a marriage that ended in bitterness or dwindled into boredom. So it is not surprising that the majority report that their second marriage is happier than their first. Perhaps the level of expectations with which people enter their second marriage is lower. The young bride expects her first marriage to be an endless romance, but the woman marrying for the second time knows she is marrying a mortal and may be willing to settle for warmth and tender intimacy.

Yet the second marriage is not necessarily a pedestrian union. There is often a sense of rejuvenation, of late flowering. As one woman put it: "To divorce is to die back to the root; this new marriage is like a second spring, and the new self that is growing from the old roots continually surprises me. Sometimes I feel like my own ghost, watching myself develop."

As Paracelsus observed more than four centuries ago: "Anyone who imagines that all fruits ripen at the same time as the strawberries knows nothing about grapes."

References

Corry, John. 1973. "Desperately Sad Men of New York." *San Francisco Chronicle: This World* (December 9):21. © 1973 by the New York Times Company. Reprinted by permission.

Cuber, John F., and Peggy B. Harroff. 1965. *The Significant Americans: A Study of Sexual Behavior among the Affluent.* New York: Appleton-Century-Crofts.

Despert, J. Louise, M.D. 1953. *Children of Divorce.* Garden City, N.Y.: Doubleday & Company.

Fast, I., and A. C. Cain. 1966. "The Stepparent Role: Potential for Disturbances in Family Functioning." *American Journal of Orthopsychiatry* (April):485–491.

Goode, William J. 1956. *After Divorce.* New York: The Free Press.

———. 1964. *The Family.* Englewood Cliffs, N.J.: Prentice-Hall, © 1964.

Harris, Tom. 1971. "Dad's County Support Bill Is Small." *San Jose Mercury-News* (March 13):59.

Mowatt, Marian H. 1972. "Group Psychotherapy for Stepfathers and Their Wives." *Psychotherapy: Theory, Research and Practice* (Winter):328–331.

Sullivan, Harry Stack, M.D. 1956. *Clinical Studies in Psychiatry.* New York: W. W. Norton & Company.

U.S. Bureau of the Census. 1972. *Census of Population: 1970 Marital Status, Final Report.* Washington, D.C.: U.S. Government Printing Office.

U.S. Public Health Service. 1967. *Divorce Statistics Analyses, United States: 1963.* Washington, D.C.: U.S. Government Printing Office.

_____. 1970. *Children of Divorced Couples: United States, Selected Years.* Washington, *Postmarital roles*
D.C.: U.S. Government Printing Office.
_____. April 1973. *Divorces: Analysis of Changes, United States 1969.* Washington,
D.C.: U.S. Government Printing Office.
_____. December 1973. *Remarriages, United States.* Washington, D.C.: U.S. Government Printing Office.

Suggested readings

Bowerman, Charles E., and Donald P. Irish. 1962. "Some Relationships of Stepchildren to Their Parents." *Journal of Marriage and the Family* 24 (May):113–121. A summary and analysis of research on the relationships between children and stepparents. Overall, the adjustment of children to stepparents is shown to be poorer than their adjustment to biological parents of the same sex. When compared with children with a dead parent, the children of divorce tend to have both the best and the worst adjustment to stepparents.

Hetherington, E. Mavis. 1973. "Girls without Fathers." *Psychology Today* 6 (February):47–52. A research study of adolescent girls whose fathers were absent from the family owing either to death or to divorce. The results indicate that girls who grow up without fathers tend to display inappropriate patterns of behavior in relating to males, although they show no difficulty relating to females. Girls raised without fathers tended to be either excessively shy with men or compulsively seductive, with differences noted between girls whose parents were divorced and those whose fathers had died.

Hunt, Morton M. 1966. *The World of the Formerly Married.* New York: McGraw-Hill Book Company. This is a perceptive account of the subculture of the divorced. The book is based on participant observation in social functions of the divorced in various parts of the United States, on interviews with some 200 separated or divorced persons, and on responses to a lengthy questionnaire.

467

Part Five

Emerging marital patterns and some alternatives

17

The corporate "family": man, wife, and corporation

Never yet had K. seen vocation and life so interlaced as here, so interlaced that sometimes one might think that they had exchanged places. What importance, for example, had the power, merely formal up till now, which Klamm exercised over K.'s services, compared with the very real power which Klamm possessed in K.'s bedroom. So it came about that while a light and frivolous bearing, a certain deliberate carelessness was sufficient when one came in direct contact with the authorities, one needed in everything else the greatest caution, and had to look around on every side before one made a single step.

Franz Kafka (1949:76–77)

Thus Kafka described life in *The Castle;* the control exercised by the fictional Klamm would have pleased the real-life executive whom William H. Whyte quotes as lamenting: "We control a man's environment in business and we lose it entirely when he crosses the threshold of his home" (1952:32). This executive was determined to remedy the situation: "Management, therefore, has a challenge and an obligation to deliberately plan and create a favorable, constructive attitude on the part of the wife that will liberate her husband's total energies for the job" (1952:32).

The corporate "family" and personal identity

The assumptions of American culture have been that the first loyalty of a man should be to his wife and children, that other claims on him should be secondary. But farther back in our cultural heritage the extended family or the clan was paramount, and the conjugal family was only a subunit in the larger whole. It was the clan that commanded a man's first and deepest loyalty. The modern corporation may liken itself to a family, and viewing the conjugal units to which its employees belong as subsidiary to the total corporate structure, make the kind of demand on an employee's energies and loyalty that the clan once made.

The claims the clan made on a man rested on blood ties and identity: the core of a man's self-image was that he was a Campbell, an Appin Stewart, a MacRob. The claims of the modern corporation are based on the employee's identification with the corporate "family" he has joined. The American male who identifies with his profession may typically say, "I am a doctor," "I am a lawyer," or "I am a plumber," when asked the standard question, "What do you do?" But many American men are beginning to identify with their corporate employer rather than with a profession, and will answer, "I am with IBM," or "I am with GE," or whatever corporate giant has hired their talents.

One man belongs to his corporation in much the same way that another belongs to the Marine Corps: he is a member of the Team. This identification with his outfit is less a product of indoctrination than of a man's inner need for a sense of personal worth based on accomplishment. We Americans learn to evaluate ourselves in terms of achievement, and few men are able to achieve a *personal* success in contemporary America.

American social structure was never completely open, but enough men made the journey from log cabin to mansion in the nineteenth century to keep the myth intact. In the latter part of the twentieth century, however, relatively few men are able to carve out a financial empire for themselves, or to become famous because of a single-handed exploit. For most Americans, feeling that one is "getting somewhere" means being promoted within a bureaucratic or corporate structure. To rise in contemporary America means typically to rise within the corporation or to move up the ranks of a governmental hierarchy: the military, the departments of the federal or state governments, a state university system.

472

There is little *individual* achievement in our society any more. Most spectacular advances in medicine, in space, and in biochemical research are made by a cooperating team, with a large organization (or the federal government) financing and sustaining their efforts. Even the astronauts are only the most visible members of their team. Pride in the achievements of one's team replaces pride in purely personal achievement for most of us.

The corporate "family": man, wife, and corporation

Probably no American would be content to base his self-esteem solely on the success of his employer; it is only when he *identifies* with his employer, when he can speak of the entire corporation or agency as *We* and can think of spectacular new developments as *Ours*, that he can feel a sense of pride in the victories of his company or department. The team spirit may be fostered by the corporation for its own ends, but it could not exist unless the individual had an inner need to identify with a large and powerful entity. C. Wright Mills observed:

> In identifying with a firm, the young executive can sometimes line up his career expectations with it, and so identify his own future with that of the firm's. But lower down the ranks, the identification has more to do with security and prestige than with expectations of success. In either case, of course, such feelings can be exploited in the interests of business loyalties (1951:244).

As indicated in earlier chapters, the status and identity of many American women are derived from the occupation of their husbands. As some women learn to think of themselves as the doctor's wife or the minister's wife, so many more American women are coming to regard themselves as army wives, faculty wives, or corporate wives. If the husband's sense of personal worth is derived from the accomplishments of his "team," and the wife's self-esteem and social status are derived from her husband's accomplishments, clearly she, too, has a stake in the success of the "team." She often comes to think of herself as a part of the "corporate family," an identification with her husband's employer that some corporations try to encourage. It is not, then, a simple struggle between wife and corporation for the primary devotion of the husband-employee. The corporate wife (or the army wife, or the faculty wife) is in the position of the woman who has married into a wealthy old family and finds herself both pleased by having the family name, with the security and prestige it offers her, and resentful of the claims that the larger "family" makes on her husband.

The functions of the corporate "family"

All the employees of the corporation and their wives and children may consider themselves a kind of pseudo-kindred. As one corporate wife explained it to me, "I think of them that way all the time. They're our fellow

473

IBM'ers." Another woman, whose husband is in the managerial cadres of General Electric, commented that she regarded other people "who are GE" as "sort of part of the family, you feel, a sort of distant cousin." Such feelings are encouraged by the corporations. Whyte quotes IBM's Thomas Watson as saying, "Our wives are all part of the business. We started with just a few hundred people in 1914 and decided that no matter how large we grew we would carry it on in the family spirit. We always refer to our people as the 'IBM Family' and we mean the wives and children as well as the man" (Whyte 1952:46).

Men are often inclined to believe that they do not take the idea of the corporate "family" seriously, and affect a mixture of amusement and chagrin when taking part in whatever solidarity ceremonies are required by their corporation. Yet one man who had been with a corporate giant for fifteen years, and had finally quit to take a better job with a smaller firm, admitted to me that he felt a deep sense of loss. He was experiencing a crisis of identity and a sense of having "left home," as he put it, that surprised him. Sophisticated to the point of cynicism, he still felt anxious about cutting his ties with the corporation: "Quitting was like biting through my own umbilical cord, and I feel lost!"

Most large American corporations offer their salaried, white-collar employees privileges that the unions have had to wring from them for blue-collar workers: pensions, health plans, recreational facilities, educational opportunities. As a family educates its children in the hope that they will achieve success and reflect favorably on the family name, so the great corporations educate their "children." One corporate wife reported, "If you have genius kids, why you're in. Harvey Williams—you know Harvey? One of his sons is going to Stanford on one of our [Our Firm's] very generous scholarships." (All of the names used from this series of interviews are fictional, to protect the privacy of very real persons.)

Fathers are educated even more frequently than sons. Another corporate wife commented:

> [Our Firm] has the ultimate in this. If you're good enough, you can take *full* time off to go to college. And often people who do take advantage of this go zooming right up in the company. Lou Wood went back to Cal—he had three children and [Our Firm] took care of everything. He's done very well in the company since then, and he's still a young man.

On the same subject, another corporate wife observed:

> Jim was commenting that if he'd realized that companies had programs like this, he wouldn't have gone into the military. He went into the Air Force because he wanted *somebody* to put him through graduate school, and if he had gone with [Our Firm] then, they would have done what the military did, but without all that.

474

In effect, corporations are assuming the educational and protective functions that the extended family or clan once performed. The term *corporate family* is sometimes used to refer to the powerful clans of Confucian China. Dorothy Blitsten describes the functions of these "great" families as follows:

The corporate "family": man, wife, and corporation

> In the past a highly centralized government did not reach into distant regions effectively. The development and control of natural resources, armed protection against invaders, police services, and most other public services had to be supplied locally. Individual families could not perform these functions, but families united into corporate organizations could and did ...
>
> The clans included or indirectly benefited small families in their districts, but they were dominated by the "great" families that owned large estates, ran large business enterprises, and manned the Civil Service ... Maintenance and control of the local militia, village schools, and roads and bridges; public recreation; poor relief, and the maintenance of genealogical records and ancestral temples were typically their responsibility ... millions of Chinese who were without the protection of a clan lived precariously at best and on a subsistence level for the most part ... The operational units of the clans were their large extended families whose members dominated life in the villages, controlled a large proportion of the economic resources of Chinese society, constituted the largest segment of the educated class, and attended the Imperial Court. (Blitsten 1963:105–106)

If the analogy is not pressed too far, the corporate family of Confucian China and the corporate "family" of industrial America have much in common. Our corporate "families" develop and control natural resources, often provide local public services, operate large enterprises, and provide recreational facilities, pensions, and the maintenance of employee records, if not ancestral temples. And just as the millions of Chinese who were without the protection of such a clan had only a precarious existence, so increasingly those Americans who are the "hard-core unemployed," and thus without the protection of a corporate "family," have a precarious, subsistence-level existence.

Like the ancient Chinese great families, the modern American corporate "families" are presumed to be immortal. "Great" families could be broken and scattered if there were a major crop failure and several years of famine and disease; corporate "families" can go bankrupt. But the expectation is that, barring some catastrophe, the corporate "family" will never die. The individual is mortal and the conjugal family is ephemeral, but as members of a "great" family, people could look forward to a secure old age, supported by sons and nephews. In comparable fashion, the man who becomes part of an American corporate "family" in his youth can expect to be provided for in his latter days by a pension plan, for while he is growing older the corporation will be growing larger and stronger. If a man lacks faith in the future of his corporation, he will presumably look for another job.

475

Like the Confucian great family, the corporate "family" provides
security for the persons under its protection. The wives, as well as the
employees themselves, can feel a sense of security. One corporate wife
commented: "One of the things that [Our Firm] does, if a husband dies,
they see to it that the wife has a job, they really do. They *make* jobs for
people that don't have any skills, hardly, to sell." As a woman might once
have been grateful for the protection and shelter offered by the powerful
lord who stood at the apex of her husband's family, so many corporate
wives in America today are grateful for the security the corporation offers
to them as well as to their husbands.

Yet the price of such security is conformity, or at least a keen awareness of how one's actions may reflect on the family name and honor or,
in the corporate "family," on the corporate image. Those members of the
corporate "family" who meet the public are under the greatest pressure
to conform to the company image. One corporate wife reports: "People
in sales at [Our Firm] are absolutely tied up and wrapped. They can't wear
colored shirts, for example, they really, honest-to-God can't."

Even the man buried in the research laboratories of a large corporate
enterprise may feel subtle pressures toward conformity to the company
image. Another wife recalled:

> That was one of the funny things when Jim first came to [Our Firm].
> He was a scientist, not a salesman, and he used to wear bow ties. He
> thought he was being quite daring because *nobody* at [Our Firm] wore
> bow ties. The funny thing was, when those two bow ties wore out, he
> never bought any more.

During a period of economic recession, the pressures to conform are
heavier, for even highly skilled technical employees can be readily replaced. Dean Robert Weatherall, director of placement at Massachusetts
Institute of Technology, is quoted by the *New York Times* as saying that in
the tight job market of 1970 nonconforming graduates were having the
most difficulty finding jobs:

> We have many more students these days with long hair, who are used to
> working in blue jeans and sandals. They're not willing to compromise their
> individuality in order to get a job, but they're finding this a difficult year to
> make a stand on clothing or hair. Last year the firms needed their talents so
> badly they were willing to endure some of these personal traits. Now, there's
> such competition for the jobs, the firms can choose what they consider the
> "normal" applicants.   (Rice 1970:103–104)

Unlike the Confucian great family, the corporate "family" does not
exist solely to serve the people who are "family" members. Few American
corporations are intended to be nonprofit enterprises, and in times of

recession some members of the team are dropped; among the common euphemisms are "surplused" and "temporarily furloughed, pending recall" (Rice 1970:28). During the 1960s, most large corporations and the smaller ones that they had spun off could afford to keep large numbers of engineers and technical specialists on their payrolls from contract to contract. There was a general sense that an employee's tenure with a firm was indefinite, provided he conformed basically to the role expectations of the corporation. The recession of the 1970s led not only to the discharge of marginal and new employees, but also to the firing of skilled specialists who had been with their firms for twenty years or more. These were employees whose education and experience entitled them to high salaries, and suddenly many corporations, especially those in the aerospace industry, could not afford their talents.

Scientists, engineers, and executives who had been accustomed to high incomes and upper-middle-class status have found themselves unemployed. Some have continued to cling to the hope of a new job in some other corporation, and others have turned to teaching or even to blue-collar jobs. Berkeley Rice, writing in the *New York Times Magazine* in November of 1970, quotes one former corporate scientist, now a high school teacher, as saying: "I still feel that in other people's eyes there's less prestige in this job. When I used to tell people I was a nuclear physicist they were impressed. Now, when I tell them I'm a high school teacher, I still can't say it with the same feeling of pride" (1970:103).

However, some of these men have found that the effects on themselves and their families have not been entirely negative. Rice quotes an electrical engineer turned carpenter as observing: "As you plummet out of the corporate cloud, you suddenly discover that you've never really had time to develop penetrating relationships with your wife and children. The same with your friends. You see them once a week for cocktails or a dinner party, but you don't really know them. I've learned that what matters is people, rather than things" (1970:103).

The corporate employee as a family man

The former engineer quoted above had held a high management post in a subsidiary of a large corporation. His experience of having little time for family and friends may be typical for the upper ranks of corporate scientists and managers, but not for the white-collar employees who are the majority. The middle-aged man in the lower echelons of the corporate structure typically thinks of himself as a "family man." He values his job because it means security for his family, and he takes a certain pride in the accomplishments of the corporate team to which he belongs. But he has typically ceased striving (after the initial period of youthful optimism when every American dreams of rising). He is the kind of man who cuts the grass every Saturday and organizes a Little League ball team.

477

His identity centers on his familial roles. Both husband and father, he does not regard these as two possibly conflicting roles, but rather as one compound role. His relationship to his wife is permeated by the fact that she is also the mother of his children; they are likely to call each other "Mother" and "Daddy" as soon as the first child is born. According to Lee Rainwater:

> In the lower-middle class the relations of husband and wife are focused more sharply than in the upper-middle class on familial function, and there tends to be more emphasis on the family as a whole than on their personal relationships. While in the upper-middle class the husband-wife relationship stands somewhat apart from their common relationship to their children, in the lower-middle class the emphasis tends to be on the total family, and the way in which husbands and wives talk about their life together suggests that children enter much more completely into their thinking about their life together. (Rainwater 1965:57)

For such men, the corporation offers protection for their families and opportunities for their children. They are likely to use the family recreational facilities that the corporation provides, to take advantage of the educational programs for their children, and to be grateful for them. For the man who has settled into a limited but secure job in the corporate structure, there is no conflict between the corporation and his family.

The man whose upward movement in the corporation (or other large organization) has carried him into the managerial or research ranks, where his talents are worth upward of $25,000 a year, is often a "family man" only in the narrow sense that he has a wife and children. His family is more often subordinated to his career than the reverse. If asked, he would probably say that it is for the good of his wife and children that he strives; that is the expected answer. But his self-image is centered on his career. If he begins to feel that he is "burned out" (something that used to happen only to painters and poets), he turns to the psychiatrist in fear that he is dissolving as a person. His home is a refuge from the arena, but he gets restless if confined at home too long.

The man who is rising in the corporate ranks either in management or in research has a very different perception of his family roles than does the lower-level employee. John Cuber and Peggy Harroff report that "when some of these men talk about home and family they suggest an image of a feudal manor house: it is a place of protection, a base from which the expedition moves out and to which it returns for replenishment" (1965:117). The wife's role is centered on home and children; she manages the household like a medieval chatelaine while her husband is in the city or flying to the coast for a conference or to Europe for a meeting. But she must also be a sensitive wife, attuned to the subtle demands her husband's career makes of their home—and of her.

Describing the family life of many of the "significant" Americans they interviewed, Cuber and Harroff observe:

The corporate "family": man, wife, and corporation

> To many career men the home is almost an adjunct to the job. It is not simply that he needs it as a place to entertain—although this can be important. It is a status symbol, at once evidence of his past successes and a recommendation to support his bid for more. The organization man in many corporations and in some of the independent professions says that he is practically required to maintain a "certain kind" of home. He often has to trade on his home and family as he does on his personality. "It's all part of a package which you present to your public."   (Cuber and Harroff 1965:117)

Having the right kind of wife can be essential to promotion in the managerial ranks. A bachelor may find that he is at a disadvantage. Cuber and Harroff quote an executive who told them: "I can tell you why *I* got married! I was getting to the place where I had to. I'd gone up in the corporation as far as I could as a single man. Why they're so prejudiced in favor of married men, I'll never know" (1965:108).

Ritual food and borrowed prestige

One of the reasons that corporations favor married men in management is that entertainment of subordinates and their wives is part of the executive's role. A bachelor can give a dinner party, but the subordinate's wives may be uneasy about the example of bachelor life that their husband is observing, and the boss's wife has the traditional role of hostess.

As one corporate wife whose husband had recently been promoted to a managerial position told me:

If you're an individual contributor, which we have been all these years, there is just no demand socially. [Notice her use of the first person plural to describe her husband's role in the corporation, which is clearly perceived by her as a joint role.] You can pick your friends and do your entertaining as you want it. Then when you start up management, there is more pressure. My husband was in research until six months ago. Now I can see where there are going to be some other demands made at his level. When you're a manager, you're expected to entertain the people who work for you. The first thing that hit me, when he took over this job from this other man, he said: "Well, *we* are expected to put on a picnic for the families in *our* group. Do you want to organize it?" You know, that was the first social demand, and I thought, "Um hum! Now what else will there be, when we're just getting our feet wet in this?"

Another corporate wife commented: "Nobody would *tell* you that you are

Skillfully conducted ceremonial entertaining is a means of enhancing group solidarity and the prestige and influence of the host. From the viewpoint of the corporation the feelings of self-esteem that are enhanced by such ritual comsumption of food and drink are important for "company morale." The corporate wife whose husband has risen to head a division is expected to become an adept hostess.

expected to entertain. You just inherit things that have been done before. You are sensitive to what has been."

The ritual of exchange carried out at a ceremonial meal is a time-honored way of establishing social bonds, as Claude Levi-Strauss (1957) has pointed out. When skillfully conducted, such ceremonial meals are a means of enhancing group solidarity and the prestige and influence of the host at the same time. Reciprocity is expected among equals. But the corporate executive and his wife also entertain subordinates, and it would be presumptuous for the subordinate's wife to return the invitation. If a high executive is traveling, a ranking subordinate may be his host, but under most other circumstances an invitation from a subordinate's wife would suggest that she felt herself the equal of the boss's wife, which would be an embarrassing blunder.

This entertainment pattern derives from a long American tradition. In rural America, the major holidays were occasions for ceremonial feasting by relatives. The dominant and most prosperous members of the older generation were always the hosts and provided the meat and most of the other food and drink. Younger family members came to the dinner bearing food of a ceremonial nature—mince pies or other delicacies—that they did not expect to eat themselves, but to exchange for a piece of the pie made by a sister-in-law or a cousin. The younger generation did not invite the older to come to their house for holiday dinners until the old people were no longer householders, but had become aged dependents. It was the mark of the ranking adult male of the kindred to be host on such occasions (which is the reason why in-laws still quarrel about which set of parents will entertain the young married couple and their children on Thanksgiving and Christmas).

The owner of a small business in an earlier America entertained his subordinates in a similar manner, and being invited to his home on festive occasions—perhaps not Christmas, which is a family occasion, but maybe a New Year's eggnog reception or some other holiday affair—was the mark of a salaried member of the business "family," a subordinate but nonetheless someone who was of sufficient rank to be a guest in the home of the owner. The wage-worker was not invited to eat from his employer's table, but was sent a gift—often food, with its ritual associations—as a gesture of *noblesse oblige.*

Such customs have survived in modified form, and the employee who is invited to the home of a corporate superior knows that he has reached a certain status in the corporation, perhaps is being looked over for possible promotion. Giving and attending such dinner parties, whether formal dinners with damask and crystal or informal displays of opulence on the terrace beside the pool, has little to do with people liking one another or enjoying one another's company. Nor did our forebears like all the cousins and in-laws they invited to a holiday dinner. People were invited because they were relatives; in similar fashion, the corporate wife invites people who stand in a particular position in her husband's firm: a promotion or a transfer would alter the guest list.

The junior members of the group come to dine, not because they like the boss and his wife (they may, or they may not; it is not really relevant to the function of such dinners), but because to refuse the invitation would be a rebuff that only a man about to quit his job would dare. However, they derive a certain borrowed prestige from the dinner. As Mills describes it: "Salaried employees have been associated with entrepreneurs, and later with higher-ups in the managerial cadre, and they have borrowed prestige from both . . . Today, in big city as well as small town, white-collar workers continue to borrow such prestige" (1951:242).

From the viewpoint of the corporation, the feelings of self-esteem that are enhanced by such ceremonial consumption of food and drink are important for "company morale." Such intangible benefits keep employees loyal to the team and wanting to rise in the corporation. The corporate wife whose husband has risen to be head of his division or even of his subdivision is expected to become an adept hostess for such ritual dinners. This role is often coveted by the wives of the junior executives, who would like to play the gracious hostess. Such wives are likely to feel a vested interest in their husbands' promotions, quite apart from the salary increase it may bring.

481

The role of the corporate wife: keeper of the retreat

Seeing that the home itself and the family life-style are part of the "package" that will ensure her husband's promotion—and thus improve her own status—is a central part of the wife's role in the upper middle class generally, and of the role of the high-ranking corporate employee's wife particularly. The wife of the rising corporate executive must create an atmosphere as well as a home. The home serves as a backdrop for her husband's personality—and her own—when they entertain his corporate associates. The basis of prestige has become more subtle and intangible than in the days when conspicuous display was enough. The wife must create a mood not only of elegance but also of a life-style that can give her husband an air of intensity or *élan.* (*Prestige,* by the way, is a word derived from Latin roots meaning either to blindfold or to dazzle.)

Another function of the corporate wife is that of nurturing the psyche as well as the physical being of her husband. In a study conducted for *Fortune* magazine, William H. Whyte asked corporate executives, corporate wives, and corporation psychologists about the role of the corporate wife. Both the wives who responded to Whyte's inquiries and the psychologists agreed that the wife's role needs to be that of "a 'stabilizer'—the keeper of the retreat, the one who rests and rejuvenates the man for the next day's battle . . . Above all, wives emphasize, they have to be good listeners" (1952:33).

As the wife of a rising engineer in a large electronics corporation described it to me:

> When Tom leaves his work he would just as soon leave his work there. Except the gripes, or "I'm tired," or "I've had it today." But otherwise, he wants to change his interests, and he wants what I've read or something interesting. He doesn't want to come home and talk about engineering. But he wants to gloat when something marvelous has happened—he's found what was the matter with a project that he's worked on for weeks, or whatever.
>
> And if he talks about one thing one week that is on his mind and the next week you ask him about it, Gee! He thinks you're marvelous! You don't have to be superhuman intellectually, but if you remember that point that was bothering him last week and ask him about it, I mean he feels in communication.

For the rest, the role of the corporate wife as seen by the corporation is essentially a negative one: it is not what she does, but what she refrains from doing that matters. According to Whyte, both management and corporate wives tend to agree that a good wife cannot help her husband as much as the wrong kind of wife can harm him, and that "the good wife is good by *not* doing things—by *not* complaining when her husband works late, by *not* fussing when a transfer is coming up; by *not* engaging in

482

controversial activity" (1952:32). This negative role is probably the most pervasive in the corporation, for it applies not only to the wives of men who are rising but also to the vast majority of corporate wives who are married to men who will never be managers, who will never need to entertain, and who will seldom be under pressure.

Whyte concluded that the large American corporations were in general agreement on what kind of wife is ideal for a man in the junior or middle ranks of management: "In her simplest terms she is a wife who (1) is highly adaptable, (2) is highly gregarious, (3) realizes her husband belongs to the corporation" (1952:32). From the viewpoint of the corporation, the employee's wife is a potential ally, not a rival. If a particular wife does not choose to play the game, the corporation may simply sidetrack her husband, put him into a job where his wife will not be an embarrassment. But the woman who is adroit at the role of the corporate wife is considered an asset to the firm as well as to her husband, and will enhance his chances for promotion.

The women who have begun to rise to managerial roles in the corporate structure find that they are hampered by the fact that few husbands are willing to take on the role expected of the corporate spouse. Although many men have come to accept the concept of dual careers in marriage, few are willing to define themselves in terms of their wife's career. The satellite role is unacceptable to most men. The man whose wife is a rising executive may be willing to attend the cocktail parties, dinners, and other social functions that are required by his wife's career, and he may accept the fact that she will be traveling on business. But he is unlikely to be prepared to play the keeper of the retreat, the gracious host, or to make their home a backdrop for his wife's business entertaining. A common compromise is for the couple to hire a housekeeper, and for business entertaining to be catered: additional expenses that add to the burden of the female executive. It will cost her more to play the role than it costs her male colleague who has a wife.

Three wives view the corporation: notes from a casebook

The relationship between man, wife, and corporation does not seem to have changed much in the twenty years since Whyte wrote about "the wife problem." The women participating in the following taped conversation are all corporate wives. The husbands of these women actually work for three different major corporations. To ensure the anonymity of these women, these three corporations will be referred to as if they were one, The Big Corporation: TBC. Other than such changes to protect privacy, the women speak for themselves.

The woman referred to as the First Wife is married to a white-collar corporate employee who has a secure but dead-end middle-management job. She and her husband are lower middle class in marital role expectations, and have lives centered on their large family. He is a family man who

483

has a job rather than a career. TBC provides this man and his family with the security that an extended family or a clan might have provided for his remote ancestors.

The Second Wife is married to a man who is rising in TBC. He has moved into management and has hopes of further promotion. This couple is entering the upper middle class, indeed probably already qualifies for this class level in terms of occupation, income, residence, and education. The husband is career-oriented and his wife is proud of his achievements; she feels she has a part to play in his rise and urges him on. Her attitude toward TBC is a combination of pride in its corporate achievements and a feeling that TBC offers her husband both security and challenge—attitudes that undoubtedly have had a positive effect on her husband's career.

The Third Wife is married to a man who also seems to be rising, but she has begun to resent the demands that TBC makes on his time and is particularly resentful of the sustained pressure under which her husband works. Unless she is able to conceal her feelings from her husband's superiors—and their wives—she may well cause her husband to be shunted into a dead-end position. If the pressures on him eased because of this, this wife might welcome such a transfer. This couple qualify at present for upper-middle-class status, which would probably not be altered if the husband rose no further.

There aren't many places at the top

First Wife: My husband and I long ago discussed that he would never be too aggressive in his job, because he does not want a higher level job and I don't want him to have it, because we've known enough people—we've been married fifteen years—and we've met enough people who are at the higher levels and I wouldn't want to trade places with them, I honestly wouldn't.

We have a large family and we decided that we would rather spend the next, say, ten years primarily raising our family and doing things with our family—camping and so forth—things with the children. So my husband has refused other jobs that would be quite a bit higher-paying but would involve traveling and possibly even more time on the job. He has refrained from doing this because he does not want to spend time out of the home and away from his family. Fine. I'm willing to settle for that, too.

Second Wife: Will he—when you have your family raised and he has, say, fifteen more years to go—will he, do you think, be unhappy that he didn't gain the goal he could have? Or do you think he will be fulfilled?

First Wife: I don't know. I think he feels fulfilled right now with his job.

Second Wife: But they hit a certain age limit and they see retirement in sight, and sometimes men become very pessimistic if they haven't pushed or done as much as they could have. I think maybe this is one

"My husband and I long ago discussed that he would never be too aggressive in his job. . . . We have a large family and we decided that we would rather spend the next, say, ten years primarily raising our family and doing things with our family —camping and so forth—things with the children. So my husband has refused other jobs that would be quite a bit higher-paying but would involve traveling . . . he does not want to spend time out of the home and away from his family. Fine. I'm willing to settle for that, too."

of the reasons women say it is hard to get a man through his forties, because he can see ahead and see the next twenty years and wonder, you know, where he is going to end up. And he's not happy if he's not far enough along, or if he's not doing something that he really likes and wants to be doing for the next twenty or twenty-five years. *First Wife:* But maybe that man isn't quite as ambitious or competitive as another man, and he may be extremely happy, saying, "I had a good life, I enjoyed my family, I like the way things went, and that's life." Life's awfully short, anyway.

Third Wife: Well, what if you have a family that you really aren't proud of? That would be a reason for getting upset, it seems to me.

Second Wife: My husband is very ambitious and he would like to go as high as he possibly could. We kind of laugh and joke about this, because we've always just automatically assumed he'll go right up— he's very ambitious. It makes him happy and if he feels he's not moving along, he gets very unhappy. So, I mean, as far as I'm concerned, the sky's the limit, go ahead. But I haven't—I don't know all

485

the problems yet. It may be when I get them I wouldn't be able to handle them—I'm sure I wouldn't be the best entertainer in the world but, you know, I'm willing to try.

Third Wife: There aren't that many places at the top, I don't think, and there are many, many qualified and capable people.

First Wife: Will said that there was someone who got a terrific promotion and he was quite tiny. And Will said someone made the catty remark that *he* wouldn't get up to the very top because they want big, athletic, impressive men at their top to *look* like leaders. And I wondered if this was a lot of baloney or if maybe there was some truth to it.

Second Wife: Well, we are going for images now and not just in politics.

Third Wife: I really think the eager beavers get promoted, the ones who at least appear to be eager beavers. I'm thinking of one now at TBC who just got a $12,000 a year *raise* and a great promotion and all this and he's—well, I don't know what's going to happen to him because I think he's getting way out of his depth, but he *looks* like an eager beaver.

First Wife: He won't last, though.

Third Wife: Well, I don't know, he's charming. And he's been able to carry this off for years. You see, what happens is that if you get high enough you have people working for you and if you're smart enough to choose the right people—if you're smart enough to recognize the *sharp* people and *use* them—

Second Wife: Isn't that called "executive ability"?

Third Wife: Perhaps.

You're part of the TEAM and you are under pressure

Second Wife: Two years ago Hal won an award and they have an award dinner each year for TBC and they bring the wife and the husband back to New York and they have a big dinner at the Waldorf and we got to go to that two years ago. Wonderful dinner! All the bigwigs were there—Dick and so on. And it's quite nice. They put you up in the Waldorf Monday night and Tuesday night, and I think it's really very, very nice. There's the recognition, plus you have a chance to, you know, *meet* people that you've heard are way up in TBC and you get to see them, and you also get an idea what TBC is doing because they explain the inventions. They have movies and they give it in simple language for the wives to understand. It's kind of interesting, plus it's recognition for your husband, and that's—

Third Wife: I think it's all well and good for TBC to say that they appreciate it when they finally get the system or whatever it has been on the market and they're getting huge royalties and what not, and then they stand up at some dinner and they thank the wives and

"They stand up at some dinner and thank the wives and children. But that doesn't compensate for the three years, maybe, or more, where your children have grown so far past—their father isn't there to help them with projects, or to see interesting highlights in their life . . ."

children, you know. But that doesn't compensate for the three years, maybe, or more, where your children have grown so far past—their father isn't there to help *them* with projects, or be there to see interesting highlights in their life, and you—you're strained, your marriage sometimes is strained, because he's always—you know—we have to walk around on broken eggs because father's exhausted, he's tired, he's under a lot of pressure, and he can't do, you know, the normal things that a man at home can do.

First Wife: I've heard this from lots of TBC'ers and I've heard it about other companies, too. I'm sure it exists in all our companies.

Second Wife: But I don't think it's a *continual* thing. I was gone for three weeks and I came back to a husband who was in budgeting. First time he's ever taken a million dollars and budgeted it for the next year. OK, all I saw was the back of his head for one solid week—every night—but he said, "Now, this will soon be over." He has to do it all day long and he has to do it nights—he has a deadline. Well, so you say, "All right, when it's over, it's over, and then we can go along on a normal life again." But I don't stand there and say, "Oh, when are you going to be through?" and make him nervous, because he has to do it.

Third Wife: I would like to say a few things, though. I agree to a certain extent, but I think that TBC has, in certain areas, relied a great deal on overtime that is not reimbursed for people—and it is not overtime that goes on for a week, or for months, but it goes on for years, and they sort of make this as a study and you're part of the Team and you've got to do it and you're under pressure and your husband is under pressure, and I've been through this where it lasted almost three years. And you get to the point where you're both rather dissatisfied with this type of life, and if your husband still enjoys what he's doing and he still feels that there's some purpose, he will carry it on, but you get very upset after awhile when you only see him on Sunday and then he's pooped and he's out, you know, maybe three nights a week working.

First Wife: I appreciate the good living that we have from TBC and I can't complain too much, but I can also see where many wives *do* gripe, and they go right up to the top, many of them and let them know, "What the heck are you doing? My husband's gone all the time—"

Second Wife: But he would say that the company doesn't ask this. I mean, it's probably an immediate superior that's setting this thing up.

Third Wife: Oh, no, because their schedules are what keep them going, and when they make a schedule that this system will be ready for shipment and ready to work, boy, that is it and the whole world has to turn in and see that it goes, so they're not going to worry about what—if she's *very* unsatisfied, they may, if he's not really that important, they may—you know—

Second Wife: He can be replaced!

Third Wife: Yeah, that's the thing, so they're not going to do very much about it. We've had this experience, where we put in lots and lots of overtime, I mean it wasn't months, it was *years,* and it gets to you after awhile, you know. Ralph says there are many departments that operate under this high pressure constantly, they're always working overtime. Somebody else sets up the schedule and you're expected to go through with it.

Second Wife: But the regulations are that if you work overtime and you are a professional person who is not paid for overtime, that you may have that time off.

Third Wife: You have to ask to take it, though. It's granted, but very grudgingly, and it's a day at a time. You never, I mean just *never,* get back all that time.

Second Wife: I think any man will take it for awhile. I mean, he's that loyal to his company. He wants that deadline met, too.

Third Wife: But they set extremely unrealistic deadlines, and the only way they're going to know they are unrealistic is if the darn thing isn't finished. You know, if you just don't do it.

First Wife: Sometimes people misjudge the amount of time—they want to look good. Like the engineers—project engineers and this sort of thing—want to look good, and so they say they'll get it out in six months or a year, whatever it is, and they have been very unrealistic in their time estimates.

Second Wife: Well, I think there are pressures and pressures. Some people work well under a certain amount of pressure, if they're doing something they really, really enjoy and they feel will go someplace and will be a contribution, and that they will get something out of it, too. This is a competitive business. If one company can do a job faster and better than the other place, they'll get the contract. There's a lot of money involved.

Third Wife: No matter how many marriages get destroyed on the way!

Second Wife: That's competition!

She MAKES the move a pleasant one

First Wife: I don't think my husband would just go on, year after year—he wouldn't let his job interfere with his family life to that extent. I think he'd find another job. There's always opportunities in other companies, I mean, there's so much mobility now, and there are many people leaving TBC all the time.

Second Wife: There's a lot of sideways job-skipping in corporations. You can change jobs without being promoted.

First Wife: Will's had three chances for promotion—all in the East— and he won't even talk about them. He just says, "I don't want my family to live in the East, period."

Second Wife: Well, I think the well-adjusted wife will say, "If it's for your betterment, let's move." And she *makes* the move a pleasant one. Which—sure, you may hate it. But I think that if your husband wants it badly enough, that comes first. Some wives just say, "I absolutely will not move," and are that stubborn, and the poor man will suffer because of it.

Third Wife: What if you had a job, too? I mean, not like my job, a teacher, where I can change, but what if you had a job—

Second Wife: I'm just old-fashioned enough to think that *he* comes first.

Third Wife: I think it depends on where you're being sent, too. Some areas might be more upsetting than others. We just heard in Washington—my husband was working for the week at a division outside Washington—evidently someone got to some Congressman, and they had part of the contract transferred to the facility in Junction City, Alabama, and one hundred-fifty employees refused to go, and I don't blame them. Now I don't know whether they left TBC or just what, but many people would not wish to move to the South and to a rural area like that.

Second Wife: People who feel that way are as bigoted as Southerners

489

are, to my way of thinking. I lived two years in the South and I wouldn't like to go back, but I think there could be a real challenge there, you know.

First Wife: Well, I'm not looking for any great challenges. I'm looking for a nice, smooth ride!

References

Blitsten, Dorothy R. 1963. *The World of the Family.* New York: Random House.

Cuber, John F., and Peggy B. Harroff. 1965. *The Significant Americans: A Study of Sexual Behavior among the Affluent.* New York: Appleton-Century-Crofts.

Kafka, Franz. 1949. *The Castle.* New York: Alfred A. Knopf.

Levi-Strauss, Claude. 1957. "The Principle of Reciprocity." In *Sociological Theory,* edited by Lewis A. Coser and Bernard Rosenberg, pp. 84–94. New York: The Macmillan Company.

Mills, C. Wright. 1951. *White Collar: The American Middle Classes.* New York: Oxford University Press.

Rainwater, Lee. 1965. *Family Design: Marital Sexuality, Family Size, and Contraception.* Chicago: Aldine Publishing Company.

Rice, Berkeley. 1970. "Down and Out along Route 128." *New York Times Magazine* (November 1):28–29, 93–104. © 1970 by The New York Times Company. Reprinted by permission.

Whyte, William H., Jr. 1952. "The Wife Problem." *Life* 32 (January 7):32–48.

Suggested readings

Cuber, John F., with Peggy B. Harroff. 1965. *The Significant Americans.* New York: Appleton-Century. Available in paper as *Sex and the Significant Americans.* An inquiry into sexual behavior and marriage among decision makers, policy makers, and other highly educated and successful Americans. The authors interviewed prominent doctors, businessmen, lawyers, diplomats, ranking military officers, and the wives, former wives, or widows of same for this study. They also interviewed some women who were prominent and successful in their own right. Because of the career achievement criteria, most of these people were no longer young, but most were vigorous and active and in their middle years. The marital patterns that Cuber and Harroff discern among these "significant Americans" (such as "utilitarian marriage," "conflict-habituated marriage," and "intrinsic marriage") and the analysis of these patterns form an illuminating study of marriage and sex among upper-middle-class Americans.

Whyte, William H., Jr. 1956. *The Organization Man.* New York: Simon and Schuster. The classic work on the members of the new social class that has emerged in twentieth-century America. As Whyte observes: "This [book] is about the organization man. If the term is vague, it is because I can think of no other way to describe the people I am talking about. They are not the workers, nor are they the white-collar people in the usual, clerk sense of the word. These people only work for The Organization. The ones I am talking about *belong* to it as well. They are the ones of our middle class who have left home, spiritually as well as physically, to take the vows of organization life, and it is they who are the mind and soul of our great self-perpetuating institutions. Only a few are top managers or ever will be ... But they are the dominant members of our society, nonetheless."

The corporate "family": man, wife, and corporation

18 Middle American families

Upper-middle class men see their homes as expressions of themselves to a much greater extent than working class men; for them the home and the activities that go on in it are expressions of their personalities and of their social status. Working class men are much more likely to perceive the home as a place women maintain to take care of their children, and to provide bed, board, and a TV set for their husbands. Lower-middle class men often share the conceptions described for upper-middle class men, but they also are more likely to see the home as a kind of refuge maintained for them by their wives with much less emphasis on the home as an expression of their own selves (other than of their ability to contribute financially and participate in money decisions about what should be done).

Lee Rainwater (1965:55)

The social class in which we were raised provided us with a set of expectations about the way in which men and women should relate as husbands and wives, as fathers and mothers. These expectations act as filters through which we perceive and judge the behavior not only of ourselves, but of others. Because we have been raised to believe that social-class differences are not quite nice, and should be glossed over in the name of democratic consensus, we have a tendency to assume that the values and expectations of our own social class are universally shared. Thus it is that we tend to assume that the kind of marriage we would like must be the only pattern for a happy marriage, when in fact it may be the pattern of marriage that is preferred within one social class only.

There has been a cherished myth that America is a society without class distinctions. The elimination of hereditary class status was among the founding principles of American democracy. Yet all of us are aware of differences in income, prestige, and life-style between American families. The differences between very rich families and the very poor are readily apparent; the differences between the middle levels of American social-class structure are more subtle, but they are there. These social-class differences involve more than the relative income, power, and prestige of families; there are also differences in family structure, in marital role expectations, in sex roles, and in family goals between the various social classes in America. Some of these differences are created by the circumstances of life at a particular income and occupational level. Other social-class differences reflect patterns of family life and sex roles that emerged to fit the circumstances of life in other times, other places, but have persisted through community, ethnic, or religious tradition.

Social-class distinctions were more sharply drawn in America in the past than they are today. At the time of the American Revolution, there was a sharp class line between southern planters and subsistence farmers, between the owners of Yankee trading ships and merchant seamen. Most nineteenth-century Americans belonged to a class that can best be described as the working poor. Yet in the early nineteenth century, eight out of ten American families owned the farm or small shop from which the family earned its living (Dobriner 1963:39). Before the Civil War, the majority of American families were poor subsistence farmers (like those described in Chapter 1). It was not until after the Civil War that the number of industrial workers without any income-producing property began to grow. By the 1890s, after the initial period of rapid industrialization in the United States, the U.S. Bureau of the Census estimated that 9 percent of the families in America owned 71 percent of the wealth. There was a social chasm between this wealthy elite and the vast majority of American families.

The federal income tax (made possible by a constitutional amendment passed shortly before World War I), federal and state inheritance taxes, and laws limiting interlocking trusts have reduced the ability of

families to retain great wealth through several generations or to transfer
families

positions of great power to their children by inheritance (a point discussed at some length in Chapter 6). However, there remain a handful of extremely wealthy American families, constituting a small upper class. A few of these families also retain great power. This American upper class is subdivided by informal but strong social boundaries into established upperclass families and new upper-class families, on the basis of how many generations of the family have occupied positions of power and wealth.

The most salient social transformation of the last half-century in America has been the rise of a large middle class. Although many of the small businessmen and professionals of the nineteenth century belonged to the middle class (middle in the sense that it stood between the wealthy elite and the poor farmers and workers), it was not until approximately the time of World War I that the middle class began to grow in numbers, influence, and affluence. Inflation and recession in the 1970s have dimmed the visions of affluence that characterized the 1960s, but the real income of the average American family is still several times that of the average American family before World War I. Even the level of living that characterized the average American family in the years immediately before World War II would today be considered the threshold of poverty.

Middle-American families: white-collar, middle classes

It is perhaps most accurate to speak of the American middle class in the plural, for there are a cluster of distinct subclasses with differing life-styles that constitute the American middle classes. Families that owned business firms were the largest component of the American middle class in the nineteenth century. Small businessmen and their families remain a recognizable element within the contemporary American middle classes. Whether they are upper-middle-class or lower-middle-class depends primarily on the annual income of the family and the size and financial stability of the family business. Families making a living from a marginal Mom and Pop enterprise constitute the bottom fringe of this segment of the American middle classes. At the upper edge of this group, which is sometimes referred to as the "old" middle class, are families that have owned profitable business firms for several generations and, in addition to their comparatively high income, have traditional class standing as the founding families of small cities and smaller towns in America. Such families often constitute a small-town elite.

Self-employed professionals were as much a part of the nineteenth-century American middle class as were the small businessmen. Professionals have often been included in the "old" middle class on the basis of lineage as well as on the basis of occupation. In the past, the majority of professionals were the sons of prosperous middle-class families. There were two reasons for this. First, the cost of a professional education was

495

a barrier to the sons and daughters of poor families (although a bright, poor boy with unusually high ambition might be able to work his way through college and a professional postgraduate school). Thus, to some degree, the sons of affluent families were overrepresented among professionals because they were the ones with the opportunity to acquire a professional education. The other reason why most professionals have come from "old" middle-class families is that such families have considered it the obligation of the parental generation to provide for their sons either an opening in the family business or a professional education. A prosperous family-owned business might be able to support two or three families at a respectable middle-class level, but a family might have more sons than the family firm could support in an appropriate manner. It was expected that surplus sons would be given a professional education so that they, too, could make a living that would be commensurate with the family's standing in the community. Thus it was that until after World War II most doctors, lawyers, and college professors in America were upper-middle-class both by occupation and by lineage.

Although the number of Americans in the "old" middle class has grown in absolute terms, this class represents a smaller proportion of the American class structure today than it did in the nineteenth century. In 1870 the "old" middle class constituted approximately one third of the labor force, but by 1940 it represented only 20 percent of the labor force (Mills 1951:63). What is sometimes called the "new" middle class (white-collar employees) has been the dynamic factor in the American class structure in the last century. William Dobriner observed that "from 1870 to 1940 the new middle class grew three times faster than the working class, eight times faster than the number of enterprisers (old middle class) and two-and-a-half times faster than the middle class as a whole" (1963:-40).

After World War II, the numbers of clerks, accountants, personnel officers, computer programmers, bank tellers, laboratory technicians, middle managers, and other white-collar employees of both corporations and government agencies grew to be an even greater proportion of the American labor force. The growth of bureaucracy meant the growth of the white-collar middle class. The middle classes—both "old" and "new"—presently constitute approximately 40 percent of American families. At the time of the 1970 census, 41.8 percent of American married men reported middle-class occupations: professionals, technical workers, managers, administrators, sales workers, clerical workers (U.S. Bureau of the Census 1972:142).

It is no longer possible to draw a class line between owners and workers, because many owners have small businesses and low incomes, while most corporate executives are seldom owners in the old sense of the word. A distinction that is more useful for purposes of differentiating social-class levels is that between upper middle and lower middle class. This distinction is based primarily on the relative power and prestige of the occupation of the male head of household and on annual family in- come. *Middle American families*

Although nearly half of the men in the labor force have working wives, and the wife's income is often a significant factor in the level of living the family can enjoy, it is the occupation of the husband that is the primary determinant of the social-class placement of the family. If the husband is present in the home, he is assumed to be the head of the household. Even if his wife is working and he is unemployed, the husband is considered to be the head of household, legally and demographically. If a woman's income and the prestige of her job are higher than those of her husband, there is a certain status ambiguity, but it is still the husband's occupation that is the dominant factor determining the status placement of the family in the community. As noted in Chapter 1, this insistence on the husband's role as head of household and on the husband's occupation as the source of the status placement of the family may change as more women achieve high prestige from professional careers.

Job title and salary range are the basis for many subtle but pervasive social distinctions: who is expected to entertain business associates, who is invited to what functions, who is expected to take work and worry home from the office, and who is not. Within the group of professionals, the line between upper middle class and lower middle class is drawn on the basis of the relative prestige of the profession (doctors and lawyers have more prestige than nurses and teachers, for example) and on annual income.

At the time of the U.S. Census in 1970, information was gathered on marital status, occupation, and annual earnings. The decade between age forty-five and age fifty-four is presumably the period in a man's life when his income is the highest it will ever be. The mean annual income reported by all white, married men between the ages of forty-five and fifty-four years was $10,853 (U.S. Bureau of the Census 1972:227). Those who were professional or technical workers reported annual incomes that averaged $16,174; managers and administrators reported a mean annual income of $15,389. Although regional living costs differ, an annual income of $25,-000 is probably the income threshold of the upper middle class. Although the average income for professional, technical, and managerial workers was below this level, it is probable that one third or more of the men in these occupational groups would have qualified for upper-middle-class status on the basis of the means test.

White married men between the ages of forty-five and fifty-four who were sales workers in 1970 reported a mean annual income of $12,464, and those who were clerical workers reported a mean annual income of $9,360. Most of the men in both of these occupational categories would be considered lower-middle-class, both in terms of occupational prestige and in terms of the means test.

Although the most salient distinctions between upper-middle-class families and lower-middle-class families are differences in income and in the relative prestige and power associated with the occupation of the head **497** of the family, there are other, more subtle differences between upper-middle-class and lower-middle-class family life. There are differences in family goals, marital roles, and sex-role expectations. Some of these differences were explored in the preceding chapter dealing with the family and the corporation.

Perhaps the major difference in personal and family goals between the upper middle and the lower middle classes is the question of the primacy of family or career. In the upper middle class, the head of the household has a career, and his family is often an adjunct to that career. Although a man's wife and children benefit from his career in a variety of ways, such as living standard, social status, and all that such social and economic advantages imply, it is his career that typically receives primary consideration when there is a conflict between his professional and familial roles. If there is some life-and-death emergency, the family comes first; otherwise, his career does. The upper-middle-class wife expects to cope with any problems that her husband's career decisions may create for the family, such as moving across the continent and relocating when her husband receives a promotion involving a transfer from New York to California.

In the lower middle class, the head of the household has a job, not a career. The job is seldom a major source of personal fulfillment (this may be due more to the nature of the job than to his personal value priorities). The family is the focus of the energies, interest, and future planning of both husband and wife, and is a major source of personal fulfillment. There are, of course, men in the upper middle class who derive great satisfaction from their families and men in the lower middle class who are depressed because their jobs are unfulfilling, and who would like to be able to find a more rewarding career regardless of the demands it might make on their time or their family. But on balance, one of the distinctions between these two middle-class groups is that the upper-middle-class male is more oriented to his career, and the lower-middle-class male is more oriented to his family.

It is at least sometimes the case that the value placed on career versus the value placed on family has determined the class status, and not the other way around. The men who rise to upper-middle-class positions are clearly more ambitious, but not necessarily more able, than those who settle into middle-level, dead-end jobs. The latter may be less qualified, or they may have chosen to place family before career, as did the husband of the "First Wife" who was quoted in Chapter 17. This woman's husband has sufficient education to qualify for a job with a higher salary and higher status than he presently holds, and has in fact turned down offers of promotion (which would have required that his family relocate to an unfamiliar region of the United States where they have no relatives or friends). His lower-middle-class status is a matter of choice, made on the basis of personal and family priorities, not the result of lack of ability or opportunity. His wife is supportive of his decision.

Middle-American families: blue-collar, working class

In the last quarter of a century, there has been a rapid rise in the income of skilled workers, many of whom now have more in common with the lower middle class than with the poorest members of the working class. Since the 1950s it has been customary to differentiate between white-collar workers (who form part of the middle class) and blue-collar workers (the working class). These terms originated in an era when the clothing of male workers was more uniform than it is today. They were intended to convey the distinction between the kind of occupation that required a man to wear the office uniform of suit, white shirt, and tie and the kind of occupation that required a man to wear heavy work clothing (including the traditional blue chambray work shirt). The office worker may now wear more casual clothing, and blue denims and coveralls may have had a season as high fashion attire, but the occupational distinctions for which *white collar* and *blue collar* were a kind of shorthand remain. The blue-collar worker typically has manual skills and manipulates things; the white-collar worker typically has interpersonal, verbal, or mathematical skills and manipulates people, paper, or numbers.

At the time of the 1970 Census, white, married men between the ages of forty-five and fifty-four years who were listed as craftsmen reported a mean annual income of $9,238, close to the average income reported by clerical workers. If only those with high school educations are considered, the craftsmen reported a slightly higher annual income than the clerical workers: $9,901 for craftsmen with a high school education, compared with $9,173 for clerical workers with a high school education. Transport operatives (truckers, bus drivers, taxi drivers, and so on) reported annual earnings of $8,174 on the average. "Operatives, except transport" (a group that includes most factory workers) reported a mean annual income of $7,905. Service workers had an average annual income of $7,351 (U.S. Bureau of Census 1972:Table 9). All of these groups of workers are part of the blue-collar working class, although small subgroups within these categories clearly qualify on the basis of income, education, and occupational prestige for lower-middle- or upper-middle-class status (for example, included among "transport operatives" are a small group of airline pilots, whose annual income may be more than $60,000 and who usually have a college education).

Laborers (except farm) reported an average annual income of $6,771 in 1970. (As in the preceding section, the income figures are for white, married men in the age group between forty-five and fifty-four years.) Depending on the size of the family, this income is still above the poverty level, although many members of this occupational group struggle to maintain a level of living that they can regard as "decent." Farm laborers and farm foremen reported average annual incomes of $4,718. Most laborers and their families are clearly "working poor," and would not be considered part of the middle class.

Thus, the income levels of the average blue-collar worker are still below those of the average white-collar worker, although the range of income overlaps and the highest paid blue-collar workers enjoy incomes that are equal to or higher than those of many white-collar workers. (In the spring of 1976, the streetsweepers of San Francisco were on strike—along with other city workers—for higher salaries: those streetsweepers had incomes of more than $16,000 per year, plus fringe benefits.)

But income is not the only determinant of a family's social-class status. The relative prestige of the occupation of the male head of the household and his level of education are also criteria of class status. There is still some difference in the relative prestige of the blue-collar worker and that of the white-collar worker, although this difference in prestige is fading as the income differential is lessened. A desk job may seem more dignified than certain manual occupations. It is also more sedentary, and stereotypes seem to be changing.

Part of the reason for the lingering prestige of the white-collar worker is attributable to the fact that typically he has more education than the blue-collar worker. However, the educational difference between the two classes is declining among the younger age groups. The expansion of community college and junior college systems offering technical programs at minimal cost has resulted in a rising educational level among skilled workers. Moreover, the current glut of college graduates in a time of high unemployment has created a new subgroup: the "overeducated" unemployed or underemployed. Many recent college graduates have turned to crafts (or even to driving a taxi) because there are few jobs available for someone with a new baccalaureate degree in, for example, medieval history.

The rising income and education of skilled manual workers relative to white-collar workers has created a certain amount of status inconsistency with regard to such factors as income, education, and occupation. The streetsweepers of San Francisco now earn more than an assistant professor at the universities in San Francisco; the longshoremen have higher incomes than the high school teachers. But college professors and high school teachers are required to have many more years of education than streetsweepers or longshoremen, and they still have higher prestige.

Whether or not blue-collar workers are middle-class by the usual socioeconomic criteria, many have come to think of themselves as middle-class, or simply as "middle-American," a phrase that seems to have replaced "the common man." (Perhaps none of us wants to consider ourselves common any more, having come to use the term only in its pejorative sense.) Americans have tended to avoid the term *working-class* and to think of themselves as *middle-class*, which has a more equalitarian ring. Many blue-collar workers have now clearly become middle-class, in terms of income and education. They are those middle Americans whose chosen symbols are the hard hat and the flag decal.

Until about fifty years ago, the typical American family was a farm **501** family, for there were still more farmers in the labor force than workers in any other occupational category (nearly one third of the labor force in 1920 were farmers). By 1970, however, farmers represented only 3.1 percent of all married American men, and farm laborers only an additional 1.2 percent (U.S. Bureau of the Census 1972:142). But 53.9 percent of married men of all ages and races reported occupations that would be considered blue-collar in 1970. The urban, blue-collar worker and his family have clearly replaced the farm family as the typical American family.

One of the reasons that so many blue-collar families are middle-income families today is that many, perhaps most, are dual-income families. All of the above income figures are based on the income of the male head of household only. But a high and growing proportion of married women are in the labor force in America. The employed wife was discussed in some detail in Chapter 1. To summarize briefly: in 1890 only 4.5 percent of the married American women whose husbands were present in the home were in the labor force (as other than unpaid family workers—a majority of women were in this category, whether on the farm or in a family-owned business enterprise). By 1940, on the eve of American involvement in World War II, the proportion of wives in the labor force had increased to 15.4 percent. Participation of women in the labor force rose markedly during World War II. Production demands for weapons and military equipment were high, and millions of men had been withdrawn from the labor force to serve in the armed forces.

Conventional wisdom has it that, after World War II, American women left the factories to have large families. The birth rate did remain high for a decade or so after the war, and some women did drop out of the labor force to have children. But in 1948, 22.0 percent of married women (with husband present in the home) were in the labor force, nearly one third more than in 1940. In 1957 the birth rate began a long decline. By 1958, 30.2 percent of married women were in the labor force; in 1968 that proportion had increased to 38.3 percent of all married women, and by 1970 it had reached 42.2 percent (U.S. Bureau of Labor Statistics 1974:58). Because this is a percentage of *all* married women with husband present in the home, the population base on which the percentage is computed includes young married women with children under school age, women in their thirties and forties with children of school age only, older women who have no children left at home, and women past the age of retirement.

The life cycle has a pronounced effect on the employment opportunities of women. If only those women who had children between the ages of six and seventeen (school age) and husband present in the home are considered (which probably means women in the age group between the late twenties and the early forties), 50.1 percent were employed outside the home in 1973 (U.S. Bureau of Labor Statistics 1974:58). Thus many families presently enjoy a middle-income living standard because there is more than one wage earner in the family. Even so, the fact that so many working-class families have arrived at middle-income (if not middle-class) *Middle American* status is one of the significant social phenomena of our time. *families*

Conjugal roles and social class

The central axis of the American family is the relationship between husband and wife: the conjugal relationship. (This may seem obvious, but it is not universal. There have been societies in which the central axis of the family has been the filial relationship between father and sons, rather than the conjugal relationship.) There must be at least a minimal reciprocity in conjugal roles, or the marriage will fall apart. There are basically two forms that role reciprocity between husband and wife can take: both can develop similar skills and share activities, or each can develop skills that complement the skills of the other, and divide responsibilities. Because marriage has multiple functions, it is possible for husband and wife to develop complementary skills and a division of labor in some areas of family life and to develop shared skills and joint or interchangeable tasks in other areas of their life together.

Various researchers (Elizabeth Bott, Lee Rainwater, Mirra Komarovsky, Marc Fried) have found that families with the most segregated conjugal role relationships are families in which the husband has a manual occupation, and that the families that have the most fully shared conjugal role relationships are ones in which the husband has a professional or semiprofessional occupation. But there are examples of both kinds of conjugal role relationships at all social-class levels. Social class is one factor, but not the only one, determining the kind of conjugal role relationship a couple develops.

There is another intervening variable determining conjugal role relationships, and this is the social network in which the couple participates. Families in which there is a high degree of segregation in the roles of husband and wife tend to be families that participate in a close-knit social network: that is, many of their friends, neighbors, and relatives know one another. This is the kind of situation that prevails in small, rural communities, but it is also found in urban, working-class neighborhoods. Families with the highest degree of segregation in conjugal roles live in stable neighborhoods, where people have grown up together and have continued living in the same neighborhood after marriage. When a man and woman raised in such a neighborhood marry, each has his or her own network of friends and relatives of the same sex, people who have been close all their lives. The emotional investment each has in his or her social network is high. Although the husband and wife may have highly segregated conjugal roles, each shares activities with these significant others outside the marriage. This is most obvious in recreational patterns: the blue-collar husband is likely to go out with his male friends; the wife is more likely to visit relatives, sometimes neighbors. Husband and wife do

503

not expect to have the ease and familiarity with each other that they find with a close friend or a relative of the same sex.

In contrast, families with joint conjugal role relationships, in which most activities are shared, tend to be families with a loose-knit social network: that is, people with whom they interact seldom know one another. These families typically live in mixed neighborhoods with a high population turnover. If either husband or wife has moved before marriage from the area in which he or she was raised (as someone who has been to the university to prepare for a professional career is likely to have done), it is likely that this spouse had a loose-knit network of friends and acquaintances before marriage. After marriage, a couple who are mobile socially and economically tend to move again, and to meet new people who do not know their old friends. Residential mobility tends to facilitate social mobility. Discontinuous social relationships make it easier for a family to enter higher social-class strata to which income and occupation may give them access. Old friends and even relatives who have remained in the social-class level of their origin may be seen by the upwardly mobile family only on the occasion of some special reunion. This is essentially the point made in Chapter 2: continuity and intimacy are important conjugal functions in a mobile population, because there is no longer a network of relatives and life-long friends to fill these functions.

In a study of families in Boston's West End, Fried (1973) found that:

> Working-class people more often appear to sustain segregated role relationships in marriage while higher status people more often demand and develop shared marital role relationships .... The differences in ideology are greater than the differences in performance and social class differences in performance in many marital role relationships are not maintained through the life cycle.   (Fried 1973:127–128)

This means simply that while many working-class husbands do help their wives with household tasks, the ideology of their social class makes them embarrassed to be seen working in the kitchen or folding laundry. Conversely, while many middle-class husbands express an ideal of shared responsibility for the household, many of them do not, in fact, participate more in the routine household tasks than do their blue-collar counterparts. Moreover, there is an age difference. The middle-class husbands seem most likely to participate equally in the household chores in the early years of marriage, but gradually turn more of the household maintenance over to their wives.

The degree to which conjugal role relationships are segregated or shared varies with the life cycle, in part because most functions that remain to marriage and family tend to wax and wane in urgency with the life cycle. The most obvious examples are the procreating and childrearing functions, often the primary focus of a young married couple's life together. These functions cease to involve the married couple by middle age.

504   However, if some differences in conjugal roles are related to the functional imperatives of a stage in the family life cycle, other differences are related to the circumstances of life at a particular social-class level. For example, Fried (1973:123) found that the working-class women in his Boston sample tended to perceive ability to support the family as the most important characteristic of an ideal husband, while middle-class women tended to consider characteristics that enhance interpersonal responsiveness the most important attributes of an ideal husband. The difference in social-class role image derives in some measure from the uncertainty of employment and income among the working class. The greater job security enjoyed by the white-collar worker may mean that his wife can take for granted that her husband will be able to provide adequately for his family, and be more concerned about his interpersonal skills.

Although both working-class and middle-class men in Fried's sample mentioned management of family and household tasks as the most important characteristics of the ideal wife, there were social-class differences in the marital role expectations of men as well as women.

> Men and women in higher status positions gave greater emphasis to interpersonal relationships within the family while those in lower social class statuses more often gave primacy to household and caretaking roles. Similarly, people in higher status positions more often saw a successful marriage as one in which there was considerable love, reciprocity, and tenderness between husband and wife, while people in lower status positions, accepting the inevitability of conflict, more readily viewed a successful marriage as one in which the husband and wife were ready to compromise and recognize the needs of the other partner. (Fried 1973:124).

There are a number of differences in social-class subcultures that are related to differences in conjugal roles. For instance, there are differences in the age at which people expect to marry. Both men and women raised in middle-class families expect to postpone marriage until they have completed some years of college (not all do, but this is the expectation). In contrast, most working-class women expect to marry shortly after graduation from high school, if not sooner (Fried 1973:122). The tendency of working-class women to marry while still in their teens may be a factor in the tendency of working-class wives to accept more segregated marital roles, for their experience before marriage with the world outside of the home is more limited.

Among the working-class families, the roles of husbands and wives are defined as more task-oriented than among lower-middle-class families. Among working-class Americans, the husband and wife are functionally dependent on each other, rather than emotionally dependent on each other. She takes pride in having a husband who is "steady" and a "good provider," and he is proud of having a wife who is a "good housekeeper" and can "manage the kids." The working class does not expect conjugal roles to be emotionally supportive. The husband is likely to derive much

505

of his emotional support from the men who are his companions, in the tradition of the farmer and laborer of the nineteenth century. The wife's major emotional ties are likely to be to her mother and other close female relatives.

The women of the working class visit their relatives frequently, especially their mothers. Komarovsky found that approximately two out of three wives in her working-class sample whose mothers lived in the same city saw their mothers several times a week, or daily. Among those women who had been married for less than seven years, 92 percent saw their mothers several times a week or daily, if the mother lived in the same city (Komarovsky 1967:243). Two thirds of the husbands and wives in her sample had been raised in the same or a neighboring community, and thus there tended to be residential stability and a close-knit social network. Komarovsky reports that in nearly one out of five of the marriages she studied, the husband had wanted to move out of the community at some time after marriage, but had been resisted successfully by the wife, who did not want to move away from her relatives (1967:242–243).

With the years, the social participation of the working-class family tends to diminish, particularly for the poorer members of this class. Men and women of the working class are less likely than middle-class persons to utilize the cultural and recreational resources of their community. With the birth of children, social participation of the wife tends to become limited to visits to relatives and some contact with neighbors. The younger men of the working class may retain an active social life with their male friends for some years after marriage, but with the growth of family responsibilities and with the approach of middle age, social involvement for the men tends to diminish. Komarovsky reports:

> Many couples in their late thirties, especially among the less-educated, seem almost to have withdrawn from life. There they sit in front of the television set: "What's there to say? We both see it." "If you had two extra hours every day, how would you like to spend them?" asked the interviewer, and a man mused: "This would make the evening awfully long and tiring if you're watching T.V." (Komarovsky 1967:341)

The couple sitting side by side in front of the television set may remain isolated in their separate worlds. The woman may express a desire for more communication with her husband but, in the working class, verbal skills are considered feminine skills, and the image of the strong, silent male remains a barrier to marital communication.

Social-class norms tend to act as filters through which we perceive the behavior of others. To the educated, middle-class person, those conjugal roles that involve joint participation in activities and shared responsibilities seem to be a necessary foundation for a successful marriage. But there are positive and negative potentials in both shared and segregated conjugal role relationships. Shared conjugal roles may have greater potential

506

The woman may express a desire for more communication with her husband, but, in the working class, verbal skills are considered feminine skills and the image of the strong, silent male remains a barrier to marital communication.

for mutual fulfillment, but they are also more likely to lead to competition between husband and wife or to absorption of the individual in a "rubber-fence" marriage.

Segregated conjugal roles may leave husband and wife with little to say to each other, coexisting in an emotionally barren marriage. Yet segregated conjugal roles have the potential of giving both husband and wife a sense of being an individual with a separate existence, some life apart from marital interaction, and a sphere of responsibility in which he or she is dominant. Segregated role relationships are a means of limiting marital conflict, although shared conjugal role relationships have greater potential for mutual need satisfaction. Affection may be a component of either shared or segregated conjugal role relationships.

Social-class differences in parental roles

Working-class families tend to have more children than middle-class families. This may be related to the tendency for working-class women to marry younger (one factor in higher fertility rates), but it is also related to the tendency for middle-class couples to postpone children for a few years after marriage. The difference in family size is another example of different social-class expectations. Fried found that among the couples in his Boston study within the age group between twenty and thirty-four "only 12 percent of the people in higher social class positions had three

507

or more children, while 51 percent of those in lower social class positions had families this large" (1973:122). Fried notes:

> Children appear to be more crucial for family life in the working class than in the middle class. The reasons for this are not entirely clear. It may well be that only with the presence of children can working-class husbands and wives depersonalize the unfamiliar intimacy between the sexes and mitigate the conflict potential inherent in two-person interaction. Conversely, for many middle-class people, marriage is predicated on a companionship ideal and the birth of children is readily experienced as an intrusion, a disruption of the harmony between husband and wife. (Fried 1973:122–123)

In the upper-middle-class family, the relationship between husband and wife is to some degree independent of their mutual relationship to their children. They interact as husband and wife, and they also interact as mother and father of their children. In the lower-middle-class family, however, the focus is more on the total family and less on the conjugal relationship as such. Rainwater notes that the way in which lower-middle-class husbands and wives talk about their life together suggests that children are an integral part of their relationship. In this respect, lower-middle-class, white-collar families more closely resemble working-class, blue-collar families than upper-middle-class families. Husbands and wives in the lower middle class tend to think of themselves in terms of family status (as do husbands and wives in blue-collar families) and thus to accept the division of labor that accompanies complementary rather than shared roles. This does not mean that lower-middle-class families have highly segregated conjugal roles; on the contrary, this is a social class in which the married couple are together a great deal of the time. Rainwater points out that:

> Lower-middle class husbands and wives expect to be together much of the time and there is little of the separate social participation common in the lower class, but they are together as husband and wife, often as father and mother, rather than simply as persons who share and value their life together. Thus, there is a subtle element of social distance between spouses that most upper-middle class couples seek to overcome with their emphasis on joint interests and participation. (Rainwater 1965:42)

The role of the father in the socialization of his child probably differs more between social classes in America than does the role of the mother, although in part the difference is created by what the mother expects the father's role to be. Numerous studies over the last several decades have indicated that the expectations and values involved in childrearing differ markedly between social classes in America. In the earlier studies (about 1930), it was found that middle-class parents were more restrictive than were working-class parents of that time. However, by the 1950s the middle-class parents had become more permissive than working-class

508

parents. Most of the changes took place in middle-class childrearing prac- *Middle American*
tices, and can be explained (at least in part) by the greater tendency of *families*
middle-class mothers to read and be influenced by books on childrearing
and by their pediatrician, whereas the working-class mother tends to rely
on the advice of her own mother and other female relatives.

The working-class mother has thus tended to take a more traditional
approach to childrearing, to retain a concern with obedience that is part
of the traditional attitude toward children. A "good" child is an obedient
child in the working class (and in much of the lower middle class). Melvin
Kohn reports: "We, too, found that working-class parents value obedience, neatness, and cleanliness more highly than do middle-class parents,
and that middle-class parents in turn value curiosity, happiness, consideration, and— most importantly— self control more highly than do working-
class parents" (1963:285).

Some sociologists have tried to explain the difference in the parental
expectations by examining the occupational requirements of the working
class and contrasting these with the occupational requirements of the
white-collar and professional middle classes. It may also be the case that
in their views of children, as in some of their other attitudes, members of
the working class are simply more traditional. Among the remnants of our
Puritan heritage is the idea that a willful child is a sinful child. The belief
that it is the parents' clear duty to discipline a defiant child is still prevalent
among the American working class (and among families whose ethnic
ancestry may be far removed from Puritan origins). Working-class children may have their mouths washed out with soap, for example, because
they used profane, obscene, or abusive language in speaking to their
parents.

The basic differences in parental values between the classes in America reflect the concern of working-class parents that their children may
become "wild" and come to a disastrous end if they are not disciplined
with a firm hand in childhood. Because this is a class whose sons are more
likely to be arrested for delinquent behavior than are rich men's sons and
whose daughters are more likely to be "ruined" by pregnancy out of
wedlock (richer girls are more likely to have an abortion), the fears of
working-class parents are not without some foundation.

In working-class families, the roles of the husband-and-father and of
the wife-and-mother are more sharply segregated than in the middle
classes. The mother's role is almost always more emotionally supportive.
The father expects to provide for his children and may expect to be the
ultimate disciplinarian in the family, but it is the mother's task to raise the
children. Commenting on the ramifications that class differences in parental values have for the father's role, Kohn observes:

> Middle-class mothers want their husbands to be supportive of the children
> (especially of sons) with their responsibility for imposing constraints being
> of decidedly secondary importance; working-class mothers look to their
> husbands to be considerably more directive—support is accorded far less

509

importance and constraint far more [*support* is used here in an emotional, not economic context]. Most middle-class fathers agree with their wives and play a role close to what their wives would have them play. Many working-class fathers, on the other hand, do not. It is not that they see the constraining role as less important than do their wives, but that many of them see no reason why they should have to shoulder the responsibility. From their point of view, the important thing is that the child be taught what limits he must not transgress. It does not much matter who does the teaching, and since mother has primary responsibility for child care, the job should be hers.   (Kohn 1963:288–289)

Middle-class parents, especially upper-middle-class parents, tend to be less concerned that their children be obedient, and more concerned that their children learn to be self-controlled and self-directed. Such self-direction is seen as part of a healthy emotional development, which includes creativity and responsive interpersonal skills. Typically, the mother takes responsibility for most of the young child's care, but both parents are concerned with the emotional and social development of the child, especially with the development of a child of their own sex. Middle-class fathers are thus more likely to be concerned with the social and emotional development of their sons than are working-class fathers. A middle-class boy is unlikely to learn an occupational role from his father, but his father is likely to play with him during his leisure hours and to be a significant other in the boy's emotional development. And a father of this class is also likely to play an important role in the emotional development of his daughter, something his great-grandfather may not have done so well.

The lingering prudery: sex and the workingman's wife

As blue-collar workers become more middle-class in both income and education, their norms seem to be moving toward those prevailing in the white-collar middle class. But the working poor have tended to cling to attitudes toward masculinity, femininity, and sexuality that parallel attitudes that prevailed in nineteenth-century America. According to Rainwater (1964:457), the view of marital sexuality among the working poor can be summarized as: "Sex is a man's pleasure and a woman's duty." He reports that over half (54 percent) of the poorest and least educated of the workingmen's wives in his sample made statements indicating strong negative feelings about sexual relations with their husbands. In contrast, less than one third (31 percent) of the "upper-lower-class" wives interviewed expressed a rejection of sexual relations in marriage (these are the women in the middle-income, blue-collar families), and only 14 percent of the middle-class wives in his sample reported negative attitudes toward marital sexuality.

Rainwater found a significant relationship between class level and sexual attitudes: the more affluent and educated women regarded marital sex more positively; the poorest and least educated wives were likely to be the most negative about sex, even with their husbands (1964:457). Komarovsky also found that education was a highly significant factor in the attitudes of blue-collar wives toward sexual relations with their husbands. She reports that "some 15 percent assert that the wife's duty is 'to give it to her husband whether she likes it or not' .... All the women in this 15 percent have less than a high school education. The high school graduates, on the other hand, tend to regard such submission less as a moral duty than as a necessary evil, or as an expression of sympathy for their husband's needs" (Komarovsky 1967:83). Whether viewed as duty or compassion, intercourse was seen by these blue-collar wives more as a matter of their husband's needs than of their own sexuality. Fear of unwanted pregnancy may have been a major element in the negative attitudes toward sex held by these workingmen's wives. Women of this social class were among the last American women to have access to adequate contraception (see the discussion in Chapter 4). In the absence of effective contraception, negative attitudes toward sex have been functional attitudes for women to whom an unplanned pregnancy often presented an economic burden and sometimes a health crisis.

Length of marriage seems to be another factor influencing sexual attitudes. According to Rainwater, some of the women who expressed negative attitudes toward marital intercourse commented that "earlier in marriage they had sometimes enjoyed intercourse but that now, with many children and other preoccupations, would just as soon do without it" (1964:461). The women who had negative feelings about sex reported various avoidance techniques, ranging from feigned illness to deliberately provoked quarrels that they expected would end with the husband leaving for the tavern. However, these women recognized the risks incurred by a wife who refuses her husband too often, and most indicated that they usually submitted to his advances. It seems likely that those wives who feel deep repugnance about sex and at the same time are highly anxious about the consequences of rejecting their husbands sexually are less aware of provoking a quarrel to avoid intercourse and more often self-righteous about the presumed subject of the quarrel; they probably also suffer more from sudden headaches.

Extremely negative views toward sex are often inculcated in girls of the working class as a means of keeping them virginal until marriage. Men of this class still tend to think of women as belonging to two groups: those who are "easy" and those a man marries. A nubile daughter is thus a worry to parents of this class, who are anxious to see her safely married to a "steady" man—that is, to a hard-working, good provider. Among the working poor, as in nineteenth-century America, an eligible young man is one who has an adequate income and a secure future, and an eligible girl is still a *virgin*.

Many women of this class are employed, but employment is not seen as an alternative to marriage. A girl may work until she marries, until her husband's wages are adequate to support the family, or until she becomes pregnant. But her major role in life is perceived as that of wife-and-mother, and to become the woman she is raised to want to be, she must

511

marry. In this class, to marry well requires that a woman remain a virgin. This accounts for the restrictions that parents place on girls whose brothers are granted the freedom of the streets.

According to Rainwater, many women in his sample of working-poor wives reported that their wedding night was a rude awakening, a traumatic experience bearing little resemblance to what they had romantically imagined (1960:60–64) The woman raised to be prudish may be shocked and repelled by her initial intercourse. The working-class husband who has married such a girl probably chose her because she seemed to be a "good" girl (having been raised in the same subculture, typically he shares its sexual norms). He may not be dismayed by the reluctant behavior of his bride. Rainwater reports that "the wife's modesty and reticence are not necessarily disapproved by her new husband; he may value them as an indication that she is still virgin and that she is not 'oversexed' " (1964:-460). A wife of the working class who is highly interested in sex is atypical and regarded as not quite "nice." To the upper middle class she would seem uninhibited; to her class peers she is "oversexed" and viewed with as much disdain as the man who is "undersexed." Conversely, to millions of working-class Americans, little stigma attaches to the wife who is unable to derive pleasure from sex, so long as she is compliant and never refuses her husband.

This is a class that is suspicious of erotic finesse; Rainwater's studies indicate that the working-poor husband tends to have a fear of stimulating "unnatural" impulses in his wife that could "lead her to look for a lover" (1964:458). This fear "is often given as a reason for not stimulating her too much or developing her sensual capacities through long or elaborated lovemaking" (Rainwater 1964:458). However, Komarovsky found that a large number of the blue-collar husbands in her sample "expressed concern with the sexual responsiveness of their wives and held themselves responsible for it" (1967:84). The middle-class sexual attitudes are filtering down the class structure. Commenting on his sexual relations with his wife, one of the men interviewed for Komarovsky's study said: "She is always there when I want her. She really likes it as women go .... Of course, I try to do a pretty good job at that like everything else" (1967:98). Of this man's wife, Komarovsky says, "Even if she derived no pleasure from sexual relations, she would submit from expediency and a sense of duty. As it is, sex is not only a physical pleasure but a factor alleviating her sense of isolation from her husband" (1967:98).

Once she has overcome initial repugnance, the workingman's bride may find the sexual relationship a means of enhancing intimacy with her husband. But with pregnancy, the bride of this class often begins to turn more to her mother and other female relatives, and her husband turns back to the male world. As the working-class bride begins to "settle down," she comes to fit more closely the role of wife as perceived by her mother, aunts, and sisters (which is precisely what this group means by "settling down"). Her closed female network does not tend to regard the role of wife as that of passionate sexual partner. Komarovsky reports the comments of a twenty-three-year-old wife: "She had been surprised at the beginning that sex was as nice as it was and she wondered how she got along without it for so long. It's hard to believe, she remarked, that what her mother and sister tell her 'about it wearing off after awhile' can be true" (1967:101). Because the good opinion of a small group of female relatives is the major source of her self-esteem, the working-class wife comes to center her self-image on her housekeeping functions rather than on her sexual role. The praises of her female relatives are elicited by a well-scrubbed house filled with well-scrubbed children. She is deeply chagrined if one of these significant "others" catches her with her house in disarray.

Finding her sexual role almost tangential to her close female network's definition of a "good wife," and not having been raised to expect to enjoy sexual relations, the working-class wife is likely to return after a few years to negative feelings about sex. Rainwater observes that in this class, "girls growing up are not encouraged to internalize a role as interested sexual partner, but are taught instead a complex of modesty, reticence, and rejection of sexual interests which continues into marriage" (1964:464).

After the early years of marriage, there seems to be a tendency for the sexual relationship in a working-class marriage to become little more than a routine release of sexual tensions for the husband and a dutiful obligation for his wife. Rainwater concludes that "there is not only a decrease in frequency, but also a tendency to relegate intercourse more and more to the category of satisfying the husband's biological need, and for whatever sense of mutuality has existed to wither" (1964:464). Such marriages are not necessarily unhappy by the norms of the working class, however. And because these sexual norms tend to be strongly supported by the religious norms of the working class, many of whom belong to conservative or fundamentalist faiths, these marriages are likely to be considered good by those who are involved in them.

The birds and the pussycats:
self-image, woman's role, and social class

Within each social-class subculture there are shared assumptions about what constitutes a good marriage, a good wife, a good woman. Each of us acquires such images in childhood, and continues to modify and refine them throughout life. Our own family, the families of relatives, the families of friends, the families of neighbors—marriages and people within a similar social-class context, for the most part—provide points of reference and comparison. The social-class context provides what the sociologist calls a "frame of reference." Social-class norms are not the only frame of reference within which self-image and sex roles are defined. A set of expectations and norms involving marriage and sex roles may be shared by an ethnic group across class lines. Within a class or ethnic subculture there may be a sharp difference in expectation that follows generational lines, with older women and younger women having different expectations of marriage, and of themselves.

Helena Lopata (1971) analyzed the conflicts and contradictions in the role expectations of urban and suburban housewives in the Chicago area. She found that a woman's attitudes toward her role changed during the life cycle, and that the stages of the life cycle had different meanings for women from different social-class backgrounds. Women who espouse traditional views of the role of wife and mother seem to assume that they will spend the rest of their lives totally involved with the home and with family relations. This view was most characteristic of the lower-middle-class woman living in an urban setting who tended to be hesitant about involvement in the world outside the home. The traditional feminine role requires a passive stance, and is circumscribed by emotionally charged norms. Lopata (1971:36) found the most vocal discontent with this role expressed by wealthier, upper-middle-class women who lived in a suburban setting.

In a study of the concept of the female role in middle-class American families, Anne Steinmann (1963) found two distinct conceptions of that role. The traditional view is "that concept held by the woman who conceives of herself as the 'other,' the counterpoint of the man and children in her life . . . . Her distinguishing feature is that she fulfills herself by proxy" (1963:277). In contrast to this traditional view is the more modern, liberated outlook, in which the woman "strives to fulfill herself directly by realizing her own potentialities . . . . Her distinguishing feature is that she seeks fulfillment through her own accomplishments" (1963:277).

Susan Grumich (1972) studied the female role perspectives of women from two suburban communities, one working-class and the other upper-middle-class, in the southern part of the San Francisco Bay area. One of these communities is a small city that was originally a rural trading center. In the 1950s, automobile assembly plants were located nearby, and these have come to dominate the local economy. For two decades, suburban tract homes have surrounded what was once a small town. Grumich drew her working-class sample from two census tracts in this community. The median household income for one of these tracts was $7,500, for the other, $8,500 (most of the men were auto production or maintenance workers). Less than 12 percent of the households had incomes over $10,-000 per year. The census information did not indicate what proportion of families had more than one wage earner, but national averages are for more than 40 percent of wives to be gainfully employed, and many of the women in this suburban, working-class community did in fact work outside the home. Most of the women were high school graduates. Approximately three out of every four families in this working-class suburb owned their homes. This was a stable, relatively homogeneous, working-class population (the census data indicated a low percentage of either black or Mexican-American families, so ethnic variables were unlikely to have distorted the study).

514
The second community that Grumich selected for comparison was

The world of the workingman's wife centers on her home and does not extend far beyond her family circle. Her perception of self in the context of familial roles is essentially the traditional feminine self-image: the woman who is a satellite of her husband, who lives by proxy, and tries to realize her dreams through her children.

located on the other side of the heavily industrialized valley, in the foothills of the coastal mountain range. This community was once a small village surrounded by summer homes, but it has become a residential area for upper-middle-class professional and managerial families. Again, there was evidence of a high degree of homogeneity in the community: 45 percent of the families reported incomes between $10,000 and $19,000 annually (most of the rest had higher incomes). Most of the wives had college educations, and few were employed.

Grumich's study involved responses to standardized role-inventory questions and projective tests, designed to reveal whether the women held traditional or more liberated role images as ideal norms and as a self-image. Although many of the working-class women did in fact work outside the home, nearly two thirds of them omitted any reference to occupational roles in response to role-inventory questions. They mentioned that they were wives, mothers, Catholics or Protestants, but they did not bother to list their paid occupation in the role inventory. In contrast, although few of the upper-middle-class wives in the community in the foothills were presently employed, many of them included a professional role they had once played among their responses to the question, "Who Am I?" Three out of four of the women who did *not* mention "housewife" among their roles were from this upper-middle-class group.

The working-class woman's perception of herself in the world has much in common with that of the lower-middle-class woman, but differs sharply from the self-perception of the upper-middle-class woman. The

515

world of the workingman's wife—like that of the lower-middle-class woman—centers on her home and does not extend far beyond her family circle. The perception of self in the context of familial roles is essentially the traditional female self-image: the woman who is a satellite of her husband, who lives by proxy, and tries to realize her dreams through her children. Having projected so much of her self onto the significant others in her life, she needs to remain close to them to be able to experience, even vicariously, the most valued potential in herself.

Rainwater and his associates asked women to give their reactions to a series of projective tests, including pictures and descriptions of hypothetical situations. They report:

> We asked our respondents to tell us what they would most and least like to be turned into if a magician were to change them into something other than a human being. The most common type of working-class response was along these lines:
>
> > A dog, because it is so faithful.
> > A French poodle, it's well fed, brushed and people pet it.
> > A house bird because of the love people give it.
> > The bed my children lay on so I could still be close to them.
> > A house, so I could watch people's lives and be close to home.
> > A fairy, so I could watch over the kids and other people.
>
> Two-thirds of the working-class women gave responses which indicate a desire to continue to be with people, to nurture them, to be nurtured by them, or to have power over them. Only one-third of the middle-class women gave such responses. Instead, they were more likely to give responses which represent a desire to escape, or simply for contentment all by one's self:
>
> > A bird because it can fly wherever it wants and see the world.
> > A cloud because it is so light and frothy and free.
> > A cow so I could just lie around and eat grass.
> > A flower that blooms for years.
>
> The middle-class women are able to use this chance to fantasy about what they might otherwise be, and often think only of themselves in such a fantasy. The working-class women still prefer to see themselves closely tied to people and they don't so often want to "get away from it all." (Rainwater et al. 1959:49)

In seeking to determine the self-image and the perception of women's roles held by her respondents, Grumich included the question that Rainwater and his associates had asked: "If a magician would change you into something other than a human being, what would you like to be?" The answers varied widely, yet there were clusters of responses that marked perceptible differences between the self-images of the upper-middle-class women and the working-class women. The working-class women gave responses that were strikingly similar to those Rainwater had obtained from workingmen's wives nearly fifteen years earlier. Grumich reports that working-class women in her sample gave responses that were typically centered on family and home. Often, these women expressed a desire to be changed into a beloved family pet: "Cat—sleep and sun myself all day and be loved by everyone in the family." Some expressed the desire to be an expensive and pampered cat: a Persian cat with a satin cushion. Grumich notes that although there was a variety of responses, "working-class women generally expressed the wish to stay in their homes, to be small and passive house pets, and to remain near their families" (1972:170). A few of the working-class women dismissed the question as "nonsense," and gave such answers as, "Nothing. All I want to be is a better wife and mother." (1972:169).

In contrast, the upper-middle-class women in Grumich's study tended to give "answers containing images of freedom, independence, flying, or getting away" (1972:169). These responses, again, were similar to those that Rainwater had reported for the upper-middle-class women in his earlier study. One typical response to the question regarding metamorphosis was that of the upper-middle-class woman who indicated she would like to become: "A song bird. Because he gives off joy and beauty. He isn't earthbound. He lives fairly independently of men. He lives close to nature. He is beholden to no one, harms no one" (1972:169).

There were no significant differences between the self-image and role perceptions of women thirty-five years of age and older and those of women thirty-four years of age and younger. Apparently the basic attitudes and role expectations inculcated by social-class norms persist through time and the life cycle.

Considering that most of the occupations open to women with only a high school education tend to be repetitive, dead-end jobs, perhaps it is not surprising that most of the working-class women have chosen familial roles rather than occupational roles as the core of their self-image. By the standards of all social classes, the social and emotional rewards accorded to *mother* are higher than those granted to the grocery checker, the sales clerk, or the member of the typing pool. A woman who works only to help support her family until her husband gets a better job, or until the workers at the auto plant are recalled from lay-off, might well omit her job from the description of herself in response to the open-ended question, "Who Am I?" The view of femininity expressed by the working-class women was most often the passive, "other" role, counterpoint to the masculine role played by their husbands. This is a role that all of the working-class women could play with some success, and thus a role from which they were able to derive personal satisfaction. It might be noted, however, that the indolent, pampered pussycat that so often appeared as the ideal metamorphosis for the workingman's wife tends to be proudly independent: a cat never grovels, or licks the master's foot.

In contrast to the workingman's wife, the well-educated upper-middle-class woman seems to be expressing a high level of frustration. She has been raised expecting to participate actively in society and to find rewards outside familial roles through social and professional achievement. The professional education that many of these women had enjoyed had become a salient part of their self-image, one that they retained even though they were no longer actively engaged in their profession. Many of these women mentioned their roles as teacher, nurse, even concert pianist, only to reveal later that it had been a decade or more since they had been able to play such a role. The responses of such women were filled with wistful thoughts of what might have been. These women seemed to have lingering regrets at having abandoned their professional careers for the domestic life, and their sense of entrapment in a gilded cage was expressed in a variety of ways. Grumich notes that "these feelings of cultural imprisonment and truncated ambitions can best be expressed by a particularly articulate upper-middle-class woman herself, as she answers the question, 'Who Am I'?" (1972:186–187):

> I am a foundation to other
> A wet rope drying in the sun
> A symphony locked in a room
> I am a breeze sending inspiration
> A conciliator, a humanitarian
> A secretary, A delivery service
> A servant, A lover, A mother
> A promoter of the sunset and sunrise
> A star that belongs to the galaxy of life
> A seed sprouting through the earth
> A bird migrating to a freer place
> A sack full of toys, looking for a chimney
> A racing car breaking its remote control
> A child seeing the circus for the first time
> A visitor who wants to help others
> A heater that hungers for fuel
> A leader who directs others
> A collector cherishing the roses
> Grateful for the privilege of being a Woman, yet scampering
> To be recognized for *the person I am.*

References

Bott, Elizabeth. 1957. *Family and Social Network.* London: Tavistock Publications.

Dobriner, William M. 1963. *Class in Suburbia.* Englewood Cliffs, N.J.: Prentice-Hall.

Fried, Marc. 1973. *The World of the Urban Working Class.* Cambridge, Mass.: Harvard University Press.

Fromm, Erich. 1941. *Escape from Freedom.* New York: Holt, Rinehart and Winston.

Grumich, Susan. 1972. "Women in Limbo: Social Class and Life Cycle Perspectives of Feminine Roles." Unpublished Master's Thesis, San Jose State University.

Hollingshed, August B. 1950. "Class Differences in Family Stability." *Annals of the American Academy of Political and Social Science* 171:39–46.

Kohn, Melvin L. 1963. "Social Class and Parent-Child Relationships: An Interpre- Middle American
families tation." *American Journal of Sociology* 68 (January):471–480.

Komarovsky, Mirra. 1967. *Blue-Collar Marriage*, rev. ed. New York: Random House.

Lopata, Helena Zaniecki. 1971. *Occupation: Housewife*. New York: Oxford University Press.

Mills, C. Wright. 1951. *White Collar: The American Middle Class*. New York: Oxford University Press.

Rainwater, Lee. 1960. *And the Poor Get Children: Sex, Contraception, and Family Planning in the Working Class*. Chicago: Quadrangle Books.

_____. 1964. "Marital Sexuality in Four Cultures of Poverty." *Journal of Marriage and the Family* 26 (November):457–466.

_____. 1965. *Family Design: Marital Sexuality, Family Size, and Contraception*. Chicago: Aldine Publishing Company.

Rainwater, Lee, Richard P. Coleman, and Gerald Handel. 1959. *Workingman's Wife*. New York: Oceania Publications.

Steinmann, Anne. 1963. "A Study of the Concept of the Feminine Role of Fifty-One Middle-Class American Families." *Genetic Psychology Monographs* 62:275–277

U.S. Bureau of the Census. 1972. *Census of Population: 1970 Marital Status, Final Report*. Washington, D.C.: U.S. Government Printing Office.

U.S. Bureau of Labor Statistics. 1974. *Handbook of Labor Statistics, 1974*. Washington, D.C.: U.S. Government Printing Office.

Suggested readings

Dobriner, William M. 1963. *Class in Suburbia*. Englewood Cliffs, N.J.: Prentice-Hall. Paper. A study of American class structure and the suburbs that includes both a theoretical discussion of social-class structure and empirical descriptions of white-collar and blue-collar suburbs. Topics covered include the images of suburbia, the faces of the middle class, the flight to the suburbs, and the search for community.

Fried, Marc. 1973. *The World of the Urban Working Class*. Cambridge, Mass.: Harvard University Press. A study of the working-class families of the West End of Boston, based on data gathered shortly before the fifty acres that constituted this urban neighborhood were leveled for urban renewal. Dislocation and relocation and community life in the working class are studied; for present purposes, the chapter on family roles and relationships in the urban working class is most relevant.

Komarovsky, Mirra. 1967. *Blue-Collar Marriage*. New York: Vintage Books, a division of Random House. Paper. An in-depth study of blue-collar families in an American industrial city in a north-central state. Because the focus is on class rather than ethnic patterns, the sample was drawn to include primarily native-born, white, Protestant families in which the head of household was a blue-collar worker. Komarovsky analyzes such aspects of marital relationships as conjugal role expectations, sexual norms, barriers to marital communication, patterns of marital dominance, and kinship relations.

19 The family in poverty

[*Their*] *deep pessimism about human nature, their bedrock conviction that most people will do ill when it is in their interest, that doing ill is more natural than doing good, interacts with the normal contingencies of life that make doing good very difficult. Parents feel that luck more than anything else determines whether their children grow up conforming to their ideas of goodness. They hope that their children will have luck, but in time they become increasingly desperate and then increasingly hopeless.*

Lee Rainwater (1970:222–223)

Many low-income families consist of an aged husband and wife, downwardly mobile and poor because of age and infirmity. These older people may be hungry and ill-housed, but their family patterns are still those of the class in which they have spent most of their lives. This chapter is not about them. Nor is it about the young couples who are struggling to begin marriage on a low income. Most young couples in America come from middle-class or working-class backgrounds, and have marital role expectations that reflect the family and class in which they were raised, including the expectation that their family income will rise.

Nor is this a chapter about families coping with temporary unemployment or temporary underemployment, although such families face real problems, particularly in a period of both high unemployment and inflation. The unemployed man who has been part of the middle class or the working class all his life retains the expectations of his class regarding marital roles and what constitutes a "decent" life-style for a family. Such expectations make the familial roles of an unemployed husband and father difficult, and the period of his unemployment a time of strain and family crisis. But middle-class or working-class attitudes and expectations are useful attributes in helping him get another job, almost as important as his skills and prior experience. There is a gulf between the life-styles of families coping with temporary unemployment and those for whom unemployment is chronic.

This is a chapter about families trapped in poverty, about chronic dependence and what poverty does to marriage and family relationships. People who are chronically dependent may learn to cope with life, but in ways that limit their ability to escape from poverty. It is the family patterns of this group that are the focus of this chapter: impoverished families headed by people who are at best semiskilled and semiliterate, who are employed part-time or seasonally, or chronically unemployed, and who have never had any experience—or any real hope—of living in any other way. They have been down so long that they have acquired a fixed view of the world from that position. Their life-style puts peculiar strains on marriage, not simply because the grocery money is short, but because the way of approaching the world that enables these people to survive is antithetical to what the middle-class and the working-class Americans regard as a normal married life.

Making do with string

Families who are trapped in poverty constitute what S. M. Miller (1964) refers to as the "unstable poor." Their instability has several dimensions: occupation (the head of the family is chronically unemployed or only employed part-time and marginally); income (sporadic as well as low); family structure (often broken, frequently mother-centered). They live in deteriorated housing, in urban areas more often than in rural areas. These families have little or no earned income, and thus live in a state of chronic dependency, although not all qualify for welfare. They come from all ethnic backgrounds and all racial backgrounds. Although the majority are white, minority groups, particularly blacks, are overrepresented in proportion to their total numbers in the population.

As Miller describes the situation of such families: "A number of forces can lead individuals into chronic dependence. *'Lower-class' life is crisis-life, constantly trying to 'make-do' with string where rope is needed.* Anything can break the string. Illness is one of the most important—'Got a job but I got sick and lost it'; 'We managed until the baby got sick' " (1964:13; emphasis in the original).

In 1974 there were 7.3 million American families (approximately 13 percent of all American families) with annual incomes below the poverty threshold, according to the federal government (U.S. Bureau of the Census 1975:1). The federal government classifies families as living at or below the poverty level by using the poverty index adopted by a federal interagency committee in 1969. This poverty index is used for determining eligibility for a number of welfare programs.

The poverty index provides a number of "poverty thresholds" that are adjusted to allow for such factors as the size of the family, sex and age of the family head, the number of children in the family, and farm or nonfarm residence. The threshold of poverty for a farm family is set at 85 percent of the nonfarm level (the assumption is that a farm family will be able to grow a portion of its own food and in other ways be more self-sufficient than a nonfarm family). The range of income levels thus derived separates poverty from a minimally adequate level of living (and often determines whether or not a family qualifies for some form of assistance). It is revised each year to take account of changes in the consumer price index, a federal index that reflects the cost of living (U.S. Bureau of the Census 1972:Appendix 12). When the poverty index was devised in 1969, the poverty threshold for a nonfarm family of four was $3,743; by 1974, it had risen to $5,038.

An annual income figure may blur some important distinctions involving the nature of the income. The life-style of a family, including its ability to budget and plan its expenditures, will be affected by whether family income is sporadic or regular, predictable or unpredictable, and whether its source is employment, unemployment benefits, a pension, Social Security, or welfare. It has been estimated that between 35 and 50 percent of the poorest families in America have *no* family member in the labor force (Keyserling 1961)—the major reason why they are impoverished. Most families trapped in poverty are headed by an adult—male or female—who is unskilled or at best semiskilled, and thus unable to compete for the kind of job that could lift the family out of poverty.

Many stable, low-income American families live in rural areas. Families living on marginal farms are often among the most deprived, in spite of the romantic assumptions about farm life cherished by urban Americans. There are also rural nonfarm families among the impoverished. These people live in hamlets along the back roads of America. The interstate highways bypass these towns, towns that were once trading centers for the surrounding farmers, or ferry landings before the bridge was built, or mill towns before all the timber was cut. Appalachia has become almost synonymous with rural poverty, but numerous other areas of the United States, such as the upper peninsula of Michigan or the backwoods of Maine or Arkansas, also have a high proportion of rural poor. The rural poor tend to have a stable family structure and a stable, if low, income. They are likely to have some land for a garden and perhaps a few chickens and a cow or goat. They get by, one winter at a time. Their life-style is essentially that of the working class, of which they are the poorest fringe.

Most of the rural poor are white. Some are members of an ethnic minority, living in ethnic enclaves. Others are nonwhite, frequently living in racial enclaves. There is general awareness among contemporary Americans that urban centers have segregated "barrios" or "ghettos." The urban ethnic neighborhood of working-class people of a given national origin has been featured in the media. But it is less generally known that there are rural racial or ethnic enclaves. Members of other groups are often perceived narrowly in such isolated rural communities, defined in stereotypes or in terms of the occasional representative of that other race or different ethnic group who happens to be visible. A rural black enclave in Texas was described as follows by a former resident, as he knew it about thirty years ago:

> Beat Five is and was the most rural of the rural. Then as now there wasn't the slightest concept of convenience as known in any modern urban or suburban area. Everyone farmed for a living. Some were sharecroppers while others owned their own plots of 100 to 400 acres. The crops were diversified—that is, people raised food for themselves, feed for the livestock, and market items such as cotton, beans, and of course cattle. The farms in Beat Five would be called ranches in California or maybe even ranches in Texas if you are not near Kings County.
>
> The social structure was very simple. One could hardly distinguish the landowners from the sharecroppers. The main social institutions were church and school. Both had black trustees. Contact with white people was minimal in Beat Five. I recall only one white resident. The white resident of Beat Five was old lady Lulie. She lived near a branch of Nails Creek in a one-room log structure. She didn't farm or ranch. She had no visible income but she did own a jackass, which was her basic mode of travel. When one saw her, one got the impression that she wore all of her clothes all of the time. If you were down wind from her you, would know that she was coming. She dipped snuff, smoked a pipe, and lived off her black neighbors.
>
> Business and industry were all but nonexistent. The Sheppards

ran a processing mill for sugar cane. The grinder was driven by one oxpower. Isaac Patrick owned a store that wasn't more than an enlarged smokehouse in size. Ted Donovan owned a large store by smokehouse standards, and Jessie McFarland owned a store and a truck that he used to haul cotton and turkeys as well as people. In Beat Five everyone helped everyone else. If your house or barn burned down everyone would help rebuild. Everyone cut wood, chopped cotton, branded livestock, everyone made meal, cured leather and furs, butchered and smoked meat. In most cases, women didn't plough or bust broncos or brand cattle, but in many cases they did, and in most cases they cooked unless there was an invalid male on hand.

In Beat Five the family was the primary unit. On the other hand, it was difficult to determine where the extended family ended. Most of the action of the community was across the board to each community member.

Many of the urban poor are recent migrants, or the children of migrants, from such segregated rural enclaves. The United States made the transition from an agrarian to an industrial society shortly after the turn of this century. In the last two or three decades our society has made a second transition, to industrial agriculture. The family farm has been gradually displaced by agribusiness. This is a point made in some detail in Chapter 1. The transition to industrial agriculture has created a new wave of displaced people from rural areas.

Some of our urban poor were once field hands, but have been displaced by mechanical cotton pickers and chemical weed killers (hardly anyone "chops" cotton anymore). Some of our urban poor were once tenant farmers, but were evicted when small holdings were consolidated into large, corporate-owned farms. Some of them may have inherited a small farm but piled mortgage on mortgage to buy seed and fertilizer, and never got out of debt. Life may have been so hard where they were living that they came to the city looking for something better. People have been doing that since the first drought-weary farmers moved to the early cities along the Nile Valley (where they were soon enslaved).

Some of our urban poor came from the rural villages of Puerto Rico, some from the mountain villages of Mexico. Some are migrants from the hills of Appalachia, or from marginal farms in the South or West. Some of them came to the slums of great cities directly. Some of them paused first in the run-down neighborhoods of a smaller city nearer to their origins. But in the not too distant past, most of the urban poor or their immediate ancestors were part of the rural poor. Most of these people left the land because industrial agriculture offers little except seasonal work for the unskilled farm laborer.

These displaced rural Americans of all races came to the city because times were hard in the country, and they hoped to find work. Even if they

525

*Displaced rural Americans of all races came to the city because times were hard in
the country and they hoped to find work. Even if they cannot find work, they stay,
surviving on welfare or the help of kinfolk. A few go back, but there is little for
them to return to in rural America. Whether in the rural area or in the city, they
have few usable skills and no capital. They are willing to work, but our society no
longer needs their labor.*

cannot find work, they stay, surviving on welfare or the help of kinfolk. A
few go back, but there is little for them to return to in rural America.
Whether in the rural area or in the city, they have few usable skills and no
capital. They are willing to work, but our society no longer needs their
labor.

In the city, rural migrants find that jobs are available only to those
who possess urban skills: literacy, knowledge of machinery, knowledge of
how to order their lives to fit the timeclock. The rural migrants seldom
have such skills. Their children may acquire them, but the conditions of
slum life do not facilitate the adaptation. What the children do learn is how
to survive on the streets of the ghetto. This is the focus of the very poor:
survival.

The work ethic and the chronically dependent

The downwardly mobile, the rural migrants, the urban dwellers trapped
at the bottom, all those who have nothing in a culture where property is
still considered the supreme proof of personal worth, survive by creating
a subculture with a different set of expectations. Each generation raised
in poverty finds it more difficult to break through the barriers of class
culture. Poverty passed from generation to generation tends to create a

526

self-sealing system, for the behavior that makes it possible to survive in poverty effectively prevents entry into the larger society.

Before the development of industrial technology, the poor (who were then the majority) were seen as the unfortunate children of God, Who had placed them in a humble station to try their souls. But as the merchants and manufacturers rose from humble birth to wealth and power, the accident of birth was no longer perceived as the unalterable will of God. The basis of the prestige claims of the rising middle class was that a man was what he made himself. The station to which he rose—or to which he dropped—indicated his worth. (For a woman, the corollary was upward mobility by marriage.) By the eighteenth century, as the middle class became dominant in numbers and power, the prevailing view of the poor came to be that they were undeserving for the most part, with exceptions made for pious cripples, chaste widows, and orphans who were meek and industrious. These last were expected to rise in the world by dint of good habits; if they did not, they were shortly relegated to the ranks of the slothful, indolent poor.

Such attitudes derive from the seventeenth and eighteenth century and from the pattern of norms that Max Weber termed the Protestant Ethic. However, a similar set of values developed in the same era in predominantly Catholic countries (such as France) that had a rising merchant and manufacturing class. It is essentially a *work ethic*. The value system was transported to America early: "He who does not work, neither shall he eat" is the legendary dictum attributed to the founder of Jamestown. The work ethic meant that there should be no privileged class who lived by the labor of others. The idle rich and the idle poor were scorned alike.

The strength of such values lies in the belief that all men should have equal opportunity to rise in the world; the negative aspect is the belief that any man who does not rise has only himself to blame. (Women have tended to be denied the opportunity to rise, and spared the blame if they did not.) These beliefs form an interlocking system, and one cannot long exist without the other. Middle-class American culture is still rooted in these values. It is thus oriented to striving for the future, which means that its norms include thrift, diligence, and self-denial in the present, to ensure future reward. The mortgage slowly paid off, with the diminishing debt marked each month in the little blue book; the insurance plan that will send the children to college some day; the retirement plan the corporation offers the husband in his twenties as an inducement to join the firm: all the planning and budgeting today for a tomorrow free of debt. But such planning requires that next month's income, next year's income, be certain and predictable. It requires a regular salary and some form of job security, whether through a union, civil service, tenure, or some other guarantee that as long as the worker does what is reasonably expected, he will be able to keep his job.

The people who live in poverty because of sporadic employment or chronic unemployment know no such security. Sporadic earnings mean long periods of deprivation, punctuated by brief spurts of indulgence. People with such a pattern of employment are oriented to today. Each day brings the necessity of finding food for the children and perhaps a pair of shoes, and the minor victory of staving off eviction for now, for today. And there is only today, for who can tell what may happen tomorrow? And when this day brings—as it sometimes does—a windfall, it is a glorious day and means a giddy trip through the market with a cart full of luxuries; it means splurging on a new television set, a record player, a watch. The bleak interval before the next bit of good fortune will be survived somehow, a day at a time, if necessary by pawning that same television set, record player, and watch—and perhaps her wedding ring. Such goods are the tangible assets of the very poor.

Children raised in poverty tend to feel that there is not much they can do to determine the course of their lives, that luck will mean the difference between living as they see their family live and having the incredible income that a big league ballplayer, a boxing champion, or a popular musician can enjoy (a gigantic windfall). Adults who are past the point of dreaming of instant fame can view the lucky number, the long-shot horse, the winning contest entry as their only means of escape from poverty. Such fatalism is based on the life experience of the very poor. One is lucky or unlucky; life seems that simple. This is the reason why the very poor cannot believe that the middle-class Americans have *earned* their affluence. The successful are viewed as merely the lucky ones who have no special right to their property, no particular claim to honor; they merely held the winning number, so to speak.

Nor is the successful musician or artist or ballplayer seen as especially deserving of praise for hard work or talent; in the view from poverty, these people, too, were simply lucky. It is hard for the very poor to believe that talent or hard work prevail, for the life experience of the very poor involves much overlooked talent, much hard work that has gone unrewarded. It seems to the poor that Fate simply smiles on someone, for no particular reason, and that someone cuts a record that sells a million copies, or holds the winning sweepstakes ticket. If luck brings reward, then the great mass of the unrewarded can go on hoping that their luck will change. For fatalism is, at the last, a form of hope: the only hope for a person who has no skills, no education, no powerful family, no highly placed friends, and only ordinary talent.

In contrast, the life experience of the middle-class American teaches him that he *can* affect the course of his own life. If he works hard and applies himself at school, he firmly believes that the reward will be a job somewhere in the professional or managerial cadre. Once there, he expects his performance to have a great deal to do with his future prospects. The idea of Free Will (a concept that was elaborated in the seventeenth century as part of the Protestant Ethic) makes sense to him, and he wants to believe it. "I am the master of my fate, I am the captain of my soul."

Here is the very credo of the "self-made man." But if he comes early to a dead-end job, he can only regard his lack of achievement as a personal failure.

The children of the slums are not likely to extricate themselves from poverty unless they grab onto the middle-class belief that they *can* alter the course of their own lives. This is the only basis on which it could make sense to finish high school when the courses seem unrelated to the world in which they live. (That such courses may be related to a world they have never known is a proposition they can accept only on faith and the evidence of television.) Only if they feel that they can shape their own future will they be willing to give up present pleasures for a tomorrow that they have learned to regard with apprehension. But if affirming middle-class values represents the lever by which the children of poverty can pry themselves out of the slum, such affirmation is a lever with a cutting edge: suppose they fail? The young man or woman who is unable to escape from poverty may find it less damaging to self-esteem to reject middle-class values, to believe "I never had a chance."

To the very poor, the world beyond their immediate neighborhood is a strange place in which anything can happen, and probably for the worse. The people from that world beyond who enter the slum by day with briefcases all seem to belong to the same, alien *They.* To the woman raised in the slum, the middle-class professionals who come to her door—the social workers, the probation officers, the poverty program organizers—all seem to have much in common with the agent who collects the rent, the officer bearing an eviction notice, the loan shark, the shyster salesman. Similar in dress, speech, manner, all represent Authority to her—and Trouble. She is suspicious of the well-dressed stranger at her door, afraid that someone is trying to take advantage of her—again—and is likely to react with the unspoken questions, "Why are you being nice to me—what do you want?"

The welfare mother

According to the Women's Bureau of the U.S. Department of Labor (1975:25), 62 percent of the mothers who did not have husbands present in the home (women who were widowed, divorced, separated, or never married) were working or looking for work in March of 1974. This rate of participation in the labor force is significantly higher than that for mothers with husbands present in the home, only 43 percent of whom were in the labor force in that same month. Still, even this high rate of labor force participation means that somewhat more than one third (38 percent) of American mothers without husbands were out of the labor force. Some of these women received alimony or child-support payments, some received survivors benefits, some received financial assistance from parents or other relatives. But many mothers who were heads of families were on welfare.

529

The image of the welfare mother that emerges from letters to the editor is that of a woman who makes a career of bearing illegitimate children in order to collect welfare payments. This image has little foundation in reality. In a study of illegitimacy and the AFDC (Aid to Families with Dependent Children) program in an urban, industrial county in the San Francisco Bay area, Kermit Wiltse and Robert Roberts (1966) focused on illegitimacy within the AFDC population, particularly on the question of repetitive out-of-wedlock childbearing. Of the total population of AFDC mothers in that county, at that time, Wiltse and Roberts found that over half of the women had *only legitimate* children. Of the 47 percent who had ever born a child out of wedlock, over half had legitimate children as well. Wiltse and Roberts observed:

> Of all the AFDC mothers who had borne illegitimate children nearly two-thirds had been married at some time in their lives, and whether or not they have been married at some time is not closely related to race or to number of out-of-wedlock children they may have borne. The important point to emphasize is that the bearers of illegitimate children are not set apart as a group who never marry.   (Wiltse and Roberts 1966:227)

There were 448 women in the sample who had borne illegitimate children, and these women had a total of 1,976 children, both legitimate and illegitimate. More than one third of these children (34.7 percent) were legitimate. The AFDC mothers who had only one illegitimate child constituted 49.9 percent of all those who had illegitimate children. Women with two illegitimate children made up 22.7 percent of the total. Only 14.7 percent had four or more illegitimate children. The women with four or more illegitimate children were, predictably, the oldest group, an average thirty-three years of age. But, as Wiltse and Roberts point out, the women with only one illegitimate child were, on the average, twenty-seven years of age; they were not young girls on their way to repeated illegitimacy.

Of the group of AFDC mothers studied by Wiltse and Roberts, approximately 37 percent were white, and most of the rest were black. Few of these women were native Californians: 88.2 percent were born in other states. Most of the black women came from the South. Approximately one third of the white AFDC mothers came from California, one third from the South, and one-third from all other sections of the United States. This group of welfare mothers was, then, primarily composed of women who had migrated to California, but not necessarily in order to receive welfare. Most of these women had been in California for several years before seeking welfare assistance. The group with the shortest period of residence before receiving aid was the group of black mothers with four or more illegitimate children, and these women had lived in California an average of five years before receiving aid. The group with the longest residence before receiving aid were the white mothers with one illegitimate child, and that group averaged eleven years of California residence before receiving aid.

The AFDC mothers studied by Wiltse and Roberts tended to have few skills and little education. Those with illegitimate children had, on the average, a tenth-grade education, with the black women slightly better-educated than the white. Only 37 percent of the AFDC mothers with illegitimate children had never been employed. Of the 63 percent who had been employed at some time, most had held only unskilled jobs. Among the black women, most had held jobs as domestic workers. Few of the white women in the study had been employed as domestics.

It should be noted that these findings apply only to the AFDC population in one county in California in 1966; even the same county at another time might show a different pattern. However, the findings of some other studies (for example, the study by Greenleigh of the AFDC program in Cook County, Illinois) are similar enough to suggest that the career unwed mother is the exception. Most women with illegitimate children marry at some time in their lives, and most of these women also have legitimate children. Most AFDC mothers with illegitimate children work or have worked at some time, but most are unskilled and poorly educated by the standards of our society.

Most are surprised at finding themselves on welfare, and most struggle to find an alternative means of supporting their children. Because this struggle involves sporadic employment, most go through a period of trying to become financially independent while still requiring financial assistance. For some, this means "cheating" on welfare. Susan Berman (1974) reports on some of these welfare mothers:

> They do earn more income than they are allowed on welfare. And they don't report it. Their lives are day to day struggles to provide for their children. They can't afford luxuries like a diaper service, new blue jeans or meat. They keep low profiles and live in constant fear that their chiseling will be discovered and that somehow their children will be taken from them. The women are real, their names are not.
>
> ... Carol is twenty-six and has a three year old son. She lives alone with her son in Bernal Heights and devotes her days to a community school which Bobby attends.
>
> Carol is angry at the way children are treated in society. She feels that the total responsibility for future generations falls on the mother and that society offers almost no support at all.
>
> She has a country fresh look to her, long blonde hair and is wearing a skirt, blouse and platform clogs. When she talks about "how society rips mothers off" her face flushes and her voice raises in anger.
>
> "I have a college degree from a Midwestern university. I got pregnant my senior year and finished school throwing up. My parents were very moral and religious and I couldn't go to them. My father was a tool and die maker and everyone knew us in the town.

531

*A day care center similar to the one where "Carol" works, not for pay, but so that
her son can attend. The cooperative day care center has many advantages, but it
may seem a trap to the single mother. "There is no money to get a baby sitter so
that I can train for anything and the only way I can afford to have him in the
community school is to work there everyday. It's a cycle."*

"I was living with a man eleven years older than me and he said, 'Don't
have an abortion.' By the time we broke up, it was too late.

"I decided to have the baby and give it up for adoption. By this time I was
living with friends in Napa. I'd take long showers and say, I can't offer this
baby anything, I must give it up. Then I would start crying and I'd pat myself
on the shoulder and say, there, there, you can keep your baby. I knew it would
get a good home being a White Anglo-Saxon Protestant baby but I wanted
it.

"When the baby was born, they told me he might be retarded. I looked
at Bobby for three weeks while he was going through the tests and knew I
loved him and that I wanted to keep him.

"I had gone on welfare to have him and decided to move to San Francisco
and look for a job. I called the welfare office and asked if they would pay for
a baby sitter for a week while I looked for a job. They said no. I said, 'But
don't you want me to work to get off welfare?' They said they weren't allowed
to pay for babysitters. I had worked in a hospital as a clerk and as an orderly.
But I couldn't afford anyone to stay with Bobby.

"It was a day to day struggle to raise him that first year. I couldn't afford
disposable diapers and never had enough money to wash the clothes more
than twice a week. Do you know what it's like to have to go dirty? . . . I had

to borrow. Just rent, food, and a few clothes for him plus car expenses, many of them to go to the doctor and see if he was retarded (he wasn't) took up my welfare check.

"To stretch the check further, a friend and I tried to rent a house together. Whenever we said we were two single women with children, doors slammed in our faces. And they slam the doors in your face if you say you are on welfare.

"We live alone and rent and food money just about takes up my check. We haven't had a vacation in four years but this year I've saved a little money to take Bobby to Yosemite.

"I cheat any way I can. If I take a typing job for one day and am away from the community school I never report it. If a friend helps me during the summer when Bobby doesn't go to child care, I deduct as much as I would have had to pay.

"I'm embarrassed about being on welfare but I don't know what else I can do. My parents look at it as being on relief. And when I see people working in terrible jobs, like secretaries or minor bureaucrats whose taxes are paying my welfare, I feel really awful.

"But there is no money to get a baby sitter so that I can train for anything and the only way I can afford to have him in the community school is to work there everyday. It's a cycle.   (Berman 1974:12–15)

The isolation of this young welfare mother and the problem of having no one to leave her child with while she finds work are difficulties faced by many young mothers who were raised in the middle classes. Through a chain of circumstance they find themselves on welfare, but that same set of circumstances has cut them off from their families. Among people raised in poverty, kinship ties and mutual assistance have developed as patterns to help single mothers cope.

The mother-centered family

In 1974, of all families with incomes below the threshold of poverty, 1,054,000 (14.4 percent) were headed by a white woman and 1,024,000 (14.0 percent) were headed by a black woman (U.S. Bureau of the Census 1975:17). More than one out of every four impoverished families in America is headed by a woman, and poor families with a female head are about evenly divided between white and black.

The network of kinship among women sustains the very poor. The ties may or may not include affection; always there is the strong bond of mutual need and a recognition that while one may need more now, perhaps another day may bring illness or misfortune to the other. Reciprocity, mutual assistance, emotional support, counseling, all are part of the mother's role with her children. The woman of this impoverished class is more mother than wife as long as she lives.

The young wife who has been raised in poverty regards her mother as the only reassuring fixture in a threatening world. She may idolize her mother or fear her, but in either case, if she runs out of food it is her

533

mother to whom she will turn first. The abandoned wife or the unmarried mother—the distinction being slender in this class—often lives with her mother, taking care of younger brothers and sisters along with her own children while her mother works. Or the grandmother may take care of the children while the younger woman works. If the mother is dead or distant, or if there is deep conflict between mother and daughter, an aunt or older sister is likely to become a surrogate mother. It is a solution to the needs of two families in which the women must be providers as well as nurturing mothers.

The husband in this class is likely to consider the deep tie between his wife and his mother-in-law natural, even though he may resent the influence his mother-in-law has in his home. The wife adheres to her mother and other close female relatives because this is the greatest security she knows. She learned in childhood that husbands come and go. Continued emotional dependence on her mother and the fear that her husband may leave her—a fear that borders on expectation—increase the probability that he *will* abandon her. The women form a close group to which the husband, by the very fact of his masculinity, can never belong. He is a tolerated outsider in his own household, particularly if the couple live with the wife's mother.

Typically, a bride of this class is reluctant to move too far from her mother. Often an impoverished young couple cannot afford an apartment of their own and must begin their married life sharing a home with the wife's mother or other relatives. The very poor cannot offer their married children the kind of financial assistance that a middle-class family often give their young married children; the poor extend the kind of mutual aid that living close together or in the same household makes possible. Yet, inevitably, the very closeness of living creates friction. If the older woman helps her daughter too much, the husband may feel that his wife is shirking her duties; if the daughter discusses marital problems in detail with her mother or reveals such things as the amount of her husband's income to her mother, the husband may regard this as a betrayal of conjugal confidence (Komarovsky 1967:118).

Because the women living in poverty, regardless of racial or ethnic group, recognize that one of the few avenues of escape open to their daughters is a good marriage (that is, a legal marriage to a man who will be able to get and keep a steady job), the mother is likely to be highly critical of a son-in-law who obviously will not be able to rise above poverty. If the girl has completed high school, urged on by a mother eager to give her the best possible chance in life, the mother may be bitter if the girl marries a high school dropout, "throws herself away" on a man very like her father.

If a struggle for power develops between a man and his mother-in-law, the man may feel at a disadvantage in terms of emotional leverage and verbal facility (words and tears are a woman's weapons, among the chronically poor), and he may resort to physical violence. This can lead to a vicious circle of conflict, arrest for wife beating (it is usually the wife rather than the mother-in-law who gets pummeled), recriminations, further conflict, and eventual marital failure.

Yet there are some marriages in which the mother-in-law contributes to marital stability. The husband and his wife's mother may form a friendly alliance for the management of the younger woman. If the mother likes her son-in-law, she may counsel her daughter to submit and endure, to accept in good grace the lot of a poor man's wife. The husband may ask his mother-in-law to intercede: "She listens to you." Or he may be grateful that his mother-in-law is willing to handle his wife's complaints and listen to her chatter (Komarovsky 1967:270–274).

The emotional isolation of the husband from his wife derives from and contributes to her dependence on her mother. The couple of this class seldom forms a tight conjugal unit. Another source of the relative emotional isolation between husband and wife among the chronically dependent poor is the curious (to the middle-class American) fact that neither the man nor the woman may feel that they chose to marry (Besner 1966:16). Their marriage was something that just happened, in their view, like most events in their lives. The fatalism that runs through the world view of this class touches marriage, too. There is a sense that it was inevitable: perhaps it was lucky, perhaps it was not, but it was "in the cards." There are few long courtships among those who live in poverty. Boy meets girl and after a brief flirtation one moves in with the other, with or without benefit of clergy.

In his pioneering studies of the black family, E. Franklin Frazier (1939) described four family forms. One, the *maternal family* as he called it, Frazier attributed to slavery and the life style of the rural South. The other three forms he identified had different origins, but all had in common a patriarchal structure. Frazier argued that the patriarchal form enabled the families that had this structure to adjust better to the urban environment and to rise to become the black middle class. Those blacks who had the rural tradition with its maternal family structure, according to Frazier, were not able to make an adequate transition to city life and, unable to cope, became dependent on charity. Frazier thus saw the dependency and poverty of the poor black family as a result of the maternal family structure, the heritage of slavery.

Oscar Lewis (1965) also found the mother-centered family related to poverty, but in his view, the mother-centered family is a result of the conditions of *urban* poverty. Lewis describes a trend toward mother-centered families among the very poor regardless of racial or ethnic origins (1965:xlvii). Elizabeth Herzog points out that in "poverty studies that deal directly or predominantly with white subjects ... again and again one reads descriptions of the lower class that sound exactly like patterns often ascribed to lower-lower Negroes—and often ... ascribed to the heritage of slavery" (1963:397).

Andrew and Amy Billingsley (1966) describe three variants of a "ma-

535

triarchal" family pattern among lower-class black families: the first is a pattern in which there is not and never was a husband resident in the home, and the unwed mother lives either by herself or (the more common pattern) with her mother or other relatives. The second pattern is one in which "there is a temporary father, or, a series of temporary fathers to children of a single mother" (1966:150). According to the Billingsleys, this pattern is like the first in being typically "matrilocal" (residence with the mother's kin), although the woman may live at one time or another in a residence provided by one of her "husbands." The third matriarchal form that the Billingsleys describe is one where "there is a stable father in the family but where the mother is still the dominant authority figure. This often occurs where 'weak' fathers have an unstable and precarious relationship to the labor market and are not able to either support their families or to exercise their parental authority" (1966:150). If this last is indeed a variant of the matriarchal family, then it would have to follow that there are only matriarchal families living in our inner-city slums.

Such terms as *matriarchal* and *matrilocal* have formal anthropological meanings that make them, strictly speaking, applicable in our society only to some American Indian tribes. In a matriarchal family there *is* a male authority figure: the mother's brother. Every man has a well-defined role with his own children and an important role as disciplinarian and authority figure with his sister's children. Where this pattern survives on the reservation, it assuredly is not a symptom of family disintegration.

Throughout the rest of American society, however, the father is expected to be the head of the family and to provide support and a place of residence: role expectations that are remnants of an earlier patriarchal and patrilocal tendency in the cultures that fed into the American mainstream and in the various ethnic subcultures that are still discernible within it: Mexican-American, Chinese-American, Italian-American, Polish-American, and so on. Nor is the expectation that a man should support his family absent in the black community. As Frazier noted, it is the pattern of the black middle class. That the husband and father should support his family is not only expected in the black community, it is the reality for a majority of black families.

The woman who must be the sole support of her family bears a heavy burden. The problems of the mother-centered family do not derive from the way women play familial roles among the very poor. The problem is rather that most men trapped in poverty have difficulty playing any familial role. The mother-centered family is a form of coping with this reality; it is "making do with string."

The marginal husband

The husband in the chronically dependent family presents a paradox: he is at once feared and powerless. To understand why, it is necessary to look at the cultural patterns of which his role is a vestige. As indicated above,

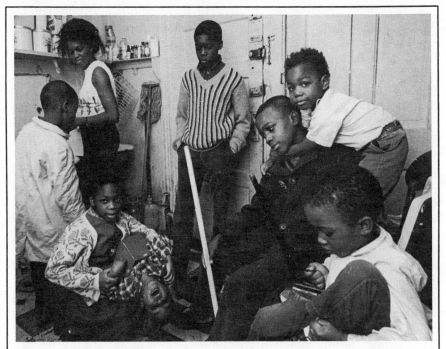

The woman who must be the sole support of her family bears a heavy burden. The problems of the mother-centered family do not derive from the way women play familial roles among the very poor. The problem is rather that most men trapped in poverty have difficulty playing any familial role. The mother-centered family is a form of coping with this reality; it is "making do with string."

most of the people who live in the urban slums are either migrants from rural areas or the descendants of such migrants. The family patterns of rural communities are a buttress against the shattering impact of poverty. But such family patterns seldom remain intact when people are transplanted to the rotting core of cities.

Among the rural poor, husband and wife have highly segregated roles that complement each other without much overlapping. The man and his sons, and perhaps his brothers and uncles, do the heavy work in the fields. If the women and younger children work in the fields, picking or weeding or hoeing, they usually do so while the men are working another field. The woman's role involves both productive labor (gardening, caring for poultry, picking cotton) and maintenance chores (caring for the house and children, cooking for the men). The husband is dominant and likely to be a heavy-handed disciplinarian; the wife and mother is the source of affection and emotional security: roles that are close to those played by the workingman and his wife, with the added conservatism of semiliterate or illiterate people who must rely on tradition.

537

For many urban poor, these were the traditional family patterns "down home," wherever that may have been. Some families living in the slums of Chicago, Cincinnati, or Detroit once farmed a few gullied acres in the "piney woods" South, living in weathered houses with long front porches and crumbling brick chimneys, houses built of green pine boards, long shrunken in the summer sun. The cracks between the boards let in flies and mosquitoes in summer. Newspapers tacked up on the inside helped cover the cracks, but the wind came through the newspaper in winter, and even in the south of Georgia it is cold on a January morning when the frost lies white on the red clay road.

Not all these poor farmers were black. Many were white men—with faces and necks burned a dull brick-red by the sun under which they labored. Their women were shapeless from childbearing and a diet of grits and greens and salt pork. They wore faded print dresses to which children clung, children with runny red eyes and pinched faces, barefoot children in a land of hookworm. Men, women, and children—walled in by self-perpetuating ignorance, suspicious of strangers. But certain of one thing: they were white.

To their bitter surprise, when these people moved into the slums of northern cities, they discovered that they were regarded as drunken, thieving, brawling, people at the bottom: the spot the blacks had occupied "down home." Lumped with displaced miners from Appalachia, the dispossessed red-dirt farmers from the southern flatlands find they are classed as "hillbillies," white, Anglo-Saxon, Protestant, but "hard-core" poor.

Farming or mining was the way of life for the men, but the skills to which they were raised do not transfer readily to the industrial world of the city. Semiliterate, they cannot fill out application forms or understand the instructions on a machine if they find a factory job; used to hand implements, they do not understand complicated machinery. And there is a growing paucity of semiskilled jobs as factories install automated assembly lines. It is difficult for these men even to enjoy the simple pastimes of the traditional men's culture in which they were raised. As Hal Bruno described the men of Chicago's "hillbilly" section:

> There's a difference in social mores that can get a man into trouble in the city. If you fight with your wife, for example, annoyed neighbors will call the police. At the end of the day down home, the workingman and his friend passed a jug around as they sat on the front porch to watch the sunset. There's no porch in Chicago, so they chip in for a six-pack of beer and settle down on the curb in front of a Wilson Avenue saloon. A squad car goes by and the policemen order the curbstone drinkers to move along. They protest that they aren't doing anything wrong, so the cops give them a routine frisking and come up with a couple of hunting knives. Every able-bodied man carried one down home, but it's against the law in the city and they're hauled off to jail for carrying concealed weapons. (Bruno 1964:29)

538

"Down home" it was given that a man—especially a white man—was superior. It was not what he had accomplished that made him superior; it was what he was born to be. The fact of his sex and his race gave him *ascribed* status. In the confused world of the city slum, in which *the labor and the leisure of the men's world he knew are no longer relevant,* he has no role, only the ascribed status. He is still a man, but the only way he can assert his male dominance is in occasional violent outbursts.

Male dominance is equally evident among Puerto Rican and Mexican slum families, where there is a name for it: *machismo,* the cult of Super Male. The same underlying pattern is found among the black families of urban slum ghettos. Herzog says, "There may be differences in the degree and expression of the sex war and the cult of masculine superiority among Negroes and whites on the lowest socioeconomic level. Nevertheless, the similarities are striking" (1963:400).

Because so much attention has been paid to the fact that the black family is mother-centered, it has not always been noted that there is a countervailing theme of male superiority. As Herzog observes: "If the women are the dominant sex among low-income Negroes, the women do not know it. On that score, one of them remarked, 'I've often heard a woman wish she was a man, but I never heard a man wish he was a woman' " (1963:400).

In *Tally's Corner,* a study of black "streetcorner" men, Elliot Liebow (1967) indicates that the black wife wants her husband to support the family and, more than that, wants him to assert his status as head of the family. She may provoke her husband deliberately into a violent assertion of his status:

The husband who sometimes responds to this testing and challenging by slapping his wife's face or putting his fist in her mouth is frequently surprised at the satisfactory results. He does not understand—or does not admit to understanding—the woman's motives and may attribute them to some vague impulse to masochism latent in women. Leroy, for example, was getting ready to take his leave from the streetcorner. He said he was going home to see what "Mouth" (Charlene) wanted. She probably wanted a whipping, he said; she seems to beg him to beat her. Afterwards, she's "tame as a baby, sweet as she can be."

Then he told of how, the day before, Charlene beat on him with a broomstick, daring him to slap her, but he simply walked out because he knew this would hurt her more than a whipping. Doubtless, it did. For Charlene, like Lorena, wanted some tangible evidence that her husband cared about her, about them as a family, and that he was willing to fight to establish and protect his (nominal) status as head of the family. She openly envied Shirley who, when things were going tolerably well for her and Richard, took pleasure in boasting to Charlene, Lorena, and other women that Richard pushed her around, insisted she stay off the street, and enforced the rule that she be up early every morning, dress the children, and clean the house. For

539

evidence of this kind of concern, Charlene would gladly pay the price of a slap in the face or a pushing around. All too often, however, Leroy declined to accept the challenge, or accepting it, was himself reduced, like John, to tears of shame, helplessness, and defeat.

Thus, marriage is an occasion of failure. To stay married is to live with your failure, to be confronted by it day in and day out. It is to live in a world whose standards of manliness are forever beyond one's reach, where one is continuously tested and challenged and continually found wanting. In self-defense, the husband retreats to the streetcorner. Here, where the measure of man is considerably smaller, and where weaknesses are somehow turned upside down and almost magically transformed into strengths, he can be, once again, a man among men. (Liebow 1967:134–136)

The traditional cultures from which the people of the urban slums came had mother-centered families in one sense: home was the woman's domain and the mother was the emotional center and balance wheel of the family. Her role within the home and as an additional provider could remain intact when the family moved to the city. But the complementary role of her husband as economic provider and task leader has been lopped off by social and technological change; economically, the husband and father has been replaced by the Welfare Department. He is a marginal man in his own family.

Liebow makes it quite clear that the ideal for the poor black man—and woman—is that the husband should support his family, but that it is not always possible for the black husband to realize this goal:

The primacy ascribed to financial support derives from two analytically separable sources of value: the simple use value, in and of itself, of supporting and maintaining the lives of one's wife and children; and the expressive or symbolic value associated with providing this support. Men and women both agree that providing financial support has a weightiness that goes beyond its simple use value. One of the men was talking to several others, derogating someone he didn't particularly care for. "But one thing you got to say," he conceded, "when he was living with her, he stone took care of her and the children."

By itself, the plain fact of supporting one's wife and children defines the principal obligation of a husband. But the expressive value carried by the providing of this support elevates the husband to manliness. He who provides for his wife and children has gone a long way toward meeting his obligations to his family as he sees them. Drinking, gambling, or seeing other women may detract from but cannot, by themselves, nullify his performance. Both as husband and father, he has gone a long way toward proving himself a man.

Few married men, however, do in fact support their families over sustained periods of time. Money is chronically in short supply and chronically a source of dissension in the home. (Liebow 1967:130–131)

A man who has been unable to find anything but temporary employment at low pay, and not even this kind of job for months, a man who sits

A man who has been unable to find anything but temporary employment at low pay, and not even this kind of job for months, a man who has reached the point where he can no longer make himself wait in line for a job interview because he has been turned away so often that defeat is an almost palpable presence that walks beside him, a man who sees the welfare check or his wife's meager earnings support the children—and himself—may feel that if he leaves home, at least he will not be a burden.

in front of the television set and waits for another day to pass, a man who has reached the point where he can no longer make himself wait in line for a job interview because he has been turned away so often that defeat is an almost palpable presence that walks beside him, a man who sees the welfare check or his wife's meager earnings support the children—and himself—may feel that if he leaves at least he will not be a burden.

Marriage versus consensual union

The middle classes may be largely unaware of the values and the norms of poverty, but the very poor are quite cognizant of middle-class values even if such values do not seem to apply to life in the slums. Grade school teachers are predominantly middle-class, whatever their ethnic origins, and the pupils in a slum school learn what the teacher expects, whether or not they apply it to themselves. The mass media, especially television, bring the dominant values into the deteriorated apartments and converted barracks and concrete monoliths that house the poor. And so it is that the slum dweller will often give the responses that middle-class social workers, teachers, and poll takers seem to expect, for one of the maxims of the

541

poor is that it is safest to say what those in authority want to hear. For this reason, although they will usually say that marriage is the most desirable form of sexual union, a large proportion of the very poor live in the more flexible consensual union (Rodman 1964).

The common-law marriage, where it is still recognized by law, is as difficult to leave as a marriage that has had all of the blessings of church and state. But what most people have in mind when they refer to common-law marriage is more accurately described as a consensual union. The latter is as easily dissolved as it is formed. This is the reason why the larger society frowns on such unions, and the reason why the people who live in poverty often prefer them.

The middle classes stress the value of a stable marriage and view each marriage, on the wedding day, as a mating until death. But divorce does provide a release from those marriages that prove to have been a gross mismatch—for those who can afford divorce, which the people of poverty usually cannot. To people who have no money for legal fees, who see the courts as the enemy camp, a divorce may seem an impossibility. The greater freedom to enter and leave relationships that the consensual union provides may seem preferable to a legal marriage, for a variety of reasons.

Temporary separations are common among the very poor, and often for reasons that have little to do with the relationship between husband and wife. The poor spend more time in jail than do the affluent. Without going into the matter of why they have higher arrest and conviction rates, it may be noted that prison, too, is part of the way of life of many of the unstable, urban poor, and that being in the "slammer" is not a disgrace forever among these people. It is viewed with somewhat the same inevitability that the middle classes regard an occasional traffic ticket. If the couple are legally married, the wife and children may find the years that the husband and father spends in prison years of real hardship. The woman is not free to acquire another spouse (or may be afraid of the possible consequences of doing so when the time comes that her husband is free again).

Or a husband may leave to seek a job elsewhere, if he cannot find employment where the family lives. Word of mouth may bring the hope of a job in some distant city, and a man can travel more cheaply by himself. If the job works out he can send for his family, but often it does not and he drifts for awhile. Whether he has deserted or not may become difficult to determine; not even he may know for sure. While the husband is gone to seek employment, his family may have to move in with relatives to survive. Usually, they move in with the woman's relatives. If they had gone with the husband and no job had been forthcoming, they would have been stranded among strangers; reluctance to leave the comparative security of the network of female relatives is a major reason why the wife usually stays behind. It is her mother, not her husband, who promises the best hope of feeding the children.

If the union is a consensual one, the woman is free to form a new relationship with a man who is present and can contribute to her support, and the former "husband" is also free to set up a new relationship where he is (assuming he is not in prison). Lewis comments that, "to men who have no steady jobs or other sources of income, who do not own property and have no wealth to pass on to their children, who are present-time oriented and who want to avoid the expense and legal difficulties involved in formal marriage and divorce, free unions or consensual marriage makes a lot of sense" (1965:xlvi).

It may not be surprising to the middle class that a man might wish to avoid the obligations of marriage; the notion accords with the middle-class image of the poor. But surely the woman would want the protection of a legal union? In the middle-class view, it is the man who provides for the woman, and marriage is thus a source of security for women and children. In the reality of poverty, it is often the woman who must provide for herself, her children, and her man, even though the expectation here, too, is that it is the husband who should provide. For people who live in chronic poverty it is often the case that women can find employment when there is none for men. Yet as indicated above, the women of this impoverished class are subservient; men still have authority simply because they are male—and because they are stronger. A wife may provoke her husband, but she may well have real fear of a broken nose or a broken jaw if she gets too assertive. So a poor woman may feel that it is safer, all things considered, not to be legally married. A husband might insist on his right to her wages or to such personal effects as she may acquire: a television set or used living room furniture that could be pawned or sold or put up as collateral for a loan. Lewis notes:

> Women will often turn down offers of marriage because they feel it ties them down to men who are immature, punishing and generally unreliable. Women feel that consensual union gives them a better break; it gives them some of the freedom and flexibility that men have. By not giving the fathers of their children legal status as husbands, the women have a stronger claim on their children if they decide to leave their men. (Lewis 1965:xlvi)

Commenting on family patterns among the poor of Trinidad, Hyman Rodman describes three forms of union that closely parallel the three "matriarchal" forms that the Billingsleys note among poor American black families. However, Rodman uses the terms employed by the people involved to describe these relationships: "friending" (a relationship of some duration that does not involve cohabitation); "living" (consensual union); and "married" (1964:66). Rodman contends that using the terms applied by the people involved avoids the built-in bias of middle-class labels and is essential to "a better understanding of what I regard as a major middle-class misconception of lower-class families—viewing cer-

543

Emerging marital patterns and some alternatives

tain patterns as *problems* when, in reality, they can as easily be viewed as *solutions*" (1964:66).

For many of the people trapped below the poverty line, the consensual union is seen as a solution. For the totally impoverished, even a consensual union may not be economically feasible, and "friending," combined with the custom of two generations of women living together and caring for their children, may be a solution to the problem of how to have some family life—and some sex—even though very poor. There are indications that sexual activity follows a pattern similar to the consumption of food among the poverty-stricken: long periods of deprivation alleviated by brief periods of indulgence.

To the middle-class observer, the very poor often seem to be without morals or even scruples. But the slum has its own code. The norms are not middle-class norms, but they exist. A study of low-income families made in Washington, D.C., suggests that there are some basic marital norms that the very poor take for granted (which is the basic test for a norm: the assumption that "everyone" acts the same way and makes the same value judgments). Herzog summarized these axioms as follows:

> The first is that a good marriage is far better than no marriage. The second is that a bad marriage is far worse than no marriage. The third is that for a girl to bear a child out of wedlock is unfortunate, but does not necessarily impair her chances for a good marriage. (Herzog 1963:398)

There are social classes in which marriage is important because it confers legitimacy upon the children of the union. In these classes, legitimacy is important because there are property rights to be transmitted, positions of hereditary power to be handed down the legitimate line. These classes do not live in the inner-city slums. As Rodman observes (1964:65): "words like *promiscuity, illegitimacy,* and *desertion* are not part of the lower-class vocabulary," and, he contends, it is "inaccurate to describe lower-class behavior in this way." According to Rodman, such terms carry middle-class meanings and are loaded with middle-class value judgments, and ought not to be used to describe the behaviors with which people cope with poverty. These, too, are ways of "making do with string."

References

Berman, Susan. 1974. "Why They Cheat on Welfare." *California Living Magazine* (July 7):10–15.

Besner, Arthur. 1966. "Economic Deprivation and Family Patterns." In *Low-Income Life Styles,* edited by L. M. Irelan, pp. 15–29. Washington, D.C.: U.S. Department of Health, Education, and Welfare, Welfare Administration Publication no. 14.

Billingsley, Andrew, and Amy Tate Billingsley. 1966. "Illegitimacy and Patterns of Negro Family Life." In *The Unwed Mother,* edited by Robert W. Roberts, pp. 149–151. New York: Harper & Row.

Bruno, Hal. 1964. "Chicago's Hillbilly Ghetto." *The Reporter* 30 (June 4):28–31.

Frazier, E. Franklin. 1939. *The Negro Family in the United States.* Chicago: University of Chicago Press.

Herzog, Elizabeth. 1963. "Some Assumptions about the Poor," *Social Service Review* 37 (December):389–401.

Keyserling, Leon. 1961. *Poverty and Deprivation in the United States.* Washington, D.C.: Conference on Economic Progress.

Komarovsky, Mirra. 1967. *Blue-Collar Marriage.* New York: Random House.

Lewis, Oscar. 1965. *La Vida: A Puerto Rican Family in the Culture of Poverty—San Juan and New York.* New York: Random House.

Liebow, Elliot. 1967. *Tally's Corner: A Study of Negro Streetcorner Men.* Boston: Little, Brown and Company.

Miller, S. M. 1964. "The American Lower Classes: A Typological Approach." *Social Research* 31 (Spring):1–22.

Rainwater, Lee. 1970. *Behind Ghetto Walls.* Chicago: Aldine Publishing Company.

Rodman, Hyman. 1964. "Middle-Class Misconceptions about Lower-Class Families." In *Blue-Collar World: Studies of the American Worker,* edited by Arthur B. Shostak and William Gomberg, pp. 59–69. © 1964. Reprinted by permission of Prentice-Hall, Inc., Englewood Cliffs, N.J.

U.S. Bureau of the Census. 1972. *Census of Population: 1970 Marital Status, Final Report.* Washington, D.C.: U.S. Government Printing Office.

———. 1975. *Money Income and Poverty Status of Families and Persons in the United States: 1974* (Series P-60). Washington, D.C.: U.S. Government Printing Office.

U.S. Bureau of Labor Statistics. 1974. *Handbook of Labor Statistics.* Washington, D.C.: U.S. Government Printing Office.

Wiltse, Kermit T., and Robert W. Roberts. 1966. "Illegitimacy and the AFDC Program." In *The Unwed Mother,* edited by Robert W. Roberts, pp. 218–230. New York: Harper & Row.

Women's Bureau, U.S. Department of Labor. 1975. *Handbook on Women Workers* (Bulletin 297). Washington, D.C.: U.S. Government Printing Office.

Suggested readings

Herzog, Elizabeth. 1967. *About the Poor: Some Facts and Some Fictions.* Washington, D.C.: U.S. Government Printing Office. Children's Bureau publication no. 451-1967. Paper. This publication, a collection of articles by a senior researcher at the Children's Bureau, has already been recommended as collateral reading for the chapter on marriage and legitimacy. Some of the articles are also particularly appropriate reading to accompany this chapter on the poor family, for they contain penetrating analysis of the family patterns of the very poor.

Lewis, Oscar. 1966. *La Vida.* Vintage Books, a division of Random House. Paper. The urban anthropologist who first defined and analyzed the culture of poverty describes an extended Puerto Rican family in San Juan and New York. The introductory statement presents the theoretical and analytical structure of the book. Much of the rest consists of translations of autobiographical statements by members of the Puerto Rican family. Chapter titles capture much of the flavor of the work. The autobiographical sketch by Fernanda is titled "You Can't Cover Up the Sky with Your Hand;" that by Erasmo is called "A Whore in the Morning Disgusts Me."

545

Emerging marital patterns and some alternatives   Rainwater, Lee. 1970. *Behind Ghetto Walls: Black Family Life in a Federal Slum.* Chicago: Aldine Publishing Company. A massive study of the family lives of the 10,000 blacks, children and adults, who lived in the Pruitt-Igoe housing project in St. Louis (a project that was later demolished by the federal government) formed the basis for this book. But it is not primarily a book of statistical information. Individual families are presented in case studies, and analytical chapters deal with marital roles and marital disruption, parents and children, and negro lower-class identity and culture.

20 Interracial marriage

I don't know if I ever told him or not, but I did get a lot of—from the black fellows on the campus—"You like him because he's white." But that had never occurred to me. He was just another individual as far as I was concerned. And I don't know, it was—that was sort of in the background. I am sure it was there, but it just wasn't foremost in my mind. I thought maybe there would be some problems, you know, later on after we were married, but so what?

A black woman married to
a white man

Marriages that cross racial lines, especially marriages between white and black, are still controversial in our society. Such marriages were once legally forbidden in most states and are still socially suspect. A Harris poll conducted in 1971[1] indicated that although more than three out of four respondents of all races (77 percent) in a national sample agreed that young people of different races are going to be seeing each other "socially" regardless of the opinion of their elders, there were nonetheless 40 percent who agreed that interracial marriages that produced "mixed-blood" children seemed to violate "God's law." Yet 62 percent of this national sample believed that love between "mature people" was more important to a successful marriage than any racial difference, and 70 percent believed that no law should tell a couple that they cannot marry because of racial difference.

The legal question was settled by the United States Supreme Court in the Loving decision in 1967. As we saw in Chapter 9, this decision made it clear that the right to marry is a fundamental civil right, protected by the U.S. Constitution. But there is a residue of conflicting attitudes and myths that complicate and restrict interracial marriage. That the attitudes expressed by the respondents in the Harris poll reflected myths and fears as often as experience is indicated by the finding that 55 percent of the persons interviewed did not know anyone who had even dated someone of a different race.

Racial endogamy and caste barriers

The fear of interracial marriage expressed by the white population is based in part on traditional attitudes, in part on racial pride, and in part on the fear of losing social-caste status. A society has a caste system if there is no possibility for a person from a subordinate group to penetrate a higher social level, either by achievement or by marriage. Theoretically, a caste system is completely closed. No real society has ever been completely closed, nor has one ever been completely open. But the caste structure that existed until the recent past in India is often taken as an example of a closed caste system. There were two principal means of maintaining caste lines in India: a rigid barrier to certain occupations for all but persons of appropriate caste, and caste endogamy, the requirement that persons marry only within their own caste.

In the United States there has been—and to some degree there remains—a *de facto* caste line based on race. It has been maintained in the past by occupational barriers, by the prohibition of interracial marriage, and by defining as black all children of mixed white and black ancestry. Even where interracial marriage has been legal, it has not been possible for the white spouse to confer his or her caste status on the black.

---

[1]The poll was conducted for *Life* magazine and is reported in the May 28, 1971, issue, pp. 66–67.

It is however, possible for a person of racially mixed origins to move up in terms of caste if he or she has so little black ancestry that appearance does not reveal it. But even though such persons may be able to "pass," they may feel compelled to announce their "real" racial identity, for the culture teaches them that if they do not, they are impostors, traitors to "their" race, or both. It is this custom of defining all persons with *any* black ancestry as black that keeps the racial caste system intact in America. If it disappeared, the class structure would not vanish; there would still be the rich and the poor and people with varying levels of power and influence, but the class hierarchy would no longer be cut through by a color bar.

A single black ancestor—one in eight, one in sixteen—is presumed sufficient to make an individual unacceptable as a member of the dominant white caste. This is not true of all racial mixture in America. The person who numbers one American Indian among his eight great-grandparents is not considered an Indian. He or she is considered white, although often proud of the remote connection with the Cherokee, Comanche, Apache, Sioux, or other warrior nation. (Any Indian who lived in the nineteenth century—when all our great-grandparents were born—now qualifies as a Noble Red Man: this is not, however, the status accorded to the red man's full-blooded descendants, most of whom live on the least fertile fragments of their ancestral territory and are in danger of losing even these to flood control projects.)

The American who is one-quarter Indian is likely to be classed as white for most social purposes, is likely to consider himself a member of the white community, and his children will be accepted as white. His one-quarter Indian ancestry is not much different, socially, from being one-quarter Irish (and he might well reckon himself both). However, the half-breed has a more ambiguous status, depending on his life-style and where he lives. He is usually a marginal person who may feel out of phase with both his Indian heritage and the white world; he may identify with one or the other, both or neither. (In this decade of rising Indian consciousness and activism, the half-breed seems to be identifying more often with the Indian side of his ancestry.)

The half-breed has a marginal status if his ancestry is half white and half Indian, Chinese, Japanese, Polynesian, or the like. But if he is half black, whatever his other racial heritage may be, he is considered black in our society. There are other societies where the mulatto has a separate status, a status that may be so stable that it has a subculture of its own (as in Jamaica). But in America, the mulatto is black.

The caste line in America is drawn between white (including persons with one-quarter or less Indian, Chinese, Japanese, or other ancestry) and black (including people with seven-eighths or more white, Indian, or Oriental ancestry). Asians and Indians are simply "other," outside the caste structure. Most attempts to form coalitions of nonwhite groups in the United States tend to falter, for any other nonwhite group would tend to lose caste if it made common cause with the blacks.

The caste line would gradually be erased from our society if interracial marriages were permitted by custom as well as by law, and if children of mixed parentage were always assigned to the status of their father, whatever race he might be, and whether or not the children were legitimate. The result would be a loss of separate racial identity for all before many generations had passed: a prospect that most whites have traditionally viewed as a disaster, and that some blacks in this era of rising black pride have come to view as undesirable.

The issue of interracial marriage is overlaid with political implications and emotional fervor; it is the most emotionally loaded rule of endogamy in America today. What follows is an attempt to describe the history and function of both customs and laws that prohibited interracial marriage in the past, in a manner as dispassionate and apolitical as possible.

All rules of endogamy exist in an attempt to maintain the existence of the group using them. If each generation is expected to be a replica of the preceding generation, the likelihood of duplicating the older generation is greatest if the parents are as like each other as is possible without violating the incest taboo. Brothers and sisters may be forbidden to marry, but their children may be required to marry each other—the common pattern in some primitive societies in which the pool of eligibles is limited to cross-cousins. In America, racial groups have come to be regarded as the equivalent of lineage groups. Yet even by 1930, Melville Herskovits estimated that no more than 20 percent of American negroes were of unmixed African descent (Herskovits 1930:240). It would be futile to hazard a guess as to what proportion of the white population of America is racially "pure." Racial admixture in the Old World started before King Solomon wooed the Queen of Sheba. Several Mongol invasions of Europe, prolonged contact between the Moors and southern Europeans, and at least three centuries of mixing and "passing" between three races in the Western Hemisphere make any claims to racial purity silly. But when something silly becomes sacrosanct, the social consequences are brutally real.

In a society in which lineage rather than achievement is the basis of class position and power, the upper class will lose its claim to superior position if the purity of the lineage is not maintained. In a society in which race rather than achievement is the basis for social placement, the dominant race will lose its claim to superiority unless racial "purity" is maintained. As indicated in an earlier chapter, when the question of the purity of the dominant male lineage is paramount in a society, the chastity of the wife is of great social significance. In a society stratified by race, women of the dominant race are taboo to men of the subordinate race. In *The Mind of the South*, W. J. Cash observed:

[The] Southern woman's place in the Southern mind proceeded primarily from the natural tendency of the great basic pattern of pride in superiority of race to center upon her as the perpetuator of that superiority in legitimate line, and attached itself precisely, and before everything else, to her enormous remoteness from the males of the inferior group, to the absolute taboo on any sexual approach to her by the Negro.   (Cash 1941:116)

All rules of endogamy are supposed to preserve the purity of the characteristics that set one group off from another: religious belief, ethnic or racial ancestry. The preservation of the group by its replacement with the same kind of people is the goal, and the young are pressured to marry within their own group for the sake of their children. The manifest function of racial endogamy is *racial purity of the dominant caste.* The composition of the subordinate caste does not greatly concern a dominant racial caste, for the subordinates can be largely a residual category of outcastes. If all children of mixed ancestry are assigned to the subordinate race, they will pose no threat to the dominant one. This is why all children with any black ancestry are considered black.

If the women of the dominant race were taboo to the men of the subordinate race, the converse did not have to be true. If the mother of a child of mixed ancestry belonged to the subordinate race, there was no question of the disruption of the power structure, provided that the child was illegitimate. Only the legitimate child inherits the property and power of his father. If marriage between the races is forbidden, there will be no legitimate children of mixed unions. This is why the prohibition of marriage across racial lines was more critical to the preservation of the old caste structure than the prohibition of racial mixture as such. Cash stated that:

the abolition of slavery, in destroying the rigid fixity of the black at the bottom of the scale, in throwing open to him at least the legal opportunity to advance, had inevitably opened up to the mind of every Southerner a vista at the end of which stood the overthrow of this taboo. If it was given to the black to advance at all, who could say (once more the logic of the doctrine of his inherent inferiority would not hold) that he would not one day advance the whole way and lay claim to complete equality, including, specifically, the ever crucial right of marriage?   (Cash 1941:116)

The latent function of preserving the power and privilege of the dominant white race was more honored than the manifest function of preserving racial purity. Concubinage may and often does cross racial lines; it is accepted where marriage is not, because concubinage does not confer the man's status on the woman, or legitimacy on the children of the union. Interracial marriage has long been permitted in some parts of the United States, however, and where this is the case, custom has preserved the caste line by assigning the children of such marriages to the lower caste, even though they are legitimate.

Servitude and marriage: a brief history

One of the myths to which northerners cling is the belief that from the day of the landing at Plymouth Rock the North has always been a free society, and that until the guns were stacked at Appomattox the South was always a land of slaves. But as Oscar Handlin (1957) makes clear, in the early colonial period there were several degrees of free and "unfree" in America, in the North as well as the South. Men who were born free could fall into servitude through poverty, crime, or misfortune. If a man were in debt, his goods could be sold to pay his creditors; if his goods did not suffice to pay his debts, he himself could be sold at auction for a term of years. Men who were convicted of major felonies could be sold for life, and even conviction of vagrancy or simply "absence of a fixed occupation" meant the possibility of being sold for a term of labor—in England *and* in her American colonies in the seventeenth century.

A man could sell his wife and children into servitude. Idle children were considered a disgrace to their parents. According to Handlin, "in 1646, Virginia county commissioners were authorized to send to work in the public flaxhouse two youngsters from each county kept at home by the 'fond indulgence or perverse obstinacy' of their parents. Orphans, bastards, and the offspring of servants were similarly subject to disposal at the will of officials" (1957:6).

Many English, Scottish, and Welsh immigrants who lacked money for passage to America paid by selling their labor for a fixed number of years. Both men and women became indentured servants. At the end of their term, they were free, but when the frontier was the forest just beyond the clearing and hostile Indians were ready to dispute any new settler's claim to land, the servants might prefer to sign on for another term of years.

The blacks thus entered a colonial America in which there were whites who were not free; until the last quarter of the seventeenth century the status of black bond servants was not very different from that of white bond servants, all of whom could have their contracts bartered for a profit or transferred if their master fell into debt or died. Handlin observes that: "when one remembers that the transportation of Irish servants was also known as the 'slave trade,' then it is clear that those who sold and those who bought the Negro, if they troubled to consider legal status at all, still thought of him simply as a low servant" (1957:10).

As settlements spread, markets grew, and labor became more valuable, the colonists tried to encourage immigration of workers. They preferred white servants, who spoke their language and were more like themselves. But word had gone back to England, Scotland, and Wales, via seamen on sailing vessels, that in the New World the life of a servant was hard. In an attempt to change this image and encourage immigration, the colonists began to pass laws improving the conditions under which a bond servant worked and which made it possible for him to become a free landowner himself at the end of his term of servitude.

*Stacked rifles, Petersburg, Virginia, 1865. One of the myths to which Northerners
cling is the belief that from the day of the landing at Plymouth Rock the North has
always been a free society and that until the guns were stacked at Appomattox, the
South was always a land of slaves. But in the early colonial period there were several
degrees of free and "unfree" in America, north as well as south.*

These new laws applied only to white bond servants. The black was
in communication with no one; nothing that improved his condition would
encourage his friends and relatives to come to America. "To raise the
status of Europeans by shortening their terms would ultimately increase
the available hands by inducing their compatriots to emigrate," Handlin
points out; "To reduce the Negro's term would produce an immediate
loss and no ultimate gain" (1957:16).

And so from about 1670, the laws of the various colonies began to
differentiate between the status of the white and the black bond servant.
Shortly the result in such colonies as Maryland and Virginia was that the

555

black was to serve *durante vita* (during life). The term *slave* took on a new meaning.

English law had long granted the master an interest in the marriage of his servants, and particularly in the marriage or pregnancy of his maid-servant. When a master paid the price of indenture, from his point of view he had paid in advance for a term of labor. If his bond servant died in childbirth before her term was up (maternal mortality was high in the seventeenth century), the master could not collect compensation for the remaining years of service. If she lived, her child was a drain on time and energy for which the master had paid, and would be fed from the master's table, clothed from his stores. Colonial laws thus provided fines or whippings for bastardy, and the bond servant's fine was paid by compelling her to serve beyond her original term. The father of the child, if another servant, could also be compelled to serve beyond his time of indenture to compensate the master for his loss. Once it was established that the black servant was bound for life, there obviously could be no extension of his term of service. Hence, if the father was black, all that the master could claim was the child (which meant that he had to be responsible for the child's food and lodging until he was old enough to be useful).

Problems arose when one parent was free and the other was not. This had been a knotty problem in feudal Europe, and the law had discouraged the marriage of free peasant and unfree serf because it complicated the status of the child. English law held, however, that in cases of mixed marriage the child was to inherit the status (free or unfree) of the father. Maryland adopted this rule in 1664. The result, according to Handlin, was that "unscrupulous masters instigated intercourse between their Negro males and white females which not only gave them the offspring, but, to boot, the service of the woman for the life of her husband" (1957:18). However common or uncommon this practice may have been, rumors of it discouraged the immigration of young girls from England, Scotland, and Wales.

Virginia had adopted the old bastardy law, under which the status of the child followed the status of the mother. Maryland soon changed its laws so that the status of the mother determined the status of the child. After 1691 the laws of several colonies forbade mixed marriages of slave and free; by that date, these terms had become nearly interchangeable with black and white. In these colonies the child of mixed parentage was illegitimate after this time, and inherited the slave status of the black mother (in what was the usual pattern of mixed parentage).

In the eighteenth century, new ideas about the nature of human beings, equality, and inalienable rights began to concern the educated gentry in France and England, and in the American colonies as well. These ideas were the intellectual force behind the American Revolution and had their clearest expression in the Declaration of Independence. It was difficult to reconcile such beliefs with slaveholding. There were some Americans, such as the Friends (Quakers), who ultimately decided that slavery was incompatible with human rights and should be abolished. For some of these Friends, this meant freeing their own slaves and the loss of a fortune.

There were other Americans who resolved the dilemma by deciding that the blacks were not quite human. The line between free and unfree had become a line determined by color; now in the minds of many whites it also became the boundary separating human from subhuman beings. To marry across such a gulf seemed a crime against nature.

The bloody excesses of slave uprisings in the West Indies seemed to prove the animal nature of the black. Certainly these slave uprisings raised fearful specters in the minds of American slaveholders. The blacks were not to be permitted assimilation through marriage; they would therefore remain separate and potentially dangerous. The slave quarters were enclaves from which violent horrors might rise. Out of a combination of fear and idealism came efforts to send freed slaves back to Africa. Liberia was founded, and many white Americans, including scores of southerners, contributed to what they considered a reasonable and just solution to the dilemma of what to do with the blacks.

At the end of the eighteenth century, slavery seemed to be disappearing in the United States of America. The newly ratified Constitution provided a final date after which there would be no new importation of slaves. Moreover, quite apart from the question of morality, slavery is economically unprofitable except on large landholdings that can utilize large amounts of labor in the production of a cash crop. As the nineteenth century began, there were not many such holdings in the United States. Most of the large estates the Dutch had carved out of New York had been subdivided, New England landholdings had never been large, and the southern plantations were largely confined to the tidelands area (especially around Chesapeake Bay), where rice and indigo were grown. Even tobacco seemed best-suited to production on small farms by farm families who could hire extra hands for seasonal work.

But in England the Industrial Revolution had begun, and the new steam-driven textile mills were blending cotton and linen in cheap, machine-loomed fabrics. Cotton for the looms of Manchester, England—and soon for the looms of Fall River, Massachusetts—came from India, Egypt, China, and the West Indies. Cotton came from places where human labor was so plentiful and cheap that even the long task of separating cotton fibers from cotton seeds manually could be profitable (Mantoux 1962: 201).

In Georgia, cotton grew wild. Sometimes cotton grew around the cabin door, planted by the farm wife as an ornamental plant. But labor costs were too high for cotton to be a profitable cash crop. This was true even for the slaveowner, for slaves were more expensive in the American South than in the West Indies. Then Eli Whitney, a Yankee from New Haven, invented the simple cotton gin for removing the fibers from the seeds. Suddenly there were fortunes to be made in cotton—provided that

557

the Indians could be driven out of the woods and beyond the Mississippi and that slaves could be obtained in sufficient numbers for the hand labor required to grow cotton.

The blacks who had so recently seemed an alien menace to be shipped back to Africa were suddenly perceived as valuable property in short supply. Enslaving the Indians might have seemed an obvious step, but their tribal organization was intact and they fought fiercely. The few who were enslaved were soon classed with the blacks—for slave status and black status were equated, and the child of mixed Indian and black parentage was considered black. And so the Indians were pushed west of the cotton lands, and the blacks were encouraged to breed. Any planter who had more slaves than he could use could sell the extra hands at a profit, and many masters came to regard breeding as a proper function of a female slave.

But if a high birth rate was desired in the slave quarters, it was not desired at the big house. The planter was in the position of the European aristocrat: he wanted sons enough to ensure an heir to the family estate, but too many sons would be a burden. Setting a son up in land and slaves was expensive, and dividing his holdings among numerous sons would reduce them all to small farmers. The planter wanted to found a dynasty, but he did not want too many heirs (Handlin 1957:148).

The age of prudery was developing, with its basic assumption that *ladies* had no sexual interest. This belief provided one part of the solution to the planters' dilemma. When a man built the big house in its pseudo-Greek style, he gave his wife her own bedroom with a lock on the inside of the door. He could court her gallantly, and once in awhile sweep her off her feet. But most of the time her disdain of sex served him well, for it was a check on the number of heirs. His passion was served by trips to the bordellos of New Orleans and by visits to the slave quarters.

Because they *were* Victorian in their view of sexuality, such men were likely to be ashamed of their lust. A guilty conscience often leads people to say—even to believe—that their behavior was invited by their victims. The "animal lust" of the black woman was thus posited as a useful belief, and built into the image that whites formed of blacks. Like most stereotypes, it was built on a kernel of reality, which in this case was simply that the black woman had not been inculcated with Victorian prudery.

Out of this simple fact, and the projected lust he could neither escape nor accept in himself, the white man built an exaggerated image of the sensuality of blacks. Handlin comments: "The master, drawn to the slave by her availability and repelled by consciousness of her inferiority, could purge himself of self-hatred only by locating the responsibility for the low passion in her, and in her not as an individual, but as one of a degraded race of beings" (1957:155).

Because the planter felt he wronged his wife by wenching in the slave quarters, he made amends by placing southern (white) womanhood on a pedestal. He saw the southern woman as virtue incarnate, as different from the lusty mulatto wenches as day from night—as white from black. Cash said: "There was hardly a sermon that did not begin and end with tributes to her honor, hardly a brave speech that did not open and close with the clashing of shields and the flourishing of swords for her glory. At the last, I verily believe, the ranks of the Confederacy went rolling into battle in the misty conviction that it was wholly for her that they fought" (1941:86). The black man who dared to raise his eyes and look at her too long had sullied her, and could expect to suffer.

The sexual exploitation of the black woman did not end with her legal emancipation. Long after the guns of Vicksburg were silent and the ashes of Atlanta were cold, there remained in the minds of white men a sharp division between the white woman, the cold, chaste wife, and the black woman, the sensual animal. A man may have felt guilty for his sexual affairs with black women (as much for "demeaning" himself as for exploiting her), but he did not expect legal punishment for sexual aggression against a black woman. No one else expected him to be punished for it either; white women felt a certain security in the situation, and the blacks were not yet able to protest.

In 1959 in Tallahassee, Florida, three white youths were arrested for the gang rape of a black college girl. To the astonishment of much of the community, the youths were convicted and sentenced to long prison terms. Commenting on the crime, a fragile, white-haired southern lady said to me, as she pulled on her white gloves, "I thought that was what they were for."

Interracial marriage: of time and trends

Interracial marriage has long been legal in a number of states, and since the 1967 decision by the U.S. Supreme Court in the Loving case, it is a recognized civil right. However, the custom of racial endogamy has kept the proportion of interracial marriages low. It is difficult to estimate how low, because most states that permitted interracial marriage in the past have not recorded the race of applicants for marriage licenses, or made any public record of intermarriages. Such data as are available indicate that the first half of the present century was a period in which the rate of marriage between whites and blacks was steadily declining.

Some of the most continuous data available on interracial marriage are from the city of Boston. During the years between 1900 and 1904, about 15 percent of all marriages involving blacks in Boston were to a white spouse (Heer 1966:267). But during the period from 1914 to 1918, only 5 percent of all marriages involving blacks in Boston were racially mixed. This was the most rapid drop recorded in Boston, but the trend was a consistently declining one. Although the data from other areas are sketchy, they suggest that the interracial marriage rate for Boston may have been unusually high in the past compared with that of New York, for example, and even when compared with interracial marriage rates in other cities in Massachusetts. Louis Wirth and Herbert Goldhamer (1944) suggested that strong abolitionist sentiment in Boston in the nineteenth century had made that city at one time "unusually and almost sentimentally receptive to Negroes."

There were also indications of a markedly higher tendency for black men to marry white brides that the converse. E. Franklin Frazier, in *Black Bourgeoisie,* attributed this to a pattern in which the black man of higher social-class status married a white bride from a lower class status (1962: 180). It has also been suggested that immigrant white women may have had a greater tendency to marry middle-class black men than did native-born white women, but the marriage records are too sketchy for this to be more than conjecture.

In 1960, the U.S. Census included a 5 percent sample of all households that revealed the racial ancestry of husband and wife and their respective educational levels. If we assume that education is a reliable index of social-class status, these data give some indication of the frequency with which white-black marriages involve marriage up or down in the class structure. Jessie Bernard (1966) analyzed these data for couples who reported having been married during the decade between 1950 and 1960. She found that 60.3 percent of the black men who married white women were in the same educational bracket as their wives. (For comparison, 63.7 percent of the black men with black wives had the same educational level as their wives.) Of those black men whose education differed from that of their white wives, 18.6 percent had *more* education than their wives; 21.1 percent had *less.* If once there was a tendency for black men to marry white women of lower social-class status, this seems to have disappeared.

David Heer (1966) compiled such statistics as were available from state records of interracial marriages between 1950 and 1964. These data indicate that "marriages between Negro men and white women are much more common than those between white men and Negro women" (1966: 266). In this respect, the earlier trend is confirmed. Heer adds that "most such marriages in fact appear to involve spouses from the same class position" (1966:266) and that some explanation other than the woman's willingness to exchange caste for class status will have to be offered. The earlier decline in interracial marriage seems to have been largely in the proportion of black men marrying white women, and the recent rise is also in this pattern of interracial marriage.

Changing racial distribution may be a factor in the trend toward an increase in interracial marriage. Numerous studies have indicated that there is a significant negative correlation between the proportion of *interfaith* marriages and the proportion of coreligionists in a given city. Single men who migrate to a distant city where there are few women of their own faith tend to marry outside their religious group. There seems to be no comparable research into the matter of interracial marriage and migration, although it is apparent that the immigration of male Filipino workers into California in the 1930s led to a rise in marriages between Filipino men and brides of varying racial backgrounds.

In the absence of data, we can only conjecture why there has been a reversal of the earlier declining trend in interracial marriage. It may be that the changing patterns of black migration since World War II have affected the frequency with which black men marry white women. It may be that the same social and ideological forces that created a favorable climate for racial intermarriage in abolitionist Boston in the nineteenth century have existed again in the recent past, and have made interracial marriage more emotionally and socially acceptable.

The decade of the 1960s was marked by a heightened concern about racism on the part of many young Americans, and the 1970 census indicates that this was a decade of increase in interracial marriages. There was an increase of 159 percent in marriages of white men to black women in the 1960s compared with such marriages in the 1950s. The increase between the two decades in the number of black men who married white women was even greater: 243 percent. A majority (69 percent) of interracial marriages in the 1960s were between black men and white women. Racially mixed marriages were highest among black men with high incomes: 7.5 percent of all black men who married during the period between 1960 and 1970 married a white woman, but 12.0 percent of black men with incomes over $10,000 per year in 1970 who had married during the 1960s chose white brides (U.S. Bureau of the Census 1972:283–284).

Whether the upward trend will continue in the face of rising black pride and black nationalism remains to be seen. In the Harris poll conducted in 1971, 40 percent of the blacks interviewed agreed that black men who had "any pride" would choose members of their own race to marry. Black college women report bitterness and resentment at being shunted aside by the black men on the campus for women who are white and blonde (Downs 1971). The total number of mixed marriages in the population is still small. Only 0.09 percent of all couples who married in the 1950s are racially mixed, and although the number of mixed marriages more than doubled in the 1960s, it still represented only 0.24 percent of all marriages in that decade (U.S. Bureau of the Census 1972:283–284).

"How do I love thee?" motives for interracial marriage

Most couples who enter mixed marriages insist that they have chosen this spouse for the same reasons that anyone else chooses a husband or wife: they have common interests, they fell in love, they saw the beloved as a person, not as a member of any race. Ernest Porterfield (1973) studied twenty couples with mixed marriages, and found that most gave no other reason for marriage. But there were a few exceptions. One black husband was willing to admit that his initial response to the white woman he married was that she would be "something to flaunt" (Porterfield 1973:74). This suggests the status motives that have been imputed to blacks who marry white women for many decades, but it should be noted that one of the motives for marriage that husbands of all races often have is that the

561

sexually desirable woman they marry will be something to flaunt before other men.

There is the appeal of the forbidden, which is often an element in romantic love. And there is also the appeal of the stereotype in romantic images. The black stereotype of white women is that they are more passive than black women, more desirous of pleasing their husbands. Such an image of white women may have been a factor for some of the black men in Porterfield's sample; at least three out of the sixteen black husbands of white wives interviewed admitted that they had held such a belief. However, the reverse stereotype may be an element in the attraction of white men to black women. One of the white men told Porterfield that he had been attracted to his black wife by her qualities of self-sufficiency and independence, and that he felt white women were too dependent and docile (Porterfield 1973:75).

Two of the black women in Porterfield's sample held graduate degrees, and these women had found that most black men with comparable education were not interested in them. These highly educated black women found it difficult to communicate with black men with less education than themselves. A white husband with a comparable education was their solution (Porterfield 1973:75). Sociologically viewed, this is an instance in which educational endogamy took precedence over racial endogamy. The cultural expectation is that the weighting should go the other way. However, educational endogamy is a growing factor in mate choice in America, as described in Chapter 9.

Whatever the elements involved in mate selection, there must be an opportunity to meet and to know each other, and a predisposition to find each other attractive. The following case study involving an interracial couple may help put some tangible human beings into the abstractions of white-black marriage. There are a number of reasons why this marriage may be atypical, but as a real-life example, it may counter the images created out of fear and imagination.

This is a real couple whose identity is disguised by the alteration of names, places, and a few other details. Other than such changes to protect their privacy, their story is the way they told it to me. He is white, was raised in California, holds a master's degree, is a professor at a small college. She is black, was raised in Alabama, left college for marriage in her senior year, is presently working in a civil service job. They had been married about six years at the time of the interview, and have a daughter who was about to enter school. Let the wife's name be Ginny, the husband's name Harry, and their daughter's name Laura.

Q   What were the circumstances in which you met?

Ginny: That's your story, kid, not mine [warm laugh].
Harry: I'm usually the one that tells it, too, I don't know why. I was in the army, on temporary duty at a camp where the all-army track

team was convening. On weekends we'd go in to [the city] and Ginny was going to school at the university there.

As it happened, most of the fellows on the track team were black, and as a result of my first experience at State I had been somewhat acculturated to a black way of life. I was not only quite comfortable around black fellows, but especially when it came to partying and things, I seemed to enjoy them more.

I found that especially when it came to dancing and so on that once I had learned to dance in a more soulful manner, I seemed to appreciate dancing with others who also did, and so we ended up at the co-op at the university—well, actually I had been there a couple of times, and I had made arrangements to meet another girl in the co-op.

Ginny: Not the co-op, the student union. [Like many other wives, she lets her husband tell the story, but stands ready to correct details.]

Harry: Right, student union. And there's this one little area, it's a snack bar and booths and a juke box, and a floor for dancing, and I was waiting for this other girl to come and happened to have been dancing, I think, with another girl—just someone, I don't know who.

But one of my friends was sitting at a booth with another girl, and Ginny was sitting across the table at the same booth, the other bench, and so after dancing, I walked over and I saw my friend sitting there, and I asked Ginny if she minded if I sat down at the table.

She said, "No," and kept looking out the window .... She was quite shy, and I guess it was that she wasn't as communicative as I thought she should be, and so we got to talking but she'd keep looking out the window.

And I guess it appealed to me—she was being coy, I suppose. And as it happened, when the girl that I was supposed to meet there came in, I never looked up, and I haven't spoken to her since [laugh].

My interest had been whetted, I guess, and that's the way it started. Up to that time it was just running into girls and scheming on them if that was what came up, and I wasn't interested in getting married, but I found that—it was one of those things where romantic love prevailed. Within three months we got married.

I suppose one of the reasons I got married was that I talked myself out of it a couple of other times, and so even though there were only three months in the interim between our meeting and our getting married, I felt, well, "Let's do it before I talk myself out of it again."

Ginny: Well, thanks, Honey.

Harry: Well, no—I would have been very—I think I would have been devastated if she had said no. I wanted very, very badly to get married. But the fact remains, I suppose, that it grew out of a tremendous romantic thing .... Do you want to add anything? Little things may have had more of an impact on you than they did on me.

Ginny: Well, no—no, except—the girl you were dancing with—you asked me to dance sometime—

Harry: That's right. That was about the time when I guess people were still—there were some sort of funky dances going around at that time and I had mastered them pretty well, and I guess I was the only white guy in the whole place, and as it happened, as they say, I was "good with my shit," at the time, in fact good enough that she said, "Well!"

Ginny: That's why I kept looking out the window!

Harry: Well, I got sort of funky on the dance floor [laugh] but I don't know, I think she feigned being offended. She was embarrassed though, that's true.

Ginny: No, I just didn't like to do that kind of dancing!

Harry: It wasn't that she was so much offended by the way in which I was dancing but that she was embarrassed, she was downright embarrassed, just—she had that look, you know, and it caught my fancy.

Q Did prior experience prepare you to be attracted to someone of another race?

Harry: As a matter of fact, it was really in my first year at State—I went to State on a track scholarship, and I got to be very good friends with a fellow who at that time was the school record holder in the high jump—a black fellow—and once I decided I was going to State, he and I cultivated quite a good friendship and agreed to room together.

And when we got up there we found that even though the housing people were not supposed to sanction any housing that indicated discriminatory practices, nevertheless it was true that black fellows were having a very difficult time finding places to live, and so the housing people ended up saying, "Well, OK, you guys find a place to live and then we'll approve it."

And at that time there weren't as many black students at State as there are now, and most of them were athletes. And so as it happened, Rich and I also found it very difficult to find a place and ended up staying in an apartment building where I was the only white kid. It was sort of sink or swim.

I had come from beautiful downtown Burbank, grew up in Burbank in a lily-white existence, really. I was a jazz musician for a time, and through athletics, also, I had acquaintances who were black—fellows, black fellows—none of them were close friends, though, but I was somewhat hip in the sense that my exposure to jazz and the jazz subculture gave me a certain advantage, broke me in a little.

But still, my initial exposure to a black subculture was a sink-or-swim kind of thing. And I found that the fellows were holding parties every once in awhile and I had better learn to dance if I wanted to party, and to dance soulfully, and I wasn't about to get out there and do anything if I couldn't do it well.

And so, I suppose, under that kind of pressure, where it was a total immersion, really, I learned very fast. And the more I learned, the more I enjoyed it. I got my feelings hurt, in finding that I had violated some of the more unique folkways of the black subculture but still, all in all, I learned and found that I enjoyed it very much.

By the time I met Ginny I was very, very comfortable even if I were to be the only white person, I didn't feel like an outsider. I would say that I feel more like an outsider around strange black people, simply because if they don't know me from Adam, then they don't know what kind of a gray dude I am, you know.

By the time I met Ginny—I was there with black fellows, and this was a black university—I had adapted well enough that I felt no pain in going over and asking someone to dance and getting out there and showboating and—[laughs]—that kind of thing.

Briefly, then, when they met Harry was already familiar with and comfortable in the black subculture, far more than most white people would be. His experience as a jazz musician, as an athlete, and as the only white in a black apartment house in college, had taught him some nuances of black life-style. He enjoyed the personality traits that are emphasized by the black subculture, and was thus prepared both to like and to have some understanding of Ginny. At the same time, he was readily accepted by black friends and had acquired enough skill in the style of dancing and other courtship rituals to compete successfully for her. *Once they were married, however, he took her to live in his world, for which she had no comparable preparation.* From this point on, it was Ginny who experienced "total immersion" and had to sink or swim.

Parental reactions to interracial marriage

The choice of mate may be a civil right of individuals in America, but marriage still unites families as well as a man and a woman. It is not unusual for there to be some social-class distance between the family of the bride and the family of the bridegroom, but racial difference is unusual. Because only about two marriages in a thousand cross racial lines, there are no clear patterns developed for dealing with in-laws of a different race. Marriages that cross religious boundaries are more frequent, and the in-laws of different faiths either avoid one another or avoid religious matters when ceremonial family occasions bring them together. Avoidance may be the only pattern developed for dealing with in-laws of a different race. That pattern of avoidance may include ostracizing the son-in-law or daughter-in-law, and the result is often a break with the son or daughter who has married across the racial boundary.

Even if people do not choose to maintain social relationships with their in-laws, there is still a connection by marriage, one that creates an

565

assumption of equality between the families so joined. Perhaps it is not surprising that white parents, who have the socially more prestigious status, tend to be more adamantly opposed to interracial marriage than black parents. Of the sixteen white brides studied by Porterfield, twelve reported that their parents had opposed their marriage to a black man. Only one of the four black brides had met with parental opposition to her marriage to a white man. Parental attitudes had not softened for eleven of the white brides, even though all of them had been married for at least a year and a half, and some for as long as four years. Porterfield (1973:76) reports that seven of the sixteen white brides of black men he interviewed had been rejected by their own families, had little contact with them, and in some cases were disowned.

Parents tend to be more emotionally involved with the marriage of a daughter than the marriage of a son: the daughter's marriage is still the most powerful determinant of her place in life; the son's marriage is less critical than his choice of occupation. Porterfield found that only one out of four of the white bridegrooms reported that his family had been opposed to the marriage. Almost the same proportion—three out of sixteen—of the black bridegrooms reported initial family opposition. However, acceptance of the racially different daughter-in-law into the kinship network is often incomplete. One of the white women interviewed by Porterfield reported that her black in-laws had accepted her at the outset, but had become involved in the black movement and did not accept her any more, had even forbidden her to bring the children to visit their black grandmother (Porterfield 1973:76–77).

In the case of Ginny and Harry, there is no nexus with her black family; in part this can be attributed to geographical distance, and in part to social distance. The initial opposition of Harry's white parents has gradually softened.

> *Ginny:* My mom lives in Alabama and ... I was in summer school when we decided to get married. And I called her and told her that I was going to get married, and she said, "Are you sure that's what you want to do?" and I said, "Yeah!" And she said, "Okay, go ahead."
>
> And to this day she has never seen him. She has seen pictures of him and talked to him, but she's never met him. Being an only child, I think she was a little more liberal, you know, maybe if she did put up some resistance, she may sort of push me away from her, and I don't think she wanted to do that.
>
> *Harry:* But you did get some static, certainly from your grandmother.
>
> *Ginny:* Oh, well, she doesn't count.
>
> *Harry:* And I think by your mom, or at least didn't she—from what I gather, she was worried but felt that if Ginny was convinced that she'd be happy, and that was what she was most concerned with—but I think she had her doubts. Don't you? I got this through you.
>
> *Ginny:* Maybe she did, I don't know. I've been back there twice; she

hasn't been out here only because my grandmother lives with her, and my grandmother is in her eighties and she is blind, and my mother took care of her all these years and she doesn't want to leave her alone and so she hasn't been out here. But she says she's planning on it.

Harry: Plus it's Alabama. That's one reason I haven't been back. We couldn't afford the whole bunch of us going back—Ginny has been back with Laura [their little girl]. Also ... her mom at least has depended to a certain extent upon members of the white community in this small town for her livelihood and it seemed to be the better part of valor to be discreet in keeping it from the neighbors and so on. I don't think her mom was ashamed, or anything, so much as just feeling that it was in her better interests not to divulge it, so to this day I suppose there are probably no more than a handful of people in Ginny's home town that know I'm white.

When we first made it known to my parents I was in New York. I'd been in a series of track meetings that was culminating at that time in the first Olympic trials, and so I called home and my parents were very upset, ostensibly because, to hear them tell it, they felt it was a very rash thing for me to do, particularly on such short notice, and that I still hadn't gone back to school.

When I went back to school I had been out two years, then two in the army, but the first two were just sort of running the streets, working now and then. But they were worried that I never would go back to school, and they felt that it would be even less likely that I would go back, incurring more obligations, this kind of thing.

But I think my mom especially reacted initially in a very emotional manner. I think that Ginny's being black had a part to play in it. Again it was, I think, more than anything her being convinced that we wouldn't be happy, or that I wouldn't be happy, that people would shun us, and so on, and it just wouldn't work, and this kind of thing— looking at it more through her eyes than trying to look at it through my eyes.

So initially she was pretty up-tight. She's a very high-strung woman, she always had been an emotional person, and so even when I came back out here she swore at the beginning that she didn't want to meet Ginny. She didn't want to meet her.

And I said, "Well, in that case I don't suppose you'll be seeing too much of me, if I can't bring Ginny over, I won't be coming over."

Ginny, by the way, was going back to school. We were married in August, then she went back to school and I went back to Fort Roberts, and she discovered about a month and a half into the semester that she was pregnant and so she dropped—it was her senior year—and she dropped out and took a bus out here and we set up housekeeping, and it was under those circumstances that Mom initially said, "I don't want to meet her."

But by the time Ginny got here, Mom had relented to the point where she met her and—I don't know, she wasn't hostile, she just didn't know how to act more than anything.

As things stand now, and really within a very short time after Ginny came out here, they've adjusted extremely well. At first there was the problem about what would the neighbors think when we came over, and being sensitive to, "Well, after all we have to live in this neighborhood and we're probably going to die here," and so on.

And I'm sure that Dad isn't, what you'd say, eager to let his business associates know, this kind of thing, just knowing what the reaction would be. And I can understand that, I don't really hold it against him that he wouldn't be so terribly candid in that regard.

I don't know how secretive he is, I doubt if he is terribly secretive, that's not particularly like him. But I think over the last few years they've relaxed now to the point where I doubt very much if they even reflect on it that much.

We visit, not very often, I'm just not that dutiful a son, I guess, but we go down there, and there is never any question about being welcome or anything like that, never has been.

I'm aware of interracial marriages where daughters, particularly, are disowned. There has never, never been anything like that, nothing approaching it. And as I say, things are to the point now where they have accepted her as readily as they would have anyone else.

Marital roles in an interracial marriage

Most of the interracial couples that Porterfield studied reported that they were happily married, and believed that their marriages were no different from other marriages (1973:75). Fifteen of the twenty couples indicated that they had developed an unusually intense awareness of each other's feelings because of the difference in their backgrounds. They reported occasional arguments about money, discipline of the children, division of labor, personality differences—the sort of issues that most married couples quarrel over—but insisted that there were no racial overtones. Most married couples adopt a similar avoidance of "low blows" in arguments, by tacit agreement forbidding any reference to sensitive issues that could be harmful to a relationship that both value. For the interracial couple, racial slurs are forbidden "low blows" in marital conflict.

Harry and Ginny have experienced no unusual gap in marital role expectations. Harry regards the way Ginny plays her role as the way "most young middle-class girls" would play the role of wife; Ginny regards her behavior as "the way all women are." Their quarrels are, with rare exception, devoid of any racial references.

Harry: I don't think that there is a sense of different backgrounds or this kind of thing that might in one way or another be reducible to race, because, really, I think that she is far more conventional than I am; her mother raised her in a very conventional manner. I don't know, maybe my mom tried to with me; the fact remains that she is probably far more middle-class in her orientation than I am.

Ginny: Well, I don't know—in the beginning you thought like the man was supposed to be the big thing, but later on it got to the point where the man wasn't the big thing, and I don't know—

Harry: What do you mean—that to you the man was supposed to be the big protector and breadwinner and that you were supposed to stay home and—

Ginny: Yeah, like there are certain things, like you're supposed to have the house all in order when he gets home and cook his favorite things, and stuff like this, and—

Harry: Oh, I think probably that's—you don't think that's middle-class? I think that is the way most young, middle-class girls go into marriage—

Ginny: Well, I don't associate it with the middle class because I come from the South and all women are like that. So to me it was just—you know—all a part of it. But after awhile, that sort of got old.

Between them, the specifics of role behavior seem to cause no great conflict. They do have the conflicts that are inevitable in any intimate relationship, and the question is to what extent these are aggravated by underlying racial hostilities.

Q   Are your marital conflcts racially focused?

Ginny: I don't understand.

Harry: Well, in other words, that any time we have conflicts they degenerate into some kind of a racial—do they express themselves at all on a racial level?

I remember one time, and one time only, that they did. This was—we'd only been married a few months and it was as much my fault—the whole thing was as much my fault as hers. I don't know—she was crying a lot, and doing a lot of this, and that, she was pregnant, and—

Ginny: He didn't understand—

Harry: Right, I didn't understand, you know. We had just gone to bed and she was crying about something and I turned over, and I told myself that I slapped her in the face because that is how you make people stop crying, you know, like in the movies, but I'm sure there was some resentment there, but at any rate, I didn't hit her hard, you know, I just smacked her, but she didn't stop, and that sort of confused me and everything else, and so I took my foot and I pushed her out of the bed.

Now, I may have been leaving things out here, but at any rate she jumped up and said, "You white son-of-a-bitch—if you ever do that again, I'll kill you!" And I was shocked beyond words.

And I remember it quite well, but I think she was shocked, too. She told me afterwards, "Well, I just picked the thing that would hurt you most," but I don't think she picked anything. I think it came out. I don't think she had time to select any particular thing that would get back at me; I think it was a spontaneous outburst and I was flabbergasted.

But ever since then—and believe me, we've had fights that exceed that in intensity, length, and everything else since then, and never once has a racial kind of thing found its way in at all.

As a matter of fact, I wouldn't say we have the best marriage, it's probably like most other marriages, it's become more a matter of peaceful coexistence and sometimes not so peaceful, but whatever problems we have are strictly personality problems, I think, wouldn't you agree?

Ginny: Yes—yes.

Harry: The fights, the problems that express themselves, they're personality problems, they are not even indirectly racial. I don't think I am deluding myself at all in saying that they have been personality kinds of things, that they are the archetypal kinds of problems.

If we don't make it, it will be because we're not compatible personality-wise, not because—these things never do degenerate into a kind of racial conflict. I never feel them, I never think them. There's never been the point where I've had to bite my tongue or this kind of thing. It just never comes out that way. If we don't get along at times, if we have problems, they're the standard type of problems, and don't involve race at all.

Ginny: Only when we're kidding around.

Harry: Oh, all right, "that's your people, that's my people," that kind of thing—

Ginny: "We all look alike—" This type of stuff.

Harry: And that's another thing, I think—that we can do this without ever having recriminations made by the other.

Community reaction to interracial marriage

The married couples studied by Porterfield reported that they thought of each other as black or white only when outsiders called their attention to racial difference. For the blacks, pressures toward black awareness tended to affect their relationships with white marriage partners (Porterfield 1973:75–76). Most of the negative pressures came from the white community, however. One of the white wives reported that when she and one of the other women went shopping together they were just two more white women shoppers and no one paid much attention to them, but when they took their black children with them, they were suddenly regarded as monsters. She was tired, she said, of having people hate her so much. The black women could take their racially mixed children shopping without occasioning comment (the children were regarded as black, like their mothers), only one of the reasons why the black wives of white husbands seemed to encounter less community hostility. Three out of the four couples in which the wife was black and the husband was white reported to Porterfield that they lived in predominantly white neighborhoods without overt difficulty. Most indicated that their neighbors seemed to be indifferent to them, which meant that while they had had no trouble, they also had few, if any, friends.

When I asked Ginny and Harry about their acceptance by white neighbors, they reported the same general pattern of being tolerated but ignored (except by a neighbor who tended to be drunk by the middle of the afternoon). Their initial marital adjustment was made in a college setting, for Harry did go back to school and, in fact, completed a master's degree. The campus setting was one in which their marital roles were comparable to those of married students of all racial backgrounds, and the racial difference between them had little effect on their relations to their student neighbors. When "Harry" took a teaching position their situation changed, and Ginny had to learn the role of faculty wife. To a certain extent, this is a role that can be avoided, and she seems to have chosen that alternative by taking a job that gives her an occupational identity of her own and an acceptable excuse for missing meetings of the faculty wives' bridge club.

Q   How are you accepted by the community?

Harry: Have you experienced any snubs, Ginny?
Ginny: No, but then I haven't had that much contact with the neighbors.
Harry: I think I have. I've experienced what I think were a couple of snubs, people up the street farther, up the street far enough that we don't know them, four houses, five houses, that kind of thing.

At school I find that the word got around very quickly when we moved in that there was an interracial couple in this area so that many more people know of us than we know, and there have been instances where I am quite sure—I walk to school, and people would get out of a car and walk right dead in front of me as I was walking home, and not look up, where it would be virtually impossible not to.

And I think I am the kind of person who would bend over backwards to be sure that I wasn't projecting anything on someone else and seeing things that didn't exist and would try to rationalize it in some other way before I'd do that, and yet I'm pretty sure that there

*"There are a couple of people up the street who do disapprove of our being here,
but there hasn't been any overt, active objection—no one has burned crosses."*

are a couple of people up the street who, while they haven't said anything, do disapprove of our being here, but there hasn't been any overt, active objection or anything—no one has burned crosses [laugh].

But I think you could go over three or four blocks into what is a much more working-class neighborhood, and I suspect we would have had a good deal more trouble. Whereas you find that these are people who are—well, perhaps in the lower middle classes still, but largely self-employed—the fellow across the street has a cleaning establishment, the fellow two houses up owns a camera shop in town, the fellow across the street is an entomologist and has his own bug outfit, and the guy next to him owns a filling station, or has a franchise. And the fellow over here is an engineer.

I tend to think that the socioeconomic level of the neighborhood is such that that has been one of the reasons why things have been so quiet. It's just not *in* to express your racial feelings.

I think that maybe the two most important things are the neighborhood, first of all, but second is the fact that I'm the white one, whereas were I black, given the fact that the family as a unit tends to derive its status and its image from the male member of the household—I think that were I black and she white, things might be far different. As I see it, I think that it is my status that tends to predominate when we are viewed as a household.

Ginny: Well, the first year I was here I was in it and I went, but I found it very boring, dull—they didn't do anything but sit around and play bridge and talk and I wasn't interested.

Harry: You like to play bridge.

Ginny: Yeah, but still not a steady diet of it. But I managed to go through it because I thought that was what I was expected to do, and some of the women sort of took me under their wings, you know, to make sure I got there, but then this past year I didn't even join.

Harry: You were working.

Ginny: Yeah, I was working, but even so, I don't think I would have. Simply because it's just a little gossip group, is all it is, and I didn't enjoy that, so—I've been called, every month I'm called to come to the meetings, but I don't go.

I've gone a couple of times with a friend of mine who didn't want to go alone, but I haven't been active in it. There are a few in the group who make me feel uncomfortable. They are going out of their way—but there are some who are very nice, and I think they accept me for what I am, and that's it.

But there are those, unfortunately, who come on too strong, and it's not—it's too much, and you can see right through it. I don't like that. But I haven't had too much contact this year with the people up there. I can't say that I've missed it.

I am working for the state, now. I'm a claims interviewer; I determine people's eligibility to draw unemployment insurance whenever they quit a job or are discharged or they're not able to work, and try to help them as much as possible to find other employment. Get them back to work as soon as possible. I started last April, and I've been there a little over a year, now. It can be pretty hectic sometimes, but I've stuck with it.

I had to take a test, an exam, and after taking the darn thing I felt so bad about it, because I just knew I had failed, and then when I got the notice to go in for the oral interview, I figured it was probably because I was the only qualified black person to come through here, and they just wanted to hire me on and then when they found out that he was white—I didn't tell anyone.

I think he picked me up from work or something, and somebody was asking, and you know, the word sort of got around—but I got no negative reactions at all. I don't know what they say when I'm not around, but they've all been quite—they didn't even come on like the women up at the college did. It was very different, I felt more comfortable with them, and I think they were very sincere in their relationship with me, and it's been just great down there.

Harry: I've found that attitudes on campus vary with the faculty member. I've got a number of friends over there, one of whom—I don't

573

know what his problem is, I like the guy, I don't like his wife much, nobody does, but he's gone out of the way it would seem to drag in the subject of race or ethnicity to the point where I just finally told him I was getting a little tired of it, in as good-natured way as I could.

I think he was quite taken aback by it. I think he sincerely didn't realize that he was doing anything that was offensive. It's just that it got old. I laughed and I grinned for long enough and finally I told him.

I don't mean over the course of one evening, or anything like that, but over the course of a number of months where I'd encounter him on campus and, well—little jokes or this and that. Just because I was married to a black person, it was appropriate to talk to me about race.

That was the thing you talked to Harry about, just like there are some guys that you fill the vacuum with talk about women, or something else. Well, for a couple of people, the most appropriate thing to discuss with Harry was race and mixed marriages. And in some instances these were people who wanted to make it very clear how liberal they were.

But I would say, overall, particularly the people to whom I gravitated quickly—and of course this is why—just were natural about it and took it as a matter of course. These are the people that we have the greatest contact with and see the most.

I would say that the faculty members both in my department and in other departments that we have the most to do with—most of whom are pretty young—are those that we feel comfortable with, and certainly that would be why.

For nearly all Americans, the husband's occupation determines the status placement of the family, and this husband is aware that his occupation is the determining factor in the way the household is regarded in the neighborhood. The fact that Harry is on the faculty of a college means that neighbors give them at least a passive tolerance, and the college atmosphere is one in which, as he observes, it is not "in" to express racist feelings.

Ginny seems to have escaped patronizing faculty wives by finding a job in which she was accepted as a black and as a person before the issue of mixed marriage was raised. And, unlike the faculty wives' club, where the woman's presence is determined by the status of the husband and the husband is thus somehow always in the background, Ginny's co-workers can easily ignore the fact of her marriage. She is there in her own right, and there is little reason for them to be continually aware of her marital relationship.

On balance, then, the most negative social pressure either of them seems to have encountered has been an occasional silent snub or a patronizing joke. As they are aware, however, their experience might have been very different.

Parental roles in interracial marriage

When parents, friends, and sometimes even bystanders try to dissuade a couple from marrying across racial boundaries, one of the usual arguments is the question of the children. As indicated above, American custom assigns the child of mixed racial ancestry to the subordinate race, particularly the child of black-white ancestry. Harry and Ginny have one child: a beautiful girl. Many little girls are pretty; this one is an arresting beauty. She has delicate features and milk-chocolate skin. Great beauty eases many problems; in time it may create some.

Q   How do your parents feel about their mulatto grandchild?

Harry: I'm an only child, so is Ginny, and we begot an only child, probably. And as my dad made it very clear to me, even the last time they were up—and I mean, he made it abundantly clear—because we've had our problems—that Ginny is like a daughter to them. And Laura, certainly as their granddaughter, is something that—especially my dad and she just have a thing. Just a thing that you wouldn't believe. But even my mom—the reason that my mom and Laura don't have such a thing is just because my mom isn't that demonstrative a person and never was. They've—I must say I'm very proud of them for having adjusted, especially my mom, because she's as inner-directed as they come. I've always been a much more demonstrative person than my mother. It's interesting, though, because my mom in some ways is very demonstrative, although not affectionately. My dad isn't demonstrative at all.

Q   Do the neighborhood children accept her?

Ginny: She gets out and she plays with the kids. I haven't heard her say anything—it seems like once—
Harry: When we first moved in, Billy next door, who is five or six, was over here and they were out in the kitchen somewhere and I was in the other room, and I heard him telling her a joke that involved a negro—an ethnic joke in other words—and it became quite clear that he was very conscious of the difference between them. I don't know— he probably treats her as he would any other little girl that age, though, as far as that goes.

So far as any major incident in the neighborhood, no—no one pulls their kids off the street or won't let their kids come over. We thought possibly at one time that this was true remember? Over across? Laura said something about she couldn't go over there anymore, or Terry couldn't come over here, but it turned out to be a misunderstanding on Laura's part, and I began to appreciate the whole concept of cultural paranoia, when you immediately jump to

575

"She did one day mention that one of her little friends about her age had told her that she didn't like her skin, and Laura asked her why not, and she said, 'Because it smells bad.' And so I was, of course, angry about it, but I did the best I could to maintain my cool and said, 'Well, tomorrow you go back and tell her that she is just smelling her upper lip.' You know, she got a big kick out of that."

the conclusion that it's because she's black, even though they had played together for awhile.

But as it happens, she hasn't had any problems in this neighborhood. Where she goes to nursery school, she's never—I don't think it's significant enough to her yet that she would come home and say, "Do you know what so and so said, this and that and the other thing," but she did in passing one day mention that one of her little friends about her age had told her that she didn't like her skin, and Laura asked her why not, and she said, "Because it smells bad."

And so I was, of course, angry about it, but I did the best I could to maintain my cool and said, "Well, tomorrow you go back and tell her that she is just smelling her upper lip." You know, she got a big kick out of that.

I think it's come up before, the word "nigger" has come up among some of her playmates at nursery school—and the whole idea of race. I mean these kids—it's amazing how early they become aware of it. They have all the images, all the stereotypes. Not very sophisticated yet, and yet some way or another, I don't think they quite include Laura in it, you know what I mean?

Ginny: Yeah—she's different, but—

Harry: I don't think they like negroes, but they're not down on Laura. They don't really know what a negro is, and Laura is something different. They don't see the relationship.

Q   How do you raise a black child in a white community?

Ginny: Well, there aren't any other black kids for her to play with, and that has been a concern of ours. She's asked, a couple of times she wanted to play with some black kids. And we don't have that many friends that are black, although we do have one with two girls.
Harry: Who's married to a white girl.
Ginny: Yeah [laugh]. But I don't know how I feel about her being isolated here when she's going to have to learn from other black kids, and I don't know at what point we should start this. I don't know, I think she should have had contact in growing up, but it has been so that she didn't, and hopefully we can do enough to make her be able to deal with any problems that she might have in growing up.
Harry: I didn't realize it until now, but I guess I have been much more concerned about it than Ginny has. You mention defenses. To my way of thinking, the defense she would learn from other black kids in dealing with the white world is how not to think so totally white that she can't see herself in a positive light. And that is the best defense in the world.

I think we do a great deal around here. I think . . . that we're both aware enough of the implications in terms of identity that we can do subtle little things that maybe a lot of parents wouldn't be aware of to try and build a positive identity.

I think at the moment she has an extremely good view of herself. She sees herself as pretty—of course she is, even by white standards —which makes it easier for her. In other words, although she is black and will be by social definition, her features are such that when a white person says, "Oh, what a beautiful child," they are not just making with the social amenities. And I don't know, we may find that we've gone further than we should have and raised a very vain little girl. I hope not.
Ginny: Yeah!
Harry: This bothers me. But anyway, around here, I think we are doing all that we can to build a positive self-image in terms of how she sees herself intellectually, how she sees herself aesthetically, and so on. I'm very much concerned that she doesn't have any little black kids to play with because I do want her to think black to a certain extent, to the point where she isn't going to, at any point in her life, rue what she is. And I think that so long as she continues to interact only with white kids, she's going to have a problem, if in no other way than in interacting with black kids when she gets older.

I think she may have a good deal of difficulty relating to black kids when she gets to college, when she gets old enough to have broadened her relationships, her horizons, to where she is interacting with more people, and I even went so far as to look around for something like a Montessori school, not just in order to—well, actually there probably wouldn't be any black kids there, but there darn sure aren't going to be any over here at this public grammar school that she would go to.

And so I felt for both educational reasons and in terms of identity she would still probably get a far better—have a far better educational experience at such a school, where she would undoubtedly interact with teachers who were more sensitive to that situation as well as kids who probably came from homes that were maybe more enlightened. We haven't found anything, though. At the moment, we are at an impasse.

Ginny: You know, I was just thinking—the one thing I wouldn't want her to do would be to just start thinking in terms of black and white. That's the one thing I don't want her to do. I want her to be able to see a person for what he is and evaluate him not in terms of color.

And I don't know, she is aware that she is black, and sometimes when we are out just shopping, she'll say, "We're different, hum?" And sometimes, I think I don't know if that's good. If she becomes obsessed with being—what are you shaking your head for? Well, I don't!

Harry: Well, I don't think she's obsessed by it. I think it's important that she knows she's different, that she's going to have to deal with it, there's no way of ignoring it or sweeping in under the rug.

Ginny: No! I'm not saying sweep it under the cover, but don't—

Harry: I think you're worried that she'll become a black militant, more than anything else, whereas I'm worried about just the opposite.

Ginny: No, I just don't want her to become so obsessed with being black that she may get to the point where she thinks that all whites are—

Harry: Do we approach the subject that way around here?

Ginny: No, we don't, but later on she might—

Harry: We approach it more in the manner that people come in different colors. You know, this kind of thing, "Yes, you are different and you are beautiful." And that people are beautiful and there are no universal standards for judging such things. She is becoming, as she grows older, more color-conscious, although I don't think she is attaching the kind of evaluative judgments to it that we need to worry about.

Ginny: I hope not.

Harry: But what worries me, of course, is that if she ever does, it is not going to be because we have it around here, it is going to be because of how she's taught. I'm not really worried about her ever not viewing other people in terms of who they are, what they are, but rather how she views herself. To me, that is of infinitely more importance.

The parental roles in this interracial family are complicated by the problems of raising a black child in a white middle-class milieu: the recurring necessity of interpreting—and helping the child to interpret—the responses of others, the question of how sensitized the child should be to racial identity, the difficulty of finding playmates who will be like herself. Some of these problems would be similar for any racially mixed family, some are probably similar for all black parents, some might be less complicated for a family that had more nexus with the black community. It is the relative isolation from other blacks that makes the parental burden such a demanding one in this family.

As the only black person with whom Laura has continuous contact, the mother must be Laura's model of what it means to be black as well as her model of what it means to be a woman. Even if these parents are able to find black playmates for Laura, however, she will still have the identity problems of a marginal individual, caught between two racial subcultures. Her father's awareness of this means that Laura will have a great deal of help in developing a positive self-image and a sense of identity.

The parental roles in this interracial family seem to be more affected by racial concerns than are the marital roles, as such. The marital roles played by both are fundamentally those of the class level of the family, which is that of the educated, professional middle class, and the interracial character of their marriage seems to have only a peripheral effect on their personal relationship to each other. As Harry observes, "It's probably like most other marriages, it's become more a matter of peaceful coexistence and sometimes not so peaceful, but whatever problems we have are strictly personality problems . . . they are not even indirectly racial." And yet it is possible that this, too, is a myth—a family myth that holds the marriage together.

References

Bernard, Jessie. 1966. "Notes on Educational Homogamy in Negro-White and White-Negro Marriages, 1960." *Journal of Marriage and the Family* 28 (August):274–276.

Cash, W. J. 1941. *The Mind of the South.* New York: Alfred A. Knopf.

Downs, Joan. 1971. "Black-White Dating." *Life* 70 (May 28):56–67.

Frazier, E. Franklin, 1962. *Black Bourgeoisie.* New York: Collier Books.

Handlin, Oscar. 1957. *Race and Nationality in American Life.* Boston: Little, Brown and Company.

Heer, David M. 1966. "Negro-White Marriage in the United States." *Journal of Marriage and the Family* 28 (August):262–273.

Herskovits, Melville J. 1930. *The Anthropometry of the American Negro.* New York: Columbia University Press.

Mantoux, Paul. 1962. *The Industrial Revolution in the Eighteenth Century*. New York: The Macmillan Company; London: Jonathan Cape.

Porterfield, Ernest. 1973. "Mixed Marriage." *Psychology Today* 6 (January):71–78.

U.S. Bureau of the Census. 1972. *Census of Population: 1970 Marital Status, Final Report*. Washington, D.C.: U.S. Government Printing Office.

Wirth, Louis, and Herbert Goldhamer. 1944. "The Hybrid and the Problem of Miscegenation." In *Characteristics of the American Negro*, edited by Otto Klineberg, pp. 276–280. New York: Harper & Row.

Suggested readings

Aldridge, Delores P. 1973. "The Changing Nature of Interracial Marriage in Georgia: A Research Note." *Journal of Marriage and the Family* 35 (November):641–642. A research report indicating a statistically significant increase in interracial marriage in Georgia since 1967, when legal restrictions on interracial marriage were removed. The data available were for white-nonwhite, and the author notes that the latter category includes Asians and others as well as blacks.

Heer, David M. 1974. "The Prevalence of Black-White Marriage in the United States, 1960 and 1970." *Journal of Marriage and the Family* 36 (May):246–259. Heer analyzes data on marriages between blacks and whites as reported in the 1960 and 1970 censuses of the United States. There was a substantial increase over the decade in the prevalence of such marriages in the North and West, and a substantial decline in the South. Overall, there was a sharp rise in marriages involving a black husband and a white wife, and some decline in those with a white husband and a black wife.

Monahan, Thomas P. 1973. "Marriage Across Racial Lines in Indiana." *Journal of Marriage and the Family* 35 (November):632–640. A brief summary of the history of legal restrictions on interracial marriage in Indiana is followed by a report of research based on data made available by the Indiana State Board of Health on all marriages registered in the state of Indiana for the six-year period from 1962 to 1967. The proportion of mixed marriages, the age of the bride and of the groom, and whether the marriage was the first or a remarriage for either spouse are among the research data reported.

Porterfield, Ernest. 1973. "Mixed Marriage." *Psychology Today* 6 (January):71–78. Porterfield studied twenty marriages between blacks and whites; a small sample, but the insights presented are useful and reveal something of the social backgrounds of the individuals who choose to marry across racial lines, the motives for interracial marriage, and some of the problems that these mixed couples have encountered.

580

21 The communal "family"

Nineteenth-century communalism stemmed from disenchantment with family arrangements; mid-twentieth-century dissatisfaction with both family and job gratifications creates a ready market for experiences which promise intimacy and authenticity . . .

Though the members of these communities often argue that they exist for specific ideological reasons (political, social, economic, ecological, religious, educational, psychological) we suggest that doctrine merely serves as a filter which selectively recruits and sustains people with homogeneous personal and social needs by providing meaningful extended interpersonal relations. In other words, the crucial factor behind the recent communal renaissance is a psychosocial "quest for community."

John H. Marx and David L. Ellison
(1975:446, 450)

The conjugal family, with the marital bond between husband and wife as its central axis, has been the dominant pattern of life in America since colonial times. There is an equally long history of communal alternatives, chosen by a small minority of Americans as a way of life. Since the 1960s, attention has been focused on experiments in communal living among adherents of what has been termed the counterculture. But the long tradition of utopian experiments in communal living in America began in the eighteenth century. By the latter part of the nineteenth century there were sixty or more communal movements in the United States, almost all of them founded on religious doctrine and communistic economic organization.

Utopian communities: an alternate American tradition

Communal living does not necessarily exclude the conjugal family. On the contrary, many communal groups have incorporated the conjugal family into the structure of the utopian community (the Hutterites are a highly successful example). But some communal movements have sought to abolish the conjugal family and to provide an alternative pattern of social and sexual life. Two of the best-remembered communal movements, the Shakers and the Oneida Community, expressly forbade marriage.

The Shakers were a religious movement founded by a woman and guided by women. As a group, the Shakers survived for nearly two centuries, despite a requirement of celibacy which meant that all new members had to be recruited. The sect originated in England in 1747 and was brought to the United States—or rather to colonies that were soon to become the United States—in 1774. The Shakers arrived in this country at the time of the American Revolution under the leadership of Mother Ann Lee. The Shakers believed that God is dual, both male and female, and that Mother Ann was the incarnation of the female principle. They called their movement the Millennial Church, but received the name Shakers from outsiders, because of the movements of the dance that was part of their religion of ecstasy.

The Shaker life, with its ecstatic religion, singing, dancing, and communal labor, attracted thousands of Americans. At the height of the movement there were nearly 100,000 members distributed among some 130 Shaker villages. Having abolished marriage, the Shakers lived as brothers and sisters in God. Abolition of the family and a strict requirement of celibacy meant that no children were born into the Shaker community. Thus the only way the group could perpetuate itself was through converts. The Shaker communities disappeared, one by one, as the movement gradually lost its ability to attract converts. The last Shaker community chose to stop accepting new members in the 1960s, for the few elderly Shakers remaining had concluded that the younger people willing to share their communal life were not accepting the Shaker religion.

The Oneida Community began as an experiment in spiritual equality. This communal living group was founded in Putney, Vermont, in 1846, a century after the arrival of the Shakers. Members called themselves Perfectionists, after the religious doctrine expounded by the founder of the movement, John Humphrey Noyes. They formed a collective in which private ownership was forbidden (even private ownership of clothing). Monogamous sexual privileges were considered a form of private ownership, and were also forbidden. The Perfectionists believed that romantic love led to jealousy and hypocrisy and that it was a barrier to spiritual love. They considered monogamous marriage a form of selfish exclusivity. The Perfectionists abolished marriage and the family, but did not advocate celibacy. The resulting life-style brought them into conflict with prevailing sexual norms, and also with the law. In 1847 Noyes was arrested and charged with adultery. Released on bond, he fled with a few followers to central New York State, where they settled along Oneida Creek, hence the name Oneida Colony, or Oneida Community.

The Oneida Community is one of the best-remembered of the nineteenth-century utopian communities, not because of its religious doctrine of Perfectionism and spiritual equality, or because of its eventual economic success. Oneida is remembered for its sexual innovations. Noyes developed a pattern of male and female relationships that he called *complex marriage.* This was essentially group marriage in a communal living group. Noyes coined the term *free love,* but it did not mean promiscuity in its original context. An adult male member of the Oneida Community wishing to have sexual relations with a particular adult female member was expected to make his request to a central committee of Community elders, which acted as a go-between, but was empowered to deny the request if it did not seem to be in the best interests of the Community. The woman had the right to refuse that man, or all men if she chose to remain celibate.

All members of the Oneida Community were expected to refrain from procreating until the group was able to provide adequately for child-rearing. There were no children born in this utopian community until twenty years after its founding! Members of the Oneida Community seem to have had remarkable success with the contraceptive technique advocated by Noyes: *coitus reservatus,* which means normal intercourse except that the male does not ejaculate (a technique also advocated by some Hindu sects). Until the young men could learn the necessary control, they were permitted to have sexual intercourse only with women past the menopause.

Noyes had read the works of Charles Darwin and Francis Galton and was convinced that procreation should be a carefully selective process, that only persons of superior mental and physical attributes should have children. After twenty years of deliberate childlessness, the Oneida Community began a pattern of selective procreation. By 1869 Noyes had developed the eugenic pattern of mating that he called "Stirpiculture." What that pattern of mate selection entailed has remained a secret. But it is known that a couple wishing to become parents had to apply for permission to a committee of elders of the Community. In the decade following 1869, there were fifty-eight children born in the Oneida Community (Noyes reportedly was the father of eleven of them). The "Stirpiculture" program was apparently a success eugenically, for the children as a group were remarkably healthy. They had a significantly lower infant mortality rate than prevailed among other American infants born in the 1870s. William Kephart (1961:191) notes that thirteen of the Oneida children were still living in the early 1960s, when all of them would have been past the age of ninety. For thirteen out of fifty-eight children born at Oneida to have lived to the age of ninety or more is significant evidence of the eugenic success of the Oneida experiment.

Infants born in the Oneida Community were cared for by their mothers. When the children were fifteen months old, they were transferred to a special area in the Mansion House, which was shared by all Oneida Community members. Children at Oneida were treated kindly, but not sentimentally. It was believed that there should not be exclusivity in the love between parents and children, for the same reason that exclusivity in the love between a man and a woman was forbidden. All adults were expected to love all children; all children were expected to view all adults of the community as loving parents.

Whenever a member of the Oneida Community deviated from group norms or showed signs of character weakness, a committee met with this person to discuss his or her personal weakness. These sessions followed the method developed by Noyes called *mutual criticism.* Mutual criticism seems to be the prototype of the many forms of sensitivity and encounter groups of our own time. Walter Edmonds describes the Oneida sessions as follows:

> The criticisms were administered in a purely clinical spirit. The subject sat in complete silence while each member of the committee in turn assessed his good points as well as his bad. In cases of unusual seriousness, perhaps involving the violation of a fundamental tenet of their common philosophy, the committee would be expanded to include the entire Community. (Edmonds 1948:20)

These mutual criticism sessions were not only for persons singled out by the Oneida Community as deviants. Many members in good standing asked for a mutual criticism session as a means of catharsis, a cleansing of the spirit. According to Carl Carmer: "Mutual criticisms met with enthusiastic approval. So beneficial were they considered that frequently members, feeling out of harmony, offered themselves for criticism, listened with humility, and returned to their duties refreshed and reinspired toward the perfect ideal" (1936:149).

Economic failure ended most nineteenth-century utopian experiments in communal living; the Oneida Community was an exception.

Oneida was economically successful, largely because of the remarkable steel trap that one of its members invented. The Community patented this trap, and produced it for the fur trade. This invention provided the capital for further development of crafts and industry at Oneida. It was social, not economic pressure that finally ended the Oneida experiment.

The sexual and eugenic innovations of Oneida were considered moral corruption by outsiders in the 1870s, the height of prudery in America. The attack on Oneida was led by Anthony Comstock, the moral crusader whose zeal also produced the federal legislation banning pornography and contraceptive information (as noted in Chapter 4). Comstock was outraged by the sexual practices at Oneida and by what he regarded as the practice of breeding children like cattle. The aging Noyes seems finally to have given up the struggle to create a radical form of group life. He left for Canada in June of 1879, never to return. A few months later the Community disbanded. The Oneida Community formed a joint-stock company and divided the stock among Community members, thus ending a social experiment and founding a thriving corporation.

The communal heavens of Father Divine

After World War I blacks began to move from rural communities in the South to northern cities, a migration that became a rapid flow of impoverished people during the early 1930s. Restrictive real estate covenants combined with prejudice to keep blacks out of most neighborhoods of northern cities. In New York blacks were effectively restricted to Harlem during the 1920s and 1930s. As the tide of black migrants poured into this limited area, the resulting housing shortage sent rents soaring beyond the means of most poor black families. Families moved in with relatives and friends, sometimes even with strangers. Three or four families often shared one coldwater tenement flat with the resident rats and roaches.

Jobs, like housing, were often closed to blacks. It is estimated that in 1933 fully half of Harlem's black families had applied for unemployment relief. People looking for a cleaning woman, or for someone to do odd jobs, could go to what was called the "slave market": a street corner where blacks of all ages stood in all kinds of weather, holding up penciled signs showing how little he or she would charge for an hour's work. For families that had no hope of employment, prostitution was a mode of survival. Even young children could be found on the street soliciting for their older sisters or their mothers. In this desolate setting of Harlem in 1933, Father Divine opened his 115th Street "heaven."

Father Divine was born George Baker, in about 1877, on an island in the Savannah River in Georgia. In about 1900 he became a self-ordained minister, worked out of a storefront church in Baltimore for a time, returned to Georgia, then moved to New York City with a few devoted followers in 1915. The religious doctrine of the movement was a simple one, taken from a verse in the third chapter of First Corinthians: "Know

587

ye not that ye are the Temple of God, and that the spirit of God dwelleth in you?" In the Baltimore days, Baker and his religious brethren had taken this to mean that God dwelt in each of the faithful. But in New York, Baker perceived that if each member considered himself an incarnation of the deity, there was little power held by the leader and little cohesion or discipline in the group. He watched as a group of which he had been a part, but not the leader, dissolved. Then he moved his followers and became the sole incarnate divinity in his own congregation.

A few years after his arrival in New York, Baker, by then known as Major Devine, or the Messenger, moved to Long Island. He bought a two-story, twelve-room house in Sayville and moved in with a small group of disciples as a communal living group. "Major Devine" ran an employment agency offering "reliable colored help" in weekly ads in the *Suffolk County News.* His clients were members of his flock, and he had considerable success in finding employment for them. They turned their pay over to their leader, who maintained the household. The Messenger shared sleeping quarters with his male disciples, while his wife, Sister Penny, slept in the women's dormitory. The members of what came to be known as the Peace Mission movement renounced personal property for communal living. They were expected to be celibate and to abstain totally from liquor, tobacco, drugs, cosmetics, and motion pictures.

About 1928, some ten years after the move to Long Island, the Peace Mission began to offer free Sunday dinners to potential converts and to advertise these dinners in Brooklyn and the Bronx. People came in increasing numbers, to the dismay of the Long Island community. Sister Penny directed the kitchen work, and filled the tables with platters of ham, chicken, rice, beans, hominy, corn, cheese, cake, and ice cream. By 1930 busloads of people—black and white—came for Sunday dinner. Some remained as converts. The Peace Mission had lived quietly and grown slowly for a decade. Within the year after the Sunday dinners began, they had increased from forty to ninety members. Skilled or unskilled, all members contributed their earnings to the maintenance of The Peace Mission.

In 1930 George Baker underwent a final rebirth and formally took the name of Father Divine. In 1932 Father Divine lost a highly publicized court battle with his Long Island neighbors, who had filed complaints charging that he operated a public nuisance. The jury found him guilty. The judge sentenced Father Divine to one year in jail and a $500 fine: the maximum sentence for being a convicted public nuisance. The sentencing took place on a Saturday morning; the following Wednesday the judge dropped dead, although he was only fifty years old and in apparent good health. From his jail cell Father Divine confessed, "I hated to do it."

Little more than a month later Father Divine left jail on bond while his case was appealed. The appellate court found that the trial had been conducted in a prejudicial manner and reversed the conviction. The effect of the publicity given the trial and the sudden death of the judge was electrifying. Here was a black man with apparent supernatural powers, appearing at a time and place where most black men were powerless and hopeless. The faithful believed Father Divine was a living God because they needed to believe. People began to claim they had been cured of crippling or disabling illness by Father Divine. There were many rehabilitated alcoholics and prostitutes among his followers who could testify that their lives had been redeemed by him. Soon after receiving a thundering ovation at a New York City rally, Father Divine moved back to Harlem. The year was 1933.

After three decades in which his disciples had been numbered by the dozens, Father Divine now numbered his followers by the thousands. Racial equality was a fundamental tenet of the Peace Mission movement, which at its height had between one-fourth and one-third white membership. Not all of the converts were poor. Some wealthy persons, white and black, signed their worldly possessions over to Father Divine and moved into one of the "heavens," as the communal living centers were called. At one time there were more than 170 heavens in the kingdom of Father Divine. Apartment houses and brownstone houses were rented, some were bought. In each the living quarters were set up in dormitory style, with the sexes segregated. Each had a dining hall, and the feeding of all who came to the table continued. Many came because they were hungry, but returned because they had been caught up in the spirit of the movement, whose greeting was "Peace, Father."

Sara Harris wrote (1954:21): "not only did he make it clear to his followers that he was their only God, he also went so far as to demand that they give up every loyalty except the one to himself." Parents were to give up all affection for their children, and children were to renounce all feeling for their parents. Husbands and wives were to become celibate brothers and sisters once they became "angels" and moved into the dormitories of heaven. Father Divine and his kingdom were the subject of much raw humor during the 1930s and 1940s. But Harris stated that "except for very occasional backsliders" celibacy was observed (1954:22).

> The men who join Father's movement have stopped worrying about being men and earning money to care for their wives and children. Father's fantasy world, where the kind of job a man does or the amount of money he makes just don't matter, understandably becomes an ideal world to them. Certainly, they can give up their wives and sweethearts who reminded them every hour of every day that their dark skins were badges of inferiority, preventing them from being good providers and whole men. Certainly they can give up "the lustful life" which demanded far too much ego-payment from them who could not approve themselves, because they could not hope to support the wives and sweethearts to whom they made love and the children who would result from that love. Most of these men, when they came to Father Divine, were half men in their own minds. Father gave them a chance to grow whole again. That is why they love him so. That is why they can so successfully down their lustful feelings. (Harris 1954:111)

589

In 1942 Father Divine moved from New York to Philadelphia, to avoid arrest on a contempt of court charge. He had refused to pay a judgment won by a disaffected follower who had sued to recover her life savings. The judgment was for little more than $4,000, but it was a matter of either pride or principle, and Father Divine moved out of New York State rather than pay it. The move cost him the political power he had been building in New York and the Peace Mission movement lost its momentum, although it survived another twenty years. Father Divine died on September 10, 1965, at Woodmont, his seventy-two-acre estate on Philadelphia's Main Line. The faithful believed that Father Divine had merely discarded his body, so there was no funeral. But there was no one else who could sustain the movement, no one who could claim to be a new incarnation of divinity, and membership in the Peace Mission movement dwindled rapidly.

The Peace Mission movement and similar religious communal groups formed during the 1930s provided an alternative means of survival during some of the most desperate economic times this country has known. These groups were both communal living groups and religious cults. All had charismatic leaders. *Charisma* has become an overworked word in our time, but it is appropriate in this context. It is from the Greek, meaning *gift,* and originally had a biblical meaning referring to the gift of tongues, or the gift of healing by laying on of hands. Faith healing and seemingly miraculous feeding of the poor were the means of attracting converts to these groups; communal living was both a mode of survival and the basis of community. Unlike nineteenth-century American utopian communities, those of the 1930s tended to remain in the inner city.

Communal living in the counter-culture

Some thirty-five years after Father Divine entered Harlem, another generation of Americans discovered communal living as an alternative lifestyle. Some of these communal groups were (and are) religious in nature, like most previous American communal living experiments: for example, the Children of God and the Ashrams, rural religious communes established by members of an East Indian religious sect. Some contemporary communal groups have a secular ideology that owes more to humanistic psychology than to religion (such as the Bridge Mountain Community in California). But by far the largest number of communes in this new wave of communal living were established (if such generally amorphous groups can be said to have been established) by "hippies" of the counter-culture during the latter part of the 1960s.

In the summer of 1966, the vanguard of what came to be known as the counter-culture established itself in the Haight-Ashbury district of San Francisco. From the outset the counter-culture included communal "families," some of which were involved in the production of hard-rock music (a few, quite successfully). Most of the hippie communal "families" were

590

involved in the use of LSD and related drugs, which were new in the early 1960s, at least as part of a drug subculture, and had not yet been included under laws regulating dangerous drugs.

Some of these communal living groups were structured, others were little more than "crash pads" where transients could find shelter. In the summer of 1967 there was an influx of teenage youth into the Haight. There had been nothing like that summer migration since 1849, when thousands of Americans rushed across desert and Indian country to California, afflicted with a manic frenzy called "gold fever." The young migrants of 1967 were also afflicted by a kind of manic frenzy, drawn to San Francisco by a potent combination of rock music, psychedelic drugs, sex, mysticism, and antiwar politics. Someone named them Flower Children, perhaps because of their penchant for picking the flowers of Golden Gate Park and wearing them as garlands or giving them to passing strangers. The term suggests innocents gone mad, in the tradition of Ophelia. The Flower Children arrived in the Haight in the summer of 1967, followed shortly by the tour buses. The Free Clinic opened soon after, offering treatment for drug-related problems, venereal disease, and a host of ailments that the malnourished runaways contracted in crowded and unsanitary crash pads.

On the other side of the continent, there was a parallel counter-culture movement. "Woodstock," the summer rock music festival that attracted thousands of young people to New York state, was to the eastern counter-culture what the migration of the Flower Children was on the west coast. New York City's East Village developed the same life-style of drugs, hard-rock music and crash-pad communal living that had appeared in San Francisco. University cities, such as Boston, developed neighborhoods similar to the area south of the campus in Berkeley. In the middle of the United States, cities such as Ann Arbor and Madison found their universities surrounded by satellite communities focused on the same themes of antiwar activism, drugs, rock music, mysticism, and communal living.

The similarities between these outposts of the counter-culture were not coincidental. Not only did exhaustive media coverage create models for young people inclined to imitate the life-style of the counter-culture, but perhaps more important, the members of the counter-culture tended to be transients. They moved, and the counter-culture spread with them. Some communes were nomadic, like the Hog Farm, a group that lived in converted school buses and encamped briefly in places as far apart as Arkansas and La Honda, California. (The Hog Farm went to Woodstock for the festival.) Most communes of the counter-culture were seminomadic, with a nucleus of members that moved from one old house to another in deteriorating neighborhoods of cities.

The wave of the counter-culture crested and broke, ebbing with the Vietnam War. Antiwar protest had been as central to the movement as hard-rock music and drugs. With the end of the war, the end of the draft, and the end of affluence, the counter-culture receded. Young toughs from

591

other neighborhoods in San Francisco descended on the Haight to beat, rob, and rape. Hippies were considered fair game and unlikely to complain to the police. Most of the communal "families" fled San Francisco in the early 1970s, more than a dozen of them relocating across the bay. Some communes sought land in the coastal mountains, partly in flight from the city, partly in search of a rural life-style.

Berkeley had communal "families" from the beginning of the counter-culture movement. Some of these moved to rural areas after the "People's Park" confrontation with Berkeley police in the summer of 1969, but other communal "families" moved into Berkeley in the early 1970s from as far away as New York City. The open crash pads of the late 1960s were gone by the middle of the 1970s. Jim Baumohl and Henry Miller (1974:39) report that the last two houses converted to such use in Berkeley burned down during the summer of 1971. During 1973 two loosely organized urban communes in Berkeley that had regularly accepted "crashers" disappeared, one because of internal dissension and the other because the house was condemned by the city and boarded up.

The Flower Children are gone, but there are still ragged panhandlers on the streets of university towns. The name that these people seem to have chosen for themselves is *street people*. Baumohl and Miller studied 292 street people in Berkeley, but comment:

> At any moment they could as readily be found in Cambridge, Madison, Ann Arbor, or even along the Southern California coast from Santa Barbara to San Diego. Their lifestyles in these other locations are similar to what we found in Berkeley: they panhandle, borrow from "wealthier" peers, engage in petty theft and small-time dope dealing. They sleep and eat when and where they can.   (Baumohl and Miller 1974:61)

Street people are seldom students, but they are attracted by the university ambience, which provides much that is supportive to them. The attractions include a variety of free services and the possibility of "crashing" with one of the communal living groups that can still be found on the periphery of many campus communities. Street people resemble the "sturdy beggars" of Elizabethan England. Most are young, white, and male. Most are dropouts, youths who have either run away or been thrown out by their families. Some quite literally live on the streets, sleeping in doorways or under bridges. Over half of the street people that Baumohl and Miller studied in Berkeley reported that they had no home, but found shelter by "crashing" with acquaintances they met on the street. Some of the rest shared houses, some lived in communes. Communal living is, for them, one of the few possible modes of survival. As Baumohl and Miller observe: "Communal living—for the hippie an experiment in new social forms—becomes, for the street person, a practical necessity characterized by little interpersonal commitment or satisfaction" (1974:56).

Most street people live completely outside of the economic system

and are ineligible for welfare. Most receive no support from their parents,
and the majority dropped out of school before acquiring skills that would
have made them employable. Among those who live in communes, economic necessity is a common bond. If the communal family is to survive
for any length of time, some members must assume responsibility for rent
and food, and provide leadership within the group. There are usually a few
who are able and willing to do this, but most members of the communal
family remain passively dependent. One young man described his communal living experience to me as follows:

In the commune I was living in two years ago there were three people
there paying rent, and one night I counted twenty people sleeping in
the house, and there were a couple of rooms out back. It wasn't an
unusual night, it was just that I stopped to count. Twenty people
there pretty continually and three people paying rent. There were
only a few people—and they generally seemed to be the same people
—who would move from house to house, but the scene would move
with them. It would be essentially the same commune moving, and
this nucleus of people that somehow managed to come up with
money to pay the rent and take a certain degree of responsibility to
keep the place going. When the first of the month came, they somehow found a way to do it.

Thus the necessities of life in the commune provide an opportunity for
some members to develop leadership roles. At least for them, the communal experience may serve as a transition between the dependency of
adolescence and the responsibility of adult life.

"This constant background noise of nothing happening"

In one of the cases that Baumohl and Miller present, the living arrangements of a respondent they call Tom are described: "Tom has been in
Berkeley for almost two years, living in a condemned house with the
myriad members of his communal family. The membership grows as
friends meet friends and friends of friends with nowhere to sleep. Originally from New York's East Village, the family is now rooted in Berkeley"
(1974:65).

It is not unusual for the nucleus of a communal "family" to survive
moves from house to house, from New York to Berkeley, from a college
town to a rural retreat. This nucleus of people may move just ahead of the
eviction notice, ahead of the health inspector or the building inspector, or
sometimes ahead of the law (a similarity to the founders of the Oneida
Community and to Father Divine, it might be noted). Sometimes the move
occurs because of internal rather than external pressures. If too many
strangers are "crashing," it may be easier to move the nucleus of the
communal "family" than to rid the group of unwanted persons. The fol-

593

lowing interview with a young man who was left behind when the nucleus of a communal "family" moved will serve as a narrative case in point. He called himself "Charlie Nothing."

> Why are there two of us here now when there were multiple other people here yesterday? All of those people didn't always *live* here, they were from a couple of different scenes. There was one that was over on Thirty-Fifth Avenue and that dwindled down, and now there is only one person that lives there. The property is going up for sale and they are tearing the house down. And so those people felt it was time to go search for greener pastures. They got a truck and everybody threw in what they could and started repairing the truck, trying to leave. And it was a positive thing again because they had a direction. It was so positive that they wanted to band together and start a commune in Oregon.
>
> The people that moved out of Thirty-Fifth Avenue moved here. There was another cat that was living here that had foreseen it coming and, not being able to handle it, moved out. Like he hardly knew the people. He knew them in the sense that we know all people, but still he had his own thing. He had nothing to say, he was more or less at one with the Source, at least that was his desire. And in order to do that he stayed more alone. And it was becoming very confused because there were a lot of funny things going on, really.
>
> There would be times when because of the floating in and out there were people that I did not know, and it turned from a home into Grand Central Station. Once I woke up in the morning and walked from my room to the other end of the house and there were maybe seven or eight or even nine people in the house that I didn't know at all. There are a lot of groovy things about a situation like that, but it also is awful freaky.
>
> I was more or less numb to it because I had been through it many times before. Paul hadn't and he made a remark about it before he left. He just came in and said, "What are all these people *doing* here?" just loud enough so everyone could hear him, and then finally he left.

Charlie Nothing was one of the founders of the small communal living group that had originally shared the old house. For a year or more the commune had been as successful as most counter-culture living groups. The pattern of development, growth, invasion, and collapse he described is typical of many counter-culture communal living groups. As the sole remaining member, he described the early days almost wistfully:

> The house is in my name and the electricity and all. When it came to, like *paying*, people that lived here at first came around with bread. Karen got bread from her parents, and one cat that lived here worked, and another had a certain amount of bread allotted to him.

"We invited the neighbors over, and they eventually moved in."

For a long time I didn't have any money at all, and nobody ever got uptight.

We ate really well. Everybody put in a little bit of bread. Karen, the girl, would go shopping and she'd take care of all that. Everybody would do what they could, and everybody was always trying and it always balanced out. It kept really free flowing, it was really peaceful. And it was good. Three of us went to school [at a local community college]. One was an art student and he was painting, the other one was in English, and so he had a lot of book work to do, and Karen just more or less did her thing, and that was happening.

Friends dropped in, we just sort of grooved together. But everything was always under control, not like toward the end when the record player would be going until four or five in the morning and the TV going on and different conversations, and somebody playing the guitar in another room—none of that. That just gets really outrageous, like everyone's competing to have the dominant thing happening.

We maintained it for a year. Karen worked for awhile and then she stopped working, nor did I work, and we managed by hook or crook. I planted a garden, so vegetables were no problem. We bought a large quantity of rice, and there was squid on the wharf, and we ate well. It was balanced, what we had was balanced. There was always lots of food, more than we could possibly eat. We would feed eight or nine people and still throw out food, there was that much. We invited the neighbors over, and they eventually moved in. And really, everybody had no money. It was just the idea of working together, even if it was just to get food.

The flux in membership was beginning to make the old Victorian house known as a place where long-haired transients could "crash." When the nucleus of another commune moved in temporarily, while repairing the old truck that was to take them to Oregon, the few remaining members of the original communal group were suddenly outsiders. Charlie Nothing recalls the next few months with some bitterness.

I was paying the rent and a lot of people started staying here. People were coming in and using the facilities, the washing machine, and because I had the garden the water bill was high and people were coming in and taking baths here. People that were just hitchhiking through town, they would say, "Oh, you can take a bath over at Charlie's house." And people would come here expecting to have that. It just got outrageous. And the water bill was going up. Somebody had to pay for it, and people weren't leaving dimes in the soap dish after they took a bath. Like now I have seventy-five dollars worth of utility bills I have to pay.

It started to look like everyone just lived from meal to meal. There was nothing apparently being done except the truck was being repaired a little bit every day. But there was nothing really going on, and to me it seems like you've got to be involved in doing something instead of nothing. I find it extremely hard under these conditions, because there is just this constant background noise of nothing happening.

I would walk into the room, and everyone would think that I was either not in favor of what they were doing or wanted to come along or *maybe* wanted to come along. They did not involve me in their plans, they were leaving me out, and I felt that. And so I would come in and I wouldn't know how to react to it. I would see them thinking I was uptight and then reacting as if I was uptight. By eye flashes, you know, turning away, looking at me and turning away—and not being able to look at one another because of what they were thinking. People start thinking things away from reality and everything gets ugly. I stuck it through to the end, and one by one they moved out. Everybody's gone, everybody split today.

Epilogue: Two years after the above interview, Charlie (no longer affecting the surname "Nothing") was the owner of a small but thriving vegetarian restaurant. The skills he had acquired in feeding large numbers of people inexpensively on rice and vegetables and the responsibility he had learned while struggling to pay the rent and the utility bills had been, for him, the means of transition to an adult role. Most who joined the exodus to Oregon have not fared so well.

The structure of communal "families"

Most communal "families" are open in structure and membership may be in continual flux. Such groups do not have sufficient structure to justify the term *family*, although the members may feel the need to have a family and call their group one. A house with a heavy flow of transients may acquire a reputation as a crash pad (as did the house described by Charlie Nothing). In contrast, the closed commune is usually not open to transients and may not take new members without extensive screening. Between these two extremes is the more typical communal "family," with some structure and a certain fluidity of membership.

Stanley Krippner and Don Fersh visited twenty-two communes between 1967 and 1970, in which they observed three basic organizational patterns: "(1) The secular commune which is relatively unstructured and which functions with a minimum of administration. (2) The secular commune which is relatively structured and which operates within an administrative framework. (3) The structured, highly-organized religious commune" (1972:221). Some of the communes Krippner and Fersh studied were in cities (Boston, New York, Toronto). But most were rural and the majority were on the west coast, primarily in Oregon and California. According to Krippner and Fersh, the "most stable, best-functioning communities" tend to share the following characteristics:

> monogamous sexual pairings, wide age range, religious orientation, collective leadership with structured delegation of tasks, frequent use of ritual, ecological concern, respect for individual privacy, noncompetitive achievement-orientation, regular source of income, good relationships with townspeople and local law enforcement authorities, no use of "hard" drugs (e.g. amphetamines, heroin, whiskey) and moderate use of "soft" drugs (e.g. beer, LSD-type drugs, marijuana, tobacco, wine). (Krippner and Fersh 1972:221)

It is difficult to generalize about such disparate groups, which range in philosophy from the devoutly religious to the hedonistic. But in rural communes the basic imperatives of subsistence agriculture set limits within which these experimental communal groups can create new life-styles. In rural communes the counter-culture has reached back to the sex roles of earlier subsistence agriculture. The women tend to be primarily responsible for food preparation and the making of clothing; the men tend to take primary responsibility for construction, cutting timber, and heavi-

597

er outdoor work. Gardening is often a shared endeavor, however, and anyone who has special skills is usually encouraged to use them, regardless of the sex-role identification of the task.

Most observers have noted that stable nuclear units tend to persist in rural communes, although the couple are frequently not married (or not married to each other). Bennet Berger (1971) and his research team studied rural or quasi-rural communes only. They found that a variety of nuclear units existed within these rural communal "families." There were legally married spouses and their children. There were unmarried couples with children. There were couples in which the male partner was not the father of the woman's children. On occasion, in a nuclear unit of man, woman, and child, it was the father who was the natural parent.

Childrearing in the communes of the counter-culture has been regarded primarily as a matter of interfering with the child as little as possible, a philosophy sometimes expressed as a desire to keep adults from "dumping on its head." This has meant little discipline for the children in most communes. The children tend to have few inhibitions, and to be remarkably self-reliant. They also tend to be illiterate, and most will find it difficult to make the transition back to the mainstream of American culture when they are grown. The children of the communes seem to be caught in the counter-culture much as the children of the inner city are trapped by their socialization in poverty.

The world view of the counter-culture has the same focus on the present that characterizes the very poor everywhere, and for the same pressing reason: surviving today requires all available energy. Rural communal "families" often take a longer view than urban communes, for they are less likely to be loosely structured crash pads. The communal "family" living off the land must anticipate the changing seasons and work within the rhythm of planting and reaping, which requires some orientation to the future. But those who sow do not always stay to reap, nor do those who reap where they have not sown believe they should feel grateful. The less-structured rural communes often function like summer camps, the members dispersing in the winter, leaving only a caretaker member or two, and returning with the spring.

The transient life-style of the street people encourages patterns of behavior that enable those who adopt them most completely to survive, sometimes even to flourish, within the confines of the subculture, but may block movement out of it. For street people, the rural commune may seem the only alternative. Conversely, for those who have made the exodus from the streets to the rural commune, failure of the rural commune may mean a return to the street. Many members of the counter-culture feel that all other doors are closed to them. Such communes are hardly a romantic adventure; they are often an alternative of last resort. A young woman who was one of the founders of a rural communal "family" in Oregon, and was (like most of the other members of the commune) a refugee from the crash pads of Berkeley, put it this way:

598

The less structured rural communes often function like summer camps. The members disperse in the winter, leaving only a caretaker member or two, and return with the spring.

We all came at the time we did because we didn't feel that there was anything else that we could do. For various reasons this was where we had to be, we couldn't be anywhere else, we had to make it here. There was no alternative, we couldn't go anywhere else. We were here with this piece of land and we had to make our life on it.

Many communal "families" that went to the land in search of Eden in the

599

late 1960s have disbanded. But there are still communal "families" in the isolated rural areas of many states, particularly along the west coast and in New England. And there are still communal living groups moving from urban centers to the land. Some communal "families" live on the transitional fringe where suburban development meets the unincorporated rural area. Where land is changing from agricultural use to residential use, land speculators flourish. They are sometimes willing to rent a condemned farmhouse to a communal "family" during the interval before the developer and the bulldozer arrive.

This is the pattern in Santa Cruz, California. The recently built campus of the University of California is located on the outskirts of the city, and burgeoning suburban tracts and condominiums have surrounded old farms near the campus. Old farmhouses are often occupied by a communal living group comprised of some students, some former students, and some nonstudents who have drifted down from Berkeley, or up from Santa Barbara. When the county health department or the bulldozer overtakes such groups, they tend to dissolve, but a nucleus often moves on to some other old house, sometimes to another area. One such communal living group occupied a condemned farmhouse near the Santa Cruz campus for about two years, growing an abundant garden. After some difficulty with the landlord, they made arrangements through a vanguard of members to move to an Arkansas farm as sharecroppers. In the spring of 1975 they loaded their battered van with belongings and headed for Arkansas, in an ironic reversal of the migration that brought so many battered cars filled with Arkansas sharecroppers to California some forty years ago.

The major difference between the rural communal living groups of the 1960s and those of the 1970s seems to be that the contemporary groups are less concerned with the philosophical implications of creating an alternative life-style and more concerned with the techniques of mulching gardens and making cheese from goat's milk. They know, as the rural poor have always known, that it is possible to survive in difficult economic times if one has a big garden, a few chickens and goats, and enough hands to work the land. Winter and hunger impose certain demands, and the survival of each individual is tied to the survival of the group as a functioning unit.

There is a discipline required of members of a successful commune that few seem able to develop unless there is a strong bond between group members. Those communal "families" that do not develop group solidarity and discipline dissolve in a relatively brief time. The more stable communal groups often have a religious doctrine that unifies the members, typically a blend of Eastern mysticism and Christianity, sometimes fundamental Christianity. There is a sense of sharing and trust in a religious communal "family," and a sense of pseudo-kinship, for all have been reborn as brothers and sisters in the faith.

One of the largest religious communal groups is the movement known as the Children of God. This is a fundamental Christian group,

600

practicing a form of religious communism. The Children of God initially received assistance from a television evangelist. Working among the street people, the Children of God converted hundreds of members. Early in the 1970s, the membership was estimated at approximately 2,000. The Children of God maintained a communal ranch in Texas, a smaller ranch in the Coachella Valley of California, and a Skid Row mission in Los Angeles. In 1971 the Children of God merged with a more loosely knit group of so-called street Christians in the Pacific Northwest. These street Christians had numerous urban communal houses and coffeehouses, most located in the Seattle area. The coffeehouses were a source of both funds and recruits.

Concerned parents and relatives have sought with small success to persuade their children to leave the Children of God. A few do. One of those who left the Los Angeles commune of the Children of God told John Dart, a reporter for the *Los Angeles Times:* "They really care about you and watch over you just like your own mother—better than your own mother" (Dart 1971:25). Like the followers of Father Divine, the Children of God seem to have transferred their loyalty from parents and family to their brothers and sisters in the communal movement. There is a tendency for communal movements to be antifamilistic, for if members felt the pull of competing loyalties, the movement would be weakened.

The commune as a transitional "family"

For most members of a communal "family," the communal experience is a transition between what was and what may be. As noted in an earlier chapter, the conjugal family as it has evolved in America is a good setting for the socialization of young children, but not well-suited to the needs of adolescents. For some who are caught in the limbo between childhood and adult roles, the communal "family" provides an alternative.

Not all communes are part of the counter-culture. Some structured communal living groups are created by social agencies to be half-way houses for wayward youth, or for persons who are trying to learn to live in society after a mental breakdown, or a term in prison, or after drug detoxification. The support of peers in various stages of rehabilitation and a professional staff make the half-way house an effective way-station for the individual who is trying to reenter society. That such a group is a surrogate family is usually explicit. Most such living groups are involved in some form of therapy, which tends to create intense personal bonds. Many half-way houses are sponsored by some social welfare agency, or supervised and licensed by local public health agencies. Some are voluntary associations that receive no governmental aid. Of these, Synanon is perhaps the best known, and one of the most successful.

Synanon is a communal society founded in 1958 by Charles E. Dederich, a former alcoholic and a former oil company executive. Taking Alcoholics Anonymous as a model and his $35 unemployment check for

601

capital, Dederich founded Synanon. By the 1970s Synanon was reported to have an annual cash flow totaling more than $2 million, with perhaps an additional $4 million per year in the form of donated food and materials. Synanon receives no government aid, but does receive substantial private donations. It is a sheltered community in which troubled persons, primarily addicts, can rehabilitate themselves. Although its major settlement is on Tomales Bay, on the California coast north of San Francisco, Synanon has reached out to persons across the country. On December 5, 1971, the *New York Times* reported that Synanon recruiters had persuaded more than 500 heroin addicts to leave New York City and journey to Tomales Bay for rehabilitation.

There are three cardinal rules for the members of Synanon: no use of addictive drugs (including alcohol); no smoking; no physical violence or threat of violence. The basic rehabilitation process is the Synanon game. This is a form of aggression therapy in which participants vent deep and sometimes angry feelings. (It is a contemporary parallel to the mutual criticism method developed by Noyes at Oneida for much the same cathartic and socializing effect.)

Critics accuse Synanon of being cultish and accuse Dederich of cultivating the reverence in which he is held by members. This is in the long tradition of charismatic leaders of communal movements, however. At the very least, Synanon does provide one effective way of handling addiction: life in a controlled, sequestered community where social and psychological support are continuous. The best results seem to be with those who remain in Synanon's controlled communal environment. In the last few years, this environment at Synanon has appealed to many persons who are not and have never been drug addicts. The growing community on Tomales Bay has become a haven for many people who have chosen this disciplined communal life as an alternative to family life in urban America.

A more recently established therapeutic community is the Delancey Street Foundation, founded by John Maher, former addict, former armed robber, former felon. Maher founded Delancey in 1971 in an apartment in San Francisco, with $1,000 borrowed from a loan shark. By 1976 the Delancey Street Foundation owned half a dozen mansions and apartment complexes in the San Francisco Bay area. The Delancey Street Foundation is a multiracial community of some 350 former felons, with a combined arrest record of over 2,000 arrests. There has been only *one* arrest of a resident since they came together to live at Delancey Street. Many "graduates" of the Delancey Street Foundation have returned to the larger society with friends, skills, credit, and jobs. As of 1976 the rate of recidivism (that is, return to a criminal life) was zero, according to Charles Hampden-Turner (1976), a sociologist who lived for a year as a participant observer at the Delancey Street Foundation.

The Delancey Street Foundation has refused federal funds and has become a self-supporting community through a variety of legitimate business ventures owned and operated by Delancey residents (this is in the

A "dissipation" at the Delancey Street Foundation. This is a "Waterhead Hearing." The faucet attached to the man's forehead is a symbol that he is to pour out his feelings.

tradition of the kingdom of Father Divine, whose followers also operated a wide variety of small business enterprises). In these businesses the ex-convicts of Delancey Street are able to get jobs and to acquire training on the job. The Delancey Street Foundation has a federally chartered credit union, an accredited high school, and sponsors a variety of sports and educational activities. Like Synanon, Delancey Street uses forms of aggression therapy as its primary mode of rehabilitation. There are therapeutic games, such as the Waterhead Hearings, which are a form of attack therapy. There are "Dissipations," as they are called at Delancey Street. "Dissipations" are group psychodramas in which members relive the worst moments of their lives in an attempt to dissipate the horrors of their past.

Such therapeutic communities as Synanon and the Delancey Street Foundation do not rely on professional therapists to rehabilitate drug addicts and former felons. Everyone in the community—professional, addict, or felon—is equally subject to aggression therapy. Thus there is no sharp line between patient and therapist, but rather a sense of a community of troubled persons, with different life histories and differing life chances.

Synanon is primarily a rural community, secluded from the pressures of urban life. The Delancey Street Foundation, in contrast, is an urban community set within the city and operating businesses that are successful urban commercial enterprises. What the two communal groups

603

have in common that accounts for their success in rehabilitation is the solidarity of a group that is able to perform a belated socializing function for persons who have never experienced the social and emotional support of a functioning family. Ruth Jacobs observes:

> Control and emotive ... groups ... become a socializing primary group, taking over the task incompleted, abdicated or failed by the family and bureaucratized education. Most early group therapy was a deliberate attempt to replicate the nuclear family ... Present ... groups seem more akin to extended families, once a major normative source. The groups provide a face-to-face situation in which norms may emerge through interaction and in which solidarity may develop and with it group control of the individuals.
> (Jacobs 1971:2)

It is the extended family, not the conjugal family, that is replicated by the therapeutic communal living group. The member of the therapeutic community feels group pride, one important element in social control. Another powerful control over the behavior of individual members is the sense of shame he or she would feel if any action of that member were to bring disgrace to the group. The therapeutic communal living group provides support for each individual member—social, economic, and emotional support—similar to that which comes from belonging to a large and successful extended family.

The commune as a surrogate family

The press and some of the participants refer to contemporary communal living groups as *communes*. Many members call them *communities* (the phrase *intentional community* is heard with increasing frequency). But whatever else they may be called, communal living groups with even a semblance of structure and stability are typically referred to by those who live in them as *families*. People living communally want to think of their group as a family, because they feel a need for the kind of security that a family is supposed to provide. There are many persons in our society for whom family life is not a real possibility, at least not at some point in their life-cycle. As noted in an earlier chapter, the conjugal family is ill-equipped to cope with the needs of persons who are making the transition from adolescent to adult. Familial roles may be too demanding for the personal, emotional, and financial resources of drug addicts, alcoholics, and the man or woman recently released from prison. Communal living groups functioning as surrogate extended families may meet the needs of such people better than the conjugal family.

The conjugal family is as ill-suited to the needs of the elderly as it is to the needs of adolescents. The growth of nursing homes and convalescent hospitals attests to the need for some institution other than the family to care for the aged, many of whom do not need nursing or custodial care.

Many aging persons who are not physically debilitated are no longer able to be completely independent. They may find the physical and financial burdens of maintaining a household too great, particularly after they are widowed. Going to live with a married son or daughter is an option frequently chosen by widows and widowers, but it is not a choice that is open to all or preferred by all. Many widows and widowers who must live alone gradually lose interest in living. People are social animals, and life alone is a depressing situation for most of us. This is particularly true for the aging, who have health and financial problems much greater than those faced by the young. Often they eat sporadically, in part because of the poverty in which many aging Americans live, but also because eating alone is likely to lead them to irregular eating habits. Sometimes the elderly withdraw into almost furtive life-styles out of fear of being the victims of robbery and urban violence. Sometimes they are isolates because they no longer are part of any other person's life. *The communal "family"*

Like the young, the old tend to be segregated and powerless. They are usually unemployed, often isolated. Their families may try to control them through financial dependence. If an elderly widow and a widower want to marry, they may face extreme disapproval from their grown children. For many of the same reasons that the dependent young find coping with the adult world difficult, the elderly find it difficult to cope with dominant adults. Dependent economically, relatively powerless, isolated from the world of work, diminished in physical strength, the aging may find refuge in communal living.

In 1969 James Gillies, an Orlando, Florida, businessman, created a nonprofit organization called Share-A-Home for elderly persons who do not need nursing care. By 1976 there were eight residences in the Share-A-Home network, with 112 members (Kellogg and Jaffee 1976:98). These are neither boardinghouses nor nursing homes; they are communal living groups. At Share-A-Home the members form a "family" unit set up to give them, as a group, legal authority over their own lives. They vote on new members. They hire and fire the staff of housekeepers. They plan menus and have kitchen privileges if they wish. Members pay from $274 to $400 per month, for which they receive room, three meals a day, laundry service, maid service, and the services of a car and a driver to take them shopping, to church, to the doctor.

Because Share-A-Home is a nonprofit organization, these communal living groups for the elderly are not considered boardinghouses or board-and-care homes and are not (thus far) subject to local ordinances or zoning restrictions that would apply to the latter. This has been an advantage to these communal living groups. On the other hand, because there is no resident medical staff, the Share-A-Home projects do not qualify for Medicaid or state programs that pay for care in nursing homes. In spite of this disadvantage in funding, the elderly may find living with people their own age a valid alternative to nursing home dependency.

Americans often spend more than a decade in the limbo of age, after

605

they have been deprived of active adult roles by retirement, widowhood, or infirmity. Like the adolescent faced with bewildering personal changes, the aging person enters a period of transition. A communal living group of the same generation forms a surrogate family of people who are experiencing together the many small but painful adjustments to advancing years.

The young and the old are not the only people in need of a surrogate family. As the number of single parents grows, there is a growing need for surrogate families to provide economic and social support for single parents and their children. Here is another group whose financial resources may be insufficient to maintain a household, a group of people who need the exchange of services (particularly child care) that a family structure normally makes possible. Many single parents resolve their dilemma by marrying and meeting their needs in a conventional conjugal family setting. But there are many single parents for whom marriage is not a feasible alternative or not their alternative of choice. Some of these single parents are finding that communal living groups can provide a surrogate family.

There are other single adults who are beginning to discover communal living. High rents in many cities have made it increasingly difficult for single persons to maintain a household. The loneliness of city life as well as the expense make a surrogate family attractive to people for whom marriage and the conjugal family are for some reason not available. As long as there have been cities, there have been boardinghouses. What are developing in some American cities are more than boardinghouses; they are communal living groups for middle-aged, middle-class persons. Because the term *commune* has become associated with the counter-culture, the name *intentional community* is often preferred by middle-class communal living groups. Most of these communal groups are composed of employed persons. Most of them share household expenses and many of them eat together at least once a day, but they usually do not pool income or personal possessions.

There is in Berkeley, California, a rental referral agency that specializes in communes and has about 200 listings on its books at any given time. These are communes that are looking for additional members, and the listing indicates the sort of person they hope to find. The typical communal household listed by this rental agency has four or five members and the average monthly rent required is $130. However, in advertising a vacancy the group is usually looking for more than a roommate who will pay a portion of the rent. Most of these groups do have a sense of community and do function as a surrogate family.

About fifty persons a week come into the Berkeley rental agency and pay for a three-month access to the listing of communes. Most applicants are employed but cannot afford to rent an apartment by themselves. Many prefer the social and emotional context of group living. The woman who founded this rental agency told Harriet Stix (1976), a reporter for the *Los*

Angeles Times, that although most communal households are composed of younger persons, many of the clients she is now seeing are in their forties or older. Many are recently divorced or widowed. Agency clients look over the listings, which include information about the amount of rent, the size of the room, whether the room is sunny, whether a deposit is required, whether meals are shared, whether the living group is for women only, for men only, or mixed, whether smokers are welcome, whether children or pets are permitted. The listing also notes whether the commune has a counter-culture life-style or is more conventional.

Many of the older applicants for communal living seem to prefer a house that has a mixture of young and old members—a surrogate family that includes generational differences, as a real family does. One intentional community in Berkeley described by Stix has an age range that includes two little girls, ages eight and twelve, who live with their respective mothers, and several adults who range in age from thirty-one to sixty years. Applicants for this communal "family" are screened by telephone, then invited to dinner. Every member of this intentional community has to approve the addition of a new member. Most members of this "family" have lived together for about two years and have come to regard each other as *chosen* relatives. They are looking for a house to buy together.

The high cost of housing, problems of child care for single parents, and other difficulties of maintaining a home may lead some persons to seek others to share expenses. This is not communal living in the sense that the Shakers knew it, or the Oneida Community, or the Peace Mission movement, or the Children of God. There is neither the personal involvement, nor the religious bonds, nor the commitment of personal and financial resources. Such group living is merely an adaptation to high rents, a housing shortage, inflation, and the accidents of life which have left these persons without a family. The poor have adapted to such social and economic pressures by taking in roomers, relatives or friends, for countless generations. What is new is that middle-class persons may now be finding themselves faced with the necessity of sharing housing. Downwardly mobile persons from the middle class may find it easier to accept such necessity by structuring it as an innovative life-style.

Opposition to the communal "family"

To those who have chosen communal living, that life-style is a means of resolving some problems, a way of coping. To many of their neighbors, the commune is a public nuisance. This is not a new pattern of conflict. As early as 1847 the surrounding community brought pressure on Noyes, the founder of the Oneida Community, who fled to avoid prosecution. The complaints of Long Island neighbors resulted in the arrest and conviction of Father Divine for operating a public nuisance. The Delancey Street Foundation has faced strong neighborhood opposition.

People who are sympathetic with the concept of a half-way house for **607** the rehabilitation of addicts or felons, or for the nonviolent mentally ill, are seldom pleased to see such a group located on their block. Somewhere else in the community, perhaps, but not on their street. There is often fear of the residents of therapeutic half-way houses: fear of a rising rate of burglary in the neighborhood, fear of muggings, of rape. Whether or not such fears are warranted, the anxiety is real. Because many contemporary communal living groups are outposts of the counter-culture, there is often fear that such a group will bring drug use into the neighborhood. Parents are afraid that a commune on the block will be a harmful influence on their children. To the neighbors, the life-style of the communal living group often appears to be a deliberate affront to the values and beliefs of the majority in the community.

When communal "families" moved out of the Haight-Ashbury district of San Francisco in 1970, refugees from growing violence and harassment, a number of these counter-culture communes moved across the Golden Gate Bridge to the city of San Rafael. Herbert Hotchner, the city planning director of San Rafael, is quoted in the *San Francisco Examiner and Chronicle* (July 20, 1975:A-2) as saying that neighbors objected to these transplanted communes because of "upsetting characteristics" and because of the "unconventional behavior of the occupants." Specifically, he noted nude sunbathing on lawns, replacing window shades with psychedelic pictures, and noise from motorcycles at all hours of the night.

In addition to antipathy based on personal values and life-style, the neighbors may fear that the value of their homes will decline if a commune is allowed to stay on their block. A home is usually a family's largest investment, and the economic fear is a real one. The conversion of a large old house from single-family occupancy to multiple-family use means that plumbing and wiring intended to serve the needs of one family must serve many persons. Overloaded circuits may become fire hazards; inadequate plumbing may become a health hazard. Such crowding often deteriorates a house rapidly. Change from single-family to multiple occupancy often marks the beginning of deterioration of the entire neighborhood. The people next door often sell out quickly, fleeing from their unwanted neighbors. The persons most likely to buy the house are seldom looking for a home for themselves, but more often are looking for a bargain in rental property. They are most likely to be able to rent to another, similar group. This is the classic pattern of neighborhood invasion and succession, to use the demographic terms. At the end of the transition the neighborhood often has become a cheap rooming house district, a deteriorated urban area.

Thus the fears of the neighbors of a communal living group are based on a mixture of fear for their personal safety, ideological differences, and potential economic loss. Neighbors sometimes band together to bring legal action to drive a commune from their street. In the past, charges of adultery and operating a public nuisance have been used to

pressure communal living groups into leaving a neighborhood. Today, the most common legal levers for removing a commune are fire codes, health and sanitation codes, and restricted zoning. If the neighborhood is zoned for single-family residence, a variance may be required for any other form of occupancy.

When city authorities put pressure on communal groups living in houses zoned for single-family residence, the members of such groups may argue that they *are* a single family. This argument has sometimes prevented eviction of a commune. City codes are typically somewhat ambiguous in defining a single family and have not required that all persons occupying a house be related by blood or marriage. Such codes were often written many years ago, in an era when large houses were frequently occupied by a family with servants (even the middle class had servants who lived downstairs as recently as World War I). As long as the house zoned for single-family occupancy is not being used as a commercial boarding-house or as a tourist accommodation, no variance may be required.

A number of cities and towns have become sufficiently disturbed by the presence of communal "families" to adopt a legal definition of a family that is more restrictive. Some of these new zoning ordinances have been challenged in the courts. In 1974 one of these suits reached the United States Supreme Court. This suit involved a zoning ordinance that limited housing to single-family units and permitted these to be occupied by no more than two persons unrelated by blood or marriage. The ordinance had been adopted by the village of Belle Terre on Long Island, after a house in the village had been rented by six students from the State University of New York at Stony Brook. When the landlords of the house occupied by the group of students were ordered to comply with the local zoning ordinance, the landlords and three of the students challenged the ordinance in the courts, alleging that it went beyond the constitutional powers of local government and that it violated the constitutional rights of the tenants. The landlords and tenants were upheld both by a U.S. district court and by the federal appellate court.

The village of Belle Terre appealed the case to the United States Supreme Court. In April of 1974 the Supreme Court upheld the right of a local government to ban communal living within its jurisdiction and said that the constitutional rights of the tenants were not violated by the ordinance. The majority opinion was written by Justice William O. Douglas, who said that the power of local governments in zoning matters "is not confined to elimination of filth, stench and unhealthy places," but that the power of local government is ample "to lay out zones where family values and the blessing of quiet seclusion and clean air make the area a sanctuary for people." This Supreme Court ruling cleared the way for the adoption of city ordinances restricting communal living groups. A number of cities have already passed such ordinances. Whether or not these ordinances defining what constitutes a family are strictly enforced, communal living does not seem likely to replace the conjugal family for a majority of Americans.

609

References

Baumohl, Jim, and Henry Miller. 1974. *Down and Out in Berkeley*. Berkeley, Calif.: City of Berkeley–University of California Community Affairs Committee.

Berger, Bennett, et al. 1971. "Child-Rearing Practices of the Communal Family." In *Family in Transition*, edited by Arlene S. Skolnick and Jerome H. Skolnick, pp. 509–523. Boston: Little, Brown and Company.

Carmer, Carl. 1936. *Listen for a Lonesome Drum*. New York: Farrar & Rinehart.

Dart, John. 1971. "Youths' Commune Religion Upsets Parents." *Los Angeles Times* (October 10):1, 24–25.

Edmonds, Walter D. 1948. *The First Hundred Years*. Sherrill, N.Y.: Oneida.

Hampden-Turner, Charles. 1976. *Sane Asylum: Inside the Delancey Street Foundation*. San Francisco: San Francisco Book Company.

Harris, Sara, with Harriet Crittenden. 1954. *Father Divine: Holy Husband*. Garden City, N.Y.: Doubleday & Company.

Jacobs, Ruth. 1971. "Emotive and Control Groups as Mutated New American Utopian Communities." *Journal of Applied Behavioral Science* (January) 7:2.

Kellogg, Mary Alice, and Andrew Jaffe. 1976. "Old Folks' Commune." *Newsweek* (April 19):97–98.

Kephart, William M. 1961. *The Family, Society, and the Individual*. Boston: Houghton Mifflin Company.

Krippner, Stanley, and Don Fersh. 1972. "Spontaneous Paranormal Experience among Members of Intentional Communities." In *Marriage and Family in a Decade of Change*, edited by Gwen B. Carr, pp. 220–233. Reading, Mass.: Addison-Wesley Publishing Company.

Marx, John H., and David L. Ellison. 1975. "Sensitivity Training and Communes: Contemporary Quests for Community." *Pacific Sociological Review* (October) 18:442–462.

Stix, Harriet. 1976. "Consider Yourself at Home." *Los Angeles Times* (May 9):Sec. 4, 1, 18–19.

Suggested readings

Kinkade, Kathleen. 1972. *A Walden Two Experiment: The First Five Years of Twin Oaks Community*. New York: William Morrow & Company. Illustrated. An account of a community run on lines laid down by B. F. Skinner in his utopian novel *Walden Two*. The community is located on a Virginia farm, near Richmond, and this is a brisk and candid account of commune life.

Vonnegut, Mark. 1975. *The Eden Express*. New York: Praeger. An autobiographical account by the son of a famous author. Mark Vonnegut graduated from college in 1969, then in the summer of 1970 went west to found a commune. In a valley in British Columbia he looked for the answers to "the nightmare life our society had become," but found schizophrenia. His journey into madness and back is chronicled with honesty.

Wolf, Susan, and John Rothchild. 1976. *The Children of the Counterculture*. Garden City, N.Y.: Doubleday & Company. Illustrated. A report of children raised in communes ranging from regimented religious communes to casual crash pads. The authors found that many counter-culture children are self-reliant, a few are emotionally disturbed. But most are ignored, illiterate, and unprepared for the world outside the commune.

22 The conjugal contract

The very being or legal existence of the woman is suspended during the marriage, or at least is incorporated and consolidated into that of the husband; under whose wing, protection, and cover she performs everything; and is therefore called in our law a femme couverte. *Upon this principle of a union of person in husband and wife, depend all the legal rights, duties, and disabilities that either of them acquire by marriage.*

Blackstone (1765–1769:442)

The new feminism of the 1960s and 1970s has brought an emerging consciousness among American women of the nature of traditional marital roles. Many women have been raising questions regarding the marriage contract. This is not a new concern, however. When Lucy Stone, an ardent feminist of an earlier century, married Henry Blackwell, the two joined hands in a symbolic gesture at their wedding and read aloud a statement declaring: "This act on our part implies no sanction of, nor promise of voluntary obedience to such of the present laws of marriage as refuse to recognize the wife as an independent, rational being, while they confer upon the husband an injurious and unnatural superiority" (cited in Flexner 1960:64).

The marriage contract: secure refuge or tender trap?

Marriage was once considered a "tender trap" in which women ensnared men (sex was the bait). In recent years, some women have begun to regard marriage as a snare in which they, too, are entangled. Whether marriage is a trap or a refuge is more a question of emotional perspective than of objective fact. At most it is possible to compare the relative freedom and security of the married and the unmarried, the rights and obligations of husbands and wives, and to ask what alternatives to marriage men and women may have.

Marriage is considered in the law to be a contract that creates a status. When a man and woman marry, they acquire the statuses of husband and wife, respectively. The marriage can be dissolved by divorce, annulment, or the death of one spouse, but the marital status of the individual returns to single only in the case of annulment. The divorced have a separate marital status, as do the widowed, which reflects the fact that they were once married and that marriage creates certain relationships which are not entirely dissolved with death or divorce. Both the divorced and the widowed are free to remarry if they choose, but they continue to have status rights and obligations that they would not have if they were single (including such rights and obligations as alimony for the divorced, inheritance and survivor's benefits for the widowed).

Marriage creates a series of other statuses besides those of husband and wife: father-in-law, mother-in-law, son-in-law, daughter-in-law, brother-in-law, sister-in-law. These statuses are a form of kinship. The Internal Revenue Service includes in-laws on the list of persons who may be claimed as dependents for income tax purposes, and the tax instructions state that "once any of the above relationships have been established by marriage, they will not be terminated by death or divorce." Such relationships may outlast a marriage for other than tax purposes. People often find that their in-laws continue to regard them as part of the family after the death of their spouse, and even after a divorce. *Marriage creates a kinship network.* In many ways, marriage is similar to adoption: to marry is to acquire a family.

As a contract, marriage resembles a business partnership, but one in which the rights and obligations of the two partners are unequal. Legally, marriage is a contract that creates certain rights and obligations with regard to property and financial support. These have been discussed at some length above, in the chapter dealing with marriage and money and in the chapter on divorce. To recapitulate briefly here: the English common law, on which statutes relating to marriage are based in all but eight of these United States, regarded husband and wife as one person, and that person was the husband. The quotation at the beginning of this chapter, from the *Commentaries* of Blackstone, the great English authority on the common law, states the legal situation of the wife under the common law. Under the common law, marriage gave the husband the right to control not only his own property, but that of his wife as well. In return for relinquishing her property (and the income derived from it) to her husband, the wife was to receive financial support for life. A man was obligated to provide for his wife's support during marriage, and was expected to make some provision for her support if she was granted a divorce or legal separation, or if he died.

In the nineteenth century, state laws were enacted that gave American women the right to own and control their separate property after marriage and to enter contracts in their own name. But the support obligation of the husband remained unchanged. In every state, the husband has an obligation to support his wife, an obligation that does not necessarily end with divorce. However, the wife is obligated to support her husband only if he is unable to support himself, and then only in some states. It is this unequal support obligation that leads many men to regard marriage as a trap.

On the other hand, the husband retains certain rights. He has the right to establish domicile in most states, which means both the right to choose where the couple will live and what their level of living will be. He has the control and management of property accumulated by the couple during the marriage. In community property states, the husband has the right to manage the community property in which his wife has an equal interest; in some states he may encumber community property (use it to secure a loan) without his wife's consent.

In states where marital property rights are based on the common law, the wife may have little claim to property accumulated by the couple during the years in which she has contributed to the family as a homemaker. Unless she has been able to acquire property in her own name, she may have little that is clearly her own if there is a divorce. A woman who truncates her education and marries while young, who spends the next decade or two focusing her energies on being a housewife and mother, will have few skills that would make her employable. She may find that she has little alternative to an unhappy marriage. It is this sense of being her husband's dependent without much hope of becoming self-supporting that leaves many women feeling trapped by marriage.

615

It is a tight circle: men may feel trapped by the support obligation of a husband, women may feel trapped by economic dependency. It should be noted, however, that although the support obligation of the husband is a matter of law, which would not apply if the couple were not legally married, the dependency of the wife is a matter of custom and her skills. A married woman may have a career that makes her economically independent; there is nothing in the marriage contract that says a wife must be confined to the role of housekeeper. Conversely, a woman living in a consensual union may be as dependent on her man as any wife could be, but lack the legal right to support and property (or Social Security benefits) that marriage would have given her. It is not marriage that traps a woman, it is lack of job-related skills.

Paradoxically, twenty years ago marriage was often seen as a liberating event. Marriage was the avenue by which girls were able to escape parental domination. Marriage established a young man as master in his own home. (Young, single people seldom had their own households until the 1960s.) There are still places in the United States where marriage retains this liberating effect, giving young people the right to run their own lives with full adult privileges. Marriage has come to seem confining in part because single people have been granted more economic, social, and sexual freedom than they used to have.

The conjugal contract: innovative solution or legal thicket?

It has become fashionable for couples to write their marriage vows, substituting their own words of commitment for traditional phrases having to do with obedience and fidelity. Together with a trend toward holding the wedding in a garden or meadow, these unique and personal vows tend to make marriage more a private agreement than a religious sacrament. It may be that the couple will arrive at a better understanding of what each expects of marriage and of the other through the process of composing their own vows, but their obligations to each other under the law will not be affected.

Many couples are now signing prenuptial agreements regarding the way in which the roles of husband and wife will be structured in their marriage. Although such agreements are sometimes called conjugal contracts, they are not contracts in any legal sense, and often are little more than a promise to share the household chores. A specific prenuptial agreement to share responsibility for their mutual needs and comfort may have a salutory effect on the marital relationship that develops, but it has no effect on their legal obligations to each other. (Some couples sign prenuptial agreements regarding the ownership of property that either or both possess before marriage; if developed with legal advice, such agreements have legal standing.) The legal obligations of spouses to each other are contained in the law of the state. State statutes defining marital rights and duties constitute the contract a married couple enter, whether they are

It has become fashionable for couples to write their marriage vows, substituting their own words of commitment for traditional phrases having to do with obedience and fidelity. Together with a trend toward holding the wedding in a garden or meadow, these unique and personal vows tend to make marriage more a private agreement than a religious sacrament.

aware of it or not, when the marriage certificate is signed, witnessed, and recorded at the county hall of records. Those married in another state are covered by the laws of the state where they have their legal residence.

Some women who have become identified with the feminist movement have chosen not to marry, rather than enter into the marriage contract as it is presently defined. Some men, particularly men who have had an early and unhappy marriage followed by divorce, prefer not to incur again the obligations that marriage places on the husband. Because most persons prefer to live with a person of the opposite sex, the result has been a growing number of consensual unions. "Living together" has become almost modish in some circles, and as indicated in an earlier chapter, the consensual union has long characterized impoverished Americans.

Some couples who are reluctant to enter marriage as it is presently defined by state laws, but who want to have some formal structure in their relationship, are entering into conjugal contracts. These are not merely agreements about who will wash the dishes and do the laundry on alternate weeks, or even about how child care will be divided. These are contracts involving questions of support, of ownership and management of proper-

617

ty, of common debts, and of the custody and paternity of children. Such a conjugal contract would be superseded by state laws if the couple married, so couples signing a conjugal contract tend to do so instead of marrying.

It should be emphasized that a conjugal contract is not a legal alternative to marriage. The state has preempted the right to determine the obligations and the rights of husband and wife. Persons executing conjugal contracts instead of marriage contracts are legally single. Depending on the state in which they live, such a couple may be defined by the law as living in lewd cohabitation.

A small but growing number of couples seem willing to take the risks inherent in entering a conjugal contract. It is not yet clear how such agreements will be viewed by the courts, if they are ever called upon to enforce the provisions of a conjugal contract. Private conjugal contracts could become a legal thicket, particularly with regard to property rights and the custody of children.

Living together: a case study

Russell Hurley and Mara Epstein (not their real names) had been living together for some months and wanted to make a more lasting commitment to each other. Yet for differing reasons, neither wanted to marry. Russell commented on his ambivalent feelings:

> *Russell:* I had been married before, for ten years, divorced, and my son was living with me. I was married from the time I was nineteen and was a father from the time I was twenty. I was a student and most of the time for one year I took in children to make money while I was going to school. I did all my studying at home rather than at a university library, so I had a lot of contact with the children. And I was used to living with a woman. Mara had a different kind of experience. She had been single all this time and—she could probably explain it better than I can.
>
> When we started living together we moved up to Rocky Creek and lived there throughout the whole winter. I found that I was uncomfortable with the idea of just living together. I had a profession, and the only legal definition of our relationship was "lewd cohabitation," and I didn't like that. Our relationship was neither immoral, indecent, nor lewd. And I figured I would like to have some protection for that relationship.
>
> And yet, as one who had been involved in the male liberation movement, I had thought about what I wanted and what I didn't want, and I understood the kind of bind that my ex-wife had been in as a married woman who was bound by certain rules. I didn't want to get involved in another relationship like that. Marriage has been a relationship that has contributed greatly to sexual stereotypes about what a woman is capable of doing and what a man is capable of doing.

contract*

I tend to be aggressive, I'm an Aries. I'm strong and have a lot of command of the physical world, the technical world. Mara is a Pisces, she is very withdrawn, has a lot of inner life. She has trouble dealing with things like bureaucracies or mechanical things. Although those things might be part of the stereotype of the differences between males and females, they don't have anything to do with the biological differences between us, they have to do with personality structure. Very often those kinds of things have been seen as—women are supposed to be that way. Women are supposed to be hairless. Mara is not hairless, she is hairier than I am. I would hate it if she shaved her legs.

Like many other couples who are living together without marriage, Russell and Mara found that there were certain ambiguities in their relationship. There was also some personal stress and some social embarrassment. Russell talked about their first winter together, clearly a winter of discontent.

Russell: Mara was in a tremendous depression that whole winter. Normally, when people start living together it is like a honeymoon. Well, it wasn't that way with us. We got together and Mara went through a lot of—it was a bad winter. It was cold, the house leaked all over, there was just a small part of the house we could occupy. My contract was over at that point, because I had just been hired from year to year, and the money was running out, so we were looking forward to a rather insecure future.

Mara was subject to some very severe depressions that lasted for a long time. She had just started a Ph.D. program, and she found out that it really wasn't what she wanted. Things weren't working out that way very well. And for the first time, she had to live with a noisy kid, and she is supersensitive to sound. It was in many ways a bleak winter. But somehow, by the end of it, I felt quite confirmed about wanting to live with her and stay with her.

And also, I felt a little strange around her parents, in that I was the guy she was living with. They were very open and accepting of me, but I felt awkward when we would go to Mara's folks' house, and Mara's father would introduce me to someone and say, "This is Mara's—This is—Uh—This is Russell."
Mara: No, before we even had our contract, he would introduce you as my husband.
Russell: Oh, really?
Mara: Yes.
Russell: I don't remember that. Well, no one was putting pressure on me to get married, but having been married from the time I was nineteen, it was a more comfortable way for me to relate. We were living together, and for my own part I wanted to get some kind of

legal definition in our marriage, because I wanted protection of it. I didn't want some landlord to be able to say, "Oh ho, you are not married, so therefore I can kick you out."

On the other hand, I was not interested in getting into a legal relationship that was going to have a long-term, negative effect. I didn't want to be in a relationship where the woman needed my signature. I am talking about when we go into a restaurant and Mara pays for dinner, and the waiter puts the change in front of me. Or where she is called "Mrs. Hurley." That has a debilitating effect in the long run. It is like water over a rock.

But I was more interested in getting a legal definition of our relationship than Mara was, I think, because she was more interested in just not getting married. To me, living with Mara was an unresolved feeling. If I was going to live with someone, I wanted it to be more of a commitment.

Unlike Russell, Mara had never been married. Nor had she ever before lived with a man. From her point of view, the decision to live with Russell was itself a commitment. Mara seems to have felt less social or psychological pressure than Russell to define their relationship in a contractual manner. Her reluctance to marry may have been unusually strong, but she is not unique in her generation. Asked to expand on her reasons for preferring a private conjugal contract to the normal marriage contract, Mara replied at some length:

Mara: I had never lived with anyone. That was pretty unusual for someone thirty years old from Berkeley, never to have lived with at least one man. To me, the fact that I was living with a man implied a great deal of commitment. It was not a casual thing, it was the most radical step I had ever taken. Having done that, I didn't feel this need immediately to take the next step. It was the only time I had ever lived with a man, and in terms of my feelings, and my family's, too, it was a pretty strong sign that something major had taken place.

Really, I had never felt that I had to be married. Being a student and working and in various relationships that I had with men, I never felt that I had to be married. That was not my verification of myself. If you are not married by a certain age there is somehow a sense of failure, at least that is the general feeling. In my middle twenties for a bit I felt that, but it didn't last long. And I wasn't getting anything from my mother like, "Oh when are you going to get married and give me some grandchildren?"

I never felt that marriage itself was a goal I was aspiring to, although I certainly liked to think of myself as eventually having a good marriage or a long-term relationship with someone. I had no feeling that I had to be married in order to prove that I was acceptable. I think that women are feeling this less and less, depending on the environments they live in.

By the time I did meet Russell, I had a resistance to changing my identity or my status, that I felt would be changed by marriage. I was very attached to my name, for example. It was part of my identity and it would feel strange to me to change my name. When I was younger, I think I wouldn't have been affected by it that way as much. It wasn't as if I had always given it this much thought. It was a process of long development. I felt that I would be less my own person.

I was also aware, from past relationships I had had with men, of the dangers and of the tendency of a woman to gain much of her identity through a man. Even though emotionally I felt I was beyond that point, I still didn't like to be defined by society as someone's wife, Mrs. Someone. As a single woman I would sometimes be questioned about—for instance, going to the dentist and the receptionist asking me to fill out an information sheet and saying, "Now put down the name of the person who is responsible for you, your husband or your father." You know, I was twenty-nine years old at that time, and I felt rather strange about that. Why should anyone assume that someone else was responsible for me? If it happened to me, as it did, when I was single, think what it would be like when I was married. I would not be considered to be responsible for myself, or speaking for myself.

A conjugal contract from the hall of records

Having agreed that they wanted a lasting relationship, but that they did not want to marry, Russell and Mara decided to develop a conjugal contract that would give them some definition of their relationship and some sense of permanency, but that would not be a legal marriage.

Russell: We sat down together one night and wrote down everything we wanted, everything we could think of, and we gave it to an attorney —a woman active in the woman's movement—who went over it for two months and added and changed things. At first we had thought about just getting a regular marriage license and attaching some legal riders to it which would make it say what we wanted it to say, but we found out that wouldn't hold up in court legally.

Q   Do you have a time clause in your contract? Is this a term contract to be renegotiated in five years, or ten?

Mara: No, it is for as long as we want it.
Russell: It lasts until either one of us wants to, with a notary, dissolve it. We could, with the stroke of a pen, end the thing. If there were any conflict, then it would come up before the courts in the same way that other legal conflicts come up. There would be fewer disputes because

we don't have any claim on each other's property. The only dispute would be the custody of a child.

Mara: Essentially, we have come together as single people, and remain single people legally.

The conjugal contract between Russell Hurley and Mara Epstein was signed, with members of their families as witnesses, notarized, and recorded in the county in which they live. It is on file in the county hall of records, set between two real estate transactions. The contract is a matter of public record, and Mara and Russell have agreed that reproducing it might be useful to others. It read as follows (only the names of persons have been changed):

This agreement is entered into between MARA EPSTEIN and RUSSELL HURLEY this 14th day of April 1973. Both MARA and RUSSELL reside in Rocky Creek, [name of county], State of California.

The parties hereto stipulate and declare that this agreement is made with reference to the following facts:

1. Our purpose is to make an agreement to effect a settlement of our rights and obligations in relation to one another including our respective property rights.

2. Both MARA and RUSSELL are responsible and caring adults. Each is in good health and fully capable of earning an adequate living.

3. Each of us recognizes the individuality and autonomy of the other and we enter this agreement in the belief that by sharing our responsibilities as set out here, we clarify and strengthen our relationship. NOW THEREFORE, for and in consideration of the mutual promises and covenants herein contained, the parties have agreed and do agree as follows:

1. *Mutual Property*

The following property and assets shall be designated as mutual property:

a. All personal property in the nature of houshold furniture and furnishings whenever acquired by either party.

b. All other investments, including real property which shall be designated at the time of acquisition as mutual property and held in the names of both parties.

c. All funds in the mutual bank account established according to the terms of this agreement.

d. The parties herein agree that each party shall have joint and equal rights of ownership and management of the mutual property designated in the paragraphs above.

e. A written consent, bearing the signature of both parties, shall be necessary for the sale, gift, encumbrance of or other disposition of the mutual property as further set out in Paragraph 3(c) herein.

2. *Individual Property*

The following property shall be designated as individual property:

a. All personal and real property owned by either party regardless of

622

when or how acquired, excepting that property designated as mutual property in the sections above.

b. Each party shall be the sole owner and manager of his or her individual property as designated in Paragraph 2(a) above.

3. *Mutual Debts*

a. All debts incurred for the following purposes shall be designated as mutual debts:

(1) For the food, shelter, or other necessities of life of the parties and any other persons who may become the legal responsibility of either party.

(2) For the acquisition and maintenance of any property, real or personal, designated as mutual property in the paragraphs above.

b. The parties herein agree that our above designated mutual debts shall be the joint responsibility of the parties.

c. Either party may incur a debt herein designated as a mutual debt without the consent of the other party in an amount not to exceed $500.00. The incurrence of any mutual debts over $500.00 requires the written consent of both parties.

4. *Individual Debts*

a. All other debts and obligations of the parties except those set forth in paragraph 3 above shall be designated as the individual debt of the party incurring such debt in his or her name alone.

b. Such individual debts and obligations whenever incurred shall be the sole responsibility of the party who contracts said debt or obligation.

5. *Bank Accounts*

a. The parties shall open a joint bank account in both their names such that funds can be withdrawn by either party in his or her own name alone. This account shall be designated as a mutual account.

b. Each party shall contribute funds to this account according to his or her individual income at any given time.

c. All debts and obligations designated herein as mutual debts shall be paid from this account. No funds shall be withdrawn from this account for any other purposes without the mutual consent of the parties.

d. Neither party shall withdraw a lump sum amount exceeding $500.00 in any calendar month from the mutual account without the consent of the other party.

e. Nothing in this section shall prohibit either party from opening and maintaining any other bank account for any purpose in the individual name of the party. Such accounts shall be designated as individual property pursuant to paragraph 2 above.

6. *Children*

a. MARA EPSTEIN agrees that she will institute no action of any kind concerning the person or estate of PATRICK JOHN HURLEY, son of RUSSELL HURLEY by a previous marriage.

b. RUSSELL HURLEY agrees that he will acknowledge his paternity of any child conceived or born to MARA EPSTEIN during the continuance of

623

this contract. Upon termination of this contract, the parties will settle any question concerning the custody and support of any children born to or conceived by MARA EPSTEIN during the continuance of this contract by mutual agreement. If the parties are unable to reach such agreement, either party shall have the right of issues of custody, visitation and support before a court of competent jurisdiction for resolution.

c. Both parties herein agree that they shall recognize and grant to each other equal rights regarding any children who may be born to or conceived by MARA EPSTEIN during the continuance of this contract.

7. *Powers of Attorney*

Both parties agree that they will execute mutual powers of attorney to enable each party to perform all legal acts for the other in the case of disability or prolonged absence of the other. Such powers of attorney shall be effective for the life of this contract. Upon termination of this agreement, such powers of attorney shall be withdrawn according to law.

8. *Wills*

Both parties agree to execute wills wherein each party wills, grants, devises, and bequeaths to the other party all right and interest in his or her property and assets not otherwise specifically disposed of by will or other means legally sufficient to convey property after death.

9. *Taxes*

a. The parties agree to file joint returns of federal and state income taxes if this is possible under the appropriate governing laws.

b. Regardless of the form of filing tax returns, the responsibility for payment of federal and state income taxes shall be as follows:

(1) Each party shall compute the percentage of his or her income which was contributed to the mutual bank account. The amount of taxes in the percentage computed in paragraph 9(1) above shall be designated the mutual debt of the parties and shall be paid out of the funds in the mutual bank account.

(2) The taxes owing on all income of either party which is not contributed to the mutual funds shall be designated as the individual debt and responsibility of each party.

c. That portion of any refund of state or federal income tax which is attributable to each party's contribution of income to the mutual fund shall be designated as mutual property. The remaining portion of such income tax refunds shall be divided between the parties according to their income and shall be designated as the individual property of each party.

10. *Amendment*

This contract may be amended by a writing containing the terms of such amendment and dated and signed by both parties.

11. *Termination*

This contract may be terminated at any time by mutual consent of parties in writing and signed by both parties, or by a written and signed declaration of either party.

a. Upon notice of intent to terminate this agreement the parties shall draw up a list of the mutual property and the mutual debts which exist as to the date of notice of termination. This list shall include the amount of such debts and the value of all property based on a fair market value at the time of the termination of the agreement. In the event that the list shall include any real property or other investments and the parties cannot agree on the fair market value of such property and/or investments, an appraiser mutually acceptable to the parties shall be instructed to determine the fair market value of such assets and his valuation shall be binding on the parties.

b. The mutual debts shall be paid first from the funds in the mutual bank account until it is exhausted.

c. The value of any remaining mutual debts shall be subtracted from the total value of the mutual property. The remaining sum, whether it be a debt or an asset, shall be divided equally between the parties and shall thereafter be the sole and individual responsibilty or property of each party.

d. The property designated as individual property in paragraph 2 above and the debts designated as individual debts in paragraph 4 above shall remain the sole property and responsibility of the party who acquired same.

12. Captions

The captions of paragraphs of this agreement are for reference only and are not to be construed in any way as a part of this agreement.

13. Choice of Law

The validity of this agreement or of any of its terms or provisions as well as the rights and duties of the parties hereunder shall be interpreted and construed pursuant to and in accordance with the laws of the State of California.

14. Partial Invalidity

If any term, provision, covenant, or condition of this agreement is held by a court of competent jurisdiction to be invalid, void, or unenforceable, the remainder of the provisions shall remain in full force and effect and shall in no way be affected, impaired, or invalidated.

15. Attorney's Fees

If any legal action is necessary to enforce the terms of this agreement, the prevailing party shall be entitled to reasonable attorney's fees in addition to any other relief to which he may be entitled.

Executed at Berkeley, California, the day and year in this agreement first above written.

_____

Mara Epstein

_____

Russell Hurley

Seal of Notary Public
Statement of Notary Public
Signature of Notary Public

Mara Epstein and Russell Hurley requested each of us to act as witnesses to this agreement executed by them in our presence on April 14, 1973.

_____ residing at _____
_____ residing at _____

Advantages and limitations of the conjugal contract

Both Russell and Mara had indicated that they preferred their private conjugal contract to a legal marriage, but for somewhat different reasons. I asked Mara whether she felt that the conjugal contract had allowed her to retain her sense of self and identity.

> *Mara:* Yes, I think so. Certainly given the awareness we have of this aspect of our relationship and our thoughts on it. I think even if we were legally married, we could probably still achieve the same thing, only it would take a great deal more effort. But over the long run we might get worn down by it and, as Russell says, it is like a drop of water slowly eroding something away. There is an accumulation of experiences that can be very subtle, and they can eventually alter a relationship.

> *Q   Russell, you said something about the contract making a difference to you as a professional?*

> Russell: I think it does. In any kind of profession the man is under very definite scrutiny about his marital situation. I would be regarded, by other professional men, as sloppy, loose, or incompetent, or going through a period of instability, if I don't have things all put into slots. That wasn't a big consideration for me. But it does make a difference.
>
> There is a male dichotomy that I am very aware of, either a woman is your wife or she is your sexpot. And so by definition, if I am living with a woman, obviously the reason I am living with her is because we have a trapeze and mirrors in our bedroom and we are doing all kinds of far-out sexual things. That is the male way of looking at it. Your wife is sort of Old Mom, you know, but your lover is [long whistle]. People would say, "Oh, are you and Mara married?" And we would say, "No." And then people would say, "Oh—Um hum!"
>
> The contract was as much to combat the social attitude and presuppositions that people have about living together as it was to do the thing about being married. My impression was that Mara was much more sensitive in terms of her own self-interest to the subtle dangers of being married, and I was more sensitive to the subtle dangers of being unmarried. To me, it would have had a long-term effect. Over the long term, just living together, without any definition, would have had a very demoralizing effect on me.

At this point it seemed as if the conjugal contract were a compromise between Mara's fear of marriage and Russell's discomfort with the ambiguities of a living arrangement. When asked if that had been the case, both initially agreed that it was.

Russell: Being married doesn't harm me that much as a male. It is all set up for men. I don't lose my name, I don't lose my respect, I don't have anything to lose. Marriage wasn't personally as threatening to me as it was to Mara.

Mara: I think it is interesting that in terms of statistics for the population in general, married men and single women are supposed to be the most emotionally healthy. Married women and single men tend to have the highest suicide rates, highest rates of alcoholism.

Russell: Men feel better when they are married and women feel better when they are single.

Mara: So this is an attempt to balance that off, but not to do away with the sense of commitment, or the development of couples and families, but to create some form so the woman can feel as good in it as a man.

Q   Would you say then that Mara is the major beneficiary of your conjugal contract, as opposed to a legal marriage?

Russell: I think that if we talk about us as individuals, yes. But I think since we are both equally interested in our relationship, I think the most protective, least threatening, and the best ground, the best earth, for this kind of relationship to grow in is what we arrived at. So therefore it is really in both our self-interests.

Mara: Yes, if I got dissatisfied or felt negatively about a marriage relationship, obviously it would affect him, too.

Russell: Besides, I was getting so much into men's lib or, I should say, so much into the kinds of things that men don't dare think about—like I don't like to work. I do not like to work. If I had to go to work nine to five every day at some ding-ass job, I would shoot myself in the head now. I work for myself. I don't fit into the man's world very well.

And as things were going, if I would get married and it didn't work out—well, a divorced man is trapped. If he doesn't pay up, his child support and his alimony, if he decides, "Well, Jesus, I've been working for fifteen years, I'm tired of working, I want to go out for a year," he can't do that. A woman can go to Esalen, she can do this. She can take the money her husband earns and go do all the other things. I was not interested in getting into a normal marriage relationship where I had the legal responsibility, the legal burden. For example, there is one woman I nearly married, before I met Mara. I just know what would have happened if I had married her and assumed the responsibility for all that. She had a couple of children and I had two children and an ex-wife to keep paying, and so on.

I know that I would not have been able to have developed in any of the ways which I have developed now, which I like very much, because I would have had too many duties, too many responsibilities. I think I would have started having stress problems, health problems. I would have been the one who would have had to buy all the insurance and support people even after I died, and, psychologically, that tends to bring men to the state of consciousness where they regard their wives as a burden. They regard the woman they have to support as a kind of constant harpy that pursues them to the grave and after the grave.

So I was not interested in getting into a conventional marriage, either. I don't know, I think if I look at it very objectively I would say that it is not true to say that the contract mostly benefits Mara, because what it does is relieve me of that extra burden. It makes our burdens equal. It doesn't give either of us the heavy load of economic and emotional and child support and insurance. Here is a woman that, when I die, I don't have to worry about her. She will take care of herself.

Whatever the psychological advantages or disadvantages of the conjugal contract, there are also some social and economic advantages and limitations. When asked what these might be, Russell replied as follows:

Russell: All the contract is is a mélange of all kinds of other little contracts, like mutual agreement on wills, on power of attorney, and some innovative contracts that haven't been written yet, like an agreement that I will declare my paternity of her children—
Mara: Well, I think we can do that in the contract.
Russell: That's what I say. The contract is a bunch of little contracts, and in that one she also declares that she will defend my full right as a father in any custodial dispute that might happen. Normally I would not have the same rights of custody of a mutual child, even though I declared paternity, that I would have if I were married to Mara.

Actually, this contract is written as an economic contract, a partnership between two people, but not using the partnership format, just using the regular two-party contract format. It sounds funny, but it revolves around the concept of having joint finances. It is a way of making our finances joint and also separate in any way we want, so community property is something we declare ourselves, not something the law defines, where everything she owns is mine and everything I own is hers. We don't do that. Anything we want to be community, we specify—like a house, or anything like that—and other things we don't. The second thing is that since the mutual economics is the basis of the contract, it is essentially a business arrangement, I guess [laughs].

Legally, we are single. We pay our own taxes. Our attorney says that the federal government tends to be most conservative when it comes to anything like this. We could try to file jointly and probably could make a good case for ourselves as an economic unit, but we haven't bothered. I get a better tax break as an unmarried head of household. So we file separately.

Effects of the conjugal contract on the conjugal relationship

After Russell and Mara had talked at some length about the various legal aspects of their conjugal contract, Russell turned the conversation to the effects on their personal relationship of having a conjugal contract rather than a legal marriage.

Russell: I feel that you haven't touched on the most important aspect of what we are doing. To put it in simple terms, one of the reasons that I think there has been a rigid stereotypical format of male-female intersexual relations has been the unspoken contract. I would characterize it this way: the man says, "Okay, I will take most of the burdens, I will die young, but in return, I will be the king." I get the picture of the family with a patriarchal father and a woman who is taking care of the house. Just like the last chapter of Proverbs, the perfect wife is the one who stays up burning the night oil sewing clothes for her family and obeys the husband. And I think this contract, this understanding, between men and women about what a marriage was, goes way back. It is dissolved in a relationship like ours, where we have a different ideal.

In our relationship we don't strive for, we don't have to achieve, we just simply *have* equal rights and equal responsibilities. I am not a superman and she is not an oppressed woman, we are just partners here. We find that the ways of relating between men and women change greatly, and this is what is so significant, what I wanted to bring out.

What has happened is there are some very profound changes. Number one: we don't have sexual relations very often. I don't know how to put it exactly, but the very manner of how one has a sexual relationship is different. There are psychological elements that are built into what turns on a person. A woman might be very aroused by something that she doesn't like the idea of at all. You have all this residue built up from what has been conditioned into a person. The thing that is exciting about sex is that it is an escape, it is a release, it is a way for people to assert all kinds of psychological things over, against, for, and into each other. It is a way for man to get his strokes,

629

it is a way for a woman to keep her man. It is a way for all kinds of things to happen.

And when sex becomes what it is, which is a very simple biological act and at the same time an extremely profound, subtle act that has to do with parts of human nature that aren't defined by science—what I am trying to say is that Mara and I have a different kind of relationship, sexually and emotionally and in many other ways, than a marriage relationship.

And those are the most profound things, those are the most interesting things. If people knew about them or understood what real equality in marriage means in a practical, day-to-day kind of thing— that a lot of these things, like whether a man does the dishes, that's nice, but that is not what the real meaning of it is. There is a change in a human relationship and you become no longer an erotic couple, you become a partner with someone. You become more of a sidekick. There's a spiritual element to it rather than a romantic element, and I don't think this is going to become popular. I think this marriage is for very few people. I am sounding awfully ascetic, I guess, but there is a change in the human relationship, a change in the male-female relationship, when it is no longer based on sex.

Mara: I think the point is that it gets reduced to its essential element, the kernal of what can be between two people expressed in a sexual way, but a lot of the emotional and psychological tensions and interplay and dynamics that go on that are also expressed sexually, those tend to fall away.

Q   You mean expressing power, compensating for insecurity, that sort of motive for sex?

Mara: Yes. And of course this isn't to say that this is how anyone getting into this or attempting this kind of relationship would find it happening. I don't know if I can say as surely as Russell does that it would, but I think it certainly would be a tendency. If the people are really maturing and developing psychologically and emotionally in ways that would bring them to the point where they want to make this kind of relationship, I think that might imply that they would find themselves being free of these other kinds of secondary sexual aspects of life.

Russell: If I see a woman and she is all dolled up and she is hairless and smooth and has made herself to be shaped the way she is supposed to be, and reveals herself, sure, that is a very sexy kind of thing. It's a turn-on. But I am not interested in it anymore, because I know the ramifications. I guess what I am trying to say is that I finally got sick of the idea that it was up to me to give the woman an orgasm. That was my responsibility. I was responsible for her nervous system. And I was very good at doing that, but it was up to me and they expected me to give them an orgasm. I finally got to the point where I realized that I didn't like that kind of relationship. That was another extension of the economic burden and everything else. It was a sexual burden.

Now with Mara, when we got together, she was in control of her own orgasm. She took her orgasm, wasn't dependent upon me giving it to her. I don't know how to explain it. She had been independent for so long she wasn't going to be taken care of by a man.

The basis of our relationship is that Mara is a woman that I started out just liking, liking a lot. If she commits herself to something, I can trust her with it. She is moral. She is like a man is supposed to be and most men aren't. She is a person who is a good friend to me, and that is very important in our relationship. If I had a brother and all of a sudden the brother turned into a female, that would be like my relationship with Mara. And it is not that she is trying to play the psychological role of mother, or the psychological role of incestuous sister, or the psychological role of lover, or any of these things. I don't feel the need for a lover, or the need of a mother. I feel sometimes little bits of that kind of need, but it is not a big thing, not as if it were an unmet thing.

I guess what I am trying to say is that the most important things about our relationship are not the contract and who does the dishes, but have to do with the interpersonal and the *inner*-personal ramifications of this kind of relationship. And now the affectionate part of the relationship takes prominence over the lustful part of the relationship.

Mara: I think one thing that is essential to all we are talking about is to try and determine what are the real differences and what are the culturally and environmentally conditioned differences between us. I mean not only in sexual matters, but in personality. When I was still in the kitchen earlier, Russell was giving some basic differences in our personalities that tend to coincide with the male and female stereotypes or accepted patterns. One of my main interests and concerns, even before getting together with Russell, when I was involved with the women's movement, was to try to understand what aspects of myself are natural and inherent in me, and which are culturally, environmentally, conditioned. And which things can I perhaps not change. You can only go so far, perhaps.

Marriage or the conjugal contract: what of the future?

Time was when people expected to enter into marriage as it was structured by tradition, religion, and the law. If they found marriage confining, they sought help, hoping to change themselves to adjust to marriage. Today, a growing number of Americans are seeking to change marriage, to adjust marriage to fit themselves.

631

To change the structure of marriage is also to change the functions of marriage and the nature of the conjugal relationship. As the couple interviewed above reported, one of the effects of an equal relationship between husband and wife is likely to be a change in the sexual relationship. The reasons for the reduced sexual expression are not readily explained. In part, as Russell and Mara point out, sexual activity is reduced because intercourse ceases to be an expression of dominance either through seduction or through sexual aggression against the spouse. People who have accepted that they are equals do not need to engage in conjugal power struggles.

There are perhaps other elements that mute sensuality in a relationship based on equality. Recall that Russell commented that one of the ways to describe his relationship with Mara was to say that if he had a brother and that brother had suddenly been transformed into a woman, that woman would be Mara. The kind of feeling that exists between close siblings is in some ways analogous to that which exists between a man and a woman with complete equality in their relationship. When a man and a woman are close friends and equals, there seems to be some suppression of sexual desire, almost as if an incest taboo were being observed.

Whatever the emotional process, it does seem that real equality and close friendship between spouses tend to reduce sexual activity. This need not be a problem except that we Americans tend to be hyperconscious of the amount and variety of sexual experience we have. A man or woman may try to ignore the sexual themes of our culture, but such questions as "What am I missing? Am I a desirable sexual partner still?" are almost inevitable. Recognizing that such feelings will arise from time to time, but recognizing also that they can lead to consequences we may not want (as Russell reports he does), is the best way to keep such feelings from damaging a close conjugal relationship.

The conjugal contract presented in detail as a narrative case in this chapter is not, of course, typical of all the contracts being developed. Conjugal contracts are private agreements and are as varied as the individuals drafting them. It is probable, however, that those developed with legal advice will include provisions regarding property, support obligations, paternity, and custody of children. Such matters are the crux of the marriage contract, and it is to be expected that they will be the basic elements of private conjugal contracts.

Insofar as any of these private conjugal contracts contain provisions that are contradictory to law (for example, if a man wanted to stipulate that he would not be responsible for the support of children born to his partner), they would be held invalid or unenforceable in any court test that might be brought by one of the partners, or by a creditor.

Most conjugal contracts are probably intended primarily to structure marital roles between the two persons entering the agreement, not to be enforced through legal proceedings. But couples with a private conjugal contract are not immune to the strains and pressures that may ultimately rupture a relationship. If the contract is dissolved, some disposition of property and child custody will have to be made. When children are involved, the court will make the ultimate decisions: what the couple thought was a private agreement may sooner or later be tested in a court of law.

There is some evidence to suggest that many private conjugal contracts are drawn in a manner that seeks to make the husband and wife equal partners in the relationship. Like the contract we have been examining, many provide for contribution of money in proportion to income to a mutual fund, which is managed on an equal, not a proportional basis. The effect of such provisions is to keep the partner with the higher income (most often the male) from exercising the power of the purse. Some private conjugal contracts go into detail regarding the responsibility each will have for household chores, although the one we have been examining does not. When included, such provisions are an attempt to remove the label "woman's work" from the maintenance tasks of the household.

Many of the goals of couples drafting private conjugal contracts could be achieved within a legal marriage. For example, there is nothing in the law of most states that says a woman must take her husband's name. That is a common-law right, but usually not a legal requirement. Mara could have kept her maiden name in a legal marriage, had she chosen to do so. But this couple, like some others, had philosophical reasons for wanting to avoid the existing marriage pattern, even where the law contains some flexibility.

The private conjugal contract may be a passing fad, like computer dating. But if such agreements are adopted in some form by a significant number of persons, state laws will ultimately be modified to reflect the changing structure of marital relationships. It is perhaps both proper and inevitable that the law should lag behind changing behavioral patterns of society. But it does seem probable that some reforms of family law will be enacted within the next decade that will recognize equal rights to property accumulated by the couple during marriage, reforms that will also include equal support obligations for spouses. If this happens, many of the couples who have entered into private conjugal contracts may well choose to marry, because there are certain benefits that derive from having a legally recognized relationship.

The dependency of the wife, written into present state laws, both protects and subordinates her. If she wants equality, she will have to give up her legal right to be supported by her husband. Conversely, the burden of support that present law places on the husband is also the basis for the dominance the law accords him as head of the family. If he would have his wife share the economic burden as an equal partner, he will have to give up his dominant role and assume a greater part of the burden of child care and household responsibilities. Many Americans of both sexes have already agreed that the gains of equality and autonomy are worth the loss of security or dominance.

One thing is certain: marriage as we have known it is in the midst of rapid change. Americans are currently engaged in a search for alternative forms of relationship between the sexes. But through all of this searching, it seems probable that the heterosexual, conjugal relationship is going to prevail. Americans will eventually redefine marriage, but it seems unlikely that they will abandon it.

References

Blackstone, William. 1765–1769. *Commentaries on the Law of England,* vol. I.

Flexner, Eleanor. 1959. *Century of Struggle.* Cambridge, Mass.: Belknap Press of Harvard University Press.

Suggested readings

Coffin, Patricia. 1972. "The Young Unmarrieds." In *Intimate Life Styles,* edited by Joann S. Delora and Jack R. Delora, pp. 316–317. Pacific Palisades, Calif.: Goodyear Publishing Company. Paper. Living together seems to have evolved as a stage of courtship in America, perhaps substituting for early and transitory marriages. This is a brief case study of a young college-educated couple who are living together without marriage.

Kanowitz, Leo. 1969. *Women and the Law: The Unfinished Revolution.* Albuquerque: University of New Mexico Press. Available in paper. An authoritative account by a legal scholar of the legal aspects of marriage and of sex-based discrimination. The chapters on "Law and the Married Woman" and "Law and the Single Girl" are particularly appropriate reading for this chapter.

Lyness, Judith L., and Milton E. Lipetz. 1972. "Living Together: An Alternative to Marriage." *Journal of Marriage and the Family* 34 (May):305–311. This article is focused on the implications for marriage of living together. Data on interpersonal feelings and social background were obtained from eighteen unmarried couples who were living together and from thirty-one unmarried couples who were dating but not living together. The comparisons indicate differences between the two groups, and between men and women in the group who were living together, in such personal attitudes as the desire for security in marriage and reciprocity of feelings.

Wells, Theodora, and Lee S. Christie. 1972. "Living Together: An Alternative Marriage." In *Intimate Life Styles,* edited by Joann S. Delora and Jack R. Delora, pp. 318–320. Pacific Palisades, Calif.: Goodyear Publishing Company. Paper. This short article is a "position paper" written by a middle-aged previously married couple who are living together in preference to marriage. Each has experienced conventional marital and family roles, and these are compared to the unconventional roles they now play.

Credits and acknowledgments

Aldine Publishing Company for extracts from *Family Design: Marital Sexuality, Family Size, and Contraception*, by Lee Rainwater. Copyright © 1965 by Aldine Publishing Company. Reprinted by permission of Aldine Publishing Company.

Hawthorn Books, Inc. for extracts from the book *The Significant Americans* by John F. Cuber with Peggy B. Harroff. Copyright © 1965 by Appleton-Century-Crofts. Reprinted by permission of Hawthorn Books, Inc. 260 Madison Avenue, New York, N.Y. 10016.

Holt, Rinehart and Winston for extracts from *Fundamentals of Human Sexuality*, 2nd ed., by Herant A. Katchadourian and Donald T. Lunde. Copyright © 1972, 1975 by Holt, Rinehart and Winston. Reprinted by permission of Holt, Rinehart and Winston.

Houghton Mifflin Company for "A Decade" by Amy Lowell. From *The Complete Poetical Works of Amy Lowell*. Reprinted by permission of Houghton Mifflin Company.

Little, Brown and Company for extracts from *Tally's Corner* by Elliot Liebow. Copyright © 1967 by Little, Brown and Company. Reprinted by permission of Little, Brown and Company. From *Human Sexual Inadequacy*, by William H. Masters and Virginia E. Johnson. Copyright © 1970 by Little, Brown and Company. Reprinted by permission of Little, Brown and Company.

The New York Times Company for extracts from "Down and Out Along Route 128" by Berkeley Rice from the *New York Times Magazine*. Copyright © 1970 by The New York Times Company. Reprinted by permission. From "Desperately Sad Men of New York" by John Corry. Copyright © 1973 by The New York Times Company. Reprinted by permission.

Oxford University Press for extracts from *White Collar: The American Middle Classes*, by C. Wright Mills. Copyright © 1951 by Oxford University Press. Reprinted by permission of Oxford University Press.

Random House, Inc. and Alfred A. Knopf, Inc., for extracts from *The Castle*, by Franz Kafka, trans. by Edwin and Willa Muir. Copyright © 1930, 1954 and renewed 1958

Credits and acknowledgments

by Alfred A. Knopf, Inc. Reprinted by permission of Alfred A. Knopf, Inc. From *The World of the Family*, by Dorothy R. Blitsten. Copyright © 1963 by Dorothy R. Blitsten. Reprinted by permission of Random House, Inc. From *The Mind of the South*, by W. J. Cash. Copyright © 1941 by Alfred A. Knopf, Inc. Reprinted by permission of Alfred A. Knopf, Inc. From *Blue-Collar Marriage*, by Mirra Komarovsky. Copyright © 1962, 1964, 1967 by Random House, Inc. Reprinted by permission of the publisher. From *The Tree of Culture*, by Ralph Linton. Copyright © 1955 by Adelin Linton. Reprinted by permission of Alfred A. Knopf, Inc.

San Francisco Examiner for an extract from "Why They Cheat on Welfare" by Susan Berman. Reprinted with permission from *California Living*, the magazine of the *San Francisco Sunday Examiner & Chronicle*, and by permission of Susan Berman. Copyright © 1974 San Francisco Examiner.

Sherbourne Press for extracts from *Sportin' House: A History of the New Orleans Sinners and the Birth of Jazz*, by Stephen Longstreet. Copyright © 1965 by Stephen Longstreet. Reprinted by permission of Sherbourne Press.

636

Photograph credits

Index

640